Contemporary
Social Studies:
An Essential Reader

A Volume in
Teaching and Learning Social Studies
Series Editor:
William Benedict Russell III

Contemporary Social Studies:
An Essential Reader
REVIEW BOARD

William Benedict Russell III
Editor

I would like acknowledge the following individuals for serving as reviewers for *Contemporary Social Studies: An Essential Reader*. All chapters underwent a rigorous double-blind peer review. All reviewers are listed below.

Contemporary Social Studies: An Essential Reader

William Benedict Russell III
University of Central Florida

INFORMATION AGE PUBLISHING, INC.
Charlotte, NC • www.infoagepub.com

Library of Congress Cataloging-in-Publication Data

Contemporary social studies : an essential reader / William Benedict Russell III, editor.
    p. cm. – (Teaching and learning social studies book series)
  Includes bibliographical references and index.
  ISBN 978-1-61735-671-1 (pbk.) – ISBN 978-1-61735-672-8 (hardcover) –
ISBN 978-1-61735-673-5 (ebook)
1. Social sciences–Study and teaching. 2. Citizenship–Study and
teaching. 3. Multicultural education. I. Russell, William B.
  LB1584.C64 2012
  300.71–dc23
                                        2011043682

CONTENTS

SECTION II

CURRICULUM, CONTENT, & STANDARDS

SECTION III

DIVERSITY & PERSPECTIVE

SECTION IV

PEDAGOGY

SECTION V

MEDIA, TECHNOLOGY, AND TEACHER EDUCATION

ACKNOWLEDGMENTS

I would like to express a sincere thank you to my family (Catie, William, Juliet, and Olivia) for their support. Additionally, I would like to thank the chapter authors for the many inspiring and thought provoking chapters and the chapter reviewers for their attention to detail and dedication to the field of social studies.

CHAPTER 1

CONTEMPORARY SOCIAL STUDIES

Issues, Perspectives, and Thoughts

William Benedict Russell III

Questions Unite, Answers Divide

—Elie Wiesel

What is social studies? What is the purpose of social studies? Like many questions, the answer is not always clear or simple. Within the field of social studies the questions are not the issue, but instead it is the answers to the questions that are the issue. These two questions or should I say, the answers to these two questions have contributed to social studies literature and its identity or lack of one. Social studies is a unique field. It is a field that has been searching for a clear and cohesive identity. The search for this cohesive identity has been challenged by the various definitions and rationales for social studies. As the focus on twenty-first century education becomes more prominent, it is an appropriate time to examine the contemporary state of social studies. What is the contemporary state of social studies? How did we get here? What will social studies look like in the fu-

Contemporary Social Studies: An Essential Reader, pages 1–4 ture? These questions are common and the chapters in this volume provide insight with regard to the various sub-fields of social studies.

What is social studies? The National Council for the Social Studies defines the social studies as, "the integrated study of the social sciences and humanities to promote civic competence. Within the school program, social studies provides coordinated, systematic study drawing upon such disciplines as anthropology, archaeology, economics, geography, history, law, philosophy, political science, psychology, religion, and sociology, as well as appropriate content from the humanities, mathematics, and natural sciences" (NCSS, 2010).

What is the purpose of social studies? The National Council for the Social Studies states that "the primary purpose of social studies is to help young people develop the ability to make informed and reasoned decisions for the public good as citizens of a culturally diverse, democratic society in an interdependent world" (NCSS, 2010).

Although the National Council for the Social Studies definition and purpose statement is the most commonly used and accepted, there are alternative definitions and purpose statements that are common to many of the critical areas of social studies. Throughout the history of social studies numerous scholars have provided differing definitions of social studies and statements regarding the purpose and approach of social studies. The chapters included in the volume provide various perspectives related to social studies, including its contemporary state and its purpose.

This volume includes twenty-eight scholarly chapters discussing relevant contempotary issues of importance to social studies. The twenty-eight chapters are divide into five sections. Section I: Purpose and Approach, includes chapters that discuss relevant contemporary issues related to various perspectives on the purpose and approach of social studies. This section begins with a chapter by Ellen Santora. Santora examines Parker's perspective of democratic education and recasts it by integrating multicultural, democratic, global and citizenship education with critical pedagogy. In the following chapter, Jonathan Miller-Lane suggests that there is a way through existing disagreements into a vision of democratic education curriculum that supports the next evolution of social studies education. Chapter four, by Merry Merryfield, discusses global education and its place in a changing and interconnected world. Merryfield's chapter is followed by Anatoli Rapoport's discussion of global citizenship and its place in social studies curriculum in chapter five. Chapter six, by Stewart Waters and William B. Russell III, discusses character education and its role as the foundation of citizenship education.

Beyond the purpose and approach discussion, Section II: Curriculum, Content, and Standards, provide readers with an array of chapters that discuss the relevant contemporary issues related to the social studies curriculum, content, and standards. In chapter seven, Keith Barton discusses history and the key elements of history curriculum for successfully learning and teaching history. Chapter eight, by Reese Todd, examines Geography Education and its vital role in the social studies curriculum. In chapter nine, Kevin Vinson, E. Wayne Ross, and Melissa Wilson discuss the state of standards based education and its impact on social studies education. Vinson, Ross, and Wilson are followed by Beverly Bisland, who examines standardized testing and its impact on elementary social studies instruction in chapter ten.

Issues and topics related to diversity are examined in Section III: Diversity and Perspective. Section III begins with chapter eleven, by Paul Fitchett and Tina Heafner, which analyzes cultural responsive social studies teaching. Chapter twelve, by Prentice Chandler and Douglas McKnight examines the critical area of race in the social studies. J. B. Mayo, Jr. follows the chapter on race with a critical discussion of GLBTQ issues in the social studies. In chapter fourteen, Christine Woyshner, provides an insightful examination of gender and social studies. Following Woyshner's chapter on gender, Tim Lintner and Windy Schweder examine special education and social studies and how to effectively bridge the gap. In chapter sixteen, Jason O'Brien examines the hot topic issue of English Language Learners (ELLs) and social studies.

Section IV: Pedagogy, examines contemporary social studies pedagogy and its relevance. In chapter 17, Michelle Reidel and Christine Draper discuss the critical topic of reading in the social studies. In chapter 18, Kyle Greenwalt and Patrick Leahy examine history pedagogy for the 21st century. Greenwalt and Leahy's chapter is followed by Christy Folsom's discussion of teaching social studies for intellectual and emotional learning in chapter nineteen. In chapter twenty, Anne-Lise Halvorsen explores facilitating discussions in the social studies classroom. Halvorsen's chapter is followed by Brad Burenheide's discussion of experiential learning in the social studies in chapter twenty-one. Section IV is concluded with a chapter by Thomas Turner, Jeremiah Clabough, Sarah Philpot, & Lance McConkey that discusses an array of pedagogical topics relevant for teaching social studies.

The section on pedagogy is followed by Section V: Media, Technology, and Teacher Education. This section begins with a chapter by Cameron White and Trenia Walker exploring the role of pop culture and media in the social studies. In chapter twenty-four, David Hicks, Stephanie van Hover, Elizabeth Yeager Washington, and John Lee examine Internet literacy and its role in promoting active citizenship. Chapter twenty-five, by Joe O'Brien, explores civic learning in a participatory media rich environment. The final three chapters of this section pertain to teacher education. Chapter twenty-six, by Lydiah Nganga and John Kambutu discusses broadening social studies by incorporating global education into a teacher education program.

Nganga and Kambutu's chapter is followed by John Strutz and Kevin Hessberg's discussion of teacher thinking, observation, and reflection in teacher development in chapter twenty-seven. This section concludes with a chapter by Jesus Gracia, Paula McMillen, and David To. The chapter discusses a research study that examines the impact of a capstone course in a social studies Master's program in the age of accountability and testing.

The chapters included in this volume represent the vast of amount of relevant topics related to contemporary social studies. Social studies is a broad field, and with that, social studies lends itself very easily to the debate over definition, approach, purpose, content, etc. These various perspectives have provided much scholarly focus and some would argue that the lack of cohesion it is good for the field of social studies. On the other hand, others would argue that the lack of cohesion has and continues to open the door to political and academic attacks. No matter your stance, this collection of chapters, provides an array of scholarly perspectives that represent issues relevant to contemporary social studies. This volume serves as a foundation for dialog and scholarship as the field of social studies moves deeper into the 21st century. Additionally, the scholarly examination of contemporary issues discussed in this volume promote an ongoing discussion about the field of social studies that will improve research, teaching, and service in the social studies.

REFERENCE

National Council for the Social Studies. (2010). *National curriculum standards for Social Studies*. Retrieved May 3, 2011 from the World Wide Web: www.ncss.org.

SECTION I

PURPOSE AND APPROACH

CHAPTER 2

21st CENTURY DEMOCRATIC SOCIAL AND CITIZENSHIP EDUCATION

A Hybrid Perspective

Ellen Durrigan Santora

Shirley Sherrod was asked to leave her position as Georgia State Director of Rural Development, United States Department of Agriculture. Her discomforting experience helps us to understand a number of important themes critical in the preparation of students as participating citizens in a democratic society and interdependent world. Sherrod rose to celebrity status when a decontextualized video clip of a speech she gave to a N.A.A.C.P. convention moved first to YouTube®, then national radio and finally prime-time television. A conservative blogger, wishing to tarnish the reputation of the N.A.A.C.P., used the clip to suggest that Sherrod, an African American in her 1986 capacity in the Georgia Office of the Federation of Southern Cooperatives, had refused to help a white farmer secure a loan. Instantly media pundits circulated the story. Sherrod, who had already brought this

Contemporary Social Studies: An Essential Reader, pages 7–31
Copyright © 2012 by Information Age Publishing

to the attention of her employer, was subsequently fired from her position. She was renounced by the N.A.A.C.P. and exploited by news commentators. Nonetheless, once officials viewed the entire 43-minute video, they exonerated Sherrod, praised her for sharing the story of how she struggled against her own bitterness and memories of subjugation and humiliation, and offered her a job as a racial conciliator with the Department of Agriculture. According to the *New York Times*, this case follows a "familiar pattern in American life, in which anyone who even tries to talk about race risks public outrage and humiliation" (Bai, 2010).

Democratic educators must have been shocked at the nation's inability to engage in dialogue with a public figure who chose to speak from an aesthetic, personal understanding about how her views had been transformed by what Giroux (1988) calls reflexive interrogation.[1] What is also overlooked in this episode is the failure of the media and government to understand how Sherrod's experiences worked in intertextual and sometimes contradictory ways to construct a "double consciousness" and the ability to see and act in hybrid ways, or ways that are informed by multifaceted cultural and civic lenses.

Democracy is an ambitious, complex and on-going project based on the idea that a democratic frame of mind is not natural but rather comes through a process of education—one that, according to Parker (2008) is not only pedagogical (e.g., Banks, 1997a; Cohen, 1986/1994) but also philosophical (Dewey, 1916; Greene, n.d.; Nodding, 1999), historical (e.g., Crocco & Davis, 2002; Crocco & Davis, 1999), sociological (e.g., Apple, 1993; Beane & Apple, 1995), cultural (e.g., Gay, 2000; Ladson-Billings, 2004), and critical (e.g., Cherryholmes, 1988; Hursh & Ross, 2000). This chapter draws on these disciplines in interdependent, fluid and hybrid ways, moving between disciplines and theories to construct an experiential and natural framework for researching and teaching 21st century democratic social education.

Gutman (1987) contends that schools are morally obligated "to give all children an education adequate to take advantage of their political status as citizens" (p. 288) while the evidence points to decreased classroom attention to democratic education. This is especially salient when we consider that a paradox exists in teaching students about democratic citizenship given that we are unable to resolve problems relevant to democracy within our own classrooms. To approach these problems, Parker (2003) suggests that we need to bring the discourses of multicultural and citizenship education together into a more coherent conceptual understanding of democratic citizenship education that responds in fluid yet meaningful ways to students' diverse experiences and needs. My research in and out of k-12 classrooms fosters a belief that, in doing this, we also need to blend liberal/progressive, constructivist, and more radical/critical theories of democratic social and citizenship education.

My purpose here is to recast Parker's perspective by integrating multi-cultural, democratic, global and citizenship education with critical pedagogy in middle through adult social education.[2] As the chapter proceeds, I will discuss contemporary challenges to democratic education, prominent themes concerning how we prepare students for participation in a pluralistic democracy and interdependent world and possibilities that have emerged from the literature describing transformative democratic citizenship education. Throughout, I contend that inclusion, identity, dialogue, and deliberation constitute interlaced strands from which we might weave a new, more hybrid understanding of democratic social and citizenship education. I hope these ideas will raise questions, elicit experiences, initiate deep conversations, and stimulate creative thinking about actions that will move us beyond traditional methods of promoting democratic social and citizenship education to those that attend locally and globally to participative citizenship and especially to the work of social justice.

CHALLENGES TO DEMOCRATIC SOCIAL EDUCATION

Regardless of the new social studies framework's (National Council for the Social Studies, 2010) reiteration that the primary purpose of social education is "to help young people make informed and reasoned decisions for the public good as citizens of a culturally diverse, democratic society in an interdependent world" (p. i), democratic education is framed within larger sociopolitical debates about the best type of education for all students. Parker (1997) argues that segregation, tracking, ability grouping, sexism, and a focus merely on the political perspectives of democracy present major obstacles to democratic education. Within these larger structural problems is an agenda that confronts and often defeats teachers in their classroom roles as democratic social educators. No Child Left Behind (NCLB), the standards and assessment movement, and its consequences in terms of "funding, autonomy, and privilege" (Segall, 2003 p. 289) pose three related challenges to democratic social education. While standards, testing and accountability have been complex and persistent issues in the history of social education, we cannot be deterred from being proactive in combating their potential to constrain teachers' curriculum choices and students' opportunities to engage in pluralistic and transformative dialogue. The first challenge we need to confront is the marginalization of social studies and thus democratic education as a result of NCLB (see, e.g., Jones, Jones, & Hargrove, 2003; Jones et al., 1999; O'Connor, Haefner, & Groce, 2007). The second is a decrease in policy makers' and administrators' attention to the inclusion of children with diverse abilities and perspectives in all classes (see, e.g., Au, 2007, 2009a; Hoeft, 2007). The third relates to the standards and assessment movement's potential for feeding the processes of teacher self-censorship. Today, some teachers, though this is far from universal, clearly feel they have neither a mandate nor time to attend to outcomes related to informed, engaged, and transformative citizenship (see, e.g., Agee, 2004; Au, 2009b, 2010; Bigelow, 1999; Gay, 2007; Grant, 2007; Sleeter, 2008).

In a domino effect, teacher silences have the potential to silence diversity, and thus disrupt dialogic, culturally democratic engagement (see Au, 2010). Whether this is a form of teacher self-censorship, censorship directly imposed by administrative policy, or censorship anchored in discourses of cynicism (see Agee, 2004), it can interrupt the project and processes of democratic social education.

To form a backdrop for my discussion of key contemporary strands in the tapestry of democratic social and citizenship education, in the ensuing section, I will describe what I mean by democracy and democratic education and suggest a few key challenges implicit in these definitions. While this discussion is neither comprehensive nor inclusive, it grounds, without pre-empting, the remainder of this chapter.

DEMOCRACY AND DEMOCRATIC SOCIAL EDUCATION

Because of its need to respond to existing interdependent realities, a genuine, fluid, and dynamic democracy is elusive. Its meanings are highly contested and vary from nation to nation, indeed from community to community, group to group and generation to generation. It is, at once, a political, social and, some would argue, economic process. It is "fragile and unstable" (Stanley, 2000, p. 69). At its foundation, however, democracy constitutes and is constituted by ways of being and living with others. With interconnectivity and dialogue at the core of his understanding of democracy, John Dewey argues that "a democracy is more than a form of government; it is primarily a mode of associated living, of conjoint communicated experience" (Dewey, 1916, p. 87). Parker also engages an associationist perspective when he suggests, as Banks (1996) writes in his Forward to *Educating the Democratic Mind*, that democracy is a mode of living with others "marked by popular sovereignty rather than authoritarianism, genuine cultural pluralism rather than oppression in the name of political unity, and a fundamental commitment to liberty, law, justice, and equality as the moral ground of social life" (p. xi). Also, consistent with Dewey's thinking, Stanley (2000) says that democracy is a way of life that requires "practical judgment" (pp. 69–72).

In the 1930s, as a reaction to the developing politics of assimilation, the intercultural education movement revitalized the term "cultural democracy." Then, as now, cultural freedom, or freedom to engage in one's primary culture, was fundamental to cultural democracy (Banks, 1997a). In tune with contemporary challenges, cultural democracy now refers to a social and political environment that respects, engages, and ultimately integrates diversity to develop expanded communities in pursuit of common interests (Pang, Gay, & Stanley, 1995; Welch, 1991). Adherents to the ideals of a cultural democracy believe that individuals and groups have a right to inhabit hybrid spaces, to be bicultural and multicultural in a pluralistic democracy.

Like democracy, democratic education cannot be defined in a static way. Rather it is a "way of being" and a moral imperative in classrooms that focus on understanding and improving interpersonal and intercultural relationships and the world condition (Dewey, 1916; Mitchell, 2001). According to Dewey (1916), education for democracy moves social relationships and a belief in the need for social change to the forefront.

> [O]ne cannot share in intercourse with others without learning—without getting a broader point of view and perceiving things of which one would otherwise be ignorant.... [T]he school becomes ... a miniature community and one in close interaction with other modes of associated experience beyond schools walls. (p. 360)

Often cited as a key challenge for educators is deciding whether democratic social education should emphasize patriotism and the knowledge needed to maintain the status quo or should promote citizenship for critical thinking and the transformation of selves and society (Hursh & Ross, 2000; Parker, 2003; Ross & Marker, 2009; Tupper, 2009). Because democratic educators and researchers often confront state and national standards that define social education more as an accumulation of knowledge to be assessed rather than a way to involve students as citizens of their communities, they must, with great resolve, allocate time for community building, active inquiry, deliberation, and social and political action. Another challenge is ensuring that students understand and act on the fact that this nation, and indeed the world, is both many and one. Students need opportunities to explore both our sameness and our difference. They need to see in the ubiquitous notion of community both *unity* and diversity and understand that the essence of community is *e pluribus unum*.

Democratic education also challenges the social educator to avoid universal ways of thinking, to challenge metanarratives, and to model with learners how to use informed critiques to negotiate shared understandings. Banks (1997a) wants teachers and students to challenge metanarratives, and especially those suggesting that we are a nation that consistently lives up to our political and social ideals. Finally educators and researchers of democratic education are summoned to create a conversation between national and global, world-centered perspectives. "It is critical that students learn from the knowledge and experiences of people who, because of their race, gender, class, culture, national origin, religious or political beliefs, are ignored, stereotyped, or marginalized" (Merryfield, 2001, p. 187).

INTERLACED STRANDS OF DEMOCRATIC EDUCATION IN THEORY, RESEARCH AND PRACTICE

Meeting the many challenges of a postmodern world, theory and research have generated four interlaced strands of transformative democratic social education. Together, these have the potential to create a new tapestry of hybrid meanings. *Inclusion* of students in democratic communities of inquiry and action is prominent particularly within discourses of diversity and dis/ability studies. Concern with *identity* has been a consistent theme in sociocultural and multicultural literature but is relatively new to discourses of democratic education (see Rubin, 2007). *Dialogue,* emerging in sociocultural and postmodernist theories, has the potential to transform the way we view discussion and seminars as democratic practices, and *deliberation* is a historically prominent construct within social education, one that is given a new twist when considered within feminist constructions of dialogue and democracy.

Inclusive Communities

As a concept integral to democratic social and citizenship education, inclusion is, at once, both simple and complex. Overwhelmingly researchers agree that it is a critical element in preparing students who have positive civic identities and who are willing to engage in civic activities for purposes of social justice (e.g., Buendia, Meacham, & Noffke, 2000; Flanagan, Stoppa, Syvertsen, & Stout, 2010; Flanagan, Cumsille, Gill, & Gallay, 2007; Noffke, 2000). Building inclusive communities begins with an awareness and willingness to act on students' need to belong, to make a positive contribution in reciprocal learning situations. An inclusive community is more however: it is an environment in which *all* students actively engage with each other; diversity is negotiated and integrated rather than used as a device for sorting, labeling, and differentiating students; and difference is a catalyst for critical inquiry, solidarity and praxis.

Bickmore (1993) sounded one of the earliest alerts to the complexity of inclusion for social educators. Based on her qualitative study of California classrooms, she found that teachers interpret inclusion in two ways: inclusion of students in dialogue and discussion and inclusion of knowledge drawn from diverse sociocultural positions. Parker (2008) offers a similar perspective of democratic citizenship education saying that it has two interconnected dimensions: political engagement and democratic enlightenment, suggesting that students need to "do" as well as "know" democracy. These interwoven ideas are intrinsic to my conceptualization of inclusive communities.

Contrary to popular conceptions of inclusive communities, I am not referring to classes designed specifically to support special education. *Inclusion*,[3] instead, suggests that we adhere to a broad definition, one that encompasses those who are outside the norm, as defined by the dominant group. Sapon-Shevin (1999) puts it this way: "Inclusion means we *all* belong; it means not having to fight for a chance to be part of a classroom or school community; it means that *all* children are accepted" (p. 4). [4] Villa and Thousand (2000) make this appropriate to social education. They argue that inclusion is a commitment to embracing *all* students and providing and protecting each member's inalienable right to be a fully participating member of the classroom community.[5] While neither Dewey nor his colleagues had in mind children who had serious learning disabilities—children who would had been labeled "retarded,"[6] he reminds us that the most essential function of schools is to train *all* children to be active participants in democratic communities. Thus schools should be constituted so that "[t] he intermingling of . . . different races, differing religions, and unlike customs creates for all a new and broader environment" (Dewey, 1916, p. 21).

Schools and classrooms that function like mini-democracies begin by constructing inclusive communities. Acknowledging the argument that community and democracy may not always be mutually supportive and that our nation and schools can be constituted by competing communities (Perlstein, 1996), I define a community as a group of people who are united by a common purpose with the contributions of each member being valued, respected, weighed and negotiated in ways that galvanize the group's identity.

As an ideal, school communities promote an ethic of caring and interpersonal responsibility, positive interaction and interdependence among students. Howard (2001) asserts that building "connection" is essential to democratic communities. Having a sense of "connection" generates a "common link and lasting bond between individuals" (p. 524). Building reciprocal trust and a belief that we are all in this together promotes members' interdependence and especially their sense of mutual responsibility (Santora, 2003). To do this, democratic social educators need to provide opportunities within the curriculum for students to connect their autobiographical experiences with the experiences of others in, as well as outside, their educational communities. This allows learners, including teachers committed to learning with their students, to construct new understandings of themselves and their roles in these communities (Hemings, 2000).

Learning, Constructing and Listening to Identity

Long excluded from discourses of democratic citizenship education and community building has been the idea of cultural, social, and transnational identities (Houser & Kuzmic, 2001). Democratic social educators and researchers need to understand and plan within complex, multiple, situated and shifting identities. Young people reciprocally create meaning and construct identities, a sense of who they are in the world, using a variety of dynamic, context-specific markers including ethnicity, language, family history, nationality, religion, race, class, gender, ability and sexual orientation (Asher, 2005; Houser & Kuzmic, 2001; Rubin, 2007; Santora, 2003). The overlapping nature of these is distinct for students from different groups. In classroom communities, culturally and socioeconomically diverse learners frequently encounter challenging spaces where their cultural and racial identities and ways of knowing meet, are disturbed and perhaps even shifted by perspectives that differ from their own (Santora, 2007). Identity formation is thus a continual process of negotiating and resolving conflicting experiences.

To sustain them through these shifts, learners need to listen and learn deeply about self and others—developing a profound sense of their multiple, complex and connected identities. This means: 1) affirming who they are and how they are connected to their immediate as well as enduring social and institutional contexts, 2) understanding that identity formation is a dynamic multi-faceted process, 3) seeing their lived experiences as intricately connected to the experiences of others, and 4) realizing that others may impose socially constructed identities on them.[7]

For educators and researchers this means two things. First they should deconstruct their own identities to better understand the hybrid spaces where cultures, histories, and geographies intersect. They need to understand how, even though they may work for social transformation, they are also part of the systems and structures they wish to expose (Asher, 2005). Second, they are obliged to place student experiences and the sharing of those experiences at the center of research and learning. Such a move pushes both at the barriers that have consistently isolated some students and the boundaries of traditional social and citizenship education. Learners' shared understandings of the connections between their own lives and the lives of those about them are fundamental to the development of empathy, cross-cultural competency, communicative ethics, hybridity and the skills necessary for critical, participative and transformative citizenship in a culturally diverse society and interdependent world.

Within our challenging demographic landscapes, centering students' voices means listening to, probing, and piecing together their everyday stories, for the hybrid narratives that reveal who they are. This is not just a project for the researcher but is one for all community members. Probing social, cultural, and civic identities means recognizing, as DuBois (1903/1989) did, the possibility that students have a double consciousness,[8] or a transnational, transcultural or hybrid identity. Many children, particularly children of color, ethnic minorities, and children living in poverty, grow up looking at the world almost exclusively through the lenses of family, neighborhood and popular cultures while also engaging with people and institutions that represent the dominant culture. To hear their voices and understand the meaning of living in multiple realities, Merryfield (2001) suggests that teachers avail themselves of opportunities to move within and across cultures, experiencing the borderlands so that they might assist students in doing the same.

Taking up discourses of diverse civic identities is particularly important in social and citizenship education classes. In her study of civic identity and its development and engagement in diverse school communities, Rubin (2007) found that secondary students from a predominantly white, middle-class school generally had experiences that were congruent with democratic ideals; however the lived experiences of many students, particularly students of color from low income communities, conflicted with what they were learning in school about American ideals. This echoes Epstein's (2000) interpretive study in which she found that students' sociocultural backgrounds, specifically their racialized identities, significantly influenced their reactions to historical pictures related to race relations in American history. She also asserts that adolescents' ideas about national history influence the beliefs and the meanings they attach to democracy and equality (Epstein, 1998). Thus attention to students' context-influenced identities as well as dialogic involvement with relevant political and historical issues may assist them to become more reflective about their interconnected worldviews. It may also help them to see themselves as interrelated actors in local and global affairs—a necessary precursor to civic growth and solidarity.

Creating hybrid democratic spaces in classrooms signifies moving beyond particularistic thinking about identity to understand the commingling of cultures and texts in shaping identities. Those who work in the area of democratic social and citizenship education need, therefore, to facilitate not only superficial perspective takings but also a critical understanding of the contextualized and mediated ways in which we think about and construct who we are as well as who the other is.

Dialogue

According to Darling-Hammond (1997), "Repairing the torn social fabric that increasingly arrays one group against another will require creating an inclusive social dialogue in which individuals can converse from a public space that brings together diverse experiences and points of view" (p. 6).

Dialogue is defined as a communicative act between or among multiple participants and/or texts. Burbules (1993) writes that the dialogic encounter is both symbiotic and synergistic and "participants are *caught up*; they are *absorbed*" (p. 21). To prepare students as other-centered citizens, educators also need to move dialogue to the center of their instructional practices, creating a third space where students mingle their voices and their emotions with each other's and with the content of social education. We can learn much about preparing students as citizens who engage in dialogue and public discourse from Bakhtin's (1981) literary theory and Freire's (1970) *Pedagogy of the Oppressed.*

Deriving his beliefs from religious and aesthetic definitions of dialogue, Bakhtin posits that dialogue, as an intersubjective and ethical engagement, is primarily a transformative exercise (Hirschkop, 1999). Occurring during the reading of virtually any type of text, auditory, visual, or kinesthetic, it is much more than discussion; it is a deep engagement with texts where understanding and response "are dialectically merged and mutually condition each other" (Hirschkop, 1999, p. 282). Within the dialogic process teachers and students need to be particularly mindful of the concept of *heteroglossia* or diverse and sometimes contradictory social viewpoints or voices orchestrated within a given text. Given this, any text is thus the reflection of previous texts in dialogue with each other, the writer/speaker/artist, and the reader—that is they embody and anticipate polyvocality.

Dialogue is not only intertextual, it is also interpersonal. Using a Bakhtinian (1986) perspective means creating hybrid spaces for educators and students to engage in "active responsive understanding" (p. 71) as they seek empathy with each other's worldviews. This means that no one Discourse (see Gee, 1999) or metanarrative can dominate classroom dialogue. Authentic dialogue within zones of cultural contact takes into account the multiple and complex cultural connotations of words as well as the context in which those words are used and their meanings are negotiated and, in doing so, helps students to develop critical, reflexive thinking skills needed for transformative participation in a pluralistic world. According to Stewart (2010), culturally responsive pedagogy (see Gay, 2000) provides a means through which teachers can orchestrate the heteroglossia of culturally and racially diverse classrooms. While this is no easy task, Freire (2005) says, "It is in experiencing the differences that we discover ourselves as individuals" (p. 127).

Freire (1970) helps us to see this in the context of critical democratic citizenship education when he says that there can be no true dialogue without *praxis.* "Thus, to speak a true word is to transform the world" (p. 68); the rest of what humans say is "idle chatter" (p. 68), or words deprived of reflection and action and words intended only to denounce, not transform, the world. Dialogue takes students beyond experiencing and into reflection on the meaning of experience thus having the potential to change each individual's frames of reference.

Authentic dialogue is the encounter of people committed to the "common task of learning and acting" (Freire, 1970, p. 71). It is the practice of equity and democracy; it exists within a community that shares a belief in the ability of humankind to engage in the existential process of becoming. It is a "horizontal relationship" of mutual trust and hope that cannot exist without a critical consciousness, a sense of one's relationship to the world and one's power, one's social responsibility, to create and re-create its cultures in more democratized ways. Educators and researchers cannot engage in true dialogue with students without first tearing down the barriers of dominance and authority that accompany banking models of education. Students cannot engage in dialogue with each other until they remove barriers of status and privilege based on perceived hierarchies of individual difference (see Cohen, 1986/1994). Dialogue would, thus, be an essential precursor to that which, in the parlance of citizenship education, is called deliberation.

Deliberation

Deliberation is often presented as a genre of discussion, but it would seem to be more than that. Gutman (1987) suggests that the primary goal of democratic education should be to prepare students for and engage them in deliberation while Mansbridge (1991) reminds us that in ancient times, democracy *was* deliberative democracy. Often considered the basic activity of democratic communities, deliberation is the principle means through which democratic ideals are advanced. Supported by dialogue, deliberation forges relationships as students work together to study and unravel the threads of a shared problem, engage in real value conflicts, articulate diverse and creative possibilities, disentangle the knots of different perspectives, decide on a fair and informed course of action, and make a collective moral commitment to that action. Going beyond Parker's (2008) definition, this definition suggests that deliberation is enlightened political engagement.

In their definitions of *deliberation*, many educators have emphasized it as a discussion strategy for collective argumentation guided by principles of evidence and counter-evidence, logic, coherency, respectful debate, and reflective and informed judgment with the possibility that participants might modify their original stance (see Preskill, 1997). These definitions may focus on equal participation and a full-range of perspectives resulting in a "rationally motivated consensus" (Gastill, 1993, p. 25). The nested way through which these definitions of *deliberation* have evolved, however, comes with cautionary notes. Brice (2002) suggests an emphasis on the rules and procedures of deliberation may actually inhibit the impromptu nature of deliberative talk or the way that students naturally interact with each other. It may also circumvent the complexity of deep involvement with the disparate texts and multiple perspectives of controversial public issues. Mansbridge (1991) also cautions us to guard against deliberation becoming a "mask for domination," or "subtle forms of control" (p. 123) where subordinate groups either cannot find a voice with which to speak, or when they do, they are not heard. Research in K-12 classrooms lends credence to this belief (e.g., Beck, 2003; Brice, 2002; Hemings, 2000; Santora, 2007). Mary Parker Follett writing in the first half of the 20th century, promoted the idea of collaborative power, favoring the deliberate integration of ideas over compromise. In "compromise" she saw winners and losers; in integration she saw unity without uniformity (Mansbridge, 1991). Walter Parker seems to confirm this when he says that a deliberative democracy would encourage its citizens to think "with and across their differences" (Parker, 2008, p. 71), and Mansbridge (1991) reinforces it when she says that deliberation should push participants to think about their self-interest differently—to see their own interests tied to the broader interests of the community, to "transform 'I' into 'we'" (p. 123). Parker (2003) writes that "... deliberation is not only a means to an end, but an end in itself, for it creates a particular kind of democratic public culture among the deliberators" (p. 80). It is an important means through which students learn and develop as individuals and as a group.

From the perspective of critical theory, including feminist theories, integrating or synthesizing ideas in equitable and socially just ways implies having a critical consciousness. Too often "critical thinking" is framed within theories of liberal democratic education as the ability to distinguish the illogicality of arguments or errors in the process of making rational judgments. While these may be very useful skills, and certainly should not be lightly dismissed, critical theorists argue that they are often an attempt to purge emotional thinking from public spaces. I suggest, instead, that deliberation should foster a healthy balance between emotional sensitivity and critical thinking. Freire (1970) helps us to understand this when he discusses the difference between problem solving, which he says is the stance taken by technocrats, and problematizing, which is critical engagement with the historical, cultural, social and political realities within which we live. I prefer, therefore, to use the concept of critical consciousness which refers to the goal of problematization—that of deep investigation resulting in a profound understanding of one's own place or role in the human condition and a willingness to intervene in its unveiled reality. Essential to this is the ability to grapple with questions not only of power and authority in society but also of life purposes, human dignity, freedom, and social responsibility (Kegan, 1982; Kincheloe, 2001). Thus just as dialogue is an existential necessity, to be in the world, having a critical consciousness ties one to the need to act on that world.

One of the primary goals of deliberation, according to Mansbridge (1991), is solidarity, which she defines as "principled commitment" (p. 130).

> Good deliberation produces, along with good solutions, the emotional and intellectual resources to accept hard decisions....Deliberation that accords respect to all participants and rests outcomes on reasons and points of view that stand up under questioning generates outcomes that even opponents can respect. (p.125)

In this reconceptualization of *deliberation* we find a way to raise students' consciousness about social injustices as well as to encourage them to engage in emancipatory or transformative action (Freire, 1970). Meant to free students to define themselves as individuals and as a group and to see and act in unity with their place in the world, deliberation has the potential to become an egalitarian and collective pedagogy of hope and possibilities.

HYBRID POSSIBILITIES

As a focal point in thinking about the nexus of social, citizenship, multicultural and global education, *hybridity* is an ubiquitous concept residing in a number of disciplines and theoretical perspectives. Largely supported by sociocultural, poststructural and postcolonial theory, it provides a heuristic for pushing at boundaries and opening up spaces for dialogue and deliberation across the conflict-ridden territory of shared citizenship. In educational settings, it is most often used to characterize complex understandings that result from the intentional process of construction and reconstruction of knowledge through dialogue. However *hybrid* also refers to the ideas themselves—ideas that are intentionally constructed in a classroom as well as the protracted, destabilizing and unintentionally generated ideas that result from practical ideational negotiation within the daily contact zones of difference and conflict (Gutierrez, Baquedano-López, Alvarez, & Chiu, 1999; Ladson-Billings, 2005; McCarthy, 2005; Pratt, 1991). The uses of hybridity that most closely align with democratic social education are those in discourses of global citizenship and postcolonial theory where hybridity refers to the mingling of concepts and ideas that emerge from "conflict, accommodation, borrowing, and rethinking across diverse people's experiences, knowledge and world views" (Merryfield, 2001, p. 189). As such, understanding hybrid practices enriches our understanding of the dialogism between unity and diversity.

As a concept that defies dichotomies and self/other distinctions, hybridity may provide a key to constructing a more stable democracy and supporting it through the consistent, yet critical, integration of multiple perspectives of students, teachers, researchers and texts. It is not a matter of finding the one best approach; rather, hybridity challenges us to value variation and push for the inclusion of multiple theories and traditions as we attempt to adjust to the needs of all learners. Hybridity is, therefore, a rich construct for reconstructing a field that has been moribund with didactic methods, claims of universal knowledge, and beliefs about the superiority of Eurocentric ideals. In this chapter, the simple idea of connecting discourses of liberal citizenship education, critical multiculturalism, critical pedagogy, disabilities studies, literary theory, and critical global education and bringing them to the problem of redefining democratic social education calls for the construction of a hybrid theoretical lens for organizing research and learning.

The tapestry created by weaving the strands of inclusion, identity, dialogue, and deliberation together is replete with layers of explanations that ask scholars and democratic educators to consider classrooms as hybrid spaces that merge often-conflicting cultures and perspectives from school, home, neighborhoods, and popular culture. These hybrid spaces bring together different knowledges, identities, discourses, relationships and resources. In conceptualizing hybrid spaces, Moje et al. (2004) write that, "people in any given community draw on multiple resources or funds to make sense of the world." She goes on to note that "being 'in-between' (Bhabha, 1994, p. 1) several different funds of knowledge and Discourse can be both productive and constraining in terms of one's literate, social, and cultural practices—and ultimately one's identity development" (p. 42).

Torres-Guzmán (2011) asks these questions: "How can we reconstruct citizenship in ways that entertain the cultural and linguistic hybridities of different communities? How might this open up spaces for the different communities to participate in civil societies" (p. 10). Educators and researchers need to model the creation of third spaces of openness and fluidity where learners give free rein to the messiness of reworking ideas. Our hope is that this will encourage the emergence of hybrid or expanded dispositions and understandings of what it means to be a participant in a democratic community of social learners. However, many well-intentioned and otherwise competent democratic educators and researchers are stymied in the process of constructing these spaces. While I neither have the answers nor do I want to offer prescriptive methods for how to make room for hybridity, I think that the integration of aesthetics into democratic social and citizenship education suggests possibilities and the hope that we can promote a more inclusive, hybrid democracy and interdependent world.

Aesthetics, coming to us largely through philosophy of education and educational theory, emphasizes the oneness felt with texts and with audiences and the ways in which this can evoke personal change. It has the potential to create hybrid spaces for the practice of what it means to be a world citizen with democratic forbearance. Dewey (1934), Slattery (1995), Greene (n.d.), and Eisner (1991) urge us to consider engaging students in aesthetic experiences, experiences that emphasize the intersubjective quality of all meaning and foster better interpersonal understanding, hybrid perspectives and a deep sense of identity consciousness. Dewey (1934), perhaps, offers the most cogent rationale for aesthetics in democratic social education when he writes, "In the end, works of art are the only media of complete and unhindered communication between man and man [sic]" (p. 105). Viewing or participating in deep ways avails students of an intersubjective experience.

Let's contemplate, for a moment, how important intersubjectivity is to democratic social education. In describing Bakhtin's stance, Hirschkop (1999) writes that "intersubjectivity and the experiences of solidarity, fulfillment and the integrity of a life story [are] essential to a civil form of existence" (p. 42); and Greene (n.d.) tells us that "those who can engage reflectively and authentically with the arts may be awakened in startling ways to the scars and flaws of our society and may be awakened to transform" (p. 1). Essential to aesthetics for democratic citizenship in a pluralistic world is an emphasis on the personal change that takes place as a result of the aesthetic engagement, the feeling of solidarity, or oneness with the "artist," as well as with others who engage, in community, with the art form (Cherryholmes, 1994, p. 16). Implicitly considering art as a metaphor for texts that have the power to elicit deep engagement, Slattery (1995) characterizes the aesthetic experience as follows:

> [It is] the experience of disturbance, perturbation, contemporaneousness, or synthetical moments [that] will inspire students to read, to research, to explore, to learn, to meditate, and to expand their understanding of the initial experience. It will also ignite a passion for justice and compassion. (p. 214)

This is not easy and the best of educators miss opportunities for aesthetic engagement. Simon (2001), studying classes in a variety of school settings, puts forth the idea that young people, by their very nature, need opportunities and encouragement to respond deeply, critically and aesthetically to relevant moral and existential questions that arise in the course of articulated school curricula. Through her analysis of moral discussions in science, English, and social studies classes, however, she finds that teachers place boundaries around discussions that often prevent students from deep engagement with each other, with texts and thus deep immersion in moral issues. In my own study of collaboration in a culturally diverse seventh grade, I found that the teacher's cultural identity, her lack of professional preparation, prescriptive teaching orientation, inadequate modeling and contradictory professional frameworks stood in the way of her intention to foster deep democratic engagement (Santora, 2000).

Emphasizing the interconnections between aesthetics, diversity, and social action, Tyson (2002) describes the importance of young people aesthetically experiencing culturally relevant literature to the collective formation of a critical, social and civic consciousness and active civic identities. The participants in her study consistently connected written texts with their lived experiences and discussed social change in their families, classroom, and communities; they developed a sense of how this could change their futures. As a result of their deep dialogic engagement, students were inspired to create their own "laboratory of social justice" (Peterson as cited in Tyson, 2002), an after-school club that encouraged them to see themselves as agents of social change and thereby, to develop a positive civic identity.

The power of aesthetics for deep democratic citizenship education is profoundly evident in the performance aspect of the "Opportunity Gap" Project documented in *Echoes of Brown* (Fine, 2004). For the second year of their summer institute, project leaders recruited a "radically diverse" group of thirteen young people interested in writing, performing arts, and social in/justice. Following the lure of performance scholarship, these students not only addressed the history of *Brown v. Board of Education* and issues of power, privilege and structural practices that support oppression, but also created a place where their multiple identities collectively, collaboratively, and comfortably became part of a tapestry of original research. Youth used their specific perspectives and talents to write, choreograph and perform hybrid artistic representations of their findings and conclusions. They involved their audiences in spoken-word poetry and stunned them with a powerful multimedia performance. Students and researchers as well as the content they studied were transformed through engagement with critical history, structural inequality, and the performing arts. Thus developing a transformative consciousness within the context of democratic social and citizenship education is both something students learn and something they do in aesthetic engagement with literature, the arts, and relevant social, political, moral and existential questions.

In each of these cases, students entered into rich dialogue and reconceptualized deliberation to arrive at hybrid solutions to persisting problems. They subsequently undertook collective action that led to a transformative consciousness—one that identified with the challenges of social justice. They fulfilled the promises of democratic social education by "being with each other in an inquiry, about being in and creating hybridity ..." (Torres-Guzmán, 2011, p. 4).

IMPLICATIONS AND CONCLUSIONS

Because social and citizenship education should be grounded in social and global learning and interaction that immerses students in the world around them, it can potentially shape the future in transformative ways. Educators who consistently pursue a hybrid democratic model need an open curriculum that acknowledges the important role of students in its co-development. As the starting point for critical inquiry, learners need opportunities to explore their connections with others and to use those connections to give meaning to their own identities. The mutual responsibility, then, of teachers, researchers, and students is to create spaces where everyone shares his or her voice and experiences and actively invites others to engage in dialogue and deliberation. However, creating hybrid spaces where students can both learn the ideals of and participate as citizens in a transformative democracy within an institutional context of segregation, homogeneity, ability grouping, high levels of accountability, and systemic sociopolitical conflict is not easy. Those who are committed democratic educators need to be relentless in their attention to the tangled processes of democratic education and especially to the strands discussed in this chapter: 1) engaging ALL learners in interactive ways; 2) putting learners' experiences and identities at the forefront of the curriculum; 3) using reflexive questioning strategies that model deep dialogic and inclusive engagement between learners and learners and texts; 4) providing opportunities for learners to engage in dialogic inquiry and deliberation; and 5) making room for aesthetic praxis with its potential for creating hybrid spaces that can transform participants' worlds.

This research interweaves progressive citizenship education, critical multicultural education, critical pedagogy and postcolonial global perspectives. In the process it has reached beyond these theoretical positions to find a shared space—one that provides opportunities for learners to practice the intentional negotiation of ideas in collective, collaborative and deliberative settings, to recognize the unintentional ideational negotiations that have helped to shape their civic perspectives and identities and to use these understandings to change their world.

Prior to this, little has been done within the field of social studies and citizenship education that explores either third or hybrid spaces in classrooms, and this is especially unsettling when we consider significant studies in literacy (e.g., Gutierrez, Baquedano-López, Alvarez, & Chiu, 1999), and science (e.g., Barton, Tan, & Rivet, 2008). Exceptions to this, however, include Brice's (2002) study of small group deliberative discourse. Using a sociolinguistic lens she analyzes intertextual talk related to global issues finding that, in democratic discourse, students negotiated how knowledge is viewed, the value attached to intertextual connections, and the rhetoric

that is most appropriate for presenting findings. In the process of their deliberations, students appropriated and linked information from a variety of
school-based and outside sources. While this study explores the third spaces
of learning in classrooms and epistemological negotiation and acknowledges that the negotiation of social norms is an important part of deliberative
discourse, it falls short of looking at the intercultural ways in which students
negotiate meaning. It is essentially, as the title says, about "task, text, and
talk." Rubin, in her study of students engaged in large-group discussions
of key documents in understanding American civic ideals, also falls short
of looking at the inclusive nature of deliberation. Finally because Tyson's
study was centered on African American students, while quite informative
about the creation of hybrid spaces that bring institutional and personal
contexts together, it sheds little light on the ways in which heterogeneity
shapes deliberative discourse. None of these studies truly focuses on the hybrid nature of cultures, identities, epistemologies, knowledge, tasks, texts,
and talk.

This review, then, and its focus on inclusion, identity, dialogue, deliberation, and hybridity suggest a number of nascent areas for future research.
Most important, would be the need to inquire into the ways in which learners, including their teachers, negotiate intercultural understandings in
small and large group deliberations both in classrooms and in extracurricular civic projects. It seems vital to explore how participants engage in
cross-ability, cross-cultural, cross-ethnic, cross-racial, cross-gender and cross-
class dialogue, negotiation and deliberation. When teachers attempt to
create democratic, heterogeneous, hybrid spaces in their classrooms, what
do these spaces look like? In those spaces, how do participants give meaning to a range of texts? What interactions actually occur? How do students
attach meanings to those interactions? What are students learning about
our democratic ideals? What are they learning about how to participate
in democratic deliberations? How are students with different abilities and
from different ethnicities, races, genders, sexualities, and classes included
in these spaces? Or are they included? How do the interactions and negotiations, which transpire within these deliberations, shape student identities?
Not all situations present deliberation in its best light. What are the flaws?
What conditions lie beneath the flaws and what can we learn from the flaws
and the conditions that support them? These are but a few of the burning
questions.

As I have already said, I hope this review suggests more—that it will elicit
experiences, initiate intense conversations, and stimulate creative thinking
about actions that will move us beyond traditional methods of promoting
democratic social and citizenship education. I also hope that it will promote democratic social and citizenship education that attends locally and
globally to the creation of hybrid spaces where learners share who they are,

listen intently to the personal narratives of others, understand how their stories are interlaced, and develop collective narratives or hybrid stories of their interconnected experiences. It is also my hope that they will use their shared understandings to engage in participative citizenship and especially to pursue the work of social justice.

Because democracy is situated in social and global interaction, social education teachers and researchers play a distinct role in forging its future. Their role is to respond to the dynamic and complex reality of democracy and to create spaces for students' voices, orchestrate students' experiences, use reflexive questioning strategies, involve students in collaborative inquiry and problem solving that focuses on recognizing and acting in opposition to hierarchical and colonial relationships, disrupt ethnocentric and hegemonic ways of knowing, and expand student understanding of what it means to be part of a pluralistic democratic community and to act as responsible citizens of an interdependent world community.

NOTES

1. Reflexive interrogation is introspection that piques awareness of how status hierarchies and social positions shape the way people view their worlds.

2. I recognize the overwhelming need to globalize our understanding of democracy and democratic education. However in order to provide a more focused review, I have purposely chosen to limit my discussion to theory, research and teaching situated within the United States.

3. Italics throughout this paragraph are mine and where they lie within quotations, do not appear in the originals.

4. Emphasis is my own and does not appear in the original.

5. I recognize that more conventional definitions are used in mainstream theories and research related to democratic education, however many multiculturalists are embracing a broader definition that includes not only those of different races, ethnicities, genders, and sexual orientations, but also those with different academic needs and abilities (see Sleeter & Grant, 1994, p. 181). This seems imperative because: 1) those with different abilities are marginalized by the more "normal" in society (Abberley, 1987); 2) students who have demonstrated lower academic achievement are tracked into mind-numbing classes that emphasize rote memorization (Oakes, 1985); 3) multiple intelligence theory draws our attention to the diverse ways in which people are "intelligent" (Gardner, 1993); 4) research and theory related to inclusive practices

shift our perspective from one that focuses on disability to one that looks at all students as having different needs and abilities (see, e.g., Hoeft & Santora, 2008); 5) PL 94-142, while still quite controversial, requires that all students be educated within the least restrictive environments; 6) about 90 percent of all students classified as disabled are only mildly disabled (Banks, 1997b); 7) more and more students with disabilities are included in general education settings; and 8) most important, inclusion of *all* makes classrooms true microcosms of our pluralistic democracy (see Dewey, 1916).

6. During late 19th and early 20th centuries, medical texts began to describe children with "retarded mental development," "retarded children" and "mentally retarded patients." By the mid-20th Century, this was considered the appropriate way to sort and name children with special learning needs. Despite compulsory education laws that had been in place since 1918, many children with disabilities were routinely excluded from public schools.

7. For more on how learners internalize identities that others have already assigned to them see *Learning Identity: The Joint Emergence of Social Identification and Academic Learning* (Wortham, 2006). Cohen (1986/1994) also speaks to this, although she places it within the construct of "status."

8. DuBois (1903/1989) says this about double consciousness: "It is a peculiar sensation, this double-consciousness, this sense of always looking at one's self through the eyes of others, of measuring one's soul by the tape of a world that looks on in amused contempt and pity. One ever feels his twoness—an American, a Negro; two souls, two thoughts, two unreconciled strivings..." (p. 5). One impulse pulls for a person to become part of the mainstream society and the other to reject it. Today, the term is used to describe a person whose identity has different and sometimes contradictory facets.

REFERENCES

Abberley, P. (1987). The concept of oppression and the development of a social theory of disability. *Disability, Handicap, and Society, 2,* 5–20.

Agee, J. (2004). Negotiating a teaching identity: An African American teacher's struggle to teach in test-driven contexts. *Teachers College Record, 106*(4), 747–774.

Apple, M. W. (1993). *Official knowledge: Democratic education in a conservative age.* New York: Routledge.

Asher, N. (2005). At the interstices: Engaging postcolonial and feminist perspectives for a multicultural education pedagogy in the South. *Teachers College Record, 107*(5), 1079–1106.

Au, W. (2007). High-stakes testing and curricular control: A qualitative metasynthesis. *Educational Researcher, 36*(5), 258–267.

Au, W. (2009a). *Unequal by design: High stakes testing and the standardization of inequality.* New York: Routledge.

Au, W. (2009b). High stakes testing and discursive control: The triple bind for non-standard student identities. *Multicultural Perspectives, 11*(2), 65–71.

Au, W. (2010). The idiocy of policy: The anti-democratic curriculum of high-stakes testing. *Critical Education, 1*(1), 1–15.

Bai, M. (2010, July 24). Race: Still too hot to touch. *New York Times.* Retrieved July 25, 2010, from *http://www.nyt.com*

Bakhtin, M. M. (1981). *The dialogic imagination: Four essays by M.M. Bakhtin* (C. Emerson & M. Holquist, Trans.). Austin: University of Texas Press.

Bakhtin, M. M. (1986). The problem of speech genres (V. McGee, Trans.). In C. Emerson & M. Holquist (Eds.), *Speech genres and other late essays* (pp. 60–102). Austin, TX: University of Texas Press.

Banks, J. A. (1996). Forward. In W. C. Parker (Ed.), *Educating the democratic mind* (pp. xi–xiii). Albany, NY: State University of New York Press.

Banks, J. A. (1997a). *Educating citizens in a multicultural society.* New York: Teachers College Press.

Banks, J. A. (Ed.). (1997b). *Multicultural education: Issues and perspectives* (3rd ed.). Boston: Allyn and Bacon.

Barton, A. C., Tan, E., & Rivet, A. (2008). Creating hybrid spaces for engaging school science among urban middle school girls. *American Educational Research Journal, 45*(1), 68–103.

Beane, J., & Apple, M.W. (Eds.). (1995). *Democratic schools.* Alexandria, VA: Association for Supervision and Curriculum Development.

Beck, T. A. (2003). "If He Murdered Someone, He Shouldn't Get a Lawyer": Engaging young children in civics deliberation. *Theory and Research in Social Education, 31*(3), 326–346.

Bhabha, H. K. (1994). *The location of culture.* New York: Routledge.

Bickmore, K. (1993). Learning inclusion/inclusion in learning: Citizenship education for a pluralistic society. *Theory and Research in Social Education, 21*(4), 341–384.

Bigelow, B. (1999). Why standardized tests threaten multiculturalism. *Educational Leadership, 56*(7), 37–40.

Brice, L. (2002). Deliberative discourse enacted: Task, text, and talk. *Theory and Research in Social Education, 30*(1), 66–87.

Buendia, E., Meacham, S., & Noffke, S. E. (2000). Community, displacement and inquiry. In D. W. Hursh & E. W. Ross (Eds.), *Democratic social education: Social studies for social change* (pp. 166–188). New York: Falmer Press.

Burbules, N. C. (1993). *Dialogue in teaching.* New York: Teachers College Press.

Cherryholmes, C. H. (1988). *Power and criticism: Poststructural investigations in education.* New York: Teachers College Press.

Cherryholmes, C. H. (1994). More notes on pragmatism. *Educational Researcher, 23*(1), 16–18.

Cohen, E. G. (1986/1994). *Designing groupwork: Strategies for the heterogeneous classroom* (2nd ed.). New York: Teachers College Press.

Crocco, M. S., & Davis, O. L. (Eds.). (2002). *Building a legacy: Women in social education, 1784–1984.* Washington, D.C.: National Council for the Social Studies.

Crocco, M. S., & Davis, O. L., Jr. (Eds.). (1999). *"Bending the future to their will": Civic women, social education and democracy.* Lanham, MD: Roman & Littlefield.

Darling-Hammond, L. (1997). *The right to learn: A blueprint for creating schools that work.* San Francisco: Jossey-Bass.

Dewey, J. (1916). *Democracy and education.* New York: Free Press.

Dewey, J. (1934). *Art as experience.* New York: Minton, Balch and Company.

DuBois, W. E. B. (1903/1989). *The souls of black folks.* New York: Penguin Group.

Eisner, E. (1991). *The enlightened eye: Qualitative inquiry and the enhancement of educational practice.* New York: Macmillan.

Epstein, T. (1998). Deconstructing differences in African American and European American adolescents' perspectives on U.S. history. *Curriculum Inquiry, 28,* 397–423.

Epstein, T. (2000). Adolescents' perspectives on racial diversity in U.S. history: Case studies from an urban classroom. *American Educational Research Journal, 37*(1), 185–214.

Fine, M. (2004). Introduction. In M. Fine, R. A. Roberts & M. E. Torre (Eds.), *Echoes of Brown, 50 Years Later: A spoken word, dance, and video performance* (Vol. 2010). New York: Teachers College Press.

Flanagan, C., Stoppa, T., Syvertsen, A. K., & Stout, M. (2010). School and social trust. In L. R. Sherrod, J. Torney-Purta, & C. A. Flanagan (Eds.), *Handbook of research on civic engagement of youth* (pp. 307–330). New York: John Wiley and Sons.

Flanagan, C. A., Cumsille, P., Gill, S., & Gallay, L. S. (2007). School and community climates and civic commitments: Patterns for ethnic minority and majority students. *Journal of Educational Psychology, 99*(2), 421–431.

Freire, P. (1970). *Pedagogy of the oppressed.* New York: Continuum.

Freire, P. (2005). *Teachers as cultural workers: Letters to those who dare teach.* Boulder, CO: Westview Press.

Gardner, H. (1993). *Multiple intelligences: The theory in practice.* New York: Basic Books.

Gastill, J. (1993). *Democracy in small groups.* Philadelphia: New Society Publishers.

Gay, G. (2000). *Culturally responsive teaching: Theory, research, and practice.* New York: Teachers College Press.

Gay, G. (2007). The rhetoric and reality of NCLB. *Race, Ethnicity, and Education, 10*(3), 279–293.

Gee, J. P. (1999). *An introduction to discourse analysis: Theory and method.* New York: Routledge.

Giroux, H. (1988). *Teachers as intellectuals: Toward a critical pedagogy of learning.* Hadley, MA: Bergin & Garvey.

Grant, S. G. (2007). High-stakes testing: How are social studies teachers responding. *Social Education, 71*(5), 250–254.

Greene, M. (n.d.). Democratic vistas: Renewing a perspective. Retrieved May 28, 2010, from *http://www.maxinegreene.org/articles.php*

Gutierrez, K. D., Baquedano-López, P., Alvarez, H. H., & Chiu, M. M. (1999). Building a culture of collaboration through hybrid language practices. *Theory into Practice, 38,* 87–93.

Gutman, A. (1987). *Democratic education.* Princeton: Princeton University Press.

Hemings, A. (2000). High school democratic dialogues: Possibilities for praxis. *American Educational Research Journal, 37*(1), 67–91.

Hirschkop, K. (1999). *Mikhail Bakhtin: An aesthetic for democracy.* New York: Oxford University Press.

Hoeft, D. (2007). *Educational practices within smaller learning environments: A qualitative inquiry of including all learners in a high school career academy.* Unpublished doctoral dissertation, University of Rochester, Rochester, NY.

Hoeft, D., & Santora, E. (2008, April). *Practicing academic, civic, and social responsibility in an inclusive school-within-school career academy class.* Paper presented at the annual meeting of the American Educational Research Association, New York, NY. Retrieved July 7, 2010, from http://www.rochester.edu/warner/papers/index.html

Houser, N. O., & Kuzmic, J. J. (2001). Ethical citizenship in a postmodern world: Toward a more connected approach to social education for the twenty-first century. *Theory and Research in Social Education, 29*(3), 431–461.

Howard, T. C. (2001). Connection and democracy. *Theory and Research in Social Education, 29*(3), 524–531.

Hursh, D. W., & Ross, E. W. (Eds.). (2000). *Democratic social education: Social studies for social change.* New York: Falmer Press.

Jones, G. M., Jones, B. D., & Hargrove, T. Y. (2003). *The unintended consequences of high-stakes testing.* New York: Rowman & Littlefield.

Jones, M. G., Jones, B. D., Hardin, B., Chapman, L., Yarbrough, T., & Davis, M. (1999). Impact of high-stakes testing on teachers and students in North Carolina [Electronic Version]. *Phi Delta Kappan,* 81, 199–203. Retrieved September 26, 2010, from http://www.questia.com.

Kegan, R. (1982). *The evolving self: Problem and process in human development.* Cambridge, MA: Harvard University Press.

Kincheloe, J. L. (2001). *Getting beyond the facts: Teaching social studies/social sciences in the twenty-first century* (2nd. ed.). New York: Peter Lang.

Ladson-Billings, G. (2004). Culture versus citizenship. In J. A. Banks (Ed.), *Diversity and citizenship education: Global perspectives* (pp. 99–126). San Francisco: Jossey-Bass.

Ladson-Billings, G., & Donnor, J. (2005). The moral activist role of critical race theory scholarship. In N. K. Denzin & Y. Lincoln (Eds.), *The Sage handbook of qualitative research* (3rd ed., pp. 279–301). Thousand Oaks, CA: Sage Publications.

Mansbridge, J. (1991). Democracy, deliberation, & the experience of women. In B. Murchland (Ed.), *Higher education and the practice of democratic politics* (pp. 122–135). Dayton, OH: Kettering Foundation.

McCarthy, C. (2005). English rustic in black skin: Post-colonial education, cultural hybridity and racial identity in the new century. *Policy Futures in Education, 3*(4), 413–422.

Merryfield, M. M. (2001). Moving the center of global education: From imperial world views that divide the world to double consciousness, contrapunctal pedagogy, hybridity, and cross-cultural competence. In W. B. Stanley (Ed.), *Critical issues in social studies research for the 21st century* (pp. 179–207). Greenwich, CT: Information Age Publishing.

Mitchell, K. (2001). Education for democratic citizenship: Transnationalism, multiculturalism, and the limits of liberalism. *Harvard Education Review, 71*(1), 51–79.

Moje, E. B., Ciechanowski, K. M., Kramer, K., Ellis, L., Carrillo, R., & Collazo, T. (2004). Working toward third space in content area literacy: An examination of funds of knowledge and discourse. *Reading Research Quarterly, 39,* 38–72.

National Council for the Social Studies. (2010). *National curriculum standards for social studies: A framework for teaching, learning and assessment.* Washington, D.C.: Author.

Nodding, N. (1999). Renewing democracy in schools [Electronic Version]. *Phi Delta Kappan,* 80, 1. Retrieved September 21, 2010, from http://www.questia.com.

Noffke, S. E. (2000). Identity, community and democracy in the "New Social Order." In D. W. Hursh & E. W. Ross (Eds.), *Democratic social education* (pp. 73–83). New York: Falmer Press.

O'Connor, K. A., Haefner, T., & Groce, E. (2007). Advocating for social studies: Documenting the decline and doing something about it. *Social Education, 71*(5), 255–260.

Oakes, J. (1985). *Keeping track: How schools structure inequality.* New Haven, CT: Yale University Press.

Pang, V. O., Gay, G., & Stanley, W. B. (1995). Expanding conceptions of community and civic competence for a multicultural society. *Theory and Research in Social Education, 23*(4), 302–331.

Parker, W. C. (1997). Democracy and difference. *Theory and Research in Social Education, 25*(2), 220–234.

Parker, W. C. (2003). *Teaching democracy: Unity and diversity in public life.* New York: Teachers College Press.

Parker, W. C. (2008). Knowing and doing in democratic citizenship education. In L. S. Levstik & C. A. Tyson (Eds.), *Handbook of research in social studies education* (pp. 65–80). New York: Routledge.

Perlstein, D. (1996). Community and democracy in American schools. *Teachers College Record, 97*(4), 625–650.

Pratt, M. L. (1991). Arts of the contact zone. In *Profession 91* (pp. 33–40). New York: Modern Language Association.

Preskill, S. (1997). Discussion, schooling and the struggle for democracy. *The Journal of Social Studies Research, 25*(3), 316–345.

Ross, E. W., & Marker, P. M. (2009). Guest editor's introduction—Social studies teacher education: Dare we teach for democracy? [Electronic Version]. *Teachers Education Quarterly,* 36. Retrieved October 20, 2010, from *http://www.thefreelibrary.com*

Rubin, B. (2007). "There's still not justice" : Youth civic identity development amid distinct school and community contexts. *Teachers College Record, 109*(2), 449–481.

Santora, E. D. (2000, April). *Weaving the tapestry of classroom culture: The personal, professional and pedagogical.* Paper presented at the Annual Meeting of the American Educational Research Association, New Orleans, LA.

Santora, E. D. (2003). Social Studies, solidarity and a sense of self. *The Social Studies, 94*(6), 251–256.

Santora, E. D. (2007). *"Challenging Spaces" : Sites for the reproduction, construction and transformation of identities and knowledge.* Paper presented at the annual meeting of the American Educational Research Association, New York, NY. Retrieved November 30, 2010, from *https://urresearch.rochester.edu/viewInstitutionalCollection.action?collectionId=81*

Sapon-Shevin, M. (1999). *Because we can change the world.* Boston: Allyn & Bacon.

Segall, A. (2003). Teachers' perceptions of the impact of state-mandated standardized testing: The Michigan Educational Assessment Program (MEAP) as a case study of consequences. *Theory and Research in Social Education, 31*(3), 287–325.

Simon, K. G. (2001). *Moral questions in the classroom: How to get kids to think deeply about real life and their schoolwork.* New Haven, CT: Yale University Press.

Slattery, P. (1995). *Curriculum development in the postmodern era.* New York: Garland.

Sleeter, C. E. (2008). Teaching for democracy in an age of corporatocracy. *Teachers College Record, 110*(1), 139–159.

Sleeter, C. E., & Grant, C. A. (1994). *Making choices for multicultural education: Five approaches to race, class, and gender* (2nd ed.). New York: Macmillan.

Stanley, W. B. (2000). Curriculum and the social order. In D. W. Hursh & E. W. Ross (Eds.), *Democratic social education: Social studies for social change.* New York: Falmer Press.

Stewart, T. S. (2010). A dialogic pedagogy: Looking to Mikhail Bakhtin for alternatives to standards period teaching practices. *Critical Education, 1*(6), 1–20.

Torres-Guzmán, M. (2011). Renaissance, sharing, and belonging: A messy language of hope [Electronic Version]. *Teachers College Record, 113,* 10–11. Retrieved November 10, 2010, from *http://www.tcrecord.org*

Tupper, J. (2009). Unsafe waters, stolen sisters, and social studies: Troubling democracy and the meta-narrative of universal citizenship [Electronic Version]. *Teachers Education Quarterly, 36.* Retrieved October 20, 2010, from *http://www. thefreelibrary.com/Unsafe+waters%2c+stolen+sisters%2c+and+social+studies%3a+troubling...-a0206465275*

Tyson, C. A. (2002). "Get up offa that thing": African American middle school students respond to literature to develop a framework for understanding social action. *Theory and Research in Social Education, 30*(1), 42–65.

Villa, R., & Thousand, J. (2000). *Restructuring for caring and effective education: Piecing the puzzle together.* Baltimore: Paul H. Brookes Publishing Company.

Welch, S. D. (1991). An ethic of solidarity and difference. In H. Giroux (Ed.), *Postmodernism, feminism, and cultural politics* (pp. 83–99). Albany, NY: State University of New York Press.

Wortham, S. (2006). *Learning identity: The joint emergence of social identification and academic learning.* New York: Cambridge University Press.

CHAPTER 3

TOWARDS AN INCLUSIVE DEFINITION OF DEMOCRATIC EDUCATION

Jonathan Miller-Lane

INTRODUCTION

Democratic education is an example of what W. B. Gallie (1964) termed "an essentially contested concept." Gallie used the term to denote a concept whose meaning would always be disputed due to its inherent complexity, its vulnerability to historical circumstances, and the presence of ardent advocates for diverse perspectives. Yet, despite the difficulty of defining essentially contested concepts, Gallie argued that the effort was worthwhile because the fact that it was so vigorously contested was an indication of the importance of the concept itself. Thus, while in the pages that follow, I define and propose a direction for democratic education that consciously leans towards inclusivity and synthesis, I do so knowing full well that this is neither the first, nor the last, word on the subject.

Contemporary Social Studies: An Essential Reader, pages 33–55
Copyright © 2012 by Information Age Publishing

My basic argument is that one is more likely to be successful in designing an education program to foster the development of citizens who are ready to engage a multicultural, democratic society if the definition of democratic education is broad enough to include various approaches to democratic education while remaining sufficiently precise to be meaningful. I offer a broad definition of democratic education intended to encourage the search for common ground rather than feed the impulse to parse differences. One other advantage of a broad definition is that it reaches out and includes allies who are working hard on similar issues, but in locations beyond traditional classroom walls and, as a result, are often unrecognized by social studies educators.

Second, the pursuit of an education program to foster the development of citizens who are ready to engage a multicultural society is more likely to successful it is grounded in an appreciation that current efforts are just the most recent of a series of historical debates in Western society regarding the proper scope and sequence of liberal education. This historical awareness also promotes a certain humility reminding teachers and scholars alike that one's point of view is unlikely to be brand new. Furthermore, curricular debates concerning, for example, whether the curriculum should focus on the great books of the past, or the important questions of the present, have obscured important areas of agreement regarding the larger purpose of social studies and democratic education in the United States, which is to prepare students for a vibrant, democratic, and diverse society.

In section I, I provide a definition of democratic education grounded in three critical attributes. In section II, I offer an historical overview of liberal education and link it to the modern debates concerning the shape of social studies education. Leaning heavily on the work of educational historians such as Davidson (1907) and Kimball (1986, 2000), I propose the education program of Isocrates the Orator as a useful compromise position. Then, in section III, I discuss two types of embodied education programs that offer underappreciated examples of democratic education: outdoor education programs, and martial arts programs that are designed to support school-based learning. I conclude by suggesting that if social studies educators assume a more inclusive, historical view of democratic education and are willing to look beyond the school grounds, they will find opportunities for collaboration that will strengthen efforts to foster an engaged citizenry. I am suggesting that there is a way through existing, and often, hardened disagreements into a vision of democratic education curriculum that supports the next evolution of social studies education.

SECTION I: A DEFINITION OF DEMOCRATIC EDUCATION

Democratic Education: A purposeful form of education that provides individuals with the skills, knowledge and attitudes necessary for their continued, self-directed growth as individuals, and the skills, knowledge and attitudes they need to contribute to and, define the public good.

Democratic education is purposeful because it is grounded in the belief that citizens are made, not born, and that to "make" citizens one needs qualified teachers capable of mobilizing both a diverse student body and public controversies (Parker, 2003, 2011). The idea that citizens are shaped through education has been with us since Plato's *Republic* and was present early on in our own history. Thomas Jefferson sought to include a provision for public education as an amendment to the Constitution because he believed that education played an essential role in the development of citizens. Horace Mann, as Secretary of the Massachusetts Board of Education from 1837-1848 (the first such position in the United States), also championed the importance of public education in transforming what he described as a random collection of immigrants into a citizenry with a shared allegiance to a common democracy. Underlying *The Social Studies Wars* that Evans (2004) chronicles, lies the basic assumption that *how* we educate our students matters, and that democratic education must be purposeful to be meaningful.

The belief that democratic education must also provide an individual with the ability to continually direct his or her own development draws intentionally from Dewey's (1938) theory of experience as outlined in *Experience and Education*. Dewey argued that before one launches into a discussion of what one should teach and why, one needs to be clear about the nature of an educative experience. What makes one experience educative and another mis-educative? Dewey's disarmingly simple answer was that educative experiences are those that lead to further growth—to the ability of the individual to direct his or her own learning in a manner that fosters continued growth. However, it is important to keep in mind that this simple definition was offered as part of a broader claim that freedom was not simply the absence of external control, but, rather, the presence of an internal locus of control. It would not, for example, make much of a difference to remove the restrictions of totalitarianism if individuals did not know how to direct their own behavior in a constructive manner. Thus, it was not enough to be anti-traditional, or anti-authoritarian in one's approach to teaching and learning. One had to be pro-something and that something, argued Dewey, should be the development of an individual's ability to determine for him or herself whether an experience was educative or not. If an education system committed to the preservation and renewal of democratic life did not develop this capacity in students, argued Dewey, the potential for democracy's preservation and renewal were greatly diminished.

Dewey (1938) also stressed the important role that teachers played in this process of helping students develop their own internal locus of control. His theory of experience existed under the assumption stated earlier that citizens are made not born. If one simply removes the physical and intellectual restrictions of traditional schooling and allows students to move freely around a classroom following every impulse they might have, one has entirely missed the point:

> It may be a loss rather than a gain to escape from the control of another person only to find one's conduct dictated by immediate whim and caprice; that is, at the mercy of impulses into whose formation intelligent judgment has not entered. A person whose conduct is controlled in this way has at most only the illusion of freedom. Actually, he is directed by forces over which he has no command (p. 95).

Thus, the role of the teacher is to direct a child's impulses in a manner that encourages the student to assess the meaning and purpose of what he or she is doing. The most important word in two of Dewey's popular early essays, *The Child _and_ the Curriculum* and *The School _and_ Society* (emphasis added) is the word "and." The teacher's job was neither to stand and transmit nor sit back and watch. The idea of the "guide on the side" is also too simplistic. In order to play the complex role of democracy's midwife, a teacher had to be fully versed in the history of the society for which the child was being prepared to enter as a citizen. A curriculum should be sufficiently purposeful to provide direction and ensure that a child learns the knowledge and skills needed to be successful and yet flexible enough to accommodate a student's particular interest. As James Baldwin (1963/1985) wrote in a *Talk to Teachers*, the purpose of education is to enable a person to "make his own decisions, to say to himself this is white or this is black, to decide for himself whether there is a God in heaven or not. To ask questions of the universe, and then learn to live with those questions, is the way he achieves his own identity" (p. 326).

This second attribute of democratic education and its emphasis on the development of self-directed development also distinguishes democratic education from less desirable forms of education such as education for fascism. As Kneller (1941) noted in his history of education under WWII Germany, individuals in a fascist system are purposefully educated for obedience, not self-directed development. In *Mein Kampf,* Hitler (1933/2010) used a broad stroke when speaking about education, but character education had a unique definition under National Socialism—each youth was to learn the unique contribution he or she could make to the community. Under National Socialism, an individual's full expression of his or her unique self could only be realized by fulfilling his or her duties to the state; instead of self expression, the individual was required to embrace state expression. Self-directed learners were to be re-educated, not held up as models. Thus, emphasizing the importance of developing an internal locus of control also helps clarify what a program of democratic education is *not* doing.

Democratic education is also characterized by its commitment to foster individuals who are able to contribute to and shape the definition of the public good. Although fascists and democrats share a commitment to the public good, the individual participates in a fascist system only as instructed and plays no role in determining the shape and definition of the public good. In contrast, as Parker (2003), Banks (1997), Gay (2000), hooks (1994), Howard (2010), Chapman and Hobbell (2010) and many others have argued, unless diverse voices have an equal role in the meaningful deliberations that set the course of a society, then genuine democracy remains chimerical. Thus, democratic education curricula should not simply provide opportunities for students to volunteer in community service organizations. They should also provide students with opportunities to examine the conditions that have created the inequities. Why do we have soup kitchens? Why is wealth distributed the way it is? Should we privatize the care of our nation's highways? Does it matter if national defense is sub-contracted? The answers to these questions determine the relationship between citizens and their government and determine the boundaries between individual liberties and common rights, as well as the common spaces we share as citizens. Democratic education must provide the skills, knowledge and attitudes that enable any citizen, who chooses to do so, to participate in civic life.

Although this definition of democratic education is broad in scope, it is sufficiently discrete to be meaningful: A purposeful form of education, that provides individuals with the skills, knowledge and attitudes necessary for their continued, self-directed growth as individuals; and with the skills, knowledge and attitudes that they need to be able to help define the public good. What is important is that an education program be committed to these three outcomes and not whether it adopts an approach involving great books or great questions or a mixture of both.

SECTION II: THE ORIGINS OF LIBERAL EDUCATION AND CONTEMPORARY SOCIAL STUDIES

In this section, I argue that current disagreements over the scope and sequence of social studies education and definitions of democratic education are a modern expression of a much older debate surrounding the purpose of a liberal education. The ancient debate that emerged in Athens during the fifth century B.C.E was first embodied in three different, education programs. These three programs are associated, respectively, with the Sophists, Socrates, and Isocrates. A historical understanding of this older debate regarding the proper form of liberal education provides an essential perspective for today's discussion. In addition, an understanding of this long-standing disagreement regarding liberal education suggests that a final resolution is unlikely and may, in fact, be counter-productive.

The Association of American Colleges & Universities (AAC&U) (2002) defines liberal education as follows:

> A philosophy of education that empowers individuals, liberates the mind from ignorance, and cultivates social responsibility. Characterized by challenging encounters with important issues, and more a way of studying than specific content, liberal education can occur at all types of colleges and universities.

This definition of 'liberal education' shares essential attributes with the definition of democratic education I provided above. Liberal education is clearly a purposeful approach to education. The idea of "empowering individuals" included in the AAC&U statement above assumes that individuals can direct their own educational development. The combination of "cultivating social responsibility" and "challenging encounters with important issues" seems intended to ensure that students are able to engage in public deliberations that shape the public good. The AAC&U statement argues that the goal of liberal education is not to cover a specific list of topics, but to encourage a certain way of studying or investigating issues and problems.

Levine (2006) has argued that the idea of a liberal education reached "generative depth in the educational century of Athens from about 450-350 BCE" (p. 13). During this century the contributions of Socrates, Plato and Aristotle changed what was a conception of education as the preservation and memorization of the epic poets into a model of education that continues to influence contemporary liberal arts colleges as well as K-12 democratic education in the United States. The story that is generally told is that each of these philosophers contributed something unique and essential to the intellectual tradition of Western education and that they are the founding fathers of liberal and democratic education in the West. Yet, while the impact of Socrates, Plato and Aristotle on the intellectual tradition of Western Civilization is unquestionable, the notion that we have simply inherited their conception of a liberal education is a gross oversimplification that ignores important curricular debates (Davidson 1907; Kimball, 1986).

The Standard Story Regarding the Origins of Liberal Education

Nussbaum (1997) helps to clarify the initial contribution of Socrates, Plato, and Aristotle. She argues that the "distinctive contribution of Socrates was to bring unrelenting philosophical argument to bear on issues of communal concern" (Nussbaum 1997, p. 20). For such unrelenting skepticism,

Socrates was accused of corrupting the youth of Athens by fostering an attitude of uncertainty regarding the Greek pantheon and sentenced to death. During his trial and defense, which Plato recorded in the *Apology*, Socrates argued that all he had ever said was that he was motivated by an unquenchable desire to know more. In the *Crito*, Socrates explains that he had spent his whole life arguing that it was the role of the citizen to do his best to ensure that the laws of a city were just. While he disagreed with the decision, since his death sentence was achieved in a democratic manner, he had to accept the sentence even though he firmly believed that the jury had misunderstood the intent of his actions. Thus, argues Nussbaum, the unrelenting desire to understand how and why one lives as one does, along with a commitment to the rule of law that serves as the foundation of a democratic society characterize the Socratic contribution to liberal education.

From Plato, the second of the three Greek founders of liberal education, we receive a more complete vision for an education system as well as numerous examples of how dialogue could be used as an instructional tool. One does not have to agree with Plato's vision of philosopher kings as the appropriate rulers of a society, nor with his restrictive vision for what people can and should be educated to do, in order to appreciate the complexity and nuance of his arguments. Plato's *Republic*, taken as a whole, still challenges anyone interested in developing education in and for democratic life precisely because timeless issues are engaged in a thoughtful and rigorous manner. One such example, that also embodies the use of dialogue as a teaching tool, is found in Book One of Plato's *Republic* in which Socrates and a group of his friends explore the meaning of justice. In *Cultivating Humanity*, Nussbaum (1997) provides a marvelous analysis of this conversation which both illustrates the power of Socratic conversations to investigate complex, political and moral issues and how this type of conversation can be used by a thoughtful teacher. The *Symposium* and *Meno* also offer two dialogues that model how argument and disagreement can be constructively engaged to inform individuals' understanding of timeless contested concepts such as the meaning of love and virtue. Thus, from Plato we inherit not only a complex vision of the ideal education of citizens and leaders, but a concerted effort to honor the pedagogical approach of Socrates.

Aristotle, the third Athenian philosopher who is generally considered to be an essential founder of liberal education is credited with distinguishing between a curriculum suited for the servile classes and one suited for the development of free men (Levine, 2006)[1]. The former, illiberal education focused on the development of specific work-related skills while the latter, liberal education, stressed the development of human beings who possessed a broader appreciation of human learning and the ability to both

---

[1] Of course, the collection of Aristotle's works that survived are extensive. A full discussion of his contribution to the shape of modern education far exceeds the limits of this chapter.

investigate and discuss the nature of that learning. Aristotle argued that a free person should be motivated to learn something for its own sake (that is, for its intrinsic value) and not solely because it might have some future utility. Although citizens needed to have practical skills what was most important was that they be educated in a system that fostered their ability to make reasoned, independent decisions as it was this decision making ability that was essential for the free, male citizens who were to lead the city. Building on this Aristotelian definition, the education of 'free men' became the model for how the elite should be educated and this distinction between liberal and illiberal education remained influential into the twentieth century (Levine, 2006).

Challenging the Common Narrative Regarding the Origins of Liberal Education

Although the above summary reflects the general understanding regarding the origins of liberal education, historians of education such as Kimball (1986), Muir (2005), and DePew & Poulakas (2004) have argued that this understanding is incomplete and inaccurate. Kimball (1986) claims that after the disintegration of the Attic-Ionian aristocracy and the emergence of democracy in the fifth century B.C.E. in Athens, three principal groups emerged with programs of education to replace what had been a system of education based on the recitation of Homeric and epic poetry. The first program of education that emerged came to be identified with a group of 'wise men,' or sophists such as Gorgias, Protagoras, Prodicus and Hippias. These men stressed the skills of composing, delivering and analyzing speech, as being the most important in a democratic city-state in which every decision was determined in public forums. Instead of emphasizing a study of the past or engaging in critical speculation they focused on the ability to speak eloquently on any topic. The sophists came to be known, sometimes derogatively, as skilled speechmakers.

A second approach to preparing citizens to participate in the city-state was developed by Plato, "who, looking back to Socrates' never ending quest for truth, regarded intellectual culture and philosophy as the ideal for the education of the citizen" (Kimball, 1986, p. 17). Plato co-opted the Homeric ideal of arête and redefined it to mean the pursuit of highest knowledge through contemplation and inquiry. But, contrary to modern public perception, it was not this school that shaped the scope and development of liberal education in Western society, argues Kimball. It was, instead, a program of education championed by Isocrates, a neglected contemporary of Plato, who disagreed with both the Sophists and Plato, and sought a middle ground that valued both the skills of oratory and of critical speculation.

Isocrates argued that the Sophists relied excessively on rhetorical displays and did not attend sufficiently to the need to develop character and ethics. He was also profoundly skeptical of the dialectical search for truth that Socrates and Plato valued. Isocrates stressed the importance of oratory, not for reasons of argumentation, but because "to speak well and to think right" was the highest expression of the civic ideal. He believed that speculative philosophy without effective speech was pointless. The only way to know if a philosopher truly had something to say was to hear him speak. Eloquence mattered because it was how one expressed one's learning and understanding. Until a person was asked to speak one had no way of knowing what he or she truly understood. For Isocrates and, later, for the Roman senator Cicero, the Orator represented an ideal marriage of eloquence and knowledge. Isocrates claimed that the Sophists cared more about eloquence than about developing character and deep knowledge. Socrates and Plato, on the other hand, were too engaged in pure speculation that was disconnected from any historical context. The Orator would stand between these extremes, drawing from past examples to critically engage the issues of the day in an ethical and virtuous manner (Marsh, 2010).

In the centuries that followed, Kimball (1986) argues that it was Isocrates' program of education that prevailed over both Plato and the Sophists for two reasons. First, Isocrates' emphasis on studying the past fit well with an educational tradition based on Homer and other epic poets. While Plato's educational program had sought to banish such cherished traditions from the ideal republic, Isocrates' program of education was more inclusive recognizing the importance of tradition as the source of contemporary life while stressing the importance of critical inquiry to solve contemporary problems. Second, the oratorical skills that Isocrates valued and sought to foster proved useful in a variety of settings over time, from the Greek city-state to the Roman senate to medieval disputations to the thesis defenses that were typical of colonial colleges in the United States (Kimball, 1986). An approach to the development of these skills that was grounded in a commitment to preserve the best from the past was appealing. While a study of Plato and Aristotle were always considered essential elements of any liberal arts curriculum, their pursuit of critical speculation was only a small part of the curriculum. Isocrates' ideal Orator was someone who could recite important texts of the past while critiquing contemporary problems. It is this model that has had the greatest impact on the development of liberal education (DePew & Poulakas, 2004; Kimball, 1986) and that still offers a compelling model for the organization of democratic education today.

Three Athenian Programs of Liberal education and the "Social Studies Wars" of the 20th Century.

Many scholars have analyzed the history of social studies education (Barr, Barth, & Shermis, 1977; Cherryholmes, 1980; Evans, 2004; Hahn, 2003; Miller-Lane, Howard, & Halagao, 2007; Nelson, 1995; Parker, 1996; Smith,

Palmer, & Correia, 1958; Stanley, 2001; Thornton, 1996; Vanaria, 1958.) In this section, instead of reworking that ground, I suggest that the ancient debates surrounding the purpose of liberal education represented in the arguments of the Sophists, Socrates and Isocrates, may provide a useful framework for understanding the 20th Century debates regarding the proper scope and sequence of social studies education (see Figure 3.1).

In Figure 3.1, I compare the three Athenian models of liberal education with different 20th Century social studies curricular reform efforts. To be sure, Figure 3.1 risks oversimplifying the complex and contentious debates regarding the proper scope and sequence of social studies education. There is also insufficient space to recognize the role of "interest groups" Kliebard (2004), who struggle and battle over how and what should be taught. The real world is far more nuanced than Figure 3.1 might imply. However, the

FIGURE 3.1. Historical Comparison of Three Athenian Debates Surrounding the Purpose of Liberal Education and Selected Exemplars of 20th Century Reform Efforts in Democratic Education

	Athenian Example	Selected Exemplars of 20th Century Reform Efforts in Democratic Education
STATUS QUO	Sophists: Eloquence for the purpose of participating in public affairs	• *The Committee of Ten (1894)* of the National Education Association. • *The Report of the Eight (1909)* from the American Historical Association. • Barr, Barth and Shermis (1977), *"citizenship transmitters."* • E. D. Hirsch (1988), *Cultural Literacy*. • "Current Issues" class.
CRITICAL ANALYSIS	Socrates: Critical speculation/inquiry in the service of the search for truth. Challenge, rather than revere, accepted standards	• George Counts (1932), *Shall the schools build a new social order*. • Harold Rugg (1931), *Problems of American Culture*. • Apple (1975), *The Hidden Curriculum*. • Hooks, (1994), *Teaching to transgress*. • Giroux (2001), *Theory and resistance in education*. • Ross and DeLeon (2010), *Critical theories, radical pedagogies and social education*.
SYNTHESIS	Isocrates: Eloquence and inquiry combined in the service of solving problems.	• *1916 Report on The Social Studies* from the Social Studies Committee of the National Educational Association. • Dewey (1938), *Education and experience*. • *Man: A course of study*. (Bruner, 1960) • Parker (2003), *Teaching democracy*. • Banks (2004), *Handbook of research on multicultural education*.

comparison is still useful and clarifies my main point—that the tensions that first became apparent in Ancient Athens regarding how to educate citizens in and for democratic life are still, broadly speaking, the fault lines of contemporary debate within the field of democratic education.

As Figure 3.1 summarizes, because the Sophists thought it was important for citizens to be able to participate in political life, they stressed the skills of oratory that they believed were essential for participating in the rough and tumble debates of the Athenian assembly. The goal of the Sophists was full participation in, not reform of, the system. In the top right column, matching this status quo model, are the two earliest efforts to organize the study of history in secondary schools: *The Committee of Ten* organized by the National Education Association (1894) and *The Report of the Eight* by the American Historical Association (1909). As Evans (2004) writes, these early efforts were the work of white, male, academic historians, "elites ensconced in an ivory tower, disconnected from the masses, not educators with a broad conception of social purpose" (p. 20). Thus, they are examples of what Barr, Barth & Shermis (1977) called "citizenship transmitters" who seek to promote a curriculum that supports the status quo of American society. The emphasis of these early programs was preparing a citizenry for the existing society—a society that was understood to be worth perpetuating fully and completely.

One can think of an uncritical "current issues class," as a contemporary example of the status quo attempt to provide preparation for broad engagement in society. Like the Sophists, the skills developed in a current issues class are useful, but they are disconnected from any commitment to critically examine why some skills, or some knowledge, is needed more than others, and who might be better able to succeed within the current system and why. In this top row, I have also placed E. D. Hirsch's (1988) well-known list of what every educated citizen needs to know. While Hirsch is emphasizing knowledge, and not public speaking, the basic assumption is similar—the purpose of the curriculum is to prepare students to engage the present without critique.

The antithesis of the Sophists, or status quo, approach is the commitment to critical speculation that Socrates championed and is represented, in the modern social studies context, by what is often called, "Critical Inquiry" (Barr, Barth, & Shermis, 1977.) The goal of critical inquiry is to interrogate the inequities of the status quo and encourage teachers to use the time and space of the public school classroom to explore remedies for those inequities. George Counts (1932) and Harold Rugg (1931) are two twentieth century examples of scholars who urged teachers to imagine schools as an essential site for building a new social order and to use the curriculum to purposefully educate students to be critical of the status quo. Michael Apple's (1975) essay on the "Hidden Curriculum" of schooling also fits in this tradition. Bell hooks (1994) and Harold Giroux (2001) are two examples of scholars working in the area of critical theory who have been unremitting in their efforts to reveal, what they argue, are the devastating injustices embedded in schools. The work of DeLeon and Ross (2010), in which they call on democratic educators to engage in critical analysis of the unjust material conditions of contemporary society, also fit here. Advocates of critical inquiry and reform argue that the schools, as bureaucratic institutions, seek to sustain their own structures rather than serve as cauldrons of democracy's renewal. This anesthetizing tendency of the school structure or the "daily grind" as Phillip Jackson (1968) called it, must be consciously and relentlessly challenged.

The synthesis of these two views is where, I would argue, Isocrates's education program rightly fits along with Parker's (2003) project of non-idiotic, enlightened political engagement, Miller-Lane, Howard and Halago's (2007) concept of civic multicultural competence, and James Banks' (2004) decades long effort to sharpen and broaden the lens through which social studies looks at American history and culture. Dewey (1936) argued in *Experience and Education* that education should be, "the intelligently directed development of the possibilities inherent in ordinary experience" (p. 89). This idea encapsulates the synthesis approach that argues that students should be educated so that they are able to examine the conditions in which they live and direct their lives in a manner that ensures they are able to continue to grow as individuals and as citizens in a larger, interdependent society.

Dewey (1938) argued that it was pointless to remove the forces of external control if an individual did not have a well-developed locus of self-control. He wrote, "The ideal aim of education is creation of power of self-control" (Dewey, 1938, p. 64). The synthesis approach seeks to provide the skills that the Sophists stressed with the confidence and ability to speak one's mind and challenge authority that the critical reformers advocated without the latter's tendency to believe that they already know the exact solutions that should be enacted. The Isocratean approach is, in a sense, a middle way—one that prepares an individual to make his or her own choice. This is also why I have included the 1916 *Report on the Social Studies* of the National Education Association's Committee on the Reorganization of Secondary Schools in this row. As Evans (2004) argues, despite its many shortcomings, the Report sought to provide a middle ground in calling for curriculum that stressed both the study of history and an examination of social issues that laid the groundwork for Rugg (1932) and Counts (1932) more radical reform efforts.

In his effort to analyze the various efforts at democratic education, Parker (2003) argued that within the field of social studies education, political conservatives have generally stressed the need to learn about past achievements while political liberals have focused on teaching the skills and disposition individuals need to critique and remedy the inequities of the status quo. Put within the context of the ancient Athenian debate I am using here, one can argue that conservatives are more like the Sophists and the reformers are more in line with what Socrates would have wanted to see. However, Parker has argued that both socialization and critique are necessary to preserve and renew a democracy. Students need to know how a democracy works and the history of this particular democracy in the United States in order to be able to determine whether it is meeting its potential. Attempts to "devise a theory that overcomes the natural tensions between the two are futile and unnecessary" (Parker, 1996, p. 16). The urge to overcome these tensions is futile precisely because it is the tension itself that fuels the best teaching—both questions and texts are needed to answer the question: How should we live and what sources shall we use to inform our answer? By arguing that Counts (1930) was wrong, that, in fact, schools cannot build a new social order for a whole host of reasons, does not mean that good education that fosters critical inquiry and a study of injustice cannot take place inside of schools (Parker, 2011). The Isocratic position described above reflects this dynamic compromise and challenges educators to engage each other in the process of deciding which historic texts from the past should be used, and how the skills of oratory should be taught so that students have the knowledge and capacity to effectively engage in public life as a citizen.

SECTION III: EMBODYING THE ATTRIBUTES OF DEMOCRATIC EDUCATION: OUTDOOR EDUCATION AND SCHOOL-BASED MARTIAL ARTS PROGRAMS

In Section I, I identified three critical attributes of democratic education. In Section II, I provided an historical overview of the debates surrounding the meaning and purpose of liberal education and argued that contemporary debates within social studies are older than we think. Rather than try to resolve any one of these particular arguments, we should try to sustain the very creative and dynamic tension that the disagreements make possible. The contested nature of the concept of democratic education can be a strength, if the parties involved in the discussion seek not to win a fight, but to find an honorable compromise. In that same spirit of opening up to possibility, rather than narrowing into definitional battles, in this section, I explore two areas of somatic education that share a commitment to the critical attributes of democratic education outlined in section I. I refer to them as somatic education (soma—from the Greek word meaning body) because both outdoor education and martial arts programs stress engaging a student's body and mind. Figure 3.2 provides a schema for this comparison.

The left column of Figure 3.2 contains the three attributes of democratic education: A purposeful form of education that fosters self-directed learning that leads to an interest in, and ability to, engage in deliberations that shape the public good. The middle column addresses the characteristics of outdoor education programs centered on the idea of positive youth development (PYD). The right column of Figure 3.2 compares the critical attributes of democratic education with martial arts based education programs.

Outdoor education and the critical attributes of democratic education

Outdoor education programs that foster Positive Youth Development (PYD) provide youth with six types of resources: supportive relationships, appropriate structure, opportunities for belonging and skill building, positive social norms, and support for efficacy (Catalano et al., 2004; Westrich et al., 2011). To do this, many of these programs create what Slater (1984) called a "temporary community," that is, a purposefully created experience for a specific group of people that is brought together for a limited period of time. Summer camps are good examples of temporary communities. Many of them are organized around specific themes and have carefully planned activities designed to foster a particular kind of group experience. Smith, Steel, and Gidlow (2010) have argued that the temporary community created during a summer camp program can foster the type of affective-based behaviors that civic educators also promote.

FIGURE 3.2. Comparison of Democratic Education with Outdoor Education and Martial Arts Based Education Programs

	Outdoor Education: Positive Youth Development	**Martial Arts Based Education Programs**
Critical Attributes of Democratic Education		
Purposive	Creation of 'temporary communities' in which ideal behavior is fostered.	Taught as a life-long "path" of study not as a means of developing fighting skills. Opposite of Hollywood stereotype.
Self-directed	Development of internal locus of control through group oriented activities that challenge individual limits—physical challenges are presented and reflected upon as metaphors for responding to emotional or spiritual challenges beyond the camp.	Development of internal locus of control through repeatedly choosing to refrain from attacks and anti-social behavior through engaging in physical conflict simulations and being required to choose carefully controlled, constructive response.
Public Minded	The self-conscious creation of temporary communities is done to provide a model for behavior for life beyond the camp experience.	Explicit purpose is to more effectively interact with others outside the dojo/training hall. The training space is intended to serve as practice ground for development of etiquette.

Slater (1984) coined the term "temporary community" to highlight both the potential and the limits of a purposefully created experience. A classroom and a summer camp are characterized by the presence of a group of people that is brought together only temporarily. Thus, the long-term impact of the experience is limited and uncertain. Yet, because the group does form a community, the norms of behavior that are created and the way they are sustained can be a model for how individuals might interact permanently. If the rules of the temporary community promote mindfulness, slowing the rush to judgment, and honoring the perspectives of others, one has created a temporary community that has many of the key attributes of democratic life.

The second critical attribute of democratic education, self-directed learning, can also be fostered in outdoor education programs. Wojcikiewicz and Mural (2006) describe how a Deweyan framework informed their teaching of sailing:

> We believe that the first challenge for outdoor and adventure educators who wish to follow Dewey's path is to understand that Dewey's concept of experience was both specific and demanding, and that it is not necessarily fulfilled just through exciting and unusual activities in exotic settings… Dewey's system requires a knowledgeable teacher or instructor. It requires the careful shaping of an environment that is both pedagogical and purposeful, one that allows interested students to be engaged in their work, to make choices, and to explore ends. It requires authority structures that operate within the meaningful discipline of the activity. It requires attention to future activities and experiences. Indeed, to operate a program, or even an activity, that fits all Dewey's criteria and leads to the developmental outcomes he specifies is no simple task (p. 117).

Reading this summary it is easy to forget that the authors are talking about constructing a program to teach sailing. Yet, their commitment to the idea of continued growth, to helping students determine what experiences are educative and which are not, is evident. Learning how to sail may well be practical or illiberal in the original Aristotelian sense of the word, but the organizers of this program are doing so with a liberal intent.

The third characteristic of democratic education (the concern for and ability to engage the public good) can also be addressed in outdoor education programs if the connection is thoughtfully made during follow-up discussions. Sammet (2010) reported on one program of outdoor education that had long lasting effects on the ability of young, female participants to reject relational aggression in favor of adopting an attitude of engagement with others' interests and concerns. Passerli, Hall and Anderson (2010) have also reported on the impact of a strengths based approach to outdoor and adventure education. They argue that such an approach fosters the kind of self-confidence needed to engage in public life.

Closer to the school grounds, Waldstein and Reiher (2001), in their survey of the impact of service learning activities found that such experiences had a positive impact on students' interest in and willingness to engage in public affairs. Shinn and Yoshikawa (2008) suggest that any program that seeks to foster Positive Youth Development, whether explicitly linked to school activities or not, should elicit community involvement in all stages of planning, implementation and follow up. Community involvement has been shown to increase the likelihood that the gains found during the activity are sustained over the long term. In sum, there is growing research that suggests outdoor educators are concerned with the critical attributes of democratic education.

Martial Arts Education Programs and the Critical Attributes of Democratic Education

The right column of Figure 3.2 compares the critical attributes of democratic education with martial arts based, education programs. These martial arts programs are important and relevant to democratic education because of the manner in which they try to address the anti-social behaviors that threaten or limit the potential for some youth to participate effectively in civic life. In their review of two decades of school shootings, Kimmel and Mahler (2003) found that it was a particular boy code that led to both the brutal teasing and insults that shooters had often experienced. These young men believed physical violence was the only means through which they would be recognized as individuals with efficacy. Thus, their experience of intense, verbal abuse, often caused by the fact that the shooters did not meet some standard of maleness in the eyes of the abusers, led the victims to act in a violent manner that the victims believed would affirm their masculinity. The belief that the ability to inflict physical violence is the only means to fully express masculinity, and to be recognized by others, impairs the ability of these young men to develop healthy interpersonal relationships and to become productive citizens (Hagan & Foster, 2001).

Research on the impact of training in the martial art of Aikido has suggested intriguing possibilities for martial arts based education programs. Contrary to mainstream images of the martial arts, Aikido practitioners reject combat and competition and choose instead to respond to an aggressive attack from another person with the utmost care and compassion. Rather than respond to an attack violently, Aikido practitioners utilize circular and blending movements to diffuse an attack—and do so without harming the aggressor (Dobson & Miller, 1993; Saotome, 1993; Stevens, 2001). Aikido has been used successfully to affect significant positive change in the behavior of severely emotionally disturbed students. In one intervention, designed to reduce disruptive classroom behavior and verbal and physical assaultive behavior, students who enrolled in a twelve-week training program that integrated form practice with presentation and discussion of the philosophy of Aikido demonstrated improvement in their ability to self-monitor and de-escalate situations that could lead to violence (Edelman 1994). Aikido has also been found to be a successful way to cultivate empathy (Chew, 1995). Learning how to physically connect with a partner in Aikido training has helped some individuals to connect with adversaries "off the mat" as well (Oberg, 1991). Martin (2004) has found that Aikido offers an effective means to teach children conflict resolution skills through the body. The opportunity to role-play real-life conflicts and practice de-escalating and managing conflicts before they become violent has been found to make a difference in youth's ability to develop an internal locus of control and engage others constructively (Goldstein & Glick, 1998).

Overall, martial arts programs in school settings have had varied success over the years in helping students develop the ability to identify and redirect violent responses to stressful situations (Howard, Flora & Griffin, 1995; Winkle & Ozmun, 2003). Those programs that have been successful have stressed four elements. First, there must be explicit connections between the traditional philosophy of the martial art and the physical teachings (Lakes & Hoyt, 2004). Second, the instructor must demonstrate and require of all participants a commitment to self-respect and respect for others. Third, calming techniques should be integrated with physical practice. Fourth, the instructor must demonstrate genuine interest and concern for each student (Zivin et al., 2001). If these four elements are not central to the martial arts based education program, the intervention may not only fail, it may actually increase the delinquency of participants (Trulson, 1986). Martial arts interventions that address violent or anti-social behavior are most effective when the philosophy is explicitly taught along with the techniques (Dykhuizen, 2000; Edelman, 1994; Lakes & Hoyt, 2004; Miller-Lane & Selover, 2008). Longer interventions have a far greater likelihood of having an impact on the participants. In addition, programs that involved a variety of community providers, established clear standards of behavior, and recognized individual's progress were common characteristics of successful programs (Catalano et al., 2004).

In summary, there is a steadily growing body of evidence that suggests there are good reasons for social studies educators to reach out to colleagues who are working with their students in out-of school settings. Both outdoor and martial arts based education programs that are purposefully and explicitly developed to foster an internal locus of control share two of three critical attributes of democratic education. Yet, the third attribute is essential—unless these programs also foster an interest in, and the ability to effectively engage the deliberations that shape the public good they cannot be called democratic education programs. The research is promising that these programs can and do embody this attribute. Yet, as Trulson (1986) noted, the activity must be combined with reflection and analysis of the greater purpose of the 'temporary community' to ensure its democratic contribution. Like any democratic education project, students need to know the purpose of the activity and how it relates to the larger mission of fostering a democratic citizenry if they are going to reap the full benefits.

SECTION IV: SUMMARY

If social studies educators assume a more inclusive, historical view of democratic education and a broader willingness to look beyond the school grounds, they will discover opportunities for collaboration that will strengthen efforts to foster an engaged citizenry. Rather than seek to rarefy differences within the field, I have sought, in this chapter, to widen the lens through which we examine the meaning and purpose of democratic education and included a discussion of outdoor education and martial arts based education programs as examples of where allies are hard at work. Those educators who emphasize the importance of contemporary issues and critical reform may fear that allowing a compromise on "classic texts" will limit the self-directed development of an individual. However, examining these texts can sometimes enhance an individual's ability to engage in the kind of critical analysis that reformers advocate.

In *Paradoxes of education in a republic*, Eva Brann (2001) wrote that the "human wisdom" of Socrates was "to know one knows nothing, and to know it in two ways: as a highly specifiable lack and irrepressible longing" (p. 163). She argued that by reading the ancient Greek texts that feature Socrates in this role, students come to understand the importance of assuming such a role in their own lives. In the same essay, Brann stressed that a Socratic longing for knowledge invariably leads to a search to determine what is true. Whether reading a "classic" book or a contemporary author, the most important question to ask is, "Is this true?" It is the act of questioning, rather than the assimilation of an existing body of knowledge, that characterizes the Socratic contribution and, one learns this, Brann argues, through reading the best that one can find from the past. Asking of these older texts, "Is this true?" ensures that the contemporary student is not simply downloading an ancient tome into her brain in a pdf format, immutable to change, but is instead engaging in a dynamic and critical conversation with some of the greatest minds that have ever lived.

Writing in a very different era and from a very different vantage point, W.E.B. Du Bois (1903/2005) made a similar argument in *The Souls of Black Folk*. At the end of the chapter entitled, "The Education of Black Men," DuBois wrote:

> I sit with Shakespeare and he winces not. Across the color line I move arm and arm with Balzac and Dumas, where smiling men and welcoming women glide in gilded halls. From out the caves of evening that swing between the strong-limbed earth and the tracery of the stars, I summon Aristotle and Aurelius and *what soul I will* and they come all graciously with no scorn nor condescension. So, wed with Truth, I dwell above the Veil (p. 82, emphasis added).

Thus, does one of the great American intellectuals of the twentieth century, who happened to be African American, write about the power of the "classics" to inform his search for truth. DuBois approached the reading of the "classics" not as a self-imposed act of oppression, but as a source of liberation. Like anyone else, DuBois read the classics to gain a better understanding of the civilization in which he had found himself 'thrown,' and to explore what a particular intellectual tradition might offer to enhance his understanding of the human experience. DuBois was able to summon "what soul I will" because he had such authors at his mind's grasp to summon. We all enter a world not of our own making and if democratic educators are interested in helping students understand their world, is it really so hard to imagine that reading authors like Socrates, Aurelius and DuBois would inform their understanding. The Isocratic commitment to engage in the critical issues that citizens face ensures that this undertaking will not be a pedantic recitation of fetishized texts.

The critical attributes of democratic education offered in this chapter demand that any education program must purposively support students' ability to engage the world—not some future world, but this one, here and now. We need books *and* questions. We need citizens skilled at public speaking and fearless in their willingness to challenge injustice in a public forum. The attributes presented in this chapter are also intended to remind us that there are democratic education programs taking place beyond the walls of the classroom, where much of public life is lived.

REFERENCES

Apple, M. (1975). The hidden curriculum and the nature of conflict. In W. C. Parker (Ed.), *Educating the democratic mind*. Albany, NY: State University of NY Press.

American Historical Association. (1909). *The study of history in elementary schools: The report of the Committee of Eight*. New York: Charles Scribner's Sons.

Association of American Colleges and Universities (2002). *Greater expectations: A new vision for learning as America goes to college*. Washington, D.C.: AAC&U.

Baldwin, J. (1963/1985). The price of the ticket, collected non-fiction 1948–1985. New York, NY: Saint Martins Press.

Banks, J. A. (1997). *Educating citizens in a multicultural society*. New York: Teachers College Press.

Barr, R., Barth, J., & Shermis, S. (1977). *Defining the social studies*. Washington, D.C.: The National Council for The Social Studies.

Brann, E. (2001). *The paradoxes of education in a republic*. Chicago, IL: University of Chicago Press.

Catalano, R. F., Berglund, L., Ryan, J. A. M., Lonczak, H. S., & Hawkins, J. D. (2004). *Positive youth development in the United States: Research findings on evaluations of positive youth development programs. Annals of the American Academy of Political and Social Science, Positive development: Realizing the potential of youth* (vol. 591, pp. 98–124). Thousand Oaks, CA: Sage Publications.

Chapman, T., & Hobbell, N. (2010). *Social justice across the curriculum: The practice of freedom*. New York, NY: Routledge.

Cherryholmes, C. H. (1980). Social knowledge and citizenship education: Two views of truth and criticism. *Curriculum Inquiry, 10*, 115–151.

Chew, P. G. L. (1995). Aikido politics in interview interaction. *Linguistics and Education, 7*(3), 201–220.

Davidson, T. (1907). *Aristotle and ancient educational ideals*. New York, NY: Charles Scribner's Sons.

DeLeon, A. P., & Ross, E. W. (2010). *Critical theories, radical pedagogies and social education*. Rotterdam, Netherlands: Sense Publishers.

Depew, D., & Poulakos, T. (Eds.). (2004) *Isocrates and civic education*. Austin, TX: University of Texas Press.

Dewey, J. (1938). *Experience and education*. New York, NY: Collier Books.

Dobson, T., & Miller, V. (1993). *Aikido in everyday life*. Berkeley, CA: North Atlantic Books.

DuBois, W. E. B. (1903/2007). *The souls of black folk*. New York, NY: Cosimo Classics.

Dykhuizen, G. C. (2000). Training in culture: The case of Aikido education and meaning-making outcomes in Japan and the United States. *International Journal of Intercultural Relations, 24*, 741–761.

Edelman, A. (1994). *The implementation of a video-enhanced Aikido-based school violence prevention training program to reduce disruptive and assaultive behaviors among emotionally disturbed adolescents*. Practicum report presented in partial fulfillment of Ed.D, NOVA Southeastern University.

Evans, R. W. (2004). *The social studies wars*. New York, NY. Teachers College Press.

Ferber, T., Gaines, E., & Goodman, C. (2005). *Positive youth development: State strategies.* Washington, D.C.: National Conference of State Legislatures.

Gallie, W. B. (1964). *Philosophy and the historical understanding.* London, UK: Chatto and Windus.

Gay, G. (2000). *Culturally responsive teaching: Theory, research and practice.* New York, NY: Teachers College Press.

Goldstein, A., Glick, B. & Gibbs, J. (1998). *Aggression replacement training: A Comprehensive Intervention for Aggressive Youth.* Champaign, IL: Research Press.

Hagan, J., Foster, H. (2001). Youth violence and the end of adolescence. *American Sociological Review, 66*(6), 874–899. Accessed: 26/01/2010 11:54: http://www.jstor.org/stable/3088877.

Hahn, C. L. (2003). Civic education in the U.S.: Recent trends and future challenges. *Basic Education, 47*(5), 3–9.

Hirsch, E. D. (1988). *Cultural literacy: What every American needs to know.* New York, NY: Vintage Books.

Hitler, A. (1939/2010). *Mein Kampf.* Murhpy, J. (Trans.) Boring, OR: CPA Book Publishing.

Howard, K. A., Flora, A., & Griffin M. (1995). Violence-prevention programs in schools: State of the science and implications for future research. *Applied and Preventive Psychology, 8*(3), 197–215.

Howard, T. (2010). *Why race and culture matter in schools: Closing the achievement gap in America's classrooms.* New York, NY: Teachers College Press.

Kimball, B. (1986). *Orators and philosophers: A history of the idea of a liberal education.* New York, NY: Teachers College Press.

Jackson, P. (1968). The daily grind. In D. Flinders & S. Thornton (Eds.), *The curriculum studies reader* (3rd ed.). New York, NY: Routledge.

Kimball, B. (1986). *Orators and Philosophers: A history of the idea of liberal education.* New York, NY: Teachers College Press.

Kimball, B., & Paris, D. C. (2000). Liberal education: An overlapping pragmatic consensus. *Journal of Curriculum Studies, 32,* 143–158.

Kimmel, M. S., & Mahler, M. (2003). Adolescent masculinity, homophobia, and violence: Random school shootings, 1982–2001. *American Behavioral Scientist, 46*(10), 31439–1458.

Kneller, G. F. (1941). *The educational philosophy of national socialism.* New Haven, CT: Published for the Department of education, Yale University by the Yale University Press.

Lakes, K. D., & Hoyt, W. T. (2004). Promoting self-regulation through school-based martial arts training. *Applied Developmental Psychology, 25,* 283–302.

Levine, D. (2006). *Powers of the mind: The reinvention of liberal learning in America.* Chicago, IL: University of Chicago Press.

Martin, P. (2004). Conflict resolution using transactional analysis and Aikido [Special issue]. *Transactional Analysis Journal: Transactional Analysis and Education, 34*(3), 229–242.

Marsh, C. (2010). Millenia of discord: The controversial educational program of Isocrates. *Theory and Research in Education, 8*(3), 289–303.

Miller-Lane, J., Howard, T., & Halagao, P. E. (2007). Civic multicultural competence: Searching for common ground for democratic education. *Theory & Research in Social Education, 35*(4), 551–573.

Miller-Lane, J., & Selover, G. (2008). Teaching constructive disagreement for a loyal opposition, somatically. *Social Studies Research and Practice, 3*(3).

Muir J. R. (2005). Is our history of educational philosophy mostly wrong? The case of Isocrates. *Theory and Research in Education 3,* 165–95.

Nussbaum, M. C. (1997). *Cultivating humanity: A classical defense of reform in liberal education.* Boston, MA: Harvard University Press.

Oberg, E. (1991). Aikido: Being present in the learning experience. *Journal of Experiential Education, 14*(3), 54–56.

Parker, W. (2003). *Teaching democracy: Unity and diversity in public life.* New York, NY: Teachers College Press.

Parker, W. C. (1996). *Educating the democratic mind.* Albany, NY: State University of New York Press.

Parker, W. C. (2011) (Ed.) *Social studies today: Research and practice.* New York: Routledge.

Passarelli, A. Hall, E., & Anderson, M. (2010). A strength-based approach to outdoor and adventure education: Possibilities for personal growth. *Journal of Experiential Education, 33*(2) 120–135.

Rouse, W. H. D. (Ed.) (1956). *The great dialogues of Plato.* New York, NY: Mentor Books.

Sack, S. (1962). Liberal education: What was it? What is it? *History of Education Quarterly, 2*(4) 210–224.

Sammet, K. (2010). Relationships matter: Adolescent girls and relational development in adventure education. *Journal of Experiential Education, 33*(2) 151–165.

Saotome, M. (1993). *Aikido and the harmony of nature.* Boston, MA: Shambhala Press.

Shinn, M., & Yoshikawa, H. (2008). (Eds.). *The power of social settings: Promoting youth development by changing schools and community programs.* New York: Oxford University Press.

Slater, T. (1984). *The temporary community: Organized camping for urban society.* Sutherland, NSW: Albatross Books.

Smith, E. F. , Steel, G., & Gidlow, B. (2010). The temporary community: Student experience of school-based outdoor education programmes. *Journal of Experiential Education, 33*(2) 136–150.

Stanley, W. B. (Ed.). (2001). *Critical issues in social studies research for the 21ˢᵗ century.* Charlotte, NC: Information Age Press.

Stevens, J. (2001). *The philosophy of Aikido.* Tokyo, Japan: Kodansha International.

Trulson, M. E. (1986). Martial arts training: A novel "cure" for juvenile delinquency. *Human Relations, 39*(12), 1131–1141.

Twemlow, S. W., & Sacco, F. C. (1998). The application of traditional martial arts practice and theory to the treatment of violent adolescents. *Adolescence, 33*(131), 505–18.

Waldstein, F. A., & Reiher, T. C. (2001). Service-learning and students' personal and civic development. *Journal of Experiential Education, 24*(1), 77–103.

Westrich, L., London, R. A., Stokes-Guinan, K., Mallonee, A., & McLaughlin, M.W. (2011). *Playworks: Promoting positive youth development in low-income elementary school.* Stanford, CA: John Gardner Center of Stanford University

Winkle, J. M., & Ozmun, J. C., (2003). Martial arts: An exciting addition to the physical education curriculum. *Journal of Physical Education, Recreation & Dance,* 74.

Wojcikiewicz, S. K., & Mural, Z. B. (2010). A Deweyian framework for youth development in experiential education: Perspectives from sail training and sailing instruction. *Journal of Experiential Education, 33*(2), 105–119.

Shinn, M., & Yoshikawa, H. (2008). (Eds.). Toward positive youth development: Transforming schools and community programs. New York: Oxford University Press.

Zivin, G., Hassan, N., DePaula, G., Monti, D., Harlan, C., Hossain, K., & Patterson, K., (2001). An effective approach to violence prevention: traditional martial arts in middle school. *Adolescence, 36*(143), 443–59.

CHAPTER 4

GLOBAL EDUCATION

Responding to a Changing World

Merry M. Merryfield

Globalization is *the* issue of the 21st century as it shapes all aspects of our lives. New communication technologies and global information networks ensure that whether people are in Beirut, Berlin or Boston, most will learn about world events—a new epidemic, a bombing, or the results of the World Cup—in their daily news. Global financial systems and multinational agreements along with the actions of transnational companies have created global markets for goods, services and labor so that there are Japanese auto plants in Tennessee, American pharmaceutical companies in China, and tech support in India and Ireland for computers made in Taiwan and Korea and used in Europe and Canada. Issues related to clean water; sustainable fisheries, air pollution, toxic waste disposal, and biodiversity have become global in scope and require nations to work together. Movement of millions of people has created new patterns of diversity within and across countries and the need for cross-cultural skills and knowledge if people are to learn to work and live together. Ideas old and new—self-determination, terrorism, Internet protests, biodiversity or women's rights—flow across borders

Contemporary Social Studies: An Essential Reader, pages 57–76
Copyright © 2012 by Information Age Publishing
All rights of reproduction in any form reserved.

and regions. Our students are growing up as citizens of the US *and the world* as their futures are linked to people and issues across the planet.

CONCEPTUALIZING GLOBAL PERSPECTIVES IN EDUCATION

What is the role of education in a globally interconnected world? How do teachers ensure that students understand their place as actors on a dynamic and changing world stage? How do students learn to make decisions and engage locally and globally as citizens of the U.S. and members of the world community? Global education, the field of study developed to meet these goals, aims to "develop in youth the knowledge, skills, and attitudes needed to live effectively in a world possessing limited natural resources and characterized by ethnic diversity, cultural pluralism, and increasing interdependence" (National Council for the Social Studies, 2005). Developed by social scientists and educators during the Cold War, global education has been grounded in two constructs that have set it apart from other ways of teaching about the world: perspective consciousness and global interconnectedness (Anderson, 1979, Becker, 1979, Hanvey, 1976). Other elements of global education, such as the study of deep culture, global issues and global systems, and the development of globalization through time and space have developed from these core constructs.

Perspective consciousness is "the recognition or awareness on the part of the individual that he or she has a view of the world that is not universally shared, that this view of the world has been and continues to be shaped by influences that often escape conscious detection, and that others have views of the world that are profoundly different" (Hanvey, 1976). How can students come to understand why people from different nations (or even within a nation) perceive an event or issue in conflicting ways? Although patterns of thinking may change over time, culture and experience always shape how humans make sense of their world. When students acquire skills in perspective consciousness, they can begin to develop understanding and empathy for people in different circumstances and identify reasons for cultural conflicts (Case, 1993; Merryfield & Wilson, 2005).

In developing knowledge of global interconnectedness, students learn how they are linked economically, politically, culturally, environmentally and technologically to people and places around the world (Adams & Carfagna, 2006; Anderson, 1979; Diaz et al, 1999). They see how they are dependent on people who grow or make products they value, and they recognize how their generation's decisions as consumers affect people and environments across the planet. They come to recognize how small changes in one region (ethnic conflict, new technologies, and political alliances) can bring about global changes over time (Pike & Selby, 1995).

Perspective consciousness and global interconnectedness contribute to the development of worldmindedness, habits of the mind that foster student abilities to process new knowledge within a global context. Perspective consciousness and global interconnectedness enrich the social studies as students learn to examine events and issues within a global framework and inquire into the ideas and experiences of diverse people, especially those people who have little power.

From these basic constructs educators began to infuse global perspectives into the social studies through the study of cultural universals, global systems (economic, political, ecological, and technological), global issues, global history (including the acceleration of interdependence over time, antecedents to current issues, and contact and borrowing among cultures) and cross-cultural awareness (Alger & Harf, 1986; Anderson, 1979; Kniep, 1986; Wilson, 1982). Over the last decade, global education has incorporated elements of perceptual learning, citizenship education, experiential learning, electronic technologies, and issues of equity and social justice (Banks et al., 2005; Bigelow & Peterson, 2002; Gaudelli, 2003; Kirkwood, 2010; Noddings, 2005; Peters, 2009; Subedi, 2010). In contrast to the substantive dimension of knowledge about the world, the inner dimension of global education focuses on understanding of self, one's own beliefs and values, and habits of the mind such as openmindedness, resistance to stereotyping, and anticipation of complexity (Abdullahi, 2010; Case, 1993; Pike, 2000).

As more global educators have advocated learning from the experiences, ideas, and knowledge of people who are poor, oppressed, or in opposition to people in power, global education has increased representation of marginalized peoples, their issues and concerns through a pedagogy for social justice (Abdullahi, 2010; Banks et al, 2005; Bigelow & Peterson, 2002; Gaudelli, 2003; Subedi, 2010; Tan, 2004). Today global educators ensure that students learn from people whose experience and knowledge differ from dominant discourse (Adams & Carfagna, 2006; Apple & Buras, 2006; Pang, 2005, Peters, 2009).

GLOBAL EDUCATION IN THE SOCIAL STUDIES TODAY

Global educators have developed a number of approaches to help elementary, middle and high school students perceive the world as an interconnected system. Introduction to global geography or world studies may begin with students examining images of Earth from space, mapping the products they use every day from other world regions, or tracing how historical events from politics in ancient Greece to trade over the Silk Road to Japanese expansionism in the 20th century continue to influence their lives today. The study of global interdependence leads to the need to understand diverse cultures, cultural interactions, and human conflicts. In the sections that follow several strategies are explicated that teachers use to infuse global perspectives into the social studies through different grade levels and courses. Elements of global education can unify diverse time periods and world regions and center students' study of local issues within a global framework (Merryfield & Wilson, 2005).

It is also important to recognize that since it usually develops within a state or local context, global education may address different regional or international connections (with Mexico in Southern California, for example), economic realities (agri-business in the MidWest, shipping in Long Beach, NAFTA in many states) or political acts (such as terrorist attacks, peace-keeping and military alliances). The goals of global education are dynamic and change over time. In the post-Cold War era the major goals of global education in the United States focus more on understanding the complexities of today's world, the increasing interconnectedness of diverse peoples, and the search for social justice and human rights (Adams & Carfagna, 2006; Tan 2004).

MAKING CONNECTIONS ACROSS TIME AND SPACE

Increasingly global interconnectedness characterizes life on planet earth in the 21st century. In historical studies students can compare the relative isolation of other time periods with the steady increase of connectivity over the last century. Only in the last few decades have we seen global transformation of access to global information as new technologies bring major events and ideas immediately into the lives of people across the planet. If something significant happens today in Indonesia or Italy, much of the world will know about it within a day if not hours. Unlike previous generations, many of the world's peoples literally viewed the same images of the 9/11 attacks, the Beijing Olympics, or the effects of hurricane Katrina on New Orleans. As seen in Tunisia and Egypt, people not only see what is happening in other countries but may be inspired to use new tech tools such as Facebook or smart phones to work towards their own political change.

Global connectedness brings us more than news. Economically it may bring new investments in our communities and contribute to jobs and economic opportunities. Americans can enjoy fresh fruit and vegetables in our grocery stories every month of the year and even those of us in Columbus, Ohio, can eat fresh tuna caught a thousand miles away. Politically global interconnectedness may reduce loss of life from ethnic or religious conflicts (think peacekeepers in Kosovo) and bring people of many nations together to address common problems (the Kyoto Accord). Advocacy groups from Greenpeace to the World Council of Churches and Amnesty International now work across world regions. Scientifically it can provide people access to new medicines, inventions, or technologies that improve mortality or safety. Cultural interconnectedness enriches our lives with new philosophies, literature, food and fashion and leads to hybrid constructions of art and music or rethinking of assumptions about violence, gender, or age (Adams & Carfagna, 2006).

Of course these benefits are not equitably distributed across regions, nations or individuals. Many people have experienced job losses as companies move operations to find lower labor costs or less environmental regulation. New transportation technologies and the global movement of people and products have precipitated new epidemics (the spread of AIDS and bird flu, for example) and the acceleration of environmental degradation and loss of wildlife as once inaccessible land, water and other resources become accessible for exploitation. The world faces new challenges from the globalization of trade in illegal drugs and weapons as well as human trafficking. Perhaps the most worrisome attributes of globalization are its unpredictability and the loss of control that nations and individuals feel as changes take place (Sassen, 1996).

Global interconnectedness is taught both within and across historical periods. For example, teachers may teach economic connections across regions around the same time period by having students examine the realities of the slave trade in Europe, the Middle East, Africa and North and South America during the 1700-1800s so that they can place the North American experience within a global framework. Geography teachers often teach interconnectedness of events and issues to help students appreciate how culture affects environmental changes. Events in Middle Eastern history can inform student understanding of current Shia/Sunni and Persian/Arab conflicts. Teachers also focus on how political ideas and military or economic innovations from one world region changed people's lives in other regions: the effects of the Chinese inventions of the compass and gunpowder on Europeans, the spread of Christianity from Europe to Latin America, or the growth of fascism that led to a world war. Cultural diffusion is often taught in U.S. History through the study of how immigrants, refugees, and people who were enslaved brought with them their beliefs, expertise, and customs which in turn influenced the development of what it means to be American. Below are some concepts, enduring understandings, and teaching ideas related to teaching global interconnectedness.

Major concepts in making connections across time and space may include:

- *Cultural Diffusion:* The process by which cultures expand and change over time and place.
- *Hybridity:* The mixing of ideas, language, or ways of living that result when two or more cultures encounter each other peaceably or through conflict.

- *Historical Antecedents:* Using historical frameworks to inform contemporary realities.
- *Economic Interdependence:* The ways in which people across the planet depend to some degree on the economic decisions and actions of people, organizations and governments in other parts of the world.
- *Ecological Interdependence:* The ways in which people's decisions and lives affect and are affected by changes in the natural or physical world (water, land, air, natural resources, and the biodiversity of plants and animals).

Enduring understandings, the big ideas we want students to remember as adults, may include:

1. Ideas, beliefs, and values from many cultures across hundreds of years have shaped and will continue to shape our identities, our communities, and our nation.
2. Our lives are connected to global systems—economic, political, social, technological and ecological—that provide both opportunities and constraints.
3. Although we may more readily notice cultural, economic or political differences across nation-states or world regions, there are significant commonalities shared across the human experience and issues shared by people across the planet.
4. As contributors to popular culture and consumers with considerable purchasing power, young Americans are influencing jobs, lifestyles and environmental changes happening right now across the planet.

These concepts and enduring understandings can be integrated into the social studies through the disciplines (geography and its comparisons across regions, history and its antecedents to today's realities, economic and political connections past and present) and through interdisciplinary approaches that help students recognize how the world already shapes their daily lives and how they, even as young children, affect people and places across the planet. The teaching ideas outlined below come practicing teachers, some of whom developed them while taking one of my face to face or online global education courses from 2000–2010; others come from my research in teachers' classrooms from 2001–2009. These social studies teachers have developed many ways to make global connections across time and space.

Teaching Idea: Global Perspectives on Influence and Change

In a culminating activity called "Influencing the World" students selected people from their study of world history whom they believed had a significant influence on the world. Working in groups of two, students researched their choices and created a campaign for the person. Their campaigns had to be based on historical connections across both time periods and world regions. They competed to win the title, "#1 in Changing the World." Although choices in this project have changed somewhat over time, there are usually some people chosen who are known for their aggression or conquest (Cleopatra, Julius Caesar, Attila the Hun, Genghis Khan, Adolph Hitler, Osama Bin-Laden), political leaders of different backgrounds (George Washington, Queen Victoria, Joseph Stalin, Mohandas Gandhi, Franklin Roosevelt, Indira Gandhi, Martin Luther King, Rosa Parks, Mao Zedong, Zhou Enlai, Deng Xiaoping, Nelson Mandela), religious leaders (Jesus, Mohammed, Martin Luther, Pope John XXIII, Siddhartha Gautama, Mother Teresa), and inventors, scientists, and entrepreneurs (Issac Newton, Charles Darwin, Marie Curie, Andrew Carnegie, Bill Gates). In follow-up discussions, students mapped out how cultural norms and issues of the era created or obfuscated opportunities for influence across time and space.

Teaching Idea: Architecture Across Time and Cultures

The study of things people build can demonstrate both connections across world regions and connections across time. In this activity a teacher chose three global themes for students to examine across several time periods:

1. The characteristics of buildings that signify wealth and power (this website of castles in Japan inspired his choice http://www.japan-guide.com/e/e2296.html);
2. walls (from ancient walled cities to China's Great Wall to the Berlin Wall to walls being constructed in Israel or even walls proposed for the US/Mexican border); and
3. religious buildings (from shrines to cathedrals). As students compiled images the class covered a classroom wall with pictures that documented cultural universals—similarities in buildings across diverse cultures over hundreds of years. The project affected student thinking as what they originally perceived as differences changed to an appreciation of how people across cultures have shared many assumptions about buildings and walls and how ideas about buildings have been shaped and reshaped by cross-cultural interaction and conflict.

Teaching Idea: Timelines

Historical timelines are often used to trace events over a country or a region's history. In this lesson students came to appreciate cultural influences on historical thinking by comparing timelines developed in different world regions. When students examined and compared http://www-chaos.umd.edu/history/time_line.html, a timeline of Chinese history with http://www.humanities-interactive.org/splendors/timeline.htm, a Pre-Columbian timeline they found that different criteria were used to decide what belongs in an historical timeline. This finding led to further research on how cultural values can be identified by examining past and present timelines developed in a variety of countries. The activity ended with a discussion of why American timelines rarely include art, music or literature when they appear frequently in timelines developed in other parts of the world.

RECOGNIZING HOW CULTURE AFFECTS PERCEPTION AND INTERACTION

As the world has become increasingly interconnected, experiences with people of diverse cultures have come to characterize our lives. The flattening of global transportation and communication systems has accelerated regional and global movement of peoples who seek better economic opportunities next door or across the ocean. Others move seeking freedom from religious persecution, ethnic strife or political repression—a traditional theme in U.S. History that has taken on new characteristics today. The old ties of colonialism have created new global highways. From Algerians in France to Pakistanis in Britain to Koreans in Japan, people from former empires are now "colonizing" the mother country. As cultural diversity increases in neighborhoods, schools, and workplaces, there is a profound need for students to develop intercultural competence, the ability to communicate and work effectively with people of many cultures. Intercultural competence begins with an understanding of how culture shapes people's identities, values, beliefs, and actions.

Until recently the study of world cultures has been centered on traditional customs and ways of living, scenes of family and public life, well-known places, and artifacts unique to the culture. We can all reflect on a time in school where we studied or perhaps taught culture through a film on daily life (on Dutch farms showcasing windmills, dikes, and wooden shoes), food (eating French crepes), celebrations (Chinese New Year), clothes (Japanese kimonos), music (listening to Ghanaian drums), famous places (photos of Red Square), or artifacts (passing around prayer beads from Saudi Arabia). There are several problems when culture learning is restricted to this approach.

First, a focus on "pure" or "traditional" cultural attributes (traditional dance, music, food, clothes, holidays or lifestyles) misleads students as it is not what they would actually see if they visited the country today and interacted with young people in that country's cities and rural areas.[1] Such content does not prepare young Americans for the realities of global social change and the multicultural nature of most countries around the world.

By choosing cultural "purity' over cultural synthesis, hybridity or global connections, we are omitting one of the great demographic and societal trends of the last fifty years—multiculturalism.

When today's teachers teach that the British people are white Anglo-Saxons they are denying their students access to current demographics as Britain today has considerable ethnic, racial and religious diversity. Do we really want to wait until a British Muslim makes the evening news before we teach young people about British citizens of a South Asia heritage? Most nations today are multicultural through movement of people into the country or because of long-standing minority cultures and sub-cultures. In order to understand their world, our students need to appreciate Muslim minorities in China, Peruvian citizens of Japanese ancestry, and the complexity of indigenous peoples, mestizos and citizens of European descent in Central America.

Second, the traditional culture approach reduces culture study to surface culture and fails to teach the patterns of beliefs and norms of behavior that make up internal culture, the essence of people's identity and worldviews (see Figure 4.1).

Although surface culture can be an entertaining way to study other societies, students also need to study internal culture if they are to understand their world today. When used exclusively, the surface approach to culture

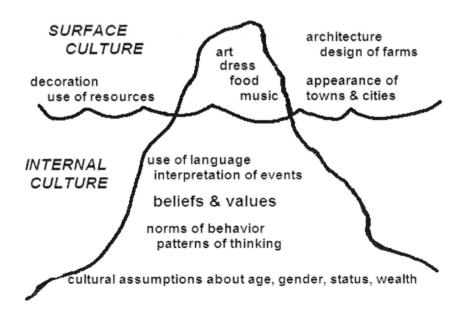

FIGURE 4.1 Culture as an Iceberg. From Merryfield & Wilson, 2005, p. 42.

denies students the opportunity to acquire cross-cultural understanding, practice perspective-taking and develop skills in communicating and working with people from other cultures.

Internal culture provides a framework for acquiring knowledge that prepares students for authentic cross-cultural interaction. Interaction is critical in global education as we assume that young people today need to learn to work effectively with people different from themselves. So culture study is not merely an academic exercise where customs are learned for a paper and pencil test. It is the development of usable knowledge that will be authentically assessed as students interact with people from many cultures during their lifetimes.

People may make different choices and hold different opinions from others in their culture, yet there are patterns of thinking that to some degree shape a society's assumptions and norms of behavior. Below are some of the elements that shape human behavior. These elements are adapted from Craig Storti's work (1999).

Case studies, simulations, cultural assimilators and authentic cross-cultural experiences are used to develop student understanding of internal culture. These resources can build skills in analyzing how cultural thought patterns affect people's communication and interaction. Craig Storti's (1999) *Figuring Foreigners Out* has a series of activities in which student identify their own cultural norms on a continuum from the extremes of individualist to collectivist (and other patterns of thought such as those above) and then compare them to norms in a dozen other cultures. His dialogues, similar in structure to the teaching idea below, demonstrate how differences in thought patterns can create significant cultural misunderstandings.

Major concepts in recognizing how culture influences perception and interaction could include:

- *Surface v. Internal Culture:* Attributes of surface culture include clothes, music, and celebration of holidays. Internal culture provides a framework of beliefs and values that shape norms of behavior and styles of communication and interaction.
- *Cultural Assumptions:* People interpret new information or experiences through their cultural lenses that provide a structure for making sense of and judging events, issues, and people.

Enduring understandings may include:

1. Societies see their world through cultural lenses that shape how they think, make decisions and take action.
2. Confusion, misunderstandings, and conflict can result when people do not know or appreciate other people's beliefs, values and norms of behavior.

FIGURE 4.2. Elements of Internal Culture

Elements of Internal Culture	Explanation and Effects on Patterns of Behavior.
Concept of Self from individualist to collectivist	The more a culture is individualistic, the more people are expected to look after themselves. Individualist cultures value independence and self-reliance. They work hard for recognition. Children are taught to take care of themselves. In collectivist cultures identity is the function of one's group. Students or employees do not want to stand out. The group demands harmony and loyalty, and, in return, looks after its members their whole lives.
Uncertainty Avoidance from low to high	The more a culture has high uncertainty avoidance, the more people want structure, rules, and strict codes of behavior. People in cultures characterized by high uncertainty avoidance are active, aggressive, security-seeking and intolerant. Cultures with weak uncertainty avoidance are contemplative and do not want a lot of rules. They are accepting of personal risk, and relatively tolerant.
Time Monochronic to Polychronic	The more monochronic a culture is, the more time is a valued resource. People take deadlines and schedules very seriously. Getting to class on time is more important that stopping to greet a friend. People do one thing at a time and finish one task before beginning another. People stay in line to wait their turn. Polychronic cultures bend time to meet needs. Schedules and deadlines are flexible. People will get there when they can but human relationships are more important than time. People can work on many tasks and interact with several people at the same time. People don't stand in line.
Responsibility Universalist to Particularist	The more universalist a culture is, the more people know what's right is always right. There are no exceptions. Fair treatment means everyone is treated the same. Favoritism and nepotism are frowned on. People succeed because of what they do. In particularist cultures, there are no absolutes. What is right depends on the situation. Fair means treating everyone uniquely, and people know everything is not fair. Favoritism is the norm because the system is not fair. Whom you know is more important than your performance.
Importance of Face from little to very important	In cultures where face is very important, people want to preserve harmony and are likely to say whatever makes the other person feel good. Strengthening interpersonal relations is more important than the telling the truth. In cultures where face is less important, telling the truth is more valued than worrying about someone's feelings. People say no or confront people when they need to do so.
Degree of Directness from indirect to direct	The more a culture is direct, the more people say what they think. And when they say yes, they mean it. In a culture that values more indirect styles, people must read between the lines. People suggest or hint at what they think or take some action that lets someone know that there is a problem. People may say "yes" when they mean "maybe" or "no" as it is more polite to agree.

These concepts and enduring understandings can be integrated into the social studies through the study of past civilizations, contemporary world cultures, and human conflict. Shared beliefs, values and norms of behavior can be examined historically within the contexts of ethnic identity (the Moors in medieval Spain, the Han in 20th century China), racial identity (white settlers in 19th century South Africa), religious identity (Jews in the Soviet Union) and through the intersection of multiple identities. It is important that students understand that shared cultural norms and language are what make some people Japanese and others Iranian, Palestinian, French Canadian or Jamaican.

Teaching Idea: Patterns of Communication Matter

Culture influences the ways in which we communicate both verbally and non-verbally. In this lesson students discussed the thinking patterns from Sorti's work (as described above) and then analyzed the dialogue below. They identified the cultural misunderstandings and then hypothesized what element/s of internal culture needed to be understood to communicate well across these cultures.

Dialogue # 1: It's Okay
Marcus: So what did Masa say about the research?
J.J.: It's okay. He says it is okay.
Marcus: Did you ask him about the references?
J.J.: Yes, I told we could not get the references done last night.
Marcus: And what did he say?
J.J.: He said, "Okay" and then starting talking about the PowerPoint.
Marcus: I guess he can work around it.

The students' explanation of the cultural misunderstanding: Marcus and J.J. are interpreting Masa's comments based on their own direct communication norms. They say what they are thinking so they assume Masa is also telling them what he thinks. However, Masa, who comes from a culture that values understatement and indirect styles, does not want to show his disappointment that they have not completed their work. He changed the subject abruptly, indicating that he finds the conversation embarrassing and uncomfortable. The boys assume Masa will finish the work while he assumes from the statement "we are sorry" that they feel badly about falling behind and will hurry to get it done.

Teaching Idea: Cultural Assumptions Underlie Interactions

Case studies or vignettes are often useful in making students aware of how misunderstandings can arise when people are operating from different cultural assumptions. By presenting two or more sides, teachers can teach the value of anticipating multiple constructions and interpretations of everyday events. This activity began with a role play of the event and then groups of students identified the cultural assumptions that led Ms. Gomez, Kim and Beatriz to interpret this incident in different ways.

The class developed this explanation:

> This is an example of how cultural misunderstandings can result when some-one from a monochronic culture interacts with someone from a polychronic culture. Ms. Gomez feels comfortable interacting with several people at the same time. She would feel badly if someone came up to her, and she did not greet them. Kim, however, comes from a monochronic culture and expects her teachers to finish working with her before they talk to other people. She thinks Ms Gomez ignored her and resents the other student not waiting her turn.

FIGURE 4.3. Cultural Assumptions

The Visible Incident at Park Middle School for the Role Play	Kim's Interpretation	Beatriz's Interpretation	Ms. Gomez's Interpretation
Ms. Gomez is monitoring students as they practice basketball skills during PE. Kim, a student, comes up and asks her about trying outs for the team. Beatriz, another student, follows and asks Ms. Gomez about her baby daughter. Ms. Elvan, an assistant coach, happens along and joins in the conversation about the baby. Kim speaks harshly to Beatriz, and then runs off to the locker room. Ms. Gomez looks puzzled. Beatriz and Ms. Elvan look upset.	I saw that Ms. Gomez wasn't doing anything so I thought it would be a good time to ask her about trying out for the team. I wanted to talk to her alone as it is nobody's business, and I wasn't sure what she would say as I don't know her very well. Then Beatriz rushes up and interrupts to ask some dumb question about a baby. Ms. Gomez starts talking to her. Then Ms. Elvan comes and it is like I am not there. And I was there first. I told Beatriz to leave off but I was also mad at Ms. Gomez. Maybe she doesn't like me?	I saw Kim go up to talk to Ms. Gomez and so I thought it would be a good time to ask her about her new baby. She goes to our church, and I know the baby is going to be baptized soon. All the sudden Kim gets all huffy and tells me to get lost. What is wrong with her? She was so rude.	In 5th period the girls were practicing baskets when Kim came over to see me. She asked about b-ball tryouts and then seemed to get really angry at Beatriz over something. I don't know what her problem is, but she needs to calm down. I don't appreciate her using bad language and running off.

Several publications of Intercultural Press www.interculturalpress.com offer dialogues, case studies, and culture-specific information that can help students become familiar with cultural thought patterns and test their skills through activities in cross-cultural interaction. It is important that social studies students recognize how cultural differences affect the ways in which people make judgments, ask questions, interpret body language, develop expectations, and interact with others.

DECOLONIZING IMPERIAL WORLDVIEWS

For over five centuries European scientists, naturalists, ethnographers, historians, geographers, journalists, painters and poets captured what was being learned through exploration, trade, and colonization and organized it for the education of their countrymen (Willinsky, 1998). Literature written by explorers and settlers, visual images from sketches, paintings and photos, plants, animals, and even humans were brought back to Europe for exhibition and study. The vast body of new information and artifacts that came with empire emerged as new knowledge (and new disciplines) to explain other cultures and the diversity of the natural world. Many of the West's treasured institutions— zoos, botanical gardens, libraries and museums—organized this new knowledge and displayed it.

Historically American knowledge about the world is rooted in European scholarship that emerged as "new" lands were explored and "new" peoples encountered, converted, enslaved or conquered. Along with Mercator's maps and "Dr. Livingstone, I presume," Americans absorbed and passed on (and some would say Americanized) many British assumptions about the world and its people that developed during exploration and conquest. These remnants of empire foster a mindset which conflicts in significant ways with a global perspective (Apple & Buras, 2006).

Imperial worldviews have several characteristics that may sound familiar to those of us in the social studies. First there is always a framework of opposition in which the world's peoples are divided, organized and described. Whether the terms are The Orient/The West, civilized/uncivilized, First World/Third World, free/communist or industrialized/developing nations, imperial worldviews demand an "us"–usually the white middle class descendants of Western Europeans and a "them," the Others who are divided from Americans by their cultures, skin colors, languages, religions, politics, or other differences. These "us and them" divisions often imply "we" are superior, just as the British assumed they were superior to the people they discovered in other parts of the world. The divisions may support xenophobia ("you can't trust those xxx") and have been used in the past as a rationale for enslaving, civilizing, removing, interring, or repressing others.

We can see the inheritance of imperial worldviews when students are taught to focus on differences between Americans and other peoples. In decolonizing the social studies students learn to balance the study of cultural differences with an appreciation of cultural commonalities and hybridity, the ways in which cultures change as they borrow and adapt over time (Apple & Buras, 2006; Willinsky, 1998).

Second, in the not so recent past U.S. and world history courses were often organized by European diffusionism, a way of centering history on the European diaspora (Willinsky, 1998). The history of the world unfolded according to where Europeans explored or colonized. Students did not study African history or Latin American history until the time period when Europeans arrived. Even when European diffusionism does include the study of Africa or Asia, it does so through European eyes, scholarship and primary sources. So the "opening" of Japan would be taught through Perry's construction of that event. The Boxer rebellion would be taught from a European historical context despite 5000 years of Chinese history.

There has been considerable attention over the last 20 years to teaching about the explorations of Columbus from European and Indian perspectives. However, we still have many social studies courses today where students only study Korean, Cuban or Vietnamese history during the time periods when Europeans or Americans were present. Such organization cannot prepare young people to understand today's global age as students need to learn about the world from a global perspective.

Third, imperialist thought and scholarship were inherently racist and contributed to the teaching of racialized identities and white superiority while ignoring or denigrating Africans and African Americans as well as Asians, Native Americans and others (Apple & Buras, 2006; Willinsky, 1998). It is important for students to recognize that people with power decide what is taught about the world. They also decide who has the credentials to create new knowledge. Although American social studies has come a long way in infusing the experiences, perspectives, literature, and knowledge of African Americans and other people of color, we still have a long way to go in teaching the perspectives of people in other world regions. The problem has been compounded by reliance upon American and European scholars and writers as though students would not gain understanding by reading history and literature written by scholars representing the other 94% of the world's population.

It is important for students to recognize that decolonizing the social studies is ultimately the recognition of how power affects knowledge. Students can examine how mainstream academic knowledge in other countries is influenced by those who hold power. In a global issues class students could examine recent attacks by Chinese and Koreans on the omission of war crimes and comfort women in Japanese textbooks or the imprisoning of a

Turk who wrote about the Armenian genocide. Such research can also explore how changes in power may lead to new knowledge, changes in taboos for public knowledge, or revisionist history. The intersections of power and knowledge provide insights into the breakup of the Soviet Union or changes in South African history since Mandela came to power. Power also shapes public knowledge through control over the media and the persecution of reporters in many countries.

One of my favorite lessons is called "the Meeting on the Congo," where without their knowing it I give half my students a page written by a European explorer and the other half a page written by an African chief about a real historical event on the Congo River. I introduce the lesson as an example of how one can teach about perspective consciousness and ask them to circle words that demonstrate the author's perspective on this historic meeting. After they complete the reading we talk about how to identify the author's perspective. Within minutes conflicting perspectives have been shared and the students are confused, then questioning. Eventually someone says 'we aren't reading the same account!' Then as they place the two accounts of the same event side by side, an intriguing discussion emerges on why they never have read accounts of African history written by Africans. Of course the outcomes of such activities are dependent on students learning to value other points of view.

Major concepts in examining relationships between mainstream knowledge and power.

- *Imperial World Views.* Patterns of thinking that developed as empires expanded.
- *Mainstream Academic Knowledge.* Knowledge taught in most public institutions that is sanctioned by the government and groups in power.

Enduring understandings may include:

1. People with political, economic and social power shape a nation's mainstream academic knowledge.
2. Created within cultural and political contexts, knowledge reflects assumptions, values, and perspectives of its time and place.

These concepts and enduring understandings can be integrated into the social studies through the inclusion of multiple perspectives and primary sources written by people in other countries. Above all the recognition of the inheritance of imperial worldviews and the relationships between power and knowledge relies upon skills in critical thinking. Students need to be able to identify unstated assumptions, detect bias, and anticipate relationships between power and knowledge.

Teaching Idea: Terrorists or Freedom Fighters?

In order to teach complex views of European colonialism and African nationalism, a teacher had his students study both European and African constructions of independence movements in Kenya and South Africa. For example, they read Kenyatta's speech in 1952 *The Kenyan African Union is not the Mau Mau* http://www.fordham.edu/halsall/mod/1952kenyatta-kau1.html for its ideas on nationalism and self-determination and compared it with British ideas on colonial rule and "Mau Mau" insurgents. The students examined ideas of the African National Congress in South Africa http://www.anc.org.za/show.php?include=docs/const/2007/const2007.html with those of the apartheid regime. To increase the complexity of their understanding, the teacher also included relevant speeches and documents from Algeria and the Belgian Congo so that his students recognized that there were different outcomes of colonial rule and diverse approaches to African nationalism.

Teaching Idea: Rethinking the World through Maps

In this lesson students analyzed maps, along with histories and literature, to trace changes in European thinking as they interacted with people in Africa, Asia and the Americas. Students catalogued how maps were used to depict unexplored lands, valued objects, animals, other cultures, and fears.

> **Resources:** See http://www.collectionscanada.ca/education/008-3070-e.html
> http://www.ibiblio.org/expo/1492.exhibit/Intro.html   http://web.reed.
> edu/resources/library/maps/ and http://www.library.yale.edu/MapColl/
> oldsite/map/oldies.html

Teaching Idea: In Black and White

To understand how people have developed ideas about race, students analyzed selections of literature from different time periods that depict white authors' perspectives on African and African American women and African and African American perspectives on white women. Included were selections from Europeans' writing about African women, African women writers' descriptions of whites, white American literature on African American women and African American women's writing about white women. See http://www.wmich.edu/dialogues/themes/africanwomen.html for resources on African women writers. Students identified changes over time and some surprising commonalities across races.

CONCLUSION

Social studies teachers are developing many strategies to prepare American students for their transcultural and interconnected world. Using 21st century technologies, students are developing the skills needed to access, evaluate and use global information from multiple points of view to inform their decisions and actions. Recognizing the implications of increasing cross-cultural interactions, teachers are teaching world cultures with skills and content that prepare young people to understand, communicate and interact with people different from themselves.

Through the study of local/global connections, the scholarship of people in other countries, and attention to current events and issues facing the planet, students are learning to see themselves and their communities within a global context. They are becoming openminded and worldminded with an appreciation of the complexity, interconnectedness, and syncrety of the global human experience.

ENDNOTE

1. In the last decade I have served as a consultant for two publishers of social studies textbooks and for Disney Publications in what the Director has termed Disney's first serious book about the world for students of middle school age (*Our World* published by Disney in 2005). In each consultancy five to ten of my international students from Europe, Asia, Africa and Latin America worked with me to review text and images and offer recommendations. The most consistent advice we gave all three companies was: your books do not depict other cultures accurately. About two of very three photos were either very dated (up to 40 years old), of unusual customs practiced by very few or only in the past, of tourist attractions Westerners admire, or of animals (especially for Africa and Asia). The international students often could not recognize their own countries and would ask me, "where do they get this information? and why are they using these old photos?" We found few photos of cities for Africa and the Middle East despite high rates of urbanization, and almost all photos of farming outside of Europe showed no mechanization despite the Green Revolution. The text accompanying the images almost always ignored societal changes and current issues within the countries. Can you imagine reading an Italian or Japanese or South African text's chapter on American culture and seeing so much misinformation that you don't recognize your own country? One of my students suggested that the US should be taught about through cowboys and Appalachian farmers (as typical jobs), Disney World and Times Square, (the tourist section), statistics on crime rates (something bad), and photos of people locked away in old folks homes (pick on anything that looks strange) to capture a comparable distortion of what was done to his country.

REFERENCES

Abdullahi, S. A. (2010). Rethinking global education in the twenty-first century. In J. Zajda (Ed.), *Global pedagogies: Schooling for the future.* New York: Springer.

Adams, J. M., & Carfagna, A. (2006). *Coming of age in a globalized world.* Bloomfield, CT: Kumarian Press.

Alger, C. F., & Harf, J. E. (1986). Global education: Why? For whom? About what? In R. E. Freeman (Ed.), *Promising practices in global education: A handbook with case studies* (pp. 1–13). New York: The National Council on Foreign Language and International Studies.

Anderson, L. (1979). *Schooling for citizenship in a global age: An exploration of the meaning and significance of global education.* Bloomington, IN: Social Studies Development Center.

Apple, M. W., & Buras, K. L. (2006). *The subaltern speaks.* New York: Routledge.

Banks, J. A., Banks, C. A. M., Cortes, C., Hahn, C. L., Merryfield, M. M., Moodley, K. A., Murphy-Shigematsu, S., Audrey Osler, A., Caryn Park, C., & Parker, W.A. (2005). *Democracy and diversity: Principles and concepts for educating students in a global age.* Seattle: Center for Multicultural Education.

Becker, J. M., (Ed.) (1979). *Schooling for a global age.* New York: McGraw-Hill.

Bigelow, B., & Peterson, B. (Eds.). (2002). *Rethinking globalization.* Milwaukee, WI: Rethinking Schools.

Case, R. (1993). Key elements of a global perspective. *Social Education, 57,* 318–325.

Diaz, C., Massialas, B. G., & Xanthopoulos, J. A. (1999). *Global perspectives for educators.* Boston: Allyn & Bacon.

Gaudelli, W. (2003). *World class: Teaching and learning in global times.* Mahwah, NJ: Lawrence Erlbaum.

Hanvey, R. G. (1976). *An attainable global perspective.* Denver, CO: The Center for Teaching International Relations, The University of Denver.

Kirkwood, T. F. (Ed.). (2010). *Visions in global education.* New York: Peter Lang.

Kniep, W. M. (1986). Defining a global education by its content. *Social Education, 50,* 437–466.

Merryfield, M. M., & Wilson, A. (2005). *Social studies and the world.* Silver Spring, MD: The National Council for the Social Studies.

National Council for the Social Studies. (2005). *Position statement on global education.* Silver Spring, MD: National Council for the Social Studies.

Noddings, N. (Ed.). (2005). *Educating citizens for global awareness.* New York: Teachers College Press.

Pang, V. O. (2005). *Multicultural education: A caring reflective approach.* Second edition. McGraw-Hill: Boston.

Peters, L. (2009). *Global education: Using technology to bring the world to your students.* Washington D.C.: International Society for Technology in Education.

Pike, G. (2000). Global education and national identity. *Theory Into Practice, 39*(2), 64–73.

Pike, G., & Selby, D. (1995). *Reconnecting from national to global curriculum.* Toronto: International Institute for Global Education, University of Toronto.

Sassen, S. (1996). *Losing control? Sovereignty in an age of globalization.* New York: Columbia University Press.,

Storti, C. (1999). *Figuring foreigners out.* Yarmouth. ME; Intercultural Press.

Subedi, B. (Ed.). (2010). *Critical global perspectives: Rethinking knowledge about global societies.* Charlotte, NC: Information Age.

Tan, K.C. (2004). *Justice without borders.* Cambridge: Cambridge University Press.

Willinsky, J. (1998). *Learning to divide the world.* Minneapolis: MN: University of Minnesota Press.

Wilson, A. (1982). Cross-cultural experiential learning for teachers. *Theory Into Practice 21,* 184–192.

CHAPTER 5

THE PLACE OF GLOBAL CITIZENSHIP IN THE SOCIAL STUDIES CURRICULUM

Anatoli Rapoport

Citizenship has always been the focal point of social studies since the concept and term appeared in the early 1900s. In 1906, Thomas Jesse Jones, who ten years later chaired the Committee on Social Studies of the Commission of Reorganization of Secondary Education, wrote that important components of the Hampton curriculum were "... the essentials of good home, the duties and responsibilities of citizenship, the cost and meaning of education, the place of labor, and the importance of thrift" (Lybarger, 1983, p. 457). Thus, more than a century ago one of the most disputable concepts, citizenship, became inseparably linked to one of the most vulnerable areas in education, social studies. Historically, citizenship evolved into a concept that expanded well beyond its primary meaning. As an increasingly contested construct, citizenship is placed at the center of political, ideological, and cultural debates. This is because citizenship is seen as a virtue that can be actively practiced by society members to resist increasing political apathy and indifference among voters, because it is the measure that helps exercise individual rights against a well visible hand of either

Contemporary Social Studies: An Essential Reader, pages 77–95
Copyright © 2012 by Information Age Publishing
All rights of reproduction in any form reserved.

market or government, and because citizenship is perceived as a means of minority struggle to achieve desirable equality and status. Citizenship is a multifaceted multifunctional construct that is difficult to define in a traditional manner. Marshall's (1950) theory of historical progression of citizenship based on the development of civil, political, and social rights well describes the chronological development of the concept, but it is no longer sufficient to encompass all aspects and characteristics of citizenship as it is understood in the 21st century. Marshall's theory has been challenged by a rising number of competing models of citizenship (Carter, 2006) that are usually conceptualized and interpreted through various discourses.

The discursive framework-based approach, in which the model of citizenship is determined by both context and involved agents (Abowitz & Harnish, 2006), has become a primary systemic instrument in citizenship model classification. Until recently, at least one aspect of citizenship was almost universally accepted: citizenship has been interpreted through an individual relationship with a nation state when loyalty to the state and building a common identity were at the core of citizenship education (Lawson & Scott, 2002). To be a citizen implied that a person, at a minimum, had a number of responsibilities to the state and to other members of the community and, at the same time, enjoyed rights that the state awarded him or her as compensation for fulfilling their responsibilities. The raising wave of what is routinely called globalization and unification profoundly influenced the very notion of citizenship by not only infusing a more distinct global perspective but also by challenging the core principles and foundations of citizenship as idiosyncratically nation or nation-state related concepts. The areas of rights, responsibilities, duties, or privileges are expanding and multiplying so that an individual's expectation of loyalty, commitment, and belonging is no longer limited to a living place or nation but also comes from a sense of belonging to a more expanded community, to the world (McIntosh, 2005). This expanded model of citizenship is increasingly becoming a center of scholars' attention. In turn, it has come to be seen as an umbrella model for several sub-models: global citizenship, cosmopolitan citizenship, supra-national citizenship, or transnational citizenship.

The purpose of this chapter is to demonstrate that the social studies curriculum is the primary space for global citizenship education. The chapter begins with a brief overview of global citizenship debates and their implication on education. Then, the attitude to global citizenship education among educators in the United States and abroad will be discussed. Finally, some methodological aspects of providing global citizenship framework in the social studies classroom will be outlined.

GLOBAL CITIZENSHIP? IS IT REAL?

Social science scholars and the corporate world have been discussing the global citizenship phenomenon for a long time. However, school practitioners, particularly in the United States, are not very vocal about it. We hear much about global aspects of citizenship at conferences but not in classrooms. What makes the concept of global citizenship so controversial? It is necessary to note that this concept is still not universally accepted. Much of the criticism is related to its social and political aspects. Wood (2008) denounces global citizenship because citizenship is a technology of governance rather than "an unambiguously emancipatory, empowering institution" (p. 25) and there are no formal political structures at the global level that citizenship could be a part of. Noddings (2005) explains the difficulty to define global citizenship by pointing out that there is no global government to which we owe allegiance and there are no international laws that are enacted without nations' endorsement. An absence of relevant global institutions together with disbelief in global ethics or in the role of an individual in global affairs are the primary reasons why people are skeptical of global citizenship, contends Dower (2003). However, many theorists do not consider the absence of a global governing body a serious obstacle for global citizenship because it simply shifts the focus from law to politics (Delanty, 2002). The emerging global civil society faces several accusations itself: that it is terminologically ambiguous, that its supporters uncritically apply nation-state phenomena to global processes, and that it undermines democracy by weakening the democratic institutions of nation-states (Corry, 2006). Armstrong (2006) argues that the supposedly "global" elements of global citizenship are much less universal and transcendent. Miller (in Carter, 2006, p. 5) calls the idea of global citizenship utopian because "the conditions for global citizenship do not exist and the term is therefore at best metaphorical." Although the role of the nation-state in citizenship education is constantly changing as a consequence of both sub-national and supra-national forces (Barr, 2005; Ramirez, 1997), the potentially pervasive role of the nation-state in the construction of global citizenship remains problematic due to unresolved tensions in cultural and value-oriented perspectives between Western and non-Western countries (White & Openshaw, 2002).

Another reason for debates, mostly theoretical, about global citizenship is the absence of consensus of what global citizenship entails. Most authors identify several factors that cause an increased interest in supra-national models of citizenship and consequent changes in citizenship education. The most noticeable among them are globalization, increasing cultural and social diversity, erosion of traditional nation-state related models of citizenship, creation of supra-national governing bodies, codification of international human rights, proliferation of transnational non-governmental organizations, and the rise of such phenomena as global ethics, global consciousness, and global law, to name a few (Banks, 2004; Dower, 2003; Gaudelli, 2009; Myers, 2006; Stromquist, 2009). We cannot use a traditional technical definition of citizenship to describe global citizenship, for there is no global government that defines the status of a global citizen. To avoid the "global government" problem, some authors suggest an associational approach (Lagos, 2002; Steenbergen, 1994) in which global citizenship is not defined by legal bureaucratic sanctions but by individuals' associations with the place or polity where they reside, work, or spend time. The European Union is an example of such an association. Noddings (2005) suggests that global citizen is the one who is concerned with the welfare of a nation, region, or globe; concerned with the well-being of particular physical places; who is interested in social as well as economic justice; and who supports world peace. McIntosh (2005) proposes a more emotional definition that involves affection, respect, care, curiosity, and concern for well-being of all living beings. She associates global citizenship with habits and capacities of mind, heart, body, and soul that "have to do with working for and preserving a network of relationship and connection across lines of difference and distinctness, while keeping and deepening a sense of one's own identity and integrity" (p. 23). Dower (2003) argues that the status of a global citizen is made up of three components: (a) normative—as global citizens, we have certain duties that extend to all human beings; (b) existential—we all are members of the global community, whether institutional or quasi-political in character; and (c) aspirational—as global citizens, we expect basic values to be realized more fully that requires strengthening communities, institutions, and legal frameworks.

Although the term global citizen is relatively new, the idea that it represents has occupied minds for centuries. Like any big idea, global citizenship is ostensibly interpreted by people differently due to people's own ideologies and contexts. Thus, a discourse, as a primary locus where ideology, language and context intersect and where meanings are negotiated and crystallized, becomes a space in which to look for definitions. Discursive typologization is helpful in that it avoids one-dimensional definitions and describes global citizenship as a multifaceted concept. Gaudelli (2009) employed heuristics to define five different discourses of global citizenship: (a) neoliberal, where a global citizen is still affiliated nationally but is governed by a universal market conception; (b) national, where civic identity is a social compact between the nation and the citizen; (c) Marxist, which bases global citizenship on class, primarily proletarian, collectives that transcend national borders; (d) world justice and governance that rationalizes global citizenship through global human rights, international law, and global civil society; and (e) cosmopolitan, whose framework of global citizenship includes matters of value, morality and humane treatment. Stromquist (2009) organized her analysis around major features of the global model of citizenship, which are: (a) proponents, (b) fundamental perspective, (c) key objectives, (d) driving forces, (e) values, (f) governance, and (g) beneficiaries. The four discourses that help understand those features are:

- World Culture. This discourse is based on sociological perspectives and holds that a global culture is emerging characterized by diversity as well as ubiquitous recognition of human rights.
- New-Era Realism. Based on political perspectives, this discourse is formed by the idea that global citizenship is a hegemonic attempt of a few world players, particularly the United States, to create a world order to mask their self-interests.
- Corporate Citizenship. This discourse, based on economic perspectives, posits corporations as new world citizens that do not respect national borders, whose "transnational liberalism is sponsored by governing elites and informed by principles of trade liberalization and corporative advantage" (p. 13).
- Planetary Vessel. This discourse, stemming from grassroots groups, acknowledges concern for universal human rights and recognizes new global problems that transcend national borders, such as environment, health, sustainability, peace, and security.

So, is global citizenship a utopian theory, a phantom, a theoretical construct existing only in the minds of theoreticians, or a real status that all humans can enjoy? On the one hand, citizenship as a form of membership possesses such a feature as exclusiveness—one is excluded from a traditionally understood citizenship "club" if he or she does not possess attributes artificially constructed by "club management". This archaic hegemonic idea of exclusiveness served well in the times of the emergence of new nations and new nation-states. On the other hand, as citizenship increasingly comes to be understood as shared rights, both human and civil, that all individuals should enjoy; as shared responsibilities of all human beings for survival of the planet, a clean environment, and a sustainable future; and as a collection of ethical principles and values that all humans embrace regardless of their cultural, ethnic, or religious backgrounds, the idea of citizenship that is shared and acknowledged by all humans is gaining strength.

We can say that the global citizenship model emulates many national citizenship models in which people acquire citizenship status automatically by the virtue of the circumstances of their birth. All those born in the United States are automatically American citizens, but it is the task of the society (parents, school, institutions) to fully socialize a legal citizen into a *national* citizen. Following this logic, all human beings are legal global citizens by birth, and it is the task of the society to fully socialize them into *global* citizens, or, in other words, to make them aware of their global citizenship status. In general, the problem of global citizenship is no longer whether or not it exists but rather how citizens should exercise their global status. This problem can be rephrased in the following way: What should parents, schools, and institutions do to help young people become aware of their status as not only local or national citizens but also as global citizens and particularly, how can we make all people, young and old alike, active global citizens?

GLOBAL CITIZENSHIP EDUCATION IN THE UNITED STATES

The attitude toward global citizenship and consequently toward global citizenship education in the United States is complicated. Besides the general reasons discussed earlier, such as the vagueness of the term, the absence of global governance, or the allegedly damaging effect on democratic development, the advance of global citizenship education in the United States has faced very specific challenges that are largely the result of political history and long-lasting debates about the place and role of the United States in the world. The ever contested and debated concepts of globalization, citizenship, and education on American soil, fertilized by isolationism, exceptionalism, decentralism, and individualism, acquire new nuances and meanings.

Since the 1990s, much of the world—particularly developing countries—has viewed globalization as a new hegemonic endeavor, as a new attempt of "encroaching imperialism" of the West, particularly the United States, to recolonize the world. In our metaphorically determined world, globalization for many in developing countries has become a symbol of poverty, injustice, and cultural degradation, and so has the United States that epitomizes this global phenomenon (Lal, 2004; Stromquist, 2009). Gradually, globalization has become synonymous to Americanization. Like all paradigmatic changes of such scale, globalization is a very controversial and ambiguous process that has both advantages and disadvantages. Questionable international policy of the United States, immediately linked by some shrewd politicians to the outcomes of globalization, also contributed to the negative image of both the United States and globalization. Ironically, in the United States, where the traditions of isolationism are still strong, globalization is perceived by many, mostly in conservative circles, as a conspiracy launched by some mythical world government, usually personified by the United Nations, against core American values. Myers (2006) noted that the paradox of globalization in the United States is that we fear the same threat that the rest of the world blames us for: that globalization "is causing us to lose our national identity and the 'American way of life,' and that regional free-trade pacts are eliminating local jobs" (p. 371). As a result, the complex, ambiguous, controversial, and provocative concept of globalization is either ignored in many US schools or presented solely through the economic interdependence framework. Teachers are sometimes instructed not to touch upon the concept of globalization due mostly to its controversial nature (Rapoport, 2010). It is not surprising, therefore, that by 2009 globalization was mentioned in the social studies standards of only 15 states (Rapoport, 2009). However, in most recently revised and updated social studies standards, globalization is presented both as an economic concept and as a more ubiquitous and nuanced phenomenon, which is a promising sign.

A discussion about citizenship education would seem incomplete without mentioning patriotism. Patriotism has long been one of the major components of citizenship education. Moreover, patriotism is sometimes viewed by many, including many educators, as the centerpiece of citizenship and thus, the main purpose of citizenship education (Finn, 2007; Fonte, 1997; Ravitch, 2006). Patriotism is usually described as a special affinity one has toward their country, a "sense of positive identification with and feelings of affective attachment to one's country" (Schatz, Staub, & Levine, 1999, p. 53), "the civic devotion toward the state as a political entity ...while expressing commitment toward it" (Kashti, 1997, p. 152), or "a kind of psychological disposition underlying the specific feelings, attitudes, and forms of behavior focused on one's country" (Reykowsi, 1997, p. 108).

Social constructs such as patriotism are vulnerable because they only exist in human consciousness and not in the physical world; therefore, if one is to feel patriotic, one must be regularly reminded of it. As Johnson (1997) put it, "Patriots are manufactured by the system of which they are members" (p. 79). If nationalism was formed and supported through the development and propagation of national myths, metaphoric symbols, rituals, and ceremonies, then patriotism, that Kashti (1997) called "state nationalism" (p. 155) is the purposeful exploitation of individuals' "primordial link to territory and society" (Janowitz 1983). Because this process involves the initiation, development, interpretation, negotiation, and reevaluation of the "collective system of meanings" (Reykowski, 1997, p. 109), control over the means of socialization, of which education is the most significant component, is crucial. This explains why in many countries, particularly in those where governments experience minimal or no civic control, those in power are so careful and particular about the systemic approach to promoting patriotism or, in other words, to centrally controlled patriotic education.

In most cases, patriotism is conceptualized in its traditional meaning. This is particularly true in the United States where, on the one hand, schooling disproportionately favors national identity over learning about the world and, on the other hand, teachers can be accused of being unpatriotic when they promote critical discussion of government policy (Loewen, 1996; Myers, 2006; White & Openshaw, 2002). However, the traditional meaning of patriotism has been challenged more and more often (Apple, 2002; Branson, 2002; Merry, 2009; Nussbaum, 1994), and the idea of patriotism as a more inclusive construct, particularly in regard to multicultural and intercultural discourses, is becoming more acceptable. "A useful definition of patriotism," noted Akhmad and Szpara (2005) "should not hinge on the legal status in a polity but embrace citizens' allegiance to universal human values, democratic ideals, and the human rights and dignity of all people in the world" (p. 10).

CURRICULUM INSECURITY OF GLOBAL CITIZENSHIP: EVERYWHERE AND NOWHERE

The obstacles to global citizenship and global citizenship education described earlier are the result of general ideological and cultural realities and tensions in the society. Together with pro-global forces, these extra-systemic contextual elements are a part of a macrosystem (Bronnfonbrenner, 1979) that directly influences education. However, a number of intro-systemic factors within education potentially hold back the development of global citizenship education in schools. Among those intra-educational obstacles are a lack of pre-service teacher preparation, insufficient curricular and methodological guidance, a lack of interest in and sometimes intentional ignoring of global education among legislators, and an absence of citizenship-related topics at global-themed teacher professional development seminars.

Research conducted among pre-service and in-service teachers demonstrates that teachers are usually oblivious about curricular content materials or instructional strategies related to global citizenship or other supra-national models of citizenship (Gallavan, 2008; Gaudelli, 2009; Myers, 2006; Rapoport, 2010; Robbins, Francis, & Elliot, 2003; Yamashita, 2006). A survey among 187 teacher training and education program graduates in Wales demonstrated that although 76 percent of graduates thought that global citizenship should have a high priority in the secondary school curriculum, only 35 percent felt confident to contribute to a whole school approach global citizenship (Robbins, Francis, & Elliot, 2003). A study in England reported that 700 teachers rated education for global citizenship as important, but had little confidence in their ability to teach it (Davis *et al.* in Yamashita, 2006). The majority of teacher candidates from a mid-South university in the United States wanted to teach their students to be world citizens, but many also felt unprepared by their teacher education programs or field experiences (Gallavan, 2008). Ironically, the highly decentralized system of education that prides itself on the ability to immediately respond to curricular needs of educators failed to adequately react to real needs of schools and justified concerns of teachers. State social studies standards are an example of such failure. The development and implementation of state content standards possess their own dynamics that explain, in part, why standards lag behind real life. This is particularly the case in social studies where the rapidly changing world dictates its own pace incompatible with other areas of education. This may be a reason why in 2008 social studies standards of only two states, Maryland and Mississippi, contained the term *global citizen* (Rapoport, 2009). Standards play a twofold role: they are a channel of political influence of the society on education and at the same time, they are the major document that guides curricular policy. By ignoring such powerful concepts as globalization or global citizenship, standards developers and state boards of education send a mixed message to social studies educators. Instead, one reads about "informed, responsible, and participating citizens at the ...international level," "responsible citizens and active participants in ...global society," "productive, informed citizens in a global society, " or "capable citizens in a culturally diverse and interdependent world." Such euphemistic descriptors are ambivalent and shift the focus. Mixed messages like these in a prescriptive curricular document eventually turn into neglect to a very important concept in the classroom. Additionally, teachers lack academic freedom, curricular justification and support if they decide to include elements of global citizenship education into their curricula. Under the pressure of omnipresent accountability that, as many practitioners know, usually means that what is not tested is not taught, topics related to global citizenship are buried under more "necessary" materials. As a result, many teachers lack the confidence needed to translate their generally positive attitude toward global citizenship education into classroom practices (Merryfield, 1998, 2000; Schweisfurth, 2006) and tend to rationalize the unfamiliar concept of global citizenship through more familiar concepts and discourses (Schweisfurth, 2006).

Despite all challenges, the global citizenship model is no longer a foreign concept. A number of schools choose global citizenship as the basis of their curricula. Concurrently, theorists and practical educators offer more and more global citizenship curricula that are based on their unique visions of global and citizenship education. After the analysis of numerous documents on international education, Collins, Czarra, and Smith (1998) identified categories of global challenges, issues, and problems that are fundamental for improved teaching about international dimensions and global citizenship. The most employed categories are *change* and *interdependence.* The other ten categories are: (a) conflict and its control, (b) economic systems, (c) global belief systems, (d) human rights and social justice, (e) planet management, (f) political systems, (g) population, (h) race and ethnicity, (i) technocratic revolution, and (j) sustainable development. The curriculum developed by Oxfam (2006), first published in 1997 and later revised and updated, identifies global themes that present a rationale for three key components for teaching responsible global citizenship:

- Knowledge and understanding (themes: social justice and equity, diversity, globalization and interdependence, sustainable development, and peace and conflict)
- Skills (themes: critical thinking, ability to argue effectively, ability to challenge justice and inequality, respect for people and things, and cooperation and conflict resolution)
- Values and attitudes (themes: sense of identity and self-esteem, empathy, commitment to social justice and equity, respect to diversity, concern for the environment, and belief that people can make a difference).

After an analysis of various approaches to global education in the United States, Myers (2006) argued that global citizenship education should be considered as an additional layer for developing democratic citizenship rather than an alternative curriculum to civics. He suggested three curricular topics for a global-oriented citizenship education: (a) international human rights as the foundation of global citizenship, (b) the reconciliation of the universal and the local, and (c) political action beyond the national state (376). Gaudelli (2009) stated that existing global citizenship curricula are determined by the five discourses discussed earlier. To enhance the curriculum theorizing and implementation, he suggested that global citizenship curricula should include two epistemic elements, namely hermeneutics and dialogue and placed self-awareness. Instead of "developing curriculum which falsely suggests that there is wide agreement about ideas of what it means to be a global citizen and how one learns to be one" (p. 79), hermeneutics will help to engage students in an active dialogue around competing worldviews on global citizenship. By the same token, placed self-awareness or placed being can help students recognize the particularity of their places and how they are permeated with social meanings by those who live there and beyond them (Helfenbine, 2006).

Vigorous debates about the essence of global citizenship, its curricular content, and pedagogical implementation, leave little space in our highly compartmentalized system of education for a basic question: Where does global citizenship education belong? We routinely say that citizenship education is a multi-component system that involves a number of agencies—the government, community, media, parents, peers, and school—which all have their share in socializing a child, in making a child a responsible and informed citizen. However, who particularly should be doing the work? Which agency is best equipped to provide conditions, space, and guidance for developing knowledge, skills, and dispositions needed to educate globally-minded citizens? It seems that school can play the leading role in this process, as school is designed to reflect on and to react to emerging challenges, particularly cultural, social, or ideological. It remains to be seen whether the reaction of many schools is timely and adequate, the public and educators themselves are often skeptical about it. Nevertheless, school remains the core element of the citizenship education network. But school curriculum, which is a set of ideas, texts, practices, and pedagogies, usually focuses on the disciplines. Global citizenship education, as an inherently multi- and interdisciplinary area, lacks what Gaudelli (2009) called "disciplinary heritage" (p. 78). Although each school discipline has a potential to introduce elements of citizenship in its content, and many do, the discipline-based approach nevertheless narrows a school's capacities to present any model of citizenship in its entirety. Ostensibly, global citizenship education is usually conceptualized within the frameworks of international education, global education (Davies, Evans, & Reid, 2005), multicultural education (Banks, 2004; Dunn, 2002), peace education (Smith & Fairman, 2005), human rights education (Gaudelli & Fernekes, 2004), or economic education. Practitioners are well aware that none of these approaches, with the possible exception of economic education, has yet secured a position in school curricula. Thus, global citizenship education, if taught as one of the topics within these frameworks, would become even more secondary. Such curricular insecurity discourages even those teachers who are enthusiastic about global citizenship.

GLOBAL CITIZENSHIP AND SOCIAL STUDIES CURRICULUM

Social studies seems to be the most natural and logical nexus for global citizenship education. First, social studies developed historically as a statutory citizenship education-oriented area. Although throughout most of the history of social studies citizenship has been rationalized and contextualized as a nation-related phenomenon, recent changes in social studies curricula as well as in curricular development and guiding documents have demonstrated a significant shift in expanding the components of the citizenship education paradigm. This paradigm now includes more references to global and international issues. Although such terms as *global citizen* or *world citizen* are still rarely used in classrooms, the realization that "the integration of [global and international education] is imperative for students to develop the skills, knowledge and attitudes needed for responsible participation in a democratic society and in a global community in the twenty-first century" (NCSS, 2001) is a promising sign. So are the references to the role of citizens in globalized world in a number of National Council for the Social Studies' position statements.

Second, social studies is one of the areas of education that explicitly addresses various components of global citizenship identified by many authors. Instruction in civics, psychology and sociology helps students understand how government works. Despite traditional cultural and ideological resistance against a world government in the United States, international governing bodies are a reality. A proper analysis of the role and place of existing international organizations, examples of mutual benefits that all countries, including the United States, gain from active participation in global affairs through mechanisms of international organizations, demonstration of how international governing bodies are elected and function, will help students more quickly rationalize this reality. The disciplines of history and geography provide students with historical perspectives of international relations, how a world that was once an ultimate war zone has gradually become less dangerous and more peaceful due to the development of world ethics and international law. Anthropology, geography, histories, psychology, and sociology teach students what it means to live in a multicultural world. Global citizenship education can help resolve, at least partially, the internal conflict of every democratic multicultural society: how to balance diversity of multiculturalism and uniformity of citizenship. The global citizenship model, both semantically and practically, transcends routinely understood multiculturalism and expands traditional notions of citizenship, and thus becomes a potentially more inclusive and transformative framework for sustainable democratic development (Snauwaert; 2002; Walker & Serrano, 2006). This is particularly significant for the United States where tensions between cultural groups are considerable and sometimes difficult to resolve. Global and cosmopolitan citizenship frameworks help minorities find their own voices by asserting that value variability is an asset rather than a liability. By teaching global citizenship, educators encourage minority groups to view their differences as assets, thereby empowering these groups to use their differences to advance themselves. This viewpoint helps reconsider an earlier view of education that advocated the elimination of difference as the sole path to successful democracy (Walker & Serrano, 2006). It is also particularly relevant considering the worldwide phenomenon of transnational migration and the unprecedented movement of diverse racial, cultural, ethnic, and religious groups across nation states. Undoubtedly, much has been accomplished lately for the development and spread of ideas of multiculturalism in US education compared to other countries. However, in many schools the international component of multicultural education is left solely to foreign language departments (VanFossen & Rapoport, 2003). Foreign language teachers are experts in introducing a new culture using the language framework. But it is the combination of various social science frameworks that adds a rationale to the *multi* component of multiculturalism, which includes interconnectedness, interrelation, and interdependence of cultures, let alone economics, histories, and geography that have already established themselves as primary and forefront areas in teaching about globalization.

Third, social studies provides a unique balance of knowledge, skills, and dispositions required for proper socialization of global citizens. Applying a global model in citizenship education is much more than shifting focus from local or national to global. As demonstrated by new curricula, the global citizenship model requires cardinal reinterpretation of knowledge, skills, and values. The contemporary global environment is a universe of exponentially expanding knowledge, but the nature of this new knowledge and its scope are no longer confined within one location; knowledge is becoming globally applicable. The biggest modern-era epistemic paradox is that knowledge, constructed as culturally-codified information in one place, quickly turns into globally-interpreted phenomenon shaped by myriads of other individual cultures or identities, eventually returning to its source as a new piece of knowledge. Borders, boundaries, and limits are becoming obsolete and may one day be completely ignored in the new global knowledge construction process.

The newly emerging global order also significantly impacts skills and values. Information-seeking skills, analytical skills, problem-solving, critical thinking, and conflict resolution skills are among those that are most likely to enhance global perspective. These skills are fundamentally important in developing young people's abilities to orient themselves in an expanding global community. Moreover, these skills are transferable, which means that teaching and applying them are not constrained to social studies areas. On the contrary, contemporary pedagogies in all curricular content areas are based on developing problem solving critical thinking skills. Teaching these skills makes citizenship education a truly interdisciplinary area.

Very few people question the centrality of knowledge, skills, and disposition in citizenship education. In this regard, the view of citizenship education in general and social studies education in particular as a primary tool of a child's resocialization or countersocialization (Counts, 1932/1978; Engle & Ochoa, 1988; Hursh & Ross, 2000) presents an intriguing theoretical issue: Are we resocializing our students by challenging traditional nation-oriented citizenship models or are we socializing them by making them aware that they are already global citizens? In any case, the global citizenship perspective in social studies instruction requires very specific techniques and strategies.

What does it mean to teach global citizenship? What does it mean to incorporate a global citizenship component in social studies education? How does one deconstruct global citizenship and how does one provide knowledge and develop skills and dispositions that are critical for future global citizens? How does one appropriately apply the interdisciplinary potential of global citizenship in the classroom and beyond? Social studies teachers will face these challenging questions should they agree to incorporate global and supra-national perspectives into their teaching. Stand-alone courses and programs, such as International Relations, World/Global/ International Studies, or International Perspectives have become an important part of many schools' social studies curricula. Undoubtedly, these courses provide frameworks for teaching global citizenship components. However, such courses are vulnerable: they depend on teachers' mobility, students' interests, ideological and cultural environments, and most often on funding opportunities. Budget cuts and excessive focus on testing make such courses almost non-existent in low-income communities.

Another approach to teaching global citizenship is incorporating elements of global citizenship models into existing social studies courses (Collins, 2007; Noddings, 2005; Smith & Faiman, 2005; Thornton, 2005). The curriculum integration approach is effective in that teachers use content and frameworks of every social studies area to raise issues related to global citizenship. Success of this approach depends on a number of factors that are determined by many objective reasons. Time is the most precious asset in the instructional process: teachers rarely have enough time to "cover" required materials, let alone to incorporate something new. Curricular documents are usually vague about topics of globalization and global citizenship related issues, and the absence of such curricular pressure either from programmatic documents or from the community discourages teachers from taking additional proactive steps in teaching about global citizenship. The lack of epistemic and disciplinary heritage (Gaudelli, 2009) discussed earlier is an additional obstacle to curriculum integration and negatively affects global citizenship education. However, the biggest challenge to the curriculum integration approach may be the lack of the teacher's own interest, motivation, and pedagogical knowledge of how to integrate global citizenship perspectives into social studies area instruction. The teacher's role is critical. Schools need professionals who understand the importance of global and international perspectives in citizenship education, who are interested and motivated to step outside the box, who are not afraid to challenge their own views.

Integration of a global citizenship model cannot be successful if teachers limit their instruction to passing on information about other countries, other cultures, or current events from the media. Mere passive knowledge acquisition can do more harm to teaching global citizenship than not teaching it at all. We should keep in mind that even in our globalizing world, our mentality has been shaped and continues to be shaped by traditional citizenship models and nationalistic discourses. School, and particularly a social studies classroom, is one of few places that can potentially create an environment encouraging students to think of their roles as global citizens, but this can only be done by challenging traditional perspectives and views. Social studies teachers have numerous tools in their pedagogical toolboxes that develop students' critical thinking and help challenge the status quo. All of these tools are in one way or another related to comparative method. For this reason, comparative inquiry and analysis can play a significant role in providing teachers and administrators with new visions and innovative ideas of how to incorporate global frameworks into citizenship education. By inviting students to compare practices or ideas in their communities, states, regions, or nation with practices in other communities or nations, social studies teachers design a rationale that contextualizes such constructs as global law, global ethics, and human and civil rights. Because properly organized comparison includes analysis and synthesis of juxtaposed phenomena, it provides an appropriate paradigm for higher-order thinking and also serves as an additional stimulus to learn more about students' immediate environment. Another technique, also based on comparative approach and the conflict resolution framework, is providing students with alternative perspectives or challenging students to consider an alternative perspective in their speculation, reasoning, interpretation, and argumentation. Paraphrasing Winston Churchill, we should convince students that histories are written not only by victors. Alternative look at historical events (not to confuse with alternative histories) can be very helpful for framing and contextualizing data not only in history courses but also in civics, cultural geography or sociology. Developing alternative perspective requires expanded knowledge base, a mastery of search skills, and the ability to thoughtfully reevaluate traditional views. Exploring alternative views, critiquing traditional approaches, and looking at customary things through the eyes of the others make students committed to accept the multiplicity of truths.

Woodrow Wilson once said, "We are citizens of the world. The tragedy of our times is that we do not know this." One hundred years later, it is still a tragedy. It is a tragedy because without being aware of our global status, we cannot act as responsible global citizens. It is a tragedy because people are still more divided than united. It is critical to understand that in our interdependent world being a citizen already means being a global citizen. New global contexts exert economic, political, ideological, and cultural pressure on individuals in all parts of the world. Young people will be much better equipped and prepared to meet global challenges if the school helps them better understand that they are already a part of the globalized world and members of global citizenry. Social studies teachers and many existing social studies curricula have a potential to be at the forefront of this process. After all, good citizenship is the purpose of social studies - good local, national and global citizenship.

REFERENCES

Abowitz, K. K., & Harnish, J. (2006). Contemporary discourses of citizenship. *Review of Educational Research, 76*(4), 653–690.

Ahmad, I. & Szpara, M. Y. (2005). Education for democratic citizenship and peace: Proposal for a cosmopolitan model. *Educational Studies, 38*(1), 8–23.

Apple, M. (2002). Patriotism, pedagogy, and freedom: On the educational meaning of September 11th. *Teachers College Record, 104*(8), 1760–1772.

Armstrong, C. (2006). Global civil society and the question of global citizenship. *Voluntas, 17*(4), 349–357.

Banks, J. (2004). Teaching for social justice, diversity, and citizenship in a global world. *The Educational Forum, 68*(4), 296–305.

Barr, H. (2005). Toward a model of citizenship education: Coping with differences in definition. In C. White & R. Openshaw (Eds.), *Democracy at the crossroads* (pp. 55–75). London: Lexington Books.

Branson, M. (2002). *Patriotism and civic literacy.* Paper presented at the We the People State and District Coordinators Conference, Washington, DC, June 30. (ERIC Document Reproductive Service No. ED477598)

Bronfenbrenner, U. (1979). *The ecology of human development.* Cambridge, MA: Harvard University Press.

Carter, A. (2006). *The political theory of global citizenship.* London: Routledge

Collins, H. T., Czarra, F. R., & Smith, A. F. (1998). Guidelines for global and international education: Challenges, cultures, and connections. *Social Education, 62*(5), 311–317.

Collins, (2007) *Global Citizenship for Young Children* London: Paul Chapman Publishing.

Corry, O. (2006). Global civil society and its discontents. *Voluntas, 17*(4), 303–324.

Counts, G. (1932/1978). *Dare the school build the new social order?* Southern Illinois University Press

Davies, I., Evans, M., & Reid, A. (2005). Globalizing citizenship education? A critique of "global education" and "citizenship education." *British Journal of Educational Studies, 53*(1), 66–89.

Delanty, G. (2002). *Citizenship in a global age: Society, culture, politics.* Philadelphia: Open University Press

Dower, N. (2003). *An introduction to global citizenship.* Edinburgh University Press.

Dunn, R. E. (2002). Growing good citizens with a world-centered curriculum. *Educational Leadership, 60*(2) 10–13.

Engle S. H., & Ochoa, A. S. (1988). *Education for democratic citizenship.* New York: Teachers College Press

Finn, C. E. (2007). Teaching patriotism—with conviction. In J. Westheimer & H, Zinn, (Eds.) *Pledging allegiance: The politics of patriotism in America's schools.* (pp. 95–98). New York: Teachers College Press.

Fonte, J. (1997). Post-West syndrome: When patriotism is threatened, so are the roots of democracy. *National Review,* October 27.

Gallavan, N. (2008). Examining teacher candidates' views on teaching world citizenship. *The Social Studies, 99*(6), 249–254.

Gaudelli, W. (2009). Heuristics of global citizenship discourses towards curriculum enhancement. *Journal of Curriculum Theorizing, 25*(1), 68–85.

Gaudelli, W. & Fernekes, W. (2004) Teaching about global human rights for global citizenship. *The Social Studies, 95*(1), 16–26.

Helfenbein, R. J. (2006). Space, place, and identity in the teaching of history: Using critical geography to teach teachers in the American south. In A. Segall, E. Heilman, & C. Cherryholmes (Eds.), *Social studies: The next generation* (pp. 111–124). New York: Peter Lang.

Hursh, D., & Ross, E. (2000). *Democratic social education: Social studies for social change.* New York: Falmer Press.

Janowitz, M. (1983). *The reconstruction of patriotism.* Chicago: University of Chicago Press

Johnson, G. (1997). The evolutionary roots of patriotism. In D. Bar-Tal & E. Staub (Eds.), *Patriotism in the lives of individuals and nations* (pp. 45–90). Chicago: Nelson-Hall.

Kashti, Y. (1997). Patriotism as identity and action. In D. Bar-Tal & E. Staub (Eds.) *Patriotism in the Lives of Individuals and Nations* (pp. 151–164). Chicago: Nelson-Hall

Lagos, T. (2002). *Global citizenship—Toward the definition.* Retrieved January 17, 2011 from http://events.facet.iupui.edu/events/IntercampusWorkshops/ Summer%20 Leadership%20Institute/globalcitizenship.pdf

Lal, D. (2004). *In praise of empires: Globalization and order.* Palgrave Macmillan.

Lawson, H., & Scott, D. (2002). Introduction. In D. Scott & H. Lawson (Eds.), *Citizenship education and the curriculum* (pp. 2–6). Ablex Publishing: Westport, CT

Loewen, J. (1996). *Lies my teacher told me: Everything your American History textbook got wrong.* Touchstone.

Lybarger, M. (1983). Origins of the modern social studies: 1900–1916. *History of Education Qurterly, 23*(4), 455–468.

Marshall, T. (1950). *Citizenship and Social Class and Other Essays.* Cambridge University Press.

McIntosh, P. (2005). Gender perspectives on educating for global citizenship. In N. Noddings (Ed.), *Educating citizens for global awareness* (pp. 22–39). New York: Teachers College Press.

Merry, M. (2009). Patriotism, history, and the legitimate aim of American education. *Educational Philosophy and Theory, 41*(4), 378–398.

Merryfield M. M. (1998). Pedagogy for global perspectives in education: Studies for teachers' thinking and practice. *Theory and Research in Social education, 26*(3), 342–379.

Merryfield, M, M. (2000). Why aren't teachers being prepared to teach for diversity, equity, and global interconnectedness? A study of lived experiences in the making of multicultural and global educators. *Teaching and Teacher Education 16,* 429–443.

Myers, J. (2006). Rethinking the social studies curriculum in the context of globalization: Education for global citizenship in the U.S. *Theory and Research in Social Education, 34*(3), 370–394.

NCSS (2001). *Preparing citizens for a global community.* A Position Statement of the National Council for the Social Studies. Retrieved January 22, 2011 from http://development.ncss.org/positions/global

Noddings, N. (2005). Global citizenship: Promises and problems. In N. Noddings (Ed.), *Educating Citizens for Global Awareness* (pp. 1–21). New York: Teachers College, Columbia University.

Nussbaum, M. (1994). Patriotism and cosmopolitanism. *The Boston Review, 19*(5), 3–16.

Oxfam (2006). *Cool planet for teachers: Global citizenship.* Retrieved January 18, 2011 from http://www.oxfam.org.uk/coolplanet/teachers/globciti/curric/index.htm

Ramirez, F. O. (1997). The nation-state, citizenship, and educational change: Institutionalization and globalization. In W. Cummings & McGinn, N. (Eds.), *International handbook of education and development: Preparing schools students and nations for the twenty-first century* (pp. 47–62). New York: Elsevier Science

Rapoport, A. (2009). A forgotten concept: Global citizenship education and state social studies standards. *Journal of Social Studies Research, 33*(1), 75–93.

Rapoport, A. (2010). We cannot teach what we don't know: Indiana teachers talk about global citizenship education. *Education, Citizenship and Social Justice, 5*(3), 1–11.

Ravitch, D. (2006). Should we teach patriotism, *Phi Delta Kappan, 87*(8), 579–581.

Reykowski, J. (1997). Patriotism and the collective system of meaning. In D. Bar-Tal & E. Staub (Eds.), *Patriotism in the lives of individuals and nations.* (108–128). Chicago: Nelson-Hall

Robbins, M., Francis, L. J., & Elliott, E. (2003). Attitudes toward education fpr global citizenship among trainee teachers. *Research in Education, 69*(1), 93–98.

Schatz, R. T., Staub, E., & Lavine, H. (1999). On the varieties of national attachments: Blind versus constructive patriotism. *Political Psychology, 20*(1), 151–174.

Schweisfurth, M. (2006). Education for global citizenship: Teacher agency and curricular structure in Ontario schools. *Educational Review, 58*(1), 41–50.

Smith, S. N., & Fairman, D. (2005). The integration of conflict resolution into the high school curriculum: The example of workable peace. . In N. Noddings (Ed.), *Educating citizens for global awareness* (pp. 40–56). New York: Teachers College Press

Snauwaert, D. (2002). Cosmopolitan democracy and democratic education. *Current Issues in Comparative Education, 4*(2), 5–15.

Steenbergen, B. (1994). *The condition of citizenship.* London: Sage Publications.

Stromquist, N. P. (2009). Theorizing global citizenship: Discourses, challenges, and implications for education. *Interamerican Journal of Education for Democracy, 2*(1), 6–29.

Thornton, S. J. (2005). Incorporating internationalism into the social studies curriculum. In N. Noddings (Ed.) *Educating citizens for global awareness* (pp. 81–92). New York: Teachers College Press.

VanFossen, P. & Rapoport, A. (2003) *The state of international education in Indiana secondary schools.* (Tech. Rep.). West Lafayette, Indiana. Purdue University, James F. Ackerman Center for Democratic Citizenship.

Walker, J., & Serrano, A. (2006). Formulating a cosmopolitan approach to immigration and social policy: Lessons from American (north and south) indigenous and immigrant groups. *Current issues in Comparative Education, 9*(1).

White. C., & Openshaw, R. (2002) Translating the national to the global in citizenship education. In D. Scott & H. Lawson (Eds.), *Citizenship education and the curriculum* (pp. 151–166). Westport, CT: Ablex Publishing.

Wood, P. (2008). The impossibility of global citizenship. *Brock Education*, 17, 22–37.

Yamashita, H. (2006). Global citizenship education and war: The needs of teachers and learners. *Educational Review 58*(1), 27–39.

CHAPTER 6

CHARACTER, MORAL, AND VALUES EDUCATION

The Foundation of Effective Citizenship

Stewart Waters and William Benedict Russell III

A nation, as a society, forms a moral person, and every member of it is personally responsible for his society.

—Thomas Jefferson (1743–1826)

INTRODUCTION

In 1994 the National Council for the Social Studies (NCSS) issued a new definition for social studies, declaring, "social studies is the integrated study of the social sciences and humanities to promote civic competence" (NCSS, 1994). The specific choice to include "civic competence" in the definition of social studies was not a coincidence by the board of directors. Throughout the 1980s and early 1990s there was a strong movement to bring character and citizenship education back into the classroom as educational researchers and law makers cited numerous alarming statistics meant to

Contemporary Social Studies: An Essential Reader, pages 97–116
Copyright © 2012 by Information Age Publishing
97

highlight the diminishing effect that the absence of character education in schools was having on society. NCSS increased the awareness for character and civic issues in social studies education. In fact, the National Council for the Social Studies position on these two trending issues contributed to the merged goals and presence of character and civic education in the social studies curriculum. The early 1990s was a time when social studies, character, and civics educator's all struggled to maintain a place in school curriculum's that were becoming increasingly focused on standards and high stakes assessments. NCSS would go on to solidify the relationship between character education, citizenship education, and the social studies with a position paper officially endorsing the goals of these intertwined fields in 1997. One of the most important pieces of this statement argued that:

> social studies teachers have a responsibility and a duty to refocus their classrooms on the teaching of character and civic virtue. They should not be timid or hesitant about working toward these goals. The fate of the American experiment in self-government depends in no small part on the store of civic virtue that resides in the American people. The social studies profession of this nation has a vital role to play in keeping this wellspring of civic virtue flowing. (NCSS, 1997, p. 2)

The National Council for the Social Studies (NCSS) advocates for social studies teachers to infuse character and civic lessons into the curriculum, the reality of this connection has yet to truly manifest itself in the classroom. Character education programs continue to exist in isolation from social studies curricular goals at the elementary and secondary levels. Civic lessons tend to be discussed in separation as well, normally presented in a secondary civics and/or government course. Even individual social science courses (such as U.S. History, Geography, World history, Economics, etc...) continue to operate with the absence of character and civic goals because many teachers in these disciplines view their subject as an isolated content area. Although much attention is given to the shared goals of citizenship and character education in social studies classrooms, many teachers fail to recognize or adequately infuse these vital topics into their curriculum. Many social studies teachers may be quick to dismiss these curricular goals, writing them off as just another fad that will pass with time. However, character education and citizenship education has demonstrated a growing popularity and presence in schools over the last twenty years thanks to much support from parents, the general public, and state and national policy makers. That being said, social studies teachers and teacher educators need to seriously consider the sensible and functional relationship between character, citizenship, and social studies education. As Hoge (2002) wrote:

> We are simultaneously involved in developing good individual people and strong communities of active citizens who apply their disciplinary content

knowledge to everyday events in their shared lives. We cannot do only one or the other, for good government requires good people, and good people need the lessons of history and the social sciences to exercise their freedoms appropriately and shoulder their responsibilities as members of our modern liberal democratic society. (Hoge, 2002, p. 107)

NCSS stated that the primary purpose of social studies was "to help young people develop the ability to make informed and reasoned decisions for the public good as citizens of a culturally diverse, democratic society in an interdependent world" (NCSS, 1994). The purpose of this chapter is to refocus social studies educators on the primary purpose of this field, as stated by NCSS, by offering the perspective that the key to effective citizenship lies in the conscious efforts of social studies teachers to infuse character and civic lessons into their daily teaching.

DEFINING CHARACTER AND CITIZENSHIP EDUCATION

Historically, the use of terms such as moral education, citizenship education, values education, and character education has been closely intertwined. To be sure, there are marked differences between all of the aforementioned terms, but each of them has been commonly used at various times throughout U.S. history to identify approaches to character development of young people. For instance, the Puritans and other early European settlers referred to the training of individuals for participation in society as moral education. Their approach to moral education was based on religious doctrine and children were expected to learn appropriate moral behaviors in order to be a productive and righteous member of the community. Moral education through religious studies was considered the best method for training future citizens in the U.S. well into the 19th century. However, the arrival and influx of many new immigrant groups caused the traditional religious based moral training in schools to become obsolete, mainly because these various groups did not share the same morals and religious beliefs as the Christian dominated schools (Russell & Waters, 2010). Having different cultures, values, and beliefs, the new immigrant groups pushed for the separation of church and state in schools so that their children would not have to face the indoctrination of beliefs which they did not hold.

Citizenship education refers to the enterprise of developing knowledge, values, and skills in youth for purposes of carrying out the rights and duties incumbent upon individuals in their relations within a society (Quigley & Bahmueller, 1991). Preparing students for active and productive civic engagement has been one of the traditional goals of schools, especially after the formation of our democratic republic and during periods of increasing social problems and immigration. The role of schools in this process was to instill in students a sense of civic virtue that would encourage them to develop habits that were conducive to the well being of society, while also promoting a strong sense of patriotism and other fundamental principles of American constitutional democracy.

Values education generally refers to the shift in moral instruction created during the tumultuous 1960s. During the height of the civil rights movement, character educators began contributing new research and theories about the practice of teaching values and morals. Values clarification was the major approach championed by Raths, Harmin, & Simon in their work titled, *Values and teaching*, (1966). The values clarification camp believed that transmitting values required more than simple student obedience and recognition of terms. They thought that discussion of value conflicts as witnessed in everyday life was the key to helping students understand the true meaning of values. The values clarification approach also requires the teacher to be non-judgmental of student's values choices; focusing most of their attention on posing guided questions to help students analyze values based decisions. This method would be the topic of much controversy and debate among many contemporary character education advocates, as they primarily believed in a universal set of values that should be directly transmitted, not open to discussion or debate.

Character education has been defined in a plethora of ways since its reemergence in the late 1980s and early 1990s. Several popular educators and organizations have provided definitions of character education over the years. Some of the influential figures in the contemporary character education movement include the likes of Edward Wynne, Thomas Lickona, Kevin Ryan, James Leming, and Marvin Berkowitz just to name a few. Each of the aforementioned educators has written extensively on the topic of character education since the early 1990s and all have created varying definitions of character education. Also, there are other researchers in the field of character education that have difficulty accepting the definitions and views presented by many of the advocates for contemporary character education. Educators such as Alan Lockwood, Alfie Kohn, and Alex Molnar, just to name a few, have all offered challenges, criticisms, and alternative definitions to the field of character education. There remains a great deal of debate over definitions provided by individuals on both sides of the contemporary character education movement, therefore definitions offered by the United States Department of Education and the Character Education Partnership are discussed below.

The United States Department of Education Office of Safe and Drug-Free Schools released a brochure in 2006 entitled, "Character Education…. our shared responsibility." This brochure defined character education in the following way:

Character education is a learning process that enables students and adults in a school community to understand, care about, and act on core ethical values such as respect, justice, civic virtue, and citizenship, and responsibility for self and others. Upon such core values, we form the attitudes and actions that are the hallmark of safe, healthy and informed communities that serve as the foundation of our society. (U.S. Department of Education's Office of Safe and Drug-Free Schools, 2006, p. 1)

In addition, the Character Education Partnership (CEP), a nonpartisan coalition of organizations and individuals dedicated to the moral development of our nation's youth, defines character education as the process of teaching students to know about, care about, and act upon core ethical values such as fairness, honesty, compassion, responsibility, and respect for self and others (Character Education Partnership, 1997).

CHARACTER AND CITIZENSHIP EDUCATION IN SOCIAL STUDIES

As the variety of definitions and terms associated with character and citizenship education indicate, the history of these fields enjoys a long and, at times, tumultuous place in society. Covering the history of character and citizenship education in great detail would be a gratuitous and daunting task for this chapter. Instead, a brief overview of these histories will be provided for the purpose of revealing the tradition and evolution of character and citizenship education in schools.

From the earliest days of European settlement in America, there has always been a concern for the moral development of children. Puritans, Quakers, and other early settlers all expressed a unique interest in the moral development of not only their children, but all children residing in the community. Parents were the primary people responsible for the moral training of their children, with formal schools and churches playing a rather minimal role in this task. However, once communities and colonies became more secure and stable in their new environment, some schools did begin to surface. These early schools were funded by the community and typically featured a female teacher, since females were thought to be better models of virtuous behavior during this era. Surprisingly, requirements for original teachers in these schools had very little to do with the teachers intelligence, and everything to do with the teachers character. This standard would prove to be critical in the field of education, as teachers would continually be looked to as "moral models" for their students well into the 20th century, and arguably, still to this day.

Following the revolutionary war, the new United States of America began to develop a vision for a national public school system to educate future citizens. Although there were many men who wrote about their vision of the function education should play in the new democratic republic, such men as Benjamin Franklin, James Madison, John Adams, and Thomas Jefferson all were particularly passionate about the role of moral education in schools (Hunter, 2000; Rosenberg, 1996). While many colonists still wanted the focus of education to be on religious teachings, men like Benjamin Franklin and Thomas Jefferson envisioned a slightly more secular experience in schools. However, while these two men did propose an education system built around practical education instead of religious scriptures, both men did recognize the importance of moral development in schools. Franklin discussed how reading material for children should "contain some useful instruction, whereby the understandings or morals of the youth may at the same time be improved" (Lemay, 2005, p. 501). Jefferson also believed that the strive for increased moral reasoning was a better goal for education than the direct indoctrination of values (Spring, 1990). However, Jefferson would go on to say that students not responding to this form of instruction should certainly be "trained in the habits of right and wrong" (Heslap, 1995, p. 79).

Although many of the aforementioned men did a great deal too initiate the discussion on public education in America, the person most generally associated with this development would be Horace Mann. Mann has been referred to as the "father of public schools in America" and one of the earliest champions of universal public schools. Mann viewed moral education in the schools not as an aspect of the curriculum, but the foundation upon which all other knowledge would be obtained. "Moral education is a primal necessity of social existence. The unrestrained passions of men are not only homicidal, but suicidal, and a community without a conscience would soon extinguish itself" (Mann, 1868, p. 20). Much like Thomas Jefferson, Horace Mann firmly believed that if the newly formed democracy was going to succeed, then citizens would surely have to be educated in both civic and moral principles on their path to self enlightenment. Mann directly expressed this belief by writing how "our institutions demand men, in whose hearts, great thoughts and great deeds are native, spontaneous and irrepressive" (Mann, 1838, p. 14).

While many of the earliest public schools were not based entirely on religious teachings and principles, they certainly were not devoid of this presence altogether. Bible readings in classrooms were quite common into the early 20th century. Popular textbooks of this era, like the *McGufffey Readers* and the *New England Primer,* sought to directly teach lessons in morality to students. The *McGuffey Readers* were far less religious based than the *New England Primer,* but both of these materials addressed the critical field of education in the moral domain. These lessons were expected to be accepted completely and not open to any form of discussion, debate, or analysis.

The overarching belief of the time was that children needed to learn how to behave in order for good habits and morals to develop. However, as the population and diversity of the U.S. continued to grow during the late 19th and early 20th centuries, so too did the controversy surrounding the place of teaching morality through religion. New immigrant groups arriving to America did not always share the same religious beliefs as the schools in their communities, causing many families to seek a curriculum more accommodating to their personal beliefs and values. As states and local school systems adjusted to meet the needs of a new and diverse population, the restructuring of moral instruction without the presence of religion would be the task of the 20th century.

The early 20th century witnessed a gradual shift away from moral education based on religious teachings. In its place, schools and educators began to emphasize democratic principles, an effort commonly referred to as citizenship education. It was generally believed that democratic instruction could adequately fill the void of moral instruction through religious beliefs because many of these principles were essentially the same. For instance, both democratic and religious beliefs expressed the importance of traits such as honesty, trustworthiness, caring, responsibility etc… Although many educators lobbied for a return to traditional moral instruction, schools had already began to transition into a new era of moral training. This era, lasting roughly from the 1930s–1960s, saw a decrease in moral training and an increase in the indoctrination of democratic beliefs. The events of WWII and the Cold War caused the U.S. education system to place a new emphasis on the importance of patriotism and the celebration of democracy. Mc-Clellan discussed how the years leading up to the Cold War viewed education as a "moral contest in which the values of democracy and decency were arrayed against the forces of authoritarianism and evil, and classrooms were expected to play an important role in the battle" (McClellan, 1999, p. 71). Schools were expected to promote love for America, its institutions, ideals, and form of government. This increased nationalism added superfluous fuel to the frantic paranoia of the Cold War, a time when character education was focused on teaching the evils of communism rather than addressing the moral development of youth. However, key court rulings and events during the 1960s would lead to a renewed attention to the field of character and moral education.

In 1962 and 1963, the Supreme Court made three very influential rulings that would dramatically change the field of character education. *Engel v. Vitale* (1962) was the first of the Supreme Court decisions and involved the forbidding of school prayer (Jeynes, 2010, p. 206). *Murray v. Curlett* (1963) expanded the effects of the aforementioned ruling by not only prohibiting school prayer and Bible readings, but also causing so much fear of lawsuits that schools began to drop the whole enterprise of character education (Murray, 1982). In the final of these three influential cases, the Supreme Court decided to disallow school prayer at the beginning of the school day in *Abington v. Schempp* (1963). These court decisions carried immense ramifications because schools suddenly had to cut religion from the moral instruction of students. Since morality and religion shared a long and storied past in U.S. classrooms, schools were left with the responsibility of character education without any real method for this endeavor.

Fortunately, or, unfortunately according to many character education advocates, the work of some prominent educational psychologists and professionals was on the rise in the 1960s. In 1966, Louis E. Raths, Merrill Harmin, and Sydney B. Simon published their book entitled, *Values and Teaching* (1966). This volume of work enjoyed a quick rise to popularity in public schools, then an equally quick demise. The premise of this instructional method was values clarification. On the surface, values clarification seemed to be the perfect solution for character education at the time because it was devoid of any religious influences and encouraged students to formulate their own values through analysis and reflection. However, this method was met with sharp opposition from character education professionals because values clarification assumed that all students were inherently "good" and that these morals would be revealed during well planned scenarios and exercises. These opponents consistently questioned how this method would account for negative values that may be justified by students during this process, such as lying, cheating, abuse of power, etc… Many of these claims were warranted and proponents of the values clarification model had difficulty addressing some of the fundamental flaws of this theory. Nevertheless, this method opened the doorway for new approaches to character education, most notably, moral reasoning.

Similarly to values clarification, Lawrence Kohlberg's theory on moral reasoning and advocacy for moral development in character education came under significant attacks throughout the 1970s and into the early 1990s. One of the major concerns for many educators was that Kohlberg's original theory was developed on research that studied only male students. The feminist approach to character education spawned out of this issue, citing that girls consistently reasoned at lower levels of Kohlberg's stages. Feminist approach advocates claimed that his theories and stages could not be generalized to females, and thus weakened the overall legitimacy of the moral development approach. Also, much like the values clarification approach, moral development was criticized for contradicting its stated goal of being non-indoctrinative. McClellan (1999) addresses Kohlberg's contradictions by discussing how, "his definition of stages and his assumption that higher stages were better than lower stages revealed a clear commitment to a principle of justice" (p. 85). Eventually, Kohlberg would modify some of his original positions regarding the nature of indoctrination and moral education by distinguishing between moral principles and rules. He believed that conventional moral education focused on a series of rules to shape behavior, while moral principles acted as universal guides for making moral decisions (Kohlberg, 1975, p. 50). Although Kohlberg continued to rework his moral development approach over the years to answer his critics, the method itself was never widely implemented by school teachers. However, unlike the values clarification process, Kohlberg's approach to moral education has not disappeared from the popular discourse of contemporary character education and his ideas are still a driving force in the development of new character education theories (Lockwood, 2009).

SOCIAL ISSUES CONTRIBUTING TO THE RISE OF CHARACTER EDUCATION IN SCHOOLS

While character education continued to be a topic of conversation in the overall field of education, its importance certainly dwindled during the 1960s and into the 1990s. During this time period, several social and academic developments began to occur that troubled society. Statistics and relevant news stories regarding the decadent behaviors of youths were routinely used as beacons for advocates of the character education movement, a practice still used by present day advocates. For instance, Edward Wynne and Thomas Lickona, two of the most influential writers of the contemporary character education movement, frequently attributed moral decay of the 1980s and 1990s to the lack of character education in schools. Wynne discussed the dramatic increase in divorce rates, single parent families, teenage pregnancies, murders, suicides, violent crimes, drug abuse, etc., to build a rationale for a return to character education (Wynne, 1985; Wynne, 1989; Wynne & Ryan, 1993; Wynne & Walberg, 1985). This sentiment was echoed in the work of Benninga and Wynne (1998) when they plainly stated that they wanted students to "stop killing and abusing themselves and one another at record rates" (p. 439-330). One survey of school-children in 1990 revealed that most students relied on trial-and-error in making moral decisions, and most of these decisions relied heavily upon self-interest (Cole & Genevie, 1990). In addition, Jeynes (2010) believed that school shootings played a major role in renewing society's interest in character education. Jeynes discussed how prior to the 1980s and 1990s, school shootings tended only to take place in urban settings. Since many Americans associated urban areas with crime, violence, and poverty, these school shooting stories were not always seen as a worthy component of national news coverage. However, as school shootings slowly began spreading to rural and suburban areas, the media and society began to take a national interest in these events. Take for example the tragic school shootings at Columbine High School in 1999 and

Virginia Tech in 2007. These senseless acts of intense violence and murder left many citizens concerned about the character development of young people and the future of our democratic republic.

Naturally, character education advocates do not claim that the reemergence of moral instruction will bring an end to acts of violence in schools or deviant behaviors in students. Nearly all advocates of contemporary character education recognize and acknowledge the social, political, and economic influences outside of the schools control that contributed to the perceived breaking down of morality in America. Contemporary character education was a movement birthed from social problems in which parents, educators, and government leaders all sought a logical solution to, what they considered to be, a lack of character development and morality in contemporary students. In response to these widespread concerns, contemporary character education advocates launched a massive renewal of character education in public schools during the 1990s, the likes of which our society has never seen. The following section will discuss a brief overview of contemporary character education, how it came to pass, and the effect it continues to have on the development of character education initiatives into the 21st century.

CHARACTER EDUCATION IN CONTEMPORARY SOCIAL STUDIES CLASSROOMS

The arrival of the contemporary education movement can trace its origins back to a number of important events, developments, and changes in the United States over the past 30 years. Vessels (1998) writes, "Character education regained momentum during the 1980s and 1990s because many parents, educators, and other concern citizens from various subcultures and regions of the country saw the need for prevention programs that would counter the tide of moral decline" (p. 5). If there was one thing that advocates for the return to character education learned from the values clarification era, it was that teachers could not instruct children in character development by treating them like fully mature adults. Lickona (1991) addressed this problem with values clarification when stating, "In the end, values clarification made the mistake of treating kids like grown-ups who only needed to clarify values that were already sound. It forgot that children, and a lot of adults who are still moral children, need a good deal of help in developing sound values in the first place" (p. 11). The absence of these "sound values" as Lickona phrased it, led many character educators to begin focusing on a certain set of universal character traits that could guide character education across America. This task would prove to be difficult due to the tremendous amount of political, social, economic, religious, and racial diversity that can be found in America. However, at the Aspen Summit Conference on character education in 1992, a group of dedicated educators came together in order to undertake the task of reshaping character education. This conference was organized by philanthropist Michael Josephson in an effort to coordinate a clear set of goals and a unified approach to character education. Numerous educators attended this conference from a variety of fields ranging from educational psychologists to superintendents of school boards. Notably, important researchers from the field of character education in attendance at this conference included Thomas Lickona, Kevin Ryan, and Marvin Berkowitz. The end result of this conference would be the production of a new character education program built around "the six pillars of character: trustworthiness, respect, responsibility, justice, caring, and civic virtue" (Barnhill, 1995, p. 19). The six pillars of character would be adopted by the Josephson Institute to create the Character Counts! program. The organization states that the six pillars are "ethical values that most people agree on, not politically, religiously, or culturally biased" (Character Counts! website). The Character Counts! program has consistently increased in popularity over the years and continues to be one of the most utilized programs in the field of character education.

The implications of the Aspen Summit Conference and the subsequent Character Counts! program were tremendous for advancing the cause of character education on a national scale. Perhaps the most influential aspect of this conference and the Character Counts! program was the inclusion of a specific set of character traits that should be taught to students. While many character education advocates and researchers had previously discussed the importance of "universal values," Character Counts! was one of the first approaches to contemporary character education that utilized these universal values as the foundation for their program. Former Secretary of Education and advocate for the return of character education, William Bennett, discussed the need for directly teaching character traits when stating, "if we want our children to possess the traits of character we most admire, we need to teach them what those traits are" (Bennett, 1991, p. 133). While the emphasis on specific character traits continued to evolve as a focal point for the contemporary character education movement, the election of President Bill Clinton in 1992 proved to be another turning moment for the return of character education.

A brief look into the Presidency of Bill Clinton can easily show the former chief executives affinity for character education. President Clinton's emphasis on character education in schools can be viewed in several different ways. For instance, one could interpret Clinton's importance on character education as a true concern which he felt as a moral individual, or a skillful political move by focusing his agenda on issues of major concern to the public. However one chooses to view the intentions of President Clinton in the field of character education, it was clear that character education was on the rise as a topic of national interest. During President Clinton's administration, he hosted five conferences on character education and specifically referenced the importance of character education in his state of the union address in 1996 stating, "I challenge all our schools to teach character education, to teach good values and good citizenship" (Clinton, 1996).

By 1993, one year after the Aspen Summit Conference and into the term of President Clinton, the Character Education Partnership (CEP) was formed. The Character Education Partnership would become one of the leading national organizations for contemporary character education because it advocated for a comprehensive approach to character education. The CEP mission statement discusses how this organization was formed as a "nonpartisan coalition of organizations and individuals dedicated to developing moral character and civic virtue in our nation's youth as one means of promoting a more compassionate and responsible society" (CEP, 2005). Essentially, the goal of the CEP was to create, sponsor, and advocate for quality resources, programs, and initiatives in the expanding field of character education. While the CEP did contribute a great deal to the widespread knowledge and availability of contemporary character education, the most substantial contributions would come the following year, in 1994, from the federal government.

The Partnership in Character Education Pilot Projects were authorized by Congress in 1994 in order to provide annual grants to state education agencies in partnership with one or more local educational agencies. Under this program, the Secretary of Education could distribute up to 10 grants each year. These grants were issued with the requirement that grantees implement projects that specifically incorporate character elements: caring, civic virtue and citizenship, justice and fairness, respect, responsibility, and trustworthiness (U.S. Department of Education's Office of Safe and Drug-Free Schools, 2006, p. 4). The primary function of this program was to provide actual funding to begin the process of implementing character education programs in several states. Never wanting to miss out on any opportunities to receive additional funding, several states began taking action on character education initiatives. A study of state legislation passed in contemporary character education was conducted by Glanzer and Milson (2006). In this study, the researchers analyzed and evaluated current legislative trends across all 50 states in the field of character education. This study found that 26 states had some form of legislation directly addressing character education. However, of these 26 states, 23 of them "had passed or substantially modified legislation related to character education between 1993 and 2004" (Glanzer & Milson, 2006, p. 536). The sudden increase in mandated character education clearly shows that this topic was a priority throughout society, from local communities to the executive office; character education was slowly working its way back into public schools.

Despite a great deal of growth and support for character education during the late 1990s, there continued to be some concern about the effectiveness of character education to positively impact students behavior. In 1999, the tragic school shootings at Columbine High School harshly reminded the public that, although progress had been made, much still needed to be done. The election of President Bush and the subsequent passing of the No Child Left Behind Act (2001) worked to increase federal funding for character education initiatives. This increase in funding contributed to the revision and expansion of numerous state mandated character education programs. The NCLB Act was particularly useful in expanding required character education programs from K-5, to K-12. In addition, the NCLB Act continued the practice of listing specific character traits to be addressed in character education programs. Inclusion of specific traits would prove to be influential by setting an informal standard that many states would follow when passing future mandates on character education, For instance, the state of Florida passed its first piece of state legislation requiring mandatory character education in 1999. This bill authorized character education instruction in elementary schools. In 2002, Senate bill 20E was passed which required there to be a character development program in K-12 schools by the 2004-2005 school year. The law (s. 1003.42(2)(q), F.S) stated that "each district school board shall develop or adopt a curriculum for the character development program that shall be submitted to the department for approval. The character development curriculum shall stress the qualities of patriotism, responsibility, citizenship, kindness, respect, honesty, self-control, tolerance, and cooperation" (Griesheimer & Cornett, 2002, p.3). Expanding character development requirements to the secondary level was an interesting twist to character education, mainly because prior to this time most character education programs were focused on the elementary grade levels. This could potentially be one of the reasons why secondary teachers feel less prepared to teach character education than their elementary counterparts (Milson & Mehlig, 2002). With character education expanding and securing a steady place in K-12 classrooms via federal and state legislation during the late 1990s, advocates for character development could now focus their attention on the development of new strategies and theories about how best to engage in the task of character education in elementary, middle, and high school. As a result, an unprecedented amount of research and curriculum materials related to character education, teacher preparation, and instruction began to surface.

CURRENT STATE OF CONTEMPORARY CHARACTER
EDUCATION PROGRAMS AND MATERIALS

The goal and purpose of the government funding character education initiatives was ultimately to teach students how to be effective decision makers and responsible citizens. By closely relating the goals of character education and citizenship education, advocates for contemporary character education were able to shed many concerns regarding the past precedent of connecting moral instruction to religion. Since the development of good citizens and good people have many overlapping goals and desired character traits, advocates for both character education and citizenship education willingly adopted and supported the interrelated goals of each program. Not surprisingly, increased funding and the demand for character education programs to meet the needs of state mandated character education requirements resulted in a massive outpour of new approaches to the field. While there continues to be great variety in these numerous programs, they all appear to be working towards similar goals of improving student behavior through the teaching of universal values for the purpose of creating democratically responsible citizens. In the following paragraphs, several key organizations and programs dedicated to the character development of students will be highlighted in order to provide an overview of what typical, contemporary character education are currently attempting to accomplish in the classroom.

The Character Training Institute (CTI) was founded in Oklahoma City, Oklahoma, as a non-profit organization in 1996. This institute created the *Character First!* program, which was designed around 45 character qualities. Originally, the program was developed and designed for public elementary schools in the local area. However, this program expanded in the spring of 2000 to include a middle school and high school component. Perhaps this organization had some good foresight into the events that would shortly follow, i.e. NCLB Act (2001) and the required expansion of character education to K-12. The approach to character education advocated by this program includes the:

> Character First is a leadership development program based on character that is delivered many ways—training seminars, books, magazines, curriculum, email—that focus on real-life issues at work, school, home, and the community. Our materials describe good character and talk about the attitudes a person needs in order to improve relationships and make ethical choices. This vocabulary helps colleagues challenge and applaud one another for good character. (Character First! website)

For more information about this organization and program, please visit their website at http://www.characterfirst.com/.

Character Counts! was one of the programs mentioned earlier in this section as a major influence on contemporary character education. This program was launched in 1993, following the conclusions and recommendations of the Aspen Summit Conference on character education a year earlier. Funding and organization of this project was provided by the non-profit and non-partisan Josephson Institute of Ethics, which resides in Marina Del Rey, California. The *Character Counts!* program revolves around the "Six Pillars of Character," which are trustworthiness, respect, responsibility, fairness, caring, and citizenship. This approach to character education provides an educational framework to teach universal values (the Six Pillars) and consists of a large coalition of organizations with a flexible approach to implementation. For more detailed information about this program, please visit their website at http://josephsoninstitute.org/index.html.

The Seattle Social Development Project began in 1981 to test several strategies for reducing childhood delinquency, drug abuse, and school failure. J. David Hawkins was the principal investigator of this study who utilized a longitudinal study to determine the effects of these interventions over an extended period of time. Participants have been interviewed regularly since 1985 and the focus on positive youth and adult development that drives this project continues to expand. While this project does not exactly relate to the programs previously mentioned, this project continues to be highly respected in the field of character education because of its potential to examine the long term benefits of character education lessons. For more information on this project please visit their website at http://depts.washington.edu/ssdp/index.html.

The Character Education Partnership outlines their idea of an effective character education program in its *Eleven Principles of Effective Character Education* (2005). These eleven principles claim that a truly effective character education program should:

1. Promote core ethical values as the basis of good character:
2. Define character comprehensively to include thinking, feeling, and behavior;
3. Use a comprehensive, intentional, proactive, and effective approach to character development;
4. Create a caring school community;
5. Provide students with opportunities for moral action;
6. Include a meaningful and challenging academic curriculum that respects all learners, develops their character, and helps them to succeed;
7. Strive to foster students' self-motivation;

8. Engage the school staff as a learning and moral community that shares responsibility for character education and attempts to adhere to the same core values that guide the education of students;

9. Foster shared moral leadership and long-range support of the character education initiative;

10. Engage families and community members as partners in the character building effort; and

11. Evaluate the character of schools; the school staff's functioning as character educators, and the extent to which students' manifest good character.

These 11 principles serve as the foundation of the CEP's vision for effective character education programs. Much like the *Character Counts!* approach, *The Eleven Principles of Effective Character Education* provides a myriad of flexible activities and strategies, ranging from classroom activities to staff development, that are all designed to help maximize the benefits of character education. For more information on this project please visit their website at http://www.character.org/elevenprinciples.

ANALYSIS OF CONTEMPORARY CHARACTER EDUCATION PROGRAMS AND MATERIALS

The growing number of character education programs, methods, and strategies of the contemporary movement could conceivably be one of its greatest strengths, or a major downfall. Extensive variety in content, curriculum, and pedagogy makes it difficult for teachers, school administrators, and policy makers to determine which programs will be the most effective in achieving the desired outcomes of contemporary character education. Since the Department of Education classifies character education materials as supplemental in scope, they are ineligible for consideration under the state instructional materials adoption process (Griesheimer & Cornett, 2002, p.4). This is a critical development for public school administrators and teachers, who now must choose from a wide variety of programs, all of which claim to be research proven initiatives. While many of these programs and strategies have research to validate their advocated approaches, this research should be examined critically for potential biases. As the end of the first decade in the 21st century comes to a close, the outcomes and effectiveness of many contemporary education programs remain a work in progress. Berkowitz and Bier (2005) conducted a massive research study analyzing the effectiveness of character education programs all across the United States. The findings of this study "identified 33 programs with sufficient scientific backing to demonstrate their effectiveness and numerous implementation strategies that commonly occur in such programs" (Berkowitz & Bier, 2005, p. 23). This meta-analysis of research evaluated a total of 109 research driven studies focusing on character education programs or methods. Since only 33 of the 109 programs were found to be effective, it is clear that public school administrators and teachers must carefully choose any proposed character education initiative. Despite the tremendous confusion about the overwhelming variety of available character education programs, the positive growth in character education and its programs indicate that society and teachers still, for the most part, support the presence of character education in the classroom. Since the purpose of character education is ultimately to improve the morality and decision making of future generations, teachers would be well advised to take these program initiatives seriously. Although teachers traditionally resist changes to the curriculum and their practiced pedagogy, the cost of ignoring character education mandates is far too high. As acts of student violence continue to occur with varying degrees of severity at all levels of education in the 21st century, society and legislatures will likely continue their support for character education in schools. However, this support will also bring with it an increase in expectations and accountability. The accountability push will likely bring with it a string of new problems regarding the assessment of character education programs because proving an improvement to student character development is rather difficult. If traditional forms of educational accountability, such as standardized tests, are going to potentially be applied to the realm of character education, then schools and teachers may quickly find themselves on the defensive as the winds of support for character education could easily turn into a tornado of public and legislative blame.

CONCLUSION

The focus of this chapter has been to inform readers about the connected nature of character education and citizenship education in order to extend dialogue about these two unique, but also complimentary fields. While these two fields do have some differences, the overall goals of character education and citizenship education are remarkably similar. It is with these similarities in mind that the authors of this chapter believe character education serves as the foundation or heart of citizenship education. Although citizenship is primarily focused on the development of students' knowledge about government, politics, democracy, and law; this knowledge would be useless without also developing a level of morality so that civic competencies can be exercised for the improvement of society. As Hoge (2002) effectively argued, "good democratic government is largely dependent on an informed, virtuous, and involved public, it seems clear that citizenship education actually needs a character education foundation" (Hoge, 2002, p. 106). This connection was also addressed by Howard et al. (2004) when it was contended that because character education focuses on "relations between and among individuals and among peer groups, conditions of civil society, and significant public issues, it formed the nucleus of citizenship education" (p. 189). With character education serving as the foundation of citizenship education, the two fields can mutually benefit from an increased focus on common goals in the social studies classroom. As public school curriculums become more congested with rising accountability measures, more pressure will be placed on social studies teachers specifically to address mandated character education standards in their curriculum. Evidence of this trend can be found in the state of Florida's New Generation Sunshine State Standards, which directly incorporates mandated character education goals into social studies curriculum standards. Examples of these standards include the following:

SS.2.C.2.2: Define and apply characteristics of responsible citizenship (e.g., respect, responsibility, participation, self-reliance, patriotism, honesty).

SS.1.C.3.1: Explain how decisions can be made or how conflicts might be resolved in fair and just ways (e.g., talking about problems, role playing, listening, sharing).

SS.912.E.2.2: Use a decision-making model to analyze a public policy issue affecting the student's community that incorporates defining a problem, analyzes the potential consequences, and considers the alternatives. (FLDOE Website, 2011).

The widespread support for character education initiatives at the public school level is clearly working its way directly into the social studies classroom. School programs implemented during the contemporary era of education are all subject to scrutiny and measures of accountability. In some states, it appears obvious that social studies will be the designated content area charged with the task of directly educating students in the moral domain. This broadened objective of social studies instruction requires teachers and teacher educators in this field to widen their lens when examining social studies curriculum design, pedagogy, and assessments. While some educators in this field may be hesitant to accept this task, it is important that social studies teachers take a moment to reflect on the nature of this field and what, at its core, the social studies strives to accomplish in the classroom. As the great philosopher Plato once said, "Education in virtue is the only education which deserves the name."

REFERENCES

Bennett, W. J. (1991). Moral literacy and the formation of character. In J. S. Benninga (Ed.), *Moral, character, and civic education in the elementary school.* (p. 131–138). New York: Teachers College.

Benninga, J. S., & Wynne, E .A. (1998). Keeping in-character: A time-tested solution. *Phi Delta Kappan, 79*(6) 439–445.

Berkowitz, M., & Bier, M. (2005). *What works in character education: A research-driven guide for educators.* Washington, DC. Report from the Character Education Partnership.

Character Counts! (2011, April). Retrieved from http://charactercounts.org/

Character Education Partnership. (1997, August). *Eleven principles of effective character education.* Washington, DC: Character Education Partnership.

Character Education Partnership. (2005). *Character education quality standards.* Retrieved from http://www.character.org/

Character Education Partnership. (2010, April). Retrieved from http://www.character.org/

Character Firtst! (2009, November). Retrieved from http://www.characterfirst.com/

Community of Caring. (2011, April). Retrieved from http://www.communityofcaring.org/index.html

Florida Department of Education (2011, February). Retrieved from http://www.fldoe.org/

Glanzer, P., & Milson, A. (2006). Legislating the good: A survey and evaluation of character education laws in the United States. *Educational Policy 20*(3), 525–550.

Griesheimer, D., & Cornett, J. (2002). Issue brief: Character Education. *Council for Education Policy Research and Improvement.* University of Central Florida.

Heslap, R. (1995). *Moral education for Americans.* Westport, CT: Praeger Publications.

Hoge, J. (2002). Character education, citizenship education, and the social studies. *The Social Studies, 93*(3), 103–109.

Howard, R. W., Berkowitz, M. W., & Shaeffer, E. F. (2004). Politics of character education. *Educational Policy, 18*(1), 188–216.

Hunter, J. D. (2000). *The death of character: Moral education in an age without good or evil.* New York, NY: Basic Books.

Jeynes, W. (2010). *A call for character education and prayer in the schools.* Santa Barbara, CA: Praeger.

Kohlberg, L. (1975). Moral education for a society in moral transition. *Educational Leadership, 33,* 46–54.

Lemay, L. (2005). *The life of Benjamin Franklin, Volume 1, Journalist, 1706–1730.* University of Pennsylvania Press.

Lickona, T. (1991). *Educating for character: How schools can teach respect and responsibility.* New York: Bantam.

Lickona, T. (1996). Eleven principles of effective character education. *Journal of Moral Education, 25*(1), 93–100.

Lickona, T. (2004). Character matters: How to help our children develop good judgment, integrity, and other essential virtues. New York: Touchstone.

Lockwood, A.L. (2009). *The case for character education: A developmental approach.* New York, NY: Teachers College Press.

Mann, H. (1838). Untitled editorial. *The Common School Journal 1* (November, 1838).

Mann, H. (1868). *Massachusetts Board of Education, Annual reports on education.* Boston: Horace B. Fuller.

McClellan, B. E. (1999). *Moral education in America: Schools and the shaping of character from Colonial times to the present.* New York, NY: Teachers College Press.

Milson, A. J., & Mehlig, L. M. (2002) Elementary school teachers' sense of efficacy for character education. *Journal of Educational Research, 96*(1), 47–53.

Murray, W. (1982). *My life without God.* Nashville, TN: Thomas Nelson Publishers.

NCSS. (1994). *Expectations of excellence: Curriculum standards for the social studies.* Washington, D.C.: National Council for the Social Studies.

NCSS. (1997). *Fostering civic virtue: Character education in the social studies.* Washington, D.C.: National Council for the Social Studies.

Previte, M, & Sheehan, J. (2001). The NCSS presidential addresses: 1936–1969, perspectives on the social studies. *The National Council for the Social Studies & ERIC Clearinghouse for Social Studies/Social Science Education.*

Quigley, C. N., & Bahmueller, C. F. (Eds.). (1991). *CIVITAS: A framework for civic education.* Calabasas, CA: Center for Civic Education.

Raths, L., Harmin, M., & Simon, S. (1966). *Values and teaching: Working with values in the classroom.* Columbus, OH: Charles E. Merrill.

Rosenberg, J. (1996). *A tie that binds: The concept of character formation in folk arts in education and the history of education in the United States.* Paper presented at the American Folklore Society Conference (Jacksonville, FL., 1992.)

Russell, W. & Waters, S. (2010). Cinematic citizenship: Developing citizens of character with film. *Action in Teacher Education, 32*(2), 12–23.

Spring, J. (1990). *The American school 1642–1990.* New York: Longman Inc.

U.S. Department of Education's Office of Safe and Drug Free Schools. (2006). *Character education: Our shared responsibility* (pp. 1–9).

U.S. Department of Education. (2007, February). *Index for No Child Left Behind.* Retrieved from http://www.ed.gov/nclb/index/az/index.html

U.S. Department of Education. (2009, November.) *Partnerships in character education programs.* Retrieved from http://www.ed.gov/programs/charactered/index.html

Vessels, G. G. (1998). *Character and community development: A school planning and teacher training handbook.* Westport, CT: Praeger.

Wynne, E. (1985). The great tradition in education: Transmitting moral values. *Educational Leadership, 43*(4), 4–9.

Wynne, E. (1989). Transmitting traditional values in contemporary schools. In L. P. Nucci (Ed.), *Moral development and character education* (pp. 19–36). Chicago: University of Chicago Press.

Wynne, E., & Ryan, K. (1993). *Reclaiming our schools: A handbook on teaching character, academics, and discipline* (1st ed.). New York: Merrill.

Wynne, E., & Ryan, K. (1997). *Reclaiming our schools: A handbook on teaching character, academics, and discipline* (2nd ed.). New York: Merrill.

Wynne, E., & Walberg, H.J. (1985). The complementary goals of character development and academic excellence. *Educational Leadership, 43*(4), 15–18.

SECTION II

CURRICULUM, CONTENT, & STANDARDS

CHAPTER 7

HISTORY

From Learning Narratives to Thinking Historically

Keith C. Barton

History is taught in schools throughout the world, although the precise nature of the curriculum—topics covered, grade levels required, and so on—varies from country to country. In most places, though, school history emphasizes narratives, often those related to the nation, and the student's job is to remember and reproduce these stories. This emphasis on remembering narratives has had two effects: Students frequently are bored by attempting to learn stories about the past (VanSledright, 2011), while at the same time the curriculum often becomes embroiled in political debates about which stories should be told about the nation (e.g., Nakou & Barca, 2010, Taylor & Guyver, 2011). In recent years a number of educators have suggested that schools should focus less on presenting particular narratives and more on engaging students in the practice of historical thinking. This includes emphasizing elements of history such as agency, perspective, and the interpretation of evidence (e.g., Barton & Levstik, 2004; Lévesque,

Contemporary Social Studies: An Essential Reader, pages 119–138
Copyright © 2012 by Information Age Publishing

2008; Seixas, 1996; VanSledright, 2011; Wineburg, 2001). This approach to history is well established in some places, but in many others it is still an innovative and little-known way of thinking about the subject. Expanding the role of historical thinking like this requires that teachers be well-prepared in their subject, that they be familiar with current scholarship in history education, and that they have a clear sense of purpose for teaching history (Barton & Levstik, 2004; Grant; 2003; VanSledright, 2011).

LEARNING HISTORICAL NARRATIVES

In most countries, the explicit objective of history education has long been for students to understand and remember specific historical narratives. These are much like narratives found in novels, plays, and movies, except of course that the people in them really existed, and the events actually happened. Yet they share key features with fictional narratives, such as characters, settings, plots, and the solution of a problem. The story of the American Revolution, for example, is one of the most commonly taught historical narratives in the United States, and usually it is presented by focusing on its narrative structure: The setting is North America after the French and Indian War; the characters are British officials and colonists of the Eastern seaboard; the central problem is the dissatisfaction of colonists with their lack of representation in Parliament, despite obligations of taxation; and the resolution is the movement for independence, leading to eventual military victory. Similarly, the story of World War II—as taught in Western Europe and many other places—is set in Europe and to lesser extent the Pacific; the characters consist of the Allied and Axis governments; the problem is the rise of Nazism and German militarism, along with Japanese aggression; and the resolution is the victory of the Allied powers during the war. Such stories may be presented in simpler or more complex forms, and their precise nature varies from country to country, but the ultimate objective is for students to remember features of the narrative. Assessments—both those created by teachers and those that are part of formal examinations—usually focus on students' memory of these stories and their ability to reproduce them in a coherent format.

Narratives and Students' Learning

History often has been criticized (and caricaturized) for the boring way in which such stories have been presented: A common stereotype—which unfortunately is rooted in reality for many students—is that history teachers stand in front of the classroom and deliver lectures recounting the details of historical stories. Such lectures are usually supplemented by textbooks in which the same narratives are laid out for students to read and remember.

One problem with such methods is that they generally fail to capture students' interest or enthusiasm: Textbooks often are poorly written, with little attention to young learners' ability to comprehend them (Paxton, 1999), and few students can attend to a lecture (even a well-delivered one) for more than a few minutes. Moreover, when methods of presentation fail to take account of students' prior knowledge, it becomes very difficult for students to integrate new knowledge into their previous frameworks of understanding, and this makes comprehension even more difficult (Donovan & Bransford, 2005). The result is that not only do students often fail to become engaged with history in school, but they fail to remember the stories that are the purpose of the curriculum in the first place (VanSledright, 2011). One extensive survey of U.S. adults found that they considered history interesting and personally relevant—except as taught in school, which they often characterized with one word: "boring" (Rosenzweig & Thelen, 1998, p. 31).

Effective teachers, however, have always found ways to make historical narratives interesting, meaningful, and comprehensible. These teachers display a high level of enthusiasm for the subject and have a good understanding of the content they aim to convey. They make the meaning and purpose of the subject clear to students rather than treating history simply as something required for graduation or promotion. And instead of relying on a literal reading of textbooks, they use a variety of well-chosen materials: not only short, well-planned lectures (involving frequent student interaction), but also trade books (including historical fiction), feature films and documentaries (Marcus, Metzger, Paxton, & Stoddard, 2010), primary sources (Gerwin & Zevin, 2010), reference works (both print and electronic), guest speakers, and field trips. Just as important, they engage students in learning activities that give them a chance to construct their own understanding of the information contained in such sources. Some of the many activities used by effective history teachers include discussion and debate; role play; displays and presentations; creation of posters, brochures, poems, artwork, music, or other creative outlets; and dialogues, simulated diary entries, and other tasks that involve looking at history through the eyes of people in the past (Levstik & Barton, 2011).

The purpose of such activities is not simply for students to have more fun—although that may be a desirable side effect—but to give them the opportunity to make sense of information by putting it into a new format. Students understand and retain information more effectively when they have to transform it (Smagorinsky, 2001)—by taking information from a reference source and creating a presentation, for example, or by reading an account and rewriting it from another perspective. In order for activities to achieve such goals, they must involve higher-order thinking, in which students do more than simply reproduce content; students must be analyzing, comparing, synthesizing, evaluating, and otherwise delving deeply into historical events (Newmann, 1990). Such processes are not easy, and they may fly in the face of the expectation that history simply involves memorization. In order for students to participate meaningfully in such difficult activities, teachers have to provide considerable assistance, particularly by linking new information to students' prior understanding (or giving students the opportunity to make such links), providing critical feedback on students' performances, and scaffolding their participation so that they learn more than they could on their own. Teachers can provide scaffolding by breaking tasks down into manageable but meaningful parts, modeling procedures, asking students probing questions as they work through activities, and supplying graphic organizers (or teaching students to construct their own) that aid in collecting, organizing, and drawing conclusions from historical information (Levstik & Barton, 2011).

Problems of Content Selection

Seeing history education as a matter of learning narratives, though—no matter how well-taught those are—results in some difficult and controversial problems of content selection. The content of historical narratives taught in schools has been criticized on multiple grounds, and although some of these criticisms are more controversial than others, all are rooted in the fact that school history originated to provide young people with a sense of national identity. In the United States, for example, schools strongly emphasize the origin and development of the nation throughout the span of grade levels; most of the stories found in the curriculum focus on English settlement, political independence, and constitutional developments. In the early grades this means learning about explorers, presidents, and civil rights leaders, while in other grades students encounter longer and more complicated narratives about congressional legislation, presidential elections, Supreme Court decisions, and the country's military engagements. World history, meanwhile, forms a much less prominent portion of the curriculum in the United States, with sometimes-fleeting attention in the middle grades or first years of high school, and virtually no attention in the early grades.

One effect of a curriculum that revolves around law, politics, and warfare is that history becomes "event-focused," because wars, elections, and many other political developments happen within a limited time frame—which may help to explain the traditional obsession with learning dates in history. This means that long-term changes—such as social developments, demographic changes, and economic patterns—tend to receive less attention than they deserve. Yet such changes are the focus of much contemporary historical scholarship and are crucial to understanding modern society and the nature of social processes. Chronological arrangement of the curricu-

lum, which teachers often perceive to be required, further stands in the way
of addressing long-term changes, for these often extend beyond the limits
of particular topics. Understanding the Holocaust, for example, requires
understanding much more than the events leading up to World War II; it
requires understanding the Jewish Diaspora and the long history of anti-
Semitism. Such long-term processes, though, do not fit neatly into a course
on the twentieth century or a unit on the rise of Nazism. The academic field
of world history increasingly focuses on broader patterns, developments,
and comparisons, but world history in schools still tends to focus on more
particularistic stories, such as regional developments or the rise and fall
of specific empires (Dunn, 2010)—despite the fact that it is impossible to
teach all important events in the history of the world in a year or two.

In addition, because legal and political affairs traditionally have been
the domain of elite, White men, focusing on such topics has the consequence of omitting most women, minorities, and less economically powerful groups. Because of this omission, students not only gain an incomplete
understanding of historical developments but may also fail to see the experiences of people with whom they identify—and this may make history
seem like something created by and for people unlike themselves (Barton,
2009; Epstein, 2009). History that focuses on larger social patterns and
processes, however, has the effect of including a wider range of people in
the story and thus allowing more students to see themselves in the past.
Although school history in many countries has moved in the direction of
more inclusive history, such inclusion often still amounts to little more than
a sidelight to the principal story of political and legal affairs dominated by
elite White men. And some countries, such as the Netherlands, have even
renewed their commitment to teaching a narrow and exclusionary history,
in order to shore up what is perceived as a disintegrating national identity.
As minorities and immigrants gain an increasingly dominant place in society, that is, some nations respond by using history as a way of defining what
a "real" citizen looks like, and this image intentionally reflects the kinds of
figures traditionally found in the curriculum (Grever, 2007).

Learning about the Past or Celebrating the Nation?

Moving away from a chronological, event-focused framework toward one
with a more inclusionary emphasis on long-term processes is difficult, but it
is even more difficult to abandon history that not only narrates but *celebrates*
the nation. Traditionally, history education has encouraged students both
to identify with their country and to regard it in a highly positive light. In
some countries, history is explicitly nationalist and patriotic, and little or no
room is provided to question the motives or achievements of the nation's
historical figures. Historical events selected for inclusion or omission may
be chosen because of their ability to justify contemporary political positions

(such as a Hindu-focused version of India's past) or to exonerate the nation from historical transgressions (such as Japanese aggression before World War II). In countries such as the United States, a milder but perhaps more effective version of nationalism can be found in schools: a story in which the nation appears as "imperfect but best" (Cornbleth, 1998, p. 622). Problems and mistakes may have occurred in the past, but the general trajectory of national history is a positive and progressive one; topics that might cast the nation in a fundamentally negative light are generally avoided, unless they involve issues that can be presented as having been resolved (Barton & Levstik, 2008).

In the United States, for example, teaching about slavery in North America is an accepted part of the curriculum, and this is largely uncontroversial (despite some regional variation), because that particular form of slavery no longer exists. However, teaching about continuing patterns of racism and discrimination in the more recent past are less acceptable, because these call attention to issues that have not yet been resolved. Similarly, U.S. military abuses during foreign interventions are rarely addressed in schools, both because they reflect so badly on the nation and because they deal with problems that cannot easily be dismissed as "behind us." Some people may resist history that includes more women and minorities, but the greatest outrage always has been reserved for history that acknowledges abuses committed by the government or those in other positions of power. Teachers who hope to address such episodes must be well-prepared to justify their place in understanding the nations' past (e.g., Chandler, 2006).

Narrative and Interpretation

Although less controversial, the most fundamental criticism of traditional history education is its reliance on narrative as the primary means of organizing the curriculum, because this obscures the fact that narratives are selective and interpretive. All narratives, for example, focus on certain people and events deemed worthy of study and consequently omit others; however, there is no agreed-upon criterion for making such selections. Many people, for example, consider events such as the Battle of Blair Mountain or the Matewan Massacre as crucial to understanding the evolving relationship between labor and capital in the United States; others think of them as marginal events that do little to shed light on the nation's past. In addition, narratives always involve interpretation, because identifying particular circumstances or events as the cause or consequence of others requires analysis and evaluation. For example, what caused the Renaissance in 14th-century Florence—the anti-authoritarian nature of Italian political organization, a more earthly form of thinking following the devastation of the Black Death, the artistic patronage of the Medici family, or the influx of Greek scholars following Ottoman conquest of Constantinople? Scholars have evaluated these factors (and their combined effect) differently, and there is no way of establishing a single "correct" answer. Similarly, identifying some situations as "problems," or some events as "resolutions" of those problems, involves interpretation. Native American resistance to White settlement in the American West was a problem from the perspective of settlers and the U.S. government, but from another perspective it was the settlement itself that was problematic. Narratives, then, are not found in the past, but are imposed on the past by those who interpret history (Barton & Levstik, 2004; VanSledright, 2011).

When history is presented as a narrative to be learned, however, its selective and interpretive nature is hidden from view. Others (the teacher, the textbook, the state) already have decided how to select settings and characters, interpret causes and consequences, and identify problems and resolutions; the task of the student is simply to reproduce those interpretations of selected situations. The problem with this way of approaching history is that students are left out of the selective and interpretive process (what if their selections and interpretations differ from the official ones?), and the very nature of history is disguised. History is presented as an objectively true account of the past in which interpretations appear to have the same status as facts: The fact that the U.S. stock market crashed on October 29, 1929, is treated as conceptually equivalent to the interpretation that the Great Depression resulted from a contraction in the money supply—both are simply parts of a narrative for students to understand and remember. Expecting students to remember information indiscriminately in this way, without regard for the selective and interpretive nature of historical knowledge, seriously weakens the subject's intellectual justification. Why should students simply be asked to remember the conclusions others have reached if they have no idea how they reached those conclusions, and if they have no practice in reaching conclusions of their own?

ENGAGING IN HISTORICAL THINKING

In response to dissatisfaction with history as a largely passive matter of remembering stories created by others, many educators have emphasized *historical thinking* as a goal of the subject. From this perspective, the purpose of learning history is not simply to comprehend selected narratives well enough to reproduce them on one's own, but instead to understand the very nature of historical knowledge—to know what is involved in creating historical accounts. This approach involves students not just in learning history but in *doing* history, so that they better understand how claims about the past are made and justified (Barton & Levstik, 2004; VanSledright, 2011). Although arguments in favor of historical thinking as the core of school history have been around since the nineteenth century (e.g., Bohan, 2004), modern versions of this perspective date primarily to the New Social Studies projects in the United States in the 1960s and the Schools Council History Project in the United Kingdom in the 1970s (Thornton, 2001). There are different ways of describing and explaining historical thinking, but three elements can be found in most descriptions: *perspective, agency,* and *interpretation of evidence.*

Perspective

Perspective refers to the attempt to understand historical events and circumstances from the viewpoint of the people involved in them (Davis, Yeager, & Foster, 2001). People have not always viewed the world in the same way that they do today; depending on the time period being studied, people in the past may have had very different values, attitudes, and beliefs, and students have to recognize those ways of thinking in order to be able to understand historical actions. If they assume that everyone has thought the way they do today—with the same ideas about nature, or society, or the supernatural—then they will misunderstand much of what people in history were doing, and they will mischaracterize their motives. Studying any particular time and place, then, must begin with trying to make sense of how people saw their world. This can be a difficult task, because it is not easy to move beyond one's own perspective; it may puzzle students, for example, to think that people in seventeenth-century Massachusetts believed that moles on the body were evidence of witchcraft. Similarly, it can be difficult to understand why women in many historical time periods not only accepted but actively supported what today appear as unjust restrictions on their dress, movement, decision-making, or participation in society. Students often respond to such ideas by concluding that people in the past were mentally defective or, more generously, that they simply hadn't yet "figured out" that women were the same as men, or that witches did not exist (Barton, 2008). Yet they can understand historical events only when see how people at the time considered such values and beliefs to be logical and coherent, and this is a major component of what it means to think historically.

Teaching about historical perspectives involves giving students direct experience with sources from the past. Historians do not simply guess what people in history thought; they base their conclusions on what has been left behind. When students read letters, speeches, or diary entries, it can help them see more clearly how people thought and what they valued. Such sources will never be enough to develop a complete understanding of historical perspectives, however, and they will always have to be supplemented with teachers' explanations or secondary readings, especially when studying times and places for which there are few accessible written sources. Even with more distant times, though, students can make inferences about values by examining surviving art or architecture. Their conclusions will always be filtered through their modern perspectives—just as historians' conclusions are—but this attempt to see the past as much as possible through the eyes of people at the time is a cornerstone of historical thinking.

It is important to recognize, however, that historical perspectives were never monolithic; that is, there was never a time when everyone in society shared all the same values, attitudes, and beliefs. Simplifying the range of perspectives at a given time is unavoidable when teaching, but it is nonetheless important to help students understand that people's beliefs differ *within* any society, and that these differences arise from a variety of factors—gender, ethnicity, class, religion, or social and political philosophies. In teaching about the European Middle Ages, for example, students should recognize that hierarchy was widely accepted as a part of the social order, but they should also understand alternative views such as those of John Ball, Wat Tyler, or others involved in popular uprisings. Similarly, the orthodox beliefs of the Catholic Church may have been dominant at the time, but students also need to know about the views of Cathars and Waldensians, as well as of Jews and Muslims. Indeed, much of the drama of history arises from attempts by some groups to impose their values on others, and students need to recognize this diversity of viewpoints in order to understand many historical conflicts.

Agency

The second element of historical thinking is *agency*. This refers to the who, what, and why of history—not the specific who, what, and why (those are the content of narratives), but rather the *kinds* of people, events, and causes involved in historical explanation. This begins with recognizing the fundamental fact that people in the past made decisions in pursuit of their goals. Although this sounds obvious, history is often presented as though developments were inevitable: One thing caused another, without any living, breathing people involved in the process. Yet historical events and processes are the result of decisions made by people, acting either alone or in concert, and historical thinking involves understanding how those decisions and their consequences came about. Julius Caesar decided to violate Roman law by leading his troops across the Rubicon; Woodrow Wilson chose to restrict African American employment in the federal government; Gandhi chose to engage in civil disobedience against the British government. Such decisions are made not only by famous leaders but also by unknown and unnamed members of society: U.S. families in the nineteenth century chose to have fewer children; many Irish during the Great Famine chose to emigrate to North America, Australia, or New Zealand; Germans in the 1930s chose to support, oppose, or ignore the actions of the Nazi party. If people had made different decisions, history would have turned out differently.

Understanding historical agency, then, involves analyzing who made decisions and why, as well as how they acted on those decisions, and this is a complicated undertaking. In looking at the actors in history, for example, it is important for students to understand the role of both individuals and societal institutions (such as governments or social movements). Sometimes, students overemphasize the role of individuals in bringing about historical changes: They may think of exploration of the New World in terms of the exploits of a few brave explorers, rather than in terms of political and economic competition among European powers, or they may think that racial discrimination in the United States changed because of a speech by Martin Luther King, Jr., rather than because of an organized social movement (Barton, 2008). Other times, students ignore individuals and think only in terms of abstract groups: Just as texts and teachers often do, they may speak of Pearl Harbor being attacked by "Japan," rather than by the Japanese military under the command of the ruling regime, or they may say that "Germany" resented reparations for World War I, rather than recognizing that certain political factions encouraged some German citizens to blame others (particularly Socialists, Communists, and Jews) for having agreed to reparations.

The problem with overemphasizing individuals is that students may not understand how people's actions and motivations are part of larger societal structures that channel and direct what they do. The problem with overemphasizing societal institutions, on the other hand, is that it becomes easy to blame those who were not responsible for the actions of others; students often conclude, for example, that dropping atomic bombs on Japan was justified because Japan had attacked the United States—even though the individuals who died in Hiroshima and Nagasaki were not those involved in that attack. The complicated relationships among individuals, groups, and institutions is a part of all historical analysis, and teachers have to help students understand that in any historical setting, they have to take these elements into account.

A second part of historical agency involves recognizing how people take action within situations of inequality. As noted earlier, history education has often focused on the actions of the powerful. This means that powerful groups and individuals often are portrayed as being entirely responsible for historical actions, while others are seen as having had little or no room to make decisions or carry out their desires. As a result, in most historical time periods women, minorities, the poor, the enslaved, and other nondominant groups can easily be seen as simple victims of repressive social structures. However, even within repressive societies, marginalized groups have had some room for maneuver, and they have used this to their advantage.

In the antebellum United States, for example, enslaved Africans developed vibrant cultural traditions despite the depredations of slavery, and women who were confined to the private sphere affected public life through their participation in charitable organizations and their advocacy for causes that affected domestic life. Rarely are people completely powerless or lacking in volition, and students need to analyze actions and decisions made by all segments of society, not just those who held the upper hand. Students also need to recognize that they cannot always reach conclusions about agency in historical situations by thinking in terms of later developments. Initial encounters between colonial powers and indigenous peoples, for example, were often much more equal—with more room for indigenous agency— than they later became.

It is also important for students to understand the societal structures that either enable or constrain historical actions and decisions. Sometimes students attribute more agency to historical actors than they actually had. For example, in learning about extreme situations such as slavery, apartheid, or the Holocaust, students often are incredulous that slaves, Black South Africans, or Jews and other targeted groups didn't either run away or fight back. In order to understand these situations, students need to recognize the factors that prevented escape or widespread resistance (as well as how some people did resist). Similarly, although Europeans may not have held the upper hand in their initial encounters with indigenous people, they nonetheless possessed technologies and forms of social organization that enabled them to exert increasing amounts of domination over others. At the same time, students need to identify how societal forces and institutions may have promoted the agency of less powerful segments of society, and therefore may have resulted in changes that could not have been achieved through purely individual efforts. The Civil Rights Movement in the United States, for example, depended heavily on the leadership and organizational capacities that had developed in African American churches. In approaching any historical situation, then, students need to ask, "What factors promoted the agency of different groups? What factors constrained it?"

Interpretation of Evidence

A third element of historical thinking involves the interpretation of evidence. Fundamental to any academic subject is an understanding of how knowledge in that field is developed. In history, this means learning about the kinds of historical sources available and the process of drawing conclusions from those sources. Until they study the subject in school, though— and unless they specifically focus on the interpretation of evidence—most students appear not to have given much thought to how we know what happened in the past. Younger students may believe that historical information has been handed down by word-of-mouth over the generations (reflecting their own experience hearing stories from relatives), while older ones often treat sources uncritically, with no attention to how, or for what purpose, a source was created (Barton, 2008). Yet without such understanding, the past amounts to little more than a guessing game, and students have no basis for deciding between accounts that are based on evidence and those that are pure fantasy. A major task of the history teacher, then, is to provide students with extensive experience working with historical evidence and using it to draw conclusions about the past.

This means, first of all, that students have to learn what kinds of historical evidence exist: They need to be exposed to letters, diaries, photographs, oral records, newspapers, magazines, monuments, artwork, music, artifacts, buildings, human landscapes, business records, government documents such as census records, and so on. Students can begin working with sources such as these from a very young age (in the first years of primary school), and in fact the visual and tactile qualities of much historical evidence can make them engaging to students of all ages. Teachers have to select such sources carefully, of course: Younger students won't be able to read complex written compositions from the past, and sources such as legislative documents can be practically incomprehensible even to adults. And as already noted, teaching about more distant time periods, and those for which written sources are not in English, will have to rely on translated sources, along with visual and archeological evidence. The use of historical sources will never completely dominate the history classroom, because students cannot be expected to learn everything they need to know about the past solely by working with evidence. However, original historical sources should be a frequent and consistent part of students' experience with history, so that they better understand how knowledge of the past is developed. Students don't need to examine sources for every historical assertion they encounter in the classroom, but they do need to know that some historian has done precisely that.

Students need much more than exposure to historical evidence, though: They need ongoing experience with its interpretation. When working with any original source, students need to learn to ask, "What can we learn from this? What can we not learn from it?" This means that they have to think about how the source was produced, and for what purpose, because these affect its content. Some sources aim to provide testimony of what existed or what happened at a given time: Official correspondence may report the details of a diplomatic or military encounter, for example, and a memoir or oral history may describe what life was like in the past. When working with such testimony, students have to consider what factors may have influenced the knowledge or objectivity of the person who created it: Did they have direct experience of the events or circumstances, or were they relying on someone else? How recently did they experience it? Did they have any reason to misrepresent what was going on? Just as important, they need to consider what sources of testimony were *not* created, and perhaps could not have been. Until recently, for example, written sources have been produced primarily by educated elites and reflect the experiences to which they had access; the lives of non-elites have been less likely to make it into written records. Even in more recent times, reports of some kinds of experiences are common than others. An official document reporting a military encounter in Vietnam, for instance, may record the experiences of U.S. soldiers as objectively as possible, but experiences of the affected villagers may still be missing. All these factors influence the reliability and completeness of historical testimony.

Students can come to understand basic issues of reliability and completeness relatively easily when given the chance to analyze historical sources critically. A major stumbling block in helping them understand how historical knowledge is constructed, though, is that they often treat *all* historical sources as though they were testimony—and sometimes, teachers and published materials reinforce this misconception. Students need to understand that not all historical sources were created in order to describe an event or a situation for others, and that historians do not always use sources in this way (Barton, 2005). Many sources are better thought of not as testimony, but as *relics* or *artifacts* of a time period. Physical artifacts obviously can provide direct, if limited, evidence of the past: An automobile from the 1930s, a 14th-century cathedral, or the remains of a Native American village all provide evidence of what actually existed, and questions of who created these sources and whether they were biased are irrelevant. Students need to ask what sources are likely to have remained and which have disappeared (cathedrals are more likely to endure than the homes of serfs), but this kind of bias is that which is found in the overall historical record, not in individual sources.

More confusing to many people are sources that include testimony but that are more useful as artifacts—and this is precisely the kind of evidence that is used most often by historians. For example, a magazine advertisement for an electric kitchen appliance from the 1940s may attest to its ease of use and its efficiency in preparing food. As testimony, the source is highly biased, and few conclusions could be reached about whether the device was actually easy to use or efficient. But as a historical artifact, it can provide very useful evidence: Not only does it demonstrate that the product existed at that time, but also that appliances were marketed in certain ways (to the readers of specific magazines, for example) and that particular strategies were considered effective because they appealed to important societal values of the period (such as a product's simplicity or its ability to save time); the advertisement could also provide evidence of how people at the time thought about the relationship between gender roles and domestic labor.

Similarly, a politician's speech from the 1930s would not be reliable as testimony to the effects of the New Deal, since the politician would likely be selectively interpreting facts in ways that would lead listeners to support or oppose particular programs. However, the speech could be very useful as an artifact, because it would present information on what arguments were being made by which politicians (regardless of the accuracy of those arguments) and, combined with other sources, could provide evidence of their effectiveness. This is why "unreliable" sources are especially useful as evidence of the perspectives of people at the time. Making such distinctions between what can and cannot be learned from a source is at the heart of historical interpretation.

Interpreting historical sources, however, cannot take place on its own; it is a part of the larger process of historical inquiry (Barton & Levstik, 2004; Zevin & Gerwin, 2010). An unfortunate classroom method that has cropped up in recent years is the practice of treating sources in isolation, as though one can simply look at a source and determine how reliable it is (or less often, how useful it is). The problem with this approach is that neither reliability nor usefulness can be evaluated without a specific question in mind; historical sources only become evidence with regard to the questions asked of them. Students have to begin with a question before they can evaluate whether a source provides evidence or not. For example, if they want to know about the nature of antebellum slavery in the United States, they cannot use textbooks from the 1920s as evidence, because these texts were shaped by the racial attitudes of the day are unlikely to have given a full account of the practice. However, if students want to know about racial attitudes in the 1920s, then these same textbooks become very good sources of evidence, because they illustrate how slavery was represented in schools. Yet even with a question in mind, no source is conclusive evidence on its own; students have to look at a body of evidence in order to reach conclusions about most questions—a collection of textbooks, speeches, or advertisements, or an even more varied set of sources. The practice of treating sources in isolation may be a reason that students frequently conclude that because all sources are biased, historical knowledge is impossible; if they had more experience interpreting sources within the broader context of inquiry-oriented investigations, the role of sources in reaching conclusions would become clearer.

As with effective teaching of historical narratives, engaging students in historical thinking is not easy. Most students have little previous experience considering issue of perspective, agency, and evidence (at least in a formal and systematic way), and they will need a great deal of scaffolding—the same kinds of modeling, graphic organizers, probing questions, task breakdown, and critical feedback mentioned earlier. And because historical thinking may be a new concept for most students, teachers must provide a clear sense of purpose: They have to help students understand why historical thinking is important enough to require so much attention. Without this kind of motivation, students may resist historical thinking as an unwelcome alternative to narratives. The need for a clear sense of purpose points to the critical role of teachers' professional knowledge and decision-making in history education.

THE ROLE OF THE TEACHER

Most history classrooms do not engage students in extensive historical thinking of the kind described here. Often, educators will complain that it is literally impossible to spend time on analyzing original historical sources or considering multiple perspectives because either the curriculum or the examination system requires memory of specific narratives. This observation is only partly true, because in reality, many teachers' practices are only weakly linked to either curriculum or examinations (Barton, 2011). In the United States, for example, examinations vary widely from state to state in their emphasis on the need to recall the details of historical stories (and many states have no history examinations at all), yet teaching practices are remarkably similar across the nation—and good teachers everywhere find ways to move beyond the norm despite their circumstances. Similarly, state curriculum requirements in the United States often include aspects of historical thinking—particularly the interpretation of evidence—yet many teachers neglect these objectives in favor of narrative; others teach for historical thinking even when the curriculum does not require it. Teachers' judgments about how to teach, therefore, play a critical role in changing or preserving the nature of history education.

In order for more teachers to incorporate historical thinking into their instruction, several conditions have to be met. First, teachers must recognize that engaging students in historical thinking is cognitively and pedagogically sound practice that will help students better learn the content of the curriculum. Historical thinking does not mean abandoning narrative, but deepening and enriching students' understanding of narrative. Students still need to encounter narratives about topics such as the spread of Islam, the Women's Suffrage Movement, or World War II, but by focusing on agency, perspective, and evidence they will have a better understanding of those narratives—their knowledge will be more subtle, nuanced, and complete, and they will have a better sense of the basis on which the narrative has been constructed. Except in those rare circumstances in which students literally are expected to repeat a specific narrative verbatim, the more complete understanding they gain through historical thinking will enable them to provide better answers on essays and other forms of examination.

In order to carry out such instruction, teachers need a rich knowledge base—not of everything that has ever happened in history, but of how to engage students in using historical thinking to analyze historical events and circumstances (VanSledright, 2011). This means becoming familiar with current historical interpretations and the work of historians, so that teachers can better understand the nature of historical thinking and its application to specific topics. That would involve both independent reading of current historical scholarship and attendance at professional conferences and workshops, as well as participating in networks devoted to professional inquiry and reflection. It also means becoming familiar with the considerable body of research on the nature of students' historical thinking, in order to better understand how students' prior knowledge and interests can be incorporated into instruction, as well as to anticipate difficulties and misconceptions students may have. Finally, teachers need to read works that describe the practices of ambitious and innovative teachers so that they can see realistic portrayals of classroom instruction that will help them reflect on their own situations (e.g., Grant & Gradwell, 2010; Percoco, 2001; Yeager & Davis, 2005).

Something else is needed, too: A clear sense of purpose. Good history teaching is hard work, and it requires going beyond simply explaining what's found in a textbook. In some instances, it may also require the courage to resist the expectations of students, administrators, or the wider community. Teachers—like anyone—only undertake such difficult tasks when they have a clear reason for doing so, and there are two possible reasons for engaging students in historical thinking. The first is that this kind of history education more closely resembles the academic discipline of history. Professional historians don't just read and reproduce other historians' stories; they construct such narratives (and other kinds of accounts) using the elements of historical thinking described above. If the purpose of teaching subjects in school is for students to understand disciplinary forms of knowledge, then it becomes impossible to omit perspective, agency, and the interpretation of evidence. That's just what history *is*.

Many educators may find a second purpose for engaging students in historical thinking even more motivating. Although historical thinking is clearly required to understand history as a discipline, it may also contribute to participation in a democratic society (Barton & Levstik, 2004). In order to reach judgments about public policy issues, for example, citizens need to be able to reach conclusions based on evidence—just as historians do. And whether making decisions about policy or working together with others in civil society, people must be able to understand the perspectives of those who come from backgrounds different than their own; this too is part of historical thinking. Finally, democratic participation requires a sense of agency: recognition that people can make choices, and that their choices influence the future of society. Just as people in the past made decisions that affected later times, we in the present can make decisions that will have consequences for many years to come. Without an understanding of agency, perspective, and the interpretation of evidence, young people will be ill-equipped for the responsibilities of democratic civic participation.

Thinking about history's purpose in terms of democratic participation brings up two questions that are not usually considered central to disciplinary historical thinking, but that are critical for making decisions about history's role in general education. First, what content will best prepare students for democratic life? The discipline of history provides direction on *how* to study history, but not on *what* to study—professional historians study anything and everything. But given the limited amount of time schools can devote to history, educators must make choices about which topics are most relevant and meaningful (Thornton & Barton, 2010). For example, as noted earlier, history education originated as a way of developing a sense of national identity, and so the curriculum traditionally has focused on people and events considered emblematic of the nation. But in today's pluralistic societies, new ways of thinking about content selection may be called for, and a more varied set of people and events may need to be included, so that each nation's story better reflects the diversity of its population. The need to understand historic links to other nations and societies has also become more apparent in light of the globalization of culture, politics, economics, and resource use; as a result, the isolated way in which national histories have often been taught may need to be rethought.

Teaching with an eye toward democratic participation may also encourage teachers to provide opportunities for students to deliberate moral and ethical issues in history. Democratic decision-making requires not just the analysis of information but an ability to make judgments in light of social, moral, and ethical value systems. This means not just examining what people did in the past and why, but evaluating whether they *should* have taken those actions. Although students could analyze the bombing of Hiroshima and Nagasaki by considering only the factors that motivated the Truman administration, they also could make judgments about whether the action was justified. This means that they would have to become familiar with the principles that underlie such judgments—religious precepts, conceptions of human rights, international humanitarian law, constitutional principles, just war theory, proportionality, and so on. Sometimes educators believe that students can simply be told which judgments are correct, and that students will accept those judgments. Other times they assume that students will draw inevitable moral lessons from their study of the past. (How can one learn about the Holocaust without becoming more committed to human dignity, for example?) However, there is little evidence that either the direct or indirect approach to moral judgment in history has much impact on students. A more deliberative model, on the other hand, in which students discuss how to link historical choices to explicit principles, may prepare them for the kinds of decisions expected in a democratic society (Barton & Levstik, 2008).

CONCLUSIONS

History teachers are faced with tasks that sometimes seem impossible: Teaching students about particular historical narratives, while at the same time engaging them in historical thinking; knowing how to motivate students and scaffold their participation in difficult forms of learning; remaining current with both historical scholarship and educational research; and balancing community pressure, disciplinary forms of knowledge, and the needs of a democratic society. The best teachers, though, do all these things. They see beyond the test, the textbook, and all the daily factors that make teaching so complicated, and they take pride in their ability to enhance students' understanding of important intellectual matters. They have a strong vision of what they are doing and why, and they accept responsibility for teaching a subject as difficult, and as important, as history.

REFERENCES

Barton, K. C. (2005). Primary sources in history: Breaking through the myths. *Phi Delta Kappan, 86,* 745–753.

Barton, K. C. (2008). Students' ideas about history. In L. S. Levstik & C. A. Tyson (Eds.), *Handbook of research in social studies education* (pp. 239–258). New York: Routledge.

Barton, K. C. (2009). The denial of desire: How to make history education meaningless. In L. Symcox & A. Wilschut (Eds.), *National history standards: The problem of the canon and the future of teaching history* (pp. 265–282). Greenwich, CT: Information Age Publishing.

Barton, K. C. (2011). Wars and rumors of war: Making sense of history education in the United States. In T. Taylor & R. Guyver (Eds.), *History wars in the classroom: Global perspectives.* Charlotte, NC: Information Age Publishing.

Barton, K. C., & Levstik, L. S. (2004). *Teaching history for the common good.* New York: Routledge.

Barton, K. C., & Levstik, L. S. (2008). History. In J. Arthur, C. Hahn, & I. Davies (Eds.), *Handbook of education for citizenship and democracy* (pp. 355–366). London: Sage.

Bohan, C. H. (2004). *Go to the sources: Lucy Maynard Salmon and the teaching of history.* New York: Peter Lang.

Chandler, P. T. (2006). Academic freedom: A teacher's struggle to include "other" voices in history. *Social Education, 70,* 354–357.

Cornbleth, C. (1998). An American curriculum? *Teachers College Record, 99,* 622–646.

Davis, O. L., Jr., Yeager, E. A., & Foster, S. J. (2001). *Historical empathy and perspective taking in the social studies.* Lanham, MD: Rowman & Littlefield.

Donovan, S., & Bransford, J. (Eds.). (2005). *How students learn: History in the classroom.* Washington, DC: National Research Council.

Dunn, R. E. (2010). The two world histories. In W. C. Parker (Ed.), *Social studies today: Research and practice* (pp. 183–195). New York: Routledge.

Epstein, T. L. (2009). *Interpreting national history: Race, identity, and pedagogy in classrooms.* New York: Routledge.

Gerwin, D., & Zevin, J. (2010). *Teaching U.S. history as mystery* (2nd ed.). New York: Routledge.

Grant, S. G. (2003). *History lessons: Teaching, learning, and testing in U.S. high school classrooms.* Mahwah, NJ: Lawrence Erlbaum Associates.

Grant, S. G., & Gradwell, J. M. (2010). *Teaching history with big ideas: Cases of ambitious teachers.* Lanham, MD: Rowman & Littlefield.

Grever, M. (2007). Plurality, narrative, and the history canon. In M. Grever & S. Stuurman (Eds.), *Beyond the canon: History for the twenty-first century* (pp. 31–47). New York: Palgrave Macmillan.

Lévesque, S. (2008). *Thinking historically: Educating students for the twenty-first century.* Toronto, ON: University of Toronto Press.

Levstik, L. S., & Barton, K. C. (2011). *Doing history: Investigating with children in elementary and middle schools.* (4th ed.). New York: Routledge.

Marcus, A. S., Metzger, S. A., Paxton, R. J., & Stoddard, J. D. (2010). *Teaching history with film: Strategies for secondary social studies.* New York: Routledge.

Nakou, I., & Barca, I. (Eds.) (2010). *Contemporary public debates over history education.* Charlotte, NC: Information Age Publishing.

Newmann, F. M. (1990). Higher order thinking in teaching social studies: A rationale for the assessment of classroom thoughtfulness. *Journal of Curriculum Studies, 22,* 41–56.

Paxton, R. J. (1999). A deafening silence: History textbooks and the students who read them. *Review of Educational Research, 69,* 315–339.

Percoco, J. A., (2001). *Divided we stand: Teaching about conflict in U.S. history.* Portsmouth, NH: Heinemann.

Rosenzweig, R., & Thelen, D. (1998). *The presence of the past: Popular uses of history in American life.* New York: Columbia University Press.

Seixas, P. (1996). Conceptualizing the growth of historical understanding. In D. R. Olson & N. Torrance (Eds.), *The handbook of education and human development: New models of learning. teaching. and schooling* (pp. 765–783). Cambridge, MA: Blackwell Publishers.

Smagorinsky, P. (2001). If meaning is constructed, what's it made from? Toward a cultural theory of reading. *Review of Educational Research, 71,* 133–169.

Thornton, S. J. (2001). History. In J. Brophy (Ed.), *Advances in research on teaching, Vol. 8: Subject-specific instructional methods and activities* (pp. 291–314). New York: Elsevier Science.

Thornton, S. J., & Barton, K. C. (2010). Can history stand alone? Drawbacks and blind spots of a "disciplinary" curriculum. *Teachers College Record, 112,* 2471–2495.

Taylor, T., & Guyver, R. (Eds.), (2011). *History wars in the classroom: Global perspectives.* Charlotte, NC: Information Age Publishing.

VanSledright, B. A. (2011). *The challenge of rethinking history education: On practices, theories, and policy.* New York: Routledge.

Wineburg, S. (2001). *Historical thinking and other unnatural acts: Charting the future of teaching the past.* Philadelphia: Temple University Press.

Yeager, E. A., & Davis, O. L., Jr. (Eds.) (2005). *Wise social studies teaching in an age of high-stakes testing: Essays on classroom practices and possibilities.* Greenwich, CT: Information Age Publishing.

Zevin, J., & Gerwin, D. (2010). *Teaching world history as mystery.* New York: Routledge.

CHAPTER 8

GEOGRAPHY EDUCATION

Making Sense of Our World with Spatial Relationships

Reese H. Todd

As the world grows smaller and more interdependent daily, our country's future absolutely depends on our ability to see the connections between ourselves and our global neighbors.

—Gilbert M. Grosvenor
Chairman of the Board of Trustees,
National Geographic Society (1984)

When children ask, "Are we there yet?" they are trying to make sense of where they are in time and space. Adults may not ask the same geographic question, but they do continue to organize their experiences into contexts of time and place and use that information to inform their interactions. Whether from a child's innocent perspective or from a scholarly point of view, geography education is fundamentally about people and places in the global environment. Advances in technology and new understandings of spatial thinking combine with professional review of the field during the

Contemporary Social Studies: An Essential Reader, pages 139–152
Copyright © 2012 by Information Age Publishing
　　　　　139

past two decades to provide geography educators with new tools for communicating the importance of geography in making sense of the world.

As with other fields of study, the more a person knows, the more deeply one understands the broader implications of available information. The content knowledge of the discipline of geography includes study of both physical and human characteristics of the spaces on earth and interactions among the ever-changing systems. Indeed, as National Geographic Society's President Grosvenor said, the future does depend on seeing the connections between ourselves and our global neighbors (1984) and that knowledge defines the scope and sequence of contemporary geography education. The chapter focuses on important events in the field of geography education in the past two decades with particular emphasis on *Geography for Life Standards (1994)* and its significance in shaping contemporary geography education. Five case studies describe practices of teachers and students who applied their knowledge to projects integrated into K–12 curriculum. The chapter concludes with recommendations for emphasizing the integration of knowledge and tools of the discipline keep geography education relevant for students living in the 21st century.

Geography education in the current U.S. curriculum brings together information from many sources to understand the connections of people and places around the world. Powerful geographic tools allow citizens internet access to multiple layers of spatial data simultaneously to inform decisions and solve problems. People do not have to be experts to analyze and interpret events in a holistic manner and can become engaged in discussions about common concerns as they view real time images (Shelley, 1999).

According to iconic geographer, Dr. Carl O. Sauer, "How the land and [people's] lives differ from one part of the earth to another" is what forms the basis of geographic curiosity that endures from childhood (cited in Downs, 1994). A recent global event shows how quickly our curiosity about people and places escalates, and becomes part of our experience.

Only moments after a 7.0 magnitude earthquake struck Haiti on January 12, 2010, images of the devastation began circulating around the world as people sent messages on their iPhones and posted videos on YouTube. The stories of the damage and loss of life from the natural disaster sent people of all ages to websites to learn about Haiti; a place many could not have located on a map the week before. They asked questions about the landscape, the people living there, the transportation network, and the economic resources. Citizens saw the plight of the islanders and used their social networking to spearhead relief efforts faster than the infrastructure could handle.

Added to the individual stories were interactive graphics showing causes of earthquakes and real time communication as a news team found and reported on an adoptive child's condition while the family awaited completion of adoption processes. Along with the information came questions posted on blogs and recorded on instant news feeds. People wondered "Why are relief agencies not getting aid to the people in a more timely manner? How could ordinary citizens help others caught in such a tragic situation? People could see so much data and tried to overlap the multiple sources to make sense of the situation.

Not all information was accurate or relevant. Those who sent relief supplies saw only part of the picture and assumed the transportation, governmental and non-governmental agencies, and problem-solving skills of leaders would respond in ways similar to that expected in the United States. They did not. In their report, the research committee on spatial thinking (National Research Council, 2006) described that disconnect in this way, "We have gone from a problem-rich, data-poor world to one that is both data-rich and problem-rich, but is currently lacking the capacity to bring data to bear on solving problems" (p. 32). It was a sign of changing times.

The first response of Americans was an emotional one that was grounded in a basic human response to care for the needs of others in crisis. Geography teachers who considered themselves global educators recognized the event as an opportunity to examine the experiences, knowledge, beliefs, and values that shape people's world views, what Merryfield and Wilson (2005) call perspective consciousness. She notes the importance of being aware of the effects of economic, political, cultural and environmental change for those living beyond the local community. With the awareness, American teachers and students use knowledge to challenge personal stereotypes and consider the interconnectedness of international people and cultures. Lessons using the wealth of primary documents from the time surrounding the disaster, further encouraged new perspectives while demanding increased geography knowledge of the physical and cultural landscape that created obstacles for recovery within the nation of Haiti. It was a learning task for both teachers and students in many classrooms. The need for international programs within teacher preparation programs was clear (Cushner, 2007) and a responsibility I needed to accept as a teacher educator in the university.

DEVELOPMENT OF GEOGRAPHY STANDARDS

People tried to see the connections between themselves and global neighbors, but needed geographic knowledge of physical and human systems to understand the multiple layers of factors shaping the recovery efforts School instruction and learning of geography had not adequately prepared citizens to make the connections. Geographers' various research projects had addressed the need for a well-grounded K–12 geography curriculum prior to 1994, but it was the establishment of themes and standards published in *Geography for Life: The National Standards for Geography* (1994), that was a turning point in contemporary geographic education in the United States. The document synthesized the knowledge of professional geographers into a framework of standards that educators in the United States could use for instruction, and built a case for geography in the reform movement. The next step, Downs (1994) noted, was to make the case "forcefully, frequently, and convincingly to the general public and to professional educators" (p. 175).

When *A Nation at Risk* (National Commission on Excellence in Education, 1983) hit the media with a highly charged negative review of the state of education in the United States, educators were stunned. I was teaching social studies in a middle school (grades 6–8) and asked myself, "Were we really doing such a poor job of educating young people? Were we endangering the future of the nation?" Students in the elementary and middle level classes I taught had learned extensive academic content, investigated challenging topics, and integrated detailed knowledge into multiple projects. They received recognition for their projects at state and national competitions and were admitted into excellent higher education programs. The questions and criticisms by the Report raised forced American educators to assess a broad spectrum of educational issues that led to some positive changes in curriculum and instruction standards for content areas.

In geography, over the next 10 years, a more focused educational scope and sequence emerged. *Geography for Life: National Geography Standards* was published as a guide for geography education K–12 under the leadership of the American Geographical Society, the Association of American Geographers, the National Council for Geographic Education, and the National Geographic Society. The project identified key components of excellence in geographic education. Eighteen standards were grouped into Six Essential Elements with examples of content students in the U.S. were expected to know and understand in three phases of their education, (i.e., K–4, 5–8, and 9–12). Those standards have served as a road map for curriculum development, teacher education, policy development, and research and development in geography. A revision is in press and is expected to be released in 2011.

In the 1980s, expert geographers had simplified key ideas of the field to make it easier for teachers to know what to teach in geography courses (Gersmehl, 2005). The five themes—Location, Places, Human-Environment Interaction, Regions, and Movement - were fairly easy to remember, but they did not convey to teachers the importance of the relationships between ideas. Was it enough to locate regions or should students be able to determine for themselves particular characteristics that could define the regions in other ways? Why do people live in areas prone to earthquakes or floods? What economic and political issues contribute to escalating the impact of a natural disaster? Gregg and Leinhardt (1994) suggested that listing the five themes as topics (nouns) constrained such geographic inquiry whereas a structure of organizing topics using verbs would emphasize the processes. Other educators noted that with the five themes, after memorizing disconnected facts about location and place, lessons were finished. Too often teachers left the other more complex and relational themes unexamined (Sunal, Christensen, & Haas, 1995). The process of improving geography literacy in the school curriculum continued to evolve.

A significant boost to improving geographic education came from the National Geographic Society (NGS) when Gilbert Grosvenor became president in 1989. In collaboration with professional geography organizations, President Grosvenor committed substantial funds to improve geographic education (Grosvenor, 1989; Lanken, 1996). Additionally, state geographic alliances were established in more than half of the states in the U.S. to bring together classroom teachers, geography professors and educational administrators to gain knowledge and skills for teaching geography in K–12 schools. Ongoing two-week summer institutes in different states were funded completely for participants. From these efforts, there emerged a cadre of teachers who became leaders in geography education both locally and nationally. Alliances also sent teacher representatives to National Geographic Headquarters in Washington, DC for in-depth 4-week institutes to support state curriculum development. Special programs were established that produced innovative educational materials, reached out to decision makers, and increased public awareness of geography. Geography Awareness Week and the National Geography Bee are two of those programs in existence today. As a side note, the winner of the National Geography Bee receives $50, 000 college scholarship. The Oklahoma Alliance (OKAGE) and its geographers gave me a valuable foundation for geography study in 1992 and today the Texas Alliance (TAGE) supports my work in teacher education at the university. A total of 1,572 teachers participated in one kind of geography academy or another in the summer of 1993 (Dulli, 1994).

Our traditional or heritage curriculum (Shelley, 1999) focused on learning the detailed facts about both local and distant places. A *geographically literate* person could locate exotic places accurately on a globe and provide statistical data about physical landscapes. The experts understood how these were relevant in constructing geographical concepts, but typical K–12 students were novice learners, seldom moving beyond the stacks of data they had stored in their memory (Bednarz & Petersen, 1994; Downs, 1994). Today's *geographically literate* person must understand the big picture of geography as "an integrative discipline that brings together the physical and human dimensions of the world in the study of people, places, and environments (*Geography for Life*, p. 18). Furthermore, at a personal level, Gersmehl

(2005) reminds us that a *geographically literate* person will "arrange information in ways that are fair, safe, efficient, and even beautiful" (p. 3).

ESSENTIAL ELEMENTS OF GEOGRAPHY EDUCATION

Geography for Life: National Geography Standards (1994) lists eighteen standards grouped into six categories. Each category includes fundamental geographic concepts that foster geographic literacy and understanding of the people, places, and environments in the world, and are summarized below:

1. **The World in Spatial Terms** uses maps and geographic representation tools to acquire, process, and report information from a spatial perspective. The essential element establishes a perspective for understanding where people and places are and how they are organized in the environment in relation to one another.

2. **Places and regions** as a theme recognizes common characteristics of places and then tie together in categories called regions to interpret some of the Earth's complexities. Within this theme are concepts about cultures and experiences that influence perceptions of places and regions.

3. **Physical systems** is a theme connecting geographers to physical sciences and the processes that shape the Earth's surface. These include study of climate, soils, watersheds, and ecosystems that are found in K–12 curriculum.

4. **Human systems** focuses on the patterns and processes relevant to human populations. It includes study of migrations, cultural mosaics, economic interdependence, and human settlements. Spatial networks of governance, cooperation and conflict among people are human systems studied in K–12 curriculum.

5. **Environment and society** emphasizes the relationships between the physical and human systems and the changes in use and importance of particular resources over time. Water resources and tracking communicable diseases are current issues for study within this theme.

6. **Uses of geography** is a theme that highlights the multiple applications of geographic knowledge in understanding the past, solving problems today, and planning for the future. Career opportunities for both female and male scholars with skills in using geographic tools are emerging at exponential rates.

Geographic Standards provided a working structure for educators, both novices and seasoned professional geographers. The document was a gateway for a broader conversation that included new voices from those under-represented in the past. New perspectives suggested new lines of research and sources of funding. They used technology to bridge gaps between theory and practice. Collaborative projects emerged and they were strengthened by a broader knowledge base. Learning to think spatially was one step toward more interdisciplinary collaborations and is discussed in the next section. Some case studies will follow to show how geographically-informed teachers and students put learning into practice in their communities.

Thinking Geographically Today

In addition to the geography standards research in the area of spatial thinking further connected concepts of geographic literacy to many aspects of everyday life. Packing the trunk of the car for a family trip, installing a child's safety seat, finding items on a grocery list, and arriving at the right gate at the airport are examples of spatial functions which require spatial skills to accomplish. People match sizes and shapes to available space, estimate distances and directions, and map out routes. *Spatial thinking* is often defined in terms of different disciplines, but a knowledge base in geography facilitates organizing everyday tasks and improving *spatial literacy*. To understand spatial literacy in the context of geography, we turn to research by Phil and Carol Gersmehl (2007).

Gersmehl and Gersmehl (2007) reviewed scholarship from brain research, cognitive psychology, and geography to identify eight modes of spatial thinking that support the skills for *spatial literacy*. Not surprising, several are critical to meeting the geography standards as students make comparisons and organize concepts. According to Gersmehl and Gersmehl, the modes of thinking are comparison, influence, region, hierarchy, analogy, transition, pattern, and association. They are distinct, yet overlap in application. A spatial *comparison* emphasizes places and locations and uses language such as "over," "under," and "next to." *Influence*, or aura, is a zone around an object such as the extent of the smell of a skunk's spray. *Region* refers to common conditions or connections within an area such as the semi-arid conditions common to my own region of West Texas; *hierarchy* is a spatial arrangement of nested areas of different sizes as neighborhoods within cities within states. *Analogy* is a common thinking strategy for relating unfamiliar ideas to more familiar concepts and is often used in daily expressions. "Prices are sky high" or "I am feeling on top of the world" are two expressions using spatial analogy. *Transition* is a mode of thinking that reinforces observations of changes in places and over time. The final two modes of spatial thinking described by Gersmehl and Gersmehl are *pattern* and *association*. Spatial arrangements of data, like city lights or plowed fields, are examples of *patterns* on the landscape while *association* recognizes which features are likely to be found near one another; playgrounds and schools, grain elevators and railroad tracks, or rattlesnakes and rocky terrain. The use of these elements in solving spatial problems furthers a person's skill in learning to think geographically.

Additional research on spatial thinking comes from the National Research Council's committee report thinking spatially (2006). In that piece, the committee describes four ways people process spatial information: a) by generating a representation, b) by maintaining a representation in working memory, c) by scanning a representation to attend to some of its parts, and d) by transforming a representation to a new perspective. Discussion of these processes is beyond the scope of the current project, but the document can be accessed online (http://www.nap.edu).

For some learners, these spatial aspects are already integral to their thinking; but for others, spatial awareness must be taught for students to be successful using tools and making decisions based on spatial information. Such skills are not currently part of the standard K–12 curriculum, but may be on the horizon. For example, the international New London Group (2000) is continuing to investigate an expanded view of literacy pedagogy that goes beyond verbal and visual texts. They suggest the term "multiple literacies" to convey the broader idea of what constitutes literacy within the context of cultural and social diversity. The particular elements of imagery, arts, digital representations, video, and other technologies are spatial representations as seen through the lens of geography education.

Geography educators can improve students' spatial thinking skills by paying attention to the questions they pose in their instruction (Jo, Bednarz, & Metoyer, 2010). Strong spatial thinking questions will address spatial concepts such as those modes of thinking described by Gersmehl and Gersmehl. Learners then will show what they have learned by representing the information spatially on maps, charts, graphs, or images. Finally they will engage in higher order thinking by using their spatial knowledge to discover relationships that can be used to make decisions and solve problems. The task of the teacher is to ask questions from a spatial perspective.

ACTING GEOGRAPHICALLY TODAY

The term *geospatial* is more specific than spatial. It means that the picture or the placemark or the line can be referenced to latitude and longitude map coordinates. Geospatial technology uses tools such as Geographic Information Systems (GIS), Remote Sensing, Global Positioning Systems (GPS) in fields such as agriculture, engineering, urban planning, tourism, political analysis, and marketing to analyze and make decisions based on data. Students of all ages are finding ways to use geographic knowledge and spatial skills to make decisions and solve problems with others as is evident in the following examples.

Example A: Where can we establish bat houses?

A high school class has been using Geographic Information System (GIS) to complete spatial projects for partners in the community. Recently they completed a project identifying sites for 18 bat houses for a research team. They identified the required characteristics for bat habitats, selected the parcels through ArcGIS, and layered maps with features such as parks, water sources within .25 miles of site, residential areas, and streets. They prepared presentations of their data and negotiated with local agencies to locate 10 of the 18 houses. As a result of the quality of their work, they are currently creating more detailed maps of area schools for the fire department, identifying entry ways and actual layout of classrooms (Carpenter, 2009).

Example B: What is a Watershed?

For some learners, tools of spatial learning include the integration of physical movement to make sense of geographic concepts (Schoenfeldt, 2001). National Geographic's GIANT Traveling Maps program (Beaupre, 2009) provides continent maps for schools to use in supporting geography education. The maps are printed on treated canvas that learners can walk on. They also support the use of plastic chains, sports cones, legos, and informational cards as place markers to understand physical systems, cultural practices, or land formations. The WOW! factor of each GIANT map is its size, approximately 25 × 36 feet); one continent rolls out to cover a gym floor. Teams use the lessons and materials in the accompanying instructional trunk to gain geographic knowledge and skills identified in *Geography for Life* and their own state guidelines of essential knowledge and skills. The concept of watersheds is a new lesson with the South America map and uses bingo chips and small whisk brooms to dramatize the movement of water from the tributaries to the mouth of the Amazon River. Young learners "sweep" the water from the mountains to the ocean, observing the patterns of the tributaries that provide water for the Amazon Basin watershed. They transfer that knowledge to desktop lessons, demonstrating they have met the state and national standards for their grade level.

Example C: How will our neighborhood change in ten years?

An area of my own research provides the information for this case. In a study with elementary school students, technology provided them with high resolution aerial imagery of their school neighborhood. Beginning with the local, young children learned about distance, direction, and location. They engaged in a simplified remote sensing analysis and interpretation of the data. Young learners not only identified places in the familar area, they also recognized patterns of urban development of residential areas and business locations. They predicted changes that might occur in the next ten years on the familiar landscape and the choices that must be made to sustain the school community. The second grade students created drawings to express their ideas about the future of their community. The criteria of fairness, safety, efficiency, and even beauty were evident in aerial perspectives that included hospitals, colleges, pet parks, wind power centers, and water treatment plants (Todd & Delahunty, 2007). Knowing one's place is a first step in understanding the importance of places and sustaining communities (Agnello, Todd, Lucey, & Olaniran, 2009; Todd & Agnello, 2006).

Example D: How do GIS teams support disaster relief?

When hurricane Katrina hit the Gulf Coast in 2005, a team of GIS experts from my university set up equipment in central Mississippi to collect real time satellite data and transfer the information onto maps for rescue workers to locate stranded people. Signs were down; landmarks were destroyed; streets were flooded. How would an emergency management team locate the sites of reported life-threatening situations? Satellite imagery placed over terrain maps with geographic coordinates combined with mobile phones and GPS units guided rescue workers through the first few weeks of the disaster that continues to haunt the residents of the region. Integrating knowledge about GIS from these experts is one approach we have taken to strengthen geographic literacy among students in the teacher preparation program.

Example E: Is it safe to travel to the high school playoffs?

In spring 2009 when the state coordinators cancelled state-level competitions in Texas because of the H1N1 Flu (swine flu) outbreak, teacher Penny Carpenter used the real world event to engage her high school GIS students in tracking the rapid spread of the illness. They used ArcGIS Desktop ArcMap and public county data from the state Department of Health to map the spread of cases from the border with Mexico through Texas. They wanted to know where it was and how great the threat was in their own region. After mapping the data they found that it was spreading along the highway systems, especially I-20 that runs across central Texas and they concluded that the local threat was low. Their spatial representation of the information attracted area media who reported, "Their GIS skills created a visual element that was relevant and meaningful in West Texas" (Carpenter, 2009/2010). Students had used the data to solve problems for the whole region.

Typically, some data is available in spreadsheets or tables. GIS technology often can translate it into geospatial notation so that it can be spatially represented on map to facilitate analysis and interpretation. For example, a list of numbers of registered voters in each county in the state can target sites for political campaign ads, but it is much easier to see the regions for emphasis by *spatializing* the data and displaying them on a map.

As further evidence of the changes taking place in geography education, the examples cross boundaries that existed in the past by including a balance of female and male voices, novice and seasoned geographers, and multi-disciplinary concerns. In answer to Jan Monk's (1999) question of "Whose world is it?" we can say that women, gender, children's lives, and multicultural issues are becoming more visible.

LOOKING AHEAD

Geography educators heeded Down's (1994) call to make the case for geography in curriculum reform "forcefully, frequently, and convincingly" (p. 175). As we continue to move forward, three aspects of making the case for quality geographic education emerge.

One of these aspects is a continued effort encouraging and mentoring women in geography through scholarships. In the professional activities of National Council for Geographic Education (NCGE), women have served as both leaders and mentors guiding the organization since 1994. Women in Geography gather at annual meetings to network and to support new female geography scholars in collaborative research projects. Sessions at the conference recognize outstanding contributions from people in the field. One or two sessions are scheduled in which students and colleagues pay tribute to contributions of particular mentors. In recent years, these have included noted women geographers such as Jan Monk, Sarah Bednarz, Gwenda Rice, and Michel LeVasseur.

A second way to continue making the case for geography education is through the integration of geographic knowledge and skills with other disciplines such as Science, Technology, Engineering, and Math (STEM) initiatives and community/business partners. In 2010-2011, National Geographic and Google partnered with one another in sponsoring a Teacher Institute in Mountain View, California, the headquarters of Google. As a result, educators and programmers developed GIANT Traveling Map extension lessons using a GoogleEarth platform. Participants are confident that the integration of high interest activities with the GIANT map and new interactive technology will increase student knowledge off geographic concepts and will build skills in spatial thinking that can be applied toward solving problems within communities. Increasingly, data from multiple sources can be put on maps so people can identify areas of greatest concern as they make decisions about water resources, homelessness, school populations, or spread of disease.

Another educational partnership with Google is Jerome Burg's Google Lit Trips which are multi-dimensional literacy adventures (Burg, 2010). Burg, and others who want to contribute to the interactive project, are engaged in an experiment in teaching great literature in a very different way. Using GoogleEarth, "students discover where in the world the greatest road trip stories of all time took place, and so much more" (www.googlelittrips. com). Other examples available to students include *Grapes of Wrath*, *Make Way for Ducklings*, and *The Kite Runner.*

Publications are a third way of making the case for geography education with new formats, wider circulation, online access, and a new journal. In addition to the flagship journals, *Journal of Geography*, *Annals of the American Association of Geographers*, and *Professional Geographer*, leaders recognized a need for communication about geography with classroom teachers across the curriculum. *Geography Teacher* was added to the professional resources in 2003-2004 with the classroom teacher in mind.

Not all publications are in typical journal format. Under the visionary leadership of the geography organizations, teachers and students are learning to access spatial data through interactive websites, webinars, or classroom blogs. NCGE President, Joseph Kerski, has added podcasts to further describe his vision on the organization's website.(www.ncge.org). With open access to such a broad scope of up-to-date knowledge, learners then interpret the geographic information and apply knowledge to making decisions and solving everyday issues. Memorizing locations and places will not be enough for citizens of the 21st century. The next wave of technology and communication is quickly becoming part of the lives of a new generation. Education must include geographic knowledge as a foundation for using these tools to make decisions that sustain people and places globally.

CONCLUSION

The publication of *Geography for Life* (1994) marked a turning point in geography education as it mobilized those who believed in being heard on the issue of geography education as a core discipline in K–12 curriculum. Efforts of many did make a difference and continue to influence policy at national and international venues. Technology facilitates gathering of information and communicating with others internationally almost instantly. As geography educators, we bear the responsibility of integrating geographic knowledge with the tools that best represent data in order to make informed decisions and solve problems in the interest of our global neighbors.

Geography education is all about people and places in a global environment. As with other fields of study, the more one knows, the more one understands. Everyday actions require spatial thinking—from packing the car for a road trip to finding the way out of city hall. We make observations about sizes and shapes, landmarks, and patterns. Teaching and learning the skills for success in these tasks provide students with a foundation for developing habits of mind of spatial thinking across disciplines and the critical and creative thinking skills to represent information with the most current tools.

REFERENCES

Agnello, M., Todd, R., Lucey, T., & Olaniran, B. (2009). Afghanistan and multiculturalism in Khaled Hosseini's novels: Study of place and diversity. *Multicultural Education & Technology Journal, 3,* 3–12.

Beaupre, D. (2009). *National Geographic GIANT traveling maps program.* Interview with author, September 27, 2009, San Juan, Puerto Rico.

Bednarz, R., & Petersen, J. (1994). The reform movement in geographic education: A view from the summit. *Journal of Geography, 93*(1), 61– 64.

Bednarz, S. W. (1998a). State standards: Implementing *Geography for Life. Journal of Geography, 97*(2), 83–89.

Bednarz, S. W. (1998b). *Power of geography.* Washington, DC: Geography Education National Implementation Project.

Bednarz, S. W. (2003). Nine years on: Examining implementation of the national geography standards. *Journal of Geography, 102,* 99–109.

Burg, J. (2010). *GoogleLitTrips.* Retrieved July 14, 2010, from www.googlelittrips.com

Carpenter, P. (2009). *Bat houses.* Interview with author April 23, 2010, Lubbock, TX.

Carpenter, P. (2009/2010, Winter). *Texas students use GIS to track H1N1 flu.* Retrieved October 1, 2010, from www. esri.com/news/arcnews/winter0910articles.

Cushner, K. (2007). The role of experience in the making of internationally-minded teachers. *Teacher Education Quarterly, 34*(1), 27–39.

Downs, R. (1994). Being and becoming a geographer: An agenda for geography education. *Annals of the Association of American Geographers, 84*(2), 175–191.

Dulli, R. (1994). Improving geography learning in the schools: Efforts by the National Geographic Society, *Journal of Geography, 93*(1), 55–56.

Geography Education Standards Project (1994). *Geography for life: The national geography standards.* Washington, DC: National Geographic Society Committee on Research and Exploration.

Gersmehl, P. (2005). *Teaching geography.* New York: Guilford Press.

Gersmehl, P., & Gersmehl, C. (2007). Spatial thinking by young children: Neurologic evidence for early development and "educability." *Journal of Geography, 106,* 181–191.

Gregg, M., & Leinhardt, G. (1994). Mapping out geography: An example of epistemology and education. *Review of Educational Research, 64,* 311–361.

Grosvenor, G. M. (1989, November). The case for geography education. *Educational Leadership, 47,* 29–32.

Grosvenor, G. (1984). Society and the discipline. *Professional Geographer, 36*(4), 413–418.

Gruenewald, D., & Smith, G. (Eds.). (2008). *Place-based education in the global age.* New York: Lawrence Erlbaum.

Jo, I., Bednarz, S., & Metoyer, S. (2010). Selecting and designing questions to facilitate spatial thinking. *Geography Teacher, 7*(2), 49–55.

Kerski, J. (2010). *Why geography education matters.* Retrieved November 30, 2010, from www. ncge.org

Lanken, D. (1996, November/December). The bee in Grosvenor's bonnet. *Canadian Geographic, 116,* 95–96.

Merryfield, M., & Wilson, A. (2005). *Social studies and the world: Teaching global perspectives.* Washington, DC: National Council for the Social Studies.

Monk, J. (1999). Whose world is it? *Journal of Geography, 98*(6), 250–252.

National Commission on Excellence in Education. (1983). *A nation at risk: The imperative for educational reform.* Washington, DC: NCEE.

National Research Council (2006). *Learning to think spatially.* Washington, DC: National Academies Press.

New London Group. (2000). A pedagogy of multiliteracies: Designing social future. In B. Cope & M. Kalantzis(Eds.), *Multiliteracies: Literacy learning and the design of social future.* New York: Routledge.

Schoenfeldt, M. (2001). Geography literacy and young learners. *Educational Forum, 66*(1), 26–31.

Shelley, F. (1999). Geographic education research and the changing institutional structure of American education. *Professional Geographer, 51*(4), 592–597.

Sunal, C., Christenson, L., & Haas, M. (1995). Using five themes of geography to teach about Venezuela. *The Social Studies, 86,* 169–174.

Todd, R., & Agnello, M. F. (2006). Looking at rural communities in teacher preparation: Insight into a P–12 schoolhouse. *The Social Studies, 97*(4), 178–184.

Todd, R., & Delahunty, J. (2007). A is for aerial imagery and art. *Social Studies and the Young Learner. (20)*2, 101–14.

CHAPTER 9

STANDARDS-BASED EDUCATIONAL REFORM AND SOCIAL STUDIES EDUCATION

A Critical Introduction

Kevin D. Vinson, E Wayne Ross, and Melissa B. Wilson

Making sense of contemporary US social studies education means making sense of it within the prevailing contexts of standards-based educational reform (SBER). Although social studies is not yet as standards- and test-driven as reading, mathematics, and science, it still functions within a dominant and dominating setting characterized across the country by myriad content and curriculum standards documents and high-stakes testing on the state and local levels.

In this chapter we explore social studies education and SBER from a variety of perspectives and on a variety of levels. We begin by reviewing the nature and meaning of SBER and briefly introducing its recent history, particularly vis-à-vis national public school policy work and the work of those national commissions and "blue ribbon" panels that influenced its development and evolution (e.g., The National Commission on Excellence

Contemporary Social Studies: An Essential Reader, pages 153–172
Copyright © 2012 by Information Age Publishing

in Education's [NCEE] 1983 publication *A National at Risk: The Imperative for Educational Reform*) and legislation such as President Bush's *No Child Left Behind Act* of 2001 (NCLB) and President Obama's "Race to the Top" (RTTT). Second, we frame social studies education itself within the larger milieu of SBER, focusing primarily upon the curriculum standards work of the National Council for the Social Studies (NCSS). We consider here the creation and influence of such landmark documents as *Charting a Course, Expectations of Excellence: Curriculum Standards for Social Studies,* and *National Curriculum Standards for Social Studies.* Third, we introduce and explicate the continuing debate surrounding social studies education and SBER. We present, of course, both the pro-SBER and anti-SBER perspectives. And fourth, we situate the present status of social studies education in terms of SBER, organizing the argument according to the conceptualization established and presented by Judith Pace. We conclude by considering the "big picture" of what all of this might mean for contemporary and future social studies education.

SBER: AN OVERVIEW

As we define it, SBER involves the pre-selection, by some "official" or governing educational agency, of content or curriculum standards, the acquisition or attainment of which by students and the precise teaching of which by teachers are measured by frequent high-stakes testing (high-stakes implying some type of significant consequences based on one's success via test scores and "meeting" the preset standards). Although the historical roots of contemporary SBER are long and complex, as a movement SBER really began in the wake of a number of policy documents and commission reports published during the 1980s and 1990s, beginning with the groundbreaking (though not necessarily on-target in that it is questionable whether schools cause US economic "non-competitiveness" and in light of Japan's subsequent economic decline) National Commission on Excellence in Education's (NCEE, 1983) *A Nation at Risk: The Imperative for Educational Reform*[1] and culminating in President George W. Bush's signing of the *No Child Left Behind Act* (NCLB) of 2001. It continues today under the banner of the Obama Administration's "Race to the Top" (We should note that President Obama is currently beginning an overhaul of certain aspects of NCLB; see http://www.whitehouse.gov/the-press-office/2011/09/23/remarks-president-no-child-left-behind-flexibility).

In that an exhaustive review of all of the many relevant documents and policy statements is beyond the scope and aim of this chapter, we have chosen here to focus primarily on *A Nation at Risk,* the Goals 2000: Educate America Act (1994), and the No Child Left Behind Act (2002) itself. In this chapter's conclusion we explore how these positions and laws provide a framework for understanding President Barak Obama and Secretary of Education Arne Duncan's current RTTT scheme and how RTTT represents the continuation of policies initiated by *A Nation at Risk,* Goals 2000, and NCLB. Our emphasis throughout, however, is on what all of this means for contemporary social studies.

Our argument in part is that several themes fundamental to understanding the recent development of SBER influence and structure the implications of RTTT for American schooling generally and for social studies education in particular. These themes are (1) the perceived relationships between "strong" schools and a "strong" economy (or, conversely, between "failing" schools and a "failing" economy); (2) international competition, both economically and pedagogically (generally premised on the belief that US schools are currently failing and that this will lead to a weakened US economy); (3) an emphasis on "higher" standards and accountability—both high-stakes testing and firing teachers; and (4) the "centerization" of SBER as a movement, that is its (sometimes ostensible) status as both a "conservative" and a "progressive" goal of educational policy. These themes are represented by, for instance, such current "new reformers" as Secretary Duncan and former Washington, DC public schools chancellor Michelle A. Rhee.

As *A Nation at Risk* (NCEE, 1983) famously begins:

> Our Nation is at risk. Our once unchallenged preeminence in commerce, industry, science, and technological innovation is being overtaken by competitors throughout the world. This report is concerned with only one of the many causes and dimensions of the problem, but it is the one that undergirds American prosperity, security, and civility. We report to the American people that while we can take justifiable pride in what our schools and colleges have historically accomplished and contributed to the United States and the well-being of its people, the educational foundations of our society are presently being eroded by a rising tide of mediocrity that threatens our very future as a Nation and a people. What was unimaginable a generation ago has begun to occur—others are matching and surpassing our educational attainments. (n.p.)

As the Commission saw things, American schools were threatening both the American economy and the American character by virtue of their failing. The tone of *A Nation at Risk,* an essentially conservative report, is that the Commission's views are not partisan, but are rather "American," conducive to pursuing the goals and aspirations of all of "us," especially against international educational and economic competition. Supporting such a view, that the failures of the economy are the failures of schools and teachers, was nothing short of good citizenship. According to *A Nation at Risk:*

Another dimension of the public's support offers the prospect of constructive reform. The best term to characterize it may simply be the honorable word "patriotism." Citizens know *intuitively* [italics added] what some of the best economists have shown in their research, that education is one of the chief engines of a society's material well-being. They know, too, that education is the common bond of a pluralistic society and helps tie us to other cultures around the globe. Citizens also know *in their bones* [italics added] that the safety of the United States depends principally on the wit, skill, and spirit of a self-confident people, today and tomorrow. It is, therefore, essential—especially in a period of long-term decline in educational achievement—for government at all levels to affirm its responsibility for nurturing the Nation's intellectual capital. And perhaps most important, citizens know and believe that the meaning of America to the rest of the world must be something better than it seems to many today. Americans like to think of this Nation as the preeminent country for generating the great ideas and material benefits for all mankind. The citizen is dismayed at a steady 15-year decline in industrial productivity, as one great American industry after another falls to world competition. The citizen wants the country to act on the belief, expressed in our hearings and by the large majority in the Gallup Poll, that education should be at the top of the Nation's agenda. (NCEE, 1983, n. p.)

In short, the NCEE presented an apparent "united front" against the dangers—the risks—imposed on America and its citizens by "failing" schools, and the recommendations of the Commission reflected the "imperative" of consensus-based, competitive, economics-driven, accountability-oriented school reform, and its findings, proposals, and orientations laid the groundwork for Goals 2000, NCLB, and RTTT—arguably, the entire contemporary SBER movement. Its effects, more than 25 years later, are stronger than ever.

In short, its recommendations focused on: (1) "content," requiring a greater number of credits in the "New Basics" (English, mathematics, science, social studies, computer science, and, for the "college bound," foreign languages) in order for students to graduate; (2) "standards and expectations," suggesting "that schools, colleges, and universities adopt more rigorous and measurable standards, and higher expectations, for academic performance and student conduct, and that 4-year colleges and universities raise their requirements for admission"; (3) "time," generally a longer or more "efficient" school day and year; (4) "teaching," mandating that teachers meet "higher" and "demonstrable" standards and teacher accountability; and (5) "leadership and fiscal support" relative to promoting the success of the proposed reforms. Overall, A Nation at Risk presented failing schools as a national economic emergency, as the cause of America's failure to outcompete other countries. Its views were "common sense" and universal—even apparently because of some clearly evident to the NCEE "American" DNA (*"feel it in their bones"*), "patriotic." To disagree with the

NCEE was "un-American." Schools and teachers were to blame for the ills of the nation, and it was a national necessity to approach fixing the schools as if facing an armed enemy in combat.

To a large extent, Goals 2000: The Educate America Act (1994) was a response to *A Nation at Risk* and also to the Department of Education's (1991) *America 2000*. *America 2000*, based in part on President George H. W. Bush's 1989 "Education Summit" with governors and corporate CEOs, sought to create US educational goals consistent with and derived from the concerns raised in *A Nation at Risk*. These goals were that:

1. All children in America would start school ready to learn;
2. The high school graduation rate will increase to at least 90 percent;
3. American students will leave grades four, eight, and twelve having demonstrated competency in challenging subject matter including English, mathematics, science, history, and geography [note, not social studies but a more traditional emphasis on the "basic facts" of individual subject areas]; and every school in America will ensure that all students learn to use their minds well, so they may be prepared for responsible citizenship, further learning, and productive employment in our modern economy;
4. U.S. students will be first in the world in science and mathematics achievement;
5. Every adult American will be literate and will possess the knowledge and skills necessary to compete in a global economy and exercise the rights and responsibilities of citizenship; [and]
6. Every school in America will be free of drugs and violence and will offer a disciplined environment conducive to learning. (p. 19)

These were to be achieved via a four-part strategy and an "accountability package." The strategy suggested that

1. For today's students, we must radically improve today's schools, all 110,000 of them—make them better and more accountable for results;
2. For tomorrow's students, we must invent new schools to meet the demands of a new century—a New Generation of American schools, bringing at least 535 of them into existence by 1996 and thousands by decade's end;
3. For those of us already out of school and in the work force, we must keep learning if we are to live and work successfully in today's world. A "Nation at Risk" must become a "Nation of Students"; [and]
4. For schools to succeed, we must look beyond their classrooms to our communities and families. Schools will never be much better

than the commitment of their communities. Each of our communities must become a place where learning can happen. (p. 15)

And, the fifteen-point accountability package focused largely on testing,
"differentiating" teachers (i.e., hierarchically distinguishing the "effective"
from the "ineffective" based on formal and quantitative assessments), and
school report cards, ideas that became central to what became NCLB.

Undoubtedly accountability was the keystone of NCLB, although there
were several other significant provisions. Simply, NCLB mandated: increased
accountability; more choices for students and parents; greater flexibility for
states, school districts, and schools; putting reading first; and other major
program changes, such as the consolidation of federal education spending programs and promoting drug free schools (No Child Left Behind Act
of 2001, Executive Summary, 2002). With respect to accountability, NCLB
required annual testing in reading and math from grades 3 through 8, with
"100% proficiency" reached "within 12 years." It demanded that states develop "high academic standards" and cutoff levels of AYP—"adequate" yearly progress. Schools and districts that failed in these measures were subject
to various punishments (e.g., reductions in federal funding).

In effect, NCLB put a federal stamp of approval on what was going on
already in most states—predetermined subject-by-subject content standards
to be measured by frequent high-stakes testing. This, again, was a bipartisan
attempt to "quality assure" teaching and teachers and to link, positively,
US economic performance to US students' test scores. It was the actual-
ization of all that had gone on before regarding the SBER/accountability
movement. It was, further, the impetus for a great deal of debate among
social studies educators about the national place for, and the nature of, an
authentic and meaningful social studies, especially given that social studies
education was not mentioned in the law.

The most recent federal intervention relative to SBER is President
Obama's Race to the Top initiative (US Department of Education, 2009).
In the words of the Executive Summary, RTTT is:

historic legislation designed to stimulate the economy, support job creation,
and invest in critical sectors, including education. The ARRA [American Recovery and Reinvestment Act of 2009] lays the foundation for education reform by supporting investments in innovative strategies that are most likely
to lead to improved results for students, long-term gains in school and school
system capacity, and increased productivity and effectiveness.

The ARRA provides $4.35 billion for the Race to the Top Fund, a *competitive*
[italics added] grant program designed to encourage and reward states that
are creating the conditions for education innovation and reform; achieving
significant improvement in student outcomes, including making substantial

gains in student achievement [i.e., test scores], closing achievement gaps, improving high school graduation rates, and ensuring student preparation for success in college and careers; and implementing ambitious plans in four core education reform areas:

1. Adopting standards and assessments that prepare students to succeed in college and the workplace and to *compete in the global economy* [italics added];
2. Building data systems that measure student growth and success, and inform teachers and principals about how they can improve instruction [i.e., test score-driven accountability];
3. Recruiting, developing, rewarding, and retaining effective teachers and principals, especially where they are needed most; and
4. Turning around our lowest-achieving schools.

Race to the Top will reward States that have demonstrated success in raising student achievement and have the best plans to accelerate their reforms in the future. These States will offer models for others to follow and will spread the best reform ideas across their States, and across the country. (US Department of Education, 2009, p. 2)

RTTT clearly represents the hyper-competitiveness of today's school "reform," in reality rather a return to the past. As with previous attempts (*A Nation at Risk*, NCLB) it presents itself as the result of a certain "liberal-conservative" consensus—what is in actuality, perhaps, the heart of the "new" reform (e.g., Vinson & Ross, 2003). And, of course, it is within this ongoing set of circumstances—economic competitiveness, learning *qua* test scores—that SBER and/in social studies must be understood. It is, simply, the continuation of traditional themes—blame the schools, in a "nonpartisan way," for poor US economic and "pedagogical" performance against international competitors, and so forth.

SBER AND SOCIAL STUDIES EDUCATION

The movement toward national curriculum standards, or at least a national education policy that emphasized content and accountability standards—essentially a test-and-punish regime—clearly affected the social studies. While this is most apparent in the work of the NCSS, particularly post-*A Nation at Risk* and NCLB (neither of which pays much attention to social studies education), other national, social education-oriented subject matter organizations were also moved to create their own national curriculum documents, most notably, perhaps, documents such as the Center for Civic Education's (1994) *National Standards for Civics and Government*, the Geography Education Standards Project's (1994) *Geography for Life: National Geography Standards: What Every Young American Should Know and be Able to Do*

In Geography, and the National Council on Economic Education's (1997) *Voluntary National Content Standards in Economics.* In this chapter, however, our focus is on the development of the NCSS's (2010) recently released and revised *National Curriculum Standards for Social Studies: A Framework for Teaching, Learning, and Assessment.*

The development of national social studies standards had, of course, some history prior to the NCSS's most recent standards publication. In the "modern" era, certainly such work goes back at least as far as the publication of the widely read and debated Bradley Commission on History in the Schools' (1988) report of the late 1980s. In fact, even before *A Nation at Risk* the NCSS had published "social studies curriculum guidelines" (NCSS Task Force on Curriculum Guidelines, 1971) and "statements on the essentials of the social studies" (NCSS, 1981), among other key documents. In 1989, in two of the most direct and significant precursors to the social studies profession's foray into national standards, the NCSS released "In Search of a Scope and Sequence for Social Studies" (NCSS Task Force on Scope and Sequence, 1989) and *Charting a Course: Social Studies for the 21st Century* (National Commission on Social Studies in the Schools, 1989). This "early" interest in standards-based reform on the part of the NCSS indicated (1) the growing strength of the SBER movement; (2) the "necessity" for social studies professionals and their representative organizations to participate in it; (3) the desire on the part of the NCSS that *social studies* be considered a distinct "field"—that is, it supported "social studies" rather than history, geography, economics, and civics (etc.) standards as distinctive of separate disciplines; and (4) social studies' defensiveness with respect to the burgeoning centrality of reading, writing, and mathematics; the perception that US students were historically, culturally, and socially (etc.) "illiterate" (e.g., Ravitch & Finn, 1987); and the notoriety and controversy surrounding national standards in "constituent" disciplines such as history (over, for instance, the extent to which the proposed history standards were "patriotic enough," "multicultural enough," and so on (see, e.g., Nash, Crabtree, & Dunn, 1997; National Center for History in the Schools, 1994a, 1994b).

The NCSS (NCSS Curriculum Standards Task Force, 1994) first proposed concrete national social studies curriculum standards in *Expectations of Excellence: Curriculum Standards for Social Studies,* which was followed in 2008 by a "Draft Revision" (NCSS Curriculum Standards Task Force, 2008). Its most recent effort, *National Curriculum Standards for Social Studies: A Framework for Teaching, Learning, and Assessment* (NCSS Curriculum Standards Task Force, 2010)[2], represents the culmination of decades worth of advocacy, thought, and refinement, and demonstrates the degree to which the themes we suggested previously illuminate (or not) and can be illuminated by (or not) recent SBER efforts in social studies. Here we focus upon the NCSS's most recent iteration of curriculum standards.[3]

National Curriculum Standards for Social Studies (NCSS Curriculum Standards Task Force, 2010), like its predecessors (NCSS Curriculum Standards Task Force, 1994, 2008), emphasizes the "interdisciplinary" nature of the social studies:

> [Social studies is] the *integrated* [italics added] study of the social sciences and humanities to promote civic competence. Within the school program, social studies provides coordinated, systematic study drawing upon such disciplines as anthropology, archaeology, economics, geography, history, law, philosophy, political science, psychology, religion, and sociology, as well as appropriate content from the humanities, mathematics, and natural sciences. The primary purpose of social studies is to help young people make informed and reasoned decisions for the public good as citizens of a culturally diverse, democratic society in an interdependent world. (NCSS Curriculum Studies Task Force, 2010, n. p.)

It is a document that pursues "decision making" and "problem solving" over the mere, disconnected acquisition of skills, values, and knowledges. It intends to provide an adisciplinary or anti-disciplinary or multidisciplinary "framework" for social studies curriculum, instruction, and assessment rather then a step-by-step, grade-by-grade list of content and testing goals, a framework defined by "democracy" and the interpretation of "civic issues" rather than by "competitive economics." "The aim of social studies [here] is the promotion of [interdisciplinary and deliberative] civic competence—the knowledge, intellectual processes, and democratic dispositions required of students to be active and engaged participants in civic life" (NCSS Curriculum Studies Task Force, 2010, n. p.).

> By making civic competence a central aim, NCSS emphasizes the importance of educating students who are committed to the ideas and values of democracy. Civic competence rests on this commitment to democratic values, and requires that citizens have the ability to use their knowledge about their community, nation, and world; to apply inquiry processes; and to employ skills of data collection and analysis, collaboration, decision-making, and problem-solving. Young people who are knowledgeable, skillful, and committed to democracy are necessary to sustaining and improving our democratic way of life, and participating as members of a global community.... The curriculum standards for social studies provide a framework for professional deliberation and planning about what should occur in a social studies program in grades pre-K through 12. (n. p.)

And:

> In democratic classrooms and nations, deep understanding of civic issues—such as immigration, economic problems, and foreign policy—involves several disciplines. Social studies marshals the disciplines to this civic task in various forms. These important issues can be taught in one class, often designated

"social studies," that integrates two or more disciplines. On the other hand, issues can also be taught in separate discipline-based classes (e.g., history or geography). These standards are intended to be useful regardless of organizational or instructional approach (for example, a problem-solving approach, an approach centered on controversial issues, a discipline-based approach, or some combination of approaches). Specific decisions about curriculum organization are best made at the local level. To this end, the standards provide a framework for effective social studies within various curricular perspectives....

The NCSS curriculum standards provide a framework for professional deliberation and planning about what should occur in a social studies program in grades pre-K through 12. The framework provides ten themes that represent a way of organizing knowledge about the human experience in the world. The learning expectations, at [the] early, middle, and high school levels, describe purposes, knowledge, and intellectual processes that students should exhibit in student products (both within and beyond classrooms) as the result of the social studies curriculum. These curriculum standards represent a holistic lens through which to view disciplinary content standards and state standards, as well as other curriculum planning documents. They provide the framework needed to educate students for the challenges of citizenship in a democracy. (n. p.)

This is all to be enacted through the NCSS's "Ten Themes":

1. Culture;
2. Time, continuity, and change;
3. People, places, and environments;
4. Individual development and identity;
5. Individuals, groups, and institutions;
6. Power, authority, and governance;
7. Production, distribution, and consumption;
8. Science, technology, and society;
9. Global connections; [and]
10. Civic ideals and practices. (n. p.)

Certainly there is nothing inherently wrong with these themes. Although most are discipline-specific, a few are potentially truly interdisciplinary (e.g., "global connections," "civic ideals and practices" and consistent with the traditional ideals of social studies education proper (that is, that tradition established at least as far back as 1916). What *National Curriculum Standards* represents, however, is an effort to please everyone. It also represents quite well, although, to be fair, only indirectly, the themes we have indicated (e.g., global economic competitiveness, the "(neo)liberal-(neo)conservative" alliance, accountability, etc.). Such efforts as those of the NCSS, of course, have not been undertaken without a fair share of multifaceted and wide-ranging criticism (see, e.g., Vinson, 1999; Vinson, Gibson, & Ross, 2001; Vinson & Ross, 2001).

SBER AND THE SOCIAL STUDIES: A CRITIQUE

With respect to the social studies, SBER, including *National Curriculum Standards for Social Studies,* must be understood within the context of the long-term "struggle" over the "nature" or meaning of social education (e.g., Evans, 2004; Ross, 2006). For in laying out standards an organization like the NCSS has a particular influence not only on defining social studies, but also, given the historical status of citizenship education within the social studies curriculum, defining such things as the "good" or "effective" citizen, "good character," "American" values, the connotations of "globalization," and even US national identity itself. The potential impact, therefore, of "standardizing" social studies goes beyond its implications for purpose, content selection, teaching methodologies, and assessment (although, to be fair, the NCSS does leave the specifics on content and assessment to states and local school districts).

The struggle for the modern social studies goes back at least as far as the late 1800s, and perhaps got its biggest push by way of the 1916 Report of the Committee on Social Studies of the Commission on the Reorganization of Secondary Education of the National Education Association (1916), considered by many to be a founding document of contemporary social studies education. This report was a sort of "compromise," a synthesis of multiple subjects and multiple orientations (Evans, 2004).

This struggle, these "social studies wars" (Evans, 2004), initially involved at least five sets of "combatants," including "traditional historians," "mandarins" or "advocates of social studies as social science," "social efficiency educators," "social meliorists," "Deweyan experimentalists," "social reconstructionists," and "consensus" or "eclectic" social educators. Throughout a large part of the 20th century, these groups competed, cyclically rising and falling with the times and with no group ever attaining a permanent dominance or ever completely disappearing. Yet as Evans (2004) argues, "what began as a struggle among interest groups gradually evolved into a war against progressive social studies that has strongly influenced the current and future directions of the curriculum" (p. 1), that is a battle between "traditionalists" and "progressives." The recent work of the NCSS demonstrates its consensus approach in attempting to take seriously and ameliorate the major arguments of each of these sides. In *National Curriculum Standards for Social Studies,* each of these views is represented.

To some extent *National Curriculum Standards for Social Studies,* as was the case with the original NCSS standards document, is a "new compromise," a new 1916 Report, in that it represents an effort to satisfy both tradition-alists and progressives, focusing as it does upon a traditional disciplinary framework (e.g., the theme of "culture" is clearly anthropology-based, the theme of "time, continuity, and change" is clearly history-based, the theme of "power, authority, and governance" is clearly political science-based, the theme of "production, distribution[,] and consumption" is clearly econom-ics-based, and so on) while at the same time playing to progressive social studies professionals' emphasis on inter- or non-disciplinarity (e.g., "the *in-tegrated* [italics added] study of the social sciences and the humanities to promote civic competence"). It accepts the traditional importance of tradi-tional historical, geographical, economic, and political science knowledge while at the same time highlighting the significance of decision-making, problem-solving, social issues, "relevance," and democracy. It equalizes the importance of facts, skills, and dispositions in terms of citizenship and citi-zenship education. On the whole, then, *National Curriculum Standards for Social Studies* is "traditionally progressive," or "progressively traditional," not overwhelmingly focused on the memorization of dominant historical and cultural facts, but neither completely dedicated to a "reconstructionist" or "critical" or even Deweyan approach. It is a middle-of-the-road, mainstream document. Perhaps this is both its principle strength and its principal weak-ness.

This consensus tactic has its advantages, but also leaves the NCSS open to criticism from across the socio-politico-economic-cultural-pedagogical spectrum. For example, in our view, it is good that the NCSS does not blatantly or overtly support its standards as a tool of capitalism, of wealth-driven economic "growth" and expansion. Nor does it seem to advocate its *National Curriculum Standards for Social Studies* as a weapon in any sort of fight-to-the-victory international competition, whether political, economic, or pedagogical. It makes no appeal to "fail the students and fire the teach-ers unless they submit and conform" accountability. And, it seemingly (al-though this is somewhat unclear) cares little (at least on the surface) about either "(neo)conservative" or "(neo)liberal" politics. Its subtexts, however, are less clear.

Certainly *National Curriculum Standards for Social Studies* can be and has been attacked from the right, following, for example, the thought of Lem-ing, Ellington, and Porter-Magee (2003). As Chester E. Finn, Jr. (2003) put it in his "Forward" to their *Where Did the Social Studies Go Wrong?*

> For a very long time, the deterioration of social studies in U.S. schools re-sembled the decline of the Roman Empire: protracted, inexorable, and sad, but not something one could do much about. Evidence kept accumulating that American kids were emerging from K-12 education—and then, alas, from college—with ridiculously little knowledge or understanding of their country's history, their planet's geography, their government's functioning,

or the economy's essential workings. Evidence also accumulated that, in the field of social studies itself, the lunatics had taken over the asylum. Its leaders were people who had plenty of grand degrees and impressive titles but who possessed no respect for Western civilization; who were inclined to view America's evolution as a problem for humanity rather than mankind's last, best hope; who pooh-poohed history's chronological and factual skeleton as somehow "privileging" elites and white males over the poor and oppressed; who saw the study of geography in terms of despoiling the rain forest rather than locating London or the Mississippi River on a map; who interpreted "civics" as consisting largely of political activism and "service learning" rather than understanding how laws are made and why it is important to live in a society governed by laws; who feared that serious study of economics might give unfair advantage to capitalism (just as excessive attention to democracy might lead impressionable youngsters to judge it a superior way of organizing society); and who, in any case, took for granted that children were better off learning about their neighborhoods and "community helpers" than amazing deeds by heroes and villains in distant times and faraway places. The social studies problem seemed hopeless. And so I and many others concluded that serious education reformers were well advised to put it on a raft and push it into deep water somewhere in the despoiled rain forest or maroon it on a glacier whose melting is caused by the excessive carbon dioxide emanating from prosperous societies. Put it somewhere far away and hope it will vanish. (pp. 1–2)

As ridiculous and hyperbolic as this may sound to many people (for instance, equating the present state of social studies education with and to the decline and fall of the Roman Empire? Teachers who don't want their students to know the history of their country, world geography, or how the economy works? "Lunatics?"), it is what some conservative critics think. It is a classic "straw-man" argument, though it is a major part of the "traditionalist" pedagogical worldview, including its attack on social studies and its (the traditionalist side's) support of SBER (see also Pyne, 2000).

Of course, the left can, and has, been critical as well. Generally this criticism has drawn on the scholarship of theorists such as John Dewey (1956), Paulo Freire (1970), Alfie Kohn (1999, 2000), Linda McNeil (2000), and Susan Ohanian (1999, 2002), among many others (see also Nichols & Berliner, 2007). In sum, this progressive critical perspective has been a critique that is *philosophical* (i.e., that SBER is incompatible with "appropriate," especially progressive, educational goals); *pedagogical* (i.e., that SBER represents poor teaching, learning, and assessment; see, especially, Kohn, 1999, 2000); *personal* (i.e., that SBER—especially high-stakes testing—presents students with negative, stressful, and harmful emotional, physical, and psychological experiences; see, especially, Ohanian, 1999, 2002); and *political* (i.e., that SBER represents the imposition of dominant ideologies, is hegemonic, and is socially unjust; e.g., Vinson & Ross, 2003).

In some ways the work of the NCSS reflects the best and the worst of both worlds; it satisfies everyone and no one. The mood of the times among mainstream educational "reformers" and politicians was—and *is*—one of curriculum standards and accountability, and the NCSS wanted—or "needed"—to play a role, some/any role.

Critiques of social studies SBER are much like the earlier example of the National History Standards (1994a, 1994b), for both the National History Standards and *National Curriculum Standards for Social Studies* lend themselves to criticism from both the politico-pedagogical left and the politico-pedagogical right. In the case of the National History Standards the right complained that there was not a strong enough emphasis on "traditional history"—"American" values, the "Founding Fathers." The left complained of too little attention paid to diversity, the Civil Rights Movement, and women. To some extent, the response of Nash, Crabtree, and Dunn (1997), scholars who helped to create the National History Standards, parallels what we believe to be the position of many NCSS members, including some who are generally against standardization:

> ...the simple fact [was] that the train was leaving the station. History standards were clearly on the country's agenda.... The matter boiled down to who would write them. Those who were at first reluctant about the wisdom of this enterprise soon decided that they might compromise their own best interests if they failed to join in. If the cards were being dealt, why would historians or social studies educators not want seats around the big table? (p. 158)

For the NCSS this might translate as: "Our hands were tied and we did the best that we could do; it was either 'us' or 'them'."

In fact, in many ways, *National Curriculum Standards for Social Studies* should be comprehended within the post-*A Nation at Risk* liberal-conservative consensus that formed during the earliest stages of the national curriculum standards/SBER movement. For "liberals," national curriculum standards were seen as necessary in order to promote or to help ensure fairness and equality of opportunity (i.e., by providing for all schools the same "high quality" curriculum available to students in the "finest" schools). This is still the case to the extent that the Obama Administration, the "new reformers," and the NCSS represent some segment of *modern* American liberals. For conservatives, national curriculum standards were seen as necessary in order to promote or help to ensure the teaching and learning of "traditional" facts and the "most significant" (especially) "American" knowledge, values, and culture. As Diane Ravitch (1995)[4] summarized the pro-SBER consensus:

1. Standards can improve achievement by clearly defining what is to be taught and what kind of performance is expected;

2. Standards (national, state, and local) are necessary for equality of opportunity;
3. National standards provide a valuable coordinating function [by providing coherence with respect to the various aspects of education—i.e., purpose, content selection, teaching methods, assessment, and so forth];
4. There is no reason to have different standards in different states, especially in mathematics and science, when well-developed international standards have already been created;
5. Standards and assessments provide consumer protection by supplying accurate information to students and parents; [and]
6. Standards and assessments serve as an important signaling device to students, parents, teachers, employers, and colleges. (pp. 25–27; see also Tucker & Codding, 1998)

For both sides, the point was that, overall, American students didn't know enough, American teachers didn't teach enough, American schools were letting Americans down (especially economically), and high-stakes testing/accountability was—*is*—a necessary (if not sufficient) means by which to encourage, or perhaps even to help "guarantee," American school "improvement" (and, therefore, American economic growth).

In any event, most likely the right will continue to criticize contemporary social studies education, including *National Curriculum Standards for Social Studies*, as "anti-knowledge" (whatever that means), "anti-American" (whatever that means), and "pro-lunacy" (whatever that means; see Finn, 2003). The left (ourselves included), as we have summarized it in our previous work (e.g., Ross, 1999, 2000; Vinson, 1999; Vinson & Ross, 2001, 2003; Vinson, Ross, & Welsh, 2010), will continue to argue that any effort to standardize the social studies is by definition a mechanism of "disciplinarity and deterrence," "anti-democratic," "oppressive," "inauthentic," and "anti-the collective good" (Vinson & Ross, 2003), as well as a tool of pro-capital, neo-liberal-neoconservative economics and cultural politics (e.g., Ross & Gibson, 2007). Nevertheless, at least for the foreseeable future, SBER presents the context within which social studies education—curriculum and instruction, teaching and learning, policy, teacher preparation, assessment, textbooks, and so on—*must* be both understood and critically (re)interpreted.

CONCLUSIONS: WHERE NOW?

The issues facing contemporary social studies are always complex, but perhaps never more so than in today's politico-pedagogical climate of SBER/ RTTT. On one hand, high-stakes testing and accountability schemes have narrowed schooling toward a focus upon reading and mathematics test preparation, effectively, in many places, squeezing social studies out of the (especially primary/elementary) curriculum. This, to a large extent, is simply a continuation of the "social studies on the back burner" phenomenon that Neil Houser (1995) so importantly and eloquently identified. On the other hand, many commentators argue for the inclusion of social studies in state testing programs in order that it may keep its place as a major, or "core," area of study. So, in the end, documents such as *National Curriculum Standards for Social Studies* function within a contested and dynamic space. We suppose this is par for the course when it comes to social studies. The dilemma? Whether to support testing, accountability, and standardization and be in, or whether to oppose testing, accountability, and standardization and be out. It is a "to be or not to be" problematic.

While the NCSS does not, per se, encourage high-stakes testing, many individual states have created NCSS-inspired content standards of their own and have mandated social studies testing programs. The question, in a sense, is how to "save" the social studies while resisting its standardization into a meaningless and uncritical "democratic" citizenship education (see Pace, 2007).

There are options. First, we could give in. As a field we could say national curriculum standards, accountability, high-stakes testing, and an NCLB/ RTTT mentality are inevitable and there is no reason, therefore, to try and fight. Second, we could say fine—if it's social studies under this kind of a system or no social studies at all, then we choose no social studies at all. Or, third, we could try—knowing the risks and realizing the inherent idealism here—a more authentic and significant effort of resistance; we could continue to work for the inclusion, or even the *centrality*, of powerful (e.g., National Council for the Social Studies Task Force on Standards for Teaching and Learning in the Social Studies, 2008), high quality social studies programs in all schools and for all students while simultaneously working against the dominant/dominating, conformative, and power-laden forces of current high-stakes testing and accountability regimes. The choice is ours, and the stakes are high indeed. We must (re)consider what our purpose is as (social) educators: what, how, and why we select the content we include; how to best teach social studies; and how best to assess students' social studies understandings. We must ask: what is our role (normatively and descriptively) with respect to the economy, international competition, conservative approaches masquerading as "new reform," and status quo politics? We leave the final say to our colleague Judith Pace (2007):

> Why must we save social studies education for all students? A voluminous literature, written by scholars, curriculum makers, and practitioners alike, speaks convincingly to that question. I will only add—at the risk of repeating bad news—that, internationally, public opinion of the United States, both its gov-

ernment and its people, worsens every day. The domestic and international issues facing us are so complex and pressing that, to preserve democracy as we know it, citizens must have some depth of historical, political, and cultural understanding. Making good decisions requires that. It's one thing to have a nation of diverse opinions, which is crucial for democracy, but opinion before knowledge, or without tolerance, leads to demise. We've seen more than enough evidence of that in recent years.

I [Pace] am not ready to support testing in social studies in elementary schools; we need less standardized testing, not more. (Social studies is "high stakes" in states such as Virginia, and there the press for "cultural literacy" has turned elementary school teaching into a coverage craze.) We need fewer mandates that dictate classroom schedules and scripted curricula. Policymakers must understand that subjects like social studies actually develop reading and writing skills in meaningful and enriching curricular contexts.... When teachers have resources, such as time for planning and good professional development, many become passionate and knowledgeable about teaching social studies, which goes a long way toward engaging students in powerful learning. (n. p.)

And, who among us who really thinks seriously about education and today's increasingly complex and varied social world could think differently? That is, who could reasonably disagree?

NOTES

1. Throughout this chapter our references to *A Nation at Risk* are to an on-line version that is not paginated. We, therefore, use "n.p."—no page—in our in-text citations.
2. We use here what is available from the NCSS website, www.ncss.org, in our citations and references to *National Curriculum Standards for Social Studies*. We cite quotations as n.p. (see footnote [1]).
3. The entirety of the debate over contemporary social studies, including over its content and curriculum, can—or even should—be considered within the long-term debate among advocates of various approaches to social education, the "progressive vs. traditionalist" social studies "wars," and the historical fight over the very purpose and meaning of social studies as a discipline/field (see, e.g., Evans, 2004; Ross, 2006).
4. We note that recently Diane Ravitch has changed her position on some of these kinds of issues. See, for example, Ravitch (2010).

REFERENCES

Bradley Commission on History in Schools (1988). *Building a history curriculum: Guidelines for teaching history in schools.* Washington, DC: Educational Excellence Network.

Center for Civic Education. (1994). *National standards for civics and government.* Calabasas, CA: Author.

Committee on Social Studies of the Commission on the Reorganization of Secondary Education of the National Education Association. (1916). *The social studies in secondary education.* Washington, DC: USGPO.

Department of Education. (1991). *America 2000: An education strategy sourcebook.* Washington, DC: USGPO.

Dewey, J. (1956). *The child and the curriculum/The school and society.* Chicago and London: University of Chicago Press. (Original works published 1902 and 1899)

Evans, R. W. (2004). *The social studies wars: What should we teach the children?* New York: Teachers College Press.

Finn, C. E., Jr. (2003). Forward. In J. Leming, L. Ellington, & K. Porter-Magee (Eds.), *Where did social studies go wrong?* (pp. 1–8). Washington, DC: Thomas B. Fordham Foundation.

Freire, P. (1970). *Pedagogy of the oppressed.* New York: Continuum.

Geography Education Standards Project. (1994). *Geography for life: National geography standards: What every young American should know and be able to do in geography.* Washington, DC: National Geographic Research and Exploration.

Goals 2000: Educate America Act of 1994, Pub. L. No. 103–227, 108 Stat. 124 (1994).

Houser, N. O. (1995). Social studies on the back burner: Views from the field. *Theory and Research in Social Education, 23,* 147–168.

Kohn, A. (1999). *The schools our children deserve: Moving beyond traditional classrooms and "tougher standards."* Boston: Houghton Mifflin.

Kohn, A. (2000). *The case against standardized testing: Raising the scores, ruining the schools.* New York: Heinemann.

Leming, J., Ellington, L., & Porter-Magee, K. (2003). *Where did social studies go wrong?* Washington, DC: Thomas B. Fordham Foundation.

McNeil, L. (2000). *Contradictions of school reform: Educational costs of standardized testing.* New York: Routledge.

Nash, G. B., Crabtree, C., & Dunn, R. E. (1997). *History on trial: Culture wars and the teaching of the past.* New York: Knopf.

National Center for History in the Schools. (1994a). *National standards for United States history.* Los Angeles: Author.

National Center for History in the Schools. (1994b). *National standards for world history.* Los Angeles: Author.

National Commission on Excellence in Education. (1983). *A nation at risk: The imperative for educational reform.* Washington, DC: USGPO.

National Commission on Social Studies in the Schools. (1989). *Charting a course: Social studies for the 21ˢᵗ century.* Washington, DC: A Joint Project of the American Historical Association, Carnegie Foundation, National Council for the Social Studies, and Organization of American Historians.

National Council for the Social Studies Curriculum Standards Task Force. (1994). *Expectations of excellence: Curriculum standards for social studies* (Bulletin 89). Washington, DC: National Council for the Social Studies. (Available on-line: http://www.socialstudies.org/standards/curriculum)

National Council for the Social Studies Curriculum Standards Task Force. (2008). *Expectations of excellence: Curriculum standards for social studies* (Draft Revision). Retrieved from http://www.socialstudies.org/system/files/Standards-Draft10_08.pdf

National Council for the Social Studies Curriculum Standards Task Force. (2010). *National curriculum standards for social studies: A framework for teaching, learning, and assessment.* Silver Spring, MD: National Council for the Social Studies. Retrieved from http://www.socialstudies.org/standards

National Council for the Social Studies. (1981). Statement on the essentials of the social studies. *Social Education, 45,* 162–164.

National Council for the Social Studies Task Force on Scope and Sequence. (1989). In search of a scope and sequence for social studies. *Social Education, 53,* 376–387.

National Council for the Social Studies Task Force on Standards for Teaching and Learning in the Social Studies (2008, May). *A vision of powerful teaching and learning in the social studies: Building social understanding and civic efficacy* (Position Statement). Retrieved from http://www.socialstudies.org/positions/powerful

National Council on Economic Education. (1997). *Voluntary national content standards in economics.* New York: Author.

Nichols, S. L., & Berliner, D. C. (2007). *Collateral damage: How high-stakes testing corrupts America's schools.* Cambridge, MA: Harvard University Press.

No Child Left Behind Act of 2001, Pub. L. No. 107-110, 115 Stat. 1475 (2002). Retrieved from http://www2.ed.gov/policy/elsec/leg/esea02/index.html

[The] No Child Left Behind Act of 2001 [Executive Summary]. (2002, January). Retrieved from http://www2.ed.gov/nclb/overview/intro/execsumm.pdf

Obama, B. H. (2011,23 September). *Remarks by the president on No Child Left Behind flexibility.* Retrieved from the World Wide Web http://www.whitehouse.gov/the-press-office/2011/09/23/remarks-president-no-child-left-behind-flexibility.

Ohanian, S. (1999). *One size fits few: The folly of educational standards.* New York: Heinemann.

Ohanian, S. (2002). *What happened to recess and why are our children struggling in kindergarten?* New York: McGraw-Hill.

Pace, J. L. (2007, December 19). Why we need to save (and strengthen) social studies. *Education Week,* 26–27. Retrieved from http://www.educationweek.org

Pyne, J. (2000, May). The struggle for history at the precollegiate level. *Perspectives Online, 38*(5). Retrieved from http://www.historians.org/perspectives/issues/2000/0005/0005spl4.cfm

Ravitch, D. (1995). *National standards in American education: A citizen's guide.* Washington, DC: Brookings Institution Press.

Ravitch, D. (2010). *The death and life of the great American school system: How testing and choice are undermining education.* New York: Basic Books.

Ravitch, D., & Finn, C. (1987). *What do our 17-year-olds know? A report on the first national assessment of history and literature.* New York: Harper & Row.

Ross, E. W. (1999). Resisting test mania. *Theory and Research in Social Education, 27,* 126–128.

Ross, E. W. (2000). Diverting democracy: The curriculum standards movement and social studies education. In D. W. Hursh & E. W. Ross (Eds.), *Democratic social education: Social studies for social change* (pp. 203–228). New York: Falmer. (Originally published in the International Journal of Social Education, 1996)

Ross, E. W. (Ed.). (2006). *The social studies curriculum: Purposes, problems, and possibilities.* Albany: SUNY Press.

Ross, E. W., & Gibson, R. (Eds.). (2007). *Neoliberalism and education reform.* Cresskill, NJ: Hampton Press.

Tucker, M. S., & Codding, J. B. (1998). *Standards for our schools: How to set them, measure them, and reach them.* San Francisco: Jossey-Bass.

US Department of Education. (2009). *Race to the top program: Executive summary.* Washington, DC: USGPO. Retrieved from http://www2.ed.gov/programs/racetothetop/executive-summary.pdf

Vinson, K. D. (1999). National curriculum standards and social studies education: Dewey, Freire, Foucault, and the construction of a radical critique. *Theory and Research in Social Education, 27,* 50–82.

Vinson, K. D., Gibson, R., & Ross, E. W. (2001). *High-stakes testing and standardization: The threat to authenticity.* Burlington, VT: John Dewey Project on Progressive Education/University of Vermont. Retrieved from http://www.uvm.edu/%7edewey/monographs/ProPer3n2.html

Vinson, K. D., & Ross, E. W. (2001). Social education and standards-based reform: A critique. In J. L. Kincheloe, S. Steinberg, & D. Weil (Eds.), *Schooling and standards in the United States: An encyclopedia* (pp. 909–927). New York: ABC/Clio.

Vinson, K. D., & Ross, E. W. (2003). *Image and education: Teaching in the face of the new disciplinarity.* New York: Peter Lang.

Vinson, K. D., Ross, E. W., & Welsh, J. F. (2010). Controlling images: Surveillance, spectacle, and high-stakes testing as social control. In K. K. Saltman & D. A. Gabbard (Eds.) *Education as enforcement: The militarization and corporatization of schools* (2nd ed;pp. 273–290). New York: Routledge.

CHAPTER 10

THE MARGINALIZATION OF SOCIAL STUDIES IN THE ELEMENTARY GRADES

An Overview

Beverly Milner (Lee) Bisland

The marginalization of social studies instruction in the elementary grades is a topic of intense interest to social studies educators and researchers in the United States (Bolick, et al., 2010; Boyle-Baise et al, 2008; Doppen, Misco & Patterson, 2008; Rock et al, 2006; VanFossen, 2005). In elementary schools at the beginning of the twenty-first century social studies instructional time is typically reduced in favor of language arts and math. This phenomenon is not new and has existed for decades (Houser,1995; Shaver, Davis & Helburn,1980). Recent studies indicate, however, that the reduction in social studies instruction has intensified with legislation designed to hold educators accountable for improving student learning beginning with the federal No Child Left Behind Act in 2001 (Crocco & Costigan, 2007; Fitchett & Heafner, 2010; Wills, 2007). The No Child Left Behind Act does not men-

Contemporary Social Studies: An Essential Reader, pages 173–191

tion social studies. The legislation focuses on accountability and achievement in math, reading, writing and science (Rock et al., 2006).

Typically the method for assessing student improvement is state tests. All states test language arts and math in the elementary grades, but only twelve states test for social studies learning (Quality Counts at Ten, 2006; US Dept. of Ed, 2010). Although that number is decreasing as some states, such as New York, have chosen not to test at the elementary level for budgetary reason. The test is considered too expensive to administer, although New York State will continue to administer elementary school tests in science, as well as language arts and math (APDA, NYSEd, 2010).

Recent studies of social studies teaching in elementary schools are primarily in states that do not test (Boyle-Baise et al, 2008; Doppen, Misco & Patterson, 2008: Rock et al, 2006; VanFossen, 2005). Findings show that social studies instruction has all but disappeared in the primary grades and is textbook driven in grades four to six. Because social studies instruction based on critical thinking and thoughtful analysis takes time, the curriculum is disappearing in favor of math, language arts and more recently science instruction which are tested and therefore considered a more valid use of classroom time (Crocco & Costigan, 2007; Sunal & Sunal, 2007/2008). A limited number of studies do exist of states in which elementary social studies is tested. In South Carolina, a state that tests social studies in the upper elementary grades, grades three to eight give more instructional time to social studies. Teachers reported that they needed to give more instructional time to the subject because it is tested (Heafner, Libscomb & Rock, 2006; Vogler et al., 2007). In contrast a recent comparison of North Carolina, a state that does not test and Virginia, a state that does test, shows that the amount of time spent on social studies instruction in the two states was not substantially different (Bolick et al., 2010).

Typically the most crucial concern among teachers is time. The focus of this concern is a limited amount of time to teach all subjects well. In an elementary classroom the teacher needs to teach in four major subject areas; language arts, math, science and social studies. Other concerns include administrative priorities, which often emphasize teaching subjects that are tested and the need to integrate subjects in a self-contained elementary classroom where all subjects are taught by one teacher. This practice can result in a subject, such as social studies, being subsumed into another subject, such as language arts. Additionally, the idea that a teacher will give more instructional time to a subject that is tested is critical.

PURPOSE

The purpose of this chapter is first to compare concerns about the teaching of social studies in the elementary grades across the spectrum of recent studies done at individual state and national levels since the onset of No

Child Left Behind. After looking for common themes about teaching social studies in these recent studies, I secondly compare the themes with concerns expressed in previous studies of elementary social studies from the mid- twentieth century, specifically chapters in the 1957 National Society for the Study of Education's yearbook on elementary social studies. NSSE has published yearbooks across a century in the field of education. The only yearbook dedicated to elementary social studies was published in 1957.

My purpose in this comparison is to determine if the same concerns resonate across the decades. It is clear that concerns about marginalization existed from the 1970s until the present (Hahn, 1970; Houser, 1995; Shaver, Davis & Helburn,1980), but I have chosen to investigate concerns about social studies teaching at an even earlier period, as well.

In order to compare recent work, I have chosen a group of studies that focus on teachers and administrators attitudes towards social studies instruction in the elementary grades. Some recent studies are comprehensive across grade levels and include middle school and high school, as well as elementary school (Doppen, Misco & Patterson, 2008), or focus exclusively on the secondary grades (Gerwin, 2004; Grant, 2007). My emphasis in this chapter is on studies that center on the elementary grades exclusively and whose methodology, either through quantitative questionnaires and data sources or through qualitative interviews and observations, try to determine elementary teachers' perceptions and understandings of social studies teaching, as well as, try to determine whether they have the time and opportunity to implement an inquiry based approach to social studies teaching.

Many excellent studies on the marginalization, or narrowing of the curriculum, as marginalization is sometimes called, exist. My selections are not meant to be comprehensive or a reflection on the quality of the studies selected or excluded, but an attempt to compare a representative sample of studies that ask the same types of questions. Some studies are from states where social studies is not tested in the elementary grades, such as California, Indiana, Alabama and North Carolina. Some are from states that do test in the elementary grades, such as South Carolina and Virginia (See Appendix I).

Only one study uses a large participant sample of teachers, 33,390 (Fitchett & Heafner, 2010). Three of the studies use participant samples in the hundreds; 590 (VanFossen, 2005), 320 (Rock et al, 2006) and 235 (Vogler et al.,2007). The remaining participant samples are between one hundred and three teachers. Two of the studies are national samples (Fitchett & Heafner, 2010; Russell, 2009). The other studies are either state wide or of a specific area in a particular state. Two studies are conducted in states that test social studies in elementary school, Virginia (McEachron, 2010) and South Carolina (Vogler et al, 2007).

Some recent studies have considered underlying causes for the marginalization of social studies besides testing under No Child Left Behind. Examples are the nature of teacher preparation at the university level, who actually teaches social studies methods and how it is taught (Bolick et al., 2010), the differences between social studies teaching in less advantaged schools as compared to more advantaged schools (Pace, 2008) and the nature of social studies teaching at the elementary level. This latter concern addresses the issue of social studies instruction under the guise of language arts instruction (Boyle-Baise et al, 2008; Fry, 2009; Hinde, 2009; Sunal & Sunal, 2007/2008). I will consider these issues in the discussion at the end of the chapter following the comparison of recent studies from across the country and studies from the 1950s.

CONCEPTUAL FRAMEWORK

My conceptual framework for this study includes two stances: first, social studies is critical to the education of informed citizens and should be used as the unifying whole for the elementary school curriculum (NCSS, 2010; Parker, 1996) and second, elementary school teachers would be more likely to teach social studies with an inquiry based approach, if this approach is modeled for them within their teacher preparation programs. Additionally the use of inquiry is more likely if they are allowed to use this methodology to teach within the time allocations of the elementary school day and administrative dictates of time usage in their individual schools and districts (Boyle-Baise etal, 2008; Levstik & Barton, 2001; Sunal & Sunal, 2007/2008).

Research Questions

The following questions guide this overview:

- How much instructional time is given to social studies during a typical elementary school day? Does the amount of instructional time differ between primary (K–2) and intermediate (3–5) grades?
- How is social studies regarded, prioritized and supported in comparison to the other main subject areas of language arts, math and science
- How is social studies taught?
- How was social studies in the elementary school regarded a half a century ago? How is the attitude towards social studies different from today's attitudes?

DISCUSSION

How much instructional time is allocated to social studies in the elementary classroom and what are the differences between grade levels?

To the question of how much instructional time is allocated to social studies in the typical elementary school day, the answer is very little. All of the studies that I selected either investigated this question or considered it in their discussions. All concluded that social studies is taught far less than either language arts or math.

The National Council for the Social Studies recommends that an hour a day be spent on social studies instruction which equals five hours a week or twenty percent of instructional time (NCSS,1994). None of the studies I considered showed that social studies was being taught to this extent, except when social studies was taught in a full integration with other subjects (Pace, 2008) or in the South Carolina example (Vogler et al, 2007) when social studies was taught over forty-five minutes a day in some classrooms. Uniformly the studies demonstrated that social studies in the primary grades is taught only occasionally, if at all, and although it is taught in the intermediate grades it does not meet the NCSS standards for amount of time and does not meet most state standards for time and content. In a non-departmentalized social studies setting, the studies considered in this chapter report that social studies is taught, at most, two hours per week.

The two quantitative studies that I chose only investigated time allocations. Each study spans several decades. The one national study (Fitchett & Heafner, 2010) intended to discover if the 2001 accountability legislation under No Child Left Behind impacted the time devoted to social studies. The study specific to Virginia, a state that tests social studies in the elementary grades, (McEachron,2010) intended to see, as well, if change had occurred across decades in the time allocated to social studies during the school day.

The national study used data collected by the National Center for Educational Statistics from 33,390 teachers across a span of seventeen years (Fitchett & Heafner, 2010). It found a significant decrease in instructional time in favor of math and language arts instruction after the onset of the No Child Left Behind legislation enacted in 2001. The study found, however, that slightly more instructional time was given to social studies than science, another subject where instructional time has diminished, but is included in the accountability mandates of the No Child Left Behind legislation. Fitchett and Heafner looked at the differences between the primary (K–2) and intermediate grades (3–5). Similar to most of the studies that I used, they found that more time was spent on social studies in the intermediate than the primary grades. They did not, however, specifically look at the time allocation differences between states that have a test in social studies at the elementary level and those that do not. Additionally they found that the amount of time allocated to social studies was diminishing prior to 2001 and the passage of the No Child Left Behind legislation did not begin the demise, but served to continue and hasten it.

The Virginia study of time allocation (McEachron, 2010) is a study in a state where social studies is tested at grades three, five and eight. McEachron points out, however, that the state of Virginia is considering doing away with the test at grade 3 on the basis that a third grader is too young to understand social studies concepts. In this study, administrative time schedules for academic and non-academic activities were quantified across twenty-two years. As in other studies the allocation of time was lowest for social studies and science among academic subjects. The allocations were highest for math and language arts. A slight (3 percent) increase occurred in time allocated in the primary grades after 1994. At that time, Virginia mandated testing of social studies at grade three. The amount of time did not nearly equal the time spent on language arts and math, however. An interesting finding in this study, other than the fact that testing social studies does not make a significant amount of difference in time devoted to teaching the subject, is the time allotted to non-core areas (physical education, health, art, music, library, media, technology, guidance, intervention activities) and non-academic areas (lunch, recess, opening, snack, restroom, clean up, dismissal) in the school day. These two areas exceeded social studies in time allocation. As the author rightly points out, reliance on written administrative schedules is not a true indication of classroom teaching. The information gleaned from these schedules can be enriched and deepened through teacher interviews and classroom observations.

Some of the other studies I considered show that teachers are integrating social studies into other core areas such as language arts and therefore borrowing social studies time from the time allocated to these other subject areas (Boyle-Baise etal, 2008; Fry, 2009; Holloway & Chiodo, 2009; Hutton & Burstein, 2008; Sunal & Sunal, 2007/2008). However, the key concern about this practice is how effectively social studies content, concepts and skills are being taught under the guise of another discipline. If it is taught as a by product of language arts, the social studies instruction is often haphazard and unsystematic as Boyle-Baise et al. (2008), Sunal and Sunal (2007/2008), and Brophy and Alleman (2002) suggest.

More often than not, social studies is ignored in the primary grades and the instruction that occurs in the intermediate grades is textbook driven. Findings in these studies show that social studies is taught from one to three hours a week in the intermediate grades, often alternating with science. Fry (2009) discusses the negotiations necessary with cooperating teachers in order to gain permission for student teachers to teach a fully integrated unit based on a social studies topic daily for two weeks. Initially the teachers told the pre-service teachers that they did not teach social studies and that teaching the integrated unit would not be possible within their time allocations for different subjects.

A difference from the overall finding on the primary grades was in North Carolina, where social studies was taught daily in kindergarten (Rock et al, 2006). The authors attributed this fact to the state curriculum for social studies in kindergarten which concentrates on citizenship, self-awareness and social skills. Social studies was not taught so frequently in the other primary grades that have end of year tests in other subjects. In North Carolina it was also found that social studies was taught daily in the fifth grade, but the authors speculated that this finding may be attributable to the fact that fifth grade often follows a rotating schedule where teachers specialize in subjects such as science or social studies.

The only study to show an increase in instructional time in social studies was South Carolina. This increase was attributed to end of year testing in social studies from grade three to grade eight. But instructional time was still low in the primary grades (K–2) where social studies is not tested. Some primary grades had no daily instruction whereas others had from fifteen to thirty minutes. Even though the time for social studies instruction increased, language arts and mathematics were still given priority in instructional time.

How is social studies regarded, prioritized and supported in comparison to the other main subject areas of language arts, math, and science?

The emphasis in all of the studies is on the teaching of language arts and mathematics. Student achievement is tested universally in these subject areas. In elementary classrooms across the country, as shown in these studies, instruction in these two subjects occurs in the mornings when young students are freshest and best able to concentrate. Both social studies and science, if taught at all, are taught in the afternoon when young students' attention is less focused.

Teachers in the study were not necessarily satisfied with the limited instructional time given to social studies, but felt that they are held accountable for students test scores and must concentrate on the subjects that are tested. VanFossen (2005) found that teachers perceived a lack of administrative support for implementing the social studies curriculum outlined in the Indiana state social studies standards. Also these Indiana teachers thought that the lack of state wide testing in social studies led to a lack of social studies instructional time. Rock et al. (2006) also speculated that testing would make a difference in instructional time and prioritize social studies more than it is prioritized now. However, Vogler et al. (2007) found that even though social studies is tested in grades three to eight and more time is spent on social studies instruction compared to time spent five years ago, language arts and mathematics, which are also tested, still hold higher priority than social studies or science.

Not only teachers but the schools themselves are held accountable for student achievement under an evaluation of the school's annual yearly progress. Therefore principals, who are judged on the achievement of the school's entire student body, devalue social studies, particularly in states where it is not tested (Boyle-Baise et al,. 2008; Hutton & Burstein, 2008; VanFossen, 2005; Wills, 2007). Many of the studies I chose focused on disadvantaged schools with low performance standards, where the emphasis was on increasing test scores in order to bring up the school's annual yearly progress score. The only contrast to this general finding was by Pace (2008) who contrasted teachers in schools in disadvantaged areas to teachers in schools in more advantaged suburban areas. She found the suburban teachers little affected by No Child Left Behind legislation and annual yearly progress reports. They had the autonomy and resources to teach as much social studies as they wished, often using it as the integrating core of their instruction.

How is social studies taught?

Optimally social studies should be taught through a child focused inquiry methodology in which the child brings prior knowledge to the inquiry and constructs new knowledge through an exploration of content that melds with their prior knowledge (Dewey, 1899/1969; Levstik & Barton, 2001; VanSledright, 2002; Wineburg, 1996) . Regardless of time constraints attributed to No Child Left Behind legislation and a lack of emphasis on social studies instruction, many elementary teachers do not feel comfortable teaching social studies with its emphasis on history. They often feel that they lack the background and content knowledge to teach the subject areas of social studies that include history, geography, economics and civic participation, among others (Wineburg, 1996).

These feelings of a lack of content knowledge were encountered by the researchers in the studies that I selected. All of the participants in Russell's (2009) study said that they lacked content knowledge in the basic social studies subjects of history, government, economics etc. and that they lacked knowledge of social studies methodology. For these teachers these shortcomings were a reason, as well as time constraints, for not teaching social studies. VanFossen (2005) found that elementary teachers in Indiana do not have a clear idea of what social studies is and, in contrast, what it is not. The National Council for the Social Studies has broadly defined social studies education as citizenship education. As VanFossen (2005) points out "it seems safe to conclude that one cannot teach a thing if one cannot define it" (p. 399). Therefore, elementary teachers may feel strongly that they are teaching social studies, often under the guise of language arts, when in fact they are not.

In agreement with VanFossen (2005), both Sunal and Sunal (2007/2008) and Boyle-Baise et al. (2008) found that social studies in the primary grades was seldom taught as stand-alone lessons, but typically subsumed in reading instruction and used as a short addendum to the reading story. Boyle-Baise et al. (2008) describe social studies at the primary level in Indiana as being without a systematic delivery of social studies content and concepts and simply added to reading instruction in an opportunistic manner based on happenstance. In Alabama, Sunal and Sunal (2007/2008) also found social studies in the primary grades incorporated within reading instruction and resulting in a disarticulated curriculum that does not meet either national or state social studies standards.

Many of the studies I chose (Boyle-Baise et al, 2008; Sunal & Sunal, 2007/2008; Wills, 2007) found that social studies was taught in the intermediate grades (3–6) but that instruction was typically textbook driven and consisted of the teacher "telling." Wills' (2007) and Pace's (2008) observations of fourth and fifth grade teachers in California showed how time constraints have impacted the nature of instruction in the intermediate grades. The teachers in Wills' study taught in an economically disadvantaged area with high racial and ethnic minorities and a high English language learner population. The teachers he observed over a ten month period were adept at presenting insightful inquiry based instruction to their students, but under the pressure of testing in language arts and math as the year progressed, reduced the time spent on social studies and reverted to simple reproduction of content knowledge, reduced the scope of the social studies curriculum and curtailed or eliminated opportunities to promote students' higher order thinking through inquiry. Pace (2008) found that the teachers in schools in the less advantaged areas had the same types of pressures as those teachers in Will's study. In contrast, the teachers in the more advantaged area that she studied used social studies as the "umbrella" for the curriculum and taught integrated units on immigration with an Ellis Island simulation, an oral history project with older relatives, historical fiction writing and a biography project based on famous people. As Pace notes, these teachers had a large amount of autonomy in curricular decision making plus a large amount of support in the form of staffed computer labs with internet access, two textbook sets for the whole class, multiple sets of trade books, and classroom aides for every teacher.

As these studies demonstrate, teaching social studies with an inquiry methodology that promotes questioning, higher order thinking and discovery takes time. For schools, particularly those in disadvantaged areas who are under the mandate to improve test scores in reading and mathematics under No Child Left Behind, one element they do not have is an excessive amount of instructional time.

Elementary School Social Studies in the 1950s

The 1950s are halfway between the inception of social studies in the 1930s as a curriculum that integrates the social sciences in an age appropriate manner for students and the beginnings of reports on the marginalization of social studies in the 1970s and 1980s. The National Society for the Study of Education published its only yearbook dedicated exclusively to elementary social studies in 1957. The purpose of the volume, as the editor Nelson B. Henry points out, is to "define the role of this field of study in terms of its peculiar relationship to the overall program of elementary education . . ."(p. viii) In his introduction, Ralph C. Preston foreshadows Van-Fossen's findings almost a half century later. He believes that social studies is central to the education of children but it does not hold this central position in the minds of the public or of many elementary school teachers and administrators. According to Preston many view the field of social studies as "containing elusive objectives, vague concepts and controversy concerning ends, mean and emphasis" (p. 2). A concern in the primary grades was that social studies was being replaced by the concept of "social living," so that children's development of amiable relationships fulfilled the goals of social studies. This concern is echoed in recent studies showing time devoted to social studies in kindergarten, but not as a clearly articulated curriculum based on content and concepts. Just as today, Preston calls for social studies to be used for modes of thinking, usually called higher order or critical thinking now, rather than teaching the child to remember information. He criticizes testing as being a simple measurement of how much information a child knows, which echoes today in criticism of the standardized testing program instituted under No Child Left Behind legislation.

Most telling of all is the attitude of social studies scholars fifty years ago towards the fusion, as it was called, of social studies with other subjects, such as language arts. Helen Heffernan sees social studies as the unifying whole, as she says "the warp and woof of living" (p. 122). She sees language arts as a tool for learning the content and concepts of the social studies through "observing, listening, discussing, reading and collecting, organizing, and evaluating information" (p. 122). In present practice the roles have been reversed with social studies as a byproduct of language arts and reading instruction (Boyle-Baise, 2008; Sunal & Sunal, 2007/2008).

CONCLUSIONS

It is clear that instructional time for social studies in the elementary school has continued to diminish under the constraints imposed by the No Child

Left Behind legislation of 2001. It is also clear that this reduction did not begin with No Child Left Behind but has been accelerated by it. Even though states where social studies is tested in the elementary grades report more time spent on social studies instruction in the grades that have tests, the priority for instructional time is still on language arts and math. This subject priority supports the adage that what is tested is taught and subjects considered more important are taught more.

Some of the studies indicate a continued reluctance on the part of elementary teachers to teach social studies because of perceived content and methodology inadequacies. Bolick et al (2010) point out the shortcomings of social studies methods courses at the college level where pre-service teachers do not see best practice in inquiry and constructivist methods modeled for them. Because social studies methods courses on the elementary level are not always taught by social studies specialists, often pre-service teachers see social studies modeled as an appendage to language arts. Additionally if social studies is not being taught in the elementary schools, pre-service teachers have little or no opportunity to observe modeling of best practice in an actual classroom setting.

Lost in recent years is the concept of social studies as the unifying whole, which has been articulated in the past. The concept of integration of social studies with language arts and also science has its proponents with the understanding that social studies content, concepts and skills must be taught. Hinde (2009) uses the example of a child's fiction book on penguins where the teacher asks the students to find Antarctica, where penguins live, on a map; showed them pictures of penguins and asked them to color and label a picture of a penguin. Students were not asked to integrate social studies knowledge with scientific knowledge or through investigation to give meaning or depth to their thinking about Antarctica as a penguin habitat and the penguins' acclimation to that habitat. Hinde's example shows the disarticulated and non-systematic nature of social studies instruction when integrated with language arts observed by Boyle-Baise et al (2008) and Sunal and Sunal (2007/2008).

Issues in social studies education persist across decades, not the least of which is the general public's, as well as teachers' and administrators', failure to see the value of the depositions, perceptions and critical thinking skills nurtured by the field. As shown in this overview, the failure to value social studies at the elementary level existed in the 1950s and still exists today exacerbated by the No Child Left Behind legislation. At the national, state, and local level it is critical to renew the focus on social studies as a subject that prepares citizens who can sustain a democratic society into the future. This focus can be renewed through an emphasis on the standards that exist in all states for social studies instruction combined with prioritizing social studies within the elementary school curriculum.

APPENDIX A: RESEARCH STUDIES

Study	Research Methodology	Sample Size	Findings
Fitchett & Heafner, (2010)	Quantitative: • National Center for Educational Statistics Schools and Staffing Survey	• National • 33,390 teachers across 17 years (1987–2004) • teachers in self-contained classrooms not social studies specialists	• Instruction time for social studies much less than instructional time for math and language arts put slightly more than for science. • Intermediate grade teachers (3–5) spend more subject specific time on social studies than lower grade teachers (K–2) • Although instructional time in social studies decreased significantly after the inception on No Child Left Behind it was decreasing previous to the national law
McEachron, (2010)	Quantitative: • Administrative weekly time schedules for academic and non-academic activities (1987–1993, 1999–2003, 2006–2009)	73 pre-service teachers collected the schedules in portfolios (50 (gr. 1–3), 23 (gr. 4–5) 3 separate school districts in Virginia	Time allocated to social studies is low (along with science) as compared to language arts and math • Slight increase in primary social studies after 1994 (Virginia has mandated testing in social studies in gr 3, 5 & 8) • Weekly allocation is greater at higher grade levels(90 minutes in primary grades and 3 hours in intermediate grades) • Non –core (physical education, health, art, music, library, media, technology, guidance, intervention activities) and non-academic (lunch, recess, opening, snack, restroom, clean up, dismissal) activities received more time than social studies
Russell, (2009)	Qualitative • Phone Interviews	National random sample • 20 teachers	A minimal amount of time is being spent on social studies because: • Social studies is not tested and is not part of high stakes testing to determine a child's progress • Teachers lack content knowledge

Study	Research Methodology	Sample Size	Findings
Fry, (2009)	Qualitative • Student teacher lesson plans • Supervisors observation notes • Post observation conferences • Reflective journals • Graphic representations of lesson meaningfulness created by the teachers	4 pre-service teachers • 4th gr., 3rd. gr. , 1st gr. and kindergarten Student taught in rural, disadvantaged area	Time allocated to social studies: • None in Kindergarten and first grade • Second, third & fourth grades 30 minutes 2 to 3 times a week Pre-service teachers taught an interdisciplinary lesson plan that incorporated social studies. Results: • Student joy and enthusiasm • Teacher satisfaction • Increased dislike of standardized testing
Holloway & Chiodo, (2009)	Mixed method • Survey (how often are social studies concepts taught) • Interviews (how are social studies concepts taught)	Surveyed 100 1st—5th grade teachers in one school district (Southwestern US) Interviewed ten of the survey participants	Teachers are committed to teaching social studies: • Social studies is integrated into time allocated for other subjects • Social studies without integration is allocated less than two hours per week
Boyle-Baise, Hsu, Johnson, Serriere & Stewart (2008)	Qualitative • Focus groups • Individual interviews (teachers & principals)	13 classrooms in 6 elementary schools in 3 school districts in west central Indiana • 3 kindergarten, 3 first gr., 2 second gr., 1 fourth gr., 2 fifth grade, 2 sixth grade	Very little social studies taught as stand alone lessons, but taught usually as a by product of reading • Primary: Subsumed in reading instruction often as a short note connected to a story • Upper grades: Social studies is textbook driven with an emphasis on literacy and comprehension skills Nature of social studies integration: • Opportunistic based on happenstance • Not systematic

(continued)

Study	Research Methodology	Sample Size	Findings
Pace, (2008)	Qualitative • Interviews	9 fifth grade teachers involved with professional development program in history (California—three districts)	• History and social science instruction was evident in high performing districts that allowed more teacher autonomy and were little effected by NCLB • Teachers in low performing districts were impeded in social studies teaching by the emphasis on reading and math in NCLB
Hutton & Burstein, (2008)	Mixed method • Survey with nine open ended questions • One on one interviews	24 K–5 teachers in Los Angeles county (survey) 8 of the 24 participated in one on one interviews	Teachers spend a minimal amount of time teaching history-social science compared to reading/language arts and mathematics • They are pressured to increase test scores in reading/language arts and mathematics • 44% of K–2 & 40% of 3–5 teach an hour or less per week • None teach the recommended five hours a week • Many teachers are finding creative ways to carve out time for history-social science • Closed the door and rearranged their instructional time • Integrated history-social science in thematic units with arts and science
Sunal & Sunal, (2007/2008)	Qualitative 1,540 electronic journal entries recorded the teaching of social studies in the teacher candidates' classroom placement Two questions structured the responses: • What is happening in social studies education in my classroom? • How is social studies taught?	60 teacher candidates enrolled in social studies methods courses at the same institution (Southeastern US) • 39 with K–3 placement • 21 with 4–6 placement	Social studies does not occupy a major role in the curriculum: • Disarticulated in K–3, teacher candidates did not observe social studies being taught • Textbook driven in 4–6, some classrooms did not teach social studies, others alternated with science for a limited amount of time Social studies was subsumed within reading instruction in K–3 classrooms resulting in a disarticulated curriculum that does not meet national or state social studies standards Social studies in grades 4–7 uses textbooks aligned with state and national standards • Teaching method traditional without the use of inquiry or problem solving Internet use in 4–6 was undertaken without clear social studies goals

Study	Research Methodology	Sample Size	Findings
Vogler, Lintner, Lipscomb, Knopf, Heafner & Rock, (2007)	Mixed method • Pre-service teachers surveyed elementary teachers using an interview format	235 South Carolina elementary teachers	Statewide tests in grades 3–8 include social studies Majority of teachers spend 30 minutes a day on social studies: The higher the grade level the larger amount of time spent on social studies • 0–15 in Kindergarten • 30–45 in 5th grade Study found: • A low commitment to the content of social studies as compared to other content areas • A correlation between teachers' commitment to social studies and grade level • A correlation between time spent on social studies instruction and grade level • An increase in the time spent on social studies instruction when compared to the time spent five years ago
Wills, (2007)	Qualitative • Observation • Videotaping • Interviews • Student work • Curricular materials	1 4th grade classroom 2 5th grade classrooms Title I school serves a disadvantaged community consisting of 75% Latino, 25% split between African-American and White students. 50% ELL	Emphasis on the Annual Performance Index (API) score that is focused on language arts and math Instructional time in social studies has been reduced, as has science: • Social studies instruction 70 to 80 minutes a week Result of reduction: • A reduction in the scope of the curriculum • Curtailment or elimination of opportunities to promote students' higher order thinking • Increased emphasis at times on simple reproduction of content knowledge

(continued)

Study	Research Methodology	Sample Size	Findings
Rock, Heafner, O'Connor, Passe, Oldendorf, Good & Byrd (2006)	Mixed method • Surveys • Interviews	Cooperating teachers from across North Carolina • 320 from Kindergarten through 6th grade	Study found: • Social studies taught two to three times a week (30 to 40 minutes) Daily in Kindergarten and 5th grade • Social studies ranked below language arts and math in priority among teachers but above science • Majority of teachers not satisfied with instructional time given to social studies, most spend time preparing students in the tested areas of language arts and math. Those that were satisfied with the time practiced integration of social studies.
Van Fossen (2005)	Mixed method: • Survey with one section of open ended questions	594 K–5 teachers across Indiana	Teachers spend less than 18 minutes a day on social studies Reasons for social studies marginalization in the elementary schools: • Perceived lack of administrative support for implementing state social studies standards • Lack of state wide assessments for social studies at K–5 level • Teachers lack of a clear understanding of the goals and mission of the social studies at the K–5 level.

REFERENCES

Bolick, C. M., Adams, R., & Wilcox, L. (2010). The marginalization of elementary social studies in teacher education. *Social Studies Research and Practice, 5*(2),1–22.

Boyle-Baise, M., Hsu, M-C., Johnson, S., Serriere, S., & Stewart, D. (2008). Putting reading first: Teaching social studies in elementary classrooms. *Theory and Research in Social Education, 36*(3), 233–255.

Crocco, M.S., & Costigan, A.T. (2007). The narrowing of curriculum and pedagogy in the age of accountability: Educators speak out. *Urban Education, 42*(6), 512–535.

Dewey, J. (1969/1899). *The school and society.* Chicago: University of Chicago Press.

Doppen, F., Misco,T. & Patterson, N. (2008). The State of K–12 Social Studies Instruction in Ohio. *Social Studies Research and Practice, 3*(3), 1–25.

Fitchett, P. G., & Heafner, T. L. (2010). A national perspective on the effects of high-stakes testing and standardization on elementary social studies marginalization. *Theory and Research in Social Education, 38*(1), 114–130.

Fry, S. W. (2009). On borrowed time: How four elementary preservice teachers learned to teach social studies in the nclb era. *Social Studies Research and Practice, 4*(1), 31–41.

Gerwin, D. (2004). Preservice teachers report the impact of high-stakes testing. *The Social Studies, 95*(2),71–74.

Grant, S.G. (2007). High-stakes testing: How are social studies teachers responding? *Social Education, 71*(5), 250–254.

Hahn,C. (1970). The status of the social studies in the public schools of the United States: another look. *Social Education, 49,* 220–223.

Hinde, E. (2009). Fractured social studies or integrated thinkers: The end results of curriculum integration. *Social Studies Research and Practice, 4*(5),118–127.

Holloway, J. E., & Chiodo, J. J. (2009). Social studies is being taught in the elementary school: A contrarian view. *The Journal of Social Studies Research, 33*(2), 235–261.

Heafner, T., Lipscomb, G.B., & Rock, T. (2006). To test or not to test? The role of testing in elementary social studies. A collaborative study conducted by NCPSSE and SCPSSE. *Social Studies Research and Practice, 1*(2), 145–164.

Henry, N. B. (1957). Editor's preface. In Nelson, N. B. (Ed.), *Social studies in the elementary school: The fifty-sixth yearbook of the National Society for the Study of Education, Part II* (pp. vii–viii). Chicago: The University of Chicago Press.

Houser, N. (1995). Social studies on the back burner: Views from the field. *Theory and Research in Social Education, 23*(2), 147–168.

Hutton, L. A., & Burstein, J. H. (2008). The teaching of history-social science: Left behind or behind closed doors? *Social Studies Research and Practice, 3*(1), 96–108.

Levstik, L., & Barton,K. (2001). *Doing history: Investigating with children in elementary and middle schools.* Mahwah,NJ: Lawrence Erlbaum Associates, Publishers

McEachron, G. (2010). Study of allocated social studies time in elementary classrooms in Virginia: 1987–2009. *The Journal of Social Studies Research, 34*(2), 208–228

National Council for the Social Studies.(1994). *Expectations of excellence: Curriculum standards for social studies.* Washington, DC: NCSS.

National Council for the Social Studies. (2010). *National curriculum standards for social studies: A framework for teaching, learning and assessment.* Silver Spring, MD: NCSS.

New York State Department of Education. (2008). *Manual for administrators and teachers: New York state grade 5 elementary level social studies test.* http://www.emsc.nysed.gov/osa/sam/gr5ss/det1551-08.pdf (retrieved October 4, 2010)

Pace, J. L. (2008). Inequalities in history-social science teaching under high-stakes accountability: Interviews with fifth-grade teachers in California. *Social Studies Research and Practice, 3*(1), 24–40.

Parker, W. (1996). *Educating the democratic mind.* Albany: State University of New York Press.

Preston, R. C. (1957). Introduction. In Nelson, N. B. (Ed.), *Social studies in the elementary School: The fifty-sixth yearbook of the National Society for the Study of Education, Part II* (pp. 1–3). Chicago: The University of Chicago Press.

Rock, T. C., Heafner, T., O'Connor, K., Passe, J.,Oldendorf, S., Good, A., & Byrd, S. (2006). One state closer to a national crisis: A report on elementary social studies education in North Carolina schools. *Theory and Research in Social Education, 34*(4), 455–483.

Russell, III, W. B.. (2009). Social studies, the lost curriculum: A research study of elementary teachers and the forces impacting the teaching of social studies. *Curriculum and Teaching, 24*(2), 75–86.

Shaver, J., Davis, O. L., & Helburn, S. W. (1980). The status of social studies education: Impressions from three NSF studies. *Social Education, 44,* 150–153.

Sunal, C. S., & Sunal, D. W. (2007/2008). Reports from the field: Elementary teacher candidates describe the teaching of social studies. *International Journal of Social Education, 22*(2), 29–48.

United States Department of Education, Institute of Education Sciences, National Center for Education Statistics. (2010). *Table 2.16. Social studies statewide assessment name, grade administered, and assessment type, by state: 2009–2010.* http://nces.ed.gov/programs/statereform/tab2_16.asp (retrieved October 25, 2010)

VanFossen, P. J. (2005). "Reading and math take so much time...": An overview of social studies instruction in elementary classrooms in Indiana. *Theory and Research in Social Education, 33*(3), 376–403.

VanSledright, B. A. (2002). Fifth graders investigating history in the classroom: Results from a researcher-practitioner design experiment. *The Elementary School Journal, 103,* 131–160.

Vogler, K. E., Lintner, T., Lipscomb, G. B., Knopf, H., Heafner, T. L., & Rock, T. C. (2007). Getting off the back burner: Impact of testing elementary social studies as part of a state-mandated accountability program. *Journal of Social Studies Research, 31*(2), 20–34.

Wills, J. S. (2007). Putting the squeeze on social studies: Mananging teaching dilemmas in subject areas excluded from state testing. *Teachers College Record, 109*(8),1980–2046.

Wineburg, S. S. (1996). The psychology of teaching and learning history" In D.C. Berliner & R. C. Clafee (Eds.), *Handbook of educational psychology* (pp. 423–437). New York: Simon and Schuster Macmillian.

SECTION III

DIVERSITY & PERSPECTIVE

CHAPTER 11

CULTURALLY RESPONSIVE SOCIAL STUDIES TEACHING

Models of Theory into Practice

Paul G. Fitchett and Tina L. Heafner

Since the 1970s, multiculturalism has been a staple of teacher education programs (Evans, 2004). Most commonly, multiculturalism is defined as the study of diversity and how diversity is perceived within our social institutions. In the social dynamic of schooling, we refer to it as multicultural education. James Banks (1999) notes, "Multicultural education assumes that race, ethnicity, culture, and social class are salient parts of US society" (p. 1). Within social studies education, diversity and multiculturalism are seemingly intuitive frameworks from which to build instruction (Rong, 1998). Yet, quite frequently, diversity education and social studies instructional methods are bifurcated (Villegas & Lucas, 2007; Zeichner, et al., 1998). As such, ideological tenants of diversity education such as tolerance, pluralism, and empathy are disconnected from practice. Preservice teachers receive a mixed message. On one side, they are told to uphold principles of a multicultural ethos. On the other side, candidates' pedagogical work does not

Contemporary Social Studies: An Essential Reader, pages 195–214
Copyright © 2012 by Information Age Publishing

readily translate into notions of diversity and cultural sensitivity. The disconnect between multiculturalism in theory and social studies in practice is further exacerbated by the continuing, prescriptive climate of our schooling culture (Crocco, 1998; Crocco & Costigan, 2007). Culturally responsive teaching theory and practice serves to instructionally realize multicultural dispositions in a manner accessible to classroom practitioners.

In this chapter, we present a practical definition for culturally responsive teaching with particular emphasis on the social studies. Culturally responsive practitioners recognize and react to the changing cultural dynamics of their classroom. They conceptualize social studies teaching as more than knowledge-based objectives; developing instruction that encourages inquiry, perspective-taking, and higher-order thinking (Parker, 2010; Ukpokodu, 2006; VanSledright, 2004). We offer two specific examples of culturally responsive teaching principles in practice. First, we provide a pedagogical scaffold: *Review, Reflect, and React* (3Rs) as an instructional strategy for lesson planning. Grounded in relevant social studies theory and research, 3Rs offers a practical implementation of culturally responsive teaching within the current standardization milieu. We also demonstrate the power of Professional Development School (PDS) partnerships to bridge academic institutions in order to create a culturally responsive teaching climate that fosters civic engagement among students, classroom teachers, preservice teachers, and teacher educators. In exploring future directions for culturally responsive teaching, we re-examine Stephen Thornton's (2001) "gatekeeping" heuristic towards social studies practice; acknowledging the pedagogical freedom of practitioners to enact purposeful curriculum within the realities of standardization (Crocco, 1998; Ross, 2006).

UNDERSTANDING CULTURALLY RESPONSIVE TEACHING

Defining What It Is

Research (Banks, 1999; Bohn & Sleeter, 2000; Cornbleth & Waugh, 1995; Sleeter & Grant, 1991) indicates that social studies standards, teaching, and textbooks are still very much centered upon Westernized, Eurocentric perspectives. Post-colonial and critical race theory critique of social studies curricula suggests that this biased agenda perpetuates an ideal of the non-White, non-Westerner as an inferior, backwards "other" to be culturally and economically exploited under the nation-state interests of the majority (Chandler, 2010; Subedi, 2010; Willinsky, 1998). Consequently, those marginalized in the curriculum are unable to find historical positionality—a sense of identity within the curriculum (Salinas, 2006; VanSledright, 1998). Disconnected from their schooling, students either reject the proposed curriculum or develop a misguided conceptualization of their place within society. Paradoxically, the very subject matter that is supposed to be guided by meaningful instruction and civic efficacy (National Council for the Social Studies, 2010) is instead perpetuating a curriculum of alienation and discouragement toward democratic participation.

The preeminence of the traditionalist social studies canon is further aggravated by prescriptive standardization. Margaret Smith Crocco and Arthur Costigan (2007) refer to the "narrowing of the curriculum" whereby teachers feel external pressures to cover social studies content, therefore limiting their pedagogical innovation. This behavior is also associated with the concept of "intensification" in which teachers perceive the instructional time and effort to be limited (Apple, 2004; Gerwin, 2004; Hargreaves, 1994). Not surprisingly, a large number of social studies practitioners continue to champion teacher-centered, textbook driven instruction over more inquiry-based, student-centered approaches (Ravitch & Finn, 1987; Wills, 2007; Wineburg, 2001). This essentialist pedagogical approach, symptomatic of curricular standardization, fails to resonate with the complex, lived experiences of learners. In yet another paradox, it endorses antidemocratic teaching practices while inculcating youth on explicit American values of liberty, freedom, and democracy. Banks (2008; Banks & Diem, 2008) suggests that in order for political and social democracy to be civically realized, we must endorse a "cultural democracy." The racial and ethnic identities of learners have a substantial impact on how they interpret social studies curriculum. Teachers who recognize the sociocultural differences in instructional motivation and curriculum understandings utilize culturally appropriate teaching strategies (Epstein, 2001, 2009; Ladson-Billings, 1995a; Salinas, 2006).

Moving beyond the superficiality associated with the most innocuous forms of multicultural education ignominiously referred to as "heroes and contributions" (Bohn & Sleeter, 2000; Cornbleth & Waugh, 1995), culturally responsive teaching advocates for a more transformative pedagogy that builds knowledge from the context and experience of students' lives (Freire, 2000; Moll, Amanti, Neff, & González, 1992). Thus, we define culturally responsive using Geneva Gay's (2002) five principles of cultural responsiveness: (1) developing a cultural diversity knowledge base (2) developing a culturally relevant curricula, (3) demonstrating cultural caring and building a learning community, (4) exhibiting effective cross-cultural communications, and lastly (5) delivering cultural congruity in classroom instruction. Associated with "funds of knowledge" (Ladson-Billings, 1995b; Moll, et al., 1992; Moll & Arnot-Hopffer, 2005), *developing a culturally diversity knowledge base* encourages social studies educators to counteract a deficit-model mentality by connecting to the lives of students in order to determine how their lived experiences serve to enrich their schooling. Teachers who acknowledge the cultural complexities of their students are more likely to *develop a culturally relevant curriculum.* As Ladson-Billings (1995a,b) suggests, culturally relevant teaching is more than the objectification of iconic figures of color. It includes a more democratic historical canon. Culturally-relevant practitioners champion alternative historical perspectives more inclusive of race and gender. They encourage inquiry-based instruction and historical thinking so that students may develop an authentic, critical understanding of the past (VanSledright, 2004).

Yet, culturally responsiveness offers more than content inclusiveness. Culturally responsive teachers *demonstrate cultural caring and build a learning community.* Incorporating a caring pedagogical disposition has implications for both how practitioners connect with students on a personal level and how teachers make instructional decisions. As Nell Noddings (1995) indicates, "When teachers discuss themes of care, they may become real persons to their students and so enable them to construct new knowledge" (p. 676). In a culturally responsive social studies classroom, caring discourse is often manifested as *cross-cultural communications.* Dialogue within the diverse social studies classroom encourages tolerance and models democratic principles of perspective-taking and equity of ideas (Avery, 2002; Hess, 2002, 2009; Parker, 2008). Culturally responsive teaching also endorses *culturally congruent* instruction that respects the cultural mores and values of students. As such, culturally responsive teachers recognize that the subjective lives of their students do not always fit within the objective demands of standardized social studies schooling (Hargreaves, 1994). Culturally congruent instruction acknowledges that supposed normative behaviors such as eye-contact, student dialogue, and engagement can have diverse responses (K. H. Au, 2010; Ukpokodu, 2006). As such, the culturally responsive instructors maximize students' potential by tailoring their methods in order to recognize and respect learners' values and motivations. The complexity of culturally responsive teaching might seem daunting to social studies teachers; particularly with prescriptive standards and high-stakes testing often looming overhead. As a reply, we offer insight into what is not considered culturally-responsive teaching. Then, we provide two specific, actualized examples of culturally responsive teaching in practice.

Understanding What It Is Not

To help clarify culturally responsive teaching as both a theory and a practice, we also define what culturally-responsive teaching is not. As Katherine Au (2010) notes, culturally responsive instruction is more than good teaching, "...to advocate a universal concept of good teaching may actually amount to advocating teaching from a European American or mainstream perspective" (p. 80). This notion of good teaching is further exacerbated by skewed biases that the majority White teaching population might have as they enter the classroom (Sleeter, 2001). These biases are conflated because multicultural education is still more often than not taught as separate courses in teacher education programs. Issues of diversity are interpreted as ancillary to professional development (Villegas & Lucas, 2007; Zeichner, et al., 1998); similar to the way that music, foreign language, and the arts are subsidiaries of current PK-12 education. This view of multicultural epistemology translates into the superficial "additive" heroification of non-Whites who fit (read: non-confrontational) within the grand narrative. Oversimplification of multicultural perspectives implicitly suggests that non-White, marginalized history is only worth including either as a continuum or juxtaposition to the sanctioned curriculum of the majority. As classroom teachers, simply incorporating student-centered instruction and incorporating non-White primary/secondary source documents is not enough. Culturally responsive social studies teachers offer opportunities both to understand and critique how culture is included in and excluded from the curriculum (Asher & Crocco, 2001; Crocco, 1998; Subedi, 2010).

Culturally responsive teaching does not promote victimization of marginalized peoples (Danker, 2002). Social studies teachers, in an effort to respond to the cultural of their classroom and beyond, will include alternative histories that showcase the trials and tribulations of non-White, non-male peoples. While the inclusion of such narratives is important for providing a more thorough accounting of the past, teachers should be careful not to encourage persecution-complex among students. As Crocco's (2010) self-study on teaching methods suggests, the unintended consequences of victimization can lead students to "essentialize" important values and customs; thereby furthering cultural superiority of Western ideals. The non-majority culture is viewed as damaged, lacking, and in need of salvation. This malefic compassion develops into a pseudo- "White's Burden" in which social studies teachers and students mistakenly believe that marginalized peoples must be dutifully conformed to the dominant values as has been historically the charge of public education (Spring, 2009). Culturally responsive teachers do not circumvent history's atrocities. They provide both an accounting for and a critique of how non-majority peoples are represented in the past. They do not avoid sensitive issues, rather offering historical accounts of struggle and inspiration.

Recognizing what culturally responsive teaching "is not" helps social studies educators better understand and implement culturally responsive practices in the classroom. Culturally responsive instruction is not simply good teaching. Rather, it offers culturally appropriate content and pedagogy that challenges students to critique curricular and institutional norms to better understand socio-historical meaning. Culturally responsive teaching does not exploit marginalized peoples. Instead, non-majority peoples are treated with dignity, both in the challenges that they have faced under pressure from dominant forces and in examples from which they persevere through oppressive organizations and regimes.

What is Currently Being Done

As the aforementioned rationale implies, culturally responsive teaching is a complex, volitional activity that requires pedagogical creativity, a social justice mentality, and thorough engagement from the teacher. The current climate of high stakes testing and accompanying standardization of curriculum seemingly compounds these issues. To some teachers, culturally responsive teaching might just appear to be yet another innovation that asks even more from overburdened teachers. Hargreaves (1994) in his analysis of teacher work posited that teachers' view time as a limited, fixed commodity and attempts to add yet another instructional piece to their already overwhelming workload will often be met with resistance. To other teachers, culturally responsive teaching might seem antithetical to the prescriptive environment of many social studies classrooms. Recent studies seemingly confer that social studies teachers feel pedagogically limited in their instructional options as high-stakes testing takes precedent over all other student outcomes (W. Au, 2009; Gerwin & Visone, 2006).

As social studies educators and former practitioners, we recognize the practicalities of working in an increasingly teacher-hostile environment. We attempt to reify—change from abstract to concrete—the concept of culturally responsive teaching. In providing these examples, we offer an alternative viewpoint, incorporating cultural responsiveness within standardized curriculum. As Wayne Ross (2006) suggests, social studies teachers should be made aware of the difference between the "formal," standardized curriculum and the "enacted," lived curriculum of the classroom. Moving between these two paradigms to offer a meaningful praxis of culturally responsive teaching is the goal of the subsequent models.

REVIEW, REFLECT, AND REACT: RETHINKING THE ROLE OF STANDARDS IN SOCIAL STUDIES INSTRUCTION

Research in social education has found that teachers perceive standardization as limiting their pedagogical options (Crocco & Costigan, 2007; Fitchett & Heafner, 2010; Gerwin, 2004). Consequently, social studies teachers often fall into the time-worn tradition of teacher-centric instruction that emphasizes knowledge acquisition over concept development. In addition, these standards most often emphasize a Eurocentric canon, whereby minorities are the marginalized or exploited "other" (Bohn & Sleeter, 2000; Cornbleth & Waugh, 1995; Willinsky, 1998). We argue for a dispositional sea-change in how we view the purpose and enactment of the curriculum standardization within our diverse classrooms. *Review, Reflect, and React* is a pedagogical scaffold designed to offer preservice and current social studies practitioners an archetype for providing culturally responsive teaching in a standards-driven curriculum (Fitchett, Starker, & Good, 2010).

Though commonly viewed as an anathema to diversity, standardization can offer social studies teachers a useful guide in developing instruction. Anita Bohn and Christine Sleeter (2000) suggest that standards make explicit the inherent curricular values of the dominant culture. It is within these curricular "spaces" that culturally responsive teachers should critique the implicit message being presented (Crocco, 1998). We suggest that teachers critically *review* their standards (Crocco, 1998; Sleeter & Stillman, 2005). Annad Marri's (2005) questioning framework provides a useful strategy: "1. Who is and is not participating in democracy and on whose terms? 2. How wide is the path to participation?" (p. 1037). Through standards investigation, social studies educators develop an understanding of who is situated within the curriculum and whose values/beliefs are validated. Understanding how the formal curriculum addresses or fails to address the perspectives of learners' provides opportunities to counteract the normative social studies trends in order to meet the diverse needs of students. Critiquing the standards also provides an important context for understanding how relationships of power and essentialist values are integrated into curriculum; thereby providing explicit points to counteract. In their study of preservice social studies teachers, Fitchett, Starker and Good (2010) led participants through a critical review of their standard course of study. By investigating the level of diversity inherent within their curriculum, preservice teachers strategized how they would modify their own instruction to be more inclusive of their diverse classroom communities.

Cultural responsiveness calls upon social studies educators to develop an understanding of students' learning contexts (Gay, 2000, 2002). Exploring the "funds of knowledge" (Moll, et al., 1992) attributed to learners provides teachers with positive examples of how social studies curriculum can be transformed to meet the diverse needs of students. It also avoids deficit-thinking by utilizing students' socio-cultural strengths and motivations. Contextual understanding necessitates examining the lived-experiences of students by bridging the school and the home communities. This often requires social studies teachers to make connections through their own action research such as home visits, student surveys, and informal interviews with members of the community (Fitchett, et al., 2010; Liston & Zeichner, 1990; Moll, et al., 1992). As a next step, teachers should *reflect* on how their students' knowledge and experiences coincide with the critical view of the curriculum. This pedagogical step is problematized by the desire of teachers working within a high-stakes testing climate to simultaneously survive and subvert the standardized curriculum. In a study of preservice social studies teachers, researchers noted successful culturally responsive teaching was exemplified by candidates who used community context and individualized experiences to express concepts aligned within the standardized curriculum while offering not-so-subtle critiques of how the course of study attempts to essentialize social values (Fitchett, et al., 2010).

As social studies teachers reflect on how their classroom community, they become empowered to pedagogically *react* through dynamic instruction. Gay (2002, p. 108) notes the importance of developing "culturally congruent" teaching methods. As a final step, practitioners react through instructional planning and implementation that addresses the strengths of diverse learners. More than just supplementation of non-White readings and historical examples, this approach demands that social studies practitioners embrace the varying learning styles of the students through student-centered instruction and historical perspective-taking (Ladson-Billings, 1995a; VanSledright, 2004). Drawing from the subjective lives of students in each step of instructional decision-making, culturally responsive instruction integrates the domestic (home) and institutional (school) spheres of learning (Ladson-Billings, 1995b). Culturally responsive teachers recognize the organic nature of their students' values and social perspectives (Epstein, 2001, 2009). They do not view their instructional options as fixed or driven by pacing guides. Rather, they adopt and adjust content and instruction to meet the varying needs of their learners. Contrary to the message of pedagogical passivity inherent to most social studies standards, Terrie Epstein (2009) suggests that race and identity should be at the forefront of instructional decision-making. Teachers, who react to the cultural diversity of their classroom, challenge students' historical viewpoints with alternative narratives, empower learners' sense of positionality (VanSledright, 1998, 2011) by teaching students how to historically think, and encourage deliberate discourse and dialogue on issues of race and identity.

We contend that dismissing standardization as the enemy to good social studies teaching is simplistic and impractical for twenty-first century teachers whose professional livelihood is often inextricably tied to the formal curriculum. *Read, Reflect,* and *React* offers a counterpoint to the notion that standardization by default limits cultural responsiveness by placing the onus of instructional decision-making in the hands of social studies teachers. We suggest this instructional framework as an approach, not to complacently bow to objectivist standards, but to work within the realities of the current schooling climate. Acknowledging our pluralist society and our complex cultural democracy as an evolving construct requires change from within the system as well as from without.

PROFESSIONAL DEVELOPMENT SCHOOL PARTNERSHIP: BUILDING A CULTURALLY DEMOCRATIC MODEL

Researchers (Abma, Fischetti, & Larson, 1999; Clark, 1999; Levine, 1998, 2002; Metcalfe-Turner, 1999; Pine, 2003; Teitel, 1998) tout PDSs as effective environments for teacher preparation, noting the value of collaborative partnerships which support all stakeholders and ensure preservice teachers get a real world view of teaching and learning. Abma, Fischetti, and Larson (1999) defined key functions of PDSs: improving the lives, learning and opportunities for all students, enhancing curriculum, school culture, and community connections, and preparing preservice teachers in professional, collegial environments reflective of the contents of experiences that they will encounter in their future classrooms and schools. Thus, the learning community within the PDS, while focused on preservice teachers, is concerned with the success and needs of young learners, with the ultimate goal being to affect student learning in a positive manner. Levine (2002) affirms these views by acknowledging that learning is the core of the PDS's curriculum as well as the direction of research and inquiry for preservice teachers, practitioners and university faculty. As a result, learning becomes a byproduct of the discourse and exchange among all stakeholders. This interaction breaks down traditional educational structures, since work in a PDS requires participants to relinquish their conventional roles and take on others (Levine, 1998). For example, everyone in a PDS partnership is both a teacher and a learner, so the usual hierarchies of "who teaches whom" are eliminated (Heafner & Spooner, 2008). Participants at all levels of experience and in all positions are, at times, teachers and learners. The work that university faculty do, the experiences that preservice teachers in professional education programs receive, and the professional development of practitioners is very important and integral to the success of the partnerships, but it is the work that is done to enhance those opportunities that brings about learning opportunities for PK-12 students.

Social studies methods courses often advocate for cultural responsiveness. However, the opportunities to "practice what we preach" are often few and far between. The gulf between teacher education and schools creates pedagogical internal conflicts as preservice teachers grapple with the divergence between ideology and practice. Anchoring teacher preparation in more authentic settings helps bridge these differences and existing partnerships provide a positive framework for this learner-centered focus. PDSs serve as a framework for contextualizing learning in democratic, service oriented environments while drawing upon established university-school collaborations (Rock, Heafner, & Taylor, in review). An additional attribute of PDSs is the engagement of all stakeholders in the learning process with focused common outcome goals; modeling democratic values, promoting deliberative discourse (Darling-Hammond & McLaughlin, 1995). Collaborative partnerships among school administrators, practitioners, university faculty, and teacher candidates support the collective goals of academic achievement for struggling, often marginalized, secondary students. Curriculum and experiences are centered around social justice and are, by nature, socially reconstructivist (Evans, 2004); confirming diversity, fostering equal opportunities, and challenging traditional views of school and educational hierarchies (McCall, 2004). Marilyn Cochran-Smith (2004) describes educational experiences that incorporate social justice to drive curriculum as using "principles of pedagogy" rather than "best practices," "models of teaching," or "essential teaching skills" (p. 65). She argues principles include many different models of teaching, and teaching for social justice is not so much as a practice as it is a praxis, "the interactive...shaping of theory and practice" (p. 66).

As an alternate approach to on-campus university methods instruction and in an attempt to build praxis out of experience and theory, we have developed an undergraduate social studies methods course taught in a secondary PDS that utilizes a service learning approach to teacher preparation (Heafner, Fitchett, & Averell, in development). Positioning the social studies methods course in an authentic PDS context, preservice teachers interacted weekly with practitioners and diverse students—bridging theory to practice. Embracing Gay's (2002) principles of cultural responsiveness, preservice teachers in the PDS setting framed their narratives of culture and cultural identity through reflective self-examination. Then, they explored concepts of cultural democracy and culturally responsive teaching as manifest in the PDS. Dialogue with teachers through interviews and panel discussions uncovered issues of achievement, standardization, intensification, diversity, and cultural dynamics enabling preservice teachers to develop a discourse on culturally relevant curriculum (Heafner, et al., in development). Preservice teachers worked with PDS teachers to create a tutoring program for struggling, at-risk and marginalized students enrolled in social studies classes. Collaboratively, they designed a culturally caring learning community in which preservice teachers enact curricula to support student academic achievement, self-efficacy, and self-regulation. Promoting cross-cultural, mixed socio-economic interactions, preservice teachers worked in small group and one-on-one settings with students who are disenfranchised from the curricula they passionately strive to teach. They grappled with challenges of equity, motivation, and difference to deliver cultural congruity in social studies tutoring instruction for the collective goals of promoting student educational growth as well as success on standardized tests. Through these experiences, preservice teachers encountered new ways of thinking, all of which helped them to define their perceptions of efficacy, equity and empathy.

This merger also created a nurturing learning environment for preservice teachers, while promoting civic engagement and social justice ideals (Heafner, et al., in development; Wade, 2008). Empowerment of teacher candidates in a democratic forum for professional exchange with practicing teachers and university faculty compiled with the interaction of diverse students encouraged preservice teachers' efficaciousness and empathic understanding. Teacher candidates recognized curricular applications and relationship development as strengths for overcoming personal biases and cultural disenfranchisement (Banks, 2008; Epstein, 2001, 2009; Gay, 2002). Much of preservice teachers' dispositional and values assessment occurred through systematic reflection. Candidate thinking was nurtured as they defined their cultural identity, evaluated how their cultural views impact teaching and learning, and culminated in reflective discourse with peers and practitioners (Gay & Kirkland, 2003). This reflective process became a circle of learning (Michalove, 1999); preservice teachers moved from thinking about social justice in history to community to school to self to students, making connections between teaching, learning, and social justice. Teacher candidates' reflections on learning provided evidence of engagement and growth in equity, efficacy, and empathy. Consequently, strategic partnerships, such as PDSs, served as models for cultural democratic engagement as students, teachers, university faculty, and preservice educators work together to enact social studies curriculum in meaningful ways that address state and federal mandates for achievement.

Creating an open environment, our PDS program offered an atmosphere of candid, open dialogue. Pragmatic concerns of preservice teachers were addressed by both methods instructors and current practitioners. Preservice teachers were exposed to pedagogical content knowledge to provide the professional skills to engage in transformative teaching practices (Shulman, 1987). Working with current practitioners, preservice teachers negotiated between the formal and enacted components of teaching to connect instructional theory and practice. Acknowledging that the context of instruction had a significant impact on the level of efficacy of preservice teachers (Pajares, 1996). We sought to improve teacher candidate efficacy by offering in-depth, semi-structured contact with teachers, students, and faculty on a regular basis. By housing the social studies methods course at a secondary PDS site, instructional strategies and theory were actualized as preservice teachers utilized their strategies in real world, service learning opportunities with student participants. Cumulatively, this process served to familiarize future practitioners with diverse, and often at-risk, student populations. In addition, the PDS partnership helped preservice teachers develop greater empathy for classroom learners and an understanding of equitable educational opportunities. As noted previously, the concept of cultural democracy depends on a shared acceptance of our pluralist society (Banks, 2008). However, if one lacks perspective of others, then such an understanding is not possible.

Affirming Wade's (1995, 2008) views, this PDS service learning experience, provided preservice teachers, practitioners and faculty the opportunity to develop new perspectives through engagement with diverse communities. Through student tutoring and teacher dialogue, preservice teachers developed "culturally congruent" forms of discourse and practice in order to better serve the student community (Gay, 2002). In addition, preservice teachers were challenged to confront their own stereotypes and prejudices. Preservice teachers demonstrated transformative thinking about education as they came to recognize that diverse groups of students must have equitable opportunities to learn. These learning opportunities included interaction with students from other racial, cultural, ethnic, and language groups to overcome bias (Banks, et al., 2005). The intimate tutoring experience afforded preservice teachers the chance to acknowledge the funds of knowledge that each student offers (Ladson-Billings, 1995a; Moll, et al., 1992).

WHAT NEEDS TO BE DONE IN THE FUTURE

To develop models of practice, social studies education needs to emphasize the practicalities of standardization and current schooling culture. As a dispositional tool for countermanding perceived curricular restriction, we suggest incorporating Stephen Thornton's (2001, 2005) concept of "gatekeeping;" whereby classroom teachers recognize their instructional autonomy regardless of the prescriptive nature of the formal curriculum. This ideal of gatekeeping applies to social studies teacher educators as well. Culturally responsive teaching is deliberate and rationalized. Research indicates that preservice professionals that do not agree in its dispositions retain their biases and stagnant instructional decision-making (Fitchett, et al., 2010; Sleeter, 2001). Yet, tolerance, empathy, and compassion are necessary to facilitate democracy (Banks & Diem, 2008; Parker, 2010). Social education has a responsibility to incorporate cultural-responsiveness as an integral part of democratic thinking and question the commitment towards democracy of any teacher or teacher candidate who does not recognize its importance towards achieving that civic-minded end.

Unfortunately, in many cases social studies remains on the "backburner" of the educational landscape (Houser, 1995) in favor of less critical American history/civics inculcation. In a recent study sponsored by policy think-tank American Enterprise Institute (AEI), researchers (2010) reported that out of a sample of public and private social studies only 20% of the teachers view factual information as a priority in teaching citizenship and only 67% percent of teachers rely on the textbook. To many social studies teachers and teacher educators these findings may be interpreted as welcome evidence that social studies is moving away from a narrow, Eurocentric curriculum. Yet, AEI (2010) reports these findings under an executive summary subtitle, "Teachers might be setting the bar too low for what they expect students to know about American history and government" (p. 5).

This begs an important question, "Why is there such a discrepancy between what educational policymakers and what social studies educators view as important for the field?" In order to bridge this gap, we argue that social studies, as a core content area of PK-12 schooling, needs to increase its visibility while underscoring the importance of an education that values both our democratic foundations and an ideology of equity, social justice, and cultural understandings.

Numerous studies have examined whether American classrooms are socially just and provide the context necessitating the merit of a social studies curricula. Cochran-Smith (2004), in *Against the Grain*, openly examines the inequity in schools,

> since the 1970s, disparities among racial, cultural, and linguistic groups in school achievement, high school completion rates, poverty levels, and educational resources have been identified as matters of urgent national importance (p. 1).

Exacerbated by political and economic decision-making of the 1980s and 1990s, an achievement gap between the haves and have-nots has permeated American schooling during the past three decades (Anyon, 1997; Ferguson, 2000; Kozol, 2005; Lareau, 2003). Zyngier (2008) adds that members of the educational class of have-nots have historically been disenfranchised students whose appearance, language, culture, values, communities, and family structures were in contrast to the social norm. These cultural disparities have been intensified in schools that attempt to standardize knowledge (Spring, 2009), a byproduct of high-stakes testing and accountability. In many cases, students who do not fit the profile of the dominant culture are disengaged from school because the curriculum or standardized tests are culturally exclusive. James Banks and colleagues (2005) affirmed these concerns and called for educators to re-envision how content is taught and portrayed in social studies classrooms. Often, teachers and textbooks promote an American history which is based on the experiences of the white middle class, creating a one-sided story in which the poor and people of color either play no part or are seen as side notes to the real history (Loewen, 1995, 2009). Zinn and Arnove (2004) note, "what is common to all these voices [marginalize populations] is that they have mostly been shut out of the orthodox histories, the major media, the standard textbooks, the controlled culture" (p. 24). Instead, if social studies educators value diverse racial, ethnic, and cultural perspectives, Banks et al. (2005) argue, social studies classes must become more culturally relevant, and therefore engaging to diverse audiences. In accordance with Bender-Slack and Raupach (2008), we argue standards and accountability do not have to stand in the way of teaching social justice; students can have academic success in environments that are culturally responsive. This message needs to be reiterated across social studies and history education programs.

Lastly, it would be negligent to fail to mention the substantial lack of social studies teachers of color currently teaching in US high schools. Research has long confirmed that social studies teacher are overwhelming white (Leming, 1991; Leming, Ellington, & Schug, 2006; Risinger, 1981) and that teaching staffs of individual schools are more becoming more segregated (Spring, 2009). Frances Rains (2006) and Sabrina King (1993) argue that the Westernized curriculum of social studies fails to resonate with minority teachers; thereby attracting and retaining less teachers. Culturally responsive teaching offers opportunities for potential social studies teachers of color to explore alternative historical and social narratives, providing a less alienating curriculum to engage as practitioners. The demographic dilemma is further compounded by research that suggest that teachers are self-segregating—white social studies teachers are more likely to teach white students and minority teachers are more likely to work in predominately minority-populated schools (Fitchett, 2010). Studies indicate that students' interactions with teachers of another race or ethnicity can have a positive impact on their perceptions of culture differences (Rong & Priessle, 1997). Conversely, the institutional segregation of social studies teachers and students can have negative implications for how teachers and students recognize and relate to democratic ideals. Therefore, we argue that a substantial movement towards culturally responsiveness requires not only a more diverse pedagogy, but a more diverse teacher workforce as well.

CONCLUSION

Madeline Grumet (2010, p. 66) refers to the "audit culture" that remains pervasive in American schooling. Easily recognizable in our nation's schools, it represents standardization, accountability, and current marketplace reform agendas. However, in many ways, it also has impacted teacher education. Teacher training programs are under siege from accreditation agencies, state legislatures, and even the current US Secretary of Education. This fetish with standardization has often left teacher education programs more concerned with graduating certified practitioners and less concerned about how these neophyte educators are going to impact their schooling communities. Making sure that teacher candidates have the right number of course credits, regardless of their practical application to the field, takes precedence. Consequently, culturally responsive education is segregated from instructional design and methods classes, leaving the impression that issues of diversity are too nebulous for application (Villegas & Lucas, 2007). In social studies education, this approach is incompatible to the principles of the field. The future direction of social studies education (Thornton, 2005) depends on the ability of teacher educators to bring the community into practice (*Review, Reflect, and React*) and bring the practice to the community (*PDS partnership*). We have provided two practical models for integrating culturally responsive teaching in social studies methods. Not to be viewed as a panacea for integrating cultural responsiveness, we hope that these examples will help further the discourse surrounding issues of diversity within social studies education.

REFERENCES

Abma, S., Fischetti, J., & Larson, A. (1999). The purpose of a professional development school is to make a difference: 10 years of a high school-university partnership. *Peabody Journal of Education, 73*(3/4), 254–262.

Anyon, J. (1997). *Ghetto schooling: A political economy of urban educational reform.* New York: Teachers College Press.

Apple, M. W. (2004). Controlling the work of teachers. In D. J. Flinders & S. Thornton (Eds.), *The curriculum studies reader* (pp. 183–198). New York: Routledge-Falmer.

Asher, N., & Crocco, M. S. (2001). (En)gendering multicultural identities and representations in education. *Theory & Research in Social Education, 29*(1), 129–151.

Au, K. H. (2010). Isn't culturally responsive instruction just good teaching? In W. C. Parker (Ed.), *Social studies today: Research & Practice* (pp. 77–86). New York: Routledge.

Au, W. (2009). High-stakes testing and curriculum control: A qualitative metasynthesis In D. J. Flinders & S. Thornton (Eds.), *The curriculum reader* (pp. 286–302). New York: Routledge.

Avery, P. G. (2002). Teaching tolerance: what research tells us. *Social Education, 66*(5), 270–275.

Banks, J. A. (1999). *An introduction to multicultural education.* Nedham Heights, MA: Allyn & Bacon.

Banks, J. A. (2008). Diversity, group identity, and citizenship in a global age. *Educational Researcher, 37*(3), 129–139.

Banks, J. A., Cookson, P., Gay, G., Hawley, W., Irvine, J., Nieto, S., et al. (2005). Education and diversity. *Social Education, 69*(1), 36.

Banks, J. A., & Diem, N. (2008). Diversity and citizenship education. In L. S. Levstik & C. A. Tyson (Eds.), *Handbook of research in social studies education* (pp. 137–154). New York: Routledge.

Bender-Slack, D., & Raupach, M. (2008). Negotiating standards and social justice in social studies: Educators' perspectives. *The Social Studies, 99*(6), 255–259.

Bohn, A. P., & Sleeter, C. E. (2000). Multicultural education and the standards movement: A report from the field. *Phi Kappa Delta, 82*(2), 156–159.

Chandler, P. (2010). Critical race theory and social studies: Centering the Native American experience. *Journal of Social Studies Research, 34*(1), 29–58.

Clark, R. (1999). *Effecitve professional development schools.* San Francisco, CA: Jossey Bass.

Cochran-Smith, M. (2004). *Waling the road: Race, diversity, and social justice in teacher education.* New York: Teachers College Press.

Cornbleth, C., & Waugh, D. (1995). *The great speckled bird: Multicultural poltics and education policymaking.* Mahwah, NJ: Lawrence Erlbaum Associates.

Crocco, M. S. (1998). Crafting a responsive pedagogy in an age of educational standards. *Theory and Research in Social Education, 26*(1), 123–130.

Crocco, M. S. (2010). (How) do we teach about women of the world in teacher education? In B. Subedi (Ed.), *Critical perspectivies: Rethinking knowledge about global societies* (pp. 19–38). Charlotte, NC: Information Age Publishing

Crocco, M. S., & Costigan, A. T. (2007). The narrowing of curriculum and pedagogy in the age of accountability urban educators speak out. *Urban Education, 42*(6), 512–535.

Danker, A. C. (2002). The uncertain future of multicultural studies. *Multicultural Review, 11*(2), 118–120.

Darling-Hammond, L., & McLaughlin, M. W. (1995). Policies That Support Professional Development in an Era of Reform. *The Phi Delta Kappan, 76*(8), 597–604.

Epstein, T. (2001). Racial identity and young people's perspectives on social education. *Theory into Practice, 40*(1), 42–47.

Epstein, T. (2009). *Interpreting national history.* New York: Routledge.

Evans, R. (2004). *The social studies war: What should we teach the children?* New York: Teachers College Press.

Farkas, S., & Duffett, A. M. (2010). *High schools, civics, and citizenship: What social studies teachers think and do.* Washington, DC: American Enterprise Institute for Public Policy Research.

Ferguson, A. (2000). *Bad boys: Public schooiln in the making of black masuclinity* Ann Arbor, MI: University of Michigan Press.

Fitchett, P. G. (2010). A profile of twenty-first century social studies teachers *Journal of Social Studies Research, 34*(2), 229–265.

Fitchett, P. G., & Heafner, T. L. (2010). A national perspective on the effects of high-stakes testing and standardization on elementary social studies marginalization. *Theory & Research in Social Education, 38*(1), 114–130.

Fitchett, P. G., Starker, T. V., & Good, A. J. (2010). Review, reflect, and react: A culturally responsive model for preservice secondary social studies teachers. *Social Studies Research and Practice, 5*(3), 1–20.

Freire, P. (2000). *Pedagogy of the oppressed.* New York: Continuum.

Gay, G. (2000). *Culturally responsive teaching: Theory, research, and practice.* New York: Teachers College Press.

Gay, G. (2002). Preparing for culturally responsive teaching. *Journal of Teacher Education, 53*(2), 106–116.

Gay, G., & Kirkland, K. (2003). Developing cultural critical consciousness and self-reflection in preservice teacher education. *Theory into Practice, 42*(3), 181–187.

Gerwin, D. (2004). Preservice teachers report the impact of high-stakes testing. *The Social Studies, 95*(4), 71–74.

Gerwin, D., & Visone, F. (2006). The freedom to teach: Contrasting teaching in elective and state-tested courses. *Theory & Research in Social Education, 34*(2), 259–282.

Grumet, M. R. (2010). The public expression of citizen teachers. *Journal of Teacher Education, 61*(1–2), 66–76.

Hargreaves, A. (1994). *Changing teachers, changing times: Teachers' work and culture in the postmodern age.* New York: Teachers College Press.

Heafner, T. L., Fitchett, P. G., & Averell, C. (in development). Reciprocal democratic learning environments: A PDS model for civic engagement, equality and social justice. In K. Zenkov & D. P. Corrigan (Eds.), *Professional development schools and social justice: Schools and universities partnering to make a difference.*

Heafner, T. L., & Spooner, M. (2008). Promoting learning in a professional development school: Helping students "get over the mountain." In I. N. Guadarrama, J. M. Ramsey, & J. L. Nath (Eds.), *University and School Connections: Research Studies in Professional Development Schools (Research in Professional School Development)* (Vol. 3, pp. 117–150). Charlotte, NC: Information Age Publishing.

Hess, D. E. (2002). Discussing controversial public issues in secondary social studies classrooms: Learning from skilled teachers. *Theory and Research in Social Education, 30*(1), 10–41.

Hess, D. E. (2009). *Controversy in the classroom: The democratic power of discussion.* New York: Routledge.

Houser, N. O. (1995). Social studies on the "backburner": Views from the field. *Theory & Research in Social Education, 23*(2), 147–168.

King, S. H. (1993). Why did we choose teaching careers and what will enable us to stay? Insights from one cohort of the African American teaching pool. *The Journal of Negro Education, 62*(4), 475–492.

Kozol, J. (2005). *Shame of a nation: The restoration of apartheid schooling in America.* New York: Crown Books.

Ladson-Billings, G. (1995a). But that's good teaching! The case for culturally relevant pedagogy. *Theory into Practice, 43*(3), 159–165.

Ladson-Billings, G. (1995b). Toward a theory of culturally relevant pedagogy. *American Educational Research Journal, 32*(3), 465–491.

Lareau, A. (2003). *Unequal childhoods: Class, race, and family life.* Berkley, CA: University of California Press.

Leming, J. S. (1991). Teacher characteristics and social studies education. In J. P. Shaver (Ed.), *Handbook of research on social studies teaching and learning* (pp. 222–236). New York: MacMillan.

Leming, J. S., Ellington, L., & Schug, M. (2006). The state of social studies: A national random survey of elementary and middle social studies teachers. *Social Education, 70*(5), 322–327.

Levine, M. (1998). *Designing standards that work for professional development schools.* Washington, DC: National Council for the Accreditation of Teacher Education.

Levine, M. (2002). Why invest in professional development schools? *Educational Leadership, 59*(6), 65–68.

Liston, D. P., & Zeichner, K. M. (1990). Reflective teaching and action research in preservice teacher education. *Journal of Education for Teaching, 16*(3), 235–254.

Loewen, J. W. (1995). *Lies my teacher told me: Everything your American history textbook got wrong.* New York: Simon & Schuster.

Loewen, J. W. (2009). *Teaching what really happened: How to avoid the tyranny of textbooks and get students excited about doing history* New York: Teachers College Press.

Marri, A. R. (2005). Building a framework for classroom-based multicultural democratic education: Learning from three skilled teachers. *Teachers College Record, 107*(5), 1035–1059.

McCall, A. (2004). Using poetry in social studies classes to teach about cultural diversity and social justice. *The Social Studies, 95*(4), 172–176.

Metcalfe-Turner, P. (1999). Variable definitions of professional development schools: A desire or a dillemma? *Peabody Journal of Education, 74*(3/4), 33–41.

Michalove, B. (1999). Circling in: Examining prejudice in history and in ourselves. In J. Allen (Ed.), *Class actions: Teaching for social justice in elementary and middle schools* (pp. 21–33). New York: Teachers College Press.

Moll, L. C., Amanti, C., Neff, D., & González, N. (1992). Funds of knowledge for teaching: Using a qualitative approach to connect homes and communities. *Theory into Practice, 31*(2), 132–140.

Moll, L. C., & Arnot-Hopffer, E. (2005). Sociocultural competence in teacher education. *Journal of Teacher Education, 56*(3), 242–247.

National Council for the Social Studies. (2010). About the National Council for the Social Studies. Retrieved from http://www.socialstudies.org/about

Noddings, N. (1995). Teaching themes of care. *The Phi Delta Kappan, 76*(9), 675–679.

Pajares, F. (1996). Self-efficacy beliefs in academic settings. *Review of educational research, 66*(4), 543–578.

Parker, W. C. (2008). Knowing and doing in democratic citizenship education. In L. S. Levstik & C. A. Tyson (Eds.), *Handbook of research in social studies education* (pp. 65–80). New York: Routledge.

Parker, W. C. (2010). Idiocy, puberty, and citizenship: The road ahead. In W. C. Parker (Ed.), *Social Studies Today: Research & Practice* (pp. 247–260). New York: Routledge.

Pine, G. J. (2003). Making a difference: A professional development school's impact on student learning. In D. L. Wiseman & S. L. Knight (Eds.), *Linking school-university collaboration and K–12 student outcomes* (pp. 31–47). Washington, DC: American Association of Colleges for Teacher Education.

Rains, F. V. (2006). The color of social studies: A post social studies reality check. In E. W. Ross (Ed.), *The social studies curriculum: Purposes, problems, and possibilities* (3rd ed., pp. 137–156). Albany, NY: SUNY.

Ravitch, D., & Finn, C. (1987). *What do our 17-year olds know? A report on the National Assessment of History and Literature.* New York: Harper Collins.

Risinger, C. F. (1981). The social studies teacher: A personal profile. *Social Education, 45*(6), 405–411.

Rock, T. C., Heafner, T. L., & Taylor, B. (in review). The professional development school: Fertile ground for service learning initiatives. *Social Studies Research and Practice.*

Rong, X. L. (1998). The new immigration: Challenges facing social studies. *Social Education, 62*(7), 293–299.

Rong, X. L., & Priessle, J. (1997). The continuing decline in Asian American teachers. *American Educational Research Journal, 34*(2), 267–293.

Ross, E. W. (2006). The struggle for the social studies curriculum. In E. W. Ross (Ed.), *The social studies curriculum: Purposes, problems, and possiblities* (3rd ed., pp. 17–36). Albany, NY: SUNY.

Salinas, C. (2006). Educating late arrival high school immigrant students: A call for a more democratic curriculum. *Multicultural Perspectives, 8*(1), 20–27.

Shulman, L. S. (1987). Knowledge and teaching: Foundations of the new reform. *Harvard Educational Review, 57*(1), 1–21.

Sleeter, C. E. (2001). Preparing teachers for culturally diverse schools: Research and the overwhelming presence of whitness. *Journal of Teacher Education, 52*(2), 94–106.

Sleeter, C. E., & Grant, C. E. (1991). Race, class, gender, and disability in current textbooks In M. W. Apple & L. K. Christian-Smith (Eds.), *The politics of the textbook* (pp. 78–110). New York: Routledge.

Sleeter, C. E., & Stillman, J. (2005). Standardizing knowledge in a multicultural society. *Curriculum Inquiry, 35*(1), 27–45.

Spring, J. (2009). *Deculturalization and the struggle for equality: A brief history of the education of dominated cultures in the United States* (6th ed.). New York: McGraw-Hill.

Subedi, B. (2010). Introduction: Reading the world through critical global perspectives. In B. Subedi (Ed.), *Critical global perspectives: Rethinking knowledge about global societies* (pp. 1–18). Charlotte, NC: Information Age Publishing.

Teitel, L. (1998). Professional Development schools: A literature review. In M. Levine (Ed.), *Designing standards that work for professional development schools* (pp. 33–80). Washington, DC: National Council for Accreditation of Teacher Education.

Thornton, S. (2001). Educating the educators: Rethinking the subject area and methods. *Theory into Practice, 40*(1), 72–78.

Thornton, S. (2005). *Teaching social studies that matters.* New York: Teachers College Press.

Ukpokodu, O. (2006). Essential characteristics of a culturally conscientious classroom. *Social Studies and the Young Learner, 19*(2), 4–7.

VanSledright, B. (1998). On the importance of historical positionality to thinking about and teaching history. *International Journal of Social Education, 12*(2), 1–18.

VanSledright, B. (2004). What does it mean to think historically...and how do you teach it? *Social Education, 68*(3), 230–233.

VanSledright, B. (2011). *The challenge of rethinking history education: On practices, theories, and policy.* New York: Routledge.

Villegas, A. M., & Lucas, T. (2007). The culturally responsive teacher. *Educational Leadership, 64*(6), 28–33.

Wade, R. C. (1995). Developing active citizens: Community service learning in social studies teacher education. *Social Studies 86*(3), 122–128.

Wade, R. C. (2008). Service learning. In L. S. Levstik & C. A. Tyson (Eds.), *Handbook of research in social studies education* (pp. 109–123). New York: Routledge.

Willinsky, J. (1998). *Learning to divide the world.* Minneapolis, MN: University of Minnesota Press.

Wills, J. S. (2007). Putting the squeeze on the social studies: Managing teaching dilemmas in subject areas excluded from state testing. *Teachers College Record, 109*(8), 1980–2046.

Wineburg, S. (2001). *Historical thinking and other unnatural acts.* Philadelphia, PA: Temple University Press.

Zeichner, K. M., Grant, C., Gay, G., Gillette, M., Valli, L., & Villegas, A. M. (1998). A research informed vision of good practice in multicultural education: Design principles. *Theory into Practice, 37*(2), 163–171.

Zinn, H., & Arnove, A. (2004). *Voices of a people's history of the United States.* New York: Seven Stories Press.

Zyngier, D. (2008). (Re)conceptualizing student engagement: Doing education not doing time. *Teacher and Teacher Education, 24*, 1765–1776.

CHAPTER 12

RACE AND SOCIAL STUDIES

Prentice T. Chandler and Douglas McKnight

Nations are given birth through the stories they tell to and about themselves. Even more revealing are the narratives not told, the ones the official "creation" stories deny (Castenell & Pinar, 1993). In "America," the official story often begins with the colonial Puritan "errand into the wilderness" to build a "city upon the hill" (McKnight, 2003; Miller, 1957), a narrative that generated a promise of opportunity and rewards for—as well as great threats to—those involved in the so-called divinely ordained mission of migrating to the New World under God's watchful eye. This is the story of the Anglo-European—invading, conquering, building, controlling. However, this story, nor the secularized nation stories that followed from it, ever mentions race, and in fact even refutes its importance. However, even though the concept of race has never been spoken as a theme within the official national narrative, its effect throughout "American" history has been palpable. For, the "errand into the wilderness" story has as its premise the creation and preservation of Anglo-European culture and power structures that could withstand the influx of any race or culture deemed "other" (Omi & Winant, 1994).

As is the case for all stories, race in the account of "American" national identity is but a fictional concept. In fact, in the biological sciences, the

Contemporary Social Studies: An Essential Reader, pages 215–242
Copyright © 2012 by Information Age Publishing
All rights of reproduction in any form reserved.

notion of race is meaningless. As Henry Louis Gates, Jr. (1985) declares: "Race, as a meaningful concept within the biological sciences, has long been recognized to be a fiction. When we speak of 'the white race,' or 'the black race,' 'the Jewish race,' or the 'Aryan race,' we speak in biological misnomers and, more generally, in metaphors" (p. 4). However, these metaphors, these fictions, have successfully sustained "whiteness," a cultural category that has been able to dominate and oppress, hence turning whiteness into all that is perceived as normal, and all non-whiteness as "Other." The socio-psychological effect of this is the complete lack of need to differentiate and speak of the story in terms of race, for the assumption is that the story is about what matters and "white" is all that matters. This process of creation and exclusion has found its greatest expression in institutional education, especially the social studies, which has always claimed to be the storyteller of American opportunity. "The same educational process which inspires and stimulates the oppressor with the thought that he is everything and has accomplished everything worthwhile, depresses and crushes at the same time the spark of genius in the Negro by making him feel that his race does not amount to much and will never measure up to the standards of other peoples" (Woodson, 1933/2000, p. xiii). In fact Pinar, Reynolds, Slattery, and Taubman (1995) make the point that the very "question of school curriculum is also a question about the self, the American self" (p. 330) and debates over curriculum are but ways of fighting over the meaning of the American metanarrative and who can claim ownership over it.

The power of race, specifically in terms of its exclusion, in the story of America is the backdrop for which "our" story unfolds. A cursory view of the unfolding of the American state reveals several truths about the racialized American experience. There are no historical eras within our story that are not directly touched by the power of race narratives and racism as an institutional truth—it is woven into our historical and political DNA.

Given this, it would seem that the social studies curriculum in the United States is positioned, better than any other subject than we teach in our schools, to begin to explore issues of race and the American experience. It would seem that if race and racism were to be a part of formal social education within our schools that it would fall to the social studies. Indeed the question begs to be asked: If not within the social studies, then where? In fact, what we see in theory and practice is that the power of race and all of its manifestations has been downplayed, marginalized, and ignored. Yet, some race theorists (Omi & Winant, 1994) claim that racism, instead of being an aberration in American history, is actually the norm, and that racism represents a major conceptual theme in American politics and history. By taking this stance, they are placing race, as a socially constructed way of organizing the American experience, at the center of our explanatory lens. "Indeed the idea that America was founded on the ideas of liberty and freedom, nebulous concepts at best, give way to the truth that the United States was founded primarily as a racial state, one whose primary existence was predicated on a racial class system" (Chandler, 2010, p. 29–30).

From a curricular standpoint, this particular counter-narrative can be and many times is problematic for pre-service and in-service teachers. In order to conceptualize the American narrative in a racialized way requires that students (and their teachers) resist commonsense notions received as natural and inherent in the American (re. white) collective consciousness. To navigate the American story with race as a major conceptual framework (or *the* major framework)—requires that students of history rethink the way they understand their beliefs about merit, fairness, power, and the American experience. Teachers must help students begin to let go of the notion that America was founded on "freedom" and come to terms with the fact that colonial explorations/invasions were predicated on ideas of racial superiority, that the founding documents (i.e., the Declaration of Independence and the US Constitution) created a racial state. Race has always been and will remain "at the center of the American experience" (Omi & Winant, 1994, p. 5). From the genesis of the creation of the American political state and its formal documents (i.e., the US Constitution and the Three-Fifths Compromise) to slavery, to racial apartheid, to the civil rights movement and beyond, race has operated as a social marker, serving to define human beings as members of an imagined racial group. The result of this organization has been to define one's political rights, location in the capitalist market system, positionality in the criminal justice system, citizenship status, and one's sense of identity. "The hallmark of this history has been racism, not the abstract ethos of equality . . . all can bear witness to the tragic consequences of racial oppression" (Omi & Winant, 1994, p. 1).

Yet, how is it that race has been relegated to this position within a constellation of other concerns within the curriculum of social studies? How is it that the "color-line" (DuBois, 1989) continues to haunt our nation and be so conspicuous in its absence in our formal and enacted curricula in this country? To begin to answer these questions, we will explore how race has been treated within the social studies curriculum and research.

SOCIAL STUDIES CURRICULUM RESEARCH:
WHAT HAS BEEN DONE

When it comes to addressing the problematic relationship that social studies has with race, Ladson-Billings (2003) points to three specific areas of contestation: 1) the social studies curriculum, 2) the social studies profession, and 3) social studies policies. The social studies curriculum, as currently constituted in the United States, represents a curriculum of distortion, avoidance, and contested, often contradictory, official state narratives. Given that much of the social studies curriculum is driven by the enormous power that textbook publishers have over the process (Ravitch, 2004), students are given a picture of the American polity that has been eviscerated by pressure groups on the left and the right. "The pressure groups of left and right have important points of convergence. Both right-wingers and left-wingers demand that publishers shield children from the words and ideas that contain what they deem 'wrong' models for living" (p. 79). This is an especially alarming fact given that the majority of the instruction that students receive in social studies classes around the nation are largely textbook driven (Goodlad, 1984; Ross, 2001). As Loewen (2007) has shown in *Lies My Teacher Told Me*, the experienced curriculum is indeed a raced one, one in which the narratives of America (like the events themselves) are colored by the racial status quo that exists/existed. In addition to half-truths and omissions in our texts, ethnic minorities are tokenized and Otherized, giving an incoherent, distorted picture of how groups have historically interacted with one another (Wills, 2001). A partial or incoherent race curriculum leaves students to fill in the blanks with conjecture and common sense race explanations (Loewen, 2010).

In this curricular treatment, people of color are best understood as characters in a morality play in which bad things (i.e., racism, removal) occurred, but these events are framed as being an anomaly or being necessary to arrive at our current station. Indigenous peoples are moved to the margins of the formal curriculum from the outset of how they are treated in textbooks. The treatment of American Indians (Rains, 2003) in mainstream history texts serves to distort the narrative to a point to where students can question whether Native Americans had any impact at all on the unfolding of the American polity: "Native Americans are seen as having cordial relations with whites, being obstacles for Manifest Destiny, and eventually succumbing to white progress, never to be discussed again, as though they never existed" (Chandler, 2010, p. 30). Indigenous populations are often fetishizied and stereotyped (Lintner, 2007) in ways that give the impression that the "exotic Indian" is a relic of the far away past, with no real connection to the present day, thus justifying the current racial regime of thought (Lintner, 2004). Without more accurate information on indigenous peoples, students are denied a more complete history of the first Americans and, perhaps more importantly for US history courses, their dealings with the US government (i.e., citizenship status, government treaties) (Wilkins & Lomawaima, 2001).

Similarly, African Americans are given token treatment, with accepted narratives reified at the expense of a more inclusive history of conflict and struggle. They have specific moments within the historical narrative where Black accomplishments are noted, but they, like the Native populations, are relegated to a supporting role, one that is supplementary to the dominant narrative of nationhood and imperialism (although this term is becoming unfashionable, see Blachette, 2010). And, as in the treatment of Native American history, atrocities are downplayed and whitewashed for school consumption. As Lintner (2007) points out, the importance of language is key to the understanding of how groups and their histories are understood. For instance, the debate over the new Texas history standards had as one of its focal points the argument over the usage of the term "Middle Passage." The State Board of Education preferred the term "TransAtlantic Trade" (Blanchette, 2010). The curriculum related to African Americans parallels that of other groups: a small list of accepted heroes (Martin Luther King, Jr.), events (Civil Rights), and ideas (suffrage) are allowed (Ladson-Billings, 2003). But the list of allowed historical ideas is designed to cater towards an American history that stresses the positive aspects of the narrative at the expense of the lived experience of people of color.

As we have previously discussed (Chandler, 2010), Ladson-Billings (2003) also is quick to point out that the social studies profession, the profession whose stated goal is democracy and citizenship training, is silent in the face of calls to diversify its teaching ranks as well as the nature of its inquiry; part of this failure resides in the implementation of old race theory paradigms. Ladson-Billings states, "I am sad to report that at the college and university level, social studies education remains as frozen in its old paradigms as it was in the late 1960s" (p. 5). The policies of the social studies profession are not explicitly directed towards issues of race either: no overt statement about race or racism is made in the standards that govern and organize the social studies; in fact, in the mid-1990s the NCSS eliminated the standing committee that was charged with race and racism in the social studies (Ladson-Billings, 2003). This event combined with the controversy surrounding the proposed boycott of the Anaheim meeting over Proposition 187 in California led several leading educators (Cornbleth, Ladson-Billings) interested in social studies and race to formally discontinue their association with CUFA (Ross, 1998). Marshall (2003) points out that the NCSS's *Curriculum Guidelines for Multicultural Education* intentionally excluded race and racism as subjects in the hopes that it would disappear of its own volition: "We rarely used the term race in the first edition, perhaps because of our vain hope that silence would facilitate racism's disappearance" (as cited in Marshall, 2003, p. 80). This is a prime example of how race, as a subject, in the social studies and multicultural initiatives, is rarely addressed in the research corpus or in the stated goals of practitioner intended policy documents. Rains' (2006) and Nelson and Pang's (2006) treatment of race as a formal topic in two chapters of *The Social Studies Curriculum* (Ross, 2006) represent two of the more critical pieces of research in this area. Rains' piece evaluates the gap between the stated goals of the social studies and the lived experiences of Native American students, and Nelson and Pang (2006) speak to the ways in which race, as a social category, is a construction that is not based on any standard of scientific proof. Both of these chapters serve as exemplars in looking at race with a critical lens and how it plays itself out in the field of the social studies (Chandler, 2010).

Over the past 30 years of research that can be found in the social studies, including research found in the journal *Theory and Research in Social Education* (*TRSE*) and the *Handbook of Research on Social Studies Teaching and Learning* (Shaver, 1991), the topic of race within the social studies curriculum, how teachers think about teaching this topic, and how teachers address this topic within their classrooms, is essentially *marginalized* in the literature. Three examples of how race is making its way into mainstream discussions about social studies can be found in the latest edition of the *Handbook of Research in Social Studies Education* (Levstik & Tyson, 2008), a chapter in Barton's (2006) book *Research Methods in Social Studies Education* by Cynthia Tyson on "Research, Race, and Social Education," and in a special issue of *TRSE* edited by Tyrone Howard and Cynthia Tyson (2004) that dealt specifically with "Race and the Social Studies." The *Handbook of Research in Social Studies Education* improves on the earlier edition in that it deals with race as a constructed identity and how that classification plays itself out in the spheres of citizenship, institutional racism, and diversity (Banks & Nguyen, 2008). Another exemplar of race related research and theory as it pertains to social studies education is found in the four volume *Race, Ethnicity, and Education* (Ross & Pang, 2006) series. In volumes three and four, the topics of colorblindness (Bonilla-Silva & Embrick, 2006; Milner & Ross, 2006), racial development (Dixson, 2006), racialized personal narratives (Laughter, Baker, Williams, Cearley, & Milner, 2006), race pedagogy (Lynn, 2006), and white privilege (Ayanru, Basualdo, & Fleury, 2006; Urrieta & Reidel, 2006) are discussed within the contexts of what meaning race plays in education, and how this shifting, fluid meaning manifests itself in the field of social education (Chandler, 2010).

Race theory and the study of Native American experiences in the context of social studies research have made their way into the research corpus with Lintner (2004, 2007) and Chandler's (2010) work with critical race theory. There has also been some attention given to race in three recent chapters: Epstein and Shiller's (2010) work on racial identity (in Parker [2010] *Social Studies Today*), Merryfield's (2010) work on race and representation, and Segal's (2010) work on race and teaching history (in Heilman, Amthor, & Missias [2010] *Social Studies and Diversity Education: What We Do and Why We Do It*). These three recent publications are much needed in this area in that they give insight into methodological questions of "how" to teach race within the context of social studies classrooms. These books provide possible beginning points by which the pedagogical and curricular discussion about how race plays into school and society can begin.

THE PROBLEM(S) OF TEACHING ABOUT RACE IN THE SOCIAL STUDIES

As stated by W.E.B. DuBois almost a century ago, we are indeed separated by the colorline. The American narrative claims that this line was quickly erased with the Civil War and then the Civil Rights movement, yet a closer look reveals something much different. Given the significance of race in the historical narrative of the United States, and given that this narrative forms how each school child will begin to understand his or her identity in relation to all who are "Other," it is imperative to note just how *thin* the research into race and racism is within the sphere of social studies. From the standpoint of social education research in curriculum and pedagogy, there has been what could be viewed as a shying away from difficult and highly contested issues of race in the United States, despite the foundational importance of such issues in the socio-cultural development of what it means to be an "American."

We feel there are several reasons for the dearth of research, conversation, and teaching about race. First, the potentially explosive nature of race is apparent in our history and it is a concern for teachers who attempt to teach about race. There is a real fear among teachers who have the courage and fortitude to teach about race in our public schools. There are aspects of our students' lived experiences that are diametrically opposed to anti-racist pedagogy and/or more nuanced understandings of America as a racial state; the rupturing of this narrative is, oftentimes, a point of contention with students. Second, the goal of a colorblind society, a society that "sees past race" (a philosophical argument from the Civil Rights Era), prevents teachers, students, and communities from having frank conversations about race and how race plays itself out in school settings and in our national narrative. In this construct, students and teachers alike adopt a stance that denies that race plays any role whatsoever in the collective or individual history of the United States. This is understood as being the goal to which our society should strive—equality. Third, the concept of liberal incrementalism, an idea that racial harmony is a utopian goal that is only achieved through a "slow, upward climb" prevents a break from the past in ways that would fundamentally change the way we view race as a country and as social educators. Lastly, race, as a formal topic of study within the social studies, is slighted by the tendency of education theorists and classroom teachers to deal with race as a part of a larger multicultural narrative of assimilation and societal cohesion.

Given the paucity of research on race within social studies education, NCSS (1994) *does* have statements directed at race and diversity within social studies:

> Students should be helped to construct a pluralist perspective based in diversity. This perspective involves respect for differences of opinion and preference; of race, religion, and gender; of class and ethnicity; and of culture in general. This construction should be based on the realization that differences exist among individuals and the conviction that this diversity can be positive and socially enriching. Students need to learn that the existence of cultural and philosophically differences are not "problems" to be solved; rather, they are healthy and desirable qualities of democratic community life. (pp. 6–7)

As the above statement suggests, the National Council for the Social Studies is not oblivious to the importance of race within social education. The issue is not whether or not we, as a profession, recognize race as a central factor in education and socialization, but rather how we treat the concept pedagogically in public education.

The newest iteration of the NCSS's *National Curriculum Standards for Social Studies* (2010) is also illustrative of how race is treated within the profession. In the "Introduction" to the standards, it states:

> The civic mission of social studies demands the inclusion of all students—addressing cultural, linguistic, and learning diversity that includes similarities and differences based on *race* (italics added), ethnicity, language, religion, gender, sexual orientation, exceptional learning needs, and other educationally and personally significant characteristics of learners. (p. 9)

However, in looking at the "10 Themes of Social Studies" (pp. 14–23), on which the 171 page document is based, the words "race" or "racism" are completely absent. In addition, the standards devote 93 pages to "Snapshots of Practice" in which they describe 60 classroom scenarios/lessons based around the "10 Themes" that are organized by grade level (Early Grades, Middle Grades, High School). Of the 60 "Snapshots of Practice," 6 deal with race, but only tangentially—even failing to use the word race in the lesson descriptions. Perhaps most importantly, the lessons fail to connect our racial past with the racial present.

TEACHERS' FEARS OF TEACHING ABOUT RACE

There is a one powerful psychological element that has contributed to this powerful condition of coded racialized actions—fear. The teaching of racism and the effects of racialized identities within the American narrative have been highly contested and filled with denials and defensiveness (Dei,

2006; Ladson-Billings, 1996). Researchers have found through interviews that teachers are afraid to present a curriculum of race in their classes (Chandler, 2007; Sleeter, 2005). There is a sense that to actually center the social studies curriculum around the concrete racialized effects produced by a narrative of freedom and America as having some great mission can be interpreted as questioning the very meaning that white children are supposed to take away from the American experiment (McIntyre, 1997). This condition often precludes any deep discussion that could interpret such an Anglo-American view of itself as the rightful inheritor of the mission and the American identity.

In addition to being fearful when teaching about race, many white teachers can be "out of their element" when teaching students from different backgrounds and experiences (Ladson-Billings, 1995a,b, 2000). In this way, the teacher is faced with a dual threat: the retribution that may be visited on a teacher for addressing the taboo topic of race *and* the lack of cultural competence to address race in a class where students of color are present (Duesterberg, 1999). Students within our pre-service methods courses often address this very concern. The white students express alarm that the community where they teach will not approve of their teaching about race. Their worry extends into fear of offending students of color as well as white students, or worse, sparking a race-related argument that could lead to violence. It was not that long ago that racial tension in southern high schools flared up to the point of generating physical altercations on large scales, enough to create lock downs at schools (McKnight, personal communication, 2002). A real fear exists that even exploring race history will cause many old wounds to open again and anger flow out (Ellsworth, 1997; Landsman 2001; Rosenberg, 1997; Tatum, 1997).

Other than a piecemeal treatment of multiculturalism (Sleeter, 1994) that dominates many school mission statements and conceptual frameworks, most students do not receive instruction on race during their K–12 experience. From the perspective of white, pre-service teachers, this is a problematic fact given that their college preparation for the field of education is probably not much better; this lack of instruction from the K–12 level through teacher training gives the impression to students, teachers, and society alike, that race, as a formal construct within our society, is a relic of the past, that race plays no role, whatsoever, in the lived experiences of Americans (Ladson-Billings & Tate, 1995). Ironically, when teachers refuse to interrogate race in the classroom as a part of their social education pedagogy, they are implicitly supporting the racial status quo, oftentimes using concepts like colorblindness, which serves to uphold the very racism that they claim they are against (West, 1993). Branch (2003) theorizes that when "teachers affirm that race is irrelevant either by audible words or by their silence about race, they reveal perhaps unwitting, racist assumptions that all people are alike . . . educators who refuse to see racial differences may believe erroneously that they are choosing equity" (pp.110–111).

Many teachers' avoid teaching about race for the simple fact that they do not want to be labeled a racist, others are fearful of their own ingrained notions about race and what may happen in the classroom if conversations commenced (Ellsworth, 1997; Landsman 2001; Rosenberg, 1997; Tatum, 1997), and others remember past difficulties they have had in talking or thinking about race. In short, talking about race is not a positive experience for many teachers, in or out of the classroom, so they actively avoid the subject altogether (Branch, 2003).

The very real fear that teachers have about teaching race related lessons may be, in part, rooted in the concept of racelessness (Branch, 2003). Since whites and people of color experience the world differently in racial terms, "White people rarely see acts of blatant or subtle racism, while minority people experience them all the time" (Tate, 1997, p. 219). In this way, white teachers simply do not place much importance on teaching or thinking about race because they have a different ontological experience with racism. This represents a pedagogical problem for those white teachers who attempt to teach about or represent a racial understanding to students who, in a profound sense of the word, understand racial oppression more intimately than does the teacher. Conversely, students of color are not privy to the ontological understanding(s) of whites who see the world with white supremacist eyes: "If race is not salient in the consciousness of white people, it makes sense that teaching about race would not be important to white teachers" (Branch, 2003, p. 113).

The fear (Kincheloe & Steinberg, 1998) that comes with teaching about race is not only an aspect of the K–12 classroom. In their research on pre-service social studies teachers, Urrieta and Reidel (2006) detail the anger and resistance that they faced when trying to implement race-based lessons and conversations in their classes. Through avoidance, anger, and what the researchers dub "convenient amnesia" the participants "found ways to not fully engage in a critical, multicultural, and social justice analysis of social studies education..." (p. 295). In attempting to teach their social studies education courses in this manner, the researchers attempted to cause "discomfort" in their students, a notion akin to Felman and Laub's (1992) idea of crisis. It should be noted that many teachers avoid these lessons, conversations, and pedagogical stances related to race because it may cause this same discomfort and crisis as they seek to navigate classroom teaching. The fear that teachers report when it comes to teaching about race may represent a method of survival, especially for untenured teachers (Chandler, 2009). This lack of teaching about race, whether caused by fear, raceless understandings of themselves (and Others), or anger, is troubling for all engaged in social education. Our teaching force is becoming more and more "white," while our school populations become less so (Pinar et al., 1995). Given this fact, it is imperative that colleges of education treat race critically, so that future teachers can address this issue in the classroom.

THE MYTH OF THE COLORBLIND SOCIETY

> To argue that we should be colorblind misses the point. In fact, it is an insult to human intelligence to enthuse that "we should not see color." Color is not the problem; it is the interpretation and judgments that we put on color that makes the problem (Dei, 2006, p. 26).

Another reason that race is pushed to the margins in social studies classes is the all-pervasive "colorblind perspective" that permeates American society and education (Chandler & McKnight, 2010). In this popular race trope, people are to convince themselves that they cannot notice or "see" the race of people with whom they come in contact. This is a call to avoid history, societal norms, and tradition so that each person can be treated fairly (i.e., fairness equated with sameness of treatment). In fact, what actually happens when people profess to be colorblind is a bit of mental gymnastics. Social actors see that someone is not like them (i.e., a different race), they have a mental alert that they are not supposed to notice one's race (i.e., engrained colorblindness), and then they must conduct themselves in a way that leads the "Other" to believe that they did not notice that they were a different race, followed by a performance that the actor thinks is in line with "not noticing race." In short, "the colorblind must see color in order to truly deny it" (Branch, 2003, p. 110). In their research on racism and white supremacy, Bonilla-Silva and Embrick (2006) point to the prevalence of "colorblind racism." This is a case in point of how race and racism, as social constructs, change over time and have different meanings and manifestations depending on context. Their work outlined the ways that white participants talked about people of color in ways that represented the "colorblind" philosophy. Strategies employed by participants ranged from speaking about race in abstractions, naturalizing race, decreasing the importance of racial explanations, semantic moves, framing race talk in the "long ago past," and equating the experiences of all immigrant groups. By utilizing these tactics, participants could make overtly racist commentary while simultaneously hiding behind colorblindness. In this way, the racism of 21st century educators might not be as vicious as racism of past years, but this is due to its having gone underground, its changing of words and codes. To quote Bonilla-Silva and Embrick (2006) they "don't see any color, just people" (p. 3). They continue: "What is fundamentally ideological about this new ideology is the myth that keeps all its components together: the idea that race has all but disappeared as a factor shaping the life chances of people in the United States. This myth is the central column supporting the house of colorblindness" (p. 19).

Colorblindness serves the cause of cultural taboos because it creates a situation that labels those that are conscious of race as racists (Hitchcock, 2002). "Therefore, in an effort not to be racist themselves and to treat all children equally, many white teachers try to suppress what they understand about people of color, which leads them to try not to 'see' color" (Sleeter, 2005, p. 248). Colorblind narratives and philosophies are inherently assimilationist in nature. In thinking of race in this way, race, as an organizing structure of social life, is devalued; even perceived "positive" manifestations of race, especially those characteristics that "distinguish us from one another" (Gotanda, 1995, p. 269) are also discarded. Also implicated in discussions about white privilege and the cult of racial invisibility is a dualism that simultaneously acknowledges and problematizes discussions and pedagogy related to race. As Apple (2000) writes:

> It would not be possible to understand the history, current status, and multiple effects of educational policy in the United Kingdom or the United States without placing race as a core element of one's analysis. Placing race at the center is less easy than one might expect, for one must do this with due recognition of its complexity. Race is not a stable category. What it means, how it is used and by whom, how it is mobilized in public discourse, and its role in educational...policy—all of this is contingent and historical. (p. 99)

Racelessness and adherence to the colorblind perspective, which serves to diminish the role that race plays in contemporary society, can be examined through four frames utilized by whites to justify the status quo: abstract liberalism, naturalization, cultural racism, and minimization of racism (Bonilla-Silva, 2003). Within the frame of abstract liberalism, whites give racial dialogue a moralistic and sensible tone in arguing that race does not play a role in contemporary society. It is also characterized by the notions of *individual* assessments of systemic racism and the idea that people have *choices* in social matters—choices that are not impacted by the social structure. The frame of naturalization suggests that racist attitudes and actions are biologically and/or culturally normal for persons of a certain group. By normalizing certain behaviors (i.e., only white people attending a certain church), the "myth of nonracialism" (p. 28) is maintained. Cultural racism is characterized by assigning certain behaviors (socially constructed notions) to a group of people (i.e., African Americans, Asians, etc.).

Within this mindset, racism is ignored and explained away by commonsensical ways of viewing Other groups. These assignments of supposed cultural attributes that are assumed to be essential to that group serve to explain why certain groups are in their current "situation." These white referenced behavioral assignments can be positive (i.e., Asians do well in school because they respect authority) or negative (i.e., "too many blacks on welfare") (p. 28). Lastly, minimalization of racism is the diminishing of importance assigned to the role that race plays in contemporary society. Inherent in this white supremacist logic is the notion of progress—that things in the past were far worse than they are now and that "race relations" are getting better with the passage of time (Bonilla-Silva, 2003).

LIBERAL INCREMENTALISM

> The frames of any dominant racial ideology are set paths for interpreting information and operate as cul-de-sacs because, after people invoke them, they explain racial phenomena in a predictable manner—as if they were getting on a one-way street without exits (Bonilla-Silva & Embrick, 2006, p. 5).

Liberal incrementalism is a relic of the civil rights movement in which it is believed that improving race relations will follow a linear progression over time. This notion of a steady upward climb towards a heretofore unrecognized racial harmony is used by all racial groups, to differing degrees, to explain a racial narrative of progress and hope. Essentially, liberal incrementalism represents a long standing race theory in America, and it is through this lens that some social studies teachers attempt to theorize about race (Chandler, 2009). Darder and Torres (2009) outline race in ways that differ from the individualistic, modernist concept of race. They argue that race be thought of as 1) an ideology rooted in capitalist expansion, 2) categories that mark people for participation in political and economic arenas, and 3) as a diverse construction (i.e., there are diverse and differing racisms that are historically contingent). Locating race within a matrix that assumes a systematic oppression, one that is conceptually braided with politics and economics, one that is, essentially, a moving target, problematizes the entire modern race project—especially liberal incrementalism and the "natural-ness" of race. Said (1993) points out the ways in which dominant forms of knowledge and seeing the world are predicated on a necessary *Otherizing* of oppressed people:

> These identities are today analyzed not as God-given essences. . . . In an important sense we are dealing with the formation of cultural identities understood not as essentializations...but as contrapuntal ensembles, for it is the case that no identity can ever exist by itself and without an array of opposites, negatives, oppositions: Greeks always require barbarians, and Europeans Africans, Orientals. (p. 52)

A major component of white supremacy in society and in the minds of teachers is its invisibility (McIntosh, 1997), the fact that its power is misrecognized. This helps to explain why researchers report that white teachers are oblivious to the idea of white supremacy because they view racial relations as a non-issue, and instead frame the discussion(s) around the cults of merit and social mobility (Sleeter, 2005). White resistance to unpopular racial policy represents an undying "commitment to unearned privilege for whites"—a privilege that is economic as well as social (Williams, 2003, p. 119).

Even poor whites have historically held on to the notion of their own whiteness as a form of valued property that kept them *socially* superior to blacks. It is the invisibility of this power that serves to create the hegemony that serves white supremacist discourse in contemporary American politics. Lipsitz (1998) writes, "Whiteness never has to speak its name, never has to acknowledge its role as an organizing principle in social and cultural relations" (p. 1). By being white in present-day America, people inherit the culture and heritage of the historical effects of slavery and white supremacy (Hitchcock, 2002). This is a facet of race relations that people of color seem to understand much more than whites who are blind to the power of the status quo (Lawrence & Tatum, 1997; Sue, 2003). Mills (2003) writes that the reason we (as a nation) do not see racial oppression in objective, political terms is that we see our racial choices in sterile, rational, biological terms; therefore, race seems so natural that it does not even appear on our "radar screens" (p. 170). In his study of white social studies teachers, Chandler (2007) found this personal race theorizing in the teachers he studied. In interviews, one participant claimed "And I firmly believe this, call me an idealist, call me old fashioned. I don't care who you are, where you're from, who your parents are, what color your skin, what your religion is, you have the opportunity, in this country to be successful. I firmly believe that" (p. 188).

Furthermore, white teachers often deny the importance of race as an authentic (i.e., "We're all the same") social category, professing the color-blind perspective in their classrooms (Sleeter, 2005). By claiming that we are all similar (i.e., hallmark of white supremacy) that has the impact of subordinating Other group's culture and adopting the mainstream, white culture (hooks, 1996). What is clear, however, is that researchers do not fully understand the complex issues that surface when white teachers attempt to teach or discuss the topic of race in the social studies classroom (DiPardo & Fehn, 2000).

In Kailin's (2002) ethnographic study of white teachers in the Lakeview school district, she found that white teachers see racism not as a systemic problem influencing all aspects of American life, but rather as individual problems that people have with the way they "think" about others. To them, racism was constituted in one's overt actions and comments. In addition, racism was thought to be outside the realm of their particular community, which was considered by the teachers to be liberal and very open-minded. Half of the respondents in this study revealed that they believed that racism and its manifestation in society was due to black people, rather than whites. The reasons for this line of thought ranged from white beliefs that black parents did not value education, black students came from bad home environments, black students were intimidating, black parents were racists, hallway control problems were due to black students, and that black students were allowed to "get away with stuff."

Forty percent of the white respondents felt that racism in their school district was due to the way that white staff members contributed to racism. Responses ranged from teachers and students making racist remarks, white parents being racist, white staff members treating black staff members poorly, and overall intolerance by white teachers relative to black students. Other findings attributed racism in the school district to *natural* factors such as institutional or cultural reasons. Responses ranged from the naturalness of self-segregation, to racism in school materials/curriculum. It is important to note, however, that the overwhelming majority of responses blamed either white or black people for the causes of racism, rather than the structural set-up of schooling as the culprit for racism in schools. It is an important, albeit tacitly acknowledged aspect of racism, that biological determinism plays a major role in race thought. The idea that race is a "particular human trait...biologically determined and thus consistent both for individuals and for the group they belong to" (Dei, 2006, p. 27) is a hallmark of institutional and societal racism. Other than being a category that is on problematic philosophical and biological ground (Haney-Lopez, 1995), thinking of race as fixed and natural also serves to paralyze and squelch action on the part of students, teachers, and policy makers (Ayers, 1997).

Critical race theorists reject the liberal, traditional paradigms of change that involve notions of the "civil rights crusade as a long, slow, but always upward pull; this line of thought is flawed because it fails to understand the limits of current legal paradigms to serve as catalysts for social change and because of its emphasis on incrementalism" (Ladson-Billings, 1999, p. 13). White people, and by extension white teachers, have been miseducated about the role that merit plays in so-called neutral institutions, such as schools, preventing them from capturing or understanding the structural and institutional aspects of race in society (Kailin, 2002); this white ignorance is due partly to the ways that multicultural education is framed and conceptualized in American schools. The following section will address the topic of race in the social studies through the lens of multiculturalism.

RACE GETS LOST IN THE
MULTICULTURAL EDUCATION DISCUSSION

Multiculturalism is not the philosophical transcendence of racism, only its negative recognition (Welsh, 2006, p. 92).

Many times, the discussion of race is lost among competing visions of what it means to have a multicultural society and what role schools should have in this vision (Sleeter, 2000a). Multicultural education, writ large, "has not yet become a central part of the curriculum regularly offered to all students...Many are unconvinced of its worth or its value in developing academic skills and building unified national community" (Gay, 2004, p. 316). There seems to be almost unanimous agreement among teacher educators that race should be a topic *covered* within a multicultural framework—the debate is found in the "centrality of race" in these discussions (Dixson, 2006, p. 21). In this formulation of the "race question" vis-à-vis multiculturalism, race is but one item to be considered among a constellation of other cultural considerations. This tangential treatment of race, is a main reason why so little change occurs at the curricular level (Dixson, 2006). In the rationale of the *NCSS Curriculum Guidelines for Multicultural Education* (1976/1991, A Rationale for Ethnic Pluralism and Multicultural Education), it states:

> Because ethnicity, race, and class are important in the lives of many citizens of the United States, it is essential that all members of our society develop multicultural literacy, that is, a solidly based understanding of racial, ethnic, and cultural groups and their significance in U.S. society and throughout the world.

The document also outlines "Principles of Ethnic and Cultural Diversity" in which the word race is not even used to describe these principles. In examining the actual Curriculum Guidelines for schools, of the 23 position statements, only one even mentions the word race in its title (#14: *The multicultural curriculum should include the continuous study of the cultures, historical experiences, social realities, and existential conditions of ethnic and cultural groups, including a variety of racial compositions*).

Furthermore, "NCSS has issued no position statements focusing on or alluding to either race or racism as a specific topic of impact or significance in citizenship education" (Marshall, 2003, p. 80). The *Curriculum Guidelines on Multicultural Education* (1976/1991), although they have been revised since their first issuance, still do not address the impact of race on social studies pedagogy or education (Marshall, 2003). Marshall (2003) continues:

> Version two...says nothing about the nature of racist microaggression students as well as teachers of color continue to encounter in schools and that diminish the experience for all...no discussion is included on the myriad of ways that racism manifests in schools...curriculum, policy, and community structures are complicit in perpetuating the devalued status of children and youth of color and the depleted quality of the education they receive. (p. 81)

Some scholars (e.g., Coffey, 2000) locate the problem with utilizing the multicultural lens in the ways in which we employ the word *culture*. "Culture is not simply an empirical phenomenon, and the commonsense approach to it as though it were obscures its relation to value, epistemological pursuits, and subject formation, all significant concerns for multiculturalism" (Coffey, 2000, p. 37). Multicultural education classes, in addition to ignoring race via colorblind perspectives, sometimes serve to contribute to the reproduction and duplication that they are designed to interrupt (Lesko & Bloom, 2000). Multicultural educational attempts often fail in that "the tensions between and among these differences is rarely interrogated, presuming a unity of difference," assuming that all difference is equal (Ladson-Billings & Tate, 1995, p. 178). Ladson-Billings (1995a) charges that current multicultural initiatives are doomed to the same fate as the civil rights legislation of the 1950s–1960s—that they will offer incremental, rather than radical change in educational institutions. These initiatives fail largely because they "reduce difference to pluralism and attempt to erase racial power while simultaneously holding onto inherited privilege" (Chalmers, 1997, p. 68) and because their efforts are still framed and understood in incremental, rather than substantive, change (Dixon & Rousseau, 2005). In essence, multiculturalism serves to mask the discrepancies between the lofty language of "culture" and "tolerance" to the point where culture, as a subject *in toto*, is homogenized. In this way, particularly in curriculum materials, culture finds itself situated in a narrative of tolerance, acceptance, and tokenism, thus employing multiculturalism to essentialize the peoples of the world (Mahalingam & McCarthy, 2000). This is most obvious when textbooks and other curriculum materials categorize people into units like "Asian American" and/or catalogue their "accomplishments" as part of the formal curriculum (Chandler, 2007).

Within the context of ever increasing diversity, the response to teaching about race via multiculturalism is to treat "culture" as a "preexistent, unchanging deposit, consisting of a rigidly bounded set of elite or folkloric knowledges, values, experiences, and linguistic practices specific to particular groups" rather than stress the fluid, shifting notions of culture (McCarthy Giardina, Harewood, & Park, 2005, p. 155). As our nation becomes more and more diverse, the most common response to multicultural education, and by extension social studies education, is to stifle critical (i.e., unfolding, non-essentialized) notions of race by instituting programs of cultural standardization (McCarthy et al., 2005). In social studies classrooms, teachers work within environments where particular kinds of knowledge are privileged and guarded; school structures and commonsense ways of thinking (or not thinking) about race and privilege (within the context of a multicultural mindset) can discourage and squelch open discussions about race. In addition, the community context can serve to normalize any discussions that are outside the comfort level of school employees and students, serving to safeguard dominant white images of themselves (Chalmers, 1997; DiPardo & Fehn, 2000). Race is often lost in the multicultural shuffle because the term "multicultural" is a "buzzword . . . undefined" and "tends to lie down with any perspective, any orientation. . . . It is a rather elusive and amorphous term" (West, 1993, p. 7). The ways in which multiculturalism is conceptualized may reinforce many of the strongly held beliefs based on the ways we think about diversity. In fact, the idea that race and its manifestation are permanent realities (i.e., fixed social arrangements) are in opposition to what we know about race—it is a social construction with a contingent history of its own (Welsh, 2006). In this way, race, as conceptualized by multiculturalists in the social studies, is organized as being collectivist (i.e., the power of sameness across a perceive race), relativistic (i.e., since no worldview is better than any other, then racism should be viewed in context), and deterministic (i.e., since multicultural thought reifies "culture" to be a fixed determinant in social interactions) (Welsh, 2006, 2007).

Sleeter (1999) outlines four conservative critiques of the umbrella term "multiculturalism": (1) that the term is used by radical, fringe members of society that do not represent the real needs and desires people of color; (2) that the term places extreme attention on the differences of race and ethnicity, which conservatives regard as divisive; (3) that multiculturalism is academically weaker than traditional curricula; and (4) that "multicultural education attacks the problem of minority students' underachievement by advocating exercises in self-esteem rather than hard work and by substituting 'relevance' of subjects studied for instruction in solid academics" (Sleeter, 1999, p. 269). Conservative backlash against multiculturalism may explain the reasons why the field does not approach divisive topics such as race. This aversion technique, combined with the idea that multiculturalism is a poor substitute for the canon of European knowledge, has created a weak platform for the examination of race in society. Furthermore, utilizing the framework of multiculturalism is a weak tool to teach about race because teachers oftentimes view the multicultural project as irrelevant (Sleeter, 1994).

The debate over multiculturalism is not likely to wane soon in light of the fact that the teaching force is predominantly white and is becoming increasingly less diverse (Kailin, 2002; Sleeter, 2001b, 2005). Much of the anti-multicultural forces in education use this term to denote things that are anti-Western, anti-democratic, and anti-universal (Banks, 2000). At the heart of multicultural education is the concept of *process*; its goal is to create a society that lives up to the creed of its founding. The ideals in the founding documents—the Declaration of Independence, the Constitution, the Bill of Rights—are things that we must work constantly in a process to obtain. "Consequently, within a democratic, pluralistic society, multicultural education is a continuing process that never ends" (Banks, 2000, p. 255). In a process-outcome educational system dominated by standardization of curricula and testing, a process education is under attack. Within the battle over multiculturalism and the "color line" in schools is the epistemological argument over what kind of citizen schools (i.e., social studies) should be producing. Is the goal to produce citizens who vote in elections and pay taxes or is it to produce global thinking citizens who will fight systemic inequalities and injustice (Malott & Pruyn, 2006)? The current state of the social studies (through a multicultural lens) suggests the former.

What is inherently necessary in social studies education is an examination of the structural nature of racism. Current race theorizing by teachers and many in the public takes on an individual, fractured stance, one that allows the social being to criticize racism and uphold white supremacist viewpoints (sometimes unwittingly) simultaneously. Sleeter (2005) explains:

> While a psychological analysis of racism focuses on what is in people's heads and asks how to change it, a structural analysis focuses on distribution of power and wealth across groups and on how those of European ancestry attempt to retain supremacy while groups of color try to challenge it. A structural analysis assumes that how white people view race rests on their vested interests in justifying their power and privileges. (p. 244)

To conceptualize the "race problem" in these terms is in stark contrast to the liberal incrementalism and meritocracy that is such a powerful strain of American political and educational thought. In an election year (2010) where campaign commercials in several states are stressing the "racial" (i.e., Tea Party Activists, anti-immigration forces, etc.) aspects of American life, such analysis in our social studies classrooms is needed. In fact, the "culture wars" of the 1990s have shifted to a decidedly racial tone in this new century, even as many claim that America has gone "beyond" race with the election of Barack Obama as President.

CONSIDERATIONS: WHERE TO GO FROM HERE

The past is never dead. It's not even past.
— William Faulkner, *Requiem for a Nun* (1959)

At the beginning we presented the view that a national identity is predicated upon the stories told, meaning that to a large degree identity is socially negotiated and constructed. As America has been in social studies constructed primarily as a white narrative, it will become even more important to unearth what is buried beneath such assumptions. Specifically important will be the understanding, as Frantz Fanon discussed throughout many works (1967, 1970) that there is no "white" without "black" and vice versa. The construction of one concept of color is based upon inclusions and exclusions. What is excluded, the qualities and characteristics, that one

group decides equals themselves is thrown onto an "Other." The significance in this process is the basic political point—"who gets to decide." In
America it has been the Anglo-European male who has managed to dictate
the terms of the narrative. But by doing so, as Pinar et al. (1995) reveal, the
whole history of America basically became about the "Other" on most levels
of existence:

> One cannot understand the identity of one without appreciating how it is
> implied by the other. So it is that European-Americans cannot hope to un-
> derstand themselves unless they are knowledgeable and knowing of those
> they have constructed as 'different,' as 'other.' The sequestered suburban
> white student is uninformed, unless he or she comes to understand how he
> or she is also—in the historical, cultural, indeed psychological sense—African
> American. Because 'white' does not exist apart from 'black,' the two co-exist,
> intermingle, and the repression of this knowledge stood as racialized beings;
> knowledge of who we have been, who we are, and who we will become is a
> story or text we construct. In this sense curriculum—our construction and
> reconstruction of this knowledge for conversation with the young—is racial
> text. (p. 330).

For Pinar et al. (1995) the key to this text, this story, is cultural literacy, the elemental facts of a history, geography, and so forth, of a culture.
In fact, this cultural literacy has been distorted in American curriculum
throughout its history of schooling, for the transmission of the facts has presented only that which can be constituted as Eurocentric and patriarchal.
If, as Castenell and Pinar (1993), along with Fanon (1967, 1970) claim,
that much of the story has not been told, or has only been told from white
eyes, then the other history, the history of the "other," must be revealed
and told in order for there to be some hope for American students and
their cultural knowledge and identity, even for their psychological wellness
(Pinar et al., 1995). These different stories, the one told and the one hidden must somehow come into conversation. From a curricular standpoint,
perhaps the best starting point is to acknowledge that race and its modern
manifestations has a history of its own (Ignatiev, 1995; Painter, 2010; Popkin, 1999; Takaki, 1993). Too often, teachers and their students treat the
concept of race as a God-given essence. If race has a history that has been
constructed by humans, then it can be challenged and interrogated. As
Freire (1998) reminds us our notions of citizenship, which are historically
race based (Brown & Urrietia, 2010) in the United States are but constructions that can be challenged:

> Yes, citizenship—above all in a society like ours, of such authoritarian and
> racially, sexually, and class-based discriminatory traditions—is really an inven-
> tion, a political production. In this sense, one who suffers any (or all) of the
> discriminations . . . does not enjoy the full exercise of citizenship as a peaceful

and recognized right. On the contrary, it is a right to be reached and whose conquest makes democracy grow substantively. Citizenship implies freedom. . . . Citizenship is not obtained by chance: It is a construction that, never finished, demands we fight for it. It demands commitment, political clarity, coherence, decision. For this reason a democratic education cannot be realized apart from an education of and for citizenship. (Freire, 1998, p. 90)

There seems, in denying that race has played an important role historically, to be an unavoidable dialectic between beliefs that "history matters" and impacts the present, and the belief in incremental, indisputable progress and American exceptionalism. In fact, the profession of history would cease to "matter" in the school systems, if it were not, in some sense, useful or valuable to creating "effective citizens." It is ironic then, that the same profession that argues that history is useful and that history "matters" is the same group who, when it comes to race, denies its importance in contemporary times. Oftentimes, teachers urge their students to try to make connections between the past and the present; this is perhaps a "natural" part of doing history. But this attempt at connecting the past with the present is avoided when it comes to race, in effect, denying its importance. The white supremacist argument that race does not matter because "it happened a long time ago" (Chandler, 2007) seems to suggest that the only qualifier that a subject must meet is recency (i.e., recent history matters more than older history), although this would disqualify most of the concepts that historians grapple with as a part of their professional lives. It seems that this belief in progress, particularly racial progress, is the conceptual moat surrounding the castle that is "Race in America" that prevents us from treating race, within the context of our history classes, as a proper topic for interrogation.

This is, perhaps, the nature of race in America. Space needs finding— classrooms, conferences, journals, books such as this—in the sphere of social education where scholars from all sides of the political spectrum can enter into what William Pinar (2004) has called a "complicated conversation." In this conversation, each position is carefully analyzed in terms of its assumptions and foundational theoretical principles, which would allow a beginning point by which to dialogue. At this moment in history, arguments unfortunately included usually are reduced to two extreme sides that have been deemed "left" and "right." From the so called "left" is the argument that race over determines every aspect of a person's life; on the "right" there is a disregarding that race plays a role in social life, that the US has arrived at a post-racial world with the election of Barak Obama in 2008. Both of these positions need critical analysis to show the inherent limitations of each line of thought. From that analysis, then, could come the beginning of a conversation within social education that may actually produce new knowledge that other disciplines could make use of. Unfortunately, instead of attempting to sift through and make sense of the different types of literature about race—from the traditional belief that race is a subject dealt with and solved, to the critical race understanding that race "colors" how we see everything—social studies research has been barely audible.

REFERENCES

Apple, M. (2000). Racing toward educational reform: The politics of markets and standards. In R. Mahalingam & C. McCarthy(Eds.), *Multicultural curriculum: New directions for social theory, practice, and policy* (pp. 84–107). New York: Routledge.

Ayanru, R., Basualdo, E., & Fleury, S. (2006). "If only we could find some!" The white privilege of teacher education. In E. W. Ross (Ed.), *Race, ethnicity, and education, Vol. 4: Racism and anti-racism in education* (pp. 263–278). Westport: Praeger.

Ayers, W. (1997). Racing in America. In M. Fine, L. Powell, L. Weis, & M. Wong (Eds.), *Off white: Readings in race, power, and society* (pp. 129–136). New York: Routledge.

Banks, J. A. (2000). Multicultural education and curriculum transformation. In F. W. Parkay & G. Hass (Eds.), *Curriculum planning: A contemporary approach* (pp. 254–263). Boston: Allyn & Bacon.

Banks, J. A., & Nguyen, D. (2008). Diversity and citizenship education: Historical, theoretical, and philosophical issues. In L. Levstik & C. Tyson (Eds.), *The handbook of research in social studies education* (pp. 137–151). New York: Routledge Press.

Barton, K. (Ed.). (2006). *Research methods in social studies education: Contemporary issues and perspectives.* Greenwich: Information Age.

Blanchette, S. (2010). Education or indoctrination? The development of social studies standards in Texas. *Social Education, 74*(4), 199–203.

Bonilla-Silva, E. (2003). *Racism without racists: Colorblind racism and the persistence of racial inequality in the United States.* Lanham, MD: Rowman & Littlefield Publishers.

Bonilla-Silva, E., & Embrick, D. (2006). The (white) color of color blindness in twenty-first century Amerika. In E. W. Ross (Ed.), *Race, ethnicity, and education, Vol. 4: Racism and anti-racism in education* (pp. 3–24). Westport: Praeger.

Branch, A. (2003). A look at race in the national standards for the social studies: Another bad check. In G. Ladson-Billings (Ed.), *Critical race theory perspectives on social studies: The profession, policies, and curriculum* (pp. 99–122). Greenwich, CT: Information Age Publishing.

Brown, A., & Urrieta, L. (2010). Gumbo and Menudo and the scraps of citizenship: Interest convergence and citizen-making for African Americans and Mexican Americans in U.S. education. In A. DeLeon & E. W. Ross (Eds.), *Critical theories, radical pedagogies, & social education: New perspectives for social studies education* (pp. 65–84). The Netherlands: Sense Publishers.

Castenell, Jr., L., & Pinar, W. (1993). Introduction. In L. Castenell, Jr. & W. Pinar (Eds.), *Understanding curriculum as racial text: Representations of identity and difference in education* (pp. 1–30). Albany, NY: State University of New York Press.

Chalmers, V. (1997). *White out: Multicultural performances in a progressive school.* In M. Fine, L. Powell, L. Weis, & M. Wong (Eds.), *Off white: Readings in race, power, and society* (pp. 66–78). New York: Routledge.

Chandler, P. (2007). *White teachers, social studies, and race: A case study of the intersection of teachers' habitus and pedagogy.* Ann Arbor: UMI Dissertations.

Chandler, P. (2009). Blinded by the white: White teachers, social studies, and raceless pedagogies. *Journal of Educational Thought, 43*(3), 259–288.

Chandler, P. (2010). Critical race theory and social studies: Centering the Native American experience. *The Journal of Social Studies Research, 34*(1), 29–58.

Chandler, P., & McKnight, D. (2010). The failure of social education in the United States: A critique of teaching the national story from "white" colourblind eyes. *Journal of Critical Education Policy Studies, 7*(2), 218–248.

Coffey, M. (2000). What puts the "culture" in "multiculturalism"? An analysis of culture, government, and the politics of Mexican identity. In R. Mahalingam & C. McCarthy (Eds.), *Multicultural curriculum: New directions for social theory, practice, and policy* (pp. 37–55). New York: Routledge.

Darder, A., & Torres, R. (2009). After race: An introduction. In A. Darder, M. Baltodano, & R. Torres (Eds.), *The critical pedagogy reader* (pp. 150–166). New York: Routledge.

Dei, G. J. (2006). "We cannot be color-blind": Race, antiracism, and the subversion of dominant thinking. In E. W. Ross (Ed.), *Race, ethnicity, and education, Vol. 4: Racism and anti-racism in education* (pp. 25–42). Westport: Praeger.

DiPardo, A., & Fehn, B. (2000). Depoliticizing multicultural education: The return to normalcy in a predominately white high school. *Theory and Research in Social Education. 28*(2), 170–192.

Dixon, A., & Rousseau, C. (2005). And we are still not saved: Critical race theory in education ten years later. *Race, Ethnicity, & Education, 8*(1), 7–27.

Dixson, A. (2006). What's race got to do with it? Race, racial identity development, and teacher preparation. In H. Milner & E. W. Ross (Eds.), *Race, ethnicity, and education, Vol. 3: Racial identity in education* (pp. 19–36). Westport: Praeger.

DuBois, W. E. B. (1989). *The souls of Black folk.* New York: Bantam.

Duesterberg, L. M. (1999). Theorizing race in the context of learning to teach. *Teachers College Record, 100*(4), 751–775.

Ellsworth, E. (1997). Double binds of whiteness. In M. Fine, L. Powell, L. Weis, & M. Wong (Eds.), *Off white: Readings in race, power, and society* (pp. 259–269). New York: Routledge.

Epstein, T., & Shiller, J. (2010). Race, gender, and the teaching and learning of national history. In W. Parker (Ed.), *Social studies today: Research and practice* (pp. 95–104). New York: Routledge.

Fanon, F. (1967). *Black skin, white masks.* New York: Grove Press.

Fanon, F. (1970). *A dying colonialism.* New York: Grove Press.

Faulkner, W. (1959). *Requiem for a nun.* New York: Random House.

Felman, S., & Laub, D. (1992). *Testimony: Crises of witnessing in literature, psychoanalysis, and history.* New York : Routledge.

Freire, P. (1998). *Teachers as cultural workers: Letters to those who dare to teach.* Boulder, CO: Westview Publishers.

Gates, H. (1985). Introduction of "race," writing, and difference. *Critical Inquiry, 12*(1), 1–20.

Gay, G. (2004). The importance of multicultural education. In D. Flinders & S. Thornton (Eds.), *The curriculum studies reader* (pp. 315–321). New York: Routledge.

Goodlad, J. (1984). *A place called school.* New York: McGraw-Hill.

Gotanda, N. (1995). A critique of "our constitution is colorblind." In K. Crenshaw, N. Gotanda, G. Peller, & K. Thomas (Eds.), *Critical race theory: The key writings that formed the movement* (pp. 257–275). New York: The New Press.

Haney-Lopez, I. (1995). The social construction of race. In R. Delgado (Ed.), *Critical race theory: The cutting edge* (pp. 191–203). Philadelphia, PA: Temple University Press.

Heilman, E., Amthor, R., & Missias, M. (Eds.). (2010). *Social studies and diversity education: What we do and why we do it.* New York: Routledge.

Hitchcock, J. (2002). *Lifting the white veil: An exploration of white American culture in a multicultural context.* New Jersey: Crandall, Dostie, & Douglass Books.

hooks, b. (1996). *Killing rage: Ending racism.* New York: Henry Holt & Company.

Howard, T., & Tyson, C. (Eds.). (2004). Race and the social studies [Special issue]. *Theory and research in social education, 32*(4).

Ignatiev, N. (1995). *How the Irish became white.* New York: Routledge Press.

Kailin, J. (2002). *Antiracist education: From theory to practice.* Lanham: Rowman & Littlefield Publishers.

Kincheloe, J., & Steinberg. (1998). Addressing the crisis of whiteness: Reconfiguring white identity in a pedagogy of whiteness. In J. Kincheloe, S. Steinberg, N. Rodriguez, & R. Chennault (Eds.), *White reign: Deploying whiteness in America* (pp. 3–30). New York: St. Martin Press.

Ladson-Billings, G. (1995a). But that's just good teaching! The case for culturally relevant pedagogy. *Theory Into Practice, 34(3),* 159–165.

Ladson-Billings, G. (1995b). Toward a theory of culturally relevant pedagogy. *American Educational Research Journal, 32,* 465–492.

Ladson-Billings, G. (1996). Multicultural issues in the classroom: Race, class, and gender. In R. Evans & D. Saxe (Eds.), *Handbook on teaching social issues* (pp. 101–110). Washington, DC: NCSS Publications.

Ladson-Billings, G. (1999). Just what is critical race theory and what's it doing in a *nice* field like education? In L. Parker, D. Deyhle, & S. Villenas (Eds.), *Race is . . . race isn't: Critical race theory and qualitative studies in education* (pp. 7–30). Boulder, CO: Westview Press.

Ladson-Billings, G. (2000). Racialized discourses and ethnic epistemologies. In N. Denzin & Y. Lincoln (Eds.), *Handbook of qualitative research* (2nd ed., pp. 257–277). Thousand Oaks, CA: Sage Publications.

Ladson-Billings, G. (2003). *Critical race theory: Perspectives on social studies.* Greenwich, CT: Information Age Publishing.

Ladson-Billings, G., & Tate, W. (1995). Toward a critical race theory of education. In A. Darder, M. Baltodano, & R. Torres (Eds.), *The critical pedagogy reader* (pp. 167–182). New York: Routledge.

Landsman, J. (2001). *A white teacher talks about race.* Lanham, MD: Scarecrow Publishers.

Laughter, J., Baker, A., Williams, S., Cearley, N., & Milner, H. (2006). The power of story: How personal narratives show us what teachers can do to fight racism. In H. Milner & E.W. Ross (Eds.), *Race, ethnicity, and education, Vol. 3: Racial identity in education* (pp. 147–166). Westport: Praeger.

Lawrence, S., & Tatum, B. D. (1997). White educators as allies: Moving from awareness to action. In M. Fine, L. Powell, L. Weis, & M. Wong (Eds.). *Off white: Readings in race, power, and society* (pp. 333–342). New York: Routledge.

Lesko, N., & Bloom, L. (2000). The haunting of multicultural epistemology. In R. Mahalingam & C. McCarthy (Eds.), *Multicultural curriculum: New directions for social theory, practice, and policy* (pp. 242–260). New York: Routledge.

Levstik, L., & Tyson, C. (Eds.). (2008). *The handbook of research in social studies education.* New York. Routledge Press.

Lintner, T. (2004). The savage and the slave: Critical race theory, racial stereotyping, and the teaching of American history. *Journal of Social Studies Research, 28*(1), 27–32.

Lintner, T. (2007). Critical race theory and the teaching of American history: Power, perspective, and practice. *Social Studies Research and Practice, 2*(1), 103–116.

Lipsitz, G. (1998). *The possessive investment in whiteness: How white people profit from identity politics.* Philadelphia, PA: Temple University Press.

Loewen, J. W. (2007). *Lies my teacher told me: Everything your American history textbook got wrong.* New York: Touchstone.

Loewen, J. W. (2010). *Teaching what really happened: How to avoid the tyranny of textbooks and get students excited about doing history.* New York: Teachers College.

Lynn, M. (2006). Toward a critical race pedagogy. In E. W. Ross (Ed.), *Race, ethnicity, and education, Vol. 4: Racism and anti-racism in education* (pp. 191–206). Westport: Praeger.

Mahalingam, R., & McCarthy, C. (2000). Rethinking multiculturalism and curricular knowledge for the twenty-first century. In R. Mahalingam & C. McCarthy (Eds.), *Multicultural curriculum: New directions for social theory, practice, and policy* (pp. 1–11). New York: Routledge.

Malott, C., & Pruyn, M. (2006). Marxism and critical multicultural social studies. In. E. W. Ross (Ed.), *The social studies curriculum: Purposes, problems, and possibilities* (pp. 157–170). Albany: SUNY.

Marshall, P. L. (2003). The persistent deracialization of the agenda for democratic citizenship education: Twenty years of rhetoric and unreality in social studies position statements. In G. Ladson-Billings (Ed.), *Critical race theory perspectives on social studies: The profession, policies, and curriculum* (pp. 71–98). Greenwich, CT: Information Age Publishing.

McCarthy, C., Giardina, M., Harewood, S., & Park, J. (2005). Contesting culture: Identity and curriculum dilemmas in the age of globalization ,postcolonialism, and multiplicity. In C. McCarthy, W. Crichlow, G. Dimitriadis, & N. Dolby (Eds.), *Race, identity, and representation in education* (pp. 153–166). New York: Routledge Press.

McIntosh, P. (1997). White privilege and male privilege: A personal account of coming to see correspondences through work in women's studies. In R. Delgado

& J. Stefancic (Eds.), *Critical white studies: Looking behind the mirror* (pp. 291–299). Philadelphia, PA: Temple University Press.

McIntyre, A. (1997). *Making meaning of whiteness: Exploring racial identity with white teachers.* Albany: State University of New York Press.

McKnight, D. (nd). Personal remembrance and interviews with classmates about 1977 series of fights between whites and blacks at West Monroe High School in West Monroe, Louisiana that led to police presence and fear among both blacks and whites.

McKnight, D. (2003). *Schooling, the Puritan imperative, and the molding of an American national identity: Education's errand into the wilderness.* Mahwah, NJ: Lawrence Erlbaum.

Merryfield, M. (2010). A meeting on the Congo: Race, voice, and representation. In E. Heliman, R. Amthor, & M. Missias (Eds.), *Social studies and diversity education: What we do and why we do it* (pp. 182–184). New York: Routledge.

Miller, P. (1957). *Errand into the wilderness.* Cambridge, MA, Belnap Press, Harvard.

Mills, C. W. (2003). *From class to race: Essays in white Marxism and black radicalism.* Lanham, MD: Rowman and Littlefield Publishers.

Milner, R., & Ross, E. W. (2006). The color-blind myth and why racial identity matters in education. In H. Milner & E.W. Ross (Eds.), *Race, ethnicity, and education, Vol. 3: Racial identity in education* (pp. xvii–xxvii). Westport: Praeger.

National Council for the Social Studies. (1976/1991). *Curriculum guidelines for multicultural education.* Silver Springs, MD: NCSS.

National Council for the Social Studies. (1994). *Curriculum standards for social studies: Expectations of excellence* (NCSS Bulletin 89). Silver Spring, MD: NCSS.

National Council for the Social Studies. (2010). *National curriculum standards for social studies: A framework for teaching, learning, and assessment* (NCSS Bulletin 111). Silver Spring, MD: NCSS.

Nelson, J. L., & Pang, V. O. (2006). Racism, prejudice, and the social studies curriculum. In E. W. Ross (Ed.), *The social studies curriculum: Purposes, problems, and possibilities* (pp. 115–135). Albany, NY: State University of New York Press.

Omi, M., & Winant, H. (1994). *Racial formation in the United States: From the 1960s to the 1990s.* New York: Routledge.

Painter, N. I. (2010). *The history of white people.* New York: W.W. Norton.

Parker, W.C. (Ed.). (2010). *Social studies today: Research and practice.* New York: Routledge.

Pinar, W.F. (2004). *What is curriculum theory?* Mahwah, NJ: Lawrence Erlbaum Publishers.

Pinar, W. F., Reynolds, W., Slattery, P., and Taubman, P. (1995). *Understanding curriculum.* New York: Peter Lang.

Popkin, R. H. (1999). Eighteenth century racism. In R. H. Popkin (Ed.), *The Columbia history of western philosophy* (pp. 508–515). New York: Columbia University Press.

Rains, F. (2003). To greet the dawn with open eyes: American Indians, white privilege, and the power of residual guilt in the social studies. In G. Ladson-Billings (Ed.), *Critical race theory perspectives on social studies: The profession, policies, and curriculum* (pp. 199–230). Greenwich, CT: Information Age Publishing.

Rains, F. (2006). The color of the social studies: A post-social studies reality check. In E. W. Ross (Ed.), *The social studies curriculum: Purposes, problems, and possibilities* (pp. 137–156). Albany: State University of New York Press.

Ravitch, D. (2004). *The language police: How pressure groups restrict what students learn:* New York: Vintage.

Rosenburg, P. M. (1997). Underground discourses: Exploring whiteness in teacher education. In M. Fine, L. Powell, L. Weis, & M. Wong (Eds.). *Off white: Readings in race, power, and society* (pp. 79–89). New York: Routledge.

Ross, E. W. (Ed.). (1998). Letters to the editor. *Theory & Research in Social Education, 28*(3), 306–310.

Ross, E. W. (2001). *The social studies curriculum: Purposes, problems, and possibilities.* Albany, NY: State University of New York Press.

Ross, E. W. (2006). *The social studies curriculum: Purposes, problems, and possibilities.* Albany, NY: State University of New York Press.

Ross, E. W., & Pang, V. O. (Eds.). (2006). *Race, ethnicity, and education* (Vols. 1–4). Westport: Praeger Books.

Said, E. (1993). *Culture and imperialism.* New York: Knopf.

Segal, A. (2010). Implicating race in students' learning how to teach history. In E. Heliman, R. Amthor, & M. Missias (Eds.), *Social studies and diversity education: What we do and why we do it* (pp. 185–188). New York: Routledge.

Shaver, J. P., (Ed.) (1991). *Handbook of research on social studies teaching and learning: A project of the national council for the social studies.* New York: MacMillan.

Sleeter, C. E. (1994). Resisting racial awareness: How teachers understand the social order from their racial, gender, and social class locations. In R. Martusewicz & W. Reynolds (Eds.), *Inside-out: Contemporary critical perspectives in education* (pp. 239–264). New York: St. Martin's.

Sleeter, C. E. (1999). Curriculum controversies in multicultural education. In M. J. Early & K. Rehage (Eds.), *Issues in curriculum: A selection of chapters from past NSSE yearbooks* (pp. 255–280). Chicago: University of Chicago Press.

Sleeter, C. E. (2001a). An analysis of the critiques of multicultural education. In J. Banks & C. Banks (Eds.), *Handbook of research on multicultural education* (pp. 81–94). San Francisco: Jossey-Bass.

Sleeter, C. E. (2001b). Preparing teachers for culturally diverse schools: Research and the overwhelming presence of whiteness. *Journal of Teacher Education, 52*(2), 94–106.

Sleeter, C. E. (2005). How white teachers construct race. In C. McCarthy, W. Crichlow, G. Dimitriadis, & N. Dolby (Eds.), *Race, identity, and representation in education* (pp. 243–256). New York: Routledge Press.

Sue, D. W. (2003). *Overcoming our racism: The journey to liberation.* San Francisco: Jossey-Bass Publishers.

Takaki, R. (1993). *A different mirror: A history of multicultural America.* Boston: Little, Brown, and Company.

Tate, W.F. (1997).Critical race theory and education: History, theory, and implications. In M. Apple (Ed.), *Review of research in education* (vol. 22, pp. 195–227). Washington. AERA.

Tatum, B. D. (1997). *Why are all the Black kids sitting together in the cafeteria? And other conversations about race.* United States: Perseus Books.

Urrieta, L., & Reidel, M. (2006). Avoidance, anger, and convenient amnesia: White supremacy and self-reflection in social studies teacher education. In E.W. Ross (Ed.), *Race, ethnicity, and education, Vol. 4: Racism and anti-racism in education* (pp. 278–300). Westport: Praeger.

Welsh, J. F. (2006). Rethinking particularity: Individualist perspectives on race and multiculturalism. In E.W. Ross (Ed.), *Race, ethnicity, and education, Vol. 4: Racism and anti-racism in education* (pp. 87–111). Westport: Praeger.

Welsh, J. F. (2007). *After multiculturalism: The politics of race and the dialectics of liberty.* Lanham, MD: Lexington.

West, C. (1993). *Beyond multiculturalism and eurocentricism: Prophetic thought in postmodern times.* Monroe, LA: Common Courage Press.

Williams, L. F. (2003). *The constraint of race: Legacies of white skin privilege in America.* University Park: The Pennsylvania State University Press.

Wills, J. S. (2001). Missing in interaction: Diversity, narrative, and critical multicultural social studies. *Theory and Research in Social Education 29*(1), 43–64.

Wilkins, D.E., & Lomawaima, K.T. (2001). *Uneven ground: American Indian sovereignty and federal law.* Norman: University of Oklahoma Press.

Woodson, C. G. (1933/2000). *The mis-education of the Negro.* Trenton:, NJ: Africa World Press.

CHAPTER 13

GLBTQ ISSUES IN THE SOCIAL STUDIES

J. B. Mayo, Jr.

INTRODUCTION

One of the core values of the National Council for the Social Studies is diversity and inclusiveness. Indeed the NCSS Strategic Plan (2000) states that "the organization affirms cultural diversity, combats discrimination, and recognizes multiple perspectives." Further, NCSS recognizes that some of the "emerging new realities" that social studies teachers/educators will face include issues such as tolerance, privacy, and diversity, and that these issues will play a prominent role in national news debates, classrooms, and public gatherings (NCSS Strategic Plan, 2000). Despite this recognition over ten years ago, only certain privileged forms of diversity are regularly recognized within the field: sexuality has not been a part of this group. To be fair, a handful of social studies researchers have attempted to fill this gap in the literature, creating spaces for conversations and research opportunities for newer scholars to carry the torch forward. These researchers presented their findings in a 2002 special issue of *Theory & Research in Social Education*

Contemporary Social Studies: An Essential Reader, pages 243–260
Copyright © 2012 by Information Age Publishing
All rights of reproduction in any form reserved.

(*TRSE*) entitled "Social Education and Sexual Identity: Introduction and Overview of the Issue."

This paper explores and raises questions about the ways in which secondary social studies teachers and students understand the connections between sexuality (read as sexual orientation), homophobia, and students' various expressions of gender. There is a slow but growing awareness among teachers about the curricular connections between sexuality and the social studies: Social studies teachers are including information about the roles played by Gay, Lesbian, Bisexual, Transgender, and Queer (GLBTQ) people during specific historical events/time periods and openly discussing the ongoing, national debate centered on gay marriage and Don't Ask Don't Tell. More pressing on the minds of teachers and students, however, is sexuality as it plays out in the hallways, in locker rooms, and in the spaces in schools often unsupervised by adults. Here, students police their classmates' gender expression; here, students vocalize (and sometimes enact) sexual desires; here, students enforce accepted heterosexist norms; here, students who break away from expected norms are bullied into submission. Many who refuse to bend to the will of their oppressor are injured, and some are killed (Crocco, 2002; Schmidt, 2009). This paper explores how the social studies can address these horrific outcomes directly so that the frequency of these incidents will decrease, while students' acceptance of difference increases. At a time when students are revealing their sexual orientation in public places as early as middle school (Denizet-Lewis, 2009) and choosing to express themselves in more creative, non-conforming ways, social studies educators must adapt their preparation of teachers to meet the changing (sexual) landscape of our schools.

SEXUALITY AT SCHOOL

It is truly naïve to believe that students are unaware of their sexuality (and the sexuality of others) and of the tensions it causes at school. Though the *sexuality* to which students are exposed usually takes the form of mandatory heterosexuality, this rigid stance clearly indicates to students that the perceived opposite condition, homosexuality, exists and is unacceptable. The unspoken, taken-for-granted nature of this understanding makes even the perception of being anything other than straight (i.e. gay, lesbian, bisexual, or transgendered) problematic. Students are constantly bombarded by sexual images and themes in the media, both in print and on television, the music that many of them listen to is full of sexual imagery, and many students have open access to sexual materials or themes via the Internet. At any given moment, students' chat communication via text message or status updates on social networking sites, like Facebook and MySpace, have the potential to be sexual in nature.

But one cannot simply blame the media or technology for bringing sexuality to school because it is found in the hallways, in the classrooms, at the lunch tables, and in the locker rooms at school even without the influence of these media. Though often unspoken, gender expectations and sexuality are found in the students' textbooks and are openly displayed in the innocent interactions teachers have with their students daily (Renold, 2000). When a teacher mentions the family gathering she enjoyed at a local park with her children in tow, for example, her (hetero) sexuality is part of the unspoken conversation. When students come to school in anticipation of the upcoming Homecoming assembly and the dance that will follow that evening, sexuality is part of that excitement and anxiety they may be feeling as it pertains to being asked to dance with a willing partner. Even our social studies lessons are full of examples of unspoken, but fully realized messages about sexuality. Bickmore (2002) recounts research that included a lecture on South African history, where a teacher said to the class, "Boers took their wives and children with them" (p. 201). Again, sexuality is present in this statement, but "it is easy to overlook the sexuality in [that] image because [students] assume as 'common sense' history's emphasis on male protagonists in heterosexual, married, male-dominant nuclear families" (Bickmore, 2002, p. 201). Whether it comes in the form of conversations between students and teachers, gossip among students peer groups, or seemingly neutral passages of historical prose in a textbook, sexuality exists and thrives at school. The social studies as a field, and k–12 teachers more generally, need to understand this reality and stop pretending that there is no place for sexuality in a school setting.

ENFORCEMENT OF GENDER SCRIPTS

Sexuality also exists in schools because students at a very early age become aware of and concerned about their sexual identities. As a social norm, parents often begin this process of identity formation by dressing their children in colors that carry widely-accepted, socially constructed meanings: sons are dressed in blue, the perceived "boy color," while their daughters are dressed in pink, "the softer, girlie color." Soon thereafter, children are given the "appropriate" toys and taught to adorn gender-appropriate attire. All the while, subtle and not-so-subtle messages are sent to children about big boys not crying and little girls seeking help and/or approval from male family members and friends. Given these conditions, children enter school with more than a notion about the gendered role they are supposed to play. These gender scripts come early and are reinforced by the relationships they witness among adults at school and the stories they hear from their teachers and other adults.

Most powerful, however, is the policing and enforcement of gender expectations from peers. Young boys are warned, both directly and indirectly, not to act, run, or throw "like a girl," and young girls realize early on that there is a social price to pay for being labeled too aggressive, a tomboy, or, in some settings, too athletic. By middle school, both boys and girls have learned to adopt and adapt to this enforcement of gender norms within the broader context of heterosexual behavior, even when it feels unnatural for them to do so. Bickmore (2002) states, "They generally believe that a girl 'must' have or seek a boyfriend, and a boy 'must' have a girlfriend or seek sexual relations with girls, and they know they will be tormented if they do not conform" (p. 200). One should also note the differentiated expectations of boys and girls indirectly stated above. Boys understand that they are expected to seek sex from girls, while girls understand that they must seek male companionship and simultaneously keep any sexual activity (or desire) hidden from public knowledge. Though many young people are able to live their lives beyond the gender script to which they are assigned, the pressure to conform is formidable. Thus, "the question is not *whether* to address gender and sexuality in the social studies class, since they are already present in the textbooks and in the ideas, concerns, and behavior patterns students bring with them to school" (Bickmore, 2002, p. 201). Rather the question is how *should* social studies teachers and educators help students make the most sense of the information students already have and help them correct any misinformation so that they can make the best, most well-informed decisions.

THEMATIC REVIEW OF THE LITERATURE

Given the presence of sexuality in the social studies classroom, it is important to know what leading researchers in the field have already written about this current and, still contentious, topic. Following is an extended review of the spring 2002 special edition of *TRSE* and the few other articles centered on Gay, Lesbian, Bisexual, Transgender, and Queer issues (GLBTQ) published in social studies journals prior to the special edition and since that time. Sadly, the field has been largely silent on GLBTQ issues since the special edition of *TRSE* was published earlier this decade.

THE HISTORY OF SILENCE CONTINUES

The introductory article in the 2002 special edition of *TRSE* asks the reader to consider a simple question: "Does everybody count as human?" Thornton (2002) contends that the social studies curriculum and its objectives, while obviously concerned about human beings, need to expand beyond the academic interests the subject matter generates. In considering the humanity of all, the social studies curriculum should also focus more broadly and include themes like "human rights, tolerance, justice, civic responsibility, and caring" (p. 178). Thornton believes that the social studies curriculum has, in fact, become more inclusive with its consideration of the experiences of ethnic minorities and women, but the silence remains around issues of gays and lesbians. This *silence*, however, is not the reality of public debate. At the time of Thornton's writing of a review on social studies curriculum and instruction (1994), he reported that two, hotly-contested public debates raged: gays in the military and New York City's "rainbow curriculum" (Thornton, 2002, p. 179). Both issues had (and have) direct, curricular connections to the social studies, yet little was written within the field to draw out pertinent themes, highlight potential learning opportunities, or help teachers and students engage the on-going public debate. During Thornton's "extensive" search for materials that might have informed social studies curriculum around GLBTQ issues, he "failed to find any reference to gays in the social studies literature" (p. 179). Only a reference to homosexual love in ancient Greece (Noddings, 1992) came up in Thornton's search. Further, Thornton reports that at the time of the *TRSE* special edition, only Wade (1995) and Crocco (2001) made any reference to GLBTQ issues in their writing.

Similarly, Crocco (2002) noted the lack of materials published about gender, sexuality, and the social studies. She offers a clear rationale for teachers to address these issues and make connections to the social studies curriculum: As the adults in schools, when teachers "ignore their moral responsibility to respond to bullying, threatening, object throwing, and chasing students [perceived] and labeled as gay or lesbian, they countenance a school culture that is sexist and homophobic, tacitly endorsing a worldview that sanctions school violence against those not fully accepted as citizens" (p. 221). Crocco contends that in such an environment, clear messages are sent to students about what standard of behavior is allowed toward some groups of people as compared to others. Like Thornton, she conducted a search for publications within the social students that directly addressed GLBTQ persons and issues. Though her ERIC search using key words gender, sexuality, and social studies yielded ten citations, only one focused explicitly on sexual orientation. In Wade's (1995) article, she characterized the subject as "diversity taboo" (Crocco, 2002, pp. 221–222). Clearly, both social studies researchers discovered the lack of literature centered on GLBTQ topics, issues, and people in the social studies, and they are highly critical of this finding. It is highly probable, in fact, that the lack of GLBTQ-centered literature within the social studies prompted conversations that led to the publication of the special edition of *TRSE*. An overview of the perspectives found in that themed edition is found below.

POLITICAL TOLERANCE OPENS A POTENTIAL GLBTQ SPACE

Pat Avery (2002) opens the discussion, making connections between political socialization, political tolerance, and sexual identity. She contends that though it is unrealistic to think that all citizens living in a democratic society will like each other, groups of people must respect the basic civil rights of other groups, even the rights of people with whom they fundamentally disagree. Her findings suggest, however, that young people are not socialized to consider the rights of GLBTQ people because their struggle for rights is not covered within the larger struggle for civil rights among other groups of people. In a social studies classroom that covers the Civil Rights Movement and the Women's Movement, for example, it is highly unlikely any mention, and certainly no in-depth coverage, of Gay Pride or the Stonewall Riots of 1969 is included in a larger discussion of the Gay Rights Movement. Therefore, all students are denied viewing the rights of gay citizens within a larger historical and political context. In addition, the "media, school, parents, and friends often convey the message that heterosexuality is socially acceptable, but that homosexuality is aberrant, if not immoral, behavior" (p. 192). Given that adolescents have a strong need to fit in, they are strongly influenced by perceived social norms. If being straight, athletic, and well-dressed in contemporary attire defines the norm, then adolescents will strive to be viewed as such. Further, Avery (2002) reported that students and adults focus much more on their individual rights, rather than their responsibilities. Most consider voting, serving on a jury, and obeying the law the extent to which their responsibilities lie, while few "demonstrate an understanding of the ways in which diversity of belief might enhance deliberation about pubic issues, or act to develop a better understanding of the 'common good'" (p. 193). Given their limited understanding of responsibilities combined with a socialization process that includes viewing homosexuality as outside the norm, it may not be shocking that Avery found a study (Conover & Searing, 2000), which reported that among young people living in four distinct U.S. communities, student support for the "right to be homosexual" ranked 11th in a set of 12 rights (p. 194). Despite these findings, however, Avery also reports that higher levels of education are positively correlated with tolerance. She stated, "Students who have attended college, in particular, are more likely to recognize the rights of gays and lesbians than those who have not attended college" (p. 195). Whether this phenomenon is caused by exposure to different people, opportunities in college classes to explore different perspectives more in-depth, or students' enhanced understanding of connections between abstract principles of democracy and their application to concrete situations, Avery concluded "education is one of the best predictors of general social tolerance and of tolerance for homosexuals in particular" (p. 195). When young people more fully understand one of the basic principles of democracy, majority rule with respect for minority rights, they will see that herein resides a voice for GLBTQ youth. "All young people need to recognize that they have a place in our democracy, but they also need to know and appreciate that the 'other' has a place as well" (pp. 195–196). Until social studies teachers stress that the "other" also includes GLBT and queer-identified people, the students in their classrooms will have a more difficult time heeding Avery's call.

MARGINALIZATION OF GLBTQ PEOPLE

Much of the current literature in social studies education regarding sexuality centers on the marginalization of GLBTQ people. The attention to marginalization is an effort to address the hostility toward GLBTQ persons in schools, including both teachers and students (Avery, 2002; Bickmore, 2002; Crocco, 2002; Franck, 2002; Marchman, 2002; Mayo, 2007; Oesterreich, 2002). Crocco (2002) speaks directly to the issue in her discussion about homophobia and the potential remedies social studies teachers can offer to this social ill. Because scholarship on masculinity suggests that "modern manhood has become consumed with patrolling the boundaries of sex role behavior and punishing those who deviate from these prescriptions," Crocco sites this as evidence that society has socially constructed and supports this learned behavior (p. 220). Rather than accepting that constructed gender roles and sexual identities have changed over time and thus have a history that could be engaged in the social studies classroom, the field has turned the treatment of sexuality over to the health curriculum, where "coverage focuses on the medical, psychological, and physiological aspects of this subject matter" (p. 220). So, while the social studies has remained silent on this issue, Crocco sees this as a missed opportunity, particularly since researchers in the humanities and social sciences have weighed in on issues of sexuality over the past several decades.

The silence Crocco and other social studies researchers have noted around issues of sexuality in the social studies works directly against an open, tolerant, and equitable form of citizenship education. When students become socialized to accept homophobia as the norm, "social studies teachers can expect such attitudes to color, interfere with, and undermine the teaching they do about democratic citizenship and its obligations" (Crocco, 2002, pp. 220–221). Further, if social studies teachers do nothing to curtail homophobic comments and attitudes in their classes, then students "sense of the universal obligations around respect, toleration, and inclusion" is severely undermined. For social studies teachers who believe strongly that citizenship education is a major focus, this set of circumstances necessarily extends social studies teachers' obligations beyond the classroom. As Crocco (2002) contends:

> Libraries that carry no books on gender and sexuality, athletic settings where sexist and homophobic comments are ignored, and hallways where young women and those believed to be lesbian or gay are harassed, all create a climate inimical to the support of human rights that should infuse the educational enterprise in American society. Social studies courses that avoid discussion of the gay liberation movement as part of the civil rights movement, that overlook gay issues and women's rights as "controversial" subject matter, and social studies teachers who condone abusive verbal and physical behavior towards gays and women, all contribute to a climate of intolerance that is hard to square with the demand of citizenship education in a pluralistic democracy (p. 221).

This indictment of social studies teachers indicates areas where they can have a direct influence on minimizing the degree to which homophobia is allowed to grow at school. Teachers can certainly confront and work to diminish the effects of homophobia at school, but what if they do not feel safe performing this role? What happens to teachers who identify as GLBTQ and who live in areas where sexual orientation is not part of the non-discrimination clause? What about those teachers whose personal/religious beliefs prevent them from addressing GLBTQ issues? Perhaps under these adverse conditions, one may understand why teachers would fail to take action.

Mayo (2007) investigated the lives of seven gay teachers who lived in a large southern state where teachers could be fired for living an openly gay identity at school. Each teacher stressed the need to be a proper role model for his students, which meant for most of them being perceived as a heterosexual male by his students. Not only did these men stress the need to be viewed as straight, but they insisted on acting out a dominant, hegemonic form of masculinity characterized by assertiveness, confidence, aggressiveness, and competitiveness (Connell, 1995).

Blount (2004) offers a plausible explanation for these gay teachers' belief system: "Schools have provided compelling social education for normative sexuality and gender. Schools have defined and regulated gender identities, and school board members and administrators have attempted to hire school workers who model acceptable sexuality and gender norms for their students" (p. 176). The gay teachers in this study, four of whom were social studies teachers, therefore felt compelled to enact the dominant form of masculinity, which helped them to most effectively hide their true sexual orientation.

Despite the choices made by the majority of the gay teachers in Mayo's study, there was one teacher who lived openly gay at school and chose a different form of masculinity to perform. Describing his form of teaching as *loving* and *understanding*, this individual served as a counter-example to the dominant male performances described by the other teachers in this study. This lone teacher stands as an example for others who endeavor to offer students alternatives to fitting into neatly structured gender expectations. Mayo (2007) points out that he is not "suggesting that *all* gender norms be discarded in the hopes of promoting an appreciation for diversity and freedom of expression," but he certainly believes that there is room for more than one type of masculine performance at school (p. 463). Mayo's study "reveals that individual teachers are capable of carving out spaces where alternative thinking can flourish. It is within these spaces where students' perspectives can be widely broadened, and where they can learn new lessons about accepting difference" (p. 463). If one teacher can promote the kinds of change seen in this study, then certainly the social studies, as a collective field, can do much more to expand the social education our students currently receive.

PROGRAMS AND PROJECTS THAT CENTER GLBTQ THEMES

Several programs are described in the spring 2002 edition of *TRSE* that promote the kind of change mentioned above. Generally, these programs are designed to promote social justice and teach social studies students and pre-service teachers to be tolerant as they raise awareness of GLBTQ teachers' and students' daily lived experiences. Crocco (2002) describes how in one graduate program in New York City, discussions of diversity are infused across all courses in the master's and doctoral programs. Gender and sexuality are given more focused attention in two particular courses, *Diversity and the Social Studies Curriculum* and *Women of the World: Issues in Teaching*. With the use of field notes, students' writing from specific prompts and in-depth, semi-structured interviews over a five year period, Crocco reported that five themes ran through virtually all the data:

1. Compulsory heterosexuality
2. Silence of the formal curriculum
3. White noise outside the classroom
4. Breeding grounds for homophobia
5. Close encounters of a positive kind

These findings mirror many of the sentiments found in other studies. Graduate students reported that they assumed everyone was straight in classes and that there was really no other option to be anything else. The silence that Thornton (2002) noted was supported by students reporting they had never encountered gay individuals in history classes and had never read works by gay people. As Crocco surmised, students probably had encountered both, but were never told this specific piece of information by their teachers. The "white noise" refers to the commonplace use of slurs like 'fag' and 'dyke' and the derogatory use of the term 'gay' thrown out in casual conversation and intentionally hurled at students who violated some social norm and therefore fell out of favor with their peers. Mayo (2007) also found that the use of homophobic language was commonplace and the teachers in his study rarely witnessed their colleagues doing anything to stop this behavior. One participant lamented, "It seems like 'faggot' or some other [words] like that are the last acceptable slurs you can use" at school (p. 457). But Crocco also noted that students in her program reported some changed attitudes toward GLBTQ people when friends or siblings revealed their sexual orientation (came out) to them. Personal contact with people considered the "other" helps one dismiss stereotypes and fear: individuals become human and can no longer be viewed as a category.

These findings suggest the importance of making sexual orientation part of the conversation in teacher education programs that challenge the homophobia found in schools (Crocco, 2002). Social studies teachers who have openly engaged these issues in their preparation for the classroom will be best equipped to tackle these problems at future sites of employment. Students in this program designed three 2-hour faculty development workshops as a culminating project. The goals of these workshops were to help teachers confront their personal feelings and beliefs, to help teachers "step into the shoes of gay and lesbian teenagers for a day," and create empathy and understanding among teachers with the use of specific literature about GLBTQ adolescents. According to Crocco (2002), these workshops could then be followed up by department-wide meetings to consider the ways in which sexuality and gender could be formally incorporated into the broader curriculum.

The projects described above were meant to engage future teachers in their thinking about how they might possibly encourage positive changes at school around issues of sexuality. The projects they created addressed hypothetical groups of teachers in future school settings. Other social studies researchers have written about simulations, workshops, and teaching units that engage *actual* teachers and students. McCrary (2002) discusses her findings about how adults were affected by the use of *Jeff's Story*, an interactive, web-based, narrative simulation designed to change biased beliefs about homosexuality. In this simulation, the adult participants played the role of Jeff's parents. Marchman (2002) writes about a high school Civics course he teaches, specifically about a two-week mini-unit entitled "Homophobia Prevention," which is part of a larger nine-week unit on tolerance and diversity. The unit that Marchman (2002) described has three goals: He hoped to raise awareness and understanding about heterosexism and the privileges that heterosexuals enjoy and take for granted; he hoped students "make connections between heterosexism and other forms of oppression"; and he hoped that students would understand homophobia as a social justice issue and identify actions they can take to bring homophobia to an end (p. 303). Both McCrary and Marchman reported positive outcomes as a result of the learning opportunities they presented to students and adults.

Franck (2002) reported on a school-wide plan to fight homophobia in an urban high school. He overheard a student use the term "homo" in class, and after subsequent interactions with this student realized "homophobia and heterosexism had a detrimental effect on all students in that school" (Frank, 2002, p. 276). The plan to fight homophobia began with mandatory in-service training for teachers and staff. Faculty members at the school explored approaches to deal with homophobic slurs, they discussed ways to help students understand "the weight of their words, and teachers were given a brief outline of the history of the modern gay rights struggle (Franck, 2002). This information provided teachers with a broad overview that placed their current school challenges in a wider, historical context. It also provided teachers an opportunity to learn more about the Gay Civil Rights Movement.

The next step toward fighting homophobia at this urban high school included student participation in student-centered workshops. All ninth and tenth graders participated in "Homo 101" workshops during an advisory period at school. During these workshops, students engaged in activities and discussions that centered on the harmful effects of stereotypes, and they received mini-history lessons about GLBTQ people and their ongoing struggles for equality. As the workshops progressed, students were asked to reflect upon the safety of gay students at their school, about what it might be like to have a gay teacher, and whether or not it was acceptable to hate others as long as no actions were taken. Franck (2002) reported that discussions based on these reflections were "the most rewarding part of the workshop for [him] because the more open-minded students dominated the conversations" (p. 284). He concluded that workshops, in-service training, and other "undoing homophobia" activities are essential if we hope to push school communities from a complacent stance on sexual identity issues to an active willingness to demand social justice for those individuals and groups who have been denied it for far too long.

INCLUSION OF GLBTQ INDIVIDUALS/TOPICS IN SOCIAL STUDIES CURRICULUM

Directly or indirectly, many social studies researchers have called for a more explicit inclusion of GLBTQ individuals, groups, events, and themes within the disciplines that comprise the field (Crocco, 2002; Franck, 2002;

Macintosh & Loutzenheiser, 2006; Marchman, 2002; Mayo, 2007; Mayo & Sheppard, 2010; Thornton, 2002, 2003). Though the subject matter is still considered "controversial" by her students, Crocco (2002) noted that "pedagogies of possibility exist for teaching about sexuality within the social studies. As new teachers gain[ed] comfort with their teaching environments and awake to these possibilities, they may discover openings in the curriculum for connecting to gender and sexuality" (p. 229). Franck (2002) lamented that "most teachers and curricula ignore gayness altogether, failing to note the contributions of homosexuals to society or issues specific to sexuality," but he believes strongly that "the social studies curriculum must be the place where we begin" to undo this shortcoming (pp. 284–285). In fact, he insists that a closer examination of Eleanor Roosevelt, the Harlem Renaissance, the Holocaust, and Walt Whitman's poetry are clear openings for social studies teachers to explore the impact of sexuality and individual gay people on key events and defined time periods throughout United States and World History. In all of these examples, sexuality and the impact of GLBTQ people are made more visible and more closely related to events in history that are covered routinely in social studies classrooms. This works against the idea that inclusion of sexuality is somehow peripheral to the larger body of work within the social studies.

It is Thornton (2002, 2003), however, who speaks most directly about the possibilities of including GLBTQ-themed topics to the social studies curriculum. He believes that changes to the social studies curriculum are most effective if they come in the form of modifying existing courses, rather than creating new ones. Therefore, he calls for "incremental changes, which may find readier and broader acceptance than radical ones" (Thornton, 2002, p. 181). He states candidly that this approach "falls short" of what must ultimately be done to affect the kind of transformation that is possible, but his suggestions represent a good start. Indeed, Thornton's first suggestion is that, at minimum, social studies teachers should say something about the possible sexual identities of various individuals already covered in standard social studies curriculum. Mentioning the sexual identities of people like Jane Addams, Bayard Rustin, or Alexander the Great is irrelevant if this information goes unconnected to larger questions and counter-productive if it only leads to gossip (Thornton, 2002). However, making GLBTQ people *visible* to students may be the only step possible for some teachers in certain school districts. In other scenarios, this first step could lead to more in-depth perspective taking among students.

Another, more effective, approach according to Thornton is for social studies teachers to start with topics where gay and lesbian related material has substantial relevance to the subject matter. A closer examination of ancient Greece, for example, could certainly include student inquiry into the prevalence of statues prominently depicting the male form. As Thornton suggests, teachers can discuss a number of different topics that are critical to understanding life in ancient Greece without ever mentioning homosexuality. Similarly, there are many topics already included in the standard social studies curriculum that are fertile ground for GLBTQ inclusion. A unit of study on the Civil Rights Movement would certainly be enriched by discussions about the Stonewall riots and an examination of Bayard Rustin, and any number of social studies teachers who cover various aspects of Native American culture would add another layer of depth to their lessons by including the important roles performed by Two Spirit individuals (Thornton, 2002; Mayo & Sheppard, 2010). And beyond history courses, GLBTQ-themed topics fit naturally in civics and government courses, particularly around policies concerning gays in the military and gay marriage. The social studies curriculum offers teachers many opportunities for GLBTQ inclusion "within the confines of courses that already exist" (Thornton, 2002, p. 184).

The opportunities presented within social studies curriculum, however, will go unrealized if social studies teachers do not take action. Researchers in the field have provided examples about how to introduce GLBTQ issues in teacher education programs, and they have provided a few examples of what this might like in k–12 social studies classes. Others have discussed the need to overcome the detrimental homophobia and heterosexism that run rampant in our schools, but questions remain: Will this be enough to goad social studies teachers into action? What other possible barriers exist that keep teachers from presenting GLBTQ materials in class? These are questions that warrant more in-depth investigation. In the meantime, Thornton's words remain as a call to action for all teacher-educators, curriculum specialists, teachers, and administrators, who wish to see social studies curriculum that includes the voices, experiences, and contributions of GLBTQ people. In his (2003) article in *Social Education* entitled "Silence on Gays and Lesbians in Social Studies Curriculum," he stated:

> Teachers have choices. All teachers are curricular-instructional gatekeepers—they largely decide the day-to-day curriculum and activities [that] students experience. How teachers enact curriculum, even with today's constraints such as standards and high-stakes tests, still matters both practically and ethically. Opportunities to incorporate at least some gay material into the standard curriculum exist; in many instances, all that is required is the will to call attention to aspects of standard subject matter that heretofore went unmentioned (p. 228).

This call to action, however, suggests that future scholars do more of the same in terms of helping teachers find innovative ways to connect and include GLBTQ materials to existing social studies curriculum. Perhaps the time has come for a more nuanced approach.

QUEERING THE VIEW

Schmidt (2010) offered a critical view of the discourse of sexuality found within the Spring 2002 special edition of *TRSE* and other NCSS documents. Using queer theory and critical discourse analysis as analytical tools, Schmidt uncovered how the authors of the Spring 2002 edition of TRSE unwittingly "reify [existing] social norms around sexuality and gender" (p. 319). She cites, for example that several *TRSE* authors use heteronormativity and homophobia to characterize the hostile environments found in schools (Franck, 2002; Marchman, 2002; Oesterreich, 2002). Using this characterization, however, "perpetuates the association between queer identities and negativity. Gay must be bad if the only images and discussions we can find are negative. Hence, the fear is perpetuated" (Schmidt, 2010, p. 320). Why would any student want to identify as GLBT or Q when these identities are always associated with things unpleasant? When all visible representations are negative, nuanced understandings of gender and sexuality are limited and the status quo remains in-tact.

Schmidt (2010) is also critical about how GLBTQ issues are positioned as controversial and different from the norm. If they are continuously labeled in this way, then social studies teachers will always have to wonder if including GLBTQ issues will be "too controversial" for their particular school community and carry the risk of negative consequences. Further, this characterization keeps open the debate about whether these issues are legitimate additions to various units of study. In addition, Schmidt (2010) highlights that how and when GLBTQ identities are included greatly affects the messages received by students. Several authors in the Spring 2002 edition of *TRSE* "bring voice to sexual identity when it is different from the norm, not when it is part of the norm" (p. 321). As an example, she cites how Whitman's approach to poetry is raised because he is gay, but the same emphasis is not given to Thomas Paine's writing of *Common Sense*. "Whitman, being gay, has sexuality that affects his writing; Paine, being straight, does not. Sexuality in these examples belongs only to the Other—the gay, lesbian, or bisexual person—rather than as a human attribute" (p. 321).

While legitimately critical of the articles in the spring 2002 issue of *TRSE*, Schmidt acknowledged their overall importance to the field. They explicitly bring GLBTQ issues to the foreground in the social studies and in ways previously undone. The articles cover a wide range of possible sites where the lack of attention to GLBTQ issues can be addressed: in teacher education programs and in k–12 classrooms. The articles also underscore the possibilities for further GLBTQ inclusion that have, to date, largely remained unexplored. There are certainly spaces available for the future use of queer theory in the social studies and Schmidt, herself, recognizes the redress of homophobia may rest in a reconsideration of political socialization as suggested by Avery (2002). She also noted promise in the ways that Bickmore

(2002) challenges heteronormativity "as a power struggle and an attempt to enforce norms of sexuality" (Schmidt, 2010, p. 322). The issues raised in the spring 2002 issue of TRSE have not become outdated in the eight years that have passed since it was distributed. On the contrary, they continue to be issues of great importance for social studies researchers, pre-service teachers, k–12 social studies teachers, and the students in our classrooms. The challenge remains, however, in how best to engage the issues that were raised and that remain current.

THE PROMISE OFFERED BY NUANCED SOCIAL STUDIES CURRICULUM

Though limited in number, researchers within the social studies have offered a wide array of potential entry points for the integration of GLBTQ people, themes, and topics in the curriculum. Teachers and teacher educators may continue to adopt a GLBT Studies approach, seeking out various people and themes to include in the social studies curriculum in innovative ways or they may take advantage of queer theory and challenge the existing categories that place limitations on our understanding of sexuality, identity, homophobia, and hetero-normative practices at school. This statement is not meant to carry judgment as both approaches have merit. Social studies teachers work within a wide variety of contexts around the United States, so all potential options must remain open to them, which provides the best chance for the execution of more inclusive social studies lessons. Of greatest importance, social studies teachers must use their lessons to impart a sense of acceptance for those considered different and guide students toward an overall philosophical belief in social justice. These goals can be attained if teachers normalize diverse perspectives, voices, and ways of being that are found within existing areas of study.

Students across the United States are introduced to Native Americans and the many cultures they represent early on in school. Individuals like Sacagawea, Geronimo, and Pocahontas and groups like the Navajo, Seminole, and Apache are widely recognized among school-aged children. Even if their only exposure to Native groups is within the context of European exploration to the "new" world, American expansion to the western frontier, or the challenges associated with life on reservations, students have some knowledge of Native Americans. What these students do not know, along with the vast majority of their teachers, is that within several Native groups there lived individuals who are known today as Two Spirit, people who were born with the masculine and the feminine spirit within one body (Jacobs, Thomas, & Lang, 1997; Wilson, 1996). These individuals were known by different names depending on the Native group to which they belonged and held special roles within their communities. Among the Navajo, for example, they were known as *nadleehi* (nawd-lay), and among the Dakota, they were referred to as *winkte* (win-tay). They were ceremonial leaders and dream interpreters; they were shaman/priests who acted as therapists and medical doctors; they were caretakers and teachers for the young; and they held vital economic vocations like weavers and cooks, all without the burden of infant care (Brown, 1997; Gilley, 2006; Jacobs, Thomas, & Lang, 1997; Roscoe, 1998; and Williams, 1986). Two Spirit individuals played vital, positive roles within Native American society without the negative stigma that is now attached to people who violate expected gender norms. The acceptance of Two Spirit individuals among various Native groups exemplified a worldview that went beyond simplified dichotomies. Lang (1997) wrote, "The acceptance of gender-variant individuals in Native American cultures can be seen as part of a worldview that realizes and appreciates transformation, change, and ambiguity in the world at large as well as in individuals" (p. 114). From an early age, Native children received an expanded form of social education that allowed them a wider breadth of acceptance for difference among their peers and adult community members.

As a field, the social studies has the potential to alter and expand the social learning that goes on in schools, which will empower students to be more thoughtful about their decisions and actions. Adolescents have the potential to expand the membership of their "in-groups" and the capacity to invite diverse people in, rather than push them way. Once accepted, individuals who were once ridiculed and placed on the margins, including sexual minorities and students with alternative expressions of gender, will find a space closer to the center. These outcomes will be possible when *all* students have engaged in a different form of social learning, one that expands their thinking and understanding of current, more-rigid social norms. Students' engagement with GLBTQ people within social studies lessons de-mystifies their lived experience. They become more familiar, viewed as fellow human beings instead of a "category" or a group stigmatized by specific, discreet acts that can be easily objectified and rejected. The lessons learned from traditional Native understandings of gender, gender expression, and their overall worldview will help straight-identified students accept their classmates for who they are, instead of trying to enforce conformity or tormenting their peers who are perceived as "different." Nuanced social studies lessons will not bring back the countless number of teens who have taken their lives, but if these lessons help create changes in students' thinking and help cleanse the toxic, homophobic atmospheres found in many schools, future teen suicides may be prevented. Young people who were once rejected will find acceptance, all students will learn to celebrate diversity in its many forms, and schools will move closer to promoting social justice. These positive outcomes are all possible when social studies teachers think more deeply and broaden the scope of existing social studies curricula centered on traditional Native American teaching.

REFERENCES

Avery, P. G. (2002) Political socialization, tolerance, and sexual identity. *Theory and Research in Social Education, 30*(2), 190–197.

Bickmore, K. (2002). How might social education resist heterosexism? Facing the impact of gender and sexual identity ideology on citizenship. *Theory and Research in Social Education, 30*(2), 198–216.

Blount, J. M. (2004). Same-sex desire, gender, and social education in the twentieth century. In C. Woyshner, J. Watras, & M. S. Crocco (Eds.), *Social education in the twentieth century: Curriculum and context for citizenship* (pp. 176–191). New York: Peter Lang.

Brown, L. B. (1997). *Two spirit people: American Indian lesbian women and gay men.* New York: Haworth Press, Inc.

Connell, R. W. (1995). *Masculinities.* Cambridge, UK: Polity Press.

Conover, P. J., & Searing, D. D. (2000). A political socialization perspective. In L. M. McDonnell, P. M. Timpane, & R. Benjamin (Eds.), *Rediscovering the democratic purposes of education* (pp. 91–124). Lawrence, Kansas: University of Kansas Press.

Crocco, M. S. (2001). The missing discourse about gender and sexuality in the social studies. *Theory Into Practice, 40*, 65–71.

Crocco, M. S. (2002). Homophobic hallways: Is anyone listening? *Theory and Research in Social Education, 30*(2), 217–232.

Denizet-Lewis, B. (2010, September 27). Coming out in middle school. New York Times. Retrieved from http://www.nytimes.com/2009/09/27/magazine/27out-t.html

Franck, K. C. (2002). Rethinking homophobia: Interrogating heteronormativity in an urban school. *Theory and Research in Social Education, 30*(2), 274–286.

Gilley, B. J. (2006). *Becoming two-spirit: Gay identity and social acceptance in Indian country.* Lincoln: University of Nebraska Press.

Jacobs, S., Thomas, W., & Lang, S. (1997). *Two-Spirit people: Native American gender identity, sexuality, and spirituality.* Chicago: University of Illinois Press.

Jagose, A. (1996). *Queer theory: An introduction.* New York: New York University Press.

Lang, S. (1997). Various kinds of Two-Spirit people: Gender variance and homosexuality in Native American communities. In S. E. Jacobs, W. Thomas, & S. Lang (Eds.), *Two-spirit people: Native American gender identity, sexuality, and spirituality* (pp. 100–118). Chicago: University of Illinois Press.

Macintosh, L. B. & Loutzenheiser, L. W. (2006). Queering citizenship. In G. H. Richardson & D. W. Blades (Eds.), *Troubling the canon of citizenship education* (pp. 95–102). New York: Peter Lang.

Marchman, B. K. (2002). Teaching about homophobia in a high school civics course. *Theory and Research in Social Education, 30*(2), 302–305.

Mayo, Jr., J. B. (2007). Negotiating sexual orientation and classroom practice(s) at school. *Theory and Research in Social Education, 35*(3), 447–464.

Mayo, Jr., J. B. & Sheppard, M. G. (2010). *Native American views on diversity: Lessons learned from the Two-Spirit tradition.* Manuscript submitted for publication.

McCrary, N. (2002). Investigating the use of narrative in affective learning on issues of social justice. *Theory and Research in Social Education, 30*(2), 255–273.

National Council for the Social Studies (2000). *NCSS Strategic Plan.* Retrieved from http://www.socialstudies.org/about/strateicplan

Noddings, N. (1992). Social studies and feminism. *Theory and Research in Social Education, 20,* 230–241.

Oesterreich, H. (2002). "Outing" social justice: Transforming civic education within the challenges of heteronormativity, heterosexism, and homophobia. *Theory and Research in Social Education, 30*(2), 287–301.

Renold, E. (2000). "Coming out": Gender, (hetero) sexuality, and the primary school. *Gender and Education, 12*(3), 309–326.

Roscoe, W. (1998). *Changing ones: Third and fourth genders in native North America.* New York: St. Martin's Press.

Schmidt, S. J. (2009, November). *Expanding the dialogue about gender and sexuality in the social studies.* Symposium conducted at the meeting of the College and University Faculty Assembly, Atlanta, GA.

Schmidt, S. J. (2010). Queering social studies: The role of social studies in normalizing citizens and sexuality in the common good. *Theory and Research in Social Education, 38*(3), 314–335.

Thornton, S. J. (1994). The social studies near century's end: Reconsidering patterns of curriculum and instruction. In L. Darling-Hammond (Ed.), *Review of research in education* (Vol. 20, pp. 223–254). Washington, DC: American Educational Research Association.

Thornton, S. J. (2002). Does everybody count as human? *Theory and Research in Social Education, 30*(2), 178–189.

Thornton, S. J. (2003). Silence on gays and lesbians in social studies curriculum. *Social Education, 67*(4), 226–230.

Wade, R. (1995). Diversity taboos: Religion and sexual orientation in the social studies classroom. *Social Studies and the Young Learner, 7*(4), 19–22.

Williams, W. L. (1986). *The spirit and the flesh: Sexual diversity in American Indian culture.* Boston: Beacon Press.

CHAPTER 14

GENDER AND SOCIAL STUDIES

Are We There Yet?

Christine Woyshner

The curriculum can be viewed as a journey, both within the confines of the school year and the course it takes over decades in regard to what we expect students to study and understand and the ways we expect them to participate, each of which changes over time. The biggest mistake we can make is to assume the notion of progress, that each year the curriculum becomes more sophisticated, more inclusive, and more reflective of self and society. A case-in-point is the role of gender and the social studies curriculum. Considerations of gender in the social studies curriculum have endured a rocky and uneven road, from early introduction to implementation to regression and back again, circling around and around.

Before we can address this circuitous path, however, we must define gender and social studies, as well as its parameters. What is typically meant by gender and social studies? For some it means paying greater attention to women and girls in the history curriculum. For others, it suggests noting how girls and boys, and young men and young women, are treated in social studies classes. Are boys called on more frequently than girls? Do female students like social studies more than male students? Gender and social

Contemporary Social Studies: An Essential Reader, pages 261–276
Copyright © 2012 by Information Age Publishing
261

studies encompasses these questions and many more. However, it should be noted that in recent decades, attention to gender in the social studies content areas has decreased, in part fueled by No Child Left Behind mandates, a reduction in federal funding for girls' and women's issues, and an assumption that full attention to gender in the social studies has been achieved. What had been through the 1980s a robust and growing area of research and practice—particularly in the area of teaching women's history—has now been sidelined as a less-meaningful or relevant focus of the curriculum. Moreover, attention to gender in the social studies is uneven. For instance, one may find more emphasis on gender in history than in economics and women's history is typically taught more during Women's History Month in March than any other time of the year in most classrooms.

This chapter will examine the ways that gender is addressed in social studies, discuss some common frameworks used in gender and social studies, and make recommendations for further inquiry. I focus primarily on the US context and will consider gender across the social studies content areas. In this chapter I will not, however, treat sexuality and the social studies, because that topic is addressed in a separate chapter in this volume.[1]

GENDER AND SOCIAL STUDIES

First, what is typically meant by gender in the social studies? Until the mid-to-late 1980s, sex or sex equity was how gender studies were framed in social studies and other subject areas. The shift to the use of the word "gender" connotes a move away from privileging biological determinants for differences, to encompass social, cultural, and ethnic understandings of what it means to be male or female.[2] Therefore, the use of the word "gender" instead of "sex" demonstrates an acceptance of the ways societies have conceptualized and sorted difference, and not just emphasized biological differences.

Efforts to bring gender equity to the school curriculum hold that it is important to "be fair and just toward both men and women, to show preference for neither, and concern for both" (Klein, Ortman, & Friedman, 2002). This endeavor is complicated by the understanding that teaching towards the goal of gender equity does not always mean that all students are treated exactly the same or are taught in identical ways. For instance, there is robust data on the effectiveness of girls- or women-only schools and classrooms, and these findings are more widely accepted than all-male educational settings. Nonetheless, men and women need to be represented equally in social studies textbooks and teaching materials and, ideally, boys and girls and young men and women should do equally well academically across the content areas in social studies.

Social studies curriculum in K–12, as well as teacher preparation in the content areas, needs to highlight the histories, politics, geographies, and economics of gender in relation to race, ethnicity, and socio-economic class. Teaching about diversity is a critical aspect of education for the healthy development of young people in a democracy. As Walter C. Parker (2003) explains, "diversity is ... essential to liberty; it *causes* liberty. Doing the opposite has the same effect: By attending exclusively and defensively to our diverse individual, cultural, and racial identities, we ignored the shared political identity and its context—the commonwealth—on which we rely to secure and nurture our diversity" (p. 2).[3] Therefore, if we take Parker's advice, we are at the point of attending not just to women and girls in social studies, but to gender in social studies, or the ways that our gendered differences play out in the classroom, curriculum, and society.

FRAMEWORKS IN GENDER AND SOCIAL STUDIES

The study of gender in social studies has relied upon or generated several fundamental frameworks by which to explain, identify, or trouble differences between men and women, boys and girls. Social studies researchers have sought to redefine and restructure existing paradigms to allow for gender differences in the social studies curriculum. The discussion below is not comprehensive; instead I discuss three major theoretical frameworks in gender and social studies. Others not included here are worthy of a close look, such as Margaret Smith Crocco's (2008) call for a new vision of citizenship education. Based on developments in scholarship in history, political science, and education, Crocco maintains that newer ideas around citizenship need to attend to three lines of inquiry. First, how has the history of social studies been shaped by gender and difference? Second, to what degree is social studies practice and theory shaped by gender, class, race, and sexual orientation? Finally, how can gender inform the future goals and priorities of social studies research and practice? In some cases, tropes from historical scholarship can enrich the social studies curriculum by helping students understand context as well as historians' thinking about the past. Two examples of such tropes are the "cult of true womanhood" and the separate spheres (Kerber, 1988; Welter, 1966), which can inform the teaching of US history.

The "cult of true womanhood" is a phrase used by historian Barbara Welter to refer to the nineteenth-century notion that women were expected to embody and reflect the purest virtue in every aspect of their lives. In other words, white, middle-class women were expected to be loving wives, doting mothers, and passive and pure in other realms as guided by four cardinal virtues: piety, purity, submissiveness, and domesticity (Welter, 1966, p. 152).

The separate spheres ideology of the nineteenth century speaks to the different domains of activity that were proscribed for men and women. For instance, men operated in the public sphere, which included the world of work, politics, and commerce. Women, on the other hand, were confined to the domestic, or private, sphere and all that it embodied. Teachers who incorporate gender and similar themes into the social studies curriculum need to be well-versed in these and other concepts because these ideas help students understand the social, political, and economic conditions of men and women. Moreover, a sophisticated understanding of such ideas is necessary to demonstrate how these ideas were mere contours of the times, and not reified roles for men and women. Additionally, there are three frameworks that hold particular salience for social studies, each of which I discuss below: the phase models in women's history, the care tradition, and the term "social education."

Phase Models

Scholars in the field of women's history developed the phase models in teaching and researching women's history in the early 1980s. The phase models helped identify a progression for integrating women's history to a greater degree in the social studies curriculum (see Figure 14.1). The first column shows the traditional approach to teaching history, called "male-defined history" by historian Gerda Lerner (1981) and "womanless, all-white history" by educator Peggy McIntosh (1983). Reading from left to right, the phases show how history can become more inclusive of women: adding notable women, looking at women's contributions, exploring women's oppression, and then finally redefining history to include women's ways of being and knowing. The phases should not be viewed as suggesting linear advancement, but map out different approaches that are iterative. Each phase coexists with the others, yet the end result, or fifth phase is viewed as desirable. However, the question remains as to what happens when the fifth phase is reached. In other words, if we put women at the center, is that the same as replicating the all-male approach, but with females?

More than thirty years after the phase models were introduced it is well worth asking whether they are relevant today. Some of the language used in them suggests outdated ways of thinking about men, women, and gender in history. For instance, "female-oriented consciousness" in history reflects the ethos of the women's movement of the 1970s, as does the phrase "women's ways of knowing." Today, researchers and practitioners are cautioned against assuming a monolithic perspective, such as in *all* women think a certain way. The same argument could be made for race and ethnicity. However, this researcher accepts the theoretical underpinning of the phase models, that they are helpful to refer to when considering the inclusion of women, girls, and gender in the social studies curriculum. If nothing else,

Model						
Lerner (1981)	Male-defined history	Compensatory history; missing and notable women are added	Contribution history; women's contributions to male-defined society are highlighted	Oppression framework; women's history told in terms of oppression; women on their own terms in history; e.g., suffrage	—	Female-oriented consciousness in history; experiences of women in the past are valued and become part of the interpretive framework; e.g., women's club movement; settlement houses
McIntosh (1983)	Womanless, all-white history	Corrective history, also known as the exceptional other history	—	Issues history; sexism and patriarchy serve as interpretive frameworks to women's history	Alternative starting point history; women's lives as history—there's nothing too humble to study	History redefined and reconstructed to include women's ways of being, knowing, living, and loving

Sources: From Lerner, G. (1981). The majority finds its past. New York: Oxford University Press; Tetreault, M.K.T. (1986); Integrating women's history: The case of United States history high school textbooks. The History Teacher, 19(2): 215-217; McIntosh, P. (1983). Interactive phases of curricular re-vision. Working Paper No. 124, Wellesley College, Wellesley, Mass; and Woyshner, C. (2002). Political history as women's history: Toward a more inclusive curriculum. *Theory and Research in Social Education, 30*(3), 359.

FIGURE 14.1. Phase Models in Researching and Teaching Women's History

the phases remind us to not get stuck in a holding pattern by focusing solely on one dimension of women's experience or representation, or one column in the phase model. For example, Nel Noddings (2001) has cautioned social studies educators against the "add women and stir" approach (p. 29).

Care Tradition

Perhaps most widely identified with the educational philosopher Nel Noddings (1984, 1992, 1996, 2001), the care framework has generally been used as an argument to bring gender into the social studies curriculum more fully. The care notion recognizes that throughout history "women have been charged with caregiving—with caring not only for their own families but also for the ill, elderly, and needy in their immediate communities" (Noddings, 2002, p. 51). Noddings (2002) posits that boys and girls should be educated for caregiving as well as breadwinning.

A social studies curriculum that emphasizes caregiving as well as breadwinning can include a study of homemaking. Students could examine homemaking and caregiving through history, philosophy, art, music and geography. They could investigate how homes and caregiving have changed over time and how climate and location influence the kinds of homes that are built and what activities take place in them. In response to critics who might view such a curriculum as non-intellectual, Noddings (2001) responds instead that a curriculum centered on care and homemaking is rife with "possibilities for radical social action" (p. 32), because of how identities are shaped by place and how homes become extensions of who we are. The care tradition also promotes the study of social policy and a consideration of the public-private dichotomy so often divided by gender. The reader might notice that the care tradition is similar to the last phase in Figure 14.1, in which women and their experiences are moved to the center of the curriculum. Nonetheless, Noddings' and others' recommendations to bring the care framework into the social studies curriculum have yet to be realized. The history curriculum remains focused around political and military history, as well as public life.

Social Education

The term social education has been used in recent years to consider a broader look at the field commonly referred to as social studies. Instead of a conglomeration of subjects, social education, as defined by Margaret Smith Crocco, is "teaching and learning about how individuals construct and live out their understandings social, political, and economic relations. . . and the implications of these understandings for how citizens are educated in a democracy" (1999, p. 1.). Therefore, employing the term helps account for women's heretofore low-status practice over men's high-status theory in the field. Social education allows for a broadening of the history and study of social studies because it considers the origins of women's efforts from outside of the content areas of history, geography, and economics. For example, leaders in the history of social studies are almost all men, if one looks at who wrote textbooks, served on influential curriculum committees, and led major professional organizations. However, if we employ the term social education, we can include women practitioners, club leaders, and those writing in areas not typically aligned with the traditional subject area called social studies. Even though Crocco uses the term in her historical collection of women social educators, social education has currency as we look beyond the past to consider why "feminist and gender discourses are not present in this field" (Schmeichel, 2011, p. 26). The ongoing work in social studies must take into account women, girls, and gender. This work may be accomplished through the use of these theoretical frameworks and other tropes that address gender and difference.

FINDINGS FROM RECENT RESEARCH[4]

Empirical research on gender and social studies reveals that there is much more work to be done for social studies to be more gender equitable in the classroom and on standardized assessments. Likewise, gender in the social studies needs to take into account race, ethnicity, and socio-economic class. Overall, there is little research to support scientifically proven solutions that result in gender equity in the social studies classroom and curricular materials, and textbooks are not as balanced in terms of gender, race, and ethnicity as they could be.

Gender differences in content knowledge in history and civics have improved in the last three decades. In the elementary grades, there are no statistically significant differences between boys' and girls' learning social studies topics and concepts related to food, housing, and shelter (e.g., Brophy & Alleman, 1999, 2000, 2001, 2003, 2005). In the secondary grades since 1995, males and females have been shown to be, overall, equally knowledgeable in history, geography, and civics and government as demonstrated on National Assessment of Educational Progress (NAEP) assessments. Prior to 1995, males did better on the civics and history NAEP test (Anderson et al., 1990; Applebee, Langer, & Mullis, 1987; Niemi & Junn, 1998). However, in the 1999 Civic Education Study of the International Association for the Evaluation of Educational Achievement, or IEA (Baldi, Perie, Skidmore, Greenberg, & Hahn, 2001; Torney-Purta, Lehmann, Oswald, & Schultz, 2001), researchers found no gender differences in civic knowledge. However, on some civic assessments, female students outscored male students on test items that ask students to read and interpret texts (Niemi

& Junn, 1998). These differences have been attributed to young women's facility with language and reading comprehension.

Overall, young women express interest in politics as much as young men (Hahn, 1996, 1998; Torney-Purta et al., 2001), while female students are more likely to trust government institutions, such as courts and municipal councils (Baldi et al., 2001). Female students expressed interest in being more politically and civically engaged as adults than their male peers (Torney-Purta et al., 2001). Moreover, female students' who participate in extracurricular activities in school are more likely to be civically active after they graduate (Damico, Damico, & Conway, 1998).

Gender differences do emerge in social studies content areas among the highest and lowest performing students. The 1998 NAEP studies of civics and a history assessment found that male students outnumber female students in the high-scoring categories as well as low-scoring categories (Chapin, 1998; Lutkus, et al., 1999; Niemi & Junn, 1998). The 2006 US history NAEP revealed that male students scored higher than female students at grades eight and eleven. Alarmingly, the gap between males and females at eighth grade was larger than the 1994 NAEP assessment (Lee & Weiss, 2007), which may be a consequence of the decreased attention to gender and social studies.[5]

In studies on Advanced Placement tests in United States and European history, researchers found that males outperformed females on the multiple choice test items, while females did better on the free response section of the exam (Breland, Danos, Kahn, Kubota, & Bonner, 1994). Interestingly, in a study of the AP tests in urban schools, researchers found that young women were more likely to take the US history test than young men (Eisner, 2001). How are these gender differences explained? Education researchers attribute the differences to two issues: the content of test items and the different courses that youth had taken prior to testing. In other words, historical proficiency, or lack thereof, does not explain the differences in achievement; it is explained by the gender bias of test items. For instance, test items that focused on power, control, and/or conflict are masculine content, while female content covers equality, individual liberty, social consequences of change over time, religion, and food (Kneedler, 1988; Walstad & Robson, 1997; Walter & Young, 1997).

A different pattern emerges regarding content knowledge in geography and economics. On geography assessments given in elementary and secondary schools, male students outperform female students, even though no gender differences have been found in grades for class performance (Educational Testing Service Gender Study, 1997; National Center for Education Statistics, 1994). In economics, the same pattern emerges, with male students performing better on tests than female students. However, research has revealed that the differences are generally small on the multiple-choice tests. This suggests that female students might do better with essay response items, as is noted in the research on history achievement and gender (Becker, et al., 1990).

Overall, women and gender-related topics are underrepresented in social studies materials and curricula. High-stakes testing and the accountability movement have resulted in downplaying women in the history curriculum because of the emphasis on political and economic history rather than social and cultural history (Symcox, 2002). In elementary classrooms, if social studies is taught at all, gender and women are generally overlooked (Henry, 1989). In civics and government, the picture is much worse. For example, gender is mentioned only twice in the *National Standards for Civics and Government* (Center for Civic Education, 1994). The standards explain that the woman's suffrage movement and discrimination against women could be used as examples of how citizen participation grew over time.

Social studies textbooks are not any better. Much scholarship has been produced in this area, and research on textbooks in US history, world history, civics and government, and economics has found that few women are represented and the women that are portrayed are in stereotypical roles (Hahn & Bernard-Powers, 1985). Recent studies of women in US and world history textbooks found that more women are included than had been in the past, although women are still included in superficial ways (Clark, Allard, & Mahoney, 2004; Clark, Ayton, Frechette, & Keller, 2005). Also, research has shown that textbooks employ frameworks of male dominance and patriarchy (Kuzmic, 2000). The same findings appear in studies of civic and economics textbooks; for example, in civics texts, it was found that women receive less coverage than men and women are not highlighted as role models in politics and government (Avery & Simmons, 2000/2001; Hahn & Blankenship, 1983). Teacher education textbooks in social studies do not attend to gender much either (Zittleman & Sadker, 2003).

Women and gender issues are, in general, absent from instruction in social studies classrooms. Women's history is infrequently taught (e.g., Schmurak & Ratliff, 1993), and most often women in history are addressed during the month of March. One researcher found that even when women were included in civics textbooks, teachers did not teach the information on women or draw attention to this content in the text (Hahn, 1996). When gender-related topics are addressed, it is usually women's fight for suffrage. The lack of attention to women in the curriculum could have an impact on students' choosing to study history and join history clubs, and it could potentially have an impact on their future civic engagement (Le, 1999; Sadker & Sadker, 1994).

Researchers and practitioners in social studies must also be mindful of the hidden curriculum, which may convey traditional gender stereotypes. Sometimes boys dominate the discussion in classrooms and in other instances, women may not be portrayed in posters and other educational material on the walls of social studies classrooms (Lee, Marks, & Byrd, 1994; Schmurak & Ratliff, 1993). In civics classes, young men reported that the classroom climate was less supportive of open discussion, while young women felt the climate was more open (Torney-Purta et al., 2001). The challenges brought to light in this research can be met by curricular materials, teacher preparation, and other suggestions listed below.

CURRICULAR EFFORTS AND PRESCRIPTIONS

There are many resources available to teachers who wish to integrate women's history into their classes and curriculum. The National Women's History Project (NWHP), founded in 1980, disseminates resources and materials on women's history. NWHP is a clearinghouse of materials on gender and the social studies for teachers, teacher educators, and others. The organization holds summer conferences and distributes a newsletter. Another gender and social studies venture is the Women in World History Project, which produces curriculum units for middle school students. Those interested in finding additional materials can peruse the Internet on "teaching women's history" which has a list of reputable links, such as the Smithsonian Institute and the (Howard) Zinn Educational Project.

To an extent, however, the production of materials and resources on gender and women's history for teachers and curriculum developers has decreased in recent years. As discussed above, the assumption appears to be that women, girls, and gender issues are integrated into the social studies curriculum, so there is little need to continue to produce resources. However, given the findings from empirical research discussed above, much work remains to be done. Examples of more recent efforts can be found. The NCSS recently published a bulletin on teaching women's history and literature (Chick, 2008). Another volume, *Clio in the Classroom* (Berkin, Crocco, & Winslow, 2009), seeks to share strategies for teaching women's history beyond the famous firsts and contribution history. The editors explain, "Women's history is firmly established at the college level today; nevertheless, it has made fewer inroads into the K–12 curriculum" (p. 4). In an effort to bring women's history to teachers, *Clio in the Classroom* includes content chapters that synthesize key findings in scholarship for particular eras (e.g., women in colonial and revolutionary America, and in the nineteenth and twentieth century's) and according to various themes, such as medicine, sexuality, citizenship, consumerism, law, and religion. This is followed by a series of chapters on teaching women's history, which includes such strategies and resources as visual images, technology, and oral history. The book concludes with a chapter on educational research and teaching and learning women's history.

Curriculum developers, teachers, and educational researchers can also draw on scholarship produced in the last several decades for social studies journals. The ideas put forth in the prescriptive literature address fitting women's history into a crowded curriculum (Crocco, 1997), reconsidering women's history as political history (Woyshner, 2002), and integrating ideas from art and media literacy (Woyshner, 2006). Suffrage has for a long time been a topic of interest in social studies, and it is also a staple of the prescriptive literature on social studies and gender (e.g., Crocco, 1995, Carter, 2011). More recently, women in world history has become an area of the prescriptive literature which offers suggestions for analyzing human rights issues through the study of women around the world (e.g., Baxter, et al., 2006; Crocco, 2007). This scholarship is a good place to start when considering gender in the social studies, although there are many gaps in the prescriptive literature which leaves room for additional writing on the topic. In particular, women of color are not as widely addressed as they could be, and as mentioned above, women in world history is only beginning to be explored in social studies journals. Other areas include women and gender in social studies topics beyond history, including economics, geography, and civics.

FUTURE DIRECTIONS

Given the evidence presented above, it is clear that attention needs to be paid to gender in the social studies curriculum. In addition to the curriculum ideas mentioned in the previous section, there are other ways to address gender in the social studies. Changes need to be made in social studies textbooks and curricular materials to include gender. This could mean more attention to women in history, or it could include the teaching of frameworks, such as separate spheres, social education, or the phase models. Other social studies content areas need to pay mind to gender as well. For instance, economics, world history, geography, and civics could more fully address gender-related topics and issues such as wage gaps and women's participation in public life. This attention to gender needs to take into account the diverse experiences of women and girls in relation to class, race, and ethnicity.

Next, the professional social studies organizations, such as the National Council for the Social Studies, need to be leaders in putting gender issues central to their missions and activities. They should also have a leadership and membership that is gender-balanced. Moreover, there need to be stronger connections between universities and colleges and K–12 institutions. In other words, new knowledge about research and teaching should inform K–12 social studies practice. One example is the developments in women's history that have emerged in higher education have not fully taken root in elementary and secondary social studies. Likewise, the field of geography has pursued research in gender and gender differences, while economics has been less invested in this area.

Also, structural problems in schools and classrooms that cause gender inequities need to be addressed by policy makers, teachers, and scholars. For example, the majority of elementary school teachers are women, while the majority of high school social studies teachers are men. What impact does this have on students' learning? How can we achieve greater gender balance in the elementary and secondary teaching force? Also, teacher educators in social studies need to consider gender issues in their courses and mentoring of new teachers.

Finally, further research into gender and gender equity needs to be conducted. There are few empirical studies on the benefits of gender inclusion at the elementary level in social studies. The specific content areas such as geography, economics, and civics need greater attention to research on how young men and women learn and the attitudes they have towards the various social studies content areas. Moreover, curriculum materials need to be more diversified, particularly the inclusion of women of color in the social studies curriculum.

Like the child awaiting arrival at the destination from the back seat of the station wagon, "Are we there yet?" is a familiar refrain to anyone who has ever been on a family trip. The road to increasing gender awareness in the social studies curriculum has been a long and rocky one. For at least the last four decades, if not longer, researchers, policy makers, and practitioners with a vested interest in gender and social studies have waited patiently for greater equity in the classroom, more gender-balanced curricular materials, and an education that is just and equitable toward boys and girls and men and women. We certainly are well on our way, but unfortunately are not close to arriving just yet.

ENDNOTES

1. Those interested in this topic see Margaret Smith Crocco, "The Missing Discourse about Gender and Sexuality in the Social Studies," *Theory Into Practice* 40, no. 1 (Winter 2001): 65–71.

2. While this is a bifurcated construction and there are more than two ways to construe gender, since the focus of this chapter is on gender and not sexuality, I will use the dualism throughout my discussion.

3. Emphasis in the original.

4. This section draws on research conducted for "Gender Equity in the Social Studies," a chapter I co-authored with Carole Hahn, Jane Bernard-Powers, and Margaret Smith Crocco, which was published in *Handbook of Research on Gender Equity* (Sue Klein, et al., Lawrence Erlbaum and Associates, 2007).

5. The report of the 2010 NAEP scores was not available at the time of publication of this volume.

REFERENCES

Anderson, L., Jenkins, L., Leming, J., MacDonald, W., Mullis, I., & Turner, M. J. (1990). *The civic report card.* Washington DC: U.S. Department of Education.

Applebee, A. N., Langer, J. A., & Mullis, I. (1987). Literature and U.S. history: *The instructional experience and factual knowledge of high school juniors* [Report No. 17-HL-01]. Princeton, NJ: Educational Testing Service.

Avery, P. G., & Simmons, A.M. (2000/2001). Civic life as conveyed in U.S. civics and history textbooks. *International Journal of Social Education, 15,* 105–130.

Baldi, S., Perie, M., Skidmore, D., Greenberg, E., & Hahn, C. (2001). *What democracy means to ninth-graders: U.S. results from the international IEA civic education study.* Washington, D.C., National Center for Education Statistics, U.S. Department of Education

Baxter, N. with Sproul, L., Kelly, K., & Franco, J. (Summer–Fall 2006). Teaching about women in social studies: Empowerment for all. *Social Science Docket 6*(2), 16–19.

Becker, W., Greene, W., & Rosen, S. (1990). Research on high school economic education, *AEA Papers and Proceedings, 80,* 14–22.

Berkin, C., Crocco, M.S., & Winslow, B. (2009). *Clio in the classroom: A guide for teaching US women's history.* New York: Oxford University Press.

Breland, H., Danos, D. O., Kahn, H. D., Kubota, M. Y., & Bonner, M. W. (1994). Performance versus objective testing and gender: An exploratory study of an Advanced Placement history examination. *Journal of Educational Measurement, 31*(4), 275–93.

Brophy, J., & Alleman, J. (1999). *Primary-grade students' knowledge and thinking about clothing as a cultural universal.* Spencer Foundation Report (ERIC Document #439072).

Brophy, J., & Alleman, J. (2000). Primary-grade students' knowledge and thinking about Native American and pioneer homes. *Theory and Research in Social Education, 28,* 96–120.

Brophy, J., & Alleman, J. (2001). What primary-grade students say about their ideal future homes. *Journal of Social Studies Research 25*(2), 23–35.

Brophy, J., & Alleman, J. (2003). Primary-grade students' knowledge and thinking about the supply of utilities (water, heat, and light) to modern homes. *Cognition and Instruction, 21,* 79–112.

Brophy, J., & Alleman, J. (2005). Primary grade students' knowledge and thinking about transportation. *Theory and Research in Social Education, 33,* 218–243.

Carter, C. M. (Jan./Feb. 2011). Raise up your cloth! The woman suffrage movement's second generation. *Middle Level Learning, 40,* M2–M7.

Center for Civic Education (1994). *National standards for civics and government.* Calabasas, CA: Author.

Chapin, J .R. (1998, April). *Gender and social studies learning in the 8th, 10th, and 12th grades.* Paper presented at the annual meeting of the American Educational Research Association. San Diego, CA.

Chick, K. A. (2008). *Teaching women's history through literature: Standards-based lesson plans for grades K–12.* NCSS Bulletin #107. Washington, DC: Author.

Clark, R., Allard, J., & Mahoney, T. (2004). How much of the sky? Women in American high school history textbooks from the 1960s, 1980s, and 1990s. *Social Education, 68,* 57–62.

Clark, R., Ayton, K., Frechette, N., & Keller, P. J. (2005). Women of the world, rewrite! Women in world history high school textbooks from the 1960s, 1980s, and 1990s. *Social Education, 69,* 41–47.

Crocco, M. S. (1995). The road to the vote: Women, suffrage, and the public sphere. *Social Education 59*(5), 257–264.

Crocco, M. S. (1997). Making time for women's history. . . when your survey course is already filled to overflowing. *Social Education, 61*(1), 32–37.

Crocco, M. S. (1999). Introduction. In M.S. Crocco and O.L. Davis, Jr. (Eds.), *"Bending the future to their will": Civic women, social education, and democracy.* (pp. 1–16). New York: Rowman & Littlefield Publishers, Inc.

Crocco, M. S. (November 2007). Speaking truth to power: Women's rights as human rights. *The Social Studies 98,* 257–269.

Crocco, M. S. (2008). Gender and sexuality in the social studies. In L. S. Levstik & C. A. Tyson (Eds.), *Handbook of research in social studies education,* (pp. 172–196). New York: Routledge.

Damico, A., Damico, S., & Conway, M. (1998). The democratic education of women: High school and beyond. *Women in Politics, 19,* 1–31.

Educational Testing Service (1997). *The ETS gender study: How males and females perform in educational settings.* Princeton, NJ: Author.

Eisner, C. (2001). *Advancing excellence in urban schools: A report on Advanced Placement Examinations in the Great City Schools. Council of the Great City Schools.* Washington, DC: College Board.

Hahn, C. L. (1996) Gender and political learning. *Theory and Research in Social Education, 24,* 8–35.

Hahn, C. L. (1998). *Becoming political: Comparative perspectives on citizenship education.* Albany: SUNY Press.

Hahn, C. L., & Bernard-Powers, J. (1985). Sex equity in social studies. In S. Klein (Ed.), *Handbook for achieving sex equity through education* (pp. 280–297). Baltimore, MD: Johns Hopkins University.

Hahn, C. L., & Blankenship, G. (1983). Women and economics textbooks. *Theory and Research in Social Education, 11,* 67–76.

Henry, T. (1989). Gender and the framework. *Social Studies Review 28*(2), 27–30.

Kerber, L. K. (1988). Separate spheres, female worlds, woman's place: The rhetoric of women's history. *The Journal of American History, 75(1),* 9–39.

Klein, S., Ortman, B., & Friedman, B. (2002). What is the field of gender equity in education? In J. Koch & B. Irby (Eds.), *Defining and redefining gender equity in education*, (pp. 3–29). Greenwich, CT: Information Age Publishers.

Kneedler, P. E. (1988). Differences between boys and girls on California's new statewide assessments in history/social science. *Social Studies Review, 27*(3), 96–124.

Kuzmic, J. (2000). Textbooks, knowledge, and masculinity. In N. Lesko (Ed.), *Masculinities in school* (pp. 105–126). Thousand Oaks, Sage.

Le, V. N. (1999). *Identifying differential item functioning on the NELS: 88 history achievement test: CSE Technical Report.* California State University Center for the Study of Evaluation.

Lee, V. E. Marks, H. M., & Byrd, T. (1994). Sexism in single-sex and coeducational secondary school classrooms. *Sociology of Education, 67*, 92–120.

Lee, J., & Weiss, A. (2007). *The nation's report card: US history 2006* (NCES 2007-474). US Department of Education, National Center for Educational Statistics. Washington, DC: US Government Printing Office.

Lerner, G. (1981). *The majority finds its past.* New York: Oxford University Press.

Lutkus, A. D., Weiss, A. R., Campbell, J. R., Mazzeo, J., & Lazer, S. (1999). *NAEP 1998: Civics report card for the nation.* Washington, DC: National Center for Education Statistics, US Department of Education. ED 435 583.

McIntosh, P. (1983). *Interactive phases of curricular re-vision. Working Paper No. 124.* Wellesley, Mass: Wellesley College.

National Center for Education Statistics. (1994). *NAEP 1994: Geography report card.* US Department of Education/OERI. Washington, DC: Author.

Niemi, R., & Junn, J. (1998). *Civic education: What makes students learn.* New Haven: Yale University Press.

Noddings, N. (1984). *Caring: A feminine approach to ethics and moral education.* Berkeley: University of California Press.

Noddings, N. (1992). *The challenge to care in schools: An alternative approach to education.* New York: Teachers College Press.

Noddings, N. (1996). *Caregiving: Readings in knowledge, practice, ethics, and politics.* Philadelphia: University of Pennsylvania Press.

Noddings, N. (2001). The care tradition: Beyond "add women and stir." *Theory Into Practice, 40,* 29–34.

Noddings, N. (2002). *Educating moral people: A caring alternative to character education.* New York: Teachers College Press.

Parker, W. C. (2003). *Teaching democracy: Unity and diversity in public life.* New York: Teachers College Press.

Sadker, M., & Sadker, D. (1994). *Failing at fairness.* New York: Scribners.

Schmeichel, M. (2011). Feminism, neoliberalism, and social studies. *Theory and Research in Social Education, 39(1),* 6–30.

Schmurak, C. B., & Ratliff, T. M. (1993, April). *Gender equity and gender bias in the middle school classroom.* Paper presented at the annual meeting of the American Educational Research Association, Atlanta.

Symcox, L. (2002). *Whose history? The struggle for national standards in American classrooms.* New York: Teachers College Press.

Tetreault, M. K. T. (1986). Integrating women's history: The case of United States history high school textbooks. *The History Teacher, 19*(2), 215–217.

Torney-Purta, J., Lehmann, R., Oswald, H., & Schulz, W. (2001). *Citizenship and education in twenty eight countries: Civic knowledge and engagement at age fourteen.* Amsterdam: The International Association for the Evaluation of Educational Achievement.

Walstad, W. B., & Robson, D. (1997). Differential item functioning and male-female differences on multiple-choice tests in economics. *Journal of Economic Education, 28,* 155–171.

Walter, C., & Young. B. (1997). Gender bias in Alberta social studies 30 examinations: Cause and effect. *Canadian Social Studies 31(2),* 83–86, 89.

Welter, B. (Summer, 1966). The cult of True Womanhood: 1820–1860. *American Quarterly, 18(2),* Part 1, 151–174.

Woyshner, C. (2002). Political history as women's history: Toward a more inclusive curriculum. *Theory and Research in Social Education 30(3),* 354–380.

Woyshner, C. (2006). Picturing women: Gender, images, and representation in social studies. *Social Education 70(6),* 358–362.

Zittleman, K. and Sadker, D. (2003). The unfinished gender revolution. *Educational Leadership, 40(4),* 59–63.

CHAPTER 15

BUILDING THE BRIDGE BETWEEN SOCIAL STUDIES AND SPECIAL EDUCATION

Perspectives and Practices

Timothy Lintner and Windy Schweder

THE RELATIONSHIP BETWEEN
SOCIAL STUDIES AND SPECIAL EDUCATION

In 2004, the U.S. Department of Education reported that 9.2% of our nation's student population received special education and related services, an increase of over 1% or 1 million students served between 1995 and 2004 (U.S. Department of Education, 2006). Recent legislation, such as the No Child Left Behind Act of 2001 and the Individuals with Disabilities Education Act of 2004, require school districts to include students with disabilities into statewide standardized assessments. These two acts also require districts to include students with disabilities into general education settings (Palloway, Patton, & Serna, 2008). As a result, approximately 52% (U.S. Department of Education, 2006) of students with disabilities across the coun-

Contemporary Social Studies: An Essential Reader, pages 277–292
Copyright © 2012 by Information Age Publishing

try spend over 79% of their school week in general education settings (U.S. Department of Education, 2005). Hence, there is an increasing need to provide students with disabilities appropriate services and supports.

SEMINAL LAWS IMPACTING SPECIAL EDUCATION

Individuals with Disabilities Education Act of 2004

It has been over 30 years since the initial passage of the Education for All Handicapped Children Act (EHA, Public Law 94-142), commonly referred to as the Individuals with Disabilities Education Act (IDEA). This sweeping piece of federal legislation has been amended/reauthorized three times (1982, 1990, 1997), with the latest reauthorization coming in 2004. The core provisions call for free, appropriate education for students with disabilities. Here, school districts are mandated to provide special education and related services to meet the needs of individual students. IDEA also requires that prior to a student receiving special education services, a comprehensive evaluation must be conducted. An Individualized Education Plan (IEP) is then established, outlining specific student learning goals and determining appropriate student services. Lastly, IDEA states that schools must educate students with disabilities to the greatest extent possible in a "least restrictive environment" in which the same opportunities are afforded to all students. The least restrictive environment is most often defined as a general education setting.

No Child Left Behind

An integral goal of the No Child Left Behind Act of 2001 (PL 107-110) was to find ways to better serve the most deserved of students and to foster a greater sense of school-based accountability. With regards to the increase in standardized testing and resultant accountability, the "question is not whether students with special needs will participate in a standard-based system but more appropriately concerns how well students with special needs will do in this new system" (Palloway, Patton, & Serna, 2008, p. 6). The inclusion of special needs students within the mandates of NCLB can certainly lead to greater expectations and, ultimately, greater student achievement. Yet NCLB can also run contrary to the learning goals outlined in student IEP's. As well, within this high-stakes testing environment, special needs students may in fact struggle in their attempt to meet state-sponsored standards, which can ultimately lead to more detrimental issues and outcomes (Harbin, Rous, & McLean, 2005; Ysseldyke, 2005).

Lawmakers and advocacy groups recommended that the reauthorization of the Individuals with Disabilities Education Act (IDEA) of 2004 align with the current No Child Left Behind Act (2001). As a result, IDEA (2004) and NCLB (2001) complement each other and charge all educators with the following tasks:

- Provide all students with a free and appropriate public education in their least restrictive environment.
- Collaborate with professionals and parents.
- Teach with empirically-based teaching strategies that allow all students to succeed.
- Prepare students with disabilities to take high-stakes testing.
- Provide appropriate accommodations and modifications to give students with disabilities access to the general education curriculum (Palloway et al.; Smith, 2007).

AN ABBREVIATED REVIEW OF THE LITERATURE

Seminal research by, amongst others, Bean (1994), Brownlee (1988), Curtis (1982), Hickey and Braun (1990), Ochoa and Schuster (1980), Passe and Beattie (1994), Patton, Palloway, and Cronin (1987), Tama and Martinez (1988), and Turner (1976), served to start conversations about what philosophical perceptions and pedagogical practices are both appropriate and effective in the teaching of social studies to students with disabilities. Building from this foundation, contemporary scholars (Connor & Legares, 2007; Crawford, Carnine, Harniss, Hollenbeck, & Miller, 2007; Dull & van Garderen, 2005; Fontana, 2004; Lintner & Schweder, 2008; McCoy, 2005; Scruggs, Mastropieri, & Okolo, 2008; Steele, 2007) have carried these conversations into the new millennium.

There exists a dissonance between what is deemed "good" social studies practice and what is actually taking place in classrooms (Meuwissen, 2005). Best practices in social studies and current research advocates that, by design, powerful social studies classrooms utilize practical, relevant, hands-on activities that provide broader and deeper understandings for both disabled and non-disabled students (Connor & Legares, 2007; Curtis, 1982; Dunn, 2000; Duplass, 2008; Gargiulo & Metcalf, 2010; Hope, 1996; Mastropieri & Scruggs, 2010; Peterson & Hittie, 2010; Prater, 2007). Such rich and engaging opportunities are often lost to the more "expedient" means of teaching social studies, namely lecture, note-taking, and factual recitation (Schug, Todd, & Berry, 1984; Vogler & Virtue, 2007; Zhao & Hoge, 2005). When most students indentified with disabilities access social studies classrooms that emphasize factual recall and complex textual material, this creates challenges for student and teacher alike.

Given that a pedagogical disconnect exists between theory and practice, and knowing that more and more students with disabilities are being exposed to the social studies content, the premise of this chapter is to provide a sweeping overview of the relationship between social studies and special education. Specific attention will be given to defining seminal terms and concepts, describing prevalent disabilities and, lastly, offering select strategies when teaching social studies to students with disabilities.

THE MOST PREVALENT DISABILITIES

The most common disabilities general educators find in their classrooms are learning disabilities, speech and language impairments, intellectual disabilities or mental retardation, and emotional and/or behavioral disorders. In fact, U.S. Department of Education data reported in 2005, that approximately 91% of all students' ages 6–21 served under IDEA are included in one of these four categories (U.S. Department of Education, 2006). Other Health Impairments (e.g., Attention Deficit and Attention Deficit Hyperactivity Disorder, Epilepsy) make up the fifth largest group of students with disabilities (U.S. Department of Education, 2006). These five disabilities can be re-categorized into one term known as high incidence disabilities. IDEA (2004) recognizes a total of 13 categories of disability served in public schools (see Table 15.1).

MAINSTREAMING VERSUS INCLUSION

The passage of the *Education for All Handicapped Children* act (1975) led educators to examine the notion of teaching students with disabilities alongside their typical peers. The idea of mainstreaming involved the placement of students with disabilities into general education settings for a portion of the school day. At the time, mainstreaming was considered a privilege "students could earn by demonstrating [that] their skills were adequate to function independently in general settings" (Mastropieri & Scruggs, 2007, p. 6).

The concept of mainstreaming has since undergone many transformations. In the early 1990s, special educators began referring to the placement of students with disabilities into general education settings as inclusion. Inclusion is still the most popular term used when discussing the addition of students with disabilities into general education settings. Hunt and Marshall (2006) define inclusion as the placement of a child with a disability into general education settings while providing them with the necessary supports to succeed. However, there are disagreements regarding what inclusion should look like, thus making inclusion a hot topic among educa-

TABLE 15.1. 13 Categories of Exceptionality

Federal Terms	Definition
Autism	A developmental disability affecting communication and social interaction and generally evident before age three.
Deaf-blindness	A combination of hearing and visual impairments causing communication and developmental delays so severe that there is a need for services other than those offered to students with blindness or deafness.
Developmental delay	A category reserved for children ages birth to nine who exhibit delays in one or more of the following development areas: physical, cognitive, communication, social, or emotional.
Emotional disturbance	Behavioral or emotional responses that are different from those of all norms and referent groups. This term includes schizophrenia but does not apply to children who are socially maladjusted unless it is determined that they have an emotional disturbance.
Deafness and hearing loss	A permanent or fluctuating loss in hearing.
Intellectual disability	A significantly sub-average general intellectual functioning (65 or below) that exists concurrently with deficits in adaptive behavior (e.g., daily living and socialization skills) and is manifested during the developmental period (before age 18).
Multiple disabilities	A combination of impairments that causes such severe educational needs that the student cannot be accommodated in a special education program provided for in one of the other 12 IDEA disability categories. This category does not include individuals with deaf-blindness.
Orthopedic impairment	A term referring to students with physical disabilities or physical impairments.
Other health impairment	A chronic or acute health problem causing a student to have limited strength, vitality, or alertness in the educational environment.
Specific learning disability	A disorder in one or more of the basic psychological processes involved in understanding or using language (spoken or written) that may manifest itself in an imperfect ability to listen, think, speak, read, write, spell, or to do mathematical calculations.
Speech or language impairment	A communication disorder resulting in impaired articulation (e.g., stuttering, substitution, omission) or language impairment (difficulty comprehending or producing language).
Traumatic brain injury	An acquired injury to the brain resulting from an external physical force that causes a functional disability and/or psychosocial impairment. This term does not include brain injuries that are congenital or degenerative, or brain injuries induced by birth trauma.
Blindness and vision loss	An impairment in vision that, even with correction, adversely affects a child's educational performance.

tors. Misguidedly, many educators feel that simply changing the location of a child's instruction will result in more effective instruction (Taylor, Smiley, & Richards, 2009).

SELECTED STRATEGIES AND TOOLS TO TEACH SOCIAL STUDIES TO STUDENTS WITH DISABILITIES

When teaching students—any students—rarely does one strategy or instructional tool fit all. Astute classroom teachers intuitively know that, to teach powerful social studies, the "right and relevant" strategies and instructional tools need to be employed. There are scores of creative, engaging, and meaningful ways to teach social studies. Yet the literature consistently supports five main strategies or tools that can be used when teaching social studies to students with disabilities: big ideas, peer-tutoring, classwide tutoring, graphic organizers, and universal design for learning.

Big Ideas

Big ideas are questions or generalizations that serve to anchor the content, making the "smaller bits of information" easier to understand and easier to intellectually digest (Duplass, 2008; Mastropieri & Scruggs, 2010; McLesley, Rosenberg, & Westline, 2010). Big ideas allow students to organize the content and to apply their understandings of this content by making meaningful connections between their lives and the information being presented (Brophy, Alleman, & Knighton, 2009; Crawford et al., 2007). Ultimately, a big idea allows all students an opportunity to understand social studies in the most efficient, appropriate, and accessible way (Carnine & Kame'enui, 1998).

Conceptualizing Big Ideas

Grant and Vansledright (2006) offer three cornerstones when conceptualizing a big idea. First, begin with a question or an issue of interest. This questioning affords an inventory of prior knowledge about social studies (what is known), as well as a reflection of what may be explored (what to learn more about). Ultimately, this analysis of teacher-interest should transfer into heightened student-interest as well.

Secondly, as teachers begin to generate possible big ideas, they should ask:

- What do I want my students to know or to experience?
- Why will students care about or be interested in this idea?
- What do I want my students to "do" to understand/internalize the big idea?
- What resources will I need?

- How will I know if my students understand what I want them to understand? (Grant & Vansledright, 2006, p. 14).

Lastly, recognize that teaching social studies through big ideas encourages creativity and innovation. The pedagogical possibilities are endless. The combination of teacher ability and student interest facilitates rich, expressive, creative, challenging, relevant, and appropriate social studies for all students.

Brophy, Alleman, and Knighton (2009) advocate constructing big ideas using a three-step process. A big idea can be a sweeping construct used throughout the curriculum, throughout the year. An example may be, "Sometimes making (and keeping) friends is difficult to do. We see throughout history that friendships—alliances—either grow or wilt." This sweepingly inclusive big idea anchors a recurring theme (e.g. alliances) illustrated throughout the course of the school year. Secondly, big ideas can be used at the unit-level, where a series of lesson plans are tied to a single idea. For example, a unit on slavery can be anchored with the big idea, *"The Signs of Slavery."* Here, each lesson is tied back to the big idea. At the end of the unit, students will have generated multiple understandings of precisely *how* and *why* slavery was both manifested and perpetuated. Lastly, a big idea can literally be tied to a single lesson plan. A different big idea can be used every day. Regardless of design, anchoring social studies instruction to big ideas develops connections and applications that enhance the learning opportunities of all students.

Constructing Big Ideas

Inside-Out Model: When constructing a big idea using the Inside-Out Model, the big idea is the anchor from which subsequent content is based. Thus, the big idea starts "in the middle" and subsequently moves outward, generating facts and/or insights complimentary to the core idea. Ultimately, the big idea will be surrounded by "smaller bits of information" that serve to contextualize it. An example of a big idea could be *"Immigration: Blessing or Curse?"* Contextualizing facts and/or insights could be "discrimination," "rise of urban cities," "contributions." Again, it is the big idea that anchors the content.

Outside-In Model: This model of big idea construction is simply the converse of the Inside-Out Model. Here, complimentary or contextualizing information is generated first that, when combined, begins to form a big idea. The teacher can ask, "What do you know about maps?" Students will then provide small, individualized bits of information. When sufficient information has been gathered, the big idea of *"How Do I Know Where to Go?"* is generated and explored.

Multiple-Perspectives Model: An additional model teachers can use to present big ideas in their social studies classrooms is premised on the belief that virtually any topic can be viewed from multiple perspectives (Crawford et al., 2007). Presenting social studies through multiple perspectives broadens student core knowledge, fosters tolerance, spurs critical inquiry, and facilitates a deeper, more complete and complex understanding of the issue at hand (Dulberg, 2002; Marcus & Stoddard, 2009; Morgan, 2009; Ogawa, 2001; Vansledright, 2004). Using *"Movin' On or Movin' Out: Westward Expansion"* as the big idea, multiple perspectives can be presented that illustrate the often complex and contradictory nature of Westward Expansion. These contradictions can be easily presented in a compare-contrast format.

Peer-Tutoring

The role of peer tutoring in the teaching of social studies, particularly in an inclusive classroom setting, has been shown to be a powerful and effective tool for learning (McTeer & And, 1983; Miller, 2005; Stenhoff & Lignugaris/Kraft, 2007). Peer-tutoring allows students to share information in an informal, personal, and oftentimes more relevant way. It is simply students talking to students, often in pairs or, at most, trios. Peer-tutoring can be same-age (typically contained within the same classroom or grade level), or cross-age (where older students serve as tutors to younger students).

Yet peer-tutoring is not an educational panacea. Effective peer-tutoring programs rely on both teacher-structure and teacher-assistance (when needed). Mastropieri and Scruggs (2010) offer five steps in designing an effective peer-tutoring program:

- Step 1: Establish the content. What are the most important social studies concepts students should explore?
- Step 2: Establish a tutoring plan. Procedures are designed that outline the establishment of pairings, the length of tutoring sessions, and specific guidelines concerning communicative protocols, and access to and use of materials.
- Step 3: Establish roles and behaviors. The role of tutor and tutee are clearly defined. Behavioral expectations are set.
- Step 4: Monitor performance. The teacher must collect formative and summative data on both the efficacy and academic impact of peer-tutoring. The teacher must also know when to "step in" to assist in the process.
- Step 5: Work with either the general education or special education teacher. Plan time to work collaboratively, reviewing the insights gained from peer-tutoring and, ultimately, make the programmatic changes deemed necessary.

Classwide Peer Tutoring

One of the most recommended strategies for promoting achievement of groups of diverse learners in social studies classrooms is the use of classwide peer tutoring (Greenwood, Arreaga-Mayer, Utley, Gavin, & Terry, 2001; Greenwood, Delquardri, & Hall, 1989; Mastropieri, Scruggs, & Marshak, 2008). Classwide tutoring differs from traditional peer-tutoring in two specific ways. First, the traditional pairing scheme ("stronger" student with a "weaker" student) found in peer-tutoring models is not the premise of a classwide tutoring program. In a classwide model, students can be randomly assigned with such pairings changing throughout the year. Here, all students get to interact with all class members. Secondly, the static role of tutor and tutee found in peer models is blurred; in the classwide approach, students serve in both capacities. This affords a deeper understanding of the social studies content, as students serve as both "senders and receivers." In research conducted in a seventh-grade social studies classroom, Mastropieri et al., (2008) concluded that by providing students with an opportunity to systematically question each other using unit-based "fact sheets," students, particularly those with special needs, scored higher on unit tests when classwide peer tutoring was implemented.

Graphic Organizers

The primary goal of using graphic organizers in social studies classrooms is to present the material both visually and spatially (Duplass, 2008; Gallavan & Kottler, 2007; Klemp, McBride, & Ogle, 2007; Stockard, 2001; Wilson, 2002). Graphic organizers assist students in focusing attention on, organizing, and recalling important social studies concepts. As many social studies concepts and constructs can be confusing and seemingly disconnected, using graphic organizers helps to visually structure the content making it accessible and easier to understand (McLeskey, Rosenberg, & Westling, 2010).

Arguably, the most common form of graphic organizer is the dominant/subordinate model. Here, the "dominant" theme or idea is placed in the middle. From this, "subordinate" information is either provided (by the teacher) or generated (by the student). This design is similar to the Inside-Out model of constructing and presenting big ideas referenced earlier. Another type of graphic organizer is the "top-down flow chart." In this model, the dominant theme is presented with supporting information flowing below it (e.g. the way the Three Branches of Government is often presented). Regardless of the structure, graphic organizers provide all students a simple, visually-rich, and creative way of accessing the social studies content.

Universal Design for Learning

The basic tenet of Universal Design for Learning (UDL) is accessibility. Originating in the field of architecture, the premise of UDL can be evidenced through curb cuts. Curb cuts were first designed to provide access to individuals in wheelchairs. Yet curb cuts inevitably provide access to persons pushing baby strollers, students pulling backpacks, and people who walk with a cane or crutches (Lewis & Doorlag, 2011; Salend, 2011; Thousand, Villa, & Nevin, 2007). This notion of universal accessibility was ultimately incorporated into the design and delivery of school curriculum. "The central premise of UDL is that a curriculum should include alternatives to make it accessible and appropriate for individuals with different backgrounds, learning styles, abilities, and disabilities in widely varied learning contexts" (Center for Applied Technology, 2003). When applied in educational settings, UDL assists all learners in accessing the general education curriculum and, ultimately, succeeding in inclusive classrooms (Hitchcock, 2001; Meo, 2008; Salend, 2011).

There are three conceptual cornerstones to UDL. First, teachers need to use *multiple means of representation.* Simply, teachers need to provide options in how the content is presented (Bouck, Courtad, Heutsche, Okolo, & Englert, 2009). Multiple means of representation may include visual or graphic displays, auditory formats, text-based instruction, peer support, and teacher lecture. Secondly, allow students *multiple means of expression.* Written assignments, oral or visual presentations, role playing, position papers, KWL's, compare and contrast charts, simulations, and traditional tests and/or quizzes are ways in which all students can demonstrate their understanding(s) of the social studies content (Bouck et al., 2009; Salend, 2011). Lastly, UDL provides students with *multiple means of engagement.* Instruction can be whole group, independent learning, cooperative groups, or partnering (Bouck et al., 2009). Ultimately, UDL provides choices for both students and teachers and allows all students appropriate and responsible access to the curriculum.

A fantastic program that links social studies content with UDL is the Virtual History Museum (VHM). Located at http://vhm.msu.edu/site/default. php:

> [VHM] provides supports and scaffolds to students with disabilities in an effort to increase their participation and achievement in social studies, especially United States and world history. VHM assists students in understanding social studies content through methods of analysis and interpretation of evidence and artifacts, exploring multiple perspectives, and enabling students to publish their own interpretations of events in social studies. (Bouck et al., 2009, p. 15)

VHM is a web-based "real" museum in which the teacher effectively becomes the museum's curator. The teacher culls exhibits for students to examine, interpret, and analyze. Students can create their own exhibits as well. A rich gathering of text-based and digital media are available, enabling the "curator" to design instruction and assessment to match the learning needs of all students. Ultimately, VHM helps teachers create a more responsive, flexible curriculum that engages students across a spectrum of learning styles and abilities (Bouck et al., 2009).

THE FUTURE OF SOCIAL STUDIES AND SPECIAL EDUCATION

In 1995, Neil Houser declared that social studies was on the back burner. Though one can argue if social studies has heretofore gained any prominence on the proverbial academic stove, what may be collectively agreed upon is that, from the federal government down to the elementary classroom, social studies is still relegated to the fringes of perceived importance (Heafner et al., 2006; Lintner, 2006; Zhao & Hoge, 2005). Throw into this perceptual mix special education. Railed as too expensive, lamented by general education teachers as "something else I have do," special education and social studies share many of the same practical and perceptual struggles—misperception, miscommunication, and missed opportunities.

So, where to go from here? We pose two ways that the both general and special education teachers can facilitate a more responsive and collaborative relationship between social studies and special education. First, general education teachers must become more comfortable and more confident in teaching students with disabilities. A common lament is that general education teachers "just don't know what to do" when addressing the learning needs of students with disabilities. Their pleas for help are not unfounded. Many teacher-education programs require but a single class in special education. Coupled with the push to include more students with disabilities into general education classrooms, it is no wonder that teachers generally feel underprepared and overwhelmed. We assert that general education teachers want to find appropriate ways to reach and teach all students, yet they simply don't have the "tools" by which to do so. In an effort to assuage the concerns of some general educators, we offer these suggestions:

- Read about how to teach students with disabilities. There is an abundance of text- and internet-based resources available. By reading how best to teach students with disabilities, general education teachers inevitably become a more responsive and reflective teacher of all students.

- Attend a district-sponsored workshop or a conference. Take an additional class or two in special education. The goal is to find assets within the special education community that can perceptually and pedagogically influence general education classrooms.
- Talk with school-based special education faculty. The most expedient resource for general education teachers is literally down the hall.

Secondly, in an effort to increase the pedagogical relationship between social studies and special education, we advocate adopting a co-teaching model of instruction (Kohler-Evans, 2006; Murawski & Dieker, 2008; Ploessi, Rock, Schoenfeld, & Blanks, 2010). The merits (and struggles) of co-teaching between general educators and special educators are clearly evident (Beirne-Smith, Smith, & The University of Alabama Tuscaloosa, 1997; Friend, Cook, Hurley-Chamberlain, & Shamberger, 2010; Keefe & Moore, 2004; McHatton & Daniel, 2008; Murawski, 2008). The co-teaching model is premised on shared responsibility in the design and delivery of the curriculum. Both the general education and special education teachers are present during instruction. Both alternate between the role of deliverer (actually teaching the content) and monitor (observing and/or assisting). At the end of the lesson, both teachers debrief and make modifications to the lesson as warranted. At its core, co-teaching allows both teachers to "learn what the other one does." It tightens the relationship between social studies and special education. And, ultimately, "As these two fields begin to combine their skills and talents, the outcome will be an atmosphere where problems are shared and the ultimate outcome of meeting the needs of all students will be accomplished" (Dieker, 1998, p. 65).

CONCLUSION

With inclusive classrooms firmly entrenched in the educational landscape, finding ways to reach and teach all students may never be more imperative. To create powerful social studies opportunities for all students, teachers need to be creative in their instructional design, relevant in their instructional delivery, and reflective of their educational practice. The inclusion model of classroom practice demands nothing less. Through the purposeful selection of materials, the careful incorporation of instructional strategies and tools, and the overarching belief that engaging, participatory social studies is rightfully accessible to all students, teachers can slowly build the pedagogical and practical bridge between social studies and special education. Working towards this common goal can revolutionize the way social studies is perceived and practiced.

REFERENCES

Bean, R. (1994). Adapted use of social studies textbooks in elementary classrooms: Views of classroom teachers. *Remedial and Special Education, 15*(4), 216–226.

Beirne-Smith, M., Smith, C., & The University of Alabama Tuscaloosa (1997). *Collaborative planning between general and special educators. Final report.* (ERIC Document Reproduction Service No. 411 633).

Bouck, E. C., Courtad, C. A., Heutsche, A., Okolo, C. M., & Englert, C. S. (2009). The virtual history museum: A universally designed approach to social studies curriculum. *TEACHING Exceptional Children, 42*(2), 14–20.

Brophy, J., Alleman, J., & Knighton, B. (2009). *Inside the social studies classroom.* New York: Routledge.

Brownlee, W. A. (1988). History and the learning disabled student. *History and Social Science Teacher, 24*(1), 28–29.

Carnine, D. & Kame'enui, E. J. (1998). *Effective teaching strategies that accommodate diverse learners.* Upper Saddle River, NJ: Merrill.

Center for Applied Technology (2003). *Summary of universal design for learning concepts.* Boston: Author. Retrieved June 20, 2010, from http://www.cast.org/udl/index.cfm?=7

Connor, D. J., & Legares, C. (2007). Facing high stakes in high school: 25 successful strategies from an inclusive social studies classroom. *TEACHING Exceptional Children, 40*(2), 18–27.

Crawford, D. B., Carnine, D. W., Harniss, M. K., Hollenbeck, K. I., & Miller, S. K. (2007). Effective strategies for teaching social studies. In M. D. Coyne, E. J. Kame'enui, & D.W. Carnine (Eds.), *Effective teaching strategies that accommodate diverse learners.* Upper Saddle River, NJ: Merrill.

Curtis, C. (1982). Teaching disabled students in the regular social studies classroom. *History and Social Science Teacher, 18*(1), 9–16.

Dieker, L. (1998). Rationale for co-teaching. *Social Studies Review, 37*(2), 62–65.

Dulberg, N. (2002). *Engaging in history: Empathy and perspective-taking in children's historical thinking.* (ERIC Document Reproduction Service No. ED 474 135.)

Dull, L.J., & van Garderen, D. (2005). Bringing the story back into history: Teaching social studies to children with learning disabilities. *Preventing School Failure, 49*(3), 27–31.

Dunn, M.A. (2000). Closing the book on social studies: Four classroom teachers go beyond the text. *Social Studies, 91*(3), 132–136.

Duplass, J.A. (2008). *Teaching elementary social studies: Strategies, standards, and internet resources* (2nd ed.). Boston: Houghton Mifflin.

Fontana, J. L. (2004). Social studies and students with disabilities: Current status of instruction and a review of intervention research with middle and high school students. In T. E. Scruggs & M. A. Mastropieri (Eds.), *Research in secondary schools: Advances in learning and behavioral disabilities* (Vol. 17, pp. 175–205). Oxford, US: Elsevier.

Friend, M., Cook, L., Hurley-Chamberlain, D., & Shamberger, C. (2010). Co-teaching: An illustration of the complexity and collboration in special education. *Journal of Educational & Psychological Consultation, 20*(1), 9–27.

Gallavan, N., & Kottler, E. (2007). Eight types of graphic organizers for empowering social studies students and teachers. *Social Studies, 93*(3), 117–123.

Gargiulo, R. M., & Metcalf, D. (2010). *Teaching in today's inclusive classrooms: A universal design for learning approach.* Belmont, CA: Wadsworth: Cengage Learning.

Grant, S. G., & Vansledright, B. (2006). *Elementary social studies: Constructing a powerful approach to teaching and learning* (2nd ed.). Boston: Houghton Mifflin Company.

Greenwood, C., Arreaga-Mayer, C., Utley, C., Gavin, K., & Terry, B. (2001). Classwide peer tutoring learning management system: Applications with elementary-level English language learners. *Remedial and Special Education, 22*(1), 34–47.

Greenwood, C., Delquadri, J., & Hall, H. (1989). Longitudinal effects of classwide peer tutoring. *Journal of Educational Psychology, 81*, 371–383.

Harbin, G., Rous, B., & McLean, M. (2005). Issues in designing state accountability systems. *Journal of Early Intervention, 27*(3), 137–164.

Heafner, T., Lipscomb, G., and Rock, T. (2006) To test or not to test? The role of testing in elementary social studies: A collaborative study conducted by NCPSSE and SCPSSE. *Social Studies Research and Practice, 1*(2), 145–162.

Hickey, G. M., & Braun, P. (1990). *Social studies and the disabled reader.* (ERIC Document Reproduction Service No. ED 322 080).

Hitchcock, C. (2001). Balanced instructional support and challenge in universally designed learning environments. *Journal of Special Education Technology, 16*(4), 23–30.

Hope, W. C. (1996). It's time to transform social studies teaching. *Social Studies, 87*(1), 149–151.

Houser, N. (1995). Social studies on the back burner: Views from the field. *Theory and Research in Social Education, 23*(2), 147–168.

Hunt, N., & Marshall, K. (2006). *Exceptional children and youth.* (4th ed.). Boston, MA: Houghton-Mifflin.

Keefe, E., & Moore, V. (2004). The challenge of co-teaching in inclusive classrooms at the high school level: What the teachers told us. *American Secondary Education, 32*(3), 77–88.

Kohler-Evans, P. (2006). Co-teaching: How to make this marriage work for the kids. *Education, 127*(2), 260–264.

Klemp, R., McBride, B., & Ogle, D. (2007). *Building literacy in social studies: Strategies for improving comprehension and critical thinking.* (ERIC Document Reproduction Service No. 509 065).

Lewis, R. B., & Doorlag, D.H. (2011). *Teaching students with special needs in the general education classroom* (8th ed.). Boston: Pearson.

Lintner, T. (2006). Social studies (still) on the back burner: Perceptions and practices of K–5 social studies instruction. *Journal of Social Studies Research, 30*(1), 3–8.

Lintner, T., & Schweder, W. (2008). Social studies in special education classrooms: A glimpse behind the closed door. *Journal of Social Studies Research, 32*(1), 3–9.

Marcus, A., & Stoddard, J. (2009). The inconvenient truth about teaching history with documentary films: Strategies for presenting multiple perspectives and teaching controversial issues. *Social Studies, 100*(6), 279–284.

Mastropieri, M., & Scruggs, T. (2007). *The inclusive classroom: Strategies for effective differentiated instruction* (3rd ed.). Upper Saddle River, NJ: Merrill.

Mastropieri, M., & Scruggs, T. (2010). *The inclusive classroom: Strategies for effective differentiated instruction* (4th ed.). Upper Saddle River, NJ: Merrill.

Mastropieri, M. A., Scruggs, T. E., & Marshak, L. (2008). Training teachers, parents, and peers to implement effective teaching strategies for content area learning. In T. E. Scruggs & M. A. Mastropieri (Eds.), *Personnel preparation: Advances in learning and behavioral disabilities* (vol. 21, pp. 311–329). Bingley, UK: Emerald.

McCoy, K. (2005). Strategies for teaching social studies. *Focus on Exceptional Children, 38*(3), 1–14.

McHatton, P., & Daniel, P. (2008). Co-teaching at the pre-service level: Special education majors collaborate with engligh education majors. *Teacher Education and Special Education, 31*(2), 54–67.

McLeskey, J., Rosenberg, M. S., & Westline, D. L. (2010). *Inclusion: Effective practices for all students.* Boston: Pearson.

McTeer, J., & And, O. (1983). *Peer tutoring as an instructional methodology for social studies teaching.* (ERIC Document Reproduction Service No. ED 230 477).

Meo, G. (2008). Curriculum planning for all learners: Applying universal design for learning (UDL) to a high school reading comprehension program. *Preventing School Failure, 52*(2), 21–30.

Meuwissen, K.W. (2005). Maybe someday the twain shall meet: Exploring disconnections between methods instruction and "life in the classroom." *Social Studies, 96*(6), 253–258.

Miller, M. (2005). Using peer tutoring in the classroom: Applications for students with emotional/behavioral disorders. *Beyond Behavior, 15*(1), 25–30.

Morgan, H. (2009). Picture book biographies for young children: A way to teach multiple perspectives. *Early Childhood Education Journal, 37*(3), 219–227.

Murawski, W. (2008). Five keys to co-teaching in inclusive classrooms. *School Administrator, 65*(8), 29.

Murawski, W., & Dieker, L. (2008). 50 ways to keep your co-teacher: Strategies for before, during, and after co-teaching. *TEACHING Exceptional Children, 40*(4), 40–48.

Ochoa, A. S., & Schuster, S. K. (1980). *Social studies in the mainstreamed classroom.* Boulder, CO: Social Science Educational Consortium.

Ogawa, M. (2001). *Building multiple historical perspectives: An investigation of how middle school students are influenced by different perspectives.* (ERIC Document Reproduction Service No. ED 465 685).

Palloway, E. A, Patton, J. R., & Serna, L. (2008). *Strategies for teaching learners with special needs.* (9th ed.). Upper Saddle River, NJ: Prentice Hall.

Passe, J., & Beattie, J. (1994). Social studies instruction for students with mild disabilities. *Remedial & Special Education, 15*(4), 22–27.

Patton, J. R., Polloway, E. A., & Cronin, M. E. (1987). Social studies instruction for mildly handicapped students: A review of current practices. *Social Studies, 78*(3), 131–135.

Peterson, J. M., & Hittie, M. M. (2010). *Inclusive teaching: The journey towards effective schools for all learners.* (2nd ed.). Upper Saddle River, NJ: Pearson.

Ploessi, D., Rock, M., Schoenfeld, N., & Blanks, B. (2010). On the same page: Practical techniques to enhance co-teaching interactions. *Intervention in School and Clinic, 45*(3), 158–168.

Prater, M. A. (2007). *Teaching strategies for students with mild to moderate disabilities.* Boston, MA: Pearson/Allyn & Bacon.

Salend, S. (2011). *Creating inclusive classrooms: Effective and reflective practices* (7ᵗʰ ed.). Boston: Pearson.

Schug, M. C., Todd, R. J., & Berry, R. (1984). Why kids don't like social studies. *Social Education, 48*(5), 382–387.

Scruggs, T. E., Mastropieri, M. A., & Okolo, C. M. (2008). Science and social studies for students with disabilities. *Focus on Exceptional Children, 41*(2), 1–24.

Smith, D. D. (2007). *Introduction to special education: Making a difference.* (6ᵗʰ ed.). Boston: Allyn & Bacon.

Steele, M. M. (2007). Teaching social studies to middle school students with learning problems. *Clearing House: A Journal of Educational Strategies, Issues and Ideas, 81*(5), 197–200.

Stenhoff, D., & Lingnugaris/Kraft, B. (2007). A review of the effects of peer tutoring on students with mild disabilities in a secondary setting. *Exceptional Children, 74*(1), 8–30.

Stockard, J. W. (2001). *Methods and resources for elementary and middle-school social studies.* Long Grove, IL: Waveland.

Tama, C. A., & Martinez, D. H. (1988). TELSQA and the mainstreamed LD social studies student. *Social Studies, 79*(6), 274–277.

Taylor, R. L., Smiley, L. R., Richards, S. B. (2009). *Exceptional students: Preparing teachers for the 21ˢᵗ century.* Boston: McGraw-Hill.

Thousand, J. S., Villa, R. A., & Nevin, A. I. (2007). *Differentiating instruction: Collaborative planning and teaching for universally designed learning.* Thousand Oaks: Corwin Press.

Turner, T.N. (1976). Making the social studies textbook a more effective tool for less able readers. *Social Education, 40*(1), 38–41

U.S. Department of Education (2005). *Twenty-seventh annual report to congress on the implementation of the Individuals with disabilities education act.* Washington D.C.

U.S. Department of Education (2006). *Twenty-eighth annual report to congress on the implementation of the Individuals with disabilities education act.* Washington D.C.

Wilson, E. (2002). Literature and literacy in the social studies classroom: Strategies to enhance social studies instruction. *Southern Social Studies Journal, 28*(1), 45–57.

Vansledright, B. (2004). What does it mean to think historically…and how do you teach it? *Social Education, 68*(3), 230.

Vogler, K., & Virtue, D. (2007). "Just the facts, ma'am": Teaching social studies in the era of standards and high-stakes testing. *Social Studies, 98*(2), 54–58.

Ysseldyke, J. (2005). Assessment and decision making for students with learning disabilities: What if this is as good as it gets? *Learning Disability Quarterly, 28*(2), 125–136.

Zhao, Y., & Hoge, J.D. (2005). What elementary students and teachers say about social studies. *Social Studies, 96*(5), 216–221.

CHAPTER 16

ENGLISH LANGUAGE LEARNERS (ELLS) AND SOCIAL STUDIES

Jason O'Brien

INTRODUCTION

Students who do not speak English as their first language are enrolling in ever-increasing numbers in the nation's schools. Teachers need to be equipped with the pedagogic skills and knowledge to help these students reach high levels of achievement. Social studies teachers are particularly important because current inclusion practices place multiple and diverse English Language Learners (ELLs) in regular social studies classrooms where they are expected to learn valuable citizenship skills necessary for participation in a democratic society. The following chapter is a resource for social studies educators and researchers alike who are concerned with meeting the needs of ELL students. The chapter will define and contextualize the growing numbers of ELLs in the nation's classrooms as well as discuss the importance of linguistic support for these students. Relevant research conducted in the past fifteen years will be briefly presented and the chapter concludes with several suggestions for future research regarding ELLs and social studies.

Contemporary Social Studies: An Essential Reader, pages 293–315
Copyright © 2012 by Information Age Publishing

BACKGROUND

Various terms have been used to label students in U.S. schools who are not proficient in English. Among these labels are Limited English Proficient (LEP), English Speakers of Other Languages (ESOL), and Non-Native English Speakers (NNES). Currently, the most common descriptor used by educators and researchers, and legitimized by the federal and state departments of education, is the term ELLs. By definition, ELLs are "students whose native language is a language other than English or come from environments where a language other than English is dominant" (National Center for Educational Statistics, 2003). The label itself is telling: the goal of instruction in most schools today is clearly for ELLs to learn English as quickly as possible.

However, this has not always been the case in the nation's schools. A significant ideological shift has occurred in the United States over the past 30 years. The passage of Title VII of the Elementary and Secondary Education Act of 1968 initiated a period of multilingual educative policies in which schools offered students curricular content in more than one language (Baca & Cervantes, 2004). Language education policy acknowledged the importance of maintaining the student's home language while simultaneously developing English language skills. These practices, known as *bilingual education* showed the most promise for ELLs (Lindholm-Leary & Borsato, 2002). Truly bilingual education allowed students to strengthen literacy skills in their home language and promoted transfer of these literacy and cognitive skills to English (Montecel & Cortez, 2002). Despite the multiple benefits of bilingualism, however, its cost-prohibitive nature prevented its implementation on a broad scale across the United States (Peregoy & Boyle, 2005; Spaulding, Carolino, & Amen, 2004).

In the early 1980s a conservative political climate and concerns about cultural and demographic change led to English-only movements across the country and effectively ended any widespread paradigmatic acceptance of bilingual instruction (Crawford, 1992). More recent legislation such as *No Child Left Behind* (2001), Proposition 227 in California, and other English-only legislation have solidified the emphasis on ELLs learning English as quickly as possible. While the efficacy of monolingual policies in schools is disputed, few would argue that to be successful in American schools, ELLs need to learn English.

ELL POPULATIONS IN AMERICAN SCHOOLS

The number of ELLs present in U.S. schools has grown significantly in the last several decades primarily due to immigration and higher birthrates for this population. Evidence of this growth can be found in U.S. Census data reported in 2000 which indicated that 18.4% of the population of the United States between the ages of 5–17 (i.e., school-aged children) spoke a language other than English at home (U.S. Census, 2000). In the ten-year period between the 1997 and 2007 school years, the percentage of ELLs in schools increased nationwide by 53% to more than 5.3 million students (NCELA, 2010b). Compared with other sub-groups in the nation's schools, these statistics indicate that ELLs are the fastest growing population in K–12 environments (Cruz & Thornton, 2009). On the eve of the 2010 census results, all demographic indicators have pointed to the continued growth of this group in the nation's schools.

FEDERAL AND STATE LAW IN REGARDS TO TEACHING ELLS

The policies which guide current ELL instruction find their origins in the Civil Rights Act of 1964. This legislation mandated that "no person on the ground of race, color, or national origin may be...subjected to discrimination under any program receiving federal funding" (Civil Rights Act, 1964). ELLs are protected under this law because their primary use of a language other than English is viewed as an extension of their national origin. In 1974, in the case *Lau v. Nichols*, a group of Chinese immigrants challenged the San Francisco school district and maintained that their language minority children were not receiving equal educational treatment under the provisions of Title VI of the Civil Rights Act. At this time, the school district of San Francisco had established a policy that required students to be proficient in English before they could participate in the educational programs of the schools.

The subsequent ruling by the Supreme Court is considered a landmark case in educational policy for ELLS on the scale of importance with 1954's *Brown v. Board of Education* in civil rights policies. The Supreme Court stated that "by [solely] providing students with the same facilities, textbooks, teachers, and curriculum...students who do not understand English are effectively foreclosed from any meaningful education" (*Lau v. Nichols*, 1974). The *Lau v. Nichols* decision gave the Office of Civil Rights (OCR) authority to regulate how schools were to design meaningful instruction that was responsive to the needs of ELLs (Berube, 2000).

The OCR took a reactive, rather than proactive stance in dealing with violations of *Lau v. Nichols*. The result was that while many school districts implemented some general policy for ELLs, the "policy was usually cast in vague and imprecise terms" (Walqui, 2000, p. 17) with no connection to student outcomes. To address the deficiencies of the practical application of *Lau v. Nichols*, the U.S Court of Appeals in *Castañeda v. Pickard* (1981) established guidelines to measure schools' compliance with the law. The measures taken by school had to be based on sound educational theory, implemented effectively with adequate resources, and evaluated as effective in overcoming language handicaps (*Castañeda v. Pickard, 1981*). Unfortunately for ELLs, due to political resistance and limited resources for enforcement, the "Castaeda standard" has only been applied on a small scale in K–12 environments and has had a limited effect nationwide (Crawford, 2004).

Two other lawsuits, initiated by private groups, significantly altered educational practices in two states with high populations of ELLs, Illinois and Florida. In the case of *Gomez v. Illinois State Board of Education* (1987), the Seventh Circuit Court of Appeals ruled that both state education agencies and local education agencies were required to ensure that the needs of limited-English-proficient children are met. Failure to do so could result in the state board of education being sued by a private entity. As a result of this ruling, education agencies have been forced to be more diligent in assigning teachers with ESL certification to content area courses. In Florida, the League of United Latin American Citizens (LULAC) sued the State Board of Education, alleging that ELLs' needs were not being met in the state's schools. The resulting decision, known as the "Florida Consent Decree" was enacted in August, 1990, and mandated that all K–12 public school teachers were either required to take 60 in-service hours of ELL training, or three college credits of a state-approved ELL education course (Florida Consent Decree, 1990).

In January of 2002, President George W. Bush signed the *No Child Left Behind Act* (NCLB) into law. Rather than resulting from a lawsuit, it was initiated by the federal government as a way to improve the quality of education across the nation by increasing accountability. NCLB mandated that all students, including ELLs, reach high standards by demonstrating proficiency in English language arts and mathematics by 2014 (NCLB, 2001). Under Title I regulations mandated by the U.S. Department of Education, ELLs who enter schools are tested from day one in mathematics and in reading/language arts after only ten months in school. Unfortunately, the tests used to evaluate students' academic progress are written in English, and are problematic, in terms of validity and reliability, when measuring ELLs' English or content mastery. Specifically, tests which assume English proficiency are not able to differentiate errors due to insufficient content mastery or limited English proficiency (Crawford, 2004).

One of the negative consequences of NCLB concerns specific sub-populations (e.g., ELLs) who do not make Adequate Yearly Progress (AYP) based on standardized test scores. When this occurs, schools and school districts face sanctions ranging from having to develop a comprehensive school improvement plan after failing to meet AYP initially, to the termination of teachers and closing of schools after several years of failing to meet learning goals. The ramifications of NCLB have been a significant narrowing of the curricula. Subjects which have historically been integral parts of curricula (e.g., art, music, physical education, or social studies) are given less instructional time than mathematics and language arts especially in primary and intermediate elementary grades (Abedi & Dietel, 2004).

CONTENT INSTRUCTION FOR ELLS

In the past, ELLs attended schools primarily in metropolitan areas which were considered migration "hubs" and which were home to large concentrations of non-English speakers. School districts in these areas ordinarily placed ELLs in sheltered or language-supported learning environments with other English learners and a trained English Speaker of other Languages (ESOL) specialist. Currently, most school districts utilize *mainstreaming* or *inclusion* practices for ELLs. Carrasquillo and Rodriguez (2002) describe mainstreaming as placing ELLs in content-area classrooms where the curriculum is delivered through English: often instruction is not modified to meet the needs of ELLs. According to Meltzer and Hamann (2005) there are several underlying assumptions that guide these mainstreaming practices, among these are notions by non-educators about what ELLs need, the scarcity of ESOL-trained teachers relative to demand, the growth of ELL populations, and restrictions in states regarding the time that ELLs can stay in ESOL programs.

What is clear about these policies is that they place a greater responsibility on all content area teachers who in the past were only responsible for teaching curricular content to English-speaking students. Unfortunately, data available indicate that content area teachers are largely untrained to effectively modify instruction for ELLs (Cruz & Thornton, 2009; Reeves, 2006). The ramifications of these policies will be discussed at length later in this chapter.

LANGUAGE ACQUISITION

To this point, ELLs have been described as a single group, however, while many students are classified as ELLs, they are not a homogeneous group. Kindler (2002) identified 400 distinct languages spoken in U.S. schools, with approximately 60% of those speaking Spanish as their native language. Further, the level of proficiency in both the student's home language as well as English varies widely. Some ELLs are heritage language learners whose language use is indistinguishable from that of native speakers, but many others are recent immigrants with very low fluency levels, especially with regards to academic English (Erben, 2009).

For recently arrived immigrants, the age at which they enter U.S. schools is particularly important. Immigrants who arrive later in their lives face unique challenges with academic course credit requirements and the growing pressures of exit level standardized exams required by most states (Salinas, 2006). *Late arrival immigrants*, as these students are called, are at a greater risk of academic failure not only because they have a limited time frame to acquire English language skills in the classroom prior to exit tests, but also because many are underprepared for grade level schoolwork. Prior education levels among these students vary greatly and some enter high school with less than four years of formal education in their home countries. Collier (1987) compared standardized test scores among different age groups and found that ELLs who arrive in the U.S. at ages twelve to fifteen encounter the greatest difficulty compared to their counterparts aged eight to eleven and five to seven, respectively.

Another complicating factor in teaching ELLs is the language acquisition process can vary significantly among students in the same classroom. Researchers have noted that second language acquisition is highly dependent upon a number of social and environmental factors such as fluency in their native language, overall intelligence levels, and motivation to learn (Crawford, 2004). As with other students in K–12 schools, socioeconomic status seems a particularly important factor in acquiring English language skills. Children from high-poverty, less educated backgrounds tend to need more time to acquire English (Hakuta, Butler & Witt, 2000).

While different students require different amounts of time to acquire English, some commonalities of language acquisition exist. Krashen & Terrell's (1983) seminal work created a four-tiered description of the different stages of language acquisition. In the first level, or *preproduction* stage, students produce very little English and devote considerable amounts of cognitive energy simply decoding words. The next stage is called *early production*. As the name implies, ELLs produce one- or two-word responses as their vocabulary in English grows. At the *speech emergence* stage students interact more freely with English. They have a larger receptive vocabulary (words which they understand) and a larger active vocabulary (words they can produce). At the stage of *intermediate fluency*, ELLs demonstrate near-native fluency in social communication but their academic vocabulary remains behind that of native English speakers.

The distinction between social language and academic language is important when teaching or assessing ELLs. Linguists (most notably Cummins, 1979) have further defined two classifications of language proficiency for students. These two classifications are Basic Interpersonal Skills (BICS) and Cognitive Academic Language Proficiency (CALP). BICS is social or conversational language that is used to communicate with others. This language is more concrete than abstract, and is usually supported by context clues, such as gestures, facial expressions, and body language (Cummins, 1979; Echevarria & Graves, 2010). CALP is specialized language that is used for academic purposes which includes decoding difficult vocabulary and communicating abstract ideas. As an example, learning citizenship skills and content mastery are difficult for ELLs without minimum levels of CALP.

A large body of research indicates that while BICS are ordinarily learned by students within the first two years of speaking a language, CALP may take as long as seven to ten years to master (Cummins, 1979). One of the misconceptions of content teachers regarding the process of second language acquisition (Olsen, 1997; Reeves, 2004; Walqui, 2000) is that many teachers in these studies consistently underestimated the time it takes for ELLs to acquire a sufficient level of academic English. Specifically, most teachers thought that ELLs should be able to master English within two years of entering school. If teachers believe that social language is the same as academic language, they may be presenting content in a manner which is incomprehensible for ELLs or may expect understanding of material that is beyond the ELLs' linguistic ability rather than intellectual ability. Conversely, if social studies teachers do not try to develop CALP in ELLs, these students may fall farther behind their English-speaking classmates. Several researchers have shown that many ELLs do not acquire sufficient levels of CALP through content-area instruction (August & Hakuta, 2005; August & Shanahan, 2006; Short & Fitzsimmons, 2007) and that inadequately developed CALP manifests in lower GPAs, repeating grades, and low graduation rates (Ruiz de Velasco & Fix, 2000; Suárez-Orozco & Suárez-Orozco, 2001).

These factors, as well as others, have created a significant academic achievement gap between the performance of ELLs and native speakers. Since 2001, state test results show that ELLs' school performance is far below that of other students, oftentimes 20 to 30 percentage points, and ordinarily shows little improvement across several years (Abedi & Dietel, 2004). Recalling the punitive measures that are taken against schools under NCLB as a result of low test scores, this achievement gap can have significant effects on schools and school systems. Data such as this point to the need for improved teacher preparation to work with ELLs in K–12 educational settings.

TEACHER PREPARATION AND ELLS

Given their growing presence in the nation's classrooms, one would expect that preparation to teach ELLs would be an integral part of most secondary methods courses. However, the limited data on this subject seems to indicate that this is not the case, at least in regards to social studies. Many content area teachers, including those who teach social studies, lack sufficient training or coursework to meet the needs of ELLs. In a study of 25 of the most frequently used texts by social studies teacher educators, Watson, Miller, Driver, Rutledge, and McAllister, (2005) discovered that less than one percent of the textbooks contained useable content related to the teaching of ELLs; in many cases, the topic of ELLs in the classroom was not addressed at all. Elementary methods instruction seems to follow a similar pattern. In a study conducted in New England states, Levine and Maley (2009) found that only six of thirty-one elementary syllabi examined contained any reference to teaching students who are linguistically diverse.

In an effort to address this shortcoming, Levine (2009) proposed a conceptual framework for social studies teacher educators with the following four components: *understandings, practices, dispositions,* and *vision. Understanding* refers to pre-service teachers understanding the components of social studies content which are particularly challenging for ELLs as well as understanding how ELLs' cultural values and backgrounds, as well as first language skills can provide either a resource or an impediment to learning social studies. *Practices* refers to pedagogic approaches social studies teachers can use when altering instruction to make it more culturally responsive to ELLs. *Dispositions* are "habits of thinking and action regarding teaching and children" (Hammerness, Darling-Hammond, & Bransford, 2005, p. 387) which are inextricably linked to the affective domain. Positive dispositions in teachers have been shown to affect teacher efficacy in regards to seeking out new approaches to teaching (Haberman, 1996) as well as fostering a belief that all children, regardless of background, can succeed in the classroom (Ladson-Billings, 2001).

Professional Development for Practicing Teachers

Given the lack of preparation in established teacher education programs, many states have begun offering English as a Second Language (ESL) endorsements for their content area teachers (e.g., social studies, math, science, and English). These endorsements are earned by taking a prescribed sequence of courses from an accredited college or university. As of 2003, the National Clearinghouse for English Language Acquisition & Language Instruction Educational Programs reported that 42 states and the District of Columbia offered such endorsements (National Clearinghouse for English Language Acquisition, 2003). However, other data indicate that many content area teachers, social studies included, have not taken advantage of these opportunities. In 2002, the National Center for Education Statistics reported that only 12.5% of the nation's teachers had received eight or more hours of training to teach ELLs who are present in content area classrooms (National Center for Education Statistics, 2002).

As a way to improve instruction for ELLs, many school districts have begun providing (and sometimes requiring) training for their secondary content area teachers (Berube, 2000). However, researchers have found that many secondary teachers resist this training. Gonzalez and Darling-Hammond (1997) hypothesized that "many teachers have experienced one or more sessions in which experts from outside the school present ideas in the manner of traveling salesmen" (p. 35) and that this "one shot" approach seems to lead to a general lack of teacher efficacy when teaching ELLs.

O'Brien (2011) conducted a study in one of the ten largest school districts in the nation to measure high school social studies teachers' attitudes towards training and support they received to teach ELLs in their content-area classes. Due to the enactment of the *Consent Decree* in Florida all the teachers in the district were required to have ELL training as a condition of their employment. The researcher expected that because Florida has long experienced high numbers of ELLs in content courses, teachers would have reported high levels of confidence and support when teaching ELLs. Unfortunately, comments from teachers in this study indicated perceived significant deficiencies in the training provided for teachers, both at the university level and from the school district. The training provided by the school district consisted of watching reportedly ineffective ELL training videos for a total of sixty hours, with no sustained follow-up support to help teachers implement the training in the classroom. One participant stated, "On the job would be the bulk of my training. It's like any other teacher workshop, you go there and you come back to your classroom and figure out what works" (p. 11).

Barriers for ELLs in Social Studies

To this point, we have examined general policies and training in regards to ELLs as well as the language acquisition process. Just as the language acquisition process varies among ELLs, the difficulty of teaching content areas varies across disciplines. In social studies classes, the presence of ELLs offers unique opportunities to integrate language and cultural awareness into the curriculum. However, social studies curriculum also offers significant challenges. One challenge is the structure of most social studies courses. Levstik (2008) points out that in many social studies classrooms content is presented orally or requires discussion of material. ELLs at the early stages of language acquisition have neither the listening skills nor the active vocabulary necessary to participate in these activities. Short (2002) observes that while many social studies teachers use some visual aids to help students understand content, demonstrations and hands-on materials (which facilitate comprehension for ELLs) are rarely used. These concrete activities can contextualize content and make it more relevant and understandable to ELLs and native English speakers.

Possibly the most vexing challenge for social studies teachers when teaching ELLs is the nature of the content itself. Social studies content can be more complex than, as an example, math or science, because the content reflects multiple perspectives on particular people and events, and learning goals are often difficult to measure over short terms. Although gains in social studies content knowledge can be measured with end-of-course exams, the ultimate goal of social studies instruction is to create effective citizens (Duplass, 2008), a multi-faceted goal which requires advanced use of language. Another significant challenge faced by ELLs is the difficult vocabulary terms endemic to social studies instruction. Many of these vocabulary words are highly abstract (e.g., justice, liberty, responsibility, etc.) and are subject to culturally-embedded meanings and experiences (Chamot & O'Malley, 1994). And while it would be problematic to assume that ELLs have no prior knowledge of the United States, the experiences they do have may reflect different understandings rooted in their home culture and educational systems (Szpara & Ahmad, 2007).

Another obstacle often mentioned in the literature is the nature of social studies textbooks, which have historically been an important component of social studies instruction. Dwyer (2007) analyzed textbook vocabulary according to grade level and found that the increase in the number of social studies vocabulary words by grade level exceeded other content areas including those for English and Language Arts. Brown (2007) wrote "that the narrative style of social studies texts is characterized by complex syntax, technical vocabulary, and a lack of helpful context...which ELLs find extremely challenging to read and comprehend" (p. 185). Short (1994) studied American history instruction in grades six through nine and found that many ELLs do not receive the language and academic support they need to master the vocabulary and difficult reading and writing that are common to the social studies classroom.

Given these barriers and the difficulty inherent in instruction, effective instructional modifications seem paramount in ELLs' instruction. Several researchers examined how efficacious secondary teachers were at modifying coursework for ELLs. Reeves (2004) and Youngs (1999) found that secondary content teachers were primarily concerned about equity issues when modifying coursework for ELLs. Specifically, they felt that altering requirements for ELLs would be unfair to the native English speaking students. This finding resonated with a study by O'Brien (2007) of 123 high school social studies teachers. In this study, one of the most common difficulties listed by teachers was "the ability to modify coursework for ELLs" (p. 80). This study also found that the major modification most often reported by teachers was simply allowing ELLs more time to complete tasks. These data point to a need for more teacher preparation to help them effectively plan and implement instruction which will be comprehensible for ELLs.

RESEARCH ON TEACHERS AND ELLS

Few areas have generated as much literature in the past 40 years as teacher expectations. Beginning with Rosenthal and Jacobson's (1968) controversial study of the self-fulfilling prophecy, teachers and researchers have long debated the importance of teacher expectations on student achievement. For ELLs, especially newly-arrived immigrants, perhaps the most important contact with native speakers is with their teachers. Brisk (1998) reported that teacher attitudes towards ELL inclusion can have a significant impact on their educational experiences and opportunities. Operating under this assumption, several qualitative studies were conducted in the late 1990s which investigated teacher attitudes towards ELLs in their content-area classes. Researchers in these studies uncovered a broad spectrum of teacher attitudes towards ELLs. For instance, teachers in some studies reported having negative attitudes (Fu, 1995; Olsen, 1997; Schmidt, 2000; Valdes, 2001) while others reported positive, welcoming attitudes (Harklau, 2000; Reeves, 2004; Verplaetse, 1998). Two consistent themes which emerged in these studies from the teachers with negative attitudes was their frustration with extra time required to teach ELLs and their lack of understanding of second language acquisition. While these teachers focused on the negative aspects of teaching a diverse group, the teachers with more positive attitudes valued the cultural diversity brought to their classrooms and showed greater empathy for their students who were working to learn English.

Teachers' classroom decision-making is important for all students and seems especially important for ELLs. Thornton (2005) posits that social studies teachers act as "gatekeepers" and makes the point that "teachers make day-to-day decisions concerning both the subject matter and the experiences to which pupils have access and the nature of the subject matter and those experiences" (p. 1). While Thornton's central thesis concerns curricula, the notion of teachers as "gatekeepers" can nonetheless be especially important for ELLs because of teachers' ability to encourage or discourage discourse, and also to choose which types of questions are asked of the students. Researchers have found that for many ELLs, their prior experiences in schools or in their native home culture may not have prepared them for questioning authority, asserting their view on a controversial topic, or even speaking in class without fear of reprisal (Szpara & Ahmand, 2006).

Researchers (Sharkey & Layzer, 2000; Verplaetse, 1998) who have studied secondary classrooms have found that ELLs are often marginalized in the classroom and their opportunities to interact are minimized, even when the classroom teachers had the best of intentions for their students. In a social studies classroom, this marginalization is the polar opposite of the goals of the instruction, in that citizenship education requires active participation. If students are not allowed to exercise their "voice" in the classroom, then early attempts at democratic participation are lost. Furthermore, Verplaetse (1998) found that the teachers in her study wanted to protect their ELLs from embarrassment so they refrained from asking difficult questions and often completed the students' answers for them. Opportunities to interact with others are critical for ELLs because language interaction plays an important part in language development. Specifically, interaction gives ELL students an opportunity to create unique language output, and forces them to manipulate components of the new language (Swain, 1985). Teachers who do not allow ELL students the opportunity to produce language, in an effort to protect them from embarrassment, are engaged in what Hatch (1992) calls a "benevolent conspiracy" (p. 67). By attempting to create a comfortable environment without checking or facilitating development of CALP or academic content knowledge, teachers effectively block access to content knowledge and language acquisition.

In a study of thirty-three high school social studies teachers in Virginia, Cho and Reich (2008) found that 70.6% of the teachers listed ELLs' lack of background knowledge as the most significant challenge to instruction. A majority of teachers (58.8%) also listed language barriers between the teacher and student to be an issue of concern. When asked about instructional modifications, almost all (90.6%) indicated that their most common practice was allowing extra time for ELLs to complete assignments. Missing from these findings were specific pedagogic techniques or modification of assignments by teachers to help make content more comprehensible for ELLs. The researchers also asked these teachers which types of training they would like to receive in the future. Ninety percent of the teachers indicated that they would like training in understanding other cultures. This contradicted earlier responses by teachers in that only 5.9% of the participants mentioned cultural differences between the teacher and ELLs as a concern. The researchers hypothesized that social studies teachers may have had a bias against selecting "cultural differences between me and my ELL" as a barrier because many valued cultural diversity in their classroom (p. 241).

O'Brien (2009) utilized survey and interview data to measure a broad range of secondary social studies teachers' attitudes towards including ELLs in their classrooms. Major concerns of teachers in this study were the inability to effectively communicate with ELLs, and the inability to modify instruction for ELLs. While more than half of the participants stated that they would welcome the inclusion of ELLs in their classes, more than three-fourths (76.5%) felt that ELLs *should not be* included in their class until they had attained a minimum level of English. A majority of teachers in this same study mentioned "diversity" or some aspect of "cross-cultural awareness" as the greatest benefit of including ELLs in their classrooms. These findings seemed to indicate that while teachers saw the benefits of having

ELLs in their classrooms, these same teachers did not see themselves as responsible for teaching students English. Unfortunately for secondary ELLs, the inclusionary practices which take place in most schools require content area teachers to teach both—subject-specific knowledge and skills as well as English language skills—simultaneously.

RESEARCH ON ELL INSTRUCTION

The remainder of this chapter will focus on what researchers, both in the field of linguistics and social studies, have found to be effective when teaching content to ELLs. While the methods and strategies reported here are not exhaustive, they are a snapshot of some best practices identified by researchers. This information is useful for practicing teachers as a way to inform their teaching, and for academics as a way to hopefully suggest lines of inquiry.

Most training for content teachers whether in university coursework or in professional development, is based on one of two theories. The first is the Cognitive Academic Language Learning Approach (CALLA) which is "an instructional model that fosters the school achievement of students who are learning through the medium of a second language" (Chamot, 1995, p. 379). The CALLA model for teaching content to ELLs relies on the explicit instruction of learning strategies, alongside content instruction. The goal of this instructional model is for ELLs to actively construct meaning using the guidance of the teacher.

The second model was created by Jana Echevarría, Mary Ellen Vogt and Deborah Short and is called Sheltered Instruction Observation Protocol (SIOP). In the SIOP Model, language and content objectives are systematically woven into the grade-level curriculum that teachers present to students through modified instruction in English. Teachers systematically develop students' CALP as part of their lessons, paying careful attention to the English learners' second language development needs (Echevarria, Vogt, & Short, 2010). While these frameworks differ slightly in methodology, both offer research-based methods for teaching content simultaneously with academic English.

Consider the following example of a social studies lesson taught using this pedagogic framework. Ordinarily, when teachers teach students about the California Gold Rush, there may be several important themes they want their students to learn during the lesson. Examples such as *push* and *pull* factors of emigration, notions of scarcity of resources causing increases in price, as well as the notion of Manifest Destiny would all be central to the lesson. Using the SIOP framework, the teacher would also work towards specific language goals. For example, two language goals might be "The student can write a complete sentences telling what it was like in the West" and "Tell how the structure of some words give clues to their meaning." The advantage of the SIOP model is that it consciously focuses the teacher and the ELL's attention on both content and language development goals during one lesson.

Culturally Responsive Instruction

Many ELLs who enter social studies classrooms come from cultures other than that of the United States. One effective response to a multicultural classroom is what Gay (2000) calls *culturally responsive pedagogy*. Teachers who are culturally responsive seek ways to validate ELLs' home language and culture. Peregoy and Boyle (2005) found that when students sense that teachers truly recognize and value their home language and culture, they are more likely to feel positive about school and learning. One way to show students that their culture is valued is to learn their cultural norms. Behaviors such as not forcing students to make eye contact or adhering to cultural practices about physical touch can all make students feel comfortable and ease the transition into American culture.

An example of effective CRP could be used while teaching about the Alamo. In history textbooks, this conflict is often taught as struggle for independence against "an autocratic foreign government, namely Mexico" (Cruz & Thornton, 2008). Mexican schools teach that this conflict was based on aggressive land acquisition by non-Spanish speaking settlers. If teachers teach this topic simply as it is commonly represented in the official curriculum, ELLs from Mexico might feel alienated if the Mexican soldiers or citizens are portrayed negatively. Teachers could show the multiple viewpoints involved in the conflict as a way to validate the actions of other groups and to show that the teacher is willing to share alternate viewpoints that are less ethnocentric. The ultimate goal is not to rewrite history, rather to teach students the diverse perspectives that exist on most social studies topics.

Visual Aids in Instruction

Another effective practice for teachers is to use realia, or real objects, to add interest and to help convey meaning. The use of real objects, charts, pictures, or photographs is an essential feature of effective instruction because it provides necessary support to contextualize learning (Dunlap & Weisman, 2006). Asking students to bring objects, drawings, or photographs related to their own family can provide an explicit link with their background knowledge, thus making the content more relevant to their experiences, and thus more comprehensible.

Graphic organizers are also an effective teaching tool that can support ELLs' understanding of difficult concepts and text (Weisman & Hansen, 2007; see also Salinas, Franquiz, & Guberman, 2006). Rather than passively answering questions on worksheets, organizers such as Venn diagrams, cause and effect charts, concept maps, drawings, images, music and videos can help students understand important concepts and understand the relationship between ideas. Graphic organizers encourage ELLs to express more complex ideas with tools that do not require elaborate written responses with syntactic or grammatical expertise. For students at the pre-production or "silent" stages of language acquisition, these organizers can be especially useful as a tool for teachers to assess student comprehension (Tannenbaum, 1996).

Student Interaction

ELLs at all levels of English acquisition can make contributions to class discussions. Obviously, students in the pre-production stages may only be able to answer simple questions with one- or two-word responses, but it is still imperative to include all students in class discussions. When utilizing lectures for whole-group instruction, content teachers should pay close attention to their rate of speech and should allow more wait time when requiring responses from ELLs. Allowing ELLs to work in collaborative groups with other ELLs is a successful strategy reported by teachers (O'Brien, 2007; Reeves, 2004). Working in small groups, especially with other ELLs who are more proficient in English and other English-speaking students, can foster a low-anxiety learning atmosphere which is particularly important to ELLs (Krashen, 1994). As students communicate with others regarding academic content, they are practicing literacy skills which can lead to better-developed CALP.

FUTURE DIRECTIONS FOR
SOCIAL STUDIES RESEARCH FOR ELLS

Today, one in five students in the United States is the child of immigrants and by 2040 that ratio is projected to increase to one in three (Hernandez, Denton, & Macartney, 2007). As the school-age population of the nation's classrooms becomes more diverse it is incumbent upon school administrators, ELL support personnel, teachers, and universities to collaborate in meeting the needs of these students. Several researchers have begun focusing their research efforts on social studies learning and ELLs (Cruz & Thornton, 2009; Janzen, 2008) as well as curricular considerations that may benefit the educational experiences of these students (Brown, 2007; Misco & Castañeda, 2009; Salinas, Sullivan & Wacker, 2007). However, researchers in the field of social studies education have much work to do. In her 2008 College and University Faculty Association (CUFA) keynote speech, Linda Levstik stated that ELLs' learning of social studies is among the most important areas which need further research (Levstik, 2008).

To these ends, teacher education programs should examine ways to more effectively prepare pre-service teachers to teach ELLs. By utilizing frameworks such as the one proposed by Levine (2009), teacher educators can measure both attitudinal changes (i.e., attitudes towards ELLs) as well as behavioral changes (i.e., instructional modifications) in future social studies teachers. Ladson-Billings (2001) has experimented with a pedagogic framework for pre-service teachers that focus' on diversity, equity, and social justice (p. xiii). Teachers in this program are expected to challenge the climate of low expectations which often exists when teaching students from diverse backgrounds. Frameworks, such as these, include affective components to allow future teachers to overcome some of the negative attitudes which researchers have reported among teachers of ELLs.

Another theoretical framework which seems particularly promising was developed by Yosso (2005) and is known as "cultural wealth theory." Embracing this theory in social studies classes can lead educators to move away from thinking of ELLs as being culturally or linguistically deficient but rather to include the wealth of knowledge that they bring into the classroom. Often, immigrants have first-hand experiences of topics only studied theoretically in American classrooms (e.g., totalitarian governments, unsafe working conditions, civil unrest, and censorship). Pedagogic models which include these students' voices may lead to higher achievement and engagement with the curricula.

Professional development for practicing teachers is another area for future study. Given the themes of resistance to teacher training that exist in the literature (Gonzalez & Darling-Hammond, 1997; Reeves, 2006), researchers can investigate different types of professional development that both increases teachers' efficacy when teaching ELLs, as well as improving learning outcomes for these students. Rather than providing one-time training, several researchers (Barnett, 2002; Milambiling, 2002, Schechter & Cummins, 2003) document the effectiveness of ongoing, sustained, and collaborative training efforts for improving teachers' ability to effectively teach ELLs. An important attribute which all have in common is the emphasis of "locally-devised, context specific solutions over the importation of solutions from other school settings" (Reeves, 2006, p. 139). Furthermore, a major goal of teacher training should be to make content area teachers understand what ESOL teachers have known for years: that teaching strategies (e.g, context clues, graphic organizers, activation of background knowledge) which benefit ELLs are helpful to *all* students.

Research to improve educational experiences of ELLs will require funding. Potential sources of funding are available through the Office of English Language Acquisition (OELA) as well as through Title I and Title III programs which set aside research dollars to address the achievement gap between ELLs and native speakers. Along with OELA, the National Clearinghouse for English Language Acquisition (NCELA) exists as a resource to scholars and researchers which seek to convey a broad range of research related to ELLs and to also provide resources "in support of an inclusive approach to high quality education for ELLs" (NCELA, 2010a).

Last, researchers might consider innovative ways to foster home-school relationships with the parents of ELLs. Scholars have found that parental involvement leads to improved student achievement, better school attendance, and reduced dropout rates for all students (Inger, 1992; Lucas, Henze, & Donato, 1990). Given the study of multiple cultures inherent in social studies instruction, these environments seem a likely place for teachers to make a focused effort to engage and involve parents of ELLs in the education of their children. Including and involving parents has the potential to demonstrate civic duty in action as teachers and schools come together with families to help them participate in a society that often marginalizes these populations.

CONCLUSION

Social studies teachers have the responsibility of preparing their students to be participatory and effective citizens. While native-born English-speaking students may learn many facets of citizenship through everyday interactions with their parents or friends, ELLs often lack these experiences with their families. They learn about citizenship through experiences in social studies classrooms. In these classes ELLs learn not only the academic and civic training necessary for participation in society as adults, but these academic expriences can also provide the avenue for social integration upon which future civic participation is built (Parker, 2001). For these reasons, with perhaps the exception of English, social studies classrooms are the most important for ELLs' success in society. To the extent that social studies teachers do not foster both linguistic development and comprehension of content, they risk stunting the growth of this ever-increasing group in American schools.

REFERENCES

Abedi, J., & Dietel, R. (2004). *Challenges in the No Child Left Behind Act for English language learners.* National Center for Research on Evaluation, Standards and Student Testing (CRESST). Retrieved February 12, 2011, from http://www.cse.ucla.edu/products/policy/cresst_policy7.pdf.

August, D., & Hakuta, K. (2005). Bilingualism and second-language learning. In M. Suárez-Orozco, C. Suárez-Orozco, & D .B. Qin (Eds.), *The new immigration: An interdisciplinary reader* (pp. 233–248). New York: Brunner-Routledge.

August, D., & Shanahan, T. (2006). *Developing literacy in second language learners: Report of the national literacy panel on language minority children and youth.* Mahwah, NJ: Lawrence Erlbaum.

Baca, L., & Cervantes, H. (2004). *The bilingual special education interface.* Upper Saddle River, NJ: Pearson Publishing.

Barnett, J. (2002). From the margins to the center: ESL as a whole school endeavor. In E. F. Cochran (Ed.), *Mainstreaming* (pp. 7–19). Alexandria, VA: Teachers of English to Speakers of Other Languages.

Berube, B. (2000). *Managing ESL programs in rural and small urban schools.* Alexandria, VA: TESOL.

Brown, C. (2007). Strategies for making social studies texts more comprehensible for English language learners. *The Social Studies, 98*(5), 185–188.

Brisk, M. (1998). *Bilingual education: From compensatory to quality schooling.* Mahwah, NJ: Lawrence Erlbaum.

Casteñada v. Pickard, (1981). 648 F.2d 989 (5th Circuit).

Carrasquillo, A., & Rodriguez, V. (2002). *Language minority students in the mainstream classroom, 2nd edition.* Boston, MA: Multilingual Matters.

Chamot, A. (1995). Learning strategies and listening comprehension. In D. Mendelsohn & J. Rubin (Eds.), *A guide for teaching of second language listening.* San Diego, CA: Dominie Press.

Chamot, A., & O'Malley. (1994). *The CALLA Handbook: Implementing the cognitive academic learning approach.* Reading, MA: Addison-Wesley.

Cho, S., & Reich, G. (2008). New immigrants, new challenges: High school social studies teachers and English language learner instruction. *The Social Studies, 99*(6), 235–242.

Civil Rights Act of 1964. (1964). 42 U.S.C. 2000d.

Collier, (1987). Age and rate of acquisition of second language for academic purposes. *TESOL Quarterly, 21*(4), 617–641.

Crawford, J. (1992). Editor's introduction. In C. Crawford (Ed.), *Language loyalties: A source book on the official English controversy* (pp.1–8). Chicago: University of Chicago Press.

Crawford, J. (2004). *No Child Left Behind: Misguided approach to school accountability for English language learners.* Washington, DC: National Association for Bilingual Education, Center on Educational Policy.

Cruz, B., & Thornton, S. (2009). *Teaching social studies to English language learners.* New York: Routledge.

Cummins, J. (1979). Linguistic interdependence and the educational development of bilingual children. *Review of Educational Research, 49*(2), 222–251.

Dunlap, C., & Weisman, E. (2006). *Helping English language learners succeed.* Huntington Beach, CA: Shell Educational.

Duplass, J. (2008). Social studies: In search of a justification. *The Social Studies Record, 47*(2), 45–51.

Dwyer, E. (2007). "The Power of Social Studies." Paper presented at the 41st annual TESOL convention and exhibit, March 21–24, in Seattle, Washington.

Echevarria, J., & Graves, A. (2010). *Sheltered content instruction: Teaching English language learners with diverse abilities* (4th ed.). Boston: Allyn & Bacon.

Echevarría, J., Vogt, M., & Short, D. (2010). *Making content comprehensible for English learners.* Boston, MA: Allyn and Bacon Publishing.

Erben, T. (2009). Orientation to English language learners. In B. Cruz & S. Thornton, *Teaching social studies to English language learners* (pp. 7–8). New York:Routledge.

Florida Consent Decree. (1990). League of United Latin American Citizens (LULAC) et al. v. State Board of Education Consent Decree, United States District Court for the Southern District of Florida, August 14, 1990.

Fu, D. (1995). *My trouble is English: Asian students and the American dream.* Portsmouth, NH: Heinemann.

Gay, G. (2000). Culturally responsive teaching: Theory, research, and practice. New York: Teachers College Press.

Gomez v. Illinois State Board of Education. (1987). 811 F2d 1030.

Gonzalez, J., & Darling-Hammond, L. (1997). *New concepts for new challenges: Professional development for teachers of immigrant youth.* McHenry, IL: Center for applied Linguistics.

Haberman, M. (1996). Selecting and preparing culturally competent teachers for urban schools. In J. Sikula, T. Butter, & E. Guyton (Eds.), *Handbook of research on teacher education* (pp. 747–760). New York: McMillan.

Hakuta, K., Butler, Y., & Witt, D. (2000). *How long does it take for English learners to attain proficiency?* Santa Barbara, CA: Linguistic Minority Research Institute.

Hammerness, K., Darling-Hammond, L., & Bransford, J. (2005). How teachers learn and develop. In L. Darling-Hammond & J. Brandsford (Eds.), *Preparing teachers for a changing world: What teachers should learn and be able to do.* San Francisco, CA: Jossey-Bass.

Harklau, L. (2000). From the 'good kids' to the 'worst': Representations of English language learners across educational settings. *TESOL Quarterly, 34*(1), 35–67.

Hatch, E. (1992). *Discourse and language education.* Cambridge, MA: Cambridge University Press.

Hernandez, D., Denton, N., & Macartney, S. (2007). *Children in immigrant families— the U.S. and 50 states: National origins, language, and early education* (Research Brief Series 2007–2011). Albany, NY: State University of New York, Child Trends Center for Social and Demographic Analysis.

Inger, M. (1992). *Increasing the school involvement of Hispanic parents. Eric Clearinghouse on Urban Education.* (Eric Document No. EDO-UD-92-3).

Janzen, J. (2008). Teaching English language learners in the content areas. *Review of Educational Research, 78*(4), 1010–1038.

Kindler, A. (2002). *Survey of the states' limited English proficient students & available educational programs and services 1999–2000 summary report.* National Clearinghouse for English language Acquisition and Language instruction Educational Programs. Washington, DC.

Krashen, S. (1994). Bilingual education and second language acquisition theory. In C. Leyba (Ed.), *Schooling and language minority students: A theoretical framework,* (pp. 47–75). Sacramento, CA: California State Department of Education.

Krashen, S., & Terrell, T. (1983). *The natural language approach: Language acquisition in the classroom.* London, UK: Prentice Hall Europe.

Ladson-Billings, G. (2001). *Crossing over to Canaan: The journey of new teachers in diverse classrooms.* San Francisco, CA: Jossey-Bass.

Lau v. Nichols (1974). 414 US 563

Levine, T. (November, 2009). *Addressing linguistic diversity in social studies methods courses: A rationale and conceptual framework.* Unpublished paper presented at the College and University Faculty Association (CUFA) conference for the National Council for the Social Studies, Atlanta, GA.

Levine, T., & Maley, C. (2009). [Patterns of practice and wisdom of practice in social studies teacher education]. Unpublished raw data.

Levstik, L. (2008). What happens in social studies classrooms? Research on K–12 social studies. In L. Levstik & C. Tyson (Eds.), *Handbook of research in social studies education,* (pp. 50–64). New York: Routledge.

Lindholm-Leary, K., & Borsato, G. (2002, May). *Impact of two-way bilingual elementary programs on students' attitudes toward school and college.* Berkeley, CA: Center for Research on Education, Diversity & Excellence.

Lucas, T., Henze, R., & Donato, R. (1990). Promoting the success Latino language-minority students: An exploratory study of six high schools. *Harvard Educational Review, (60)*,3, 315–340.

Meltzer, J., & Hamann, E. (2005). *Meeting the literacy development needs of adolescent English language learners through content-area learning. Part two: Focus on classroom teaching strategies.* Providence, RI: Education Alliance at Brown University.

Milambiling, J. (2002). Good neighbors: Mainstreaming ESL students in the rural Midwest. In E. Cochran (Ed.), *Mainstreaming,* (pp. 21–30). Alexandria, VA: Teachers of English to Speakers of Other Languages.

Misco, T., & Castañeda, M. (2009). "Now, what should I do for English language learners?": Reconceptualizing social studies curriculum design for ELLs. *Educational Horizons, 87*(3), 182–187.

Montecel, M., & Cortez, J. (2002). Successful bilingual education programs: Development and the dissemination of criteria to identify promising and exemplary practices in bilingual education at the national level. *Bilingual Research Journal, 26*(1), 1–21.

National Center for Education Statistics. (2002). *School and staffing survey 1999–2000: Overview of the data for public, private, public charter and Bureau of Indian Affairs elementary and secondary schools.* Washington, DC: U.S. Department of Education.

National Center for Education Statistics. (2003). *Characteristics of the 100 largest public elementary and secondary school districts in the U.S.: Definitions.* Washington, DC: U.S. Department of Education.

National Clearinghouse for English Language Acquisition (2003). *Policy report: Summary of findings related to LEP and SpEd-LEP students.* Washington, DC. Document number ED-00-CO-0089.

National Clearinghouse for English Language Acquisition (NCELA), (2010a). *The growing number of English learner students 1997/98–2007-08.* Retrieved September 23, 2010 from http://www.ncela.gwu.edu/files/uploads/9/growing-LEP_0708.pdf

National Clearinghouse for English Language Acquisition (NCELA), (2010b). *National Clearinghouse for English Language Acquisition homepage.* Retrieved October 6, 2010, from http://www.ncela.gwu.edu/.

No Child Left Behind Act. 20 U.S.C. § 6319 (2001).

Olsen, L. (1997). *Made in America: Immigrant students in our public schools.* New York: The New Press.

O'Brien, J. (2007). High school social studies teachers' attitudes towards the inclusion of ELL students in mainstream classes. Unpublished doctoral dissertation, University of South Florida, Tampa.

O'Brien, J. (2009). High school social studies teachers' attitudes toward English language learners. *Social Science Research & Practice, 4*(2), 36–48.

O'Brien, J. (2011). The system's broken and it's failing these kids: High school social studies teachers' attitudes towards training for ELLs. *Journal of Social Studies Research, (35)*1, 22–38.

Parker, W. (2001). Educating democratic citizens: A broad view. *Theory into Practice, 40*(1), 6–13.

Peregoy, S. & Boyle, O. (2005). *Reading, writing, and learning in ESL: A resource book for K–12 teachers.* Boston, MA: Pearson Education.

Reeves, J. (2004). 'Like everyone else': Equalizing educational opportunity for English language learners. *TESOL Quarterly, (38)*1, 43–66.

Reeves, J. (2006). Secondary teacher attitudes towards including English-language learners in mainstream classrooms. *The Journal of Educational Research, (99)*3, 131–142.

Rosenthal, R. & Jacobson, L. (1968). *Pygmalion in the classroom: Teacher expectations and student intellectual development.* New York: Holt, Rinehart, and Winston.

Ruiz de Velasco, J., & Fix, M. (2000). *Overlooked and underserved: Immigrant students in U.S. secondary schools.* Washington, DC: Urban Institute.

Salinas, C. (2006). Educating late arrival high school immigrant students: A call for a more democratic curriculum. *Multicultural Perspectives, 8*(1), 20–27.

Salinas, C., Fránquiz, & Guberman, S. (2006). Introducing historical thinking to second language learners. *The Social Studies, 97*(5), 203–207.

Salinas, C., Sullivan, C, & Wacker, T. (2007). Curriculum considerations for late-arrival high school immigrant students: Developing a critically conscious world geography studies approach to citizenship education. *Journal of Border Educational Research, 6*(2), 55–67.

Schechter, S. , & Cummins, J. (2003). *Multilingual education in practice: Using diversity as a resource.* Portsmouth, NH: Heinemann.

Schmidt, M. (2000). Teachers' attitudes toward ESL students and programs. In S. Wade (Ed.), *Inclusive education: A casebook and readings for prospective and practicing teachers* (pp. 121–128). Mahwah, NJ: Erlbaum.

Sharkey, J, & Layzer, C. (2000). Whose definition of success? Identifying factors that affect English language learners' access to academic success and resources. *TESOL Quarterly, 34*(2), 352–366.

Short, D. (1994). Expanding middle school horizons: Integrating language, culture, and social studies. *TESOL Quarterly, (28)*3, 581–608.

Short, D. (2002). Language learning in sheltered social studies classes. *TESOL Journal, 11*(1), 18–24.

Short, D., & Fitzsimmons, S. (2007). *Double the work: Challenges and solutions to acquiring language and academic literacy for adolescent English language learners.* Washington, DC: Alliance for Excellent Education.

Spaulding, S., Carolino, B., & Amen, K. (2004). *Immigrant students and secondary school reform: Compendium of best practices.* Washington, DC: Council of Chief State Officers.

Suárez-Orozco, C., & Suárez-Orozco, M. (2001). *Children of Immigration.* Cambridge, MA: Harvard University Press.

Swain, M. (1985). Communicative competence: Some roles of comprehensible input and comprehensible output in its development. In S. Gass & C. Madden (Eds.), *Input and second language acquisition* (pp. 235–257). Rowley, MA: Newbury House.

Szpara, M., & Ahmad, I. (2006, Spring). Making social studies meaningful for ELL students: Content and pedagogy in mainstream secondary classrooms. *Essays in Education, 16,* University of South Carolina Aiken.

Szpara, M., & Ahmad, I. (2007). Supporting English-language learners in social studies class: Results from a study of high school teachers. *The Social Studies, 98*(5), 189–196.

Tannenbaum, J. (1996). *Practical ideas on alternate assessment for ESL students.* ERIC Digest. ED 395 500.

Thornton, S. (2005). *Teaching social studies that matters.* New York, NY: Teachers College Press.

U.S. Census. (2000). *Language use, English ability, and linguistic isolation for the population 5 to 17 years by state.* Retrieved from http://www.census.gov/publication/cen2000/phc-t20/tab02.pdf.

Valdes, G. (2001). *Learning and not learning English: Latino students in American schools.* New York: Teachers College Press.

Verplaetse, L. (1998). How content teachers interact with English language learners. *TESOL Journal, 7*(1), 24–28.

Walqui, A. (2000). *Access and engagement: Program design and instructional approaches for immigrant students in secondary schools.* McHenry, IL: Center for Applied Linguistics.

Watson, S., Miller, T., Driver, J., Rutledge, V., & McAllister, D. (2005). English language learner representation in teacher education textbooks: A null curriculum. *Education, 126*(1), 148–157.

Weisman, E., & Hansen, L. (2007). Strategies for teaching social studies to English-language learners at the elementary level. *The Social Studies, 98*(5), 180–184.

Yosso, T. (2005). Whose culture has capital? A critical race theory discussion of community cultural wealth. *Race, Ethnicity, and Education, 8*(1), 69–91.

Youngs, C. (1999). Mainstreaming the marginalized: Secondary mainstream teachers' perceptions of ESL students. Unpublished doctoral dissertation, University of North Dakota, Grand Forks.

SECTION IV

PEDAGOGY

CHAPTER 17

READING, DEMOCRACY AND SECONDARY SOCIAL STUDIES EDUCATION

Michelle Reidel and Christine Draper

INTRODUCTION

A strong democracy depends upon the ability of the people to not only comprehend what they read but to also question and challenge it (O'Quinn, 2006). While the capacity to gather information from both print and nonprint materials is important, unaccompanied by the ability and disposition to critique and interpret these materials from a variety of perspectives, it is at best technical literacy; at worst a form of civic illiteracy (O'Quinn, 2006). It is difficult to imagine anyone in our media-saturated world developing the knowledge and skills necessary to engage in the decision-making practices required in a multicultural democratic society if they are ill-prepared

Contemporary Social Studies: An Essential Reader, pages 319–334
Copyright © 2012 by Information Age Publishing
All rights of reproduction in any form reserved.

or unable to critically read a wide variety of texts. Yet this is the exact reality facing a large number of adolescents in the United States.

The current crisis in adolescent literacy is well-documented. National Assessment of Educational Progress (NAEP) exam results from 2009 reveal that most secondary students are "reading significantly below expected levels" (National Center for Educational Statistics, 2010, p. 2). Approximately 70% of middle and high school students score at or below the "proficient" level indicating that they can decode but cannot understand or evaluate grade-level texts (NCES, 2010). For many students who are reading proficiently at the middle school level, the transition to high school brings with it discipline-specific literacy demands that they are ill-equipped to meet. The result is a precipitous decline in reading proficiency among high school students that is closely aligned with high drop-out rates (NCES, 2010). In most high school classrooms, students engage in very little sustained reading and that reading is often limited to teacher-created handouts and textbooks (Heller & Greenleaf, 2007). Recent studies by the National Endowment for the Arts (NEA) in 2004 and 2007 reveal that adolescents' reading practices outside of school are also cause for concern. In *To Read or Not to Read*, the NEA documents that "the first generation of students raised in the midst of electronic media read less—and less well—than previous generations" (2007). While adolescents' online reading of websites, blogs, email and tweets may be increasing, research suggests that Internet-based reading fosters "shallow" reading practices that do little to support the development of critical thinkers and citizens (NEA, 2007). Results from both NEA studies reveal that reading is decreasing across all social and educational groups and that this retreat from reading has negative cultural, economic and civic implications (NEA, 2004, 2007).

Social Studies educators can play an important role in reversing this alarming trend by helping their students acquire reading skills needed to actively and meaningfully participate in our democracy. The Social Studies classroom can be a powerful context to encourage students to not only read a wide variety of texts but to also question what they read (Soares & Wood, 2010; Wineburg & Martin, 2004). In this chapter we delineate the ways in which critical literacy is an important element of a vibrant and strong democracy and consider how secondary Social Studies educators can support the development of their students' reading skills. To do so, we analyze the ways in which reading instruction has traditionally been positioned in secondary education and the challenges of content area literacy. We draw upon the work of both content area literacy specialists and Social Studies educators and use insights from this literature to outline future possibilities for research, teacher education and classroom practice.

THE RELATIONSHIP BETWEEN
CRITICAL LITERACY AND DEMOCRACY

Understanding Critical Literacy

Critical literacy is often defined as reading and writing pedagogy that gives voice to oppressive experiences within oppressive social systems (Freire, 1972; Lankshear & McLaren, 1993; Lesley 2005; Shor, 1999). Within this framework, literacy is not seen as a series of skills to master, but rather as a contextualized "emerging act of consciousness and resistance" (Giroux, 1981, p. 367). Critical literacy seeks to help students understand whose interests are served and represented through both the stories we are told and the stories we tell (Janks, 2010). In doing so, students' lives and the ways in which they are socially, politically, and culturally situated become the most compelling text in any classroom (Haas-Dyson, 2001). Haas-Dyson notes that critical literacy invokes societal and local matters because "it is something we do in response to others' words and actions, including their voiced views of the social world" (p. 5). This is what enables and empowers students to understand the social construction of themselves, their fellow classmates, their family, cultures, and the world beyond the classroom.

Encouraging students to understand that knowledge is not neutral is a core dimension of critical literacy theory and practice. The key to fostering this recognition is providing students with opportunities to seek out silenced voices and perspectives and to bring them to the fore-front of understanding (Wolk, 2003). Fine (1987, p. 157) posits, "Silencing [in school] constitutes the process by which contradictory evidence, ideologies, and experiences find themselves buried, camouflaged, and discredited." Rather than silencing; issues of race, gender, power, and culture need to be brought to our students' attention. Focusing on the relationships between language, social practice, power and access helps readers move beyond the literal meaning of a text to question its origin, purpose and hidden cultural assumptions. As students learn to uncover the sociopolitical aspects of texts and recognize whose knowledge or viewpoint is being privileged, they take control over how they position themselves in relation to these messages. This awareness empowers students to imagine alternative ways of viewing their lives and their world. In doing so, critical literacy does more than just provoke students' anger at the ways in which particular voices are silenced or marginalized; it prepares them to act (Ellsworth, 1992; Lesley, 2004).

Consciously considering multiple perspectives, as well as noticing silences and the marginalization of particular voices, can meaningfully inform citizens' actions and community-building. Without the skills and inclination to approach texts from a critical stance, readers/citizens can be misinformed or manipulated. Social Studies educator Wolk (2003, p. 102) argues that if we are not teaching for critical literacy we must ask ourselves if "we are preparing the future citizens we need to make the daily decisions necessary to participate in our democracy."

Fostering Creative and Critical Engagement with Texts

All teachers, not just those teaching language arts courses, need to encourage their students to reflect on and apply their knowledge and understanding to the various texts and resources they encounter. Students need to understand and uncover the multiple realities they face in their reading, writing and day-to-day living. Educators need to support students as they work to make meaning with and from texts.

Critical literacy educators guide their students to analyze what different types of texts (written, visual, and oral) "do" to readers, viewers, or listeners and whose interests are served (or not served) by what these texts "do" (Janks, 2010). These educators also work to help students rewrite themselves and the current realities or situations they face. Pedagogically, critical literacy works to ensure students are aware of the complex inter-relationship of domination and power, social difference and identity, equity and access. To achieve this type of consciousness, readers need to be able to:

- decode the text. Work out what the text is actually saying.
- make meaning from the text. Bring one's own culture, content, context, text-use and text-structure into the active process of making meaning.
- interrogate the text. Examine its assumptions, values, and positions and understand how the text is positioning them.

Critical reading is possible when one is able to stand outside the text and to question the constructions within the text. This specifically forces the reader to ask why the writer made the choices they did, whose interests were served (or not served), and who is empowered or disempowered. Students need to understand that all texts are positioned and positioning and that every text is just one set of perspectives on the world. This is easier when we read texts that offend us; the beliefs and values presented that are different than our own gives us the critical distance to read against the texts. It becomes much more difficult to engage in resistant reading with texts that we are comfortable with or that work to serve our interests (Janks, 2010). Educators need to realize that when texts touch something considered 'sacred' to a student, critical analysis can be threatening (Janks, 1995, 2010).

There is no explicit methodology for teaching critical literacy but there are a number of classroom practices commonly utilized by educators across a variety of disciplines (Behrman, 2006). These instructional strategies include: (1) reading supplemental or multiple texts as a way to investigate the subjectivity of an author; (2) reading from a resistant perspective as a way to recognize that no text is ever 'true' in the absolute sense; (3) creating counter texts as a way to incorporate marginalized voices and perspectives; (4) engaging in dialogue about texts as a way to learn to listen to others' voices; (5) providing students with opportunities to research topics of personal interest; and (6) taking social action (Beck, 2005; Behrman, 2006; Powell, Contrell, & Adams, 2001; Wile, 2000; Wolk, 2003). In each instance readers are positioned as 'meaning makers,' critics and actors rather than as passive recipients. They are prompted to think creatively, question critically and take action (Freire & Macedo, 1987). While this type of critical engagement is vital for citizens in a multicultural democracy, there is little evidence that adolescents are reading or participating in critical literacy practices in their Social Studies classrooms.

READING INSTRUCTION IN SECONDARY SOCIAL STUDIES

Content Area Literacy

While literature advocating the integration of reading instruction into Social Studies education and providing resources to support this integration is voluminous, research on the practice of reading in Social Studies classrooms is minimal. Camperell's and Knight's 1991 review of existing research on reading instruction in Social Studies revealed that "although much has been written about how to teach reading using Social Studies material, very little progress has been made in implementing instruction" (p. 567). Sadly, two decades later, this observation continues to ring true. Though current research suggests that textbooks continue to be the most widely used resource in Social Studies classrooms, few studies consider how teachers and students use these texts (Levstik, 2008). We also know little about how other reading materials—both offline and online—are incorporated and utilized. As Camperell and Knight found in their 1991 review, much has been written over the last two decades about how to use websites, literature, primary sources and other print and web-based texts in secondary Social Studies classrooms, but we know little about if, when, and how teachers are using these materials and the reading instruction they provide for their students.

Though many Social Studies educators agree that reading can play a pivotal role in learning Social Studies content and skills; what teachers and students are reading together and how they make sense of this material remains a mystery. In order to understand this disconnect, we draw upon research by content area literacy experts and then consider the ways in which recent work on discipline-specific reading instruction offers possibilities for Social Studies educators to meaningfully integrate reading and critical literacy practices into their instruction.

Research demonstrates that the incorporation of reading instruction into Science, Math and Social Studies classrooms improves students' comprehension of content (Shanahan & Shanahan, 2008). Still, content area literacy experts have struggled for decades to convince secondary educators to embrace and implement reading instruction (Alger, 2009; Hall, 2005; Moje, 2008). In many teacher education programs, preservice teachers are required to complete a content area literacy course. Three decades of research indicates that these courses can inform secondary educators' beliefs about the importance of reading, but have little impact on actual classroom practice (Alger, 2009; Hall, 2005). Secondary educators in Alger's 2009 study, for example, employed strategies that "ameliorated the necessity for students to read text independently"— a practice Alger calls "workarounds" (p. 66). Existing research on content area literacy coursework and classroom practices reveals that teachers' beliefs and secondary school structures inform the use of workarounds and encourage secondary educators to avoid reading with their students (Alger, 2009; Hall, 2005).

Research on content area teachers' beliefs about teaching reading reveals that some educators believe that is it not their responsibility to teach reading while others believe that their students do not need reading instruction to be successful in their classrooms (Hall, 2005; Moje, 2008). Pressures to prepare students for high-stakes exams position secondary educators to focus solely on content acquisition, leaving little time to consider or integrate reading instruction into their practice (Hall, 2005; Moje, 2008). These belief systems are a major obstacle, and the traditional compartmentalized structure of most secondary schools does little to interrupt this type of thinking. Organizational structure at the secondary level reinforces the notion that reading is learned *independently* of learning content, and supports the idea that learning math, science or social studies depends upon the same generic reading practices. Finally, some content area educators do not utilize the literacy strategies and practices learned in their content area literacy courses because these strategies and practices are not aligned with values and structures of the disciplines they teach (Hall, 2005). Moje (2008) argues that content area literacy has traditionally been approached "from the standpoint of literacy theory rather than from the standpoint of the disciplinary learning theory" (p. 99). It is this disconnect that must be addressed.

Shanahan and Shanahan (2008) argue that reading in the content areas—whether biology or history or mathematics—is not a generic practice but one tied to disciplinary norms and practices. Discipline-based literacy depends upon the acquisition of content specific, sophisticated skills and interpretive practices (Damico, Baildon, Exter & Guo, 2009; Joel, Hebard, Haubner & Moran, 2010; Moje, 2008; Shanahan & Shanahan, 2008; Wineburg & Martin, 2004). As Moje notes, "literacy thus becomes an essential aspect of disciplinary practice rather than a set of strategies or tools brought into the discipline to improve reading and writing of subject matter texts" (p. 99). Recent scholarship on discipline-specific reading practices suggests that such an approach not only provides students with the skills to comprehend challenging content area texts, it also reveals how knowledge is produced in the discipline (Moje, 2008). With this insight, students are not only provided access to content area knowledge and texts, but are in a position to critique, challenge and change this knowledge (Moje, 2008).

Understanding how knowledge is constructed and which knowledge is privileged within a discipline positions students to be more than mere recipients of others' expertise. In this regard, discipline-specific reading instruction can act as a bridge to broader critical literacy practices that are not content specific. This bridge is perhaps strongest in the Social Studies, where the practice of learning to read like a historian is clearly aligned with goals and practices of critical literacy.

Learning to Read Like a Historian

In the Social Studies, most of the recent work on discipline-specific literacy focuses on history and what it means to 'read like a historian' (Damico, et al., 2009; Joel, et al., 2010, Wineburg, 2001). Wineburg's seminal text, *Historical Thinking and Other Unnatural Acts* (2001), forms the foundation of much of this research and provides a powerful portrait of historians' reading practices. Wineburg used thinkalouds to explore and document how expert historians approach text and how their practice differs from the way in which students of history typically approach texts (2001, pp. 63–89). At the core of these differences is the way in which historians focus not simply on what a text says "but what it *does*" (p. 65, emphasis added). To understand what a text does, historians not only considered the literal text and the inferred text but the subtext of everything they read (p. 65). More specifically, they not only attempt to construct an author's intentions and purpose, but consider how a text reveals an author's worldview and beliefs (pp. 65–66). In this regard historians, according to Wineburg, view texts not only as a tool used to describe the world but to also construct it (p. 66). Historians' reading practices are firmly situated within a framework that views texts as "social instruments skillfully crafted to achieve a social end" (p. 69).

Subsequent research by Wineburg and others provides Social Studies educators with a detailed portrait of the specific reading practices historians employ to understand what a text does. Sourcing, or the practice of determining the author of a text *before* reading the text, is the "first and most instinctive reading move that historians make" (Joel, et al., 2010, p. 16). As Wineburg explains, for historians "a document's attribution was not the end of the document but its beginning; sources were viewed as people, not objects, as social exchanges, not sets of propositions" (2001, p. 76). Knowing who wrote or produced a particular text, when it was created and where it was published positions historians to question rather than passively accept what they read. They immediately begin to situate the text within a particular social world and nexus of power relations. In doing so, historians begin to formulate a text's purpose.

Sourcing is the first step in the work of contextualization, another reading practice historians routinely employ (Reismann &Wineburg, 2008; Wineburg, 2001). As historians read, they utilize information in the text itself along with prior background knowledge to construct a complex portrait of the society and time period within which a text was produced. They ask questions about whose perspectives or voices are privileged and whose perspectives or voices are missing and begin to determine what they do *not* know about a particular topic, issue, event, group or individual (Wineburg, 2001; Joel, et al., 2010). The practice of contextualization prompts historians to locate other texts on the same topic, issue, event, group or individual in order to corroborate information and access diverse perspectives. Working to corroborate information, historians juxtapose multiple texts on the same topic or issue and carefully compare details and language utilized in each text in order to determine what information is most trustworthy. Evaluating claims and evidence by reading multiple texts enables historians to understand what a text does, how it positions readers and the larger political and social purposes it serves (Wineburg, 2001; Wineburg & Martin, 2004).

In many ways, the practice of reading like a historian parallels the theory and practice of critical literacy. At the heart of critical literacy practices is an approach to reading intended to prevent a reader from being manipulated by a text (Freire, 1972). Through critical literacy practices, the reader has the ability and disposition to question rather than simply accept the information they encounter and to recognize the inherent power relations within which this information is situated (McLaughlin & DeVoogd, 2004). Like the reading practices of historians, critical literacy positions readers to make sense of what a text does, not merely what it says. The practices of sourcing, contextualizing and corroborating that historians routinely employ when reading primary sources can be applied to a wide range of texts and empower readers to question and challenge whatever they read.

While strong alignment between the reading practices of historians and critical literacy suggests a smooth or seamless integration of critical reading into secondary Social Studies classrooms, the transition will not be easy. As noted above, many secondary Social Studies educators do not believe that teaching reading is their responsibility. The compartmentalized structure of most secondary schools supports this belief. Pressures to prepare students for high-stake exams position secondary Social Studies educators to focus on content acquisition and the content area literacy courses required in many teacher education programs have had minimal impact on classroom practices (Shanahan & Shanahan, 2008). At the same time, a large percentage of adolescents do not read at the proficient level while many others simply refuse to read. As students transition from elementary to middle and high school there is, what Gallagher calls, an "unfortunate shifting of reading attitudes—from enthusiasm to indifference to hostility" (2009, p. 3). Student resistance or refusal to read remains a powerful deterrent to reading instruction in secondary content area classrooms.

Currently there are a number of web-based resources, such as the Stanford History Education Group's "Reading like a Historian" curriculum, that provide secondary Social Studies teachers with resources to teach the skills of sourcing, contextualization and corroboration. While these resources are invaluable, unless the above challenges are also addressed, it will be difficult to foster the development of critical reading throughout the secondary Social Studies curriculum and in secondary Social Studies classrooms.

WHERE DO WE GO NEXT?: IMPLICATIONS FOR RESEARCH, SOCIAL STUDIES TEACHER EDUCATION AND CLASSROOM PRACTICE

Insights from Research on Adolescent Literacy

Contending with the reluctance of secondary Social Studies teachers to integrate reading instruction into their practice and the reluctance of many adolescents to read, requires a multifaceted approach. Bridging the gaps between research on discipline-specific reading practices, adolescent literacy experts, and Social Studies educators is an essential first step in this process.

At the heart of any effort to decrease secondary Social Studies educators' reluctance to fully integrate reading into their classroom practice is reaffirming the ways in which reading is integral to each academic discipline—not a separate 'basic skill.' Heller and Greenleaf (2007) contend that "generations of researchers and educators have drawn a sharp distinction between the teaching of basic skills and the teaching of academic content, with reading and writing assigned to the former" (p. 16). This distinction generates strong resistance among secondary educators who believe it is not their 'job' to teach skills that should have been acquired at the elementary level. To diminish this resistance, secondary Social Studies educators need opportunities to develop an awareness of the ways in which *they* read and make sense of a wide variety of texts. More specifically, within the context of studying history, the "hidden literacies" of the discipline can be highlighted, practiced and discussed (Heller & Greenleaf, 2007, p. 20). As the reading practices of sourcing, contextualization, and corroboration are made visible; it is easier to recognize the ways in which learning history is as much about learning to read in certain ways as it is about learning specific facts. Facilitating this shift in perspective is essential but, if it is not accompanied by an awareness of the specific needs and challenges of adolescent literacy, it may result in little change. Social studies educational researchers and teachers can learn much from our literacy colleagues that can inform both Social Studies teacher education and secondary Social Studies classroom practices.

The crisis in adolescent literacy has attracted the attention of educators, politicians, business leaders, professional organizations and advocacy groups (Heller & Greenleaf, 2007; Kamil, 2003; National Association of State Boards of Education, 2005; National Council for Teachers of English, 2006; National School Board Association, 2006). As a result, there is a growing body of research on adolescent literacy and a number of nationwide and state-level efforts to put lessons learned from this research into practice. Existing research reveals that it is most effective to teach reading comprehension strategies "while students are engaged in reading challenging, content-rich texts" (Heller & Greenleaf, 2007, p. 8) rather than teaching these skills in isolation. More importantly, students develop proficiency with these skills when "they have compelling reasons—such as the desire to make sense of interesting materials—to use them" (Heller & Greenleaf, 2007, p. 10). Given the deficits in many high school students' basic literacy skills, comprehension strategies must continue to be taught throughout the curriculum, but these are not the only reading skills that adolescents need.

Adolescents also need explicit instruction and opportunities to engage in discipline-specific reading practices in order to recognize the ways in which language and literacy practices vary between disciplines (Moje, 2008). Research suggests that adolescents can develop advanced literacy skills when learning about controversial or compelling issues and problems and when educators make connections between the cognitive, social and personal strengths students bring with them to school and content area texts (Greenleaf, Brown & Litman, 2004; Guthrie, 2004; Moje, 2008).

Finally, research on adolescents' attitudes about reading reveals that choice and access to a wide-range of high interest reading materials also plays a powerful role in the development of advanced reading skills (Gallagher, 2008; Pitcher, Martinez, Dicembre, Fewster, & McCormick, 2010). Students indicate that they "were able to understand what they chose to read and what they read on the computer" (Pitcher, et al, 2010, p. 643). More specifically, traditional classroom textbooks need to be supplemented with an array of real-world texts such as newspapers, graphic novels, zines, websites and blogs (Gallagher, 2008; Wolf, 2007).

Applying the insights above to the challenge of integrating reading instruction—and more specifically critical literacy—into secondary Social Studies classrooms, suggests a number of possible actions. First, research on adolescents' attitudes about reading indicates that choice and the use of real-world texts will foster student engagement. Much of the research on learning to read like a historian and the curriculum materials that are currently available focus on teaching the skills of sourcing, contextualization and corroboration when reading primary sources and textbooks. If we hope to overcome adolescents' resistance to reading we must then provide them with a wider range of texts and options. The critical literacy skills of sourcing, contextualization and corroboration can be taught as students read graphic novels, blogs and websites, as well as textbooks and primary sources.

The research on adolescent literacy cited above also suggests that the quality of reading materials we provide students has a significant impact not only on their motivation to read but also on the development of basic comprehension and advanced literacy skills. Challenging. Content-rich. Interesting. Compelling. Controversial. Real-world. These are the adjectives employed to describe the types of texts that both empower and engage adolescent readers. They are not adjectives used to describe the typical Social Studies textbook. Many reading experts and Social Studies educators have long maligned Social Studies textbooks yet they continue to be the most widely used resource in Social Studies classrooms (Levstik, 2008). De-centering the textbook will be an important component of integrating reading instruction into Social Studies classrooms.

Findings from research on adolescent literacy also make clear that it is essential to build connections between students' personal lives and their school texts. When these connections are not addressed, adolescents' motivation and engagement decrease (NCTE, 2006). One component of building these connections is to create bridges between students' everyday literacies and academic literacy practices. Barton (1994) points out that "everyday literacy gives a richer view of literacy which demands a new definition of literacy, a new way of thinking about what is involved in reading and writing" (p. 5). Out-of-school literacies, such as journal writing or social networking, could be utilized to teach personal response and reflection and increase awareness of differences in cultural and social meanings of political issues such as drugs, poverty, bullying or violence. Drawing upon out-of-school literacies enables teachers to understand and develop a "culturally responsive curriculum" based on their students "funds of knowledge" (Moll & Greenberg, 1990).

Each of the above will require a serious commitment to rethinking how we position reading in Social Studies educational research, teacher education and secondary Social Studies classrooms. One place to begin this work is for Social Studies educators to carefully consider the texts we share with our students and to begin to integrate a wider variety of real-world, high-interest texts into instruction. Here again we can look to our literacy colleagues for insight and support.

Text Sets as a Reading Resource in Secondary Social Studies Education

Literacy educators have long understood the ways in which literature can serve as a teaching partner, companion, informant, and question poser and, as a result, they pay close attention to the text choices they provide their students. With this in mind, they create sets of reading materials that are designed to provide students with multiple viewpoints and perspectives on the topic under study.

Text sets have traditionally been used as a way to build early readers' background knowledge and comprehension skills. A text set consists of a group of related texts of various genres and reading levels (Hamman, 1995). It is the combination of different text types and levels that encourages students to read critically and construct knowledge (Hynd, 1999). Text sets typically start with a guiding and thought-provoking book that serves as the launching point for the topic or theme. These text sets nurture critical thinking through personal connections, intertextual comparisons, and multiple means of response (Hade, 1994; Mathis, 2002). Through discussing and understanding the various materials within the text sets, students wrestle with multiple interpretations and work to reconcile divergent information and perspectives. They are also provided with opportunities to reveal and confirm who they are, what matters to them, and what they know and care about.

Moving the text set into the secondary Social Studies classroom is one way for Social Studies educators to begin to carefully consider the texts they provide for their students. It is also a context within which to teach the skills of sourcing, contextualization and corroboration and motivate adolescents to read Social Studies materials. As noted above, it is essential that text sets incorporate a wide range of genres and formats as well as web-based materials that promote student engagement. The school's librarian can also serve as a key resource in helping to develop appropriate text sets on topics that meet these requirements. Text sets in secondary Social Studies classrooms should also focus on controversial topics or issues and provide opportunities for students to draw upon their everyday literacies. It is the teacher's responsibility to ensure that a wide variety of perspectives and voices are represented through the text set—something often lacking in traditional textbooks. The juxtaposition of multiple texts provides a powerful context for secondary Social Studies educators to teach critical literacy skills. As students read and move between the texts, questions of authorship, context and trustworthiness arise that empower students to construct and challenge knowledge rather than merely receive it. In this manner, the use of text sets in secondary Social Studies classrooms can address students' resistance to reading while providing opportunities to teach and practice vital critical literacy skills.

CONCLUSION

Participating intelligently and humanely in the decision-making practices required of citizens in a multicultural democratic society depends upon the ability to locate and evaluate information from a wide variety of sources. Blindly accepting messages embedded within texts renders the power relationships inherent in these texts invisible, making it difficult to critique and engage with society or imagine alternatives (Wolk, 2003). Most adolescents in the United States are ill-prepared to read the word or the world in this manner as they struggle to comprehend academic and other real-world texts.

Many secondary Social Studies educators often avoid reading with their students or engage in 'workarounds' as a way to minimize the amount of independent reading required of students. While this is in some ways logical due to the weak reading skills of many high school students, it only perpetuates the troubling aliteracy of many students and does not prepare them to thoughtfully or meaningfully participate in our democracy. Social Studies educators and researchers have a responsibility to teach students the discipline-specific reading practices that will enable them to understand what texts do and not merely what they say. Critical literacy serves as a tool for advocacy by encouraging students to share critical questions, explore diverse perspectives, and discuss what they read. It is through these processes that "concerted efforts are being made to understand and practice reading and writing in ways that enhance the quest for democratic emancipation and for empowerment of the sub-orientated, the marginalized Other" (Lankshear & McLaren, 1993, Preface).

Dewey (1916) posited that schools should provide numerous occasions for students to not only learn about democratic ways of life but to also understand how democracy works in practice. The social studies classroom is the perfect starting point for encouraging our students to not only read controversial materials, but also to question truths, sources and evidence (Wineburg & Martin, 2004). It is through this understanding that our students become critical consumers of the multiple texts and resources they encounter throughout their daily lives.

REFERENCES

Alger, C. (2009). Content area reading strategy knowledge transfer from preservice to first-year teaching. *Journal of Adolescent & Adult Literacy, 53*(1), 60–69.

Barton, D. (1994). *Literacy: An introduction to the ecology of written language.* Oxford, UK: Blackwell.

Beck, A. S. (2005). A place for critical literacy. *Journal of Adolescent & Adult Literacy, 48*(5), 392–400.

Behrman, E. (2006). Teaching about language, power and text: A review of classroom practices that support critical literacy. *Journal of Adolescent & Adult Literacy, 49*(6), 490–498.

Camperell, K., & Knight, R. (1991). Reading research and social studies. In J. Shaver, (Ed.) *Handbook of research on social studies teaching and learning* (pp. 567–578) New York: Macmillan Publishing Company.

Damico, J., Baildon, M., Exter, M., & Guo, S. (2009/2010). Where we read from matters: Disciplinary literacy in a ninth grade social studies classrooms. *Journal of Adolescent and Adult Literacy, 53*(4), 325–335.

Dewey, J. (1916). *Democracy and Education.* Mineola, NY: Dover.

Ellsworth, E. (1992). Why doesn't this feel empowering? Working through repressive myths of critical pedagogy. In C. Luke & J. Gore (Eds.), *Feminisms and critical pedagogy* (pp. 90–119). New York: Routledge.

Fine, M. (1987). Silencing in public schools. *Language Arts, 64,*157–74.

Freire, P. (1972). *Pedagogy of the oppressed.* Harmandsworth, UK: Penguin.

Freire, P., & Macedo, D. 1987. *Literacy: Reading the word and the world.* Westport, CT: Bergen & Clavey.

Gallagher, K. (2009). *Readicide: How schools are killing reading and what you can do about it.* Portland, ME: Stenhouse Publishers

Greenelaf, C., Brown,W., & Litman, C. (2004). Apprenticing urban youth to science literacy. In D. Strickland and D. Alvermann (Eds.), *Bridging the gap: Improving literacy learning for preadolescent and adolescent learners in grades 4–12* (pp. 200–226). Newark, NJ: International Reading Association.

Giroux, H. (1981). *Ideology, culture and schooling.* London: Falmer Press.

Guthrie, J. (2004). Classroom contexts for engaged reading: An overview. In J. T. Guthrie, A. Wigfield, & K. C. Perencevich (Eds.), *Motivating reading comprehension: Concept-Oriented Reading Instruction,* (pp. 1–24). Mahwah, NJ: Erlbaum.

Haas-Dyson, A. (2001). Relational sense and textual sense in a U.S. urban classroom: The contested case of Emily, girl friend of a ninja. In B. Comber & A. Simpson (Eds.), *Negotiating critical literacies in classrooms* (pp. 3–18). Mahwah, NJ: Erlbaum.

Hade, D. (1994). Aiding and abetting the basilization of children's literature. *The New Advocate 7*(1), 41–44.

Hall, L. (2005). Teachers and content area reading: Attitudes, beliefs and change. *Teaching and Teacher Education, 21,* 403–414.

Hamman, V. (1995). Using text sets in the social studies curriculum. *Southern Social Studies Journal, 20*(3),34–43.

Heller, R., & Greenleaf, C. (2007). *Literacy instruction in the content areas: Getting to the core of middle and high school improvement.* Washington, D.C.: Alliance for Excellent Education.

Hynd, C. R. (1999). Teaching students to think critically using multiple texts in history. *Journal of Adolescent & Adult Literacy, 42*(6), 428–436.

Janks, H. (1995). *The research and development of critical language materials for use in South African secondary schools.* Unpublished doctoral thesis, Lancaster University, Lancaster.

Janks, H. (2010). *Literacy and Power.* New York, NY: Routledge.

Joel, C., Hebard, H., Haubner, J.P., & Moran, M. (2010). Reading through a disciplinary lens. *Educational Leadership, 67*(6), 12–17.

Kamil, M. (2003). *Adolescents and literacy: Reading for the 21ˢᵗ century.* Washington, D.C.: Alliance for Excellent Education.

Lankshear, C., & McLaren, P. (1993). *Critical literacy: Politics, praxis and the postmodern.* Albany: State University of New York Press.

Lesley, M. (2004/2005). Looking for critical literacy with post baccalaureate content area literacy students. *Journal of Adolescent & Adult Literacy, 48*(4), 320–334.

Levstik, L. (2008). What happens in social studies classrooms? Research on K–12 social studies. In L. Levstik & C. Tyson (Eds.) *Handbook of Research in Social Studies Education* (pp. 50–64). New York: Routledge.

Mathis, J. B. (2002). Picture book text sets: A novel approach to understanding theme. *Clearing House, 75*(3), 127–131.

McLaughlin, M., & DeVoogd, G. (2004). Looking for critical literacy as comprehension: Expanding reader response. *Journal of Adolescent & Adult Literacy, 48*(1), 52–62. doi:10.1598/JAAL.48.1.5

Moje, E. (2008). Foregrounding the disciplines in secondary literacy teaching and learning: A call for change. *Journal of Adolescent and Adult Literacy, 52*(2), 96–107.

Moll, L.C., & Greenberg, J. (1990). Creating zones of possibilities: Combining social contexts for instruction. In L.C. Moll (Ed.), *Vygotsky and education* (pp. 319–348). Cambridge: Cambridge University Press.

National Association of State Boards of Education. (2005). *Reading at risk: The state response to the crisis in adolescent literacy.* Alexandria, VA: NASBE.

National Center for Education Statistics (2010). *The nation's report card: Reading 2009* (NCES 2010-458). Institute of Education Sciences, U.S. Department of Education, Washington, D.C.

National Council of Teachers of English (2006). *NCTE principles of adolescent literacy reform: A policy research brief.* Urbana, IL: National Council of Teachers of English.

National Endowment for the Arts (2004). *Reading at risk: A survey of literacy reading in America.* Research Division Report 46. Washington, D.C.: National Endowment for the Arts.

National Endowment for the Arts (2007). *To read or not to read: A question of national consequence.* Research Division Report 47. Washington, D.C.: National Endowment for the Arts.

National School Board Association. (2006). *The next chapter: A school board guide to improving adolescent literacy.* Alexandria, VA: NSBA.

O'Quinn, E (2006). Critical Literacy in democratic education: Responding to socio-political tensions in US schools. *Journal of Adolescent and Adult Literacy, 49*(4), 260–267.

Pitcher, S. M., Martinez, G., Dicembre, E. A., Fewster, D., & McCormick, M. K. (2010) *Journal of Adult & Adolescent Literacy. 53*(8), 636–645.

Powell, R., Contrell, S., & Adams, S. (2001). Saving Black Mountain: The promise of critical literacy in a multicultural democracy. *The Reading Teacher, 54*(8), 772–781.

Reisman, A., & Wineburg, S. (2008). Teaching the skill of contextualizing in history. *The Social Studies, 99*(5), 202–207

Shanahan, T., & Shanahan, S. (2008). Teaching disciplinary literacy to adolescents: Rethinking content area literacy. *Harvard Educational Review, 78*(1), 40–59.

Shor, I. (1999). What is critical literacy? In I. Shor & C. Pari (Eds.), *Critical literacy in action* (pp. 1–30). Portsmouth, NH: Heinemann.

Soares, L.B., & Wood, K. (2010). A critical literacy perspective for teaching and learning social studies. *The Reading Teacher, 63*(6), 486–494.

Wile, J.M. (2000). A Literacy Lesson in Democratic Education. *The Social Studies, 72*, 170–177.

Wineburg, S. (2001). *Historical thinking and other unnatural acts: Charting the future of teaching the past.* Philadelphia: Temple University Press.

Wineburg, S., & Martin, D. (2004). Reading and rewriting history. *Educational Leadership, 62*(1), 42–45.

Wolf, M. (2007). *Proust and the Squid: The story and science of the reading brain.* New York: Harper Collins.

Wolk, S. (2003). Teaching for critical literacy in social studies. *The Social Studies, 94*(3), 101–106.

CHAPTER 18

SITUATING THE NATION

History Pedagogy for the 21ˢᵗ Century

Kyle A. Greenwalt and Patrick N. Leahy

If we regret the violence nations wreak on each other and sometimes on their own citizens, we must acknowledge that at present we have no more effective or alternative institution to defend and protect citizens and human rights.
—Thomas Bender, 2006, p. 298

Yet we cannot be sure whether the multiplying effects of globalizing connections are having the moral effect of spreading world civic consciousness, or, instead, facilitating the pursuit of vested interests.
—Derek Heater, 1999, p. 144

In responding to most innovations, teachers generally weigh personal and school-related factors . . . rarely do they have to actively consider national and global forces. I am suggesting, therefore, that difficulties in finding meaning in global education stem, in part, from the problems of comprehending an educa-

Contemporary Social Studies: An Essential Reader, pages 335–356
Copyright © 2012 by Information Age Publishing

tional innovation that cannot be sufficiently understood in the context of the
cultural framework within which teachers normally operate.
                                              —Graham Pike, 2000, p. 70

In his classic book on nationalism—a topic about which the author had
written extensively before—Eric Hobsbawm (1962, 1983) observed the following: "*Finally*, I cannot but add that no serious historian of nations and
nationalism can be a committed political nationalist . . . Nationalism requires too much belief in what is patently not so" (1991, p. 12). With such a
statement, we are in deep agreement—as we believe Thomas Bender would
be also, as evidenced by the above quote. Yet it is instructive to note the
change in tone in the twenty years separating Hobsbawm's text from the
more recent one of Bender.[1]

Hobsbawm's illustrious academic career spanned nearly forty years, and
throughout his work one can find an implicit but clear connection to what
Marxists have traditionally called "the national question:" How could well
entrenched nationalist loyalties best be overcome in the struggle to create
international solidarity among peoples? For Hobsbawm, "the nation" was a
delusion, and not just because nationalists "invented" traditions which they
then located in a foggy, long-ago and indeterminate past (Hobsbawm &
Ranger, 1983). Rather, nationalists were delusional because "no satisfactory
criterion can be discovered for deciding which of the many human collec-
tivities should be labeled in this way" (Hobsbawm, 1991, p. 5). So, following
Hobsbawm, this paper raises the question of what, after all, is a nation.

Contemporary social and political realities suggest that we abandon the
structural logic that would have us frame our political projects in either/
or terms (national *versus* global citizenship). Instead, diverse writers have
endorsed the practice of what Derek Heater (1999) calls "multiple citizenship." The theoretical framework underlying this chapter therefore could
be described by the following observation: While nationalism—as a political project—may require belief in what is "patently not so" (Hobsbawm,
1991, p. 12); and while globalization—however we might choose to define
it—may challenge any simple notion of sovereignty as uniquely vested in
the Westphalian nation-state[2] (Held, 1999; Scholte, 1997); national identities—as imagined communities of practice—seem more entrenched than
ever. Social studies education, perhaps now more than ever, seems caught
in the middle.

We write this chapter as curriculum researchers, ones interested not only
in the academic issues posed by the historiography of nationalism and its
relationship to globalization, but in the more particular role of the social
studies in fostering a global citizenship practice (Hanvey, 1975; Merryfield
& Wilson, 2005; Parker, Ninomiya, & Cogan, 1999). Yet to date, much of
the U.S. research done in the area of global education has not located a
clear curricular home for such an area of study (Gaudelli, 2007). Hence—

despite our considerable sympathies for an integrated, issues-centered curriculum—we tend to worry that much of the work on a global citizenship curriculum will not ever be enacted in actual flesh-and-blood classrooms (Thornton, 2005).

This chapter therefore examines the rationale for curricular readjustment in perhaps the most "sacred" subject-area of the social studies: U.S. history courses. We do this in four steps. First, we summarize and critically appraise the historiography of the nation-state as it has developed over the past 25 years. In the process, we seek to define the nation, and suggest that the dangers which come along with nationalism may, if we do not proceed with caution, be extended into global frames of being and acting.

Second, we examine the possible classroom implications of this scholarship, in particular, through recent calls from within the discipline of history itself for a transformed historical pedagogy, one that would draw less strict boundaries between "the domestic" and "the global," and historicize the nation-state in the process. In so doing, we build upon the important early work in a "globalized" U.S. history course by Merry Merryfield and Angene Wilson (2005), Stephen Thornton (2005), William Gaudelli (2007), and Helena Benitez (2001). In the process, we provide concrete examples of essential questions and topics for classroom practitioners.

Next, recognizing that such a project is not without controversy, we elaborate on a series of objections that might be raised to history teaching that seeks to break down the borders between the U.S. and the world. In each case, we provide a rationale for what we are arguing for, with reference to both academic and pedagogical considerations. Finally, in conclusion, we provide an addendum, one written as a letter to the history teachers of the twenty-first century. In it, we lay claim to our faith in the teachers of the future, and their ability to combine life-long learning with political acumen, as they confront such issues as increasing curriculum standardization and public mistrust of teachers. In the process, we draw upon the substantial body of research in global education from the past 35 years.

MODELS OF NATION-BUILDING: A PEDAGOGY OF ASSIMILATION AND EXCLUSION

Diversity had not bothered earlier centuries very much. It seemed part of the nature of things, whether from place to place or between one social group and another. But the [French] Revolution had brought with it the concept of national unity as an integral and integrating ideal at all levels, and the ideal of oneness stirred concern about its shortcoming. Diversity became imperfection, injustice, failure, something to be noted and remedied.

—Eugen Weber, 1976, p. 9

In this first section, we wish to turn to explicating two models of nations and nation-building that have been identified in the broader historiography on the topic. In doing so, we hope to further situate the stakes around which our current moment—as citizens, as educational researchers, and as teachers—revolves. That is, we view an understanding of the models of nation-building as an important lens for an informed discussion of globalization—a lens far too often overlooked, in our view—and of what such a phenomenon might mean for any project of curriculum reform.[3]

The first model of nation-building—one we shall call "vertical"—is most famously represented by the work of Benedict Anderson (1983/1992), though it has precedents in work by Eugen Weber (1976) and parallels to contemporaneous work by Ernest Gellner (1983). For Anderson (1983/1992), the nation was defined quite clearly as, "an imagined political community—and imagined as both inherently limited and sovereign" (p. 6). Anderson correctly noted that all communities, from the largest empires to the smallest tribal villages, are imagined—that is, all communities rely upon symbolically-mediated relationships between their members. In addition, all nations are imagined as limited in obvious ways, for no nation imagines itself as composed of all humanity. Finally, all nations are imagined as sovereign, thereby monopolizing the "legitimate" use of violence and obscuring alternative identity projects rooted in religion, race, and the like.

This model is considered a vertical one because it sees nation-building as a process whereby a set of culturally-similar elite bind their often diverse subjects into a united and homogenous body which shares similar modes of speaking (the elimination of local dialects), market consumption (the spread of internal markets of trade), where religion is gradually relegated to the realm of private experience (the "disenchantment" of the world), and where secular bureaucracies work to form a strong and centralized state apparati (see also Bell, 2003). Vertical nation-building is thus a project of mass homogenization. It almost always make use of an already existing state apparatus to further its aims—though, at least for Anderson (1983/1992), a "genuine, popular nationalist enthusiasm" often existed alongside the state's attempts to create and maintain such enthusiasm (p. 163).[4] In the absence of such popular enthusiasm, however, vertical models are best viewed as a type of "internal colonialism" (Hechter, 1975/1999)—a situation where a pre-existing political community is forcefully integrated a larger national community.

The second model to consider—a "horizontal" nation-building—is less well developed in the literature, but is nonetheless glimpsed across several key historiographical texts (Bell, 2003; Hechter, 2002; Marx, 1996, 2003). We believe that the general processes that the horizontal model seek to describe, though, might best be understood by turning to Edward Said,[5] and his classic text, *Orientalism*. There, Said (1978/1991) writes about the manner by which the Orient helped to define Europe "as its contrasting image, idea, personality, experience" (p. 2). That is, in these opening passages of his book, Said speaks of the imperial encounter as a western project of self-definition, a way of marking cultural boundaries between an "us" and a "them," and in the process, of establishing a supremacist western identity that would support the cultural and economic ambitions of imperialists.

Hence, nation-building works not only through attempts to include and homogenize, but to separate and divide. Anthony Marx (1996, 2003) has persuasively argued that the foundations of nation-building projects are exclusionary in origin. In turning to the case of U.S., for example, he argues that the foundations for the mass Americanization campaigns of the early twentieth century were laid though the prior creation of a legally-enforced system of racial hierarchy, wherein black Americans were targeted for exclusion by the state. As he notes:

> Agreement on a racially defined "other" as a common enemy defined and encouraged white unity . . . Although intrawhite tension remained, it was contained within a unified polity. Racial domination was repeatedly reinforced to consolidate the nation-state.[6] (1996, p. 182)

Hence, nation-building can also quite clearly be viewed through the lens of exclusion—even scapegoating.[7]

In both models, it is important to finally note, it is the public school which ultimately stood as the favored state instrument for the construction of the nation. Schools were deeply implicated in the nation-making endeavor, not least through their practices of enforcing certain language practices and historical narratives as "natural" for their "own" citizens. Indeed, the teaching of "national" history has long been one of the favored tools of nationalists. Hence, any serious attempt to institute global education within American public schools would seemingly need to rethink the way in which U.S. history courses are taught.

For if, in 1861, Massimo d'Azeglio could famously pronounce—*We have made Italy. Now we have to make Italians*—one route for doing so was compulsory public schooling. If, today, a globalized economy is a *fait accompli*, the task of defining a global citizenship and identity likewise remains ahead of us. Schooling is again likely to play a role in this process, yet that role must be carefully guarded. Despite the fact that globalization has weakened the economic and identity-forming power of nation-states, the two most favored tactics of nationalists in the past—cultural assimilation and structural exclusion as carried out by the public schools—are still powerfully at work in contemporary global society. Hence, there is a clear need to confront some of these processes through a reformed U.S. history pedagogy. It is there which we shall next turn.

THOMAS BENDER'S NEO-COMPARATIVE HISTORY:
A SAMPLE UNIT IN ACTION

Historians are to nationalism what poppy-growers in Pakistan are to heroin-addicts: we supply the essential raw material for the market.
                                                    —Eric Hobsbawm, 1992, p. 3

We send young people to Europe to see Italy, but we do not utilize Italy when it lies about the schoolhouse.
                                                    —Jane Addams, 1908/2009, p. 44

In September of 2000, on behalf of the Organization of American Historians and New York University's Project on Internationalizing the Study of American History, Thomas Bender published *The LaPietra Report*. This short but provocative work in many ways summarized for the historical profession the results of twenty-five years of research into the origins of the nation-state. It also sought to draw certain conclusions based on that research. In particular, it argued that:

> If historians have often treated the nation as self-contained and undifferentiated, it is increasingly clear that this assumption is true in neither the present nor the past. A history that recognizes the historicity of different forms of solidarity and the historical character of the project of nation-making promises to better prepare students and the public to understand and to be effective in the world we live in and will live in. (2000, sect. II, para. 4)

Bender's insight here is not so much that the discipline of history itself has a history—for the reflexivity underlying such a claim is itself essential to historiography as an important tenet of the discipline—but that *the history of history cannot be told apart from its strong relationship to the rise of the nation-state* (see also Anderson, 1983/1992; Rosenzweig & Thelen, 1998; White, 1973/1980). To speak of U.S. history, or Canadian history, or French history is indeed quite natural—yet it is the very naturalness of appending nationality to historical narratives that needs to give us pause. Bender's work in the pedagogy of history is a first step in that direction, one that curriculum workers in the social studies should be careful to consider. In this section, we would like to explore the curricular possibilities that are inherent in Bender's work, possibilities that might inform the important future work of building "forms of solidarity" that rest more firmly on global frames of reference.

While Bender has followed this work with other projects (2002), his most important scholarship might seemingly be his attempt at re-thinking the traditional American history survey text, *A Nation Among Nations: America's Place in World History* (2006). Breaking U.S. history into five separate periods, Bender's text reads like other popular texts of revisionist history we have seen used in high school classrooms and in social studies teacher education courses, by such scholars as Howard Zinn (1980/2003) and James Loewen (1995/2007).

Yet to a degree beyond those presented by Zinn and Loewen's texts, we feel that Bender's (2006) revisionist text is likely to present problems for future social studies educators. The amount of material covered in each chapter is encyclopedic, and is not guided by any larger vision of what curricular topics might show most promise for pedagogical exploration in the public school setting. For example, his chapter on the American Revolution includes not only the background context of Britain and France's rivalry for global hegemony, but includes a bewildering multiplicity of other examples of "local resistances" to colonial projects during this time period (South Africa, Haiti, Peru, Brazil, and India—among others).

Bender's (2006) text provides the type of information out of which teachers might begin to craft critical counter-narratives and unearth "subjugated knowledges"— knowledge which might eventually open up space for teachers and their students to critically interrogate and transform the present (Kincheloe, 2001). The work of critical interrogation and transformation of the present we see not only as the strongest purpose and rationale for the inclusion of the social studies in the public school curriculum, but more broadly, as the single most important goal of schooling itself. Indeed, it is exactly out of such interrogation of a globalizing present that we hope to see the emergence of an informed sense of global citizenship. Yet if such work is to happen in the U.S. history classroom, more guidance is needed towards the emerging work of the sort Bender's text represents.

Hence, we would recommend that we help teachers to use essential questions in their U.S. history courses which are not only explicitly comparative in nature, but also evaluative. Such questions, at the level of the entire course, might include the following:

1. Is the course of U.S. history "exceptional?"
2. Is the U.S., in the words of Lincoln, "the last best hope of earth?"

Historians might perhaps cringe at such questions. Yet such questions, we would argue, only make transparent the argument implicit in all too many existing U.S. history courses, which often tend to treat the history of the U.S. as one only of expanding rights and freedoms (Barton & Levstik, 1998; Cornbleth, 2002; Epstein, 2000; Wertsch & O'Connor, 1994). Indeed, as Bender (2000) himself has argued, "by contextualizing the nation and comparing it with other nations, one may better appraise the nature of its particular, even exceptional qualities, while avoiding simplistic assertions of American exceptionalism" (sect. II, para. 15). That is, then, we might launch our courses by making American exceptionalism the starting point—rather than the undisputed framework—for student exploration.

Another consideration is that the concepts used in any revised course of U.S. history would need to extend beyond those currently in use, particularly as it relates to the inclusion of foreign countries. That is, globalized narratives would need to extend beyond international armed conflict. To the degree that they are covered at all in U.S. history courses, the histories of Britain, Canada, Mexico, Spain, Germany, Russia, Cuba, Korea, China, Vietnam and Iraq tend to be included only around periods of armed conflict with the U.S.[8] The other ways in which national histories are linked—most importantly, through the circulation of goods, peoples, and ideas—therefore need to be deepened and extended in the course of student investigation. Hence, we would suggest using such paired concepts as diaspora and immigration, colonialism and resistance, trade and exploitation, peace and war, and, most importantly, given the nation-building models we have laid out above, assimilation and exclusion, as explicit organizing course themes.

Bender's (2006) own work is clear about the need to include such concepts—and they are quite helpful, we believe, on the level of the course. But as one starts to break this down into smaller curricular levels, problems related to the development of specific units and lessons emerge. Given the admittedly exploratory nature of our writing, we feel that we are only in a position to speculate about these issues—with the help, though, of the ample research about powerful teaching in the history classroom as our guide (see Barton & Levstik, 2004; Grant, 2003 for summaries of this literature). So as to ground our exploratory thinking in as concrete a curricular context as possible, we will now turn to imagining a sample unit around the American Revolution.

The concepts out of which Bender builds his exploration of the later eighteenth century are those of colonialism and local resistance. In particular, he opens the chapter by arguing for the importance of examining the diversity of local reactions to eighteenth-century colonialism, from active resistance in Haiti, Peru, and the U.S., to tacit acceptance in India and Canada. We agree that this manner of globalizing the U.S. history curriculum is a good one—that of using themes that are already present in powerful explorations of the standard U.S. curriculum. Hence, a common essential question used in many units addressing the Revolutionary War—*Were the colonists justified in their reaction to Britain?* (see Wineburg & Wilson, 1991, for this essential question in action)—would itself be appropriate for our globalized unit. For clearly, this question is itself reframed in interesting ways when students are asked to consider this question in more than one case example.

As a next step, then, any curricular deliberations would need to address the following: If the Era of Revolution is going to be explored through an additional case example, which one is pedagogically most appropriate? To answer this question, we would like to suggest two principles to guide any curricular deliberations, ones we will call interrelationship and interest. We will explain and apply each of these in turn.

The principle of interrelationship speaks to the need for topics to connect in ways that are rather obvious and clear. To gain a comparative perspective, teachers and their students will need to examine other national histories that parallel that of the U.S. in illustrative ways. And if we allow the essential question to limit our focus to British colonialism—a limiting and directing of attention that any good essential question would do—then the best comparative examples at this time period might include either the West or the East Indies, both of which were important parts of the British empire at this time, though for differing reasons, and with differing governing structures.

Let us accept this as a first step in our curricular deliberations, then, and let us further concretize our examples by focusing on a choice between either Jamaica and Bengal—both of which would provide further perspective in determining why local elites might choose to either accept or resist British rule. The next step would be to turn to the principle of interest, which would be of help in making further curricular choices by speaking to the need to ground curricular choices in our knowledge of the present. Hence, one way of going about this would be to consider the U.S.'s current geo-strategic interest in India. Studying late eighteenth-century India would allow students, then, both the chance to explore the unit's essential question in a manner that moves beyond the U.S. as the only determining case, and allows students and their teacher to explore the history of a nation-state that is currently of much general interest. This, in any case, might be one approach.

Yet we can think of nothing more important in the present than the actual flesh-and-blood students that teachers meet in their classrooms on an everyday basis—and the potential identity transformations that might come about as a result of powerful history teaching. So, rather than relying only on geo-strategic criteria—which are themselves laced with nationalist presumptions (Tye & Tye, 1992)—might not a teacher working with a group of African American students (for example) want to consider Jamaica?

Even a cursory glance at the history of that island would reveal that the white elite of Jamaica had initially supported the white North American elite in their resistance activities against the British crown. Yet this quickly changed as Jamaica's own white elite was faced with hostile resistance activities by the large, numerically-superior black population. The parallels between the slave societies in the U.S. and Jamaica therefore might provide a richer context for powerful history teaching and learning, as students explore questions such as: What is the relationship between slavery and freedom in these two colonies? How did calculations among British elite, white colonial elite, and black slaves play out in the two case examples? How did the happenings in one place affect those in the other? How does this knowledge of the past help us think about the opportunities to form new global solidarities in the present—ones that would avoid the structural dilemma of assuming that identities must be either one thing or another, either assimilated or excluded? It is around this last question that a globally-informed U.S. history would ultimately want to revolve—as it explored continuing possibilities for cross-national solidarity-building projects, ones linked to the interests and identity projects of a multitude of diverse students in our schools today.

We think that such a unit could be an important pathway to breaking down the "naturalness" of national frames of reference—an important first step towards building the type of informed global citizenship for which so many in the social studies community have called (Cogan, Grossman, & Liu, 2000; Gaudelli, 2003; Hanvey, 1975; Heilman, 2007; Merryfield & Wilson, 2005; Myers, 2006; Wilson, 1997). We say this, however, without in any way wanting to detract from the powerful teaching and learning that could and often does take place in more "traditional" units.

Likewise, we make these claims recognizing that this type of curricular thinking might be subject to all types of wrong-headed assumptions about who are students are and where their interests and allegiances actually lie. Are all African Americans interested in forming a pan-African diasporic identity? Would Hindu-Americans be more interested in studying Bengal—a territory where most inhabitants are Muslims—than Jamaica? We understand there is a deep risk here of provoking some sort of politically-correct firestorm, one of the sort that Jonathan Burack (2003) at least somewhat accurately foresaw in his own critique of the "troubling ideological agenda" of global education (p. 42).

Yet the point here *cannot* be that we teach so as to avoid controversy. Rather, such controversy might become the very fabric of good history teaching and of global education itself. As John Dewey himself pointed out (1902/2001), there are many attendant dangers in grounding curricular decisions in our knowledge of the child.[9] Yet such dangers seem to us unavoidable, unless we are to fall back into the "common sense" frameworks of the nationalists themselves. The teacher must always seek to realize that "the child and the curriculum are simply two limits which define a single process" (Dewey, 1902/2001, p. 109).

Our hope, then, is that such a unit—whether it would choose to focus on either Bengal or Jamaica—would provide a more concrete and clear home for global perspectives in the U.S. curriculum by drawing on the subject matter-based curriculum as it currently exists (Thornton, 2005). Such a project can be compared with similar attempts to globalize the curriculum—both across the entirety of the existing curriculum, as well as certain strategic subjects within it—in both the U.K. (Davies, Evans, & Reid, 2005; Ibrahim, 2005) and Canada (Schweisfurth, 2006). But at bottom, the method underlying this discussion is far from novel: let us reintroduce the comparative method in our schools, for it might serve as a helpful heuristic for crossing the borders that now divide the local from the global, the U.S. from the rest of the world.

FURTHER OBJECTIONS/FURTHER RESPONSES

What we should work toward is the generous gesture: This place means everything to us! How can we preserve and share it?
—Nel Noddings, 2005, p. 58

An informed and rigorous comparative approach would allow skilled social studies teachers the opportunity to more clearly extract the "big ideas" inherent in their traditional units while at the same time providing a more well defined space in which to analyze and discuss contemporary issues and interests. Most importantly, such an approach would start to historicize the nation by allowing students to rethink and reexamine (in our example above), its founding myths and the "exceptionalism" of its founders.

Yet we can imagine global-education critic, Jonathan Burack, were he to read this chapter, frustratedly exclaiming, as he did in his own critique of global education (2003), "it is hard to see why a separate U.S. history course of any sort ought to be provided in the first place" (p. 64). To which our response might be—"you are right, it is hard, for both contemporary global realities and the historical scholarship recommend us to do otherwise." Yet this does not mean that we would want teachers to devise curriculum that would somehow ignore the seminal role played by the United States in world history, nor that we are advocates for a stoic cosmopolitanism (Nussbaum, 2002). Indeed, in this section of the chapter, we hope to further flush out exactly these difficulties as we explore the questions of what to teach, why we teach it, and where we should teach it.

First of all, a clear limitation of the traditional treatment of foreign nations in traditional U.S. history courses is the tendency to drop the exploration of a particular country when it is no longer has a clear connection to U.S. national interests. Hence, students get a smattering of eighteenth-century Britain, nineteenth-century Mexico, and twentieth-century Vietnam. The U.S. becomes the center around which all countries orbit in this particular curricular rendering of the world—an implicit message quite problematic when viewed through the lens of global citizenship. A neo-comparative approach does not remedy this deficiency, and indeed, apart from falling into the trap of trying to "teach everything" from a non-positioned, "objective" framework—we do not see how this problem could ever be seriously addressed. An approach such as Bender's would, however, expand the basis upon which international relationships in the past are identified by moving beyond the sole theme of armed conflict. It would also stress the need to move away from a strictly narrative approach to teaching history, and would instead tend to reconceptualize U.S. history courses around those moments where the international system of nation-states was being locked into place. Powerful U.S. history teaching already tends to reorganize its curriculum into a more limited number of topical units (see Grant, 2003, pp. 16–28)—a neo-comparative approach would need to make sure that it furthers this encouraging trend.

Second of all, a neo-comparative approach would have to be flexible enough to allow for the inclusion of diverse comparative case examples. Part of this flexibility would relate to the state of actually existing pedagogical resources—the availability of classroom-appropriate primary documents, documentary films, and textbooks that may or may not exist for any particular time period (Merryfield, 1998). But this flexibility might also entail, as we suggested above, considerations of the identities of concrete classroom students, and the potentials that exist there for topics of study that could help build cross-national solidarities—along the lines of race, gender, language, religion, and any of the other social formations that are currently considered to exist "within" or "below" the nation. Indeed, from our own point of view, stoic cosmopolitanism, of the sort advocated by Martha Nussbaum (2002), makes very little sense in its suggestion that a person's overlapping identity practices—their nonsynchronicity—could ultimately be "contained by" or "grounded in" a universalist liberal-rationalist framework.[10]

Third, we understand that the project we have sketched might better be taken up in reinvigorated world history courses—ones modeled, perhaps, on the work being done by the National Center for History in the Schools (Dunn, 2002; Dunn & Vigalante, 1996) or the Advanced Placement World History program (Dunn, 2008). Yet we find the notion of a "world history" course equally as problematic in certain of its usual features as the "national" history course to which it is so closely related. Consider, for example, this description of the scope of the A.P. World History course:

> The United States is included in the course in relation to its interaction with other societies: its colonial period in the seventeenth and eighteenth centuries, the War for Independence, and its expansion. The internal politics of the United States is not covered. Coverage of the United States is limited to appropriate comparative questions and to United States involvement in global processes. (The College Board, 2009, p. 10)

While such scope for a world history course is surely better than one in which the United States' role in the world is entirely omitted, it still is left having to draw boundaries around those aspects of history which are "internal" to the nation-state, and those which depend upon global "interaction." We find such a distinction dubious, for it reinforces an organic view of the nation and "its" culture. It is to say that the boundaries between "us" and "them" are both clear and unproblematic, and that possibilities for hybridities and interstices do not exist. It should be clear by now that we wish to confront such either/or thinking.

The issue, as Nel Noddings (2005) correctly realized, must ultimately be this: "how educational strategies can use love of place to develop knowledge and skills useful in the larger world" (p. 57). We have argued for a U.S. history curriculum that acknowledges its connections to other nations and other histories—while still preserving and honoring our love of the United States, in all of its tragedy, complexity and beauty.[11] Drawing in particular on the work of Thomas Bender, we have attempted to demonstrate here the ways in which the civic imagination might be reimagined to build cross-national solidarities through rigorous examination of the past. By drawing comparisons with other nations, and by situating portions of national history *within* world history (as opposed to presenting national history alongside it), we believe that an important space is provided for students and educators to consider the connections between the global and the national, between lived experiences of the present and cultural memories of the past—all in ways which might challenge and indeed transform the taken-for-granted identities of the present.

This type of history teaching is going to be difficult. It is also going to have clear implications for the ways in which citizenship is (re)conceived. As Gaudelli (2007) has noted, "as the nation-state is reconfigured, new forms of citizenship are needed to address the fact that nations are no longer the sole locus of political belonging, obligation, and protection" (p. 480). If, then, multi-citizens, hybridized identities and reimagined solidarities appear as a herculean task of curriculum reform, they are nonetheless a future good well worth pursuing. In closing, we would like to briefly raise the question of just what type of social studies teacher might lead us into the next century.

ADDENDUM: TO THOSE WHO WILL BE EDUCATING TOMORROW'S STUDENTS FOR MULTICITIZENSHIP

When you start teaching, you do not know enough, but you are also not culturally developed enough to be a model for your students. This might be particularly true if you come from a family that never had much access to "high" culture. Even if you got a lot of "culture," is it really yours, or is it a ragbag of secondhand experiences and unexplained views? How do you help your kids build the rainbow bridges back and forth? How can you sell them on literacy if you yourself don't read much and don't enjoy books? What about your identity as a teacher? What about the struggle for democracy? You might like the picture of the teacher going out to meet the people, but what do you really have to offer? This is a harsh question, but you have a big responsibility if you are signing up as a teacher. How do you start the lifetime work of becoming a practical intellectual who can help the people progress culturally?

—Joseph Featherstone, 2003, pp. 170–171

We hope that teachers, in particular, aspiring teachers, might read this chapter. Therefore we would like to address this final section to you, the history teacher of the twenty-first century.

In the first section of this chapter, we walked you through the historical literature on nationalism. We suspect that many of the ideas presented there were not unfamiliar to you. In the next section, we walked you through the process of curriculum deliberation, as *we* might undertake it, in our roles as both social studies teachers and social studies teacher educators. In particular, we tried to suggest important concepts and essential questions, and give you some ideas about how you might approach thinking about *both* your curriculum units *and* the students to whom you would be teaching them. As you undertake this work, we recommend that you read the work of Thomas Bender, from whom our own chapter has borrowed heavily. But more importantly, we would just encourage you to read—and not just historical research, but literature drawn from across the humanities (really, whatever excites you and helps you think about your students and your teaching will do just fine).

Finally, we raised a series of objections, ones you might very well hear one day from parents, departmental colleagues, or administrators. We have tried to suggest some possible responses, but ultimately, this task is up to you. As Joseph Featherstone (2003) says, in his own quite lovely letter to an aspiring teacher, "new teachers often don't realize that there are sides to take, and that they are called upon to choose" (p. 164). Teaching is of course hard work, and the teaching of history is twice as hard (and dare we say a comparative approach makes our work three times as hard?). You will make choices, and then be called upon to explain them—and we recommend that you be prepared to revise those decisions in the light of what you learn from your students and their parents, as well as your colleagues. We wish you both courage and humility as you undertake these tasks.

In this brief letter to you, we would like to raise just a few more concluding issues, and provide some sense of the research that guides us in what we are recommending.

Now, we want to make clear that we are not in favor of piling on requirements for teachers. We are not interested in devising any new exams—for either you or your students—nor are we interested in prescribing more undergraduate coursework for those of you just beginning your career. Indeed, if anything, we agree strongly with one of the founders of global education, Robert Hanvey, who said that "the postmodern personality type . . . is not likely to be produced by educational strategies" (1975, p. 12). Loading you down with additional course requirements might backfire if it sends you the message that you have learned all you need to know in your undergraduate coursework.

One thing you might consider, if you do not already have this skill, is learning another language. (And if you grew up speaking a language other than English, by all means, continue to grow in that language as well!) Bender (2000) suggested this as a basic requirement for anyone wanting to study U.S. history in the future, because, of course, other people writing in other languages might just have something to teach us about the history of the United States. This is one reason a history teacher might learn another language, but by the far the more important reason is the ability to learn through travel, work and study in another country.

Research by Kenneth Cushner (2007) has made clear to us just how important such experiences might be in developing global-mindedness. Indeed, global educator Merry Merryfield (2000) did a fascinating study of preeminent global educators in the U.S. and found that, "the experience of living as an expatriate is frequently *the* lived experience that middle-class white teacher educators cite as turning points towards multicultural and global education" (p. 439).[12] Remember, however, there are no guarantees. Living abroad does not automatically produce global consciousness, nor does it guarantee that you will know what to do with whatever knowledge and insight you gain once you return to your classroom. That responsibility always rests with you and your own ability to design experiences for your students that can offer them the possibility to gain some of the same insights you have gained in your own travels (see Germain, 1998).

Future teachers, the responsibility to figure out the curriculum of the future is therefore yours. Know, however, that researchers have also given us a few clues about what *not* to do. One quite important notion comes from global educator Graham Pike, who did a study in which he talked with global educators in the U.K., U.S., and Canada. Pike (2000) found that "British and Canadian practitioners tend to speak in terms of interconnections between people and global systems, whereas American teachers are more likely to characterize global education as learning about a constellation of discrete countries and cultures" (p. 65). He goes on to note that "American culture is used, often without exposition of its own complexity, as the yardstick by which other cultures' similarities and differences are compared" (p. 65).

Globalizing U.S. history does not just mean that we study people outside the U.S., nor should it mean we study those less fortunate than ourselves—

for such an approach leaves unquestioned the conditions that have made some more "fortunate" than others. Global educator Merry Merryfield (2001) and educational historian John Willinsky (1998) have made just this point—so whatever you do with your students, we hope that you will be attentive to how some differences "make a difference" more than others, and help to articulate with your students why this is (Why *did* John Adams support Haitian independence while Thomas Jefferson deeply feared it and worked actively to suppress it?).

You might sometimes read calls for teachers to infuse more coverage of African, Asian or Latin American nations into their curriculum—those peoples who, admittedly, were all too invisible in the American curriculum of the past. Yet simply "covering more" will not produce the type of history instruction that the twenty-first century needs, nor will it make your classroom a more enjoyable place to learn. Merry Merryfield found something very interesting in this regard, in her study of exemplary k–12 global educators: "It is quite remarkable the degree to which students affected instruction . . . Most of these teachers were acutely responsive to student interests, abilities, behavior, and concerns" (p. 354). Globalizing the U.S. history course should not mean that we study more "there" at the expense of "here"—indeed, it just such dichotomies that must be broken down, and it is only by starting with our students' lives that such will be done.

Good luck, then. We know that there are incredible pressures on you to "cover" certain content in your courses so as to "meet the standards." But please do not feel like you have to wait around for some state committee to adopt a curriculum resolution that says the U.S. is a part of the world. For the U.S. and the world have always been joined, it is just that our history writing has not always reflected that. If you find what we are saying compelling or in the least bit interesting, just start experimenting! Infuse some unfamiliar comparisons into your units, and see if all the world might not just come of it.

ENDNOTES

1. Hobsbawm's book on nationalism, which was first printed in 1990, then reprinted in 1991, was based upon a series of lectures he gave in Belfast in 1985. As he all too briefly notes in the Preface to the 1991 edition, "the location suggested the topic" (p. vii). Indeed, it is important to recall that in the 1980s, the Irish Republic Army was actively carrying on a bombing campaign in Britain. Indeed, just seven months prior to these lectures, the IRA set off a 100-pound bomb in the Grand Hotel, in Brighton, England, where the Conservative Party was having its annual conference. Five people were killed, including a member of Parliament.

2. "Before the onset of intensified globalization several decades ago, world politics was chiefly organized on the basis of the so-called Westphalian system. The name is derived from the Peace of Westphalia (1648), which contains an early official statement of the core principles that came to dominate world affairs during the subsequent three hundred years" (Scholte, 1997, p. 19). These core principles are the division of the world into territorial states, each of which has sovereignty over its own territory, free of interference from other states.

3. It is, of course, quite possible to speak of globalization without speaking of the historical processes of nation-building. Yet we find such discussions often lack historical depth. One way nations were built was through a process of unification that tended to obliterate previous existing boundaries and identities. Given that globalization can be understood as doing the same thing on a grander scale, careful attention to the prior history of nation-building seems warranted.

4. Anderson's initial focus on popular support of the nation-building project was reconsidered in the second edition of his book, where he placed more emphasis on the colonial state's tendency to manufacture, through institutions such as the map and the museum, anti-colonial nationalist sentiments. Such an interpretation has caused consternation for some postcolonial theorists, who are keen on presenting the non-derivative nature of anti-colonial struggles. See Chatterjee, 1993; Chrisman, 2004; Gandhi, 1998.

5. We recognize that Said is not usually grouped among the theorists of the nation. Yet we find the general mechanism he lays out in his book to be so persuasive as to represent a whole line of later thinking.

6. Exclusionary nationalism not only bolsters intra-group unity by scapegoating another, but by punishing those members of its own group willing to live across group divisions. Hence, Hechter (2002) notes that the "first targets of the Serb paramilitary units that swept into multiethnic Bosnian villages were those *Serbs* who favoured ethnic integration" (italics are our own, p. 131).

7. Ultimately, both models should be employed in tandem. This is particularly the case in those nationalisms that are born as movements of resistance and liberation, as was the case in the twentieth century's anti-colonial struggles. Such struggles—what Michael Hechter has called peripheral nationalisms (2002)—employed both methods simultaneously, as local elite sought to demarcate an "indigenous" pre-colonial cultural tradition (horizontal work) around which subalterns could be made to rally (vertical work).

8. The one large exception to this claim would be England, whose people played an important part in the way the "settling" of the American continent is told in many U.S. history classrooms. Yet the mono-ancestral approach—ignoring as it does the impact of Native American, west African, Spanish, and French peoples on the formation of an "American" identity—probably does more harm for global citizenship than good.

9. "It will do harm if child-study leave in the popular mind the impression that a child of a given age has a positive equipment of purpose and interests to be cultivated just as they stand. Interests in reality are but attitudes toward possible experiences; they are not achievements; their worth is in the leverage they afford, not in the accomplishment they represent. To take the phenomena presented at a given age as in any way self-explanatory or self-contained is inevitably to result in indulgence or spoiling" (Dewey, 1902/2001, p. 112).

10. Nonsynchrony is a term used in critical race curriculum theories. It refers to the fact that "race, class and gender function in contradictory fashion in daily life; they do not reproduce themselves in any simple manner" (Pinar, Reynolds, Slattery & Taubman, 2002, p. 319). That is, there is no single identity frame that contains all others—identity is always shifting, according to the contextual features of a situation.

11. We are well aware the Noddings and others usually use the concept of "place" to refer to the "local." However, here we would return to Anderson (1983/1992): all communities are imagined, even the most "local" ones, and even those tied to very particular "places." Under certain contexts, we are quite confident the nation and its territory can be experienced as a "local place." This is not, however, to downplay the importance of what we might call "backyard" studies.

12. Merryfield (2000) is absolutely correct that there is "a profound difference between developing a double consciousness to survive a racist state and developing a consciousness of others' perspectives when the other holds no power over one's life" (p. 439). That is, being an outsider in another country mustn't lead one to believe that one better understands people whose exclusion are structural features of a national system.

REFERENCES

Addams, J. (2009). The public school and the immigrant child. In D. J. Flinders & S. J. Thornton (Eds.), *The Curriculum Studies Reader* (3rd ed., pp. 42–44). New York: Routledge.

Anderson, B. (1992). *Imagined communities: Reflections of the origin and spread of nationalism* (rev. ed.). London: Verso. (Original work published in 1983)

Barton, K. C., & Levstik, L. S. (1998). "It wasn't a good part of history": National identity and students' explanations of historical significance. *Teachers College Record, 99*(3), 478–513.

Barton, K. C., & Levstik, L.S. (2004). *Teaching history for the common good.* Mahwah, NJ: Lawrence Erlbaum Associates, Inc., Publishers.

Bell, D. A. (2003). *The cult of the nation in France: Inventing nationalism, 1680–1800.* Cambridge, MA: Harvard University Press.

Bender, T. (2000). *The LaPietra report: A report to the profession.* Retrieved November 13, 2010, from: http://www.oah.org/activities/lapietra/index.html#Anchor-20246.

Bender, T. (Ed.). (2002). *Rethinking American history in a global age.* Berkeley and Los Angeles, CA: University of California Press.

Bender, T. (2006). *A nation among nations: America's place in world history.* New York: Hill and Wang.

Benitez, H. (2001). Does it really matter how we teach? The socializing effects of a globalized U.S. history curriculum. *Theory and Research in Social Education, 29*(2), 290–307.

Burack, J. (2003). The student, the world, and the global education ideology. In J. Leming, L. Ellington, & K. Porter (Eds.), *Where did social studies go wrong?* (pp. 40–69). Washington, DC: Thomas B. Fordham Foundation.

Chatterjee, P. (1993). *The nation and its fragments: Colonial and postcolonial histories.* Princeton, NJ: Princeton University Press.

Chrisman, L. (2004). Nationalism and postcolonial studies. In N. Lazarus (Ed.), *The Cambridge companion to postcolonial literary studies* (pp. 183–198). Cambridge: Cambridge University Press.

Cogan, J. J., Grossman, D., & Liu, M. (2000). Citizenship: The democratic imagination in a global/local Context. *Social Education, 64*(1), 48–52.

College Board. (2009). *World history course description.* Retrieved October 9, 2010, from: http://apcentral.collegeboard.com/apc/public/repository/ap-world-history-course-description.pdf.

Cornbleth, C. (2002). Images of America: What youth do know about the United States. *American Educational Research Journal, 39*(2), 519–552.

Cushner, K. (2007). The role of experience in the making of internationally-minded teachers. *Teacher Education Quarterly, 34*(1), 27–39.

Davies, I., Evans, M. & Reid, A. (2005). Globalising citizenship education? A critique of global education and citizenship education. *British Journal of Educational Studies, 53*(1), 66–89.

Dewey, J. (2001). *The school and society & The child and the curriculum.* Mineola, NY: Dover Publications, Inc. (Original work published in 1902)

Dunn, R. E. (2002). Growing good citizens with a world-centered curriculum. *Educational Leadership, 60*(2), 10–13.

Dunn, R. E. (2008). The two world histories. *Social Education. 72*(5), 257–263.

Dunn, R.E. & Vigilante, D. (1996). *Bring history alive! A sourcebook for teaching world history.* Los Angeles: UCLA Book Zone/The UCLA Store.

Epstein, T. (2000). Adolescent perspectives on racial diversity in U.S. history: Case studies from an urban classroom. *American Educational Research Journal, 37*(1), 185–214.

Featherstone, J., Featherstone, L., & Featherstone, C. (2003). *"Dear Josie": Witnessing the hopes and failures of democratic education.* New York: Teachers College Press.

Gandhi, L. (1998). *Postcolonial theory: A critical introduction.* New York: Columbia University Press.

Gaudelli, W. (2003). *World class: Teaching and learning in global times.* Mahwah, NJ: Lawrence Erlbaum Associates, Publishers.

Gaudelli, W. (2007). Global courts, global judges, and a multicitizen curriculum. *Theory and Research in Social Education, 35*(3), 465–491.

Gellner, E. (1983). *Nations and nationalism.* Ithaca, NY: Cornell University Press.

Germain, M.H. (1998). *World teachers: Cultural learning and pedagogy.* Westport, CT: Bergin & Garvey.

Grant, S.G. (2003). *History lessons: Teaching, learning, and testing in U.S. high school classrooms.* Mahwah, NJ: Lawrence Erlbaum Associates, Publishers.

Hanvey, R. (1975). *An attainable global perspective.* New York: Center for War/Peace Studies.

Heater, D. (1999). *What is citizenship?* Molden, MA: Polity Press.

Hechter, M. (1999). *Internal colonialism: The Celtic fringe in British national development.* New Brunswick, NJ: Transaction Publishers. (Original work published in 1975)

Hechter, M. (2002). *Containing nationalism.* Oxford: Oxford University Press.

Heilman, E.E. (2007). (Dis)locating imaginative and ethical aims of global education. In K. Roth & I. Gur-Zeév (Eds.), *Education in the era of globalization* (pp. 83–104). Dordrecht, The Netherlands: Springer.

Held, D. (1999) The transformation of political community: Rethinking democracy in the context of globalization. In I. Shapiro & C. Hacker-Cordón (Eds.), *Democracy's edges* (pp. 84–111). Cambridge: Cambridge University Press.

Hobsbawm, E. J. (1962). *The age of revolution, 1789–1848.* New York: Mentor Books.

Hobsbawm, E. J. (1983). Mass-producing traditions: Europe, 1970–1914. In E. J. Hobsbawm & T. Ranger (Eds.), *The Invention of tradition* (pp. 263–307). Cambridge, England: Cambridge University Press.

Hobsbawm, E. J. (1991). *Nations and nationalism since 1780: Programme, myth, and reality.* Cambridge, England: Cambridge University Press.

Hobsbawm, E. J. (1992). Ethnicity and nationalism in Europe today. *Anthropology Today, 8*(1), 3–8.

Hobsbawm, E. J., & Ranger, T. (Eds.) (1983). *The invention of tradition.* Cambridge, England: Cambridge University Press.

Ibrahim, T. (2005). Global citizenship education: Mainstreaming the curriculum? *Cambridge Journal of Education, 35*(2), 177–194.

Kincheloe, J. L. (2001). *Getting beyond the facts: Teaching social studies/social sciences in the twenty-first century* (2nd ed.). New York: Peter Lang Publishing, Inc.

Loewen, J. W. (2007). *Lies my teacher told me: Everything your American history textbook got wrong* (Rev. ed.). New York: Touchstone. (Original work published in 1995)

Marx, A. W. (1996). Race-making and the nation-state. *World Politics, 48*(2), 180–208.

Marx, A. W. (2003). *Faith in nation: Exclusionary origins of nationalism.* New York: Oxford University Press.

Merryfield, M. M. (1998). Pedagogy for global perspectives in education: Studies of teachers' thinking and practice. *Theory and Research in Social Education, 26*(3), 342–79.

Merryfield, M. M. (2000). Why aren't teachers being prepared to teach for diversity, equity, and global interconnectedness? A study of lived experiences in the making of multicultural and global educators. *Teaching and Teacher Education, 16*(4), 429–43.

Merryfield, M. M. (2001). Moving the center of global education: From imperial world views that divide the world to double consciousness, contra punctual pedagogy, hybridity, and cross-cultural competence. In W. B. Stanley (Ed.), *Critical Issues in Social Studies Research for the 21ˢᵗ Century* (pp. 179–207). Greenwich, CT: Information Age Publishing.

Merryfield, M., & Wilson, A. (2005). *Social studies and the world: Teaching global perspectives.* Silver Spring, MD: National Council for the Social Studies.

Myers, J. P. (2006). Rethinking the social studies curriculum in the context of globalization: Education for global citizenship in the U.S. *Theory and Research in Social Education, 34*(3), 370–394.

Noddings, N. (2005). Place-based education to preserve the earth and its people. In N. Noddings (Ed.), *Educating citizens for global awareness* (pp. 57–68). New York:

Nussbaum, M.C. (2002). Patriotism and cosmopolitanism. In J. Cohen's (Ed.), *For Love of Country?* (pp. 3–17). Boston: Beacon Press.

Parker, W. C., Ninomiya, A., & Cogan, J. (1999). Educating world citizens: Toward multinational curriculum development. *American Educational Research Journal, 36*(2), 117–45.

Pike, G. (2000). Global education and national identity: In pursuit of meaning. *Theory into Practice, 39*(2), 64–73.

Pinar, W. F., Reynolds, W. M., Slattery, P., & Taubman, P. M. (2002). *Understanding curriculum: An introduction to the study of historical and contemporary curriculum discourses.* New York: Peter Lang Publishing, Inc.

Rosenzweig, R., & Thelen, D. (1998). *The presence of the past: Popular uses of history in American life.* New York: Columbia University Press.

Said, E. W. (1991). *Orientalism: Western conceptions of the orient.* London: Penguin Books.

Scholte, J. A. (1997). The globalization of world politics. In Baylis, J. & Smith, S. (Eds.). *The globalization of world politics: An introduction to international relations* (pp. 13–30). Oxford: Oxford University Press.

Schweisfurth, M. (2006). Education for global citizenship: Teacher agency and curricular structure in Ontario schools. *Educational Review, 58*(1), 41–50.

Thornton, S. J. (2005). Incorporating internationalism into the social studies curriculum. In N. Noddings (Ed.), *Educating citizens for global awareness* (pp. 81–92). New York: Teachers College Press.

Tye, B. B. & Tye, K. A. (1999). *Global education: A study of school change.* Orange, CA: Interdependence Press.

Weber, E. J. (1976). *Peasants into Frenchmen: The modernization of rural France, 1870–1914*. Stanford, CA: Stanford University Press.

Wertsch, J.V. & O'Connor, K. (1994). Multivoicedness in historical representation: American college students' accounts of the origins of the United States. *Journal of Narrative and Life History, 4*(4), 295–309.

White, H. (1980). *Metahistory: The historical imagination in nineteenth-century Europe*. Baltimore, MD: The John Hopkins University Press.

Willinsky, J. (1998). *Learning to divide the world: Education at empire's end*. Minneapolis, MN: The University of Minnesota Press.

Wilson, A. H. (1997). Infusing global perspectives throughout a secondary social studies program. In M. M. Merryfield, E. Jarchow, & S. Pickert (Eds.), *Preparing teachers to teach global perspectives: A handbook for teacher educators* (pp. 143–167). Thousand Oaks, CA: Corwin Press, Inc.

Wineburg, S. S. & Wilson, S. M. (1991). Models of wisdom in the teaching of history. *History Teacher, 24*(4), 395–412.

Zinn, H. (2003). *A people's history of the United States: 1492 to present*. New York: Harper Perennial. (Original work published in 1980)

CHAPTER 19

PEDAGOGICAL PARADOX OF SOCIAL STUDIES

Teaching for Intellectual and Emotional Learning

Christy Folsom

The subject of Social Studies is a pedagogical paradox. It has all the ingredients needed—passion, hate, love, treason, faulty decision-making, flawed leaders, remarkable accomplishments, and courageous citizens—for deep thinking and emotional learning to take place. Social studies provides opportunities for learning content through project work where students can express their creativity while at the same time, develop the critical thinking skills of decision making, planning, and self-evaluation. Yet, too often, social studies is taught in a way that is anything but the passionate, memorable subject it could be. Russell (2010) states that too many students hear the uninspiring words, "Read the chapter and complete the worksheet" (p. 65), instead of having the opportunity to engage in learning experiences more suited to the live-action, self-regulated, participatory drama favored by the curious YouTube generation (Pogrow, 2010).

Contemporary Social Studies: An Essential Reader, pages 357–383
Copyright © 2012 by Information Age Publishing
All rights of reproduction in any form reserved.

INVESTIGATING THE PARADOX

Investigating the paradox of how social studies content is taught in classrooms uncovers another paradox. The second paradox concerns how prospective teachers are prepared to teach social studies. Most teacher educators and researchers in the United States espouse constructivist teaching methods (Alazzi, 2008; Yilmaz, 2008). However, what progressive educators see as memorable student-centered learning opportunities that inspire students to think critically and develop a love of social studies (Dicamillo, 2010), traditional educators often see as an amalgam of ill-structured activities that lack the content that students need to become knowledgeable citizens (Ravitch, 2003; Rochester, 2003).

Many who favor traditionalist methodology point to progressive constructivist teacher education as a major reason for low performance on assessments of social studies knowledge by U. S. students (Leming, 2003; Schug, 2003). Yet, these methods are found in relatively few classrooms. In spite of the efforts of teacher educators, constructivist methods do not consistently transfer to classrooms for which they are intended (Hollingsworth, 1989). Instead, new teachers, regardless of their preparation program, often follow a "pattern of teachers transmitting information to students who are then asked to reproduce it" (Newmann, 1991, p. 324). Regardless of the preparation many teachers have received, they teach social studies in a manner focusing more on content coverage than on the processes of thinking.

Studies show that high school and college students score poorly on national assessments in social studies that focus on content (Risinger & Garcia, 1995; Rochester, 2003). At the same time that students do poorly on showing mastery of social studies content, there is little evidence that they have mastered the thinking or emotional processes of critical thinking, problem solving, creativity, ethics and social responsibility (Consortium, 2006). As Newmann (1991) points out, there are many factors of policy, curriculum, testing, and others that contribute to social studies teaching and learning that is less than optimal. Nevertheless, how can teachers learn to teach social studies in a balanced approach that gives equal attention to content and process?

This chapter looks at the contradiction in social studies teaching and addresses three questions. First, why is there not more evidence of teaching social studies content through active, thinking-rich learning experiences? The second question has two parts. If teacher educators are preparing teacher candidates in constructivist methods based in thinking, why is there so little transfer of these methods to classroom teaching? Concurrently, why do more traditional methods of teaching, focused on content coverage, not result in evidence of social studies content mastery on national assessments? Third, what is Teaching for Intellectual and Emotional Learning and how is the TIEL Curriculum Design Model being used in an urban graduate methods course to help prospective elementary teachers learn to develop social studies units and lessons that are balanced between content and the development of students' thinking and emotional processes?

DEFINITIONS

Several terms that relate to educational philosophy, educators, and curriculum will be used throughout the chapter. Those terms will be defined here for clarification.

Progressive, Constructivism, and Traditional

The terms *progressive, constructivism,* and *traditional* will be used throughout this chapter to describe teaching philosophy and methodology. Therefore, clarification of the definitions is needed before exploring the questions. *Progressive* is a broad term when applied to education that is linked to the progressive political movement that took hold at the beginning of the 20th century. One of the educational philosophies that emerged at that time was experience-based, child-centered education that promoted the development of thinking processes (Folsom, 2009).

Constructivism is a philosophy about learning and knowing (Brooks & Brooks, 1993) that has been applied to teaching. It has much in common with historical progressive education. At its core, constructivism posits that all knowledge is constructed by the learner. Characteristics of constructivist pedagogy, like progressive pedagogy, include experienced-based, student-centered learning, group dialogue, domain knowledge, student interest, choice, interdependence, cooperation, and development of student thinking and metacognition (Bailey & Pransky, 2005; Mintrop, 2004; McCombs & Whisler, as cited in Yilmaz, 2008).

Traditional pedagogy is also known by the terms scientific and behaviorist. Teacher-centered and direct-instruction are other terms used to describe traditional pedagogy (Schug, 2003). Educators who hold a traditional view of teaching maintain that there is a specific body of content knowledge that must be imparted to students (Brooks & Brooks, 1993). Traditional pedagogy is often described as transmission teaching where the learner is a more passive recipient of information than in constructivist teaching (Darling-Hammond, 1997).

Teacher Educator, Candidate, Teacher, and Student

The terms *teacher educator, teacher candidate, teacher,* and *student* will be used throughout the chapter. *Teacher educator* refers to those who teach courses in a teacher preparation program. *Teacher candidate* is used to refer to a prospective teacher who is in enrolled in a teacher preparation program. *Teacher* refers to those who are teaching in P–12 classrooms. The term *student* refers to any student in P–12.

CURRICULUM COMPONENTS

Understanding content and process within a larger structural framework can help teacher educators prepare prospective teachers with the knowledge and skills they need to achieve pedagogical balance in their practice. There are four fundamental components in curriculum development—context, content, process, and product. Together these components provide a solid structural foundation for developing units or lessons in social studies as well as other subjects.

Context refers to who the students are, where they are developmentally, what they already know, consideration for learning styles, and connections students might make to content (Chiarelott, 2006). *Content* includes the topic, facts, skills, and concepts, as well as generalizations and principles of the subject matter that is taught (Erickson, 2007).

Process is more elusive than the other components and is often considered in terms of teaching methodologies. For example, large or small group discussion, cooperative or individual learning, role-play or individual presentations are pedagogical processes teachers use in the classroom. However, process also refers to the specific thinking and social emotional processes that motivate and empower students, as well as make content memorable. When teachers understand these largely invisible processes of learning, they can consciously plan questions and learning activities that help students develop their thinking and emotional processes as they are learning content (Folsom, 2005). *Product* is a component of assessment. Product is that which the student creates, writes, or speaks that shows his or her understanding of the content that has been taught. Criteria for evaluation are another component of assessment through which the success of a product is evaluated. Understanding these components can help teachers acquire pedagogical balance between content and process.

MISSING IN SOCIAL STUDIES CLASSROOMS

Learning content through doing and thinking is not a new idea. Long before constantly-streaming, self-produced media became ubiquitous, learning academic content through doing and thinking were clearly described by educators (Beyer, 2008; Boyle-Baise & Goodman, 2009; Dewey, 1938; Hollingworth, 1926; Kilpatrick, 1918, 1934, 1936; Taba, 1962). In addition, those in the field of psychology have provided voluminous support for the active, hands-on, minds-on learning and teaching of content that lie at the heart of progressive constructivist teaching (Bandura, 1993; Sternberg, 1997; Vygotsky,1994). There is no shortage of research, materials, and suggestions for teaching social studies in ways that integrate doing and thinking with content (Levstik & Barton, 2000; Parker, 2010). Yet, notwithstanding the availability of such resources, the subject of social studies itself is sorely neglected or poorly taught in many of our schools. Why is there a lack of evidence that social studies is being taught through active, thinking and social-emotionally rich learning experiences? What are some possible reasons that we are not getting our intellectual and emotional money's worth from the teaching of social studies?

STANDARDIZED TESTING

Research has shown a continued erosion of time devoted to social studies due to the emphasis on standardized testing. In our current testing climate, put in place by No Child Left Behind (NCLB), preparing for tests in the subjects of English Language Arts and Math has usurped the time once spent teaching social studies (Bolick, Adams, & Willox, 2010; Brophy & Alleman, 2008; Misco & Shiveley, 2010). Au (2007) found in his metasynthesis of 49 studies focused on the effect of high stakes testing that curriculum has been narrowed to those subjects—math and literacy—that are consistently tested; knowledge has become increasingly fragmented as students learn "bits and pieces" (p. 264) for the tests; and teacher-centered instruction has increased. While it is difficult for students in grades 1–6 to learn social studies, if it is not being taught, it is also difficult for teacher candidates to learn to teach social studies when there are few classrooms in which to observe engaging social studies teaching and learning (Bolick et al., 2010). These conditions certainly do not support engaged, thinking and social-emotionally rich instruction in social studies and there is little relief in sight. While NCLB is being replaced by differently labeled policies, Misco and Shiveley (2010) point out that the emphasis on standardized testing is unlikely to diminish.

TEACHER PREPARATION

A second reason for the lack of active, thinking-based social studies teaching is that teachers need a deeper understanding of the complex processes that engaging, thinking and social-emotionally rich learning requires. Sarason (1982) and French and Rhoder (1992) found that teachers had not learned in their teacher education programs how to plan in ways that promote student thinking. Teachers were unable to teach and discuss thinking with students because they did not know how.

Teachers need more explicit instruction in how to develop and deliver lessons and units that weave process with content, have focused objectives and assessments, and include consciously planned questions and learning activities that promote critical and creative thinking and social emotional learning through hands-on experiential learning (Folsom, 2011; Erickson, 2007; Swartz, Costa, Beyer, Reagan, & Kallick, 2008; Tomlinson, 1999; Wiggins & McTighe, 1996).

Yet, there is little evidence that teacher education programs are adequately preparing teachers to plan social studies curriculum with deep thinking and social emotional learning consciously imbedded within content (Folsom, 2009). If teachers do not clearly understand the relationship between content and thinking processes and how to bring these elements together in lessons and units to promote active learning, social studies teaching will lack the necessary balance for students to learn in more complex ways.

TRANSFER FROM COURSEWORK TO CLASSROOM

A third reason for the lack of teaching social studies using engaging, thinking-rich methods is the challenge of transfer from what is learned in coursework to the classroom. Even when teacher educators are teaching constructivist methods that promote thinking, these methods do not necessarily transfer to the classroom. Goodlad (1990) reported that teacher candidates showed a lack of internalizing what they had learned in coursework. Teacher educators perceived that their courses had a strong influence on teacher candidates. Candidates, on the other hand, indicated that coursework had little effect on the beliefs and values concerning teaching that they held coming into their programs. Hollingsworth (1989) also found that it was difficult to change the mindset of students who had learned in more traditional ways. While those who came into teacher preparation programs with a more constructivist view of learning did better, many teachers reverted to traditional ways of teaching when they reached the classroom.

It is a matter of concern that transfer from teacher preparation coursework to K–12 classrooms is inconsistent and uneven. Yet, Darling-Hammond, in her research of seven teacher education programs, found a high rate of transfer from the knowledge and skills learned in these programs to the graduates' classrooms. Many factors were found to contribute to the high rate of transfer including support of the college and structures of the programs, while other factors relate to pedagogy.

Two of the pedagogical factors are instructive in this discussion of how to increase the transfer of pedagogical skills learned in teacher preparation programs to classrooms. First, these successful programs use *explicit* [italics are mine] strategies to help students "confront their own deep-seated beliefs and assumptions about learning and students" (Darling-Hammond, 2006, p. 41). Second, these programs use "an inquiry approach that connects theory and practice" (p. 277). Candidates learn to question their own practice and gain deep understanding of teaching strategies through consistently connecting theory to practice. Bransford, Derry, Berliner and Hammerness (2005) point out "the more that knowledge is acquired with understanding, the higher the probability that appropriate transfer will occur" (p. 70).

NEED FOR BALANCE

Balance is clearly necessary. The simplistic views of constructivism as inchoate student-centered process and traditional teaching as wheelbarrows full of facts dumped at the feet of students need to be modified so educators of both persuasions can develop learning experiences in social studies that bring together the best of both viewpoints. Many teachers learn constructivist methods for teaching social studies in their teacher education programs, yet they do not demonstrate constructivist methods in their classrooms (Hollingsworth, 1989; Newmann, 1991). At the same time, research shows that students leave social studies classrooms without a firm grasp of the facts and events that are part of social studies education (Ravitch & Finn, 1987; Risinger & Garcia, 1995).

Why have constructivist methods not consistently transferred to social studies classrooms? And, at the same time, why is mastery of specific knowledge of history and geography so limited? It seems that neither pedagogical method has been sufficiently effective.

COMMON GROUND

The common ground that lies between these two pedagogical philosophies is the thinking and social emotional processes found at the core of engaging teaching. Darling-Hammond recognizes the skills needed to teach in ways that lead to student engagement and understanding, as well as to maintain these progressive methods successfully in the classroom. In *The Right to Learn: A Blueprint for Creating Schools that Work* (1997) she says:

> Perhaps the biggest obstacle to maintaining progressive reforms is the extensive skill needed to teach both subjects and students well...they often did not

know how to fashion work that was rigorous as well as relevant, how to employ variable student-based strategies, and also teach for high levels of disciplined understanding in content areas. (p. 12)

J. Martin Rochester (2003) is a staunch supporter of traditional education and a vocal critic of progressive constructivist methods. He has little patience with what he sees as the constructivist practices that he believes undermine traditional rigor in teaching and learning. For Rochester, constructivist methods are "too airy and loosey-goosey" (Shaunessy, 2007). Yet, he points out the need for educators to integrate seemingly exclusive methodologies such as "rigor and creativity, memorization and understanding, lecturing and active engagement, learning and fun, moral clarity and values clarification" (Rochester, p. 35). To Rochester these processes are both compatible and integral to education.

There is common ground between these two different approaches to teaching and learning. Darling-Hammond (1997) recognizes the complexity of progressive constructivist teaching and the high level of pedagogical skill required to teach content and processes effectively. Rochester (2003), in spite of his strong criticism of constructivist methodology, calls for pedagogy that integrates the content focus of traditional education with the processes that are central to progressive education. For example, while student learning is a goal of educators in both philosophies, rigor, memorization, lecturing, and moral clarity could be considered characteristics associated with traditional education. Creativity, understanding, active engagement, fun, and values clarification are common characteristics of progressive education.

Yet, bringing content and process together is not an easy task. One of Dewey's (1938) greatest worries about experience-based educational methods was that educators would not or could not carry them out effectively. Dewey is both blamed and celebrated for the pedagogical methods of the progressive education movement. While many of the practices of progressive education are currently utilized in today's schools with varying degrees of quality, Dewey (1916) advocated for a balance between the content to be learned and the processes needed for learning. He stated the folly of having each act of learning dictated by a teacher, while at the same time pointing out the equally flawed teaching that "permits(s) capricious or discontinuous action in the name of spontaneous self-expression" (p. 102).

THE TIEL CURRICULUM DESIGN MODEL

The ability to balance the content ideals of traditional education with the intellectual and emotional processes of learning emphasized in progressive education is an elusive skill that teachers need to master. Yet, they often lack the knowledge and understandings of the underlying processes needed to do so. The TIEL Curriculum Design Model, Teaching for Intellectual and Emotional Learning, provides a framework that makes the invisible intellectual and social emotional processes visible. It is a powerful tool for helping teacher educators, prospective teachers, and teachers address the paradoxes of social studies by clarifying the processes that must be balanced with content in curriculum planning.

The TIEL model provides a tool of inquiry into curriculum development that bridges theory and practice. Synthesized from the work of Guilford and Dewey, the TIEL model makes explicit fundamental intellectual and social emotional processes that underlie engaging teaching and learning (Folsom, 2009). In teacher education coursework, the TIEL model helps

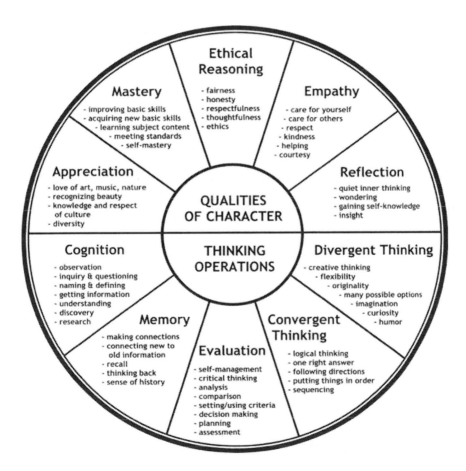

FIGURE 19.1. TIEL Curriculum Design Model

teacher candidates become conscious of these invisible, yet essential processes in planning and instruction. The TIEL Model serves as a guide that helps candidates plan lessons and units that integrate thinking and social emotional processes with content. In addition, the TIEL model helps candidates ask questions that guide self-assessment and reflection on both planning and instruction. Examples of using the TIEL model for planning and reflection are found in the section on project-based curriculum.

The model includes five fundamental thinking operations derived from Guilford's (1977) Structure of Intellect Theory. These are *cognition*—inquiry, the gathering of information, discovery, observation; *memory*—recall, connection-making; *evaluation*—critical thinking and self-management skills of decision-making, planning, and self-evaluation; *convergent thinking and production*—logical thinking, one right answer; and *divergent thinking and production*—creativity, imagination, risk-taking.

The thinking operations are complemented by five qualities of character that Dewey (1964) defined as important emotional aspects of teaching and learning. These are reflection, empathy, ethical reasoning, mastery, and appreciation. The thinking operations and qualities of character are organized into complementary color-coded pairs. The complementary pairs are cognition/reflection (pink), memory/empathy (blue), evaluation/ethical reasoning (green), convergent thinking and production/ mastery (yellow), and divergent thinking and production/appreciation (orange). The colors are based on Meeker's (1979) application of Guilford's theory to education. This wide range of thinking processes and social-emotional qualities are those described by social studies researchers and educators who identify the knowledge and skills students need to develop to take their places as well-informed, active citizens in a democracy (Alazzi, 2008; Bailey & Pransky, 2005; Engle, 1960; Folsom, 2009; Parker, 2009; Rochester, 2003; Skolnick, Dulberg & Maestre, 2004).

PROJECT-BASED LEARNING

Project-based learning provides a rich opportunity for students to master rigorous content while, at the same time, learning the wide range of thinking and social emotional processes outlined in the TIEL model (Folsom, 2009). Through project-based learning, students learn the critical thinking skills of decision-making, planning, and self-evaluation needed for citizenship in a memorable, creative way. Project-based curriculum meets the goals of both traditional and constructivist education. It provides opportunities for inquiry into a topic and planned teacher- directed lessons that focus on essential content and processes. Project-based learning includes a culminating project that gives students the opportunity to do further research, make decisions, plan, and create a product that shows their understanding and appreciation of the major concepts, facts, and skills learned throughout the unit of study.

In my social studies methods course, teacher candidates learn how to balance content and process in project-based curriculum by experiencing structured project work themselves. Candidates use the TIEL model to consciously make decisions, plan, research, design and present their own projects. After this experience, candidates learn to develop project-based curriculum units in social studies for their future students. The following description is an example of a group presentation entitled the *"The Truth about the First Thanksgiving,"* (Loewen, 2008). The Loewen projects are examples of culminating projects that students might develop at the end of a unit.

Five teacher candidates bustled at the front of the social studies methods classroom preparing to share what they had learned from studying their chapter, "The Truth about the First Thanksgiving" from the book "Lies My Teacher Told Me: Everything Your American History Textbook Got Wrong." Within a

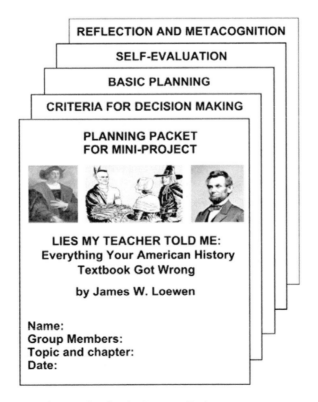

FIGURE 19.2. Student Packet for the Loewen Project.

few minutes a table was transformed with a white tablecloth, a bowl of plastic vegetables including corn on the cob, and a plate for each of the five guests who had taken their seats. The guests spanned geography and time. The first, dressed in a white bonnet made of a plastic bag tied neatly under her chin, represented the 35 Pilgrims of Massachusetts. The second guest, dressed in a long black jacket, represented the 67 other Europeans aboard the Mayflower. The third was a cantankerous representative of the Englishmen from the failed Virginia Colony. The final two guests were Native Americans. One was a representative of the Chiskiack tribe. The other was Frank James of the Wampanoag tribe, who in 1970 was invited to speak at the 350th anniversary of the Pilgrims' landing. He was prevented from giving his prepared speech after those at the Massachusetts Department of Commerce in charge of the ceremony disapproved of what he had to say.

The stage directions explained the setting: "Pilgrims and Native Americans sitting at a table celebrating the umpteenth Thanksgiving together pretending to be 'merry.'" As they ate, they remembered the past—each from the perspective of the representatives seated at the table.

As part of the Loewen Projects, each candidate used a planning packet to structure their work and reflect on the content and thinking and social-emotional processes involved in developing their projects. The planning packet includes graphic organizers for decision making, planning, self-evaluation, and metacognition (See Figure 19.2). I will refer to the Loewen Projects to explain how the TIEL model helps candidates begin to understand both the content and processes that form the foundation of project work in social studies.

COGNITION AND REFLECTION

The thinking processes that are part of the thinking operation *cognition,* help teachers think deeply about the content and how they will present it as they plan. Social studies teachers need to see planning not simply as reading from the text, sequencing information, or even organizing a series of interesting activities. Instead, they need to specifically plan what students will observe, inquire into, discover, or research in order to develop an understanding of the concepts, facts, and skills they are learning (Parker, 2009; Taba, 1962).

Teacher educators can provide general questions that will help prospective teachers plan how students will acquire content. How can the students use textbooks, primary sources, and other resources to gather information in ways that will help them develop understanding? What questions can I ask that will help them inquire into their reading? How can I elicit questions from students about this topic?

Questions about content can also be more specific. When teacher candidates learn to ask focused questions about content, they become more aware of the content they want the students to learn. The following questions are based on the social studies disciplines (Parker, 2009). What is the major problem or historical event? How did geography play a part in the events and experiences of the people? What decisions made by government leaders and/or ordinary citizens changed historical events? How did economics influence the decisions and events? How did culture affect the decisions and how did decisions affect the cultures? (Sociology and anthropology are combined for the elementary level.)

Reflection is a natural outcome of observation (Dewey, 1964), one of the components of the thinking operation *cognition.* The TIEL Curriculum Design Wheel visually reminds teachers to plan opportunities for students to reflect metacognitively on their learning. In the Loewen Project, candidates use each TIEL component on the metacognition worksheet (see figure 6) in their planning packet to reflect on their thinking and social emotional learning while developing the project. A student who immigrated to the United States from Nigeria wrote, "The project afforded me an opportunity to reflect on the true meaning of the Thanksgiving that has become an annual celebration" (Student A, Loewen Project)

Students in teacher preparation programs often spend significant time reflecting on teaching methodology (Zeichner & Liston, 1996). These opportunities reflecting on subject matter content provide examples of how to structure reflection opportunities for their students. As teachers plan, they can ask themselves the following questions. How can I have my students reflect on the information and concepts they are learning? How can learning this social studies content help students learn about themselves? How can I help students reflect on the intellectual and social-emotional processes of their learning through this social studies unit of study?

MEMORY AND EMPATHY

Memory stores information, facilitates recall, and allows us to make connections between concepts and experiences (Guilford, 1977; Jensen, 1998; Sprenger, 1999; Sternberg, 1985; Wolfe, 2001). If *memory* is the glue that allows us to use our experiences to learn, then social studies contributes to creating the glue that binds collective memory. When social studies is taught in a way that touches students' emotions (Pogrow, 2010), students build strong memories of civic knowledge that connect to our collective memory.

As candidates read the chapters in Loewen, the teacher candidates realized how little they recalled from their own social studies classes. Their experiences resembled the non-instruction described by Schug (2003) that lacks the better qualities of either teacher-directed or constructivist teaching. Since they remembered so little, the candidates began to question the effectiveness of answering end-of-chapter questions and memorizing dates and places. To illustrate, one student who studied the chapter, "*Herofication*," reflected on the process of memory saying:

> I remember learning about these figures in Social Studies. I learned about them in the "wrong and mistaken" fashion that Loewen spoke of in the chapter. In elementary school, I learned that Helen Keller was blind, deaf, and learned to read and write. In junior high school, I learned that Woodrow Wilson was president during World War I. I learned nothing else about them (Student B, Loewen Project)

The TIEL framework helps teachers recognize that memory goes well beyond the recall of information and encourages a broader range of questions that will help them plan learning experiences for their students that make content memorable. How can students connect Paul Revere's ride to something that is familiar to them? How can students develop their memory skills as we study the Declaration of Independence? What visual and/or hands-on learning will make the study of the United States Constitution memorable?

Empathy is deeply connected to memory (Jersild, 1955; Noddings, 2003). Keen (2006) defines empathy as "a vicarious, spontaneous sharing of affect, can be provoked by witnessing another's emotional state, by hearing about another's condition, or even by reading" (p. 208). Endacott (2010) points out that historical empathy involves both cognitive and affective domains. If social studies deals with our collective memory, then studying the people and events in history can increase our capacity for empathy (Skolnick et al., 2004). Empathy lies at the foundation of a nurturing and caring society, which Berman (1997) names as one of four conditions that help young people develop social responsibility and active citizenship. In an increasingly interdependent world (Gallavan, 2003), students need to have experiences that will help them understand and feel empathy for others, as well as for themselves.

In the book *Through Other Eyes* (Skolnick, Dulberg & Maestre, 2004), the authors present strategies for helping students "move from their own experience to the experience of another" (p. 4). These strategies include children's literature, family history, artifacts, writing, the arts, and 'experiencing' history. The student quoted previously wrote about how his encounter with history brought out empathy:

> I read one of Helen Keller's interviews where she talked about how her adult life is overlooked in history. This made me think back to all the times my accomplishments get overlooked and how awful that feeling is. All of my accomplishments pale in comparison to what Helen Keller has done. I could only imagine what it would feel like to have accomplished so much in your life, just to have it ignored and trivialized. (Student B, Loewen Project)

Several questions can assist teachers in helping students connect to the experiences of those from another place and time. What experiences have students had that will help them connect to the experience of a historical figure? How did the culture and time period influence the actions of an important person in history? How can I help students care deeply about their work by introducing them to those in history who had great passion for their work?

EVALUATION AND ETHICAL REASONING

The components of the thinking operation *evaluation,* decision making, planning, self-evaluation, and critical thinking, are prominent in the social studies education literature. Across the historical landscape of social studies education, scholars and practitioners alike have emphasized the need to teach students decision-making and critical thinking (Alazzi, 2008; Boyle-Baise & Goodman, 2009; Engle, 1960; Folsom, 2009; Halpern, 1998; Parker, 2009; Smith, 2009). All are skills needed by citizens to maintain a democratic society.

Democracy is a difficult, long-range project. It requires that people work together, plan, make decisions, and take action (Engle, 1960). In the classroom, project-based work in social studies provides ample opportunity to practice democratic skills while simultaneously learning the content of social studies topics (Dicamillo, 2010; Kilpatrick, 1936; Parker, 2009). The TIEL model describes the self-management skills of criteria setting, decision-making, planning, and self-evaluation that students can learn as they work on projects. When students use democratic processes through project-work, they remember the content they have learned for a number of reasons.

First, students have choices. The opportunity to make decisions about and plan their projects promotes memorable learning. The Loewen Project helps prospective teachers experience the democratic processes found in the *evaluation* operation (See Figure 19.3). They collaboratively made decisions about how they would present their chapter and the content they would share using the criteria outlined by Wiggins and McTighe (1996): What is an enduring understanding? What is important to know? What is good to be familiar with?

Second, project work gives students the opportunity to participate in setting the criteria for evaluating their projects helping students practice critical thinking based on their own work (Gallavan & Kottler, 2009). As they contribute ideas about how the finished project will be evaluated, students develop ownership of their work (Folsom, 2009). I set criteria for evaluating the projects with the candidates. When the project is completed, the candidates use the criteria to

Criteria for Decision Making

Using Criteria to Rate Ideas
Write in the problem you need to solve or the decision you need to make.

State Problem Or Decision:	

List Criteria:

List Ideas: Total

How to use this tool:
1. **List** the possible solutions or options under *List Ideas.*
2. **List** the criteria you need to consider in solving the problem or making the decision within the boxes labeled *List Criteria.*
3. **Rate** each of your ideas based on each criterion.
For example: Option for a project: Creating a drama.
Criterion: Materials. Ask yourself: Do I have the materials to make a drama?
If the idea is:

Very workable in terms of this criterion:	3 points
Somewhat workable in terms of the criterion:	2 points
Not so workable:	1 point
Not at all workable:	0 points

FIGURE 19.3. Criteria for Decision Making Grid for Loewen Project.

evaluate their finished projects. The criteria include visual, written, spoken components; information from each social studies discipline; evaluating Loewen's choices; verifying content through outside resources; increased appreciation for the people and events in the chapters; participation of all group members; and care shown through research and organization.

SELF-EVALUATION

Description of Project:

Criteria for Evaluation:

	4	3	2	1

State 3-5 things you learned about your topic that you did not know before?

How did you challenge yourself with this project?

If you could do this project again, what would you change?

FIGURE 19.4. Self-Evaluation Sheet for Loewen Project.

Third, a project for school, like the project of democracy, needs a plan. The criteria for evaluation become the foundation of the plan with additional components that include a clear description of the project, the materials needed, the steps that will be taken to complete the project, and a prediction of problems students may have in the course of their work, as well as possible solutions. The planning packet for the project contained graphic organizers for decision-making, planning, a calendar, self-evaluation, and a worksheet for metacognition based on the TIEL components (See Figure 19.5).

Project work provides opportunities for metacognition. Using the TIEL components to reflect on the thinking and emotional processes used during the unit helps candidates become aware of processes that rarely receive attention (See Figure 19.6). One candidate wrote, "During the planning of the project, everyone received a task and [a time] when to submit it." (Stu-

Basic Planning
Group Project

Who is in your group? List names, phone numbers, and email addresses.

Describe your project.

We are going to

Due Date:

Audience:

We will evaluate our project using these criteria:	4	3	2	1

The materials and resources we will need are:

FIGURE 19.5. Basic Planning Sheet for Loewen Project (page 1 of 2).

dent C, Loewen Project). This simple comment shows a consciousness of process that he can use in planning learning experiences for his future students.

Ethical reasoning, or "unswerving moral rectitude" as Dewey (1964) referred to it, is evaluation anchored by qualities of character. *Ethical reasoning* is decision-making that takes into account personal reflection, empathy for others, and appreciation for the physical and emotional environment in

Steps: Who will do what? When is it to be finished?		
Who	What	When

Problems we might have:	Possible Solutions

Timeline: Develop a calendar and plan your work.

Mon	Tues	Wed	Thurs	Fri	Sat	Sun

FIGURE 19.5. Basic Planning Sheet for Loewen Project (page 2 of 2).

which the decision is being made. Ashley (1961) stated that "the lack of a public conscience may be in part a reflection on the teaching of social studies" (p. 443).

Reflection and Metacognition

Give **explicit examples** of how, during the project and presentation you developed the following thinking operations and qualities of character.

Thinking Operations Qualities of Character	Comments
Cognition Reflection	
Memory Empathy	
Evaluation Ethical Reasoning	
Convergent Production Mastery	
Divergent Production Appreciation	

FIGURE 19.6. Reflection and Metacognition Sheet for Loewen Project.

It is important to consider how ethical reasoning should be addressed in teaching children. Munoz (2003) is explicit about the place of ethical reasoning in social studies. He states that social studies educators, like their progressive forebears, are focused on "the development of students who possess the mental faculties and moral compass to be productive citizens and capable civic leaders" (p. 20). Engle (1960) was more implicit. He stated that "to duck the question of values is to cut the heart out of decision making" (p. 10).

The Loewen Project allows candidates to question parts of the historical record not found in textbooks. One group learned about Jefferson's conflicted relationship with slavery. As they rushed to judgment, I asked them to consider the historical context in which Jefferson lived as he helped develop a new country. In one candidate's self-evaluation and reflection on the project, she listed all the things about Jefferson she had not known. As she wrote how she challenged herself with the project, she said:

> It was difficult to learn the truth about a figure that was always portrayed as patriarchic and endearing to so many. Discovering the truth actually made him more human, even though the choices he made were questionable. Trying to reconcile the fact that he could have potentially done more to end slavery, along with the good he did for our new nation, was certainly challenging. (Student E, Loewen Project)

While ethical reasoning can be a thorny issue in teaching social studies, there are questions that can help teachers consciously include it as they plan social studies units and lessons. In the course of this unit of study where can children become aware of decisions based on honesty, respect, and fairness? How can understanding context help students apply reasoned judgment as they learn about the choices made by historical figures? How can I use group project work to help students develop capacity for ethical reasoning as they work with each other?

CONVERGENT AND DIVERGENT THINKING AND PRODUCTION

The enduring argument between traditionalists and constructivists hinges, in part, on the understanding of convergent thinking and production and divergent thinking and production. Therefore, it is useful to discuss these thinking processes together in order to clarify the importance of balancing these two kinds of thinking in the classroom.

Convergent production is a kind of productive thinking that seeks for "one correct answer" as well as logical and deductive thinking (Guilford, 1977). Research shows that much of social studies teaching attributed to the traditional viewpoint focuses on this kind of thinking (Bolick et al., 2010; Russell, 2010). *Divergent production*, on the other hand, involves a broad production of information, resulting in options, alternatives, and variety (Guilford, 1977; Meeker, 1979). It is not difficult to see that those favoring a constructivist point of view tend to value divergent thinking and production. *Divergent production* includes the kind of fluent and flexible thinking students needed to succeed in today's complex society. Guilford (1968), however, cautioned about considering convergent production to be only about problems that have a correct answer since the interplay between convergent and divergent processes is necessary for creative thinking. Instead of thinking that a problem must have one right answer, the combination of convergent and divergent thinking can lead to a solution that both preserves and liberates (Hoge, 1988). For example, the teacher candidate who struggled with the circumstances of Jefferson's life considered the facts and allowed flexibility in her thinking. By using a combination of convergent and divergent thinking, she was able to preserve her respect for Jefferson's great accomplishments, while at the same time, liberating herself from the unbending thinking that belief in perfection requires.

Understanding the importance of helping students develop both convergent and divergent thinking skills encourages questions that help teachers prepare social studies lessons and units that balance the two kinds of thinking. What facts are important for students to learn about this topic, historical figure, event, or geographical location? How can I plan for students to use their creativity within this social studies unit while still explicitly learning the most important facts and concepts?

MASTERY AND APPRECIATION

While *convergent* and *divergent thinking* are important intellectual skills, each corresponds to a social-emotional characteristic that is important for students to develop. *Mastery* in social studies is often seen as answering convergent questions that include the memorization of dates, names, and facts surrounding people and events. Mastery, however, also relates to social emotional development and self-mastery. When students struggle or experience repeated failure in mastering content or process, they develop a "lack of confidence in themselves as learners" (Weiner, 1999, p. 71).

Struggle, however, is not completely to be avoided. The scaffolded struggle that students can experience through well-structured, balanced, project-based curriculum can help students build resilience and learn the importance of perseverance in achieving a goal. One candidate shared his experience about developing a skill as well as social-emotional self-mastery.

He wrote, "My presentation helped my basic communication skills. I stood in front of a class without trepidation." (Student C, Loewen Project)

Students who are not challenged intellectually in school can also experience feelings of confusion, frustration, and defeat leading to a loss of confidence that can inhibit the development of positive social-emotional characteristics (Rimm, 1986). For these students, mastering social studies concepts and facts through well-structured project work can provide an intellectual challenge as they research an area of interest, make decisions, plan, and create projects that allows them to reach beyond their grade level.

The following questions can help teachers more consciously include a balance between *mastery and appreciation* in their planning. How can I help this student develop mastery of social studies concepts in order to help him gain self-confidence as a learner? How can I plan social studies lessons, units, and projects that allow the most advanced students to achieve further mastery? How can this social studies unit help students develop an appreciation for differences in themselves and others? How can I use art and music in teaching social studies content to help students increase their appreciation of both art and history (Desai, Hamlin, & Mattson, 2010)?

CONCLUSION

The TIEL Curriculum Design model addresses the pedagogical paradoxes of social studies in several ways. First, using the TIEL model in teacher preparation coursework clarifies the thinking and social emotional processes that bring social studies content to life transforming it from dry and uninspiring to engaging, thinking-rich, and dramatic. The TIEL model helps fill the long-standing gap in teacher education in the explicit teaching of thinking and social emotional processes. The chapter shares the experiences of candidates in an urban teacher education program as they learn to consciously develop project-based curriculum by first developing their own project. They use the TIEL model as a guide to inquire into their topic, research, make decisions, plan, and self-evaluate. Second, using the TIEL model can help support transfer to the classroom by making process explicit, visibly linking theory to practice, and helping students develop understanding of process, an elusive component of curriculum design. Third, using the TIEL model with teacher candidates helps them understand the relationship between content and process. Looking closely, the curriculum components of content, the focus of traditionalist educators, and process, the focus of constructivist educators, lie at the core of the paradoxes that are found in both classrooms and social studies methods courses. Attention to *both* content and process is equally important in teaching social studies effectively and memorably. A pedagogy that balances content and process in social studies is necessary to bring the best of traditional and constructivist teaching together for the benefit of students, teachers, and the democracy-in-progress in which we live.

REFERENCES

Alazzi, K. F. (2008). Teachers' perceptions of critical thinking: A study of Jordanian secondary school social studies teachers. *The Social Studies, 99*(6), 243–249.

Ashley, C. A. (1961). Social studies. *The Canadian Journal of Economics and Political Science, 37*(4).

Au, W. (2007). High-stakes testing and curricular control: A qualitative metasynthesis. *Educational Researcher, 36*(5), 258–267.

Bailey, F., & Pransky, K. (2005). Are "other people's children" constructivist learners too? *Theory into Practice, 44*(1), p. 19–26.

Bandura, A. (1993). Perceived self-efficacy in cognitive development and functioning. *Educational Psychologist, 28*(2), 117–148.

Berman, S. (1997). *Children's social consciousness and the development of social responsibility.* Albany, NY: State University of New York Press.

Beyer, B. K. (2008). What research tells us about teaching thinking skills. *The Social Studies, 99*(5), 223–232.

Bolick, C. M., Adams, R., & Willox, L. (2010). The marginalization of elementary social studies in teacher education. *Social Studies Research and Practice, 5*(2).

Boyle-Baise, L., & Goodman, J. (2009). The influence of Harold O. Rugg: Conceptual and pedagogical considerations. *The Social Studies, 100*(1), p. 31–41.

Bransford, J., Derry, S., Berliner, D., & Hammerness, K. (with Beckett, K. L.). (2005). Theories of learning and their roles in teaching. In L. Darling-Hammond & J. Bransford (Eds.), *Preparing teachers for a changing world: What teachers should learn and be able to do* (pp. 40–87). San Francisco: Jossey-Bass.

Brooks, J. G., & Brooks, M. G. (1993). *In search of understanding: The case for constructivist classrooms.* Alexandria, VA: Association for Supervision and Curriculum Development.

Brophy, J., & Alleman, J. (2008). Early elementary social studies. In L. S. Levstik & C. A. Tyson (Eds.), *Handbook of research in social studies education* (pp. 33–49). New York: Routledge..

Chiarelott, L. (2006). *Curriculum in context.* Belmont, CA: Thomson Higher Education.

Consortium. (2006). Key Findings: Are they really ready to work? Employers' perspectives on the basic knowledge and applied skills of new entrants to the 21st century U.S. workforce (2006). Retrieved October 16, 2010 from The Partnership for 21st Century Skills website http://www.p21.org/documents/key_findings_joint.pdf

Darling-Hammond, L. (1997). *The right to learn: A blueprint for creating schools that work.* San Francisco: Jossey-Bass.

Darling-Hammond, L. (2006). *Powerful teacher education.* San Francisco: Jossey-Bass.

Desai, D., Hamlin, J., & Mattson, R. (2010). *History as art, art as history: Contemporary art and social studies education.* New York: Routledge.

Dewey, J. (1916). *Democracy and education: An introduction to the philosophy of education.* New York: The Free Press.

Dewey, J. (1938). *Experience and education.* New York: Collier Books.

Dewey, J. (1964). *John Dewey on education: Selected writings.* R.D. Archambault, Ed. Chicago: University of Chicago Press.)

Dicamillo, I. (2010). Linking teaching for understanding to practice in a U. S. history class. *The Social Studies, 101*(1), 10–17.

Endacott, J. L. (2010). Reconsidering affective engagement in historical empathy. *Theory and Research in Social Education, 38*(1), 6–49.

Engle, S. H. (1960). Decision making: The heart of social studies instruction *The Social Studies, 94*(1), 7–10. (Reprinted from *Social Education, 24*(7)).

Erickson, H. L. (2007). *Curriculum and instruction for the thinking classroom.* Thousand Oaks, CA: Corwin Press.

Folsom, C. (2005). A model for preparing teachers in a changing world: Teaching for intellectual and emotional learning (TIEL). *Teacher Education and Practice, 8*(4), 471–487.

Folsom, C. (2009). *Teaching for intellectual and emotional learning (TIEL): A model for creating powerful curriculum.* Lanham, MD: Rowman & Littlefield Education.

Folsom, C. (2011). Learning to teach the cognitive skills and emotional dispositions required in the 21st century. In D. A. Contreras (Ed.), *Psychology of thinking.* Hauppauge, NY: NOVA Publishers.

French, J. N., & Rhoder, C. (1992). *Teaching thinking skills: Theory and practice.* New York: Garland.

Gallavan, N. P. (2003). Decision making, self-efficacy, and the place of career education in elementary school social studies. *The Social Studies, 94*(1), 15–19.

Gallavan, N. P., & Kottler, E. (2009). Constructing rubrics and assessing progress collaboratively with social studies students. *The Social Studies, 100*(4), 154–159.

Goodlad, J. I. (1990). *Teachers for our nation's schools.* San Francisco: Jossey-Bass.

Guilford, J. P. (1968). *Intelligence, creativity, and their educational implications.* San Diego, CA: Robert R. Knapp.

Guilford, J. P. (1977). *Way beyond the IQ.* Buffalo, NY: Creative Education Foundation.

Halpern, D. F. (1998). Teaching critical thinking for transfer across domains. *American Psychologist, 53*(4), 449–455.

Hoge, J. D. (1988). *Civic education in schools. ERIC Digest.* Retrieved September 26, 2010 from the ERIC Digests website http://www.ericdigests.org/pre-1910/civic.htm.

Hollingsworth, S. (1989). Prior beliefs and cognitive change in learning to teach. *American Educational Research Journal, 26*(2), 160–189.

Hollingworth, L. S. (1926). *Gifted children: Their nature and nurture.* New York: MacMillan.

Jensen, E. (1998). *Teaching with the brain in mind.* Alexandria, VA: Association for Supervision and Curriculum Development.

Jersild, A. T. (1955). *When teachers face themselves.* New York: Teachers College Press.

Keen, S. (2006). A theory of narrative empathy. *Narrative, 14*(3), 207–236.

Kilpatrick, W. H. (1918). The project method. *Teachers College Record, 19*, 319–35.

Kilpatrick, W. H. (1934, October). The essentials of the Activity Movement. *Progressive Education*, 346–359.

Kilpatrick, W. H. (1936). *Remaking the curriculum.* New York: Newson.

Leming, J. S. (2003). Ignorant activists: Social change, "higher order thinking," and the failure of social studies. In J. Leming, L. Ellington, & K Porter-Magee (Eds), *Where did social studies go wrong?* (pp. 124–142). Retrieved from the Thomas B. Fordham Institute website http://www.edexcellence.net/doc/ContrariansFull.pdf .

Levstik, L .S., & Barton, K. C. (2000). *Doing history* (2nd ed.). New York: Routledge.

Loewen, J. (2008). *Lies my teacher told me: Everything your American history textbook got wrong.* New York: New Press.

Meeker, M. (1979). *A structure of intellect.* El Segundo, CA: SOI Institute.

Mintrop, H. (2004). Fostering constructivist communities of learners in the amalgamated multi-discipline of social studies. *Journal of Curriculum Studies, 36*(2), 141–158.

Misco, T., & Shiveley, J. (2010). Seeing the forest through the trees: Some renewed thinking on dispositions specific to social studies education. *The Social Studies, 101*(3), 121–127.

Munoz, J. S. (2003). Community resource mapping—An exciting tool for decision making in the social studies classroom. *The Social Studies, 94*(1), 20–22.

Newmann, F. M. (1991). Promoting higher order thinking in social studies: Overview of a study of 16 high school departments. *Theory and Research in Social Education, 19*(4), 324–340.

Noddings, N. (2003). *Happiness and education.* New York: Cambridge University Press.

Parker, W. C. (2009). *Social studies in elementary education.* New York: Pearson.

Parker, W. C. (2010). *Social studies today.* New York: Routledge.

Pogrow, S. (2010). Teaching content OUTRAGEOUSLY. *Kappa Delta Pi Record, 47*(1), 18–23.

Ravitch, D. (2003). A brief history of social studies. In J. Leming, L. Ellington, & K. Porter (Eds.), *Where did social studies go wrong?* (pp. 1–5). (ERIC Document Reproduction Service No. ED481631)

Ravitch, D., & Finn, C. E., Jr. (1987). *What do our 17-year-olds know? A report on the first national assessment of history and literature.* New York: Harper & Row.

Rimm, S. B. (1986). *Underachievement syndrome: Causes and cures.* Watertown, WI: Apple.

Risinger, F. C., & Garcia, J. (1995). National assessment and the social studies. *The Clearing House, 68*(4), 225–228.

Rochester, J. M. (2003). The training of idiots: Civic education in America's schools. In J. Leming, L. Ellington & K. Porter (Eds.), *Where did social studies go wrong?* (pp. 6–39). (ERIC Document Reproduction Service No. ED481631)

Russell, W. B., III. (2010). Teaching social studies in the 21st century: A research study of secondary social studies teachers' instructional methods and practices. *Action in Teacher Education, 32*(1), 65–72.

Sarason, S. B. (1982). *The culture of the school and the problem of change.* Boston: Allyn & Bacon.

Schug, M. C. (2003). Teacher-centered instruction: The Rodney Dangerfield of social studies. In J. Leming, L. Ellington, & K Porter-Magee (Eds), *Where did social studies go wrong?* (pp. 94–110). Retrieved from the Thomas B. Fordham Institute website http://www.edexcellence.net/doc/ContrariansFull.pdf

Shaughnessy, M. F. (2007). An interview with Dr. J. Martin Rochester: About schools, learning, and class warfare. EducationNews.org, 12/7/07. Retrieved October 9, 2010 from the Education News website *http://www.ednews.org/articles/an-interview-with-dr-j-martin-rochester-about-schools-learning-and-class-warfare.htm*

Skolnick, J., Dulberg, N., & Maestre, T. (2004). *Through other eyes: Developing empathy and multicultural perspectives in the social* studies (2nd ed.). Toronto: Pippin Publishing Corporation.

Smith, K. M. (2009). Dualism within progressive pedagogies: The dynamic nature of democratic education. *Social Studies Review*. Fall–Winter 2009.

Sprenger, M. (1999). *Learning & memory: The brain in action*. Alexandria, VA: Association for Supervision and Curriculum Development.

Sternberg, R. J. (1985). *Beyond IQ: A triarchic theory of human intelligence*. New York: Cambridge University Press.

Sternberg, R. J. (1997). Educating intelligence: Infusing the triarchic theory into school instruction. In R. J. Sternberg & E. Grigorenko (Eds.), *Intelligence, heredity, and environment* (pp. 343–362). New York: Cambridge University Press.

Swartz, R. J., Costa, A. L., Beyer, B. K., Reagan, R., & Kallick, B. (2008). *Thinking-based learning: Promoting quality student achievement in the 21st century*. New York: Teachers College Press.

Taba, H. (1962). *Curriculum development: Theory and practice*. New York: Harcourt, Brace & World.

Tomlinson, C.A. (1999). *The differentiated classroom: Responding to the needs of all learners*. Alexandria, VA: Association for Supervision and Curriculum Development.

Vygotsky, L. S. (1994). *Thought and language*. Cambridge, MA: MIT Press.

Weiner, L. (1999). *Urban teaching: The essentials*. New York: Teachers College Press.

Wiggins, G., & McTighe, J. (1996). *Understanding by design*. Alexandria, VA: Association for Supervision and Curriculum Development.

Wolfe, P. (2001). *Brain matters: Translating research into classroom practice*. Alexandria, VA: Association for Supervision and Curriculum Development.

Yilmaz, K. (2008). Social studies teachers' views of learner-centered instruction. *European Journal of Teacher Education, 31*(1), 35–53.

Zeichner, K. M., & Liston, D. P. (1996). *Reflective Teaching: An introduction*. Hillsdale, NJ: Lawrence Erlbaum.

CHAPTER 20

FACILITATING DISCUSSIONS IN SOCIAL STUDIES CLASSROOMS

Anne-Lise Halvorsen

A responsible citizen in a democracy must be able to communicate ideas and opinions in an informed, reasoned manner and to engage in discussion with people of similar and/or dissimilar views. Open, honest, exchange of ideas is a critical component of a multicultural democratic society since it helps citizens learn to tolerate perspectives different than their own and to become more knowledgeable. The ability to discuss important issues has deep roots in the history of the United States. The nation's founders believed an informed, educated citizenry was necessary for the survival of a young democracy.

Social studies educators agree upon the importance of discussion. The authors of the 2010 National Council for the Social Studies (NCSS) Curriculum Standards identify discussion as a necessary skill that helps students achieve excellence in the social studies (National Council for the Social Studies, 2010). In social studies education, discussion is more than a sustained exchange of ideas since it also involves particular instructional steps and teachable skills. Teaching discussion shows students how to propose ideas and solutions, argue for positions, and listen to others' opinions. As

Contemporary Social Studies: An Essential Reader, pages 385–398
Copyright © 2012 by Information Age Publishing

Hess (2009, p. 16) explains, discussion among people with differing perspectives builds political tolerance.

Students in most social studies classrooms (and classrooms, in general) rarely have the opportunity to participate in in-depth discussions, especially on topics where there are different (often controversial) perspectives (Avery, 2004; Kahne, Rodriguez, Smith, & Thiede, 2000; Newmann, 1990; Wilen, 1990). More often, students experience recitation style learning: the teacher asks a question, a student answers, the teacher asks another question, another student answers, and so forth (Parker & Hess, 2001). For example, the 2002 National Assessment of Educational Progress (NAEP) civics assessment in high school classrooms reported which topics were taught in social studies classes and how these topics were taught, according to students. Most students said they only completed worksheets and read textbooks. Only 19% of the students reported participating in debate or discussions (cited in Levstik, 2008, p. 59).

As far as classroom discussion in social studies, it appears there is a wide gap between theory and practice. Although educators have demonstrated that students acquire a deeper understanding of their social studies subjects through classroom discussion, many social studies learning activities are passive, requiring no interactive exchanges with classmates. Why is discussion so difficult to incorporate in classrooms at all levels in K–12 education? Why is discussion used so rarely in social studies classrooms where the ideas, values, and opinions studied offer such a rich store of discussion topics? What is needed to support teachers so they can learn to introduce and sustain civil and thoughtful classroom discussion?

By addressing these questions in a review of the literature on discussion, this chapter has two main purposes. First, to argue for the importance of classroom discussion as a pedagogical method, and second, to suggest steps educators can take to implement the method in classrooms. The chapter examines the following topics: (1) educators' definitions and uses of discussion; (2) the teacher's role in discussion; (3) the importance of discussion in social studies classes; (4) teaching discussion facilitation skills to teacher candidates; (5) challenges for teachers using discussion; and (6) areas for future research.

EDUCATORS' DEFINITIONS AND USES OF DISCUSSION

As a pedagogical method, classroom discussion is variously defined and refers to a number of teaching techniques. Discussion in social studies classes is different from discussion in other classes. Differently disciplinary processes guide the discussions in math, science, and literature classes. For example, discussion in science classes often involves disagreement about evidence, using the precise, specialized language of scientific discourse. The purpose of scientific argumentation is to promote understanding of a phenomenon or situation, and to persuade others of an idea's validity (Michaels, Shouse, & Schweingruber, 2007). In literature classes, discussions are often "dialogic discussions" in which teachers, after selecting discussion topics based upon student interest, encourage students to take independent viewpoints while trying to grasp others' perspectives (Adler & Rougle, 2005). In general, discussions come in many forms. Hess (2009) identifies five definitions of discussion proposed by experts in classroom discussion proposed by others. These definitions range from the minimalist and vague definition of "the free exchange of information among three or more participants" (Christoph & Nystrand, 2001, p. 250) to the more complex, purposeful definition of discussion as "a kind of shared inquiry the desired outcomes of which rely on the expression and consideration of diverse views" (Parker, 2003, p. 129).

Social studies education scholars use the term "discussion" to describe various forms of classroom dialogue. They distinguish this dialogue from discussions in other subjects by its emphasis on the specific skills and behaviors needed by citizens in a democracy where ideas and solutions are proposed and arguments are made for opinions and beliefs. So broad is the usage of the term, however, that it is often said to be elusive (Larson, 2000). Teachers' understanding of how to facilitate discussion is equally complex and difficult to pin down (Larson, 1997; Larson & Parker, 1996). However, Hess (2004, 2009) specifies some common, agreed-upon features of discussion: (1) a dialogue among people; (2) a particular way to reach new understandings or knowledge, whereby powerful ideas are produced through oral expression of ideas; and (3) an activity that is multi-form and multi-purpose.

Parker and Hess (2001) identify three classroom discussion formats: deliberation, seminar, and conversation. Deliberation centers on problem resolution and plans of action—choosing among the various possible responses to a problem. Seminar, where there is no "end goal," but rather increased understanding (e.g., of an idea, a theory, an issue), centers on the process for process's sake. Conversation, which occupies the "third space" between seminar and deliberation, engages students in self-reflexive discussion on the norms and methods of classroom dialogue. A sample focus question in a conversation is: "What kind of society (classroom) do we want to have?" (Parker & Hess, 2001, p. 281).

Yet another classroom discussion format is the structured deliberation of social and civic issues. Proponents of issues-centered social studies (e.g., Engle & Ochoa, 1988) believe that student debate and discussion of such public issues is the most effective way to teach students critical thinking and reflective skills. This approach is used more often at the secondary than at the elementary level, although it is possible to engage young children in discussion of issues relevant to their lives.

Harris (2002) has identified a number of discrete, assessable discussion skills for use in evaluating discussion of such public issues. He explains how to evaluate students' competence with these skills using hypothetical student responses. Among these skills, which he categorizes as either substantive or procedural, are the following: stating the issue (substantive); drawing upon foundational knowledge in the disciplines (substantive); recognizing when values are in conflict (substantive); summarizing the discussion (procedural); not interrupting (procedural); and questioning others' statements (procedural).

Each discussion format (deliberation, seminar, conversation) can be used in the elementary, middle, or high school classroom so long as thoughtful consideration is given to the level of sophistication and complexity of the discussion topics. At the lower elementary level, for example, students might deliberate on a proposed classroom rule such as "you can't say you can't play" (Paley, 1992). Since young children are interested in consequences of the rule (exclusion of others from group play), they are willing to deliberate on the rule's pros and cons and thus to negotiate group behavior. Policy is decided by group discussion. As another example, students in upper elementary, middle and high school may engage in public issue structured deliberations. Of course, teachers have to make judicious selections of public issues for discussion, considering not only the age and maturity of their students but also the community context. Discussions often focus on matters of public concern, such as an issue on the election ballot, a moral or ethical dilemma, or historical events which often have multiple (often conflicting) interpretations.

Thus, disagreement about the definitions and uses of discussion can inhibit the use of discussion (of any kind) in social studies classrooms and make it difficult to support teachers in using discussion.

THE TEACHER'S ROLE IN DISCUSSION

Researchers have noted the teacher's role in facilitating good class discussions. Hess (2004) states that good discussions generally center on a text that students have read before the discussion, involve a problem or issue that has multiple perspectives, and take place in a classroom community that values diverse perspectives and risk-taking. To guide such discussions effectively, the teacher must be well-prepared and must carefully balance his or her role in the discussion. The teacher is a discussion observer and director as well as a discussion participant. Brookfield and Preskill (1999) also describe several requirements of effective discussions that depend on the teacher. These requirements include selection of topics that are relevant and interesting to students (including topics suggested by students) and a classroom environment that encourages diverse opinions. The teacher must also take care that no voice (including his or her own) dominates the discussion.

Vivian Paley has written of her experiences as an elementary teacher who effectively facilitates discussion (Paley, 1992). Referenced earlier, as an example, she described authentic discussions on the rule "you can't say you can't play" that she led in her kindergarten classroom and in a fifth grade classroom. Since Paley wanted the students to consider alternative perspectives, she gently questioned their assertions. She said to the students: "Is it fair for children *in school* to keep another child out of play? After all, this classroom belongs to all of us. It is not a private place, like our homes" (Paley, 1992, p. 16, emphasis in the original). Her goal was that the children, as a group, would discuss the effect of the proposed rule on everyone in the classroom.

Effective discussions can occur without teacher intervention, especially at the secondary level. However, the teacher generally plays a critical role by preparing the students for the discussion, by helping them focus on the issue, by creating a classroom environment that supports civil discourse (including disagreements), by moving the discussion along, and by drawing the discussion to a close.

What factors support teachers in leading discussions effectively? They include being a strong teacher in general, recognizing that students need to be taught explicitly the skills and attitudes necessary for effective participation in discussion, and creating a classroom community that is supportive and positive, and thus a place where students feel comfortable expressing their beliefs (Hess, 2009, p. 166). However, further research is needed to better understand the other myriad factors needed for leading effective discussions.

THE IMPORTANCE OF DISCUSSION IN SOCIAL STUDIES CLASSES

Experts in the social studies identify particular skills they believe citizens in democracies need. Perhaps the most important skill is the ability and will to communicate one's opinions in an informed, reasoned manner. It is well-documented that learning to engage in substantive conversation on public issues is a critical skill for civic efficacy, defined as the readiness and willingness of people to assume citizenship responsibility (National Council for the Social Studies, 2008), and for democratic education, defined by Hess (2009) as "a form of civic education that purposely teaches young people how to *do* democracy" (p. 15, emphasis in the original). According to Avery (2004), "One of the primary ways in which students develop critical and systemic thinking skills is by engaging in substantive discussions of public issues…The ability to engage in discussions of public issues is a particularly important skill in a democratic society" (p. 45).

Discussions with participants who have diverse perspectives are particularly important in helping students develop skills for citizenship. Hess (2009) concluded:

> Engaging in discussion of public problems—as long as there are people in the group with views different from your own—builds political tolerance, teaches people, and may result in better policy decisions. Although individuals may not change their minds on issues, they better understand the opposing perspective, which in turn, helps develop individuals' tolerance for groups whose political views differ from one's own. (pp. 16–17)

Harris (2002, pp. 211–12) lists four main reasons for discussion in social studies (or "civic oral discourse," in his words). First, discussion helps students learn social studies content. Second, discussion facilitates "reciprocal thinking" whereby students learn to anticipate others' viewpoints. This is a skill considered "fundamental to democratic citizenship." Third, discussion promotes reflection on democratic values such as liberty, equality, and the consent of the governed. Fourth, discussion requires higher order thinking skills.

Social studies educators believe that discussion practice in the K–12 setting is essential to prepare students for their civic responsibility as voting adults. Parker and Hess (2001) write: "Discussion is important to understand, both as a way of knowing and a way to being together. Participation in sustained discussions of powerful questions can be both a mind-expanding and community-building endeavor" (p. 273). Moreover, besides strengthening their social studies content knowledge, discussion participation gives students the opportunity to acquire and improve communication skills (Hess, 2009). Brookfield and Preskill (1999) state: "Democracy and discussion imply a process of giving and taking, speaking and listening, describing and witnessing—all of which help expand horizons and foster mutual understanding" (p. 3).

The NCSS Curriculum Standards (National Council for the Social Studies, 2010), list discussion as a criterion for good citizenship. The Introduction to the Standards states: "…the experiences students have in their social studies classrooms should enable learners to engage in civil discourse and problem-solving, and to take informed civic action." (National Council for the Social Studies, 2010, p. 12). Of the ten "themes" that the NCSS Standards recommend as a focus for social studies, one is "Civic Ideals and Practices." This theme refers to the many "processes" related to discussion (e.g., a high school process is "to participate in the process of persuading, compromising, debating, and negotiation in the resolution of conflicts and differences" (National Council for the Social Studies, 2010, p. 64). Another "essential social studies skill and strategy" for all grade levels is "Dialogue with others who have different perspectives" (National Council for the Social Studies, 2010, p. 166).

State standards also emphasize discussion. In the Michigan Grade Level Content Expectations, the strand, "Public Discourse, Decision Making, and Citizen Involvement," states the expectation that students should know "how, when, and where to construct and express reasoned positions on public issues" (Michigan Department of Education, 2007, p. 5). Students are expected to demonstrate these skills as early as kindergarten. For example, in kindergarten children are expected to "compare their viewpoint about a classroom issue with the viewpoint of another person" and to "express a position on a classroom issue" (Michigan Department of Education, 2007, p. 13). As children advance in school, the expectations become more complex. Expectations for sixth graders ask them to: "Clearly state an issue as a question or public policy, trace the origins of an issue, analyze various perspectives, and generate and evaluate alternative resolutions. Deeply examine policy issues in group discussions and debates to make reasoned and informed decisions..." (Michigan Department of Education, 2007, p. 57). Another example comes from Virginia where a goal for all grades is for students to develop "skills in debate, discussion..." (Board of Education Commonwealth of Virginia, 2008, p. v). Students in Missouri are expected to "exchange information, questions and ideas while recognizing the perspectives of others" (Missouri Department of Elementary and Secondary Education, 2008, Performance Goals, Goal 2). Discussions can help students meet these expectations by providing opportunities for them to state their position on issues, listen to the perspectives of others, ask questions of others, and reconsider their perspectives.

TEACHING DISCUSSION FACILITATION SKILLS TO TEACHER CANDIDATES

Leading effective discussions is challenging work (Parker & Hess, 2001). Many teachers no doubt struggle with organizing and leading discussions because they themselves lack discussion skills (e.g., knowing how to start a discussion, bring a discussion back on track, ensure that multiple perspectives are voiced and heard, and summarize the key points made in a discussion). It is probable that these teachers never received training or practice in discussion. Lacking discussion knowledge and skills, they find it difficult to facilitate good discussions among their students.

In general, teacher educators have not made teaching discussion skills to pre-service teachers a priority. Too often, educators classify students as either the outgoing, talkative type who is naturally good at discussion or as the shy, quiet type who prefers to remain silent. However, as Hollander (2002) claims, discussion is a learned skill and not an innate talent or ability. Even teacher candidates who are skilled discussants may not necessarily be able to facilitate discussions in the classroom (Parker & Hess, 2001).

According to Hess (2009), in examining how students learn to discuss controversial issues "the single most important factor is the quality of a teacher's practice" (p. 53). The "quality of a teacher's practice" is a gray area, however. There is little research on the influence of social studies education on teacher knowledge and skills, including discussion facilitation skills. We do not know 1) which social studies training best prepares teacher candidates to be effective social studies teachers; or 2) which social studies teachers' knowledge and skills most benefit their students' learning. Nor do we have a clear picture of the content, instructional strategies, or assessment methods used by teacher educators.

Another challenge Parker and Hess (2001) identify is distinguishing between teaching *for* and teaching *with* discussion. Whereas teaching *for* discussion involves teaching the particular procedural dimensions of facilitating a discussion, teaching *with* discussion means teaching particular content through the instructional strategy of discussion. Parker and Hess (2001) found that participating effectively in discussions did not teach students how to lead discussions themselves: "students remembered the subject matter, not the delivery system" (Parker & Hess, 2001, p. 287).

What is particularly problematic about teaching *for* discussion is that often pre-service teachers do not appreciate the effort and planning it takes to lead classroom discussions. As Hess (2004) writes:

> ....teachers need to prepare themselves and their students for effective participation. When teaching novice teachers about discussions, I am often struck by how odd this seems to them. These new teachers believe that the best discussions are those that evolve spontaneously from the students. To the contrary, research shows that effective discussions are much more likely to occur when they are planned. (p. 155)

Based on my recent research on instructional strategies for teacher candidates, I identified several activities that have a positive influence on their discussion facilitation skills (Halvorsen, 2010). I found the following activities useful for teacher candidates in their pre-service training: 1) reading about instructional approaches using discussion; 2) watching and reflecting on videos of high-quality social studies discussions; and 3) participating in and facilitating small group discussions. These activities particularly helped develop teacher candidates' skills in the procedural dimension of leading a discussion (e.g., gathering background reading for the discussion topic, preparing guiding questions, encouraging student participation, and summarizing the discussion). However, teacher candidates continued to struggle with the substantive dimension of facilitating discussions (e.g., drawing upon foundational knowledge in the disciplines and recognizing when values are in conflict. (Halvorsen, 2010). I recommend that social studies methods courses make teaching discussion a high priority, that teacher educators explicitly teach (and have teacher candidates practice) the steps for leading discussion of substantive topics, and that teacher candidates understand the value of discussion in a democracy.

CHALLENGES FOR TEACHERS USING DISCUSSION

There are various challenges teachers face in using classroom discussion. These challenges are described here to explain why discussion is not commonly used by teachers. At the very least, highlighting these challenges may draw attention to factors inhibiting discussion. Moreover, a better understanding of these challenges may lead to ways to overcome them.

Lack of Time

Since little time in the school day is allocated to social studies (particularly at the elementary level), teachers have to use that time carefully. They have to select the instructional approaches that most efficiently meet learning outcomes. Although, as discussed above, discussion is featured in national and state content standards, such standards place much less emphasis on discussion compared to disciplinary knowledge and other skills standards.

Preparing students for the discussion and facilitating the discussion are very time-consuming activities. Discussions, even when their use is justified as time spent helping students learn disciplinary content (Hess, 2004, 2009), take large chunks of classroom time. Students need time to talk through their opinions, time to make their contributions, and time to think about new perspectives.

In another sense, discussion requires time: teacher time. Before or after discussions, the teacher has to gather the discussion materials, prepare the discussion, and assess the students' participation. Given other teaching demands, this is time many teachers do not have.

Classroom Control

Since discussion is a student-centered instructional strategy, teachers cannot always predict or direct the course the discussion will take. Good discussions require direction from the teacher (e.g., posing the topic for discussion, asking guiding questions to advance the discussion, and summarizing key points). However since discussion often requires students to express an opinion, students may surprise a teacher with their responses (in principle, a good thing). This uncertainty may make some teachers uncomfortable or nervous, especially if they are used to giving lectures or relying on reading to the class from the textbook (Hess, 2004; Simon, 2001).

Inadequate Preparation

There are teachers who perceive their lack of preparation for discussion as a challenge. They may feel they do not know discussion topics well enough and/or discussion methodology well enough (in part, because teacher programs have not prepared them). In general, few elementary teachers think they have competent expertise in either social studies topics (Levstik, 2008) or discussion skills. Teachers are particularly unprepared to lead their students in discussion of controversial topics (McBee, 1996).

Assessment

Assessment of discussion is difficult because traditional paper-and-pencil tests are incapable of assessing discussion skills. Written tests can assess students' grasp of discussion topics and their ability to defend a position using evidence and democratic reasoning. However, written tests cannot assess the students' competence in oral discourse. Although Harris (2002) identifies discrete discussion skills and presents a procedure for assessing them, most teachers have not been trained in such discussion evaluation. Moreover, we know that what is assessed is closely linked to what is taught. For that reason, teachers are disinclined to teach a skill that is not assessed according to prescribed standards.

Failure of Discussions

Some teachers fear their classroom discussions will not succeed in accomplishing the expected goals. Hess (2004, p. 152) gives four reasons that teachers are unsuccessful in facilitating effective discussions: "the tendency of teachers to talk too much, to ask inauthentic questions, as well as the lack of focus and depth in students' contributions, and the unequal participation of students." Each reason stems from a lack of teacher preparation. Simon (2001) claims teachers often talk over students in discussions and end discussions prematurely. Brookfield and Preskill (1999) devote a chapter in their book to showing teachers how to keep their discussion participation in balance.

Avoidance of Controversial Topics

Hess (2009) writes there is a "general aversion to controversy" (p. 24) in the United States and in its education system. Teachers who lead discussions on controversial topics are on the front line, facing students, parents, and communities (McBee, 1996). There is also pressure from school administrators. For example, Hess found that some administrators even told teachers to avoid teaching about the events of September 11, 2001 (Hess, 2009). In highly argumentative and divisive communities, it is unsurprising that many social studies teachers think it is inconceivable for students to discuss controversial topics in classrooms.

In summary, there are significant challenges to using discussion in social studies classes. However, research shows that some teachers are capable of overcoming these perceived hurdles and infuse their classrooms with rich discussions of often controversial topics (Hess, 2009).

AREAS FOR FUTURE RESEARCH

Social studies scholars have shown significant interest in promoting classroom discussion. Yet more research on the techniques and results of effective discussion is needed at all levels, especially at the elementary level. Specifically, research on discussion in social studies should focus on the following areas: (1) the link between discussion skills and citizenship education; (2) effective social studies pedagogy that incorporates discussion; (3) effective pre-service and in-service education that prepares K–12 teachers to teach discussion; and (4) assessment of students' discussion skills. These areas are explained next.

Social studies experts agree that discussion is an important citizenship skill, but more empirical research is needed that focuses on the link between learning to discuss and becoming a person who can engage in reasonable discourse (e.g., by clearly defining a position, by presenting evidence for a claim, by drawing upon relevant disciplinary knowledge, and by tolerating diverse perspectives). Hess's work (e.g., 2004, 2008, 2009) contributes to our understanding of the value of discussion. Longitudinal studies are now needed that follow students through various grade levels and examine the long-term classroom effects of discussion training.

Second, more models are needed on how to structure social studies classes that require students to engage in discussion. Research can help us understand which skills are developed by the various discussion formats (e.g., debate, seminar, or conversation) and which formats are grade-level appropriate. At present, social studies textbooks, which do not feature discussion as a primary pedagogical tool, tend to relegate discussion questions to the end of the chapter with little or no direction offered to teachers on how to facilitate and assess discussions.

Third, research is needed to learn which instructional strategies help teacher candidates (and practicing teachers) (1) develop discussion facilitation skills and (2) inspire them to make discussion a central component of their lessons. While in my research, I identified strategies for developing the procedural dimension of discussion, more research is needed for developing the substantive dimension (Halvorsen, 2010). To that end, researchers could study the strategies that help candidates develop the disciplinary background to facilitate discussions of social and civic issues.

Fourth, since we know the subjects tested take priority in the school curriculum, researchers could focus on measuring students' participation in discussions. Reliable and valid assessment tools are needed that can be used efficiently and effectively in group settings. Harris (2002) provides an important starting point by identifying substantive and procedural skills that can be individually assessed.

CONCLUSION

Social studies scholars have begun the important work of integrating discussion into social studies lessons. There is theoretical research on discussion formats, empirical research on discussion facilitation, and practice-oriented research on evaluations of discussion competency. There is also a good understanding of why teachers do not use discussion in their classrooms. This is a beginning.

It is agreed, not only by practitioners and theorists but also by education standards setters, that discussion is a necessary citizenship skill that should be taught. Inflammatory talk radio forums and biased, interactive websites are not substitutes for civil, empirically-based discussions. The classroom is the proper venue for teaching the principles and values of reasonable discourse, despite the hard work ahead. As Hess, (2004) concludes; "Discussion in social studies is well worth the trouble" (p. 156).

REFERENCES

Adler, M., & Rougle, E. (2005). *Building literacy through classroom discussion: Research-based strategies for developing critical readers and thoughtful writers in middle school.* New York: Scholastic.

Avery, P. G. (2004). Social studies teacher education in an era of globalization. In *Critical issues in social studies teacher education* (Susan Adler, Ed., pp. 37–57), Charlotte, NC: Information Age Publishing Inc.

Board of Education Commonwealth of Virginia (January 2008). *History and social science standards of learning for Virginia public schools.* Retrieved from http://www.doe.virginia.gov/testing/sol/standards_docs/history_socialscience/next_version/stds_all_history.pdf

Brookfield, S.D., & Preskill, S. (1999). *Discussion as a way of teaching: Tools and techniques for democratic classrooms.* San Francisco: Jossey-Bass Inc.

Christoph, J.N., & Nystrand, M. (2001). Taking risks, negotiating relationships: One teacher's transition toward a dialogic classroom. *Research in the Teaching of English,* 36, 249–285.

Engle, S., & Ochoa, A. (1988). *Education for democratic citizenship: Decision making in the social studies.* New York: Teachers College Press.

Halvorsen, A. (2010, May). *Preparing teachers/preparing citizens: Developing practices for leading discussions in the elementary classroom.* Panel paper for the annual meeting of the American Educational Research Association, Denver, CO.

Harris, D. E. (2002). Classroom assessment of civic discourse. In W. C. Parker (Ed.), *Education for democracy: Contexts, curricula, assessments* (pp. 211–232). Greenwich, CT: Information Age Publishing.

Hess, D. (2004). Discussion in social studies: Is it worth the trouble? *Social Education,* 68(2), 151–156.

Hess, D. (2008). Controversial issues and democratic discourse. In L.S. Levstik & C. A. Tyson (Eds.), *Handbook of research in social studies education* (pp. 124–136). New York: Routledge.

Hess, D. (2009). *Controversy in the classroom: The democratic power of discussion* (New York: Routledge).

Hollander, J. A. (2002). Learning to discuss: Strategies for improving the quality of class discussion. *Teaching Sociology,* 30(3), 317–327.

Kahne, J., Rodriguez, M., Smith, B., & Theide, K. (2000). Developing citizens for democracy: Assessing opportunities to learn in Chicago's social studies classrooms. *Theory and Research in Social Education,* 28(3), 311–338.

Larson, B. E. (1997). Social studies teachers' conceptions of discussion: A grounded theory study. *Theory and Research in Social Education,* 25(2), 113–136.

Larson, B. E. (2000). Classroom discussion: A method of instruction and a curriculum outcome. *Teaching and Teacher Education,* 16(5–6), 661–677.

Larson, B. E., & Parker, W. C. (1996). What is classroom discussion? A look at teachers' conceptions. *Journal of Curriculum and Supervision,* 11(2), 110–126.

Levstik, L.S. (2008). What happens in social studies classroom? Research on K–12 social studies practice. In L. S. Levstik & C. A. Tyson (Eds.) *Handbook of research in social studies education* (pp. 50–62). New York: Routledge.

McBee, R. H. (1996). Can controversial topics be taught in the early grades: The answer is yes! *Social Education,* 60(1), 38–41.

Michaels, S. Shouse. A., & Schweingruber, H. (2007). *Ready, set, SCIENCE!: Putting research to work in K–8 Science Classrooms.* Washington, DC: National Academies Press.

Michigan Department of Education (2007). *Grade level content expectations: Social studies grades K–8.* Retrieved from http://www.michigan.gov/documents/mde/SSGLCE_ 218368_7.pdf

Missouri Department of Elementary and Secondary Education (2008). *Show-Me standards social studies.* Retrieved from http://dese.mo.gov/standards/ss.html

National Council for the Social Studies (2008). A vision of powerful teaching and learning in the social studies: Building effective citizens. *Social Education,* 72(5), 277–280.

National Council for the Social Studies (2008). *A vision of powerful teaching and learning in the social studies: Building social understanding and civic efficacy.* Retrieved from http://www.socialstudies.org/positions/powerful

Newmann, F. M. (1990). Qualities of thoughtful social studies classes: An empirical profile. *Journal of Curriculum Studies, 22*(3), 253–275.

Paley, V. G. (1992). *You can't say you can't play.* Cambridge, MA: Harvard University Press.

Parker, W. C. (2003). *Teaching democracy: Unity and diversity in public life.* New York: Teacher's College Press.

Parker, W. C., & Hess, D. (2001). Teaching with and for discussion. *Teaching and Teacher Education, 17,* 273–289.

Preskill, S. (1997). Discussion, schooling, and the struggle for democracy. *Theory and Research in Social Education, 25*(3), 316–345.

Simon, K.G. (2001). *Moral questions in the classroom: How to get kids to think deeply about real life and their schoolwork.* New Haven: Yale University Press.

Wilen, W. W. (1990). Forms and phases of discussion. In W. W. Wilen (Ed.), *Teaching and learning through discussion: The theory, research and practice of the discussion method* (pp. 3–24). Springfield, IL: Charles C. Thomas.

CHAPTER 21

ENGAGEMENT IN THE SOCIAL STUDIES

Using Experiential Learning in the Social Studies Classroom

Brad Burenheide

There are a countless number of challenges facing social studies education today. A major warning has gone out to social studies educators across the country that social studies is being considered a boring subject by many students (Zhao & Hoge, 2005). There are also warnings decrying the fact that social studies has been placed on the backburner as it is not tested by NCLB (Blanchette, 2008). Additionally, the conceptualization of social studies in the future of education is going to be seriously challenged with the advent of 21st Century Skills steering much of the direction of future education and social studies in particular (Partnership for 21st Century Skills, n.d.). These challenges are going to require teachers to teach innovatively and inspiringly to reach their students who are technological natives and crave high-interest and stimulating instruction (Devaney, 2010). At the same time some of these students do not desire reading (Gallagher, 2010). Many of

Contemporary Social Studies: An Essential Reader, pages 399–419
Copyright © 2012 by Information Age Publishing
399

these students are lost in the massive curriculum that is subject to high-stakes tests (Stoskopf, 2001).

While it seems to be an impossible quagmire to wade through, there is the possibility for stimulating social studies instruction to occur. Several researchers have prompted the encouragement of social studies education throughout the curriculum to adapt methods that promote active, innovative, and experiential learning in what has slowly become a stale subject (Thornton, 2005; Yell, Scheurman, & Reynolds, 2004). The ideas of these writers will be at the heart of this chapter.

The question discussed within this chapter is how can models of experiential learning be employed in social studies instruction? In answering this question, this chapter will begin with a model of experiential learning will be explored through the lens of Kolb's theory of experiential learning (Kolb, 1984). This section will explore the four components of this theory. The chapter will then illustrate strategies and methods with how experiential learning can promote a more powerful level of learning by instituting key components that are often overlooked in traditional strategies. Experiential learning allows teachers to bring social studies to life and can be seen as the vehicle through which active learning can take place in the social studies classroom, whether it is a simulation, a primary source investigation, or a case study. The remainder of the chapter will position experiential learning in today's educational environment with strategies that promote the utilization of critical thinking as found throughout the realm of the social studies.

THE QUESTION OF ENGAGEMENT IN SOCIAL STUDIES INSTRUCTION

The question of engagement focuses on how to maximize student involvement in the learning activity. While defining engagement, Burden and Byrd (2003) call for the focusing of students on the material and learning activities rather than exploring off-task stimuli and engaging in behaviors not relevant to the learning process. This notion has been explored through a number of sources (e.g. Good & Brophy, 2008; National Research Council, 2000; Sullo, 2007). For the purposes of this exploration of engagement however, it is necessary to operationally define engagement. Burden and Byrd (2003) noted that engagement is achieved through building on the momentum of instruction and providing clear organization for learning. Schunk, Pintrich, & Meece stated engagement was a matter of addressing learning to activities that are focused upon student backgrounds, interests, and experiences which allows the student to be more autonomous in their learning (2008).

Whether taken as a matter of enhancing classroom management or encouraging students to become more involved in their learning, engagement is a vital component of learning as described in the preceding paragraph. For the purpose of this discussion, it is more appropriate to focus on engagement as it regards to the latter rather than the former consideration as Zhao and Hoge (2005) have considered it. For the purpose of this discussion then, engagement will be defined as the following:

The involvement of the learner in the educational activity as an active participant in the learning process.

This definition focuses upon the learning process providing an opportunity for the learner to actively be involved in the activity to create new schema much as the theory of constructivism discusses (Gibson & McKay, 2001; Schunk, 2008). By being an active participant in the gathering of information the student is immersed in the data collection process and through meta-cognition, learning can better take place. Engagement therefore, as defined above, allows students the opportunity to collect data, process it, analyze it, manipulate it, and develop an understanding of how this data explains the phenomenon being studied.

KOLB'S THEORY OF EXPERIENTIAL LEARNING

Experiential learning is "the process of learning where knowledge is created through the transformation of experience" (Kolb, 1984). It is focused on the active construction of knowledge and knowledge structures by transferring learning to specific situations. Thissen (2005), argued that the teacher must break from the traditional role of transmitter of knowledge to become a guide or a facilitator, thus placing the impetus of learning upon the student experiencing the learning action, or to put it another way, focusing upon student action rather than the absorbing of information and then asking the student to do something with the information (Siedner, 1978). As the teacher places students in concrete and realistic situations, the student can experience learning in a way that challenges and engages in emotional and existential ways.

Historically speaking, experiential learning is based deeply in the thoughts of John Dewey who stressed learning through experience (Dewey, 1939). As research evolved, other experiential theories developed such as those presented by Piaget (1952), Rogers (1959), Maslow (1968), and Jarvis (1987). In the advent of instructional gaming, however, Kolb's model has developed as the preferred model of experiential learning (Powell & Wells, 2002).

Kolb's theory of experiential leaning is based on the assertion that "learning is the process whereby knowledge is created through the transformation of experience" (1984, p. 38). The model has been touted as having a significant impact on student learning and has become a key theory behind instructional gaming, especially that involving simulations (Coleman, 1978; Costigan, 1984; Kolb & Lewis, 1986; Powell & Wells, 2002). Kolb's model has been described as a circular model that parallels the scientific method (Healey & Jenkins, 2000) and follows a pattern considered the reverse order of how traditional learning takes place (Dorn, 1989). The steps of Kolb's model are listed below with a brief description (Cowan, 1998; Jenkins, 1998):

1. Concrete experience—the learner experiences or does an action.
2. Reflective experience—the learner recalls, reflects, or observes what has happened.
3. Abstract conceptualization—the learner creates an explanatory theory or model, thinks about the meaning of what happened, or generalizes what was observed.
4. Active experimentation—the learner plans how to test or model the theory.

The model has several strengths that are compatible with the ideas of instructional gaming. Kolb (1984) believes the model forces students to utilize learning styles outside of their preference, which provides students with long-term benefits. The teacher as facilitator in the model (Powell & Wells, 2002) also must change the way in which material is provided to the students, which resulted in better teaching practices from K–12 to the university level (Terry, 2001).

In an article advocating Kolb's model, Healey and Jenkins (2000) saw numerous strengths to this model and how it applied to student learning. The Kolb model causes a large variety of teaching methods to be used and provides a direct connection to real world situations. It forces students to reflect on their own learning and provide feedback. Additionally, it can reach diverse learners across the various discipline areas. Finally, the model can be packaged as a single lesson, or an entire program of learning for individual students or cooperative groups. This is perhaps its greatest strength, as it allows for a broad variety of use and understanding.

Kolb's model provides a framework for experiential learning, the importance of which was foreshadowed by the following quote from the introductory commentary by Tansey and Unwin (1969):

Physicists have their ripple tanks, geographers have their wave-form tanks, and little children have their dolls and toy soldiers. Simulation is within the experience of each one of us. It is not even a new concept in the classroom in some of its forms. What is new, possibly, is the realization of the potential of the technique as an aide in education (p. 89).

The implications of this theory are rather significant. By placing students in a situation where the focus of their learning comes from what they directly experience, the student is then responsible for unpacking their thoughts and becoming familiar with their own meta-cognition. The results of this are rooted deeply in constructivism and allow for a greater understanding and depth of knowledge. In brief, constructivism allows for the learning of new knowledge by combining the material to be learned with an established schema, or knowledge possessed by the learner (Maxim, 2006). By rooting this new knowledge with previous knowledge, learners generate new understandings. With the understanding that students are able to generate new understandings by combining new information with previous knowledge, learning experiences can be framed within contextualized simulations in the classroom.

UTILIZING SIMULATIONS IN SOCIAL STUDIES INSTRUCTION

The utilization of a simulation in a classroom is an interesting and stimulating means to engage students in learning in social studies classrooms. This portion of this chapter will explore the potential for simulations to provide this stimulation for students in the classroom. To do this, the simulation will be explored and defined as an instructional tool. Next, the steps to install a simulation successfully and the key components of a successful simulation will be presented. Finally, some examples of successful implementations of simulations will be shared to provide a point of exploration for the reader.

What is a simulation? This question can be hard to answer as many teachers see different pedagogical techniques serving as a simulation of social studies content. Perhaps the best definition of a simulation is that it is a learning activity where students engage in acting out a scenario where they play a role. This role allows the student a full exploration of a topic from the role being played by asking questions, receiving feedback, and continuing to make decisions during the activity. To operationally define a simulation, a simulation "re-creates or represents an actual event or situation that causes the student to act, react, or make decisions" (Burden & Byrd, 2003). The simulation will have a purpose for the students to explore and will have a set of events or situations for the student to act, react, and make decisions (Burden & Byrd, 2003). In the process of exploring the topic from the viewpoint of a participant of a given situation, the simulation will provide a specific framework to explore the topic. This framework allows for the participant to pose questions, make decisions, and respond to results. The place where learning will often occur is in the debriefing that occurs at the conclusion of the activity (Burden & Byrd, 2003).

The necessary components needed for a successful simulation are a realistic setting, the opportunity to interact with the content, and a framework for further development with the content. By a realistic setting, it does not mean that a multitude of props are necessary to recreate and stoke an imaginary sense of being in the era being studied as the classroom provides limited means in location, resources, and material. However, it is possible to enhance the setting with some props, but this should not be the focus of the simulation. A realistic setting means that the students are given appropriate roles and a clear task to work towards. Examples of a realistic setting are found below:

- A student takes on the persona of a member of the Second Continental Congress and debates with other students the advantage of declaring independence from England.
- A student is assigned to be an ecologist and must prepare testimony to be given at a mock congressional hearing regarding the impact of acid rain on a region's ecosystem.
- Three students are given the task to create a situation map for President Lincoln to see the situation of the American Civil War in July 1863. The students will then present the situation map to "President Lincoln" played by the teacher.

The setting has to be realistic in that a role has to be something that could actually happen and that the task is authentic. An authentic task is meaningful, provides for divergent means to respond to the task, and is respectful to the dignity of the student, meaning that it has inherent worth to the student. These tasks need students to be able to interact with the content, whether it be through researching content to provide data for a component of the simulation, or by manipulating the data to setup a new situation of the situation.

The results of the student's actions in the simulation are not necessarily predetermined where there is flexibility for appropriate responses to student prompts to react to and further drive the simulation. This is the key part that increases the engagement of the strategy. Rather than having a predetermined outcome in the simulation where students can "win" the activity by gathering a predetermined number of points or achievement of goals, the actions of the student result in interaction with the content which gives the teacher the flexibility to tailor the activity to the needs of the student, their involvement with the content, and the positioning of the learning in the activity.

In terms of Kolb's Theory of Experiential learning, the simulation fits perfectly with the initial components of the theory. The initial step in the theory calls for students to experience something or begin to explore the content. This can be done via student reading of the material and organizing what they find or through direct instruction of the teacher. The key to presenting information to students in this manner comes in the second step of the theory. By having students reflect on the actions of the figure in question or the setting being studied and propose the alternatives of the historical outcome, the students are properly positioned for future study and exploration of the topic. By going through this process students are able to begin thinking of how the figures of the simulation act and interact and place themselves in the setting that has been properly established in the simulation.

Given the context of the theory above and how they can be set in the context of Kolb's theory, it is possible to give a more complete description of how they would look in the classroom:

Second Continental Congress Simulation[1]

Experience: Students encounter the historical setting of the situation the colonists find themselves in through an experience the teacher creates establishing a common knowledge base for students.

Reflection: Students weigh the relative arguments and look at what they might have decided if put in the position of a revolutionary colonist.

Testing via Simulation: Roles are assigned historical roles by the teacher and students participate in a mock debate about several different topics as occurred in the actual Continental Congress that declared independence.

Debrief: At the conclusion of the experience, the teacher leads students through a debriefing of their experience in the simulation and discuss key points brought out. The summative assessment contains an essay question where students have to weigh the merits of staying loyal to England or declaring independence.

Congressional Hearing Simulation Regarding Acid Rain[2]

Experience: Student's explore a basic reading detailing the historical and geographical problem of acid rain destroying a portion of the Black Forest in Germany. Through anecdotal evidence, most students see this as a simple solution to fix and the reading itself, which is quite limited does not go into much depth as to why it is a major problem.

---

[1] This simulation was utilized in the author's classroom and is based on a simulation created by Interact. It can be found of their website at: http://www.interact-simulations.com

[2] This simulation was created in the author's classroom. The anecdotal information provided about the experience stems from the author's experience using it in the classroom, an introductory world geography course.

Reflection: Students begin the process identifying the causes of the problem and begin to propose solutions. Again, anecdotally, little thought was given by the students as to the greater impact of simply shutting the factories down.

Testing via Simulation: The students are put in a hypothetically created setting. Emphasis is placed on the economic factors, which would result if factories were just told to shut down. The students are given a role to play and a set of realistic data, which they would have access to if they were the person in real life. Some students are assigned the role of congressional representative who would hear the testimony and others are assigned the role of individuals representing different entities who would be impacted by the decisions of Congress. A vote of the representatives concludes the activity.

Reflection: Students would analyze the results of the hearing and then place the results of the simulation in the setting of the historical event. A discussion in class resulted about the historical setting with improved understandings about the bigger picture.

Presidential Briefing Simulation in the Civil War[3]

Experience: Students had been exploring for approximately two weeks the historical events of the first half of the American Civil War with the hypothesis that the events of 1863 shaped the remainder of the war and hastened its end.

Reflection: Students are asked to put into their own words whether or not the hypothesis based upon their understanding of the events.

Testing via Simulation: Students are grouped into small groups and are given a list of thirty geographic locations to map from the American Civil War up to the end of 1863. They are then to take their map and predict with the imperfect knowledge they would have had at that time what the outcome of the war would be. The students then are assigned the role of President Lincoln's war cabinet and must brief him on the situation and share their predictions with the president in a difficult situation facing reelection in just a few short months.

Reflection: Students share their predictions after the performance. Students are then asked to defend their positions. The class then continues in completing their study of the Civil War to see if their predictions are correct and what events were the catalyst to the Union winning the war.

---

[3] This activity was based on a learning experience conducted in the author's classroom and is based off an activity created by the author and a colleague.

The key part to understanding the true learning power to the simulation is the understanding that while some answers provided by the students are better than others, it is vitally important for the teacher to suppress judgment and allow the students to explore their divergent answers. The opportunity to rethink what they find through their study is the best thing for learning to occur, much like a means of cognitive dissonance (Schunk, Pintrich, & Meece, 2008).

USING PRIMARY SOURCES IN SOCIAL STUDIES INSTRUCTION

The author has often advocated for the use of primary sources in social studies instruction as they have proven to be impactful upon student understanding in their learning (Burenheide, 2007). It is necessary to understand that primary sources are the key to getting students engaged in historical study. In a sense, there is a movement by leading researchers in history education for history to become a laboratory class where students are immersed in the handling, interpreting, and analysis of primary sources (Levstik & Barton, 2005; VanSledright, 2002; Wineburg, 2001). Along these lines, researchers have developed an understanding that history education can develop a laboratory orientation.

In the context of Kolb's theory, primary sources allow the generating and testing of hypotheses as experiential learning encourages, but by allowing students to progress through a different order of events. Rather than having students experiment at the conclusion of the activity, the experimentation comes before the reflection through the analysis of primary sources. This analysis involves students testing what they have learned and hypothesized through some form of introductory instruction. The students then create an understanding of the phenomenon being studied by proposing a hypothesis. By then digging into the primary sources, the student then tests the understanding, which involves reflection and determining if it has a reasonable and logical conclusion.

When looking at the potential for adapting history instruction to this lab orientation, one must look specifically at the styles of teaching when utilizing primary sources. Brophy and VanSledright (1997) developed a sense of how to categorize the teaching styles of teachers of history. Their conclusions led to categorizing four typologies of instruction for the history teacher to employ. While their defining of the styles indicated different versions of teaching, it can be easily understood to root each of these styles in the utilizing of primary sources. The four categories identified can be labeled: storytelling history, scientific history, reform history, and eclectic history. The eclectic teacher uses a combination of all three of the aforementioned styles. The storyteller provides students with a story of the events in a riveting narrative fashion. The scientific teacher of history provides an overview of an historical phenomenon through the exploration of primary sources, described in another manner as "doing history." Finally, the reform minded history teacher sees the discipline as a means of teaching lessons valuable to society and the students, especially dealing with issues of diversity and showing a different perspective from society. These four styles of teaching can be rooted in the utilization of primary sources, which can provide students with a greater understanding of the topic being studied and a level of engagement not found in direct instruction which often occurs in classrooms today (Zhao & Hoge, 2005).

"Primary sources, secondary sources, historiography, hermeneutics, and heuristics are to the history teacher's laboratory what nucleus, neutrons, protons, isotopes, and quarks are to the physics teacher's laboratory" (Drake & Nelson, 2009). This understanding has led to the encouragement of new methods and development of pedagogical techniques that will enable students to engage in inquiry rooted in the exploration of primary sources. This type of instruction enables students to acquire an interesting set of skills. These skills allow a student to understand historical thinking, develop historical empathy, and to be fully engaged in the historical imagination (VanSledright, 2002). To fully understand the descriptions of the utilization of primary sources, an example of each of the styles is provided below.

Storytelling: The Life of Francesco Petrarch (10th Grade World History)[4]

Introduction: Francesco Petrarch is known in history as the first modern scholar who had a major impact upon the development of the humanist school of thought during the European Renaissance (Hanover Historical Texts Project, 1995). In the figure of Petrarch, students meet the archetype of the humanist thinker who illuminated the Renaissance spirit. Students are engaged in a story of the life of the figure. The story presented by the teacher explores the scope of the life of the figure and incorporates a drawing of the figure in his library as an introduction to what life in the Renaissance may have been like for the protagonists of the era.

The Story: Students are engaged in an overview of the life of Petrarch. His childhood is wrapped in comfort and an education in law. Upon the death of a demanding father, he began a study of the humanities and earned the patronage of a Cardinal in the church. As he later acquired a public office, he began collecting manuscripts

---

[4] The example of the life of Francesco Petrarch came from a class taught by the author in his teaching career.

of classic orators and thinkers: Cicero, Livy, Pliny, Quintilian, Homer, Aristotle, and Plato. From this knowledge, his muse was sparked to write his *Letters*, a collection of fictitious letters to the greats of history as well as contemporaries. Other significant works included his love letters to the mysterious Laura in the *Canzoniere* as well as his epic poem honoring Scipio Africanus entitled *Africa*. The brief exploration of these works sum up the life of this figure. Further commentary is provided on the picture providing an overview of the life of the figure and how it is indicative of the sparse life of the wealthy during the time period. He was found dead in his study with his pen fallen from his hand head resting on his book in a dramatic and romantic image. The story ends with a quote of the figure that wraps up the life of the man:

"Nothing weighs less than a pen and nothing is more cheering…Of all earthly delights none is nobler, sweeter, more lasting and dependable than that afforded by books" (Foster, 1984).

The Investigation: After students have been introduced to the figure and have a firm understanding, the teacher asks students to explore a sampling of his writing and share impressions gathered from the reading of a few small excerpts. The excerpts were selected from the collection of the Hanover Historical Texts Project (1995), which includes some of his *Letters*. Students read the texts and then share a conclusion of what they believe humanist thought will center around. The compiled responses are then placed on the board and the class then predicts the direction of the Renaissance and changing world-views compared to what they studied during the preceding unit on the Middle Ages.

Scientific: The Age of Jackson (8th Grade American History)[5]

Introduction: The presidency of Andrew Jackson changed the face of the American presidency as he was the first man of "common stock" to attain the office of the president. In his presidency, the events that marked his term of office not only changed how the office would shape the future of the country. Students are then engaged in developing an interpretation of how this era changed the country.

The Overview of Method: At this point in the curriculum, the students had been engaged in single source interpretation, and had been given an overview of historiography and the Hegelian dialectic so that they have a basic understanding of how the discipline of his-

[5] The example of primary source investigation of the Age of Jackson came from the author's teaching of an 8th Grade American History class.

tory works. The teacher wanted to get students in the habit of fully understanding how history works and as the class was using primary source investigation on a regular basis in the classroom. At this time in the class, students were able to take multiple sources and compare and contrast them. This exercise then involved them to take a thesis statement and either agree or disagree with it based upon their evaluation of the sources.

The Investigation: After having identified the key elements of Jackson's presidency, the teacher informs students that there are to undertake a primary source activity involving a thesis statement that they are to agree or disagree with using the sources as evidence to support their opinion. The teacher was able to use a discarded textbook for a foundation for his sources. The sources were taken from *Discovering American History* (Kownslar & Frizzle, 1974). The sources included:

- Two eyewitness accounts of Jackson's Inauguration
- A campaign portrait of Jackson, 1828
- An 1832 Broadside of Jackson
- Two accounts of Jackson and the Small Capitalists
- A New Yorker's Account of Jackson
- An account of the Cherokee Indians from Henry Steele Commager's *Documents of American History* from the textbook

The thesis statement that the students were to grapple with dealt with whether or not Jackson changed the image of the President. Students then took the sources and working with their peers, analyzed the sources for information that would lead to their agreement or disagreement. The students then summarized their findings by providing their belief of the veracity of the thesis and then identifying how each of the sources led to their conclusions. Their final results are then shared with the class and a final discussion occurs regarding the net opinion of the class.

Reform: African-Americans in the "Wild West" (8th Grade American History)[6]

Introduction: As a way to try to explain the different experience that some individuals may have had in an historical period, this primary source activity had students explore a set of primary sources different than what may traditionally be accessed. As this came later in the curriculum, students were able to form their thesis statement

---

[6] As with the other lessons demonstrated in this chapter, the author utilized this in his teaching.

and performed a full research project with the resources coming from the teacher.

Rationale: At the conclusion of the year-long performance of primary source use, students are put in a situation to research a lesser known portion of American history. The African-American experience in the frontier west is less known than that of traditional cowboys and pioneers. This investigation had students explore what it was like for a group of individuals not traditionally as well known to understand the notion of diversity, in this case stressing the different perspective a group of people would have.

The Investigation: Students engaged in utilizing primary sources dealing with African-Americans in the westward expansion period. As the students went through the sources and began making comparisons between them, a preliminary working thesis is formed. Students through the experience begin to find a better understanding of historical process, but they also start to develop understandings about the difficulties encountered by African-Americans. This investigation provides students with an understanding of a different group of individuals with the desired result of empathizing with the historical figures being studied.

As might be understood through looking at this activity, the end result is the experience of students fully engaged in the study of history having developed their own interpretation of history. The full benefit of which is students developing their own understanding, combining this new knowledge to established schema, and personalize the knowledge to their own understanding. What is further important is that the knowledge generated is based upon a lens of history not fully explored before by students and oft neglected by mainstream histories. This creates an opportunity for students to fully explore the realm of historical study and embrace their own rationally thought out interpretations.

The key to understanding the use of primary sources in the classroom is how the teacher implements their use. It is important to remember that the classroom does not hold students to the same expectations that professional historians are held. The teacher provides the appropriate scaffolding and setting for students to encounter the study of history and while this may lead to limited understandings and not encompassing the vast breadth of sources that historians encounter, it meets the needs of getting students actively involved in the study of history, developing critical thinking skills, and creating some individual ownership when the study is tailored to their interests (Husbands, 1996). The idea of turning the history classroom into a lab setting is of promoting primary source instruction. By merging appropriate pedagogy with the structure of Kolb's theory, the teacher is able to promote the desired skills of primary source instruction, namely critical thinking, analysis, and the enhancement of reading and writing.

ENGAGING STUDENTS IN
CIVICS EDUCATION UNDERSTANDING

To engage students better in civics, students can engage in creating understandings of constitutional principles rather than direct instruction. Under the ruling levied in *Marbury v. Madison,* the Supreme Court became the institution in the American legal system that serves as the ultimate arbiter of issues of constitutional law. In the majority opinion of this case, Justice John Marshal noted that "the judicial power of the United states is extended to all cases arising under the Constitution...It is also not entirely unworthy of observation that, in declaring what shall be the supreme law of the land, the Constitution, itself is first mentioned, and not the laws of the United States generally, but those only which shall be made in pursuance of the Constitution, have the rank" (The Oyez Project, n.d.).

Under this system of judicial review, it becomes extremely important for students to understand the rights contained with the Constitution and the subsequent Bill of Rights as the Constitution is the ultimate law of the United States. As precedents developed, the scope of the rights of citizens has evolved over time. Thus, it becomes important for citizens to follow this evolution and how the courts currently measure these rights.

As Vontz and Leming (2003) noted, the use of Supreme Court cases lend themselves well to certain methods. But, in this specific case, it is important to realize that the method must be integrated with the content. Vontz and Lemming further suggest civics educators who utilize active and participatory strategies, analyze documents and issues, teach with relevant topics, and teach civics content relevant to democratic citizenship can best motivate students to acquire knowledge of citizenship. One of the means of doing this is through the analysis of Supreme Court cases.

The case study method of court decisions can engage students in gaining key knowledge through the analysis of important cases (Long, 1994; McDonnell, 2002). Vontz and Leming denote however that the understanding of the "bigger topics" of citizenship can be collected from the study of Supreme Court cases than the law students analyzing cases for method and specific topics of study (Vontz & Leming, 2003). These cases can allow students to investigate facts, issues, arguments, context, civic principles, and higher order thinking skills (Knapp, 1993; Leming, 1991).

While there are common strategies to dissect cases of the Supreme Court, many of them can be heavily involved and use up a large amount of time in the classroom. Hanna and Dettmer (2004) encourage the teacher when designing assessments to maintain a balance between reliability, authenticity, and economy. Reliability would be accuracy of the measurement. Authenticity deals with the real-world application of knowledge to encourage transfer of learning. Economy deals with the use of time, effort, and energy in administering the assessment. Where economy focuses on the great "enemy" of the teacher—time—the teacher must consider if the strategy is the optimal and most appropriate use of time. In their article encouraging the use of Supreme Court cases, Vontz and Leming (2003) called for the use of Socratic seminars and moot court cases to effectively analyze the thinking of the court, the institution of the case in an historical context, and by taking an active role in the participating of the activity, becoming content experts of the case. But is this the best use of time in the classroom? Does the depth of content in this instance supersede the coverage of breadth? This study intends to analyze this question by employing a strategy that employs a significant quantity of cases without sacrificing the apparent quality of learning.

Description of the Model

The "Lightning Case" method discussed in this study is rooted in a sound literature base of experiential learning. Again the strategy turns to the model presented by Kolb (1984) and advocated for by Kolb and Lewis (1986). Further exploration was conducted by Mukhamedyarova (2005), who explored the idea of interactive learning. O'Brien (2003) discussed a model for students to engage in historical prediction making. Finally, Hess (2002) and Parker (2003) illuminated the nature of controversial deliberation in the classroom and provided guidelines for teachers to follow.

Through the sources cited above, a model was constructed that causes students to be actively engaged in the analysis of cases, make predictions based upon their knowledge of the Constitution, and discuss with fellow students, albeit briefly, about their decisions and rationale. Figure 21.1 provides a visual overview of the model.

The model provides students with the opportunity to utilize several cases to develop their own conceptualization of the boundaries of liberty within society and in the "eyes of the law." The teacher provides a brief overview of

Figure 21.1. An Overview of the "Lightning Case" Model

the rights enumerated in the Constitution based upon the specific concept that will be addressed. After this introduction, several cases are presented to the student in a written or oral format with a short synopsis of the key facts of illustrative Supreme Court cases. Pending on the teacher's preference, students may be given the opportunity to deliberate with their classmates, or they will create their own decision of the case. After the court's actual decisions are shared with the students with brief rationale for their decision, students conceptualize the boundary of the right or concept discussed in the "Lightning Case" session. As an example of this model in action, figure 21.2 provides an overview of one of the sessions detailing the concept of "search and seizure."

As evident in the presentation of the model, this learning experience fits within the idea of the Kolb theory. Students experience the context of the concept being studied via the introduction to the activity and what they may already know through prior knowledge. The reflecting and conceptualizing stages of the theory occur during the action of the learning activity. The experimentation occurs at the end of the learning activity when the application of the knowledge gained occurs in either a discussion or a final case to explore their knowledge. Regardless, the setting up of the activity along the basic tenets of Kolb's Theory provides an engaging activity. The best part of which, when the teacher utilizes this theory with subject matter that interests students, the interest level of the students is piqued and produces outstanding results.

Lesson Piece	Activity of the Lesson Piece
Overview	Reading of the Fourth Amendment
Case Presentations	*Weeks v. U.S.* (1914)
	Mapp v. Ohio (1961)
	Katz v. U.S. (1967)
	Illinois v. Gates (1983)
	Nix v. Williams (1984)
	Flippo v. West Virginia (1999)
	Brigham City v. Stuart (2006)
	Hudson v. Michigan (2006)
Conceptualization	"Marzano" Organizer Detailing the Limits of Search and Seizure

Figure 21.2   Illustrative Sample of Lightning Case Session—Search and Seizure

CONCLUSION

Engagement is the key to the success of a social studies teacher. Throughout many of the author's experiences, students have been appreciative of those times when they have been pushed to understand social studies in a much deeper and higher-order of thinking. Those who are engaged find the material to be appealing, interesting, thought-provoking, and even fun (Arnold, 2000). With these benefits perceived as possible, it would behoove teachers to find those experiences where students will be immersed, situated, and placed into the context of what they are studying.

When the teachers look at the composition of their classes, they need to find ways to enhance the educational experience. When taking into account the particular learning styles of students, it becomes evident that it is necessary to adapt to student means of learning. In order to help students be engaged in the classroom, it becomes necessary for a teacher to utilize effective strategies that will maximize the learning of content. Sound pedagogy with the opportunity to implement it in a variety of learning styles enables teachers to provide instruction to a student in a means that promotes engagement.

This chapter explores engaging social studies strategies rooted in Kolb's Theory of Experiential Learning. This theory provides a tangible means for the teacher to create instructional activities that provide a basic understanding of a phenomenon, look and reflect upon that phenomenon, generate ideas for further exploration, and then test whether their assertions are correct as can be determined via the disciplines of the social studies. This presentation of ideas allows a teacher the freedom and flexibility to explore in a means where the teacher can provide the appropriate scaffolding for each individual learning style and tailor the learning experience to different levels of student ability and yet maintain a rigorous learning environment set in a stimulating setting.

The final piece of wisdom that can be gleaned from incorporating this theory into one's instruction is the role that engagement plays into the social studies classroom. As noted in the introduction, the discipline of social studies is under criticism for not providing meaningful and engaging instruction to students. It is possible for the teacher to utilize a form of instruction where the teacher is in total control of the instructional pace, content, and delivery and be successful with a high level of learning (Leming, Ellington, & Porter-Magee, 2003). It is also important to realize that this assertion cannot apply to all teachers who control the classroom. The teacher that is successful in student achievement usually has a good grasp as to what Albert North Whitehead called the "rhythm of education" by understanding the romance, precision, and generalizations of education (1929). By building the educational experience in alignment with student interest and engagement, the teacher need not give up the control of the classroom, its activities, or its learning strategies. But it is imperative for the teacher to provide the scaffolding for each student to succeed, and to be given the opportunity to be engaged, immersed, and imbued with the content. The presentation of how this can be balanced in the classroom has been demonstrated with the strategies presented in this chapter. It is necessary for the teacher to setup the learning experiences in the interesting context, so that the student will be involved in learning.

REFERENCES

Arnold, J. H. (2000). *History: A very short introduction.* Oxford: Oxford University Press.

Blanchette, S. (2008). The importance of social studies. *The Dallas Morning News.* Retrieved February 2, 2011, from http://www.dallasnews.com/sharedcontent/dws/news/city/collin/opinion/stories/DN-central_blanchette_18edi.ART.South.Edition1.462033c.html

Brophy, J., & VanSledright, B. (1997). *Teaching and learning history in the elementary school.* New York: Teacher's College Press.

Burden, P. R., & Byrd, D. M. (2003). *Methods for effective teaching.* (3rd ed.). Boston: Allyn and Bacon Publishing.

Burenheide, B. J. (2007). I can do this! Revelations on teaching with historical thinking. *The History Teacher, 41*(1), 55–62.

Coleman, J. S. (1978). Information processing and experiential processing: Two modes of learning. In R. Stadskiev (Ed.), *The handbook of simulation gaming in social education, part I: Textbook* (pp. 26–32). Tuscaloosa, AL: Institute of Higher Education Research and Services, University of Alabama.

Costigan, L. L. (1984). Debriefing. *Simulation and Games, 15,* 415–431.

Cowan, J. (1998). *On becoming an innovative university teacher: Reflection in action.* Milton Keynes, UK: Open University.

Devaney, L. (2010). Digital native need tech-rich education. *eSchool news.* Retrieved January 1, 2011, from http://www.eschoolnews.com/2010/01/26/digital-natives-need-tech-rich-education

Dewey, J. (1939). *Experience and education.* New York: Macmillan.

Dorn, D. S. (1989). Simulation games: One more tool on the pedagogical shelf. *Teaching Sociology, 17*(1), 1–18.

Drake, F. D., & Nelson, L. R. (2009). *Engagement in teaching history: Theory and practices for middle and secondary teachers* (2nd ed.). Upper Saddle River, NJ: Merrill.

Foster, K. (1984). *Petrarch: Poet and humanist.* Edinburgh: Edinburgh University Press.

Gallagher, K. (2010). Reversing readicide. *Educational Leadership, 67*(6), 36–41.

Gibson, S., & McKay, R. (2001) What constructivist theory and brain research may offer social studies. *Canadian Social Studies* online version. www.quasar,ualberta.ca/css/C55_35_4/ARConstructionist_theory.htm

Good, T. L., & Brophy, J. E. (2008). *Looking in classrooms*. (10th ed.). New York: Longman.

Hanna, G. S., & Dettmer, P. A. (2004). *Assessment for effective teaching: Using context-adaptive planning*. Boston: Pearson

Hanover Historical Texts Project. (1995). *Francis Petrarch: Selections from his correspondence*. Accessed online January 1, 2011 from: http://history.hanover.edu/texts/petrarch.htm

Healey, M., & Jenkins, A. (2000). Kolb's experiential learning theory and its application in geography and higher education. *Journal of Geography, 99*(5), 185–195.

Hess, D. E. (2002). Discussing controversial public issues in secondary social studies classroom: Learning from skilled teachers. *Theory and Research in Social Education (30)*1, 10–41.

Husbands, C. (1996). *What is history teaching?* Bristol, PA: Open University Press.

Jarvis, P. (1987). *Adult learning in the social context*. London: Croom Hilm.

Jenkins, A. (1998). *Curriculum design in geography*. Cheltenham, UK: Geography Discipline Network, Cheltenham and Gloucester College of Higher Education.

Knapp, P. (1993). Strategies for teaching law in American history. *Update on law-related education, 17,* 17–22.

Kolb, D. A. (1984). *Experiential learning: Experience as the source of learning and development*. Englewood Cliffs, NJ: Prentice-Hall.

Kolb, D. A., & Lewis, L. H. (1986). Facilitating experiential learning: Observations and reflections. In L. H. Lewis (Ed.), *Experiential and simulation techniques for teaching adults* (pp. 99–102). San Fransisco: Jossey-Bass.

Kownslar, A. O., & Frizzle, D. B. (1974). *Discovering American history* (3rd ed.). New York: Holt, Reinhart, and Winston.

Leming, J. S., Ellington, L, & Porter-Magee, K. (2003). *Where did social studies go wrong?*

Leming, R. S. (1991). Teaching the law using United States Supreme Court cases. *ERIC Digest* (September).

Levstik, L. S., & Barton, K. C. (2005). *Doing history: Investigating with children in elementary and middle schools* (3rd ed.). Mahwah, NJ: Lawrence Erlbaum Associates.

Long, G. P. (1994). *Constitutional rights of juvenile students: Lessons on sixteen Supreme Court case*. Bloomington, IN: ERIC.

Maslow, A. (1968). A critical theory of adult learning and education. *Adult education, 32,* 19–23.

Maxim, G. W. (2006). *Dynamic social studies for constructivist classrooms*. (8th ed.). Upper Saddle River, NJ: Pearson Publishing.

McDonnell, M. (2002). Making the case for the case study method. *Social Education, 66,* 68–71.

Mukhamedyarova, Z. (2005). Interactive methods of teaching as a condition for developing students' independent learning skills in Kazakhstand and the U.S. *International Education, 34*(2), 62–70.

National Research Council. (2000). *How people learn: Brain, mind, experience, and school*. Washington, D. C.: National Academy Press.

O'Brien, J. (2003). Prediction making within a historical context. *The Social Studies, 94*(6), 271–278.

The Oyez Project, Marbury v. Madison, 5 U.S. 137 (1803) Retrieved February 2, 2011, from http://oyez.org/cases/1792-1850/1803/1803_0

Parker, W. C. (2003). The deliberative approach to education for democracy: Problems and possibilities. In J. J. Patrick, G. E. Hamot, & R. S. Leming (Eds.), *Civic learning in teacher education: International perspectives on education for democracy in the preparation of teachers, Vol. 2.* (pp. 99–116). Bloomington, IN: ERIC Clearinghouse.

Partnership for 21st Century Skills. (n.d.). *Social studies literacy map.* Retrieved January 18, 201 from http://www.p21.org/images/stories/matrices/ICTmap_ss.pdf

Piaget, J. (1952). *Origins of intelligence in children.* New York: Free Press.

Powell, K., & Wells, M. (2002). The effectiveness of three experiential teaching approaches on student science learning in fifth-grade public school classrooms. *The Journal of Environmental Education, 33*(2), 33–38.

Rogers, C. R. (1959). A theory of therapy, personality, and interpersonal relationships, as developed in the client-centered framework. In S. Koch (Ed.), *Psychology: A study of a science* (Vol. 3, pp. 184–256). New York: McGraw-Hill.

Schunk, D. H. (2008). *Learning theories: An educational perspective.* (5th ed.). Upper Saddle River, NJ: Pearson Publishing.

Schunk, D. H., Pintrich, P. R., & Meece, J. L. (2008). *Motivation in education: Theory, research, and applications.* (3rd ed.). Upper Saddle River, NJ: Pearson Publishing.

Seidner, C. J. (1978). Teaching with simulations and games. In R. L. Dukes & C. J. Seidner (Eds.), *Learning with simulations and games* (pp. 11–45). Beverly Hills, CA: Sage Publications.

Sullo, R. A. (2007). *Activating the desire to learn.* Alexandria, VA: Association for Supervision and Curriculum Development.

Stoskopf, A. (2001). Reviving Clio: Inspired history teaching and learning (without high stakes tests). *Phi Delta Kappan, 82*(6), 468–473.

Tansey, P. J., & Unwin, D. (1969). *Simulation and gaming in education.* London: Methuen Educational Ltd.

Terry, M. (2001). Translating learning style theory into university teaching practices: An article based on Kolb's experiential learning model. *Journal of College Reading and Learning, 32*(1), 68–85.

Thissen, F. (2005). *Inventing a new way of learning—Constructive fundamentals of a multimedia teaching methodology.* Retrieved November 15, 2005, from the Special Interest Group for Game-Based Learning in Universities and Lifelong Learning Website: http://www.sig-glue.net.

Thornton, S. J. (2005). *Teaching social studies that matters: Curriculum for active learning.* New York: Teacher's College Press

VanSledright, B. (2002). *In search of America's past: Learning to read history in elementary schools.* New York: Teacher's College Press.

Vontz, T. S., & Leming, R. S. (2003). Using United States Supreme Court Cases to promote civic learning in social studies teacher education. *Civic learning in teacher education: International perspectives on education for democracy in the preparation of teachers, Vol. 2.* (pp. 75–98). Edited by J. J. Patrick, G. E. Hamot, & R. S. Leming). Bloomington, IN: ERIC Clearinghouse.

Whitehead, A. N. (1929). *The aims of education and other essays.* New York: MacMillan.

Wineburg, S. S. (2001). *Historical thinking and other unnatural acts: Charting the future of teaching the past.* Philadelphia: Temple University Press.

Yell, M., M., Scheurman, G., & Reynolds, K. (2004). *A link to the past: Engaging students in the study of history.* Silver Springs, MD: National Council for the Social Studies.

Zhao, Y. & Hoge, J. D. (2005). What elementary students and teachers say about social studies. *The social studies, 96*(5), 216–221.

CHAPTER 22

SOCIAL STUDIES PEDAGOGY

Thomas Turner, Jeremy Clabough,
Sarah Philpott, and Lance McConkey

INTRODUCTION

Educators and scholars in general for that matter love to use $10 words for the most fundamental of ideas. Pedagogy is one of those words. It refers to what a teacher does, the art and science of teaching, or teacher methodology. Pedagogy is a good word because it encompasses the thousand and one miracles that good teachers perform every day with the magnificence of Scheherazade. Effective pedagogy helps teachers achieve what Eisner (2006) claimed is the first satisfaction of teaching—to "introduce students to ideas they can chew on for the rest of their lives." Eisner went on to say "Great teaching traffics in enduring puzzlements, persistent dilemmas, complex conundrums, enigmatic paradoxes. "(p. 44) He argued that good teaching was not involved with certainty because certainty was a dead end. Dead ends do not engage the mind. Great ideas, according to Eisner, "have legs—They take you somewhere." (p. 44)

Up until the twentieth century, direct teaching was the principle pedagogical approach in social studies. Teachers presented information and had students read. Question and answer along with discussion were used

Contemporary Social Studies: An Essential Reader, pages 421–438
Copyright © 2012 by Information Age Publishing
All rights of reproduction in any form reserved.

421

to get feedback and as assessment tools. Direct instruction was seen as the most efficient way to transfer knowledge from those who have it to those who did not. It seemed natural as a method or process. Since the earliest civilizations people have told and listened to stories and news, processed what they heard, and then we pass it on to others. They also learned from explanations of how others did things and then applied what they heard, synthesized it, analyzed it, and evaluated it.

Presentation remains as an important form of pedagogy. The literature is filled with traits of good presenters, lecturers, and storytellers (Doyle, 2008; Felder & Brent, 2010; Gambrell & Marinak, 2009; Mohidin, 2009; Morris, 2009; Sutcliff, 2010):

1. The teacher knows his or her stuff. They have expertise, knowledge, and background. They are masters of the content.
2. The teacher is passionate about what he or she is teaching, loves his or her stuff and shows it.
3. The presenter is dynamic and excited, uses his or her voice as a tool, and is neither monotone nor singsong. Sometimes we feel we are straining to hear them. With others they bombard our senses.
4. The presentation appeals to the interests of the audience, uses dramatic devices to do so, sucks you in.
5. The presentation is focused and pointed, clear and economic. We do not like flowery, wordy presentations that drone on.
6. The presentation recognizes where we are, relates to what we know, and recognizes our background.
7. The presenter makes sense. The listener can follow the organizational patterns and even predict the nature of what is coming next.
8. The presentation holds our interest, makes us sit up and notice. Sometimes it makes us say, "I didn't know that!" or "I wish I had said that!"

The teacher is aware of and fits his or her presentation to the attention span of the audience. He or she "reads them" well and senses when to change activities direction, tempo, and volume to bring them back, when to stop, when to draw them into intimacy.

The twentieth century brought a change in social studies pedagogy. Teachers thought about and debated the right ways to teach social studies. An incisive and thorough summary of this struggle is presented in *The Social Studies Wars* (Evans, 2004). Evans concludes, rather glumly that the pattern of the century was one of struggle over both content and approaches to teaching with constant attacks from small groups of vocal critics. Advocates of different approaches ranging from recitation, to question and answer drills, to inquiry based methods, to simulations, to engaging students in problem based curriculum offered their solution as the best practice of teaching. Even the United States Senate had its say about the 1994 National History Standards and how they should be taught (Evans, 2004). Because of the outcry among educators related to the original standards, the majority of the Senate voted to eradicate the standards and the process for teaching them. Eventually, the standards were changed to acquiesce with the opponents. Controversies, like the one over standards were not new. Concerns and conflicts about pedagogy had been pervasive throughout the twentieth century. From the progressive education era through the standards movement, pedagogy had been a source of conflict.

WHAT IS PEDAGOGY?

The dictionary defines pedagogy as "the art, science or profession of teaching" (Merriam-Webster, Inc., 2003). More narrowly, the National Board for Professional Teaching Standards (1998) specifically identified content pedagogy as, "the pedagogical (teaching) skills teachers use to impart the specialized knowledge/content of their subject area(s)." Effective teachers display a wide range of skills and abilities that lead to creating a learning environment where all students feel comfortable and are sure that they can succeed both academically and personally. "This complex combination of skills and abilities are integrated in the professional teaching standards that also include essential knowledge, dispositions, and commitments that allow educators to practice at a high level."(NBPTS, 1998) Recently pedagogy has been attached to many political and theoretical dimensions. We hear about feminist pedagogy, industrial pedagogy, and most of all critical pedagogy. Critical pedagogy is aimed at changing the teacher learner relationships and raising learner's consciousness in relation to socially oppressive conditions (21st Century Schools, 2011). According to Evans (2008) advocates of critical pedagogy often think that, "critical pedagogy means the imposition of a rather dogmatic view."

Combining elements from all of these, the working definition of pedagogy embodies a set of skills and knowledge that includes perception of how students learn, how teachers perceive themselves and their relationships with students, how teachers perceive the purpose of the schools, and the methods teachers use to get students to acquire knowledge and skills. Effective pedagogy evokes passion for learning, raises more questions than it answers, challenges, and provokes. Social studies teachers have both advocated and used a number of pedagogical approaches across the centuries since the first teacher took on the first pupil. Drummond (2002) was trying to capture their essence when he compiled a list of twelve practices relevant to excellence in teaching. More recently Marzano (2004, 2007) has advocated and described research based strategies and practices. Evidence strongly indicates that effective pedagogy results when teachers translate their learning goals and objectives into practice (Evans, 2006).

In the chapter that follows, we attempt to explore and explain the role of pedagogy and pedagogical approaches in the social studies. To present pedagogy as comprehensively and objectively as possible within the limited scope of a single chapter, we think that it is important to avoid categorizing labels for types of pedagogy for the most part and reflect both the real and the ideal of social studies practice.

EFFECTIVE PEDAGOGY

Inquiry

Since the beginning of the twentieth century, social studies educators have been seeking to broaden and improve pedagogy. Among the most important developments was the inquiry movement or inquiry based learning which emerged in the late 1950s. Inquiry teaching envisioned the roles of both teacher and students in entirely different ways than they had been conceived in the past. The teacher was seen far less as an authority and much more as a guide. Students were to be encouraged to ask questions and seek the answers themselves, questions that did not have simple, single, or absolute answers. Students were also encouraged to challenge authority, to probe deeply, and to use more scientific approaches and methods. They were pushed to probe more deeply, to think at higher levels.

Among the leaders in the movement, Donald Oliver, Fred Newmann, and James Shaver worked with practicing educators in what was known as the Harvard Social Studies Project. They used the scientific method to help students solve social problems (Stern & Riley, 2001). The three created a series of pamphlets entitled the *Public Issues* series. In them, the authors used key social studies events as the backdrop for students to analyze and question social issues. Bohan and Feinberg (2008, p. 61) write that the series provided an "innovative approach to teaching social studies." Bohan and Feinberg (2008, p. 62) described a typical Harvard Social Studies Project inquiry worked through the example of a pamphlet entitled *The Railroad Era* and *The American Revolution:*

> Authors carefully portray conflicts of interests. Subsequently, students are asked to answer persisting questions of history, including making value judgments about the conflicts. Students also identify various interest groups, explain why a particular person would support or oppose the railroad, and make parallels to similar modern problems. (Bohan & Feinberg, 2008, p. 62)

This series of pamphlets provided teachers with essential tools to employ inquiry learning in their classrooms. In a sense, the pamphlets themselves were lessons in pedagogy for teachers as they provided students and teachers factual background knowledge, directions for using simulation games, case studies to analyze, value based questions, and connections to current events. This pedagogy was not teacher centered. Instead, the writers tried to create situations that evoked and encouraged student questioning. Students were prodded to craft their own opinions about social studies topics by analyzing and discussing their reasons. Students were pushed to reflect on the various conclusions of others. Of course, the prerequisite of this methodology was that the opinions of students were of value. Teachers also would have to feel comfortable leading discussions that at times could touch on controversial topics.

Zemelman, Daniels, and Hyde (2005) contended that the following qualities must be present for a successful social studies program utilizing an inquiry based pedagogy:

- Regular opportunities to investigate topics in-depth.
- Students choose own topics to investigate (this can also be done in conjunction with teacher offering a list of suggestions).
- Open questions should be explored that challenge the thinking of students.
- Real-world inquiry problems should be utilized so that students can participate in real-world issue.

The difficulties involved in building inquiry-based instruction were enormous. Teachers had seen little beyond presentation social studies. This approach required a deviation from traditional methodology with teachers taking the role of guides. The role change was as large, if not larger, challenge for students whose image of school culture was based on teachers and textbooks asking referenced closed ended questions. Unfortunately, by the end of the twentieth century, there was also an even larger barrier to using inquiry pedagogy in the social studies classroom in the form of growing emphasis on assessment.

Storytelling

Presentation or didactic teaching itself has evolved somewhat. With the greater emphasis on reading in elementary school, one of the ways that social studies has responded is with greater emphasis on story and on reading and listening skills. The great traditions of social studies teaching began with storytellers and bards who entranced and entertained, while at the same time conveying the history, values, morals, and heroes of their people. Such storytellers have succeeded in a number of ways because:

1. Facts and concepts embedded in stories are more memorable, especially long term. We remember the stories and the circumstances in which they were told.
2. Stories humanize characters and events whether past or present, give them dimensionality and make them real, not just names and stick figures in a book.
3. Stories help students to relate to historical events and people and see them as more like themselves.
4. Stories give teaching entertainment value, allowing the teacher to create incorporate suspense, adventure and humor into teaching itself.
5. Stories enrich students' vocabularies and improve their listening skills.
6. Stories teach students that passion, excitement, and truth can be found in learning.

Every historical event, person, every law, and document represents a maze of interconnected stories. Every place, every group of people, every nation or state or city, and every culture also has its origin stories, discovery stories, and a host of other stories that, taken together, comprise its history. It is our job as teachers to find and select the most important and useful stories and to tell them in the best possible way that we can. The stories embody the essence of the social sciences, the best lessons of citizenship, and the most important knowledge that we can teach.

Vocabulary Development and Concept Learning

Social studies teachers at all levels have become more cognizant of the reading and listening issues including vocabulary development and concept learning. Technology has become an important tool in this area enhanced by electronic vocabulary research, dealing with language from different periods and cultures, visualization based on verbal pictures, and speaking and writing skills.

In this dawning information age, content literacy has enormous importance. Content area reading specialists have long claimed that every teacher must be a reading teacher, but the need for reading skills to mine the rich resources of the internet must be part of next generation social studies pedagogy. Students need to be able to use many different forms of text. Technology only creates more forms of material for students to need to read.

Textbooks, trade books, and technology-based learning, including electronic texts will definitely have an impact on the social studies. The visual aids to learning as well as sound clues are going to make teaching concepts and teaching the past in general far more alive and real. Students will be more involved in shaping their instruction.

Drama

Since the time of John Dewey, drama has been an important part of social studies pedagogy. However, advocates of the value of drama related techniques became particularly vocal in the 1960s and 1970s (Shaftel & Shaftel, 1967). Role-play, socio drama, and simulation games were among the earliest strategies introduced. To these, many other drama approaches and techniques have been added. Many of the figures studied in the social studies rose to prominence and made their mark because of their ability to be dramatic, to inspire loyalty, and to generate enthusiasm. From Shakespeare to Homer, to Paul Revere, to Winston Churchill to Martin Luther King, Jr., the ability of approaches that evoke emotional involvement and response had been recognized. By the 1960s, the power of the human voice to incite emotion, help solve problems, and cast attention to learning opportunities was widely recognized. Drama, in many forms, has been used since classical times as a manner of teaching and will continue to be utilized as impactful pedagogy technique in the twenty-first century.

Why is drama a useful pedagogy in the social studies? Numerous reasons may be offered:

1. Dramatic approaches make social studies more interesting and exciting.
2. Drama brings passion and emotion to the classroom, empathy for historical characters and for people of varying cultures.
3. Drama provides opportunities for students to understand human interactions and multiple perspectives.
4. Drama helps students better comprehend textbooks and other content-area media (Rosler, 2008).

Kornfeld and Leyden (2005) pointed out that "dramatic engagement can greatly enhance students' understanding of the stories they read, adding a depth and dimension to the plot, setting, and characters that simply reading the printed words rarely accomplishes." Many might consider drama a commodity reserved for stage actors, but this performance art has many benefits as a method of teaching and is varied in type. Teachers can set the stage, so to say, in a variety of ways where students can be active participants in learning. Turner (2010) described some of the various types of dramatic techniques as follows:

- Readers' Theater—Students, in character, read either pre-written scripts or scripts they compose.
- Guided Fantasies—students sit with their eyes closed while they envision a story or place described by a reader.

- Ballet and Interpretive Dance—Students move to music to enact a plot line.
- Class Action Stories—Students read or listen to stories with key names and phrases. These words are signals for verbal and nonverbal responses.
- Mime—Students use their body to depict ideas, stories, or characters.
- Dramatic Play—Students take on roles and portray the world (i.e. playing house, pretending to be community helpers, etc.)
- Mock Trials—Students recreate trials from the past or present.
- Story Play—Students play out a known story or event. Some involve only movement while other forms involve improvised dialogue.
- Simulation Games—Students play out a problem-solving scenario in a prescribed role. Game rules limit and direct the play of characters toward particular goals.

Dramatic "play" and drama in all its forms are part of what might be termed natural pedagogy for the social studies. Young children in their play interpret their families, their neighborhoods, their imaginary life, and their world in dramatic story play. These little plays are often done in role and have simple everyday actions as plots. Primary teachers utilize this same story play by setting up centers or stations for students to play out the role of community helpers. Beginning in the elementary grades, teachers can take the drama a little further and might. For example, teachers may have students envision historical events such as the Louisiana Purchase or the signing of the Magna Carta in guided fantasies. Middle grade teachers might incite students to write and perform readers' theaters about the Spanish Inquisition, the Constitution, or other large, often somewhat abstract events. High school students could benefit from re-enacting a U.S. Supreme Court case to learn about the judicial system and deal with their concepts of justice and law.

Role-play itself is one of the oldest dramatic techniques to be utilized in the classroom. It has many potential beneficial uses in the social studies (Bolinger & Warren, 2007; Shaftel, 1970). Morris (2009) described one such benefit saying that "through role-playing, students explore places, times, and situations that they may not have directly experienced." Simulation games use role-play as part of recreating or simulating historical, political, and social problem situations and conflicts. In simulations, students assume the role of particular individuals while the teacher creates a problem scenario. Within prescribed boundaries or rules, students in the simulation games make decisions and take actions as they think the characters they are preparing would. Each tries to assume the character and act from his or her viewpoint. Burlbaw (1991) described a teacher-led simulation where students play roles of farmers, storeowners, and oil tycoons to learn about the growth of big business and railroads, says that this dramatic activity allows students to learn about definitions, concepts, and ideas in an active environment. It is through this active pedagogy that students learn about historical events or issues as they make-believe their classroom is a particular scene. Students inherently use problem-solving strategies and gain perspective about social studies issues in this type of dramatic activity.

With purposeful planning, teachers with solid classroom management skills and the ability to allow students to make the classroom a stage can employ such drama pedagogy. Such teachers become stage managers creating scenarios where students learn about and experience the emotions of social studies. A constructivist view of learning seems to promote drama in their classrooms since drama advances student engagement in content. The advent of the internet has further widened the horizons for drama with the opportunity to adapt and use online simulations, to use and create features for YouTube, Teacher Tube, social networking sites, and take virtual tours. Via television, videos, and the internet students can be in the spotlight. Technology may be in factor persuading teachers to use pedagogy where students can be center stage. The range of possibilities in the twenty-first century is exponentially greater.

Questioning

Questioning techniques flow very naturally from direct teaching, even from stories. Since teachers cannot know what is going on inside students' heads, they look to student responses to questions for indications of their thinking. Good teachers guide learning with questions serving as advanced organizers for their presentations and stories. Because they want their students to master and understand, good teachers encourage students to ask questions in order to bring clarity and extend their learning. The teachers themselves ask questions to review what they have covered and to check comprehension.

In the 1930s, Paul Hanna and Harold Rugg revolutionized the social studies providing elementary social studies curriculum frameworks built on accessing children's prior concepts and ideas (Bisland, 2009; Evans, 2008; Stern & Riley, 2001). Hanna and Rugg not only revitalized elementary and middle grade social studies curriculum, but also gave a new importance to both teacher questions and student questions in social studies pedagogy by their stress on integrating the social sciences and social justice. The inquiry movement that began in the late 1960s increased the emphasis on questions, and especially on student generated questions. A central belief of advocates of inquiry approaches supported by research was that when children explore questions in which they are genuinely interested, learning becomes intrinsically motivated (Pataray-Ching & Kavanaugh-Anderson, 1998).

Questioning as a pedagogical tool, whether the teachers or the students raise and pose the questions, has been subject to various examination and categorization across the years. Researchers and writers in the 1960s and 1970s explored questioning in the classroom distinguishing three types of questions. The three types of questions are rhetorical questions, simple recall and definitional questions, and higher order questions. Generally, research has shown that teachers ask very few higher order thinking questions. Social studies authors have constantly encouraged teachers not only to ask higher order thinking questions but also to engage students in inquiry approaches and to challenge them to ask and seek answers to such questions themselves (Beyers, 1971; Sanders, 1966; Shaftel & Shaftel, 1967).

In the last two decades of the twentieth century, thought and research related to questioning have focused more on the impact and purpose use of questioning strategies than on individual questions in isolation. Teachers have looked to strategies like the one used by news reporters referred to as the "Five W's" (Who? What? When? Where? Why?). Reading/ study skills strategies, while formulaic in nature, have also shown the importance of an overall approach to questioning as exemplified in approaches such as SQ3R (Study, Question, Read, Recite, Review) and K-W-L (What I know, What I want to know, What I have learned) (Carr & Ogle, 1987).

Socratic questioning is one questioning strategy that has been widely advocated and used in recent years. At least initially, Socratic questioning is teacher controlled with deep probing questions. Socratic questions are analytic in nature beginning with questions about purpose and direction and moving to questions that examine thoughts—their origin and meaning, and then to questions that look for the basis of thoughts (Paul & Elder, 2007).

A more holistic typology for social studies questioning strategies, though, should look at the pedagogic functions that questioning strategies of different kinds serve. The most obvious function of questions is to review information that teachers want students to recall from presentations or readings. Appropriate questioning techniques help the organization of material being examined while providing key educational skills for students such as interpreting the material and drawing inferences about cause and effect relationships.

Beyond questions, teachers need to look at the various types of discussion settings in which questioning strategies occur in the social studies classroom. These include the following, among others:

1. Formative discussions set the tone for a lesson or unit. Within them, teachers communicate or help students determine objectives. The "KWL" questions are asked and direction is set.

2. Planning discussions give students a sense of empowerment and involvement in the class. In such discussions, ideas are stressed and future activities are structured. They are useful for unit and lesson culmination and for group research and projects. Brainstorming and decision-making are often involved.

3. Issue discussions often focus on "why" and "so what" questions, on morality and ethics, and on fairness and justice. They are concerned with controversies, differing viewpoints, and the reasoning behind these viewpoints. They sometimes clarify; sometimes alter students' points of view.

4. Probing and clarification discussions tend to have an interrogation aura about them. They are teacher-controlled but student-centered. Questions are seldom simple, nor are they answerable in a single word or sentence. Nearly every initial question has follow up questions that probe the initial answers.

5. Review discussions cover factual material, concepts, and generalizations. While evaluation is the end goal, they are also useful in preparing for tests and other forms of assessment. They are summative in nature and help students crystallize and realize what they have learned and how they understand differently. Review discussions may reach back into other units and lessons.

6. Analysis and synthesis discussions alternatively take apart or put together people, documents, places, and events in order to give them more meaning and deepen understanding.

7. Valuing discussions involve questions of justice, right and wrong, good and bad, value and worth, honor and dishonor, and importance and worth. In other words, they ask students to weigh and evaluate people and their acts, motives, and decisions—in fact any and all things studied.

THE RANGE OF PEDAGOGICAL ALTERNATIVES

Reform and technology have brought a range of pedagogical alternatives into social studies teaching. These alternatives include, but are not limited to the following: teacher centered, Socratic thinking, inquiry, critical pedagogy, service learning, collaborative learning, and project based learning.

Teacher centered or presentation pedagogy: Teacher centered or presentation pedagogy is the oldest approach to teaching and functions on the undeniable premise that teachers have the skills and information that they are trying to impart to their students. This pedagogy is inherent in lecturing, storytelling, show and tell, and in using various sources that may read or observed.

Many of the uses of the most advanced technology today including Power-Point presentations, wikis, and blogs are basically presentation pedagogy.

Socratic thinking pedagogy: The purpose of Socratic questioning or Socratic thinking strategies is to get students to realize what they do and do not know. The pedagogical approach aims at producing critical thinking. Questions probe to analyze the parts of thinking. Teachers need considerable skill to develop dialogue skills.

Inquiry learning: Inquiry learning approaches are problem based and focus on students developing curiosity and questions themselves. The teacher takes a less controlling role, serving more as a guide. Students are encouraged to become learners and researchers. While the teacher still poses questions, even generates hypotheses, it is the inquiring student who is in control.

Critical pedagogy: Critical pedagogy accentuates social activism and focuses on challenging authority, accepting nothing as fact until it is satisfactorily proven to be so. Conceptual definitions, principles, axioms—all are open to attack and challenge by logic and reason. Precedent alone is never sufficient.

Service learning: While service learning is a version of project based learning, the prominent use of it as an instructional tool warrants a separate discussion. Service learning focuses on active citizenship activities. The premise is that good citizens make the world a better place by helping others, improving the school and neighborhood, and by generally becoming useful in practical ways. The students are involved in conceptualizing and designing the service learning projects as well as active in implementing them. They often involve physical labor, interaction with other people, and civic activities.

Collaborative learning: Collaborative and cooperative strategies involve students problem solving and developing projects in small groups. Each member of the group has a specific role and job within the group. Collaborative pedagogy divides the learning and gives each student a degree of teaching responsibility.

Project based or task based pedagogy: In project based or task based pedagogy, learners have a job of communicating what they are learning in some recognizable, often defined form. They do presentations, create portfolios, are actively involved in cultural journalism, or give visual forms to show their mastery of the knowledge or skill and their ability to use it.

CONTEMPORARY PEDAGOGY

Contemporary pedagogy is above all else eclectic. Social studies teachers must reflect an awareness and understanding of multiple factors including the attention span of their students, the multiple levels, rates, and styles of learning in their classes, the diversity of the society and of the student body, and the tools at hand. The constantly changing available technology also opens new pedagogical opportunity. A growing emphasis on multicultural education and global education has not only changed the curriculum but altered affective and cognitive aspects of pedagogy. The growing availability of immediate news and information, and the increasing interdependence of nations and cultures have increased geographic and cultural exchanges and interactions. Students can have real time conversations with people around the world.

Global awareness is very close to becoming a reality for everyone. At the beginning of the twentieth century, progressive pedagogy had been focused on how to Americanize immigrant children, to teach them to become citizens of America. In the new millennium, however, while ethnocentrism and nationalism are still very much a part of American culture and thinking, social studies educators are increasingly concerned with how to teach students to be citizens of a world. Learning about the differences and similarities of cultures around the world helps us all learn about the global village in which we reside. Reducing and eliminating racism and cultural prejudice is a goal.

The pedagogy of multicultural education while given less attention is as important as the curriculum content. It may range from direct teaching to research projects to Socratic discussions of current issues, to student-created projects, to hosting a cultural fair. Based on the works of Banks (2007), Bennett (2010), and Bigelow (2007), at least six major approaches to multicultural education are currently in use. These include:

- A unit approach that focuses on a particular culture (e.g. Black History Month.)
- An Integrated or inclusive history approach (inclusion of history of all groups as an overview.)
- A perspectives approach (similar to the integrated approach but with a special effort to show the point of perspectives of different groups.)
- A balanced biographical approach (teaching history through biography with a special effort to include the contributions of individuals of different ethnicities and cultures.)
- A balanced geographical approach (teaching geography with an attempt to look at all cultures and peoples.)
- A value based approach (attempting to look at social studies through "multicultural eyes.")

Multi-cultural education often incorporates progressive education goals with experience based pedagogy. Ukpokodu (2008) suggested that teachers guide students in social activism. Social activism is a type of service learning that takes the form of students investigating a problem and working to help solve the issue. In its early conceptions, service-learning projects were limited to the local community. However, in social activism, students contribute to the solving of global problems; yet do so without leaving their schools. Projects such as elementary students raising money to build a school in Afghanistan, student fund raising and lobbying Congress to create a civil rights museum close to the Lincoln Memorial, and high school students publishing and distributing voters' guides are just a few examples of service learning projects where teachers help students become socially active (Golston, 2010).

The service-learning projects described above also relate to global education. Global education is different from multicultural education in that global education wants to extend a school curriculum to extend understanding with diversity to a global perspective (NAIS, 2011; The Center for Global Education, 2011). Students should engage in activities that increase cultural awareness from citizens outside of one's borders while strengthening connections between groups in distant lands through collaborative partnerships to address specific problems in the world (NAIS, 2011). Through this process, students will gain a deeper level of tolerance and awareness of groups that share different cultural, social, and religious values than those held in a students' society.

Public awareness related to multiculturalism has increased with the creation of such events as Black History Month and Hispanic Heritage Month. This, in turn, empowers teachers to provide opportunities for students to gain perspective about their own heritage and that of others. The National Council for the Social Studies has been an enabling force with articles in *Social Education* and *Social Studies and the Young Learner* that suggest and encourage methods of teaching about cultural and global knowledge. The February/March 2010 issue of *Social Education*, for example, offer various strategies for students to learn about China with ideas ranging from teaching Chinese geography through cuisine (Lipman, 2010) to having students watch and then discuss Chinese films with sub-titles (Lee, 2010).

Through creative pedagogical practices, teachers are engaging students in active learning experiences while providing them opportunities to learn about our world. Of course, these practices are not without controversy since some critics want students to focus on the United States instead of the world.

FUTURE OF PEDAGOGY

As we enter a new millennium, social studies pedagogy and curriculum are at a pivotal point. The high stakes testing era of NCLB brought unwelcome change, as time once dedicated to the teaching of social studies was usurped in a desperate effort to improve test scores in literacy and math (McGuire, 2007). To achieve anything approaching curricular equity, social studies teachers have to teach smarter, teach better, and use their time more effectively. According to Marzano and Polluck (2004), advocates of effective research based practice; one of the three key elements to creating effective pedagogy is the use of well-designed instructional strategies. Social studies teachers in this era of high stakes testing must, more than ever depend on the use of well-planned and well-executed pedagogy to ensure the success of their students. In this section, we will look at three areas of effective social studies pedagogy: general best practices in social studies; how teachers instruct students in increasing content literacy in social studies, and the increasing use of technology in social studies.

There is a growing list of exciting opportunities for the use of technology in the social studies classroom in the twenty-first century. The continuing reduction of the price of hardware and software is a trend that is essential if this is to continue. A school district can currently purchase laptop computers for less than $500 dollars each and desktops for even less. According to the National Center for Education Statistics (2006), 99% of instructional rooms in public schools have access to the internet with 97% of those schools having access to high speed broadband internet. This widespread availability of the internet can lead to the inclusion of new internet based Web 2.0 tools in the social studies classroom. Web 2.0 tools such as wikis, blogs, and video sharing are designed to be user friendly, facilitate information sharing, and encourage collaboration within schools. They also open the possibility for communication between students from distant parts of the world. Wikis, blogs, social-networking, and video-sharing sites seem to be at the heart of the social studies classroom in the new millennium. The pedagogical use of these tools is only limited by the creativeness of the social studies teacher and students.

Technology and especially the potential to do research using the internet have revolutionary potential for the social studies. There are many tools already available for teachers online. Included among them are thousands of web quests, virtual tours of museums and historical sites, virtually inexhaustible primary documents including photos and paintings, shared activities, teaching materials, and units, a huge variety of interactive maps, computer games and simulations. Test and assessment material are also available. The internet also provides access to libraries and information sources around the world.

CONCLUSION

Teaching is ultimately an interaction between two people—a teacher and a learner. Many factors go into good pedagogy, but ultimately if we can create a caring relationship between ourselves and our students, inspire them to want to learn, make them feel that they are stakeholders in their own learning success, convince them that they can learn, show them that the content that we are trying to get them to learn is interesting, important and vital, our pedagogy will be successful.

But our pedagogy must be vital, varied, tested, and open to change. Teachers need better tools, more efficient access to a broad spectrum of interesting and significant materials, and guidance to best use their resources. The twenty-first century offers more pedagogical tools than we have ever had before. And if the technological innovations of the last quarter of the twentieth century are any indication, the next fifty years will offer even greater possibility. But social studies tomorrow, as today will depend on good teachers and good teaching. We must hold on to and create replacements for social studies teachers who love their stuff, use sound pedagogy, care about their students, and want to share the mystery, the excitement, and the importance of what we call social studies.

REFERENCES

21st Century Schools. Critical pedagogy. Retrieved Feb 8, 2011 from http://www.21stcenturyschools.com/Critical_Pedagogy.htm

Banks, J. (2007). *An introduction to multicultural education* (4th ed.). Boston, MA: Allyn & Bacon.

Bennett, C. (2010). *Comprehensive multicultural education: Theory and practice.* (7th ed.). Boston, MA: Allyn and Bacon.

Beyers, B. (1971). *Africa through Inquiry. Social Education, 35*(2), 147–153.

Bigelow, B. (2007). *Rethinking our classrooms: Teaching for equity and justice.* (revised ed.). Milwaukee, WI: Rethinking Schools Ltd.

Bisland, B. (2009). Two traditions in the social studies curriculum for the elementary grades: The textbooks of Paul R. Hanna and Harold O. Rugg. *Journal of Social Studies Research, 33*(2), 155–196.

Bohan, C. H., & Feinberg, J. R. (2008). The authors of the Harvard Social Studies Project: A retrospective analysis of Donald Oliver, Fred Newmann, and James Shaver. *Social Studies Research and Practice, 3*(2), 54–67.

Bolinger, K., & Warren, W. J. (2007). Methods practiced in social studies instruction: A review of public school teachers' strategies. *International Journal of Social Education, 22*(1), 68–84.

Burlbaw, L. M. (1991). Add a teacher-led simulation to your lecturing techniques. *Social Studies, 82*(1), 30–32.

Carr, E., & Ogle, D. (1987). K-W-L Plus: a strategy for comprehension and summarization. *Journal of Reading, 30,* 628–631.

Doyle, T. (2008). *Keys to effective lecture: Eight steps to better teaching.* Retrieved from www.ferris.edu/fctl/Teaching_and...Tips/.../Effective-Lecture.ppt.

Drummond, T. (2002). *A brief summary of the best practices in college teaching: Intended to challenge the professional development of all teachers.* Retrieved from http://webshare.northseattle.edu/eceprogram/bestprac.htm.

Eisner, E. (2006). The satisfaction of teaching. *Educational Leadership, 63* (6), 44–46.

Evans, M. (2006). Educating for citizenship: What teachers say and what teachers do. *Canadian Journal of Education, 29*(2), 410–435.

Evans, R. W. (2004). *The social studies war: What should we teach the children?* New York, NY: Teachers College Press.

Evans, R. (2008). The (Unfulfilled) Promise of Critical Pedagogy, *Journal of Social Studies Research 32*(2), 16–25.

Felder, R., & Brent, R. (2010) Teaching institute: Assessment of impact and implications for faculty development. *Journal of Engineering, 99*(2), 121–134.

Gambrell, L., & Marinak, B. (2009). Sometimes I just crave information. *Social Studies and the Young Learner, 21*(3), 4–5.

Golston, S. (2010). The civic mission of schools. *Social Education, 74*(1), 4–6.

Kornfeld, J., & Leyden, G. (2005). Acting out: Literature, drama, and connecting with history. *The Reading Teacher, 59*(3), 230–238.

Lee, T. (2010). Ten top films for teaching about China today. *Social Education, 74*(1), 49–51.

Lipman, J. (2010). Chinese geography through Chinese cuisine. *Social Education, 74*(1), 17–19.

Marzano, R. (2007). *The Art and science of teaching.* Alexandria, VA: A.S.C.D.

Marzano, R., & Polluck, J.E. (2004). *Classroom instruction that works: Research based strategies.* Englewood Cliffs, N.J.: Prentice-Hall.

McGuire, M. E. (2007). What happened to social studies? The disappearing curriculum. *Phi Delta Kappan, 88*(8), 620–624.

Merriam-Webster's Collegiate Dictionary, 11th Edition thumb-notched with Win/Mac CD-ROM and Online Subscription by Merriam-Webster (Apr 2, 2011)

Mohidin, R, et al. (2009). Effective teaching methods and lecturer characteristics: A study on accounting students at the University of Malaysia Sabah. *European Journal of Social Sciences, 8*(1), 21–30.

Morris, L. (2009). Little lectures? *Innovative Higher Education, 34,* 67–68.

NAIS. (2011). *Educating for global citizenship.* Retrieved from http://www.nais.org/about/seriesdoc.cfm?ItemNumber=148793&sn.ItemNumber=146810.

National Board for Professional Teaching Standards, (1998). Retrieved Feb 1, 2011 from http://www.intime.uni.edu/model/Portuguese_Model/teacher/teac4.html.

National Center for Education Statistics. (2006). *Technology Integration in K–12.* http://projects.coe.uga.edu/ITFoundations/index.php?title=Technology_Integration_in_K–12

Pataray-Ching, J., & Kavanaugh-Anderson, D. (1998). When children pose inquiry questions that disagree with society's beliefs. *The Educational Forum, 63*(1), 73–78.

Paul, R & Elder, L. (2007). Critical thinking: the art of Socratic questioning. *Journal of Developmental Education, 31*(1), 36–37.

Rosler, B. (2008). Process drama in one fifth-grade social studies class. *Social Studies, 99*(1), 265–272.

Sanders, N. (1966). *Classroom questions: What kinds?* New York, NY: Harper & Row Publishers.

Shaftel, F. R. (1970). Role playing: An approach to meaningful social learning. *Social Education, 34*(5), 556–559.

Shaftel, F. R., & Shaftel, G. (1967). *Role-playing for social values: Decision making the social studies.* Englewood Cliffs: NJ: Prentice-Hall.

Stern, B. S., & Riley, K. L. (2001). Reflecting on the common good: Harold Rugg and the Social Reconstructionists. *The Social Studies, 92*(2), 56–59.

Sutcliff, Mark. (2010). *What makes a good lecture: A review of some recent research findings.* Retrieved from http://webcache.googleusercontent.com/search?q=cache:6s7c-JynxYgJ:wps.pearsoned.co.uk/wps/media/objects/1187/1215876/T_L/teaching10.doc+What+makes+a+good+Lecture:+A+review+of+some+recent+research&cd=1&hl=en&ct=clnk&gl=us&lr=lang_en.

The Center for Global Education. (2011). Current Projects. Retrieved from http://globaled.us/projects.asp.

Turner, Thomas N. (2010) *Drama and storytelling in teaching: Course materials for education,* 526. (Unpublished)

Ukpokodu, O. N. (2008). Fostering national and global citizenship: an example from South Africa. *Social Studies and the Young Learner, 21*(1), 15–18.

Zemelman, S., Daniels, H., & Hyde, A. (2005). *Best practice: Today's standards for teaching and learning in America's schools* (3rd ed.). Portsmouth, NH: Heinemann.

SECTION V

MEDIA, TECHNOLOGY, AND TEACHER EDUCATION

CHAPTER 23

MEDIA AND POPULAR CULTURE

Cameron White and Trenia Walker

Media brings the world into our homes. Almost everything we know about people, places, and events comes from the media. We also rely on media for entertainment and pleasure. Popular culture has become the storyteller of our generation: these stories tell us about who we are, what we believe, and what we want to be.

—(Tyner, 2003)

INTRODUCTION

Media and popular culture offer great potential for transforming social studies. A strong argument can be made that media and popular culture are very influential among our students and in all of society. Our society has made media and popular culture a cornerstone of cultural identity. It is precisely in the diverse spaces and spheres of popular culture that most of the education that matters today is taking place on a global scale (Giroux, 2004). We do need to acknowledge that popular culture is part of our lives and is very important to our society, our citizens, and especially our chil-

Contemporary Social Studies: An Essential Reader, pages 441–465
Copyright © 2012 by Information Age Publishing

dren, regardless of the debate or which end of the spectrum one subscribes to. In a society increasingly fragmented by debate, misunderstandings, and lack of consensus, perhaps popular culture remains one of the few arenas that provide a forum for common understandings, dialog, and communication (Pasek et al., 2006).

New technologies, television, movies, music and other media often provide connections among our often disconnected citizenry. We still talk at the "water cooler" about recent pop phenomena; and thus, we owe our students opportunities for critical analysis of media and popular culture. Rather than blindly accepting the "Disneyfication" or "Simpsonizing" of our students and their lives, we should use elements of popular culture as teachable opportunities. Film, television, music, literature and other forms of popular culture can provide rich opportunities for teaching and learning (Steinberg & Kincheloe, 2004).

We cannot ignore or censor popular culture as a text / tool for social studies. If we are interested in facilitating the "great" goals of social studies such critical thinking, collaboration, democracy, efficacy, and also connect with students, then media / popular culture is a natural tool for teaching and learning. Popular culture embodies a language of both critique and possibility; a language that allows students to locate themselves in history, find their own voices, and establish convictions and compassion necessary for active citizenship (Freire & Giroux, 1989).

Many contemporary social studies educators agree that the aim of social studies is to provide students with the knowledge, skills, and attitudes needed to meaningfully engage in responsible citizenship (National Council for Social Studies [NCSS], 2010); however, there is far less agreement on the best practices to achieve those goals. Further, the directive to include learning opportunities for skills and attitudes, even though they are specifically required by many states in their social studies teaching and learning standards, is often neglected by both teachers and administrators for the more tangible (and testable) knowledge component. This approach was insured by *No Child Left Behind*, which created a low-level high-stakes testing environment (Grant, 2007).

Many schools have evolved into places where inquiry and active engagement are not encouraged (White, 2011). Diane Ravitch, a former champion for the standards and accountability movement, recently acknowledged in an article entitled "The Obsession with Testing is Nuts" that the current level of testing has actually resulted in "less education" (2010). A standardized curricula, instruction, and procedures dictate little risk-taking. Teachers and administrators have become afraid to drift from the norm. Teachers often even state that they don't have time to teach anything but the mandated curriculum. The accountability and achievement movement has severely limited what can occur in schools in the name or teaching and learning. For many students, a bland and boring social education has thus emerged (Hursh, 2008).

This environment has had a deleterious effect on students; they are disengaged, unprepared, and uninspired (Giroux, 1996). This has serious implication for public and social life in the United States given the necessity of an engaged and informed citizenry (Tupper, 2009). The current "supply-side" education approach, or the "trickle-down" of knowledge to students within an institutional environment, has undermined the schools' role in the training for democratic citizenship (Kincheloe, 2001). It is important that social studies educators recognize that in the twenty-first century, an educational setting cannot be limited to merely the classroom. Approaches to learning must be "integrated with all aspects of living, from work to entertainment to leisure" (Goldfarb, 2002, p. 21). We live in a participatory culture that requires us to contribute and produce, not merely consume (Jenkins, 2006a).

Media and popular culture, when used effectively by teachers, can help counter the negative trend and improve student engagement. If we are truly interested in students learning and applying social literacy knowledge and skills, then we must make stronger efforts toward integrating real world connections in teaching and learning. These connections allow students to develop the skills needed to construct knowledge. Media and popular culture can enhance a transformative social studies education by providing these connections.

Increasingly the nexus of power in the world can be found in media. As both cause and effect of media's power, we experience the world now primarily through popular entertainment, or popular culture (Danesi, 2008). As a result, media education and media literacy are even more important. These literacy issues are increasingly addressed in the position statements of international and national education organizations such as National Council for the Teachers of English (NCTE) and the National Council for the Social Studies (NCSS), and many states have included them into the content standards. Unfortunately, these issues have proved difficult to assess and have therefore, for the most part, been ignored (Walker, 2010). This has been the case for most of the skills and/or attitude standards in states such as Texas and Washington.

We are missing the opportunity to strengthen the preparation of young people to, as Thomas Jefferson said, assume the office of citizen. According to Jefferson, "the qualifications of self-governance are not innate. They are the result of habit and long training" (Letter 1797). Integrating popular culture into social studies teaching and learning may be an effective way to provide skill and attitude training to prepare students for productive democratic citizenship. Given the power and pervasiveness of popular culture it should no longer be written off as innocuous fluff (Walker, 2006).

Gee (2008) wrote, " young people sometimes seem to engage in deeper learning in their popular culture than they do in school, especially schools devoted to skill-and-drill in the service of passing standardized tests" (p. 1024). Popular culture belongs in the classroom as both pedagogy and text. Students should learn about, and through, popular culture.

Media and popular culture belongs in the classrooms as both pedagogy and text and can facilitate opportunities for common dialog and understanding. Popular culture often provides a context for connections to the world and sense making in the world. This dialog and common understanding in media and popular culture can be used to enhance social education (White, 2003). Again, despite the often negative view adults often have of various media and popular culture, there seems little today that we get excited over and encourages social discourse more than this form of culture. Allowing students to bring in their cultural choices as they investigate issues, make connections, construct knowledge, and engage in sense making may very well be a threat to the entrenched (Daspit & Weaver, 2000).

Media and popular culture can be used effectively as alternative texts particularly in social studies education. These alternative texts provide an opportunity for the common understandings, dialog / communication, cultural identity, motivation and context / connections. The authors will problematize their presentation of media and popular culture with contemporary concerns such as information transmission, media literacy, technology, globalization, coverage versus depth, problem solving / inquiry, and moral panics. We will provide practical applications and specific examples of current media and popular culture, focusing on critical inquiry in all areas of teaching and learning including curriculum, instruction, and assessment.

CONNECTING CONTENT AND CONTEMPORARY ISSUES

Several important concepts and themes in social studies content may be more powerfully taught (and learned) by integrating media and popular culture into instructional events. These concepts and themes include:

- Economic, market, and consumer issues
- Cultural preferences and social factors
- Ideology, dominance, and agendas
- Popular appeal and mass culture
- Moral panic and popular culture

These issues suggest using and analyzing media and popular culture in critical analysis of social concerns. They should definitely be addressed, particularly as part of the promotion of critical social education, that which promotes multiple perspectives and critical investigation. A related concern is that these issues are often employed as reasons to belittle or demean popular culture often leading to censorship.

Economic, market, and consumer issues affect the state of popular culture. The issues of mass market and what sells often dictate kind and quality of music and other popular culture. Many even suggest that the idea of mass produced culture for profit limits creativity and choice regarding options for the public. A few corporations dominate the media industry perhaps suggesting that these have become culture industries, creating our culture for us, less for creativity and pleasure sake than for corporate profits. The globalization of market ideals has often also narrowed the global media market, often at the expense of the popular culture and media in various societies (Crothers, 2007).

Related to the influence of corporations is the idea of cultural imperialism. Popular culture (at least in global sales) is dominated by the U. S. and Britain. As a result, global cultural preferences are often dominated by the United States. Societal factors also influence popular culture, which is perhaps the reason for the success of western popular culture throughout the world. Despite the power of the global popular culture industry, class and ethnicity can often provide a strong influence on trends and even sales in popular culture (Crothers, 2007).

A particular critique of popular culture is the perceived ideology often inherent within in reinforcing dominant values and the agenda of those in power. Many suggest that that which is popular only becomes accepted so as to ensure the status quo. In other words, the hegemonic powers would not allow much popular culture or media to question or challenge entrenched societal values. Despite the perceived success of this agenda, much popular music has successfully usurped the system and affected societal change.

Popular culture as one vital component is perhaps one of the few remaining avenues for possible common dialog and understanding. If nothing else, it often provides a context for connections to the world and sense making in the world. Passion and intrinsic appeal is somehow inherent in popular culture. This dialog and common understanding in popular culture and media can be used to enhance critical social studies education (White & Walker, 2008). Exploring popular culture of the times or about the times can really assist in providing context and connections for students, particularly if they are allowed to compare with their popular culture.

Perhaps the more intriguing issue regarding media and popular culture is the idea of moral panic and the threat to society. As a result, new popular culture is often subject to condemnation, censorship and regulation by those is power in schools or society at large. For example, from the early experiences in pop such as Elvis to punk to heavy metal to hip hop, music has been questioned regarding its legitimacy and impact on popular and society. Music is often viewed as promoting antisocial behavior and attitudes in popular, therefore many feel it must be controlled or at the very least ignored. Thus, application of popular music in schools is rarely found as it is perceived to do little in meeting traditional goals. What one often finds in schools is a negative reaction to kid culture in whatever form (music, video games, new technologies, etc.) through stereotypes, banning, and demeaning acts and comments. Media and popular culture as very vibrant examples not only serve as a reflection of the times, but as is evidenced from the social history of the late twentieth century, can also be very active social forces.

Economic factors, such as the recent recession and socio-economic differences, influence popular culture. The prosperity that emerged following WWII enabled music to flourish as a dynamic force. An essential component of popular culture is knowledge and awareness of music fads and trends. The economic climate of the times (whichever period one mentions) is again often reflected in the media that is popular. Economic and social issues are particularly evident in the music of the late sixties, early seventies, early and late eighties, and much of the nineties.

Technology has also provided an impetus for the development of popular culture as a societal force. Developments in the latter half of the twentieth century not only brought music to the masses, but they also enabled new and innovative sounds and techniques to be introduced. The electric guitar, synthesizers, and computers have had quite a substantial impact on the evolution of music. Television, MTV, CD's, and the internet can all be investigated regarding their influence on music, popular culture, and society. Technology has become a vital theme in society. Using technology as an agent in popular culture can really facilitate the idea of social efficacy since technology and technology issues are so prevalent in today's society. Twitter and other social media as used recently in Tunisia and Egypt are examples.

One of the most controversial issues related to the growth of music as popular culture is that of the influence of industry and the idea of corporate profits as the driving force for music. Central to issues with popular culture is the connection between marketing and popular culture in the late twentieth century to the present. Artists often provide empowering social efficacy messages, but are also subject to personal sales. This often contradictory issue can provide much fodder for debate in the teaching and learning process. Issues related to capitalism, globalization, music choices, hegemony as the driving force, marketing, and how each relates to social education could easily be integrated in schooling as we attempt to facilitate critical and active participation in society. Integrating discussions and debates regarding these issues are meaningful strategies for the classroom.

Integrating popular culture has great potential in promoting critical social education. Despite the lack of its use in schools, popular culture has had a profound effect as a force for social change. Instead of dismissing its potential, schools would be wise to work diligently on integrating popular culture into the teaching and learning process if for no other reason than that there is a desperate need to improve the perceived relevance of schooling (at least in the eyes of our young people).

POPULAR CULTURE AS PEDAGOGY: GAMES AND TELEVISION

School is un-engaging for many students today (Ravitch, 2009; White & Walker, 2008). This is especially true for students in social studies; students think that the classes are boring and the material covered is irrelevant (Hobbs, 2005; Loewen, 1995; Chiodo & Byford, 2004; Russell & Waters, 2010). Generally when it comes to learning, teachers often have to be more concerned about covering the tested content than about either the learner or the principles of democratic citizenship. Unfortunately, as the 2006 National Assessment of Educational Progress (NAEP) scores in social studies content areas such as U.S. History reveal, merely teaching the content that will be on the test is not effective. Researchers suggest that there may be a connection between students' lack of engagement with both content and learning with a lack of enjoyment in learning (Ravitch, 2010, White & Walker, 2008).

Enjoyment and motivation are linked. Student learning is contingent on a willingness to engage and to persevere, and that this will not be the case unless the learning task is considered potentially enjoyable. This will produce the motivation to begin, and once experienced as enjoyable, persistence will result. The emotional connection to the material may expedite the construction of meaning, and can be especially useful in the social studies since, as Loewen (1995) explains "[e]motion is the glue that a causes history to stick" (p. 294). Using popular culture that is important in the lives of students in a classroom is motivational for the students since it gives them a sense of ownership of both the material and the learning (Walker, 2006). Two mediums of popular culture that can be used effectively in social studies teaching and learning are video and computer games, and television.

Video and Computer Games

Play has long been considered to increase motivation in learning (Rieber, 2001). According to Gee (2003) video games are the leading form of entertainment for the K–12 generation. The Pew Research Center's Internet and American Life Project, conducted from November 1, 2007—February 5, 2008, surveyed 1,102 youth ages 12–17 about their video game habits. Researchers found that gaming in this age group is pervasive and nearly universal: 99% of the boys in the study and 97% of the girls play video games. Gaming is also social: 76% of the respondents reported playing games with others at least some of the time. In the two years since the survey was conducted by the Pew Research Center, the number of people playing games has increased according the Entertainment Software Association's (ESA) 2010 Essential Facts Report. According to the ESA study, 67% of American households play video or computer games.

Contemporary video games are long, complex, and difficult; however, as Gee (2008) points out, "if they could not be learned they could not be played and in fact it has been argued that such games recruit learning as a form of pleasure" (p. 1024). Games today require a substantial cognitive investment from players. Gamers learn to think like scientists: "hypothesize, probe the world, get a reaction, reflect on the results, and re-probe to get better results" (Gee, 2008, p. 1024). Squire (2008) warns educators that the gaming generation will have a difficult time adjusting to "traditional schooling with its grammar of teachers text as authority and student as product, when outside school this generation relives historical eras, leads civilizations, conducts forensic investigations or can earn a real wage by buying and selling virtual currencies" (p. 639).

Fuller and Jenkins (1995) explain that educators must develop an understanding of how games are transforming previous forms rather than how they fit into the traditional curriculum. Video or computer game play may provide learners the same, or even improved, skills and attitudes that are sought in the social studies classroom through traditional instructions strategies such as simulations, role-play, and cooperative group activities. Game play in *Civilization, SimCity, Rise of Nations*, and even *Oregon Trail* centers on overlapping choices and consequences. According to Parker (2009), deliberation in the decision-making process is "probably the most important foundation of democratic citizenship" (p. 73). He goes on to say that these skills are often not intrinsic and must be "taught, practiced, and learned" (p. 73). Playing games such as *Civilization* and *World of Warcraft* are highly motivational for students as well as offering opportunities to practice decision making skills. Game play decisions are taken very seriously as they may affect life and death (albeit in a virtual world). Also, players' decision making in these games alters the play and therefore results in a "real sense of agency, ownership, and control; it is their game" (Gee, 2008, p. 1025).

Researchers who were involved with the Pew Research Center's Internet and American Life Project (2008) examined specifically the question of whether civic development among young people is connected to civic gaming experiences such as "creating a virtual nation, working with others cooperatively, expanding one's social network online, and helping less experienced players play games" (np). Among those surveyed, young people reported encountering the following civic gaming experiences *at least sometimes*: 76% reported helping others; 52% reported thinking about moral or ethical issues; 44% reported learning about a problem in society; 43%

reported making decisions about how a community, city, or nation should be run; and, 30% organized or managed game or affinity groups. Further, those who have the most civic game play experiences report a much higher level of civic and political engagement than those who have not had these experiences. Among those who had the most experiences, 70% go online to get information about politics and current events compared to 55% of those who have the least number of civic game play experiences; 70% of those with the most experience have raised money for charity in the past 12 months compared to 51%; 69% are committed to civic participation compared to 57%, and 15% of those with the most civic game play experiences have participated in a protest, march, or demonstration compared to only 6% of those who have had the last civic gaming experiences. Respondents who reported playing games socially tended to be more engaged than those who played individually. Interestingly, social game play is correlated to civic engagement but only when the players are in the room together and not to online play.

In addition to democratic skill building and improved attitudes toward civic engagement, social studies educators should consider using video games to improve spatial cognition skills (Feng, Spence, & Pratt, 2007; Spence, Yu, Feng, & Marshman, 2009). Spatial cognition is particularly important to the study of geography. According to the *International Encyclopedia of the Social and Behavioral Sciences*, the use and design of maps and other geographic information products depends, in part, on human understanding of depicted spatial relations (Smelser & Baltes, 2001, p. 14772). Researchers have generally accepted that there are gender differences in spatial cognition (Kimura, 1999; Terlecki & Newcombe, 2005; Voyer, Voyer & Bryden, 1995). Feng, Spence, and Pratt (2007) found that there were no biological causes for these differences. One reason that differences in these cognitive skills are found in adults may be the differences in the play as children (Baenninger & Newcombe, 1989). Boys' game play, such as building structures and sports games, often exercise spatial abilities, while girl games generally do not. More recently, video and computer game play has been associated with improved performance on a variety of high-level spatial tasks (Law, Pellegrino, & Hunt, 1993). Many of the greatest improvements have been seen among those who play first-person shooter games (Green & Bavelier, 2007). Unfortunately, these games are more popular among males than females (Pew Research Center's Internet and American Life Project, 2008; Terlecki & Newcombe, 2005).

Spence, Yu, Feng, and Marshman (2009) conducted a research study that showed that when females and males started at the same ability level in mental rotation tasks, playing video games for ten hours a week improved both groups at the same level. They experimented with two types of video games, a puzzle game (*Tetris*) and a first-person shooter game (*Medal of*

Honor: Pacific Assault). Playing *Tetris* produced no significant changes in visual attentiveness, the primary factor underlying spatial cognition (Feng, Spence, & Pratt, 2007; Spence, Yu, Feng, & Marshman, 2009). *Tetris* players focus primarily on one object at a time. Players are not required to detect, discriminate, select, or track objects over a wide field of view (Spence, Yu, Feng, & Marshman, 2009, p. 1099). First-person shooter games on the other hand, require that players pay close attention to multiple objects. While players focus on their character's field of view, they also must be constantly aware of what is going on in the virtual world just outside their view. Players must be aware of actions and events of other characters that affect the game play. Virtual worlds also require virtual maps and players must simultaneously manage navigation screens to stay on course. Good games, according to Gee (2008), encourage players to "to think laterally (not just linearly)" (p. 1025). Spence, Yu, Feng, and Marshman (2009) found that playing complex first-person shooter type video or computer games will improve visual attentiveness, and therefore spatial cognition. These same researchers found that game play can erase gender differences in spatial cognition in adults. Even more encouraging was the finding that even non-video-game players realized large gains after only ten hours of training and play.

Social studies educators have long incorporated game activities into students' teaching and learning experiences (Devlin-Scherer & Sardone, 2010). There are classic, non-electronic simulation games such as *BafaBafa* and review games based on classic television game shows such as *Jeopardy*. Video and computer games may also be used for these classroom activities as well as and many more complex activities. Spatial thinking, often included as one of the social studies skills standards that educators are required to cover, may be taught with video games. Spatial cognition will aid students' mastery of geography skills such as map making and *cartographic* visualization skills. Educators must verify the ratings, or age-appropriateness, of the video or computer game selection as they would before using any form of media prior to using it in the classroom. Students may be asked to consider the pros and cons of the various ratings systems and the censorship implications.

Television

Many people consider broadcast television, almost since its inception, as an educative tool (Buckingham, 2007). Broadcasting opened doors to experience for viewers and was seen as reality, never as constructed. Educational researchers advocated the use of broadcasts as a valuable teaching tool for students who were disenchanted (Beastall, 2006). Buckingham (2007) writes that early research on the use of broadcasting in education cited the "magical power" of television to transfix children (p. 54). According to Scupham (1964), the "immediacy of television" was most appropriate for students who were academically challenged, those who "accept and understand life" in "concrete terms" (p. 8). Buckingham (2007) associates this view with the deficit model of the working-class child for whom television was alleged to compensate for his or her "innate limitations in intellectual ability" (p. 55). Therefore, unsurprisingly, educational broadcasting initially was far more concentrated in lower-achieving secondary schools to target perceived underachievers (Beastall, 2006; Goldfarb, 2002).

According to Goldfarb (2002) the Ford Foundation played a major role in the direction that early educational television moved. The Foundation was one of the initial supporters of using televised broadcasts in schools in the United States. Their focus was not on innovation but rather on efficiency. They sought to introduce broadcasts and standardize curriculum and pedagogy in order to reduce educational staff in the schools. Interestingly, the funding that they contributed to educational television meant that it would not stay within the confines of the schools but rather quickly infiltrated public and domestic spaces as well. This gave them a pedagogical authority outside the classroom, one that gave viewers information.

This view of broadcast television held for nearly a half century. Goldfarb (2002) suggests that this is now facing significant challenge. Television has become the "modality of choice" even in educational settings where "high levels in achievement in reading and writing are assumed to be the norm" (Goldfarb, 2002, p. 20). For social studies educators the value of the television extends beyond the belief in the magic of, and the inherent authority in, the broadcast itself. The notion that merely showing televised images to unengaged and underperforming students will communicate some real knowledge is the lowest form of pedagogical practice. Those who limit the use of broadcasts to this purpose are missing an opportunity to hone critical thinking skills, long associated with decision-making ability, a key to responsible citizenship (Parker, 2009).

Johnson (2006) writes that popular television broadcasts today are more complex than earlier versions and require viewers to develop higher levels of thinking skills in order to make sense of them. According to Johnson (2006), popular television shows have "increased the cognitive work they demand from their audience, exercising the mind in ways that would have been unheard of 30 years ago" (p. 62). For example, Johnson (2006) explains that the same cognitive skills long attributed to reading print text— "attention, patience, retention, parsing of narrative threads"—now are required to read televisual texts (p. 64). Critical engagement with television is increasing (Caughie, 2006) which requires unprecedented interactivity between broadcast and audience (Jermyn & Holmes, 2006). Engaging student in critical analysis activities such as debates, group discussions, or history fair like projects can enhance these endeavors.

The interactivity required by video and computer games is much higher than viewing broadcasts, however, there is far less passivity possible with the televisual today than ever before (Caughie, 2006; Jermyn & Holmes, 2006; Johnson, 2006. Many of the current shows require viewers to track multiple threads that run through the narrative in order to make sense of complex broadcasts. These are shows that "force you to be intelligent" (Johnson, 2006, p. 63). Johnson (2006) makes a distinction between the broadcasts that require intellectual work on the part of viewers, and intelligent shows where the words and actions of the characters express intelligence (i.e. *Big Bang Theory* and *Outsourced*). These shows require viewers to pay attention to the narrative but do not force them to remember or interact with it: "you don't challenge your mind any more than you challenge your body by watching Monday Night Football" (Johnson, 2006, p. 64). Several states include critical analysis as a social studies skills standard. Educators may use popular television shows as texts for analyzing controversial issues such as racism, sexism, classism, and so on. Contemporary television shows, especially those that are popular among young people, may increase student engagement in learning.

Even the much maligned relatively new genre, reality shows, requires audience interactivity. Viewers of shows such as *House Hunters* follow home buyers into three houses, one of which they will make an offer to purchase. The audience can invest a great deal of the show's 30-minute total broadcast time learning about the purchasers. Then viewers can compare their own personal stories and preferences to those of the home-buyers and then predict which of the three houses they will choose. In this reality show, viewers do not influence the purchasing decisions; however, in some reality shows such as *American Idol* and *The Bachelor*, viewers do get a say. In fact, they deliberate on the 'issues' at hand and get a 'vote' that influences who "wins" and who "loses" on the show. A viewer's decision-making process is often the same for choosing an 'American Idol' as it is for choosing a member of the House of Representatives, albeit with far lower consequences for a bad choice. Discussing and writing on the decision-making process for voting on these shows and in elections is definitely warranted.

Broadcasts not only have the potential for improving critical thinking and decision-making, two vital skills for civic competence, but also for connecting like-minded people into interest groups. The ability to collaborate effectively as a member of a group is a fundamental citizenship skill (Beal, Bolick, & Martorella, 2009). Fans of broadcasts often use digital technologies to form virtual communities. Fan culture, once considered to be the domain for science fiction fanatics (e.g., *Trekkies*), is now acceptable participation (Jenkins, 2006b). Fans are no longer thought to be merely "cultural dupes who passively ingest mainstream media" (Black, 2008, p. 594). Fans join others in fandom groups that then become part of the larger participatory culture (Jenkins, 2006b). Social studies teachers may ask students to extrapolate from the membership requirements for the virtual communities they belong to the rights and responsibilities of citizens in the United States. This will also offer students the opportunity to bring in their personal popular culture as examples or representations which facilitates better connection for teaching and learning.

Jenkins, et al.(2006c) explains that participatory culture is "emerging as the culture absorbs and responds to the explosion of new media technologies that make it possible for average consumers to archive, annotate, appropriate, and recirculate media content in powerful new ways" (p. 10). Today many of us, at least in the United States, are not only consumers of media but also producers. It is the interactive nature of new media is both cause and effect of participatory culture. Jermyn and Holmes (2006) point out that new technologies, especially the digital video disk (DVD) and the digital video recorder (DVR) along with multi-channel television, have changed the way we engage with film and television: "increasing numbers of viewers are being 'empowered' and encouraged to become television connoisseurs as deeply passionate, reflective, and knowledgeable about TV as film buffs are about cinema" (p. 55). They go on to explain that telephiles often invest in the texts they have become fans of, owning collections and becoming 'media historians' (Jermyn & Holmes, 2006).

In a participatory culture (one where we have a stake and increased input) it is "We the People" who make the decisions from the bottom up rather than the top down. Participatory culture erects very few barriers to prevent or discourage people from civic engagement. As a result, Gee (2004) and others point out, the new participatory cultures are ideal learning environments. He refers to these informal educative opportunities as "affinity spaces" and favors them because they are "sustained by common endeavors that bridge differences in age, class, race, gender, and educational level, and because people can participate in various ways according to their skills and interests, because they depend on peer-to-peer teaching with each participant constantly motivated to acquire new knowledge or refine their existing skills, and because they allow each participant to feel like an expert while tapping the expertise of others" (Gee, 2004, as quoted by Jenkins, 2006a, p. 177). Black (2008) points out that online affinity spaces, where more and more young people are spending their time, offer effective learning environments. One reason is because they are organized around a common interest or activity so anyone can join. Members bring a range of knowledge and understanding to the space which offers multiple opportunities for members to both teach and learn (Gee, 2004). Group membership and participation skills are major factors in responsible democratic citizenship.

Social studies teachers today have an unprecedented range of popular culture texts and genres to use in constructing teaching and learning opportunities for students. Often students have extensive educative experiences with these texts outside school and educators need to understand and appreciate the variety of social and cultural venues in which the experiences take place (Kincheloe, 2001). Educators, especially those in the social studies, must recognize these experiences as legitimate means for building the skills and attitudes of responsible citizenship and civic engagement.

POPULAR CULTURE AS TEXT

Music

Effective integration of media and popular culture in schools is definitely improving Obviously, music programs help students develop into more well-rounded human beings. An appreciation of music and art, and other media is vital for critical social education, yet often one finds that funding for the arts is the first to be cut in times of financial crisis. And now, with the emphasis increasingly placed on achievement of "essential" knowledge one often finds time for the arts being cut as well (Eisner, 2004).

There are also instances of teachers (acting in isolation mostly) who integrate popular culture into their teaching environment. Some teachers play classical or jazz as background music as students work on assignments. Others allow students to bring in examples of their own to play during these assignment times, or even as free time sharing. Perhaps the most effective use is when a teacher actually integrates music into the teaching and learning process. Some social studies teachers, for example, have used music very effectively to demonstrate historical periods. Sample music integration examples include units on music and war, music and postwar America, the labor movement and music, social issues and music, and global cultures and music.

Many of these examples, while at least using music, are teacher directed with the teachers usually choosing and demonstrating the music examples. This is definitely a first step in meaningful integration—that of modeling, but critical social efficacy necessitates more student active involvement and choice (Brooks & Brooks, 2001). Critical social efficacy requires that we engage in a more sincere effort at promoting the context and connections needed to ensure a more relevant learning experience. Allowing students to be involved in the social construction of meaning in their world is a vital step.

Keeping with social studies examples, using current events and social issues to provide context and connections for today and for the study of the past enhances the links necessary for student efficacy and empowerment.

Popular music is a natural tool for achieving these goals. But it must be students' popular music. We can demonstrate ours as examples and modeling, but again, allowing students to include theirs in the teaching and learning process takes it that needed step. Only then can we hope to facilitate critical social efficacy.

Most music genres or individual artists contain examples of songs that contain social commentary or historical references. Many people are under the assumption that social commentary in music reached its peak in the late sixties and early seventies. Punk, Hip Hop, and Grunge are genres from the eighties through today that provide considerable social commentary and historical references. And Pop still has much to say regarding social efficacy. And these are often the genres that most interest our students. While we may just not understand the music of today, we cannot become our parents and blindly dismiss its potential for critical social efficacy. Remember the early folk and rock days.

Many forms of popular culture emerge as commentary or resistance toward more mainstream culture and society. Perhaps no better example of this exists than in pop music. From its earliest days pop has been viewed as cutting edge, crossing the boundaries, and a threat to the values and morals of society. Little Richard, Elvis, the Beatles, Bob Dylan, NWA, Nirvana, Green Day, Acid—Pop, Heavy Metal, Disco, Punk, MTV, Grunge and Thrash, Rave, and Hip Hop have all witnessed their detractors and have been viewed at one time or another as threats to the basic social fabric.

Through its history, pop like all forms of popular culture has not only served as a reflection of the times, it has been a catalyst for critical social efficacy and societal change. Several themes can be used to integrate pop music into teaching and learning for social efficacy in schools. Pop music can be a very powerful theme as students investigate issues such as ethnicity and the struggle for equality, population growth, economics, technology, business and industry, efficacy and empowerment within the context of social history (White, 2003). This focus in itself would provide the necessary relevance students need to facilitate intrinsically a love of learning leading to effective social efficacy.

Perhaps the most relevant issue surrounding music (at least regarding schooling) is its role as societal force; as this relates most directly to the issue of social efficacy. Regardless of the genre, popular music remains a vibrant cultural phenomena that reflects societal issues but can also have a proactive impact. Exploring the role of music in reflecting and impacting societal change can be a very motivating experience for kids in their endeavor to make sense of the world. The idea that music can not only be a device for entertainment, but one that provides social commentary and perhaps even a "call to arms" for change enables it to be a powerful tool for social efficacy.

"New" Technologies

A recent Sunday edition of the comic strip *Pearls before Swine* is a perfect illustration of technology saturation. Rat is at the computer working on his resume. "Ping!" An email arrives that he must read. It has a YouTube attachment that must be watched. It stirs questions necessitating his consulting Wikipedia. Additional questions emerge that make a Google search also necessary. Once he has images and information, he sees the need to post an update on Facebook. While posting he receives a friend request from a person he does not know, suggesting the need for another Google search. All of this leads him to write about his findings on his blog. He finally realizes that he must get back to working on his resume and clicks back, just in time to hear "Ping!" He has received another email which takes him off again. Sound familiar? All of these new technologies can be integrated into social studies through individual, small group, or whole class projects.

The iPad, eReaders, Netbooks, iPods, and smartphones are a few of the latest technology innovations that are engulfing many parts of the world. The recent unveiling of the iPad made almost as much news as the iPhone, including front covers of major newspapers and magazines. The finding of the prototype new generation iPhone in a California bar made national news. Thus the debate continues... is all of this new stuff really making life easier, or is much of it just constant marketing so that consumers long to purchase the next new gadget? And what about video game systems, and what role will/should these new technologies have in education? Perhaps these could be questions for discussion in social studies classes.

Recent reports indicate that kids under the age of eighteen are no longer watching television, and that their first choices are video games, their cell phones, or the Internet (Johnson, 2006). These new technologies are as much popular culture as movies, music or television. In fact, these new technologies are directly affecting all the other forms of popular culture. Music is now mostly downloaded on computers and played through MP3 devices. Much the same can be said about movies and television. Many people are choosing to download favorite shows or movies from the web onto computers or iPods. The video game market makes more money than the film industry. Using these texts and tools rather than censoring them can only enhance an integration of multiple perspective and learning styles.

Technology conversations are now in the norm at the water cooler. Have you seen the new app? Did you hear about the iPhone mishap? What level did you reach on ...? Were you able to DVR ...? Have you seen the new viral video on YouTube? Many of us engage in these conversations several times daily. Technology innovation and use is now the popular culture of choice, and all other popular culture is adapting to the new technology tools. In fact, it is really often about the tools rather than the video, music, or film.

Every aspect of our lives is being affected. One example, a recent report stated that in five years, the entire population of the world will have some type of access to smartphones, essentially handheld computers integrated with a mobile telephone (National Public Radio, http://www.npr.org/, February 2011). Much of our time is now spent using new technologies. And for many of us the smartphone or iPod have become appendages, as ubiquitous as anything else in recent memory. We read and often complain about students multitasking, but we are all becoming quite adept at this at least perceived required talent of the twenty-first century. Should we celebrate this, accept it and move on? Or should we question this as some challenge to social development and meaningful human endeavor?

We better embrace new technologies now, through application and critical analysis, and social studies is a natural fit. Some students are already way beyond their teachers, and this really offers a possibility for the classroom. Embracing these new technologies rather than dismissing or censoring them can pave the way for more student-centered approaches to teaching and learning. And whether we like it or not, this is how students engage and ultimately learn.

Beyond the use of these technologies in schools, they enable critical analysis, collaboration, and debate—skills we need to embrace more. For example, these skills are vital in social studies (and society), and the theme of technology is ripe for connecting with students. What has rarely occurred in schools is using technology to focus on rights and responsibilities. What is also rarely done is to allow critical investigation of the web. Issues such as appropriateness, marketing, information as knowledge, and bias offer great learning potential, but are usually ignored or deemed inappropriate. These new technologies can also foster collaboration through problem- and project-based instruction.

What about the "issues" in integrating these new technologies in schools? Generally only the "safe" ones are allowed. SMART boards are currently the technology of choice for those who can acquire them and are viewed as safe, probably due to their being teacher-controlled. Much of the technology embraced by students is censored or banned from teaching and learning. Many schools have often only allowed very limited access to sites on the Internet. YouTube is censored, Wikipedia is banned, and web 2.0 tools are rarely integrated.

It is all about the devices—that is what the media hoopla is all about. It is what we are literally "buying" into. The smartphone wars are crazy, as new iPhone launches are societal events. At some point educators need to accept the fact that there is great potential for their use in teaching and learning. Texting, tweeting, polling, Internet access, GPS, maps, Google apps, and using other apps all have meaningful potential and offer ways that naturally connect to students. We have all read recent reports regarding the amount of texting and even tweeting occurring among young people. Texting, tweeting, and Facebook are now their communication tools of choice, each readily accessible through smartphones. The immediate future suggests increased use of them; there are already great examples of schools allowing and teachers integrating smartphones in teaching and learning activities.

Netbooks, eReaders, small laptops, and hybrid devices such as the iPad are likewise the present for many and the future for most. Many schools and even entire states are looking into using such devices to replace traditional resources such as textbooks and the one-computer classroom. Likewise, innovations such as Flip cameras, digital capability on smartphones, and numerous video uploading sites are facilitating the incredible growth of online video. Again, media hype exists with these devices as well, but the educational potential is also evident.

The Internet has resources and tools that can definitely enhance teaching and learning. Web 2.0 tools are excellent for classroom use as they generally are free and only require a computer and Internet access. Google has numerous tools that have great potential for the classroom. Beyond the information sites, Google Docs and Google Sites allow for very creative collaborative project development. Blogs, Nings, and wikis are social networking sites that can be established for classroom sharing and project development. Prezi and SlideShare are two tools that allow for online presentation development. Polls can be conducted using tools such as Poll Everywhere and PollDaddy. Screencasting can be used to demonstrate the use and analysis of websites. Each of these can be explored through web searching or finding various web 2.0 sites.

Facebook and Twitter are increasingly social media of choice (see recent reports on world crises). Recently Facebook overtook Google as the most accessed web tool in the U.S. on a daily basis. While many schools censor the use of these tools, schools and individual classes are increasingly implementing these and other social networking sites. A quick search focusing on Facebook or Twitter and "education" or "use in the classroom" results in interesting student-centered ideas. A recent cover story in *Time* magazine (May 20, 2010) dealt with the popularity of Facebook and issues tied to Internet use and privacy. These tools are often the most immediate method for many to post breaking news (Michael Jackson, Iran protests).

Focusing specifically on web 2.0 and social networking, Classroom 2.0 and other sites such as Ning for Education have been established to facilitate integration with teaching and learning. Such sites keep up with new technologies, resources, and additional links to enhance new technologies for education. They also do not steer away from the controversies and debates; they provide additional links and suggestions dealing with these issues. Even many professional education organizations are now suggesting better use of social networking in the classrooms (National School Boards Association, National Education Association, National Council for the Social Studies).

A new viral video is often the rage among students and is in the news and online almost daily (Lady Gaga is the first to have over 1 billion YouTube hits). Students are choosing this popular culture instead of television and even movies because they can be active participants. Music artists often post their new video online as a method of marketing new projects. Students are doing the same thing by posting self-made films, music videos, documentaries, and commentaries.

There are many digital video sites on the web, but YouTube is the best known. Its use is rife with controversy as there are many inappropriate videos found there. Regardless, YouTube offers many valuable resources that can be meaningful in classrooms. YouTube is used constantly by students to upload their own homemade videos and to view the latest viral video. There are many instances of schools and classrooms establishing their own YouTube channels for projects. There is also TeacherTube for more traditional educational video.

Despite the reservations, online video has great potential for the classroom, especially if it is student-centered. And there are many sites that enable the capturing of individual online video for use in the classroom such as Media Converter and Snagit. Please see the online videos listed at the end of the article. Many were developed by students focusing on technology and learning for the twenty-first century.

Perhaps the technology that is affecting current popular culture the most is video games. Video game platforms are themselves popular culture as competition is fierce between the Wii, PlayStation, and Xbox, not to mention handheld gaming devices. "Edutainment" has been used in the classroom for a long time with games such as *Oregon Trail* and *Carmen San Diego*. There are many educational video games that can be integrated meaningfully in the classroom. Examples include *SimCity*, *Civilization*, and *Quest Atlantis*. Many video games are obviously not appropriate for classroom use, but the concept and interactive nature need to be investigated.

Virtual world applications such as *The Sims* have been around for some time. Online sites such as *Second Life* offer users access to whole new worlds through personal avatars. As a result, many schools have established islands in *Second Life* for innovative learning through simulations and role play. Again, controversies exist with such tools, and as a result an education or student-based version of *Second Life* is now available online. A review of a recent game, *Red Dead Redemption*, stated that not only is it one of the best video games ever developed, but it also may be the best movie of the year. And the popularity of *Rock Band Beatles* brought generations together. Video games make more money than the film industry in this country. Ignoring them as inappropriate for the classroom is a mistake as discussions about violence, gender, marketing, skill development, and social interaction can be applied. Integrating education or theme-oriented games can also provide connections to and for students.

Downloading is a process that is now part of our lives. Increasingly, downloading popular culture such as music, movies, and books will become commonplace. Downloading sites such as iTunes are replacing our traditional ways of purchasing music. Specialty 'record and music stores' have been relegated to history, and even stores like Best Buy are cutting their inventory for CD's to almost nothing. The same can be said for books. With eReaders such as the Kindle and the iPad, print-based texts may soon be difficult to find. Google is attempting to digitize thousands of books to establish an online library. There are fewer bookstores than ever and print-based newspapers are disappearing. While this is all a bit problematic, having potential access to thousands of books on a small device is appealing, if only for its portability. Devices such as these (and laptops for all) are the future of our classrooms.

Reform is consistently the talk in education circles, and it is increasingly a focus in media and society in general. Educators are often subjected to reactionary approaches to educational reform—the next new thing is all too familiar. Debate rages regarding standards, testing, and achievement. Technology is popular culture, but it is also reforming education and impacting how students learn. New technologies and yes, even the technologies that some adults are not comfortable with, also have great potential for teaching and learning. These are the technologies that many students use on a daily basis. What will be the next new technology?

CONCLUSION

Media and popular culture can make a difference for our students in their learning experience (White & Walker, 2008). What is needed is the understanding that any society can only progress if it moves beyond transmission ideals and the status quo. We must recognize that the growing restrictions and accountability movements in the U. S. only serve to undermine participatory democracy. Harping on non-issues, prison and punishment mentality, the mythology of America as world savior, corporate and military welfare, and unbridled market globalization are antithetical to social justice. Creating a world of caring and compassion through social justice requires the cultivation of the human spirit, the nourishment of the imagination, and the impulse for self-expression (Ayers, Quinn, & Stovall, 2008).

We must not integrate media and popular culture for its own sake and to hopefully placate our troubled youth. We must provide opportunities for in-depth analysis of societal issues through media and popular culture, thus leading to social efficacy. We cannot ignore the issues regarding the economic and political factors possibly driving the choices we are given. The ideas of culture, culture icons, objectification, and social justice should be explored through in-depth inquiry, problem solving and critical thinking. Using a Disney movie or a *Simpsons* episode just because the children like them is not enough.

Teachers and others interested in social efficacy and social justice within social studies must realize that neutrality is impossible. What is important is creating a classroom atmosphere where students and teachers are empowered to question and critically analyze social studies issues and themes. It is perfectly fine to disagree, but what is important is creating opportunities for students to act on their ideas (participate as citizens in our democracy). Media and popular culture embody a language of both critique and possibility; a language that allows students to locate themselves in history, finds their own voices, and establishes convictions and compassion necessary for democratic civic courage (Browne, 2004). The concept of social efficacy is practically non-existent in our country today. This should be our goal—through the integration of popular culture in teaching for social efficacy and social justice within the education process.

Popular culture is a natural intrinsically motivating factor in our lives and should be integrated into the teaching and learning process in our schools. We are all very passionate about our likes and dislikes when it comes to popular culture. It can be a very powerful tool as we hope to develop social efficacy within our students as it allows for transformative investigation. Allowing for the investigation of issues regarding media and popular culture or using both as social and historical references can only enhance powerful social studies teaching and learning that actual involves students in discourse and dialog. What better way to engage in critical inquiry and problem solving for social efficacy than use popular culture within our schools?

As social studies educators it is time to follow Kincheloe's counsel (2001) and participate in a process of "rethinking what social studies can become, the brilliance it can produce, and the hope and insight it can provide" (p. 4). Social education can truly come alive for our students if educators allow for the integration of media and popular culture. If we are truly interested in facilitating powerful approaches in social education, then we must begin to integrate long ignored (and often demeaned) tools such as media and popular culture. What is important is creating a classroom atmosphere where students and teachers are empowered to question and critically analyze social studies issues and themes. Media and popular culture embodies a language of both critique and possibility; a language that allows students to locate themselves in history, find their own voices, and establish convictions and compassion necessary for democratic civic courage (Freire & Giroux,

1989). What better way to engage in critical inquiry and problem solving for social education than use media and popular culture in our classrooms? Infusing media and popular culture into the classroom may be one answer.

REFERENCES

Ayers, W., Quinn, T., & Stovall, D., (Eds.). (2008). *Handbook of social justice in education*. New York: Routledge.

Baenninger, M., & Newcombe, N. (1989). The role of experience in spatial test performance: A meta-analysis. *Sex Roles, 20,* 327–344.

Beal, C., Bolick, C., & Martorella, P. (2009). *Teaching social studies in middle and secondary schools*. Boston: Allyn & Bacon.

Beastall, L. (2006). Enchanting a disenchanted child: Revolutionising the means of education using information and communication technology and e-learning. *British Journal of Sociology of Education, 27*(1), 97–110.

Black, R. (2008). Just don't call them cartoons: Literacy spaces of anime, manga, and fanfiction. In J. Coiro, M. Knobel, C. Lankshear, & D. Leu (Eds.), *Handbook of Research on New Literacies* (pp. 583–610). New York: Lawrence Erlbaum Associates.

Brooks, J., & Brooks, M. (2001). *In search of understanding: The case for constructivist classrooms*. Upper Saddle River, NJ: Pearson/Prentice Hall.

Browne, R. (2004). *Popular culture across the curriculum*. Jefferson, NC: McFarland and Company.

Buckingham, D. (2007). *Beyond technology: Children's learning in the age of digital culture*. Cambridge, England, UK: Polity Press.

Caughie, J. (2006). Telephilia and distraction: Terms of engagement. *Journal of British Cinema and Television, 3*(1), 5–18.

Chiodo, J. & Byford, J. (2004). Do they really dislike social studies? A study of middle school and high school students. *The Journal of Social Studies Research, 28*(1), 16–26.

Crothers, L. (2007). *Globalization and American pop culture*. Lanham, MD: Rowman & Littlefield Publishing Group.

Danesi, M. (2008). *Popular culture [introductory perspectives]*. Lanham, MD: Rowman & Littlefield Publishing Group.

Daspit, T. & Weaver, J. (2000). *Media and popular culture and critical pedagogy*. New York: Falmer Press.

Devlin-Scherer, R., & Sardone, N. (2010). Digital simulation games for social studies classrooms. *Clearing House, 83*(4), 138–144.

Eisner, E. (2004). *The arts and the creation of mind*. New Haven, CT: Yale University press.

Entertainment Software Association (2010). *Essential facts about the computer and video game industry*. Retrieved from http://www.theesa.com/facts/pdfs/ESA_Essential_Facts_2010.PDF

Feng, J., Spence, I., & Pratt, J. (2007). Playing an action video game reduces gender differences in spatial cognition. *Psychological Science, 18*(10), 850–855.

Freire, P., & Giroux, H. (1989). Pedagogy, media and popular culture, and public life. In H. Giroux & R. Simon (Eds.), *Media and Popular Culture: Schooling and Everyday Life*. Granby, MA: Bergin and Garvey Publishers.

Fuller, M., & Jenkins, H. (1995). Nintendo and new world travel writing: A dialogue. In S. Jones (Ed.), *Cybersociety: Computer-mediated communication and community* (pp. 57–72). Thousand Oaks, CA: Sage Publications.

Gee, J. (2003). *What video games have to teach us about learning and literacy*. New York: Palgrave Macmillan.

Gee, J. (2004). *Situated language and learning: A critique of traditional schooling*. New York: Routledge.

Gee, J. (2008). Being a lion and being a soldier: Learning and games. In J. Coiro, M. Knobel, C. Lankshear, & D. Leu (Eds.), *Handbook of research on new literacies* (pp. 1023–1036). New York: Lawrence Erlbaum Associates.

Giroux, H. (1996). *Fugitive cultures: Race, violence, and youth*. New York: Routledge.

Giroux, H. (2004). *The abandoned generation*. New York, Macmillan.

Goldfarb, B. (2002). *Visual pedagogy: Media cultures in and beyond the classroom*. Durham, NC: Duke University Press.

Grant, S. (2007). High-stakes testing: How are social studies teachers responding?. *Social Education, 71*(5), 250–254.

Green, C., & Bavelier, D. (2007). Action-video-game experience alters the spatial resolution of vision. *Psychological Science, 18*, 88–94.

Hobbs, R. (2005). Media literacy and the K–12 content areas. *Yearbook of the National Society for the Study of Education, 104*(1), 74–99.

Hursh, D. (2008). *High-Stakes Testing and the Decline of Teaching and Learning: The Real Crisis in Education. Critical Education Policy and Politics #1*. Lanham, MD: Rowman & Littlefield Publishers.

Jefferson, T. (1826). *The Jefferson Cyclopedia: A Comprehensive Collection of the Views of Thomas Jefferson*. Retrieved from http://guides.lib.virginia.edu/content.php?pid=77323&sid=573588

Jenkins, H. (2006a). *Convergence culture: Where old and new media collide*. New York: New York University Press.

Jenkins, H. (2006b). *Fans, bloggers, and gamers: Exploring participatory culture*. New York: New York University Press.

Jenkins, H., Purushotma, R., Weigel, M., Clinton, K., & Robison, A. (2006c.) *Confronting the challenges of participatory culture: Media education for the 21ˢᵗ century*. John D. and Catherine T. MacArthur Foundation Reports on Digital Media and Learning. Retrieved from http://mitpress.mit.edu/books/full_pdfs/Confronting_the_Challenges.pdf

Jermyn, D., & Holmes, S. (2006). The audience is dead; long live the audience: Interactivity, 'telephilia' and the contemporary television audience. *Critical Studies in Television, 1*(1), 49–47.

Johnson, S. (2006). *Everything bad is good for you: How today's popular culture is actually making us smarter*. New York: Penguin Group.

Kimura, D. (1999). *Sex and cognition*. Cambridge, MA: MIT Press.

Kincheloe, J. (2001) *Getting beyond the facts: Teaching social studies/social sciences in the twenty-first century*. New York: Peter Lang.

Law, D., Pellegrino, J., & Hunt, E. (1993). Comparing the tortoise and the hare: Gender and experience in dynamic spatial reasoning tasks. *Psychological Science, 49*(3), 35–40.

Lingard, B., & Ladwig, J. (2001). *School reform longitudinal study: Final report* (Vol.1). Report prepared for Education Queensland by the School of Education, The University of Queensland.

Loewen, J. (1995). *Lies my teacher told me: Everything your American history textbook got wrong.* New York: New Press.

National Council for the Social Studies. (2011). *National standards for social studies.* Washington, DC: National Council for the Social Studies.

National Public Radio, http://www.npr.org/, February 2011.

Parker, W. (2009). *Social studies in elementary education.* Boston: Allyn & Bacon.

Pasek, J., Kenski, K., Romer, D., & Jamieson K. H. (2006). America's youth and community engagement: How use of mass media is related to political knowledge and civic activity among 14 to 22 year olds. *Communication Research, 33*(3), 115–135.

Pew Research Center's Internet and American Life Project. (2008). Retrieved from http://www.pewinternet.org/Reports/2008/Teens-Video-Games-and-Civics.aspx

Ravitch, D. (2010, October 4). 'The obsession with testing is nuts'. Retrieved from *Huffington Post* website http://www.huffingtonpost.com/diane-ravitch/the-obsession-withtestin_b_749512.html

Rieber, L. (2001). *Designing learning environments that excite serious play.* Proceedings of the Annual Conference of the Australian Society for Computers in Learning in Tertiary Education (ASCILITE), Melbourne, Australia, Dec. 9–12.

Ross, E. (2006.) *The social studies curriculum.* New York: SUNY press.

Russell, W., & Waters, S. (2010). Instructional methods for teaching social studies: A survey of what middle school students' like and dislike about social studies instruction. *The Journal for the Liberal Arts and Sciences, 14*(2), 7–14.

Scupham, J. (1964). *Broadcasting and education.* London, England, UK: BBC Publishing.

Smelser, N., & Baltes, P. (Eds.). (2001). *International encyclopedia of the social and behavioral sciences.* Oxford: Pergamon Press.

Spence, I., Yu, J., Feng, J., & Marshman, J. (2009). Women match men when learning a spatial skill. *Journal of Experimental Psychology: Learning, Memory, and Cognition, 35*(4), 1097–1103.

Squire, K. (2008). Video-game literacy: A literacy of expertise. In J. Coiro, M. Knobel, C. Lankshear, & D. Leu (Eds.), *Handbook of research on new literacies* (pp. 635–669). New York: Lawrence Erlbaum Associates

Steinberg, S., & Kincheloe, J. (Eds.). (2004). *Kinderculture: The corporate construction of childhood.* Boulder, CO: Westview.

Terlecki, M., & Newcombe, N. (2005). How important is the digital divide? The relation of computer and videogame usage to gender differences in mental rotation ability. *Sex Roles, 53*(5–6), 433–441.

Tupper, J. (2009). Unsafe waters, stolen sisters, and social studies: Troubling democracy and the meta-narrative of universal citizenship. *Teacher Education Quarterly, 36*(1), 77–94.

Tyner, K. (2003). Why teach media literacy? *Media Awareness Network*. Retrieved from http://www.media-awareness.ca/english/teachers/media_literacy/index. cfm

Voyer, D., Voyer, S., & Bryden, M.P. (1995). Magnitude of sex differences in spatial abilities: A meta-analysis and consideration of critical variables. *Psychological Bulletin, 117*(4), 250–270.

Walker, T. (2006). Adventures in Metropolis: Popular culture in social studies. In A. Segal, E. Heilman, & C. Cherryholmes (Eds.), *Social Studies—The next generation: Researching in the postmodern* (pp. 171–187). New York: Peter Lang.

Walker, T. (2010). The red pill: Social studies media texts, and literacies. *Learning, Media, and Technology, 35*(1), 1–14.

White, C. (2003). *True confessions: Popular culture, social efficacy and the struggle in schools.* Kresskill, NJ: Hampton Press.

White, C. & Walker, T. (2008). *Tooning in: Essays on popular culture and education.* New York: Rowman and Littlefield.

White, C. (2011). *Journeys in social education: A primer.* Rotterdam: Sense Publishers.

Willms, J. (2003). *Student engagement at school: A sense ofbelonging and participation, results from Pisa 2000,* Organization for Economic Co-operation and Development [OECD]. Retrieved from http://www.pisa.oecd.org/document/.

CHAPTER 24

INTERNET LITERACIES FOR ACTIVE CITIZENSHIP AND DEMOCRATIC LIFE

In Search of the Intersection

**David Hicks, Stephanie van Hover,
Elizabeth Yeager Washington, and John K. Lee**

The term "technology in schools" has often been viewed as an educational panacea in which students would be able to learn (almost) in spite of their teacher, and countless school reform measures have been suggested (or mandated) that advocate "state of the art" technology (see Friedman & Hicks, 2006). State of the art technology has evolved from radio and motion pictures to television, microcomputers, educational software, static web pages, and currently, Web 2.0 technologies that foster interaction and communication. For each new development, there has been a parallel prediction that its use would revolutionize teaching and learning in social studies education (see Christensen, Johnson, & Horn, 2008; Gardner, 2009). However, the promises and potential of technology have not materialized (Cuban, 2001; Martorella, 1998).

Currently, "state of the art" digital technology takes the form of the Internet, specifically Web 2.0—that is, participatory, "read-and-write" interactive technologies like MySpace, Facebook, YouTube, Flickr, Wikipedia, Blogger, Twitter, and beyond (Bull, et al., 2008; Dede, 2008; Greenhow, Robelia, & Hughes, 2009; McManus, 2005; O'Reilly, 2007). Researchers and educators are pointing to the tremendous potential of Web 2.0 to transform teaching and learning and to foster the understanding and skills, in particular literacy skills, necessary for active, engaged citizenship (e.g., Greenhow, et al., 2009; Leu, O'Byrne, Zawilinski, McVerry, & Everett-Cacopardo, 2009). At the same time, however, critical questions are being asked regarding the impact digital technologies have on the nature and quality of learning. For example, Carr (2010) suggests that our reliance on the Internet as an immediate source of easily accessible information will "make us shallower thinkers" (p. 194). He contends that the ease and speed of access to information through search engines such as Google "diminishes… the ability to know, in depth, a subject for ourselves, to construct within our own minds the rich and idiosyncratic set of connections that give rise to a singular intelligence" (Carr, 2010, p. 143). Importantly his work pays attention to and has initiated debate on the evolving effects of digital technologies on learning itself. Clearly there is an ongoing need to gain both a fuller understanding of children's uses of digital technologies within their larger everyday informal and formal educational activities, and the extent to which their use of digital technologies, like the Internet, have any connection to learning and civic participation (See Livingstone, 2010).

In his 2001 book *Oversold and Underused: Computers in the Classroom*, Larry Cuban asserted that minimal evidence existed to show that teachers and students were using technology specifically to "create better communities and build strong citizens" (p. 197). A decade later Cuban's comments and concerns continue to resonate and raise important questions for those interested in citizenship education in the 21st century. That is, with the rapid proliferation of so many creative, engaging digital technological innovations, is the relationship between digital technologies and democratic citizenship education any less opaque? Do these new Web 2.0 technologies require different ways of thinking and talking about 21st century citizenship education? And to what extent is it possible to connect ideas of 21st century digital literacy to understandings of educating for *active* democratic citizenship? In this paper, we use these questions as initiating points through which to map the complex relationship between Web 2.0 technologies, literacy in the digital age, and learning for active citizenship. Heeding Shulman's (2007) observation that "the work of both scholarship and practice progresses as a consequence of dialogue, debate, and exchange" (p. 1), we seek to initiate a generative dialogue, informed by transdisciplinary scholarship, about current understandings and descriptions of 21st century digital literacy, and the extent to which such technology ascribed literacy practices can be used to promote "active" citizenship.

WEB 2.0 AND LITERACY

Internet technology has changed rapidly over the past decade, both in terms of Web access and the nature of the Web (Greenhow, et al., 2009). Benkler (2006) contends that digital technologies themselves have afforded at least two distinct new ways to communicate beyond traditional patterns of media communication:

> The first element is the shift from a hub-and-spoke architecture with unidirectional links to the end points in the mass media, to distributed architecture with multidirectional connections among all nodes in the networked information environment. The second is the practical elimination of communication costs as a barrier to speaking across associated boundaries. (p. 212)

Such changes prompted a new term, Web 2.0, coined to describe a "shift from the presentation of material by website providers to the active co-construction of resources by communities of contributors" (Dede, 2008, p. 80). Web 2.0 technologies are considered "both a platform on which innovative technologies have been built and a space where users are as important as the content they upload and share with others" (Greenhow, et al., 2009, p. 247). Such platforms include social networks, social bookmarking, collaborative knowledge development, creative works, content aggregation and organization, feeds and tagging tools, and more Jenkins (2006) characterizes Web 2.0 as a "participatory culture" created by social interconnections, creative capabilities, and interactivity, a culture in which individuals believe their contributions and creations matter (p. 3). The lines between being a producer of material on the Internet and a consumer of that material have blurred (Richardson, 2006). Ownership of content has shifted from a small group of "experts" to growing collaborative online communities, what Dede (2008) terms a "seismic shift in epistemology" that calls for new ways of thinking about "knowledge," "teaching" and "learning" (p. 80).

Like Dede (2008), Livingstone (2008a), observes that the Internet and associated Web 2.0 technologies are beginning to push policymakers, educators, parents, and researchers to think about knowledge (and knowledge production) differently and, also, to consider what young people need to know when using the Internet. Bennett, Maton, & Kervin (2008) suggest that such a "push," however, should not be the result of succumbing to what they describe as an "academic form of moral panic" (p. 782) in terms of the type of public discourse that is clamoring for educational change to meet the needs of today's students. Livingston (2010), stresses the necessity of going beyond overgeneralizations and oversimplifications to a more thoughtful and careful considerations regarding young people's interactions and experiences with digital technologies. She notes, "If we overestimate young people's skills, we may underestimate their need for support…. Further, if we overestimate youthful skill, we may misunderstand their practices" (p. 4). In light of this, she argues that it is helpful to think about this "knowledge" in terms of literacy—that "through the concept of literacy" we can "weave together an account of basic and advanced skills, linking individual skills with social practices and crossing the boundary between formal and informal learning" (p. 102). Literacy, conceived broadly, involves the ability to think, to process information, to construct new ideas, and to organize one's thoughts. Barton and Hamilton (1998) defined literacy as "something people do," an:

> activity, located in the space between thought and text. Literacy does not reside in people's heads as a set of skills to be learned, and it does not just reside on paper, captured as texts to be analysed. Like all human activity, literacy is essentially social, and it is located in the interaction between people. (p. 7)

They assert that literacy is historically situated and purposeful, is best understood as a set of social practices, and is patterned by social institutions and power relationships (Barton & Hamilton, 1998). Barton and Hamilton (1998) conceptualized their notion of literacy as social and cultural practice while thinking about traditional forms of interaction with text—that is, reading and writing. The rise of new technologies has led to discussions of new literacies, including information literacy, media literacy, and Internet literacy (see, Buckingham 2003, 2008; Laverty, 2009; Livingstone 2008a,b; NCSS, 2009).

The definition of information literacy has evolved as the nature, form, and purpose of computing, telecommunications, and information technologies has changed over time (Laverty, 2009; Livingstone, 2008a). Information literacy emphasizes the acquisition of a set of skills—the ability to collect, access, retrieve, analyze, manage, communicate, create, convey, share, deconstruct, and donate information—as well as well developing habits of mind and engaging in ethical behavior (Laverty, 2009). According to Buckingham (2003) media literacy refers to the "knowledge skills, and competencies that are required in order to use and interpret media" (p. 36). But, he warns, media literacy (or literacy of any kind) is far from straightforward. Rather, media literacy requires critical literacy; it involves learning how to understand who created media, for what purposes, with what message, and for what audiences, as well as analyzing how these media represent the world, the symbolic meanings, text, and subtext of media (Buckingham, 2008). Buckingham (2003) notes that media cannot be separated from the "social and institutional structures in which it is situated" (p.

38) and involves a broader understanding of the social, political, economic, institutional, and intellectual influences of media within a certain time and space. Digital media have been seen as part of the broader field of media literacy (Buckingham, 2008).

The NCSS (2009) position statement on media literacy clearly reflects such an understanding:

> Media literacy includes the skill of accessing, analyzing, evaluating, creating and distributing messages as well as the cultural competencies and social skills associated with a growing participatory culture . . . Media literacy also includes analysis of ideology and power as students learn how media are used to position audience and frame public opinion.

Whereas the NCSS position statement uses the term media literacy as an umbrella concept (as does Buckingham above), the emergence of online environments—the world of Web 2.0—may well require a further iteration of how we think and talk about literacy; specifically in terms of shifting beyond notions of information literacy and media literacy (Leu, 2000; Livingstone, 2008a). Leu et al. (2009) argue that the Internet should be viewed "as a literacy issue, not a technology issue" (p. 265) and draw on N/new literacies theory. New literacies (uppercase N) is a "broader, more inclusive concept" that benefits from new research that explores "either a specific area of new literacies (lowercase n), such as the social communicative transactions occurring with text messaging...or a focused disciplinary base, such as the semiotics of multimodality in online media" (Leu, et al., 2009, p. 265). New literacies share certain elements: They are multi-faceted, subject to almost continuous change, central to full participation in a global community, and attentive to the new skills, strategies, dispositions, and social practices required by new technologies for information and communication (Leu, et al., 2009).

Livingstone (2008a), does not directly refer to N/new literacies, but rather calls for a specific and "ambitious" definition of *Internet* literacy, one that satisfies the "social, economic, cultural, and political ambitions that society has for the information society and, especially, for the so-called 'Internet generation'" (p. 102). She recognizes that traditional literacy, media literacy, and information literacy are relevant to thinking about Internet literacy, but that the unique, complex and ever-changing nature of the medium requires revisiting and recalibrating our understandings of literacy. Livingstone (2008a) defines Internet literacy as a "situated form of knowing" and as the "ability to access, understand, critique, and create information and communication content online" (p. 110). Specific skills, Livingstone (2008a) argues, include "information searching, navigation, sorting, assessing relevance, judging reliability, and identifying bias" (pp. 108–109). Internet literacy, like other forms of literacy, is not neutral, but always considered within the context of the economic, cultural, social, and political resources (or capital) that are unequally distributed. Livingstone (2008a) warns that theories of Internet literacy need to avoid technological determinism—that is, the risk of attributing an all-powerful role to technology (see, Buckingham, 2008)—and recognize the dynamic interaction between user and technology.

Livingstone (2008a) moves beyond definitions and identifies three purposes for Internet (and media and information) literacy: lifelong learning, cultural expression, and personal fulfillment; knowledge economy, competitiveness and choice; and, democracy, participation, and active citizenship (pp. 113–114). She argues:

> In a democratic society, a media and information-literate individual is more able to gain an informed opinion on matters of the day, and to be able to express their opinion individually and collectively in public, civic, and political domains, while a media and information-literate society supports a critical and inclusive public sphere. (p. 113–114)

Livingstone's (2008a) assertion that key purposes of Internet literacy are democratic participation and active citizenship reflects Greenhow, Robelia, and Hughes' (2009) contention that "new and emerging information and communication technologies, shaping and shaped by social practices, have tremendous potential to help improve individual and collective access to information, knowledge, and participation in evolving a just and democratic culture" (p. 281). However, as Simon, Corrales and Wolfensberger (2002) remind us, the Internet is neither naturally democratic nor naturally anti-democratic. An important point that was recently reiterated by Secretary of State Hilary Clinton, who, in her January 21st, 2010 remarks on Internet freedom, noted: "We stand for a single internet where all of humanity has equal access to knowledge and ideas. And we recognize that the world's information infrastructure will become what we and others make it." Indeed, the Internet does have the potential to offer democratic affordances (see Table 24.1). However it must also be remembered that the Internet in and of itself will not "naturally" increase citizens' desire for appropriate and positive speech, and the careful and appropriate sharing and discussion of political viewpoints.

The democratic characteristics and affordances of the Internet that are so often touted and revered remain fragile and precariously balanced as individuals, groups, and institutions search for ways to use the Internet to advance their own ideas and agendas at the expense of others (see Table 24.2).

What becomes clear, as Faris and Etling (2008) point out, is that "the Internet and other digital tools are merely that—tools. They are available for all, including those who seek to expand and represent democracy, those who seek to manipulate public institutions and government for their own

TABLE 24.1.   Democratic Characteristics/Affordances of Internet Technologies

Affordances of Internet Technologies
1. The Internet offers the potential for overcoming political and geographic borders as well as the government's ability to fully regulate, censor and monitor their citizens' activities in terms of locating, gathering and sharing information.
2. The Internet creates opportunities for citizens to locate, receive, and disseminate information and ideas over time and space.
3. The Internet allows/empowers citizens to access, research, disseminate/share, and broker information as well as seek out and form allegiances to support a common cause and advance political, social, and economic agendas regardless of location. The Internet removes some of the stumbling blocks to the grassroots mobilization of interest groups and minority voices. Though Gladwell (2010) suggested that it can really only create weak network ties and not deep strong network ties required for sustaining the type of civil rights activism of the 1960s.
4. The pace of change, and development of the Internet make it difficult for governments to exert total control over the nature and flow of information.
5. The Internet offers an accessible space for citizens to expect governmental agencies and businesses to share information regarding their activities and procedures. The expectation is for governments to use technology for transparency to support the common good in a more open forum.
6. The Internet shifts the nature of knowledge production from the traditional, authoritative, disciplinary divisions of knowledge that are passed down from governmental, corporate, and research institutions to a new paradigm of knowledge production that is socially distributed, application-oriented, transdisciplinary, and subject to multiple accountabilities.
7. The Internet enables a widening of the knowledge society by serving as an educational portal for people to learn and study across time and space.

Adapted from Simon, Corrales, & Wolfensberger 2002.

gain, and those who seek to seize and consolidate power. This prompts the question of who can best utilize these tools" (p. 80). Given recent works that raise concerns regarding: the *shallowness* of the internet (Carr, 2010); young peoples' every day practices interacting with digital technologies (Bennett, Maton & Kervin, 2008); the nature and quality of some young people's access to digital technologies (Bennett, Maton & Kervin, 2008; DeWitt, 2007; Leu, O'Byrne, Zawilinski, McVerry & Everett-Cacopardo, 2009); the overwhelming Babel-inducing level of information available via search engines (see Faris & Etling, 2008); and, the limited potential of digital Web 2.0 technologies to foster the type of strong, deep sustainable networks to support and foster activism for social justice (Gladwell, 2010), we suggest that education as a whole, and citizenship education in particular, is of great importance in facilitating the literacy skills needed to prepare future citizens to be ready, willing, and able to participate within the ongoing struggle

TABLE 24.2. Anti Democratic Characteristics of Internet Technologies

Anti Democratic Characteristics of Internet Technologies
1. Governments can ban, censor, or impose strict regulations on Internet providers within their own countries. It is technologically possible for governmental regimes to block their citizens from using the Internet to see certain things that are deemed offensive, corrupt, or inflammatory. Such censorship is made more difficult with the spread of cell phones that can be used to access the web and send text messages and videos. However, in January 2011 the Egyptian Government cut Internet and cell phone connectivity as part of effort to quell protests against the regime of Hosni Mubarak.
2. Issues of security, privacy and monitoring of information and ideas, even in democratic countries, have emerged in the post 9-11 era.
3. Power elites can influence the outcome of Internet searches to manage and control news and information through the use of search suppression or optimization techniques.
4. The Internet can be used a powerful portal for hate speech, incitements to violence, invasions of privacy, and cyber bullying.
5. Using the Internet as a portal for democratic education does not necessarily transform what has been taught if PowerPoint slides simply replace overhead transparencies, e-books and iPads replace textbooks, and course management sites made up of folders of documents replace three-ring binders.

Adapted from Simon, Corrales, & Wolfensberger 2002.

for, and over, information that is shared, stored and disseminated on the Internet. Such a stance itself raises a number of important questions with regard to preparing citizens for active participation in 21st century societies. To what extent can the Internet be seen as a participatory democratic space that encourages citizenship engagement, participation, and knowledge production? How can citizens be supported and encouraged to access and make critical uses of civic-oriented information? How can new technologies support more meaningful and inclusive civic discourse? How can citizens make active and creative uses of participatory media to strengthen democratic structures and protect civil liberties? And, most importantly, what does *active citizenship* look like in the age of Web 2.0?

ACTIVE CITIZENSHIP

The literature on democratic citizenship addresses the complexity of *defining* the concept of democracy and "active" citizenship, both in theory and in practice. Democracy, to Dewey (1916, 1927), largely meant a form of *active community life*—a way of being and living with others. Moreover, he emphasized that democracy entails certain habits of the mind that must be cultivated throughout citizens' lives as they participate in various institutions and groups in which they have a voice in setting goals, sharing knowledge, communicating, and taking direct action. Most importantly, Dewey envisioned democracy as a creative and constructive process for which citizens needed practical judgment, a shared fund of civic knowledge, and deliberative skills and dispositions.

Yet Dahrendorf (1997) also emphasized that citizenship is "not just an attitude of mind or even a subject of political education":

> Citizenship is above all a set of entitlements common to all members of society... I like to think of citizenship as a set of chances—life chances—that define a free society. [This] involves basic rights, equality before the law, due process, the integrity of the person, freedom of expression and association. It also involves chances of participation, universal suffrage, of course, but equally importantly market access including labour market access, and social movement in the numerous opportunities of civil society. This is what citizenship means in the full sense of the word... (Citizenship) provides an instrument for living with difference with regard to how people act with and toward other citizens, societies and cultures within a global community. (pp. 62–63)

Jones and Gaventa (2002) specifically conceptualize *active* citizenship as "the direct ways in which citizens influence and exercise control in governance" and "the direct intervention of citizens in public activities," as well as the "accountability of the state and other responsible institutions to citizens" (p. 7). This "relational dynamic" of citizenship places "obligations on both citizens and the state through participatory democratic systems ...(that) require direct connection between citizens and the state" (p. 7). This, in turn, "entails institutional reforms that enable democratic participation through the production of new forms of relationship between civil society and the state" (p. 7). They conclude, "When citizens perceive themselves as actors in governance, rather than passive beneficiaries of services and policy, they may be more able to assert their citizenship through actively seeking greater accountability...and shaping policies that affect their lives" (p. 7).

Another way of thinking about active citizenship is what Parker (2008) has called "enlightened political engagement" or "wise political action" (p. 68). Parker explained:

> Political engagement refers to the action or participation dimension of democratic citizenship, from voting to campaigning, boycotting, and protesting. Democratic enlightenment refers to the knowledge and commitments that inform this engagement: for example, knowledge of the ideals of democratic living, the ability to discern just from unjust laws and action...and the ability and commitment to deliberate public policy in cooperation with disagree-

able others. Without democratic enlightenment, participation cannot be trusted...(and) can be worse than apathy. (p. 68)

Parker reminds us that enlightened political engagement is not easy to accomplish; it is a continuous goal toward which we work with others who hold different ideas and perspectives than ourselves.

The literature also includes useful national and cross-national studies that demonstrate the variety of ways in which active citizenship can be conceptualized (e.g., Davies, 2006; Davies & Issitt, 2005; Ibrahim, 2005; Jones & Gaventa, 2002; Torney-Purta & Richardson, 2004; Torney-Purta, Lehmann, Oswald, & Schulz, 2001; Watts, 2006). Cogan and Derricott's (1998) idea of *multidimensional citizenship* is informative; it includes eight key characteristics with implications for being "active" as a *global* citizen: (1) the ability to look at and approach problems as a member of a global community; (2) the ability to work with others in a cooperative way and to take responsibility for one's role/duties in society; (3) the ability to understand, accept, appreciate and tolerate cultural differences; (4) the capacity to think in a critical and systematic way; (5) the willingness to resolve conflict in a non-violent manner; (6) the willingness to change one's lifestyle and consumption habits to protect the environment; (7) the ability to be sensitive toward and to defend human rights; and (8) the willingness and ability to participate in politics at local, national and international levels. They conclude:

> ... (The task is) to help [future] citizens recognize the global challenges which affect each of us personally and are part of our individual and social responsibility to address. Put simply, global challenges cannot be left for someone else to deal with: rather, the responsibility lies with each of us to safeguard global well-being...Twenty-first century citizenship will require active citizenship participation—citizens who view themselves as actors in the world. (p. 133)

Developing informed and active citizens has long been articulated as an essential goal of education. Dewey (1916, 1927) helped to break this ground by arguing that the school should be a democracy in microcosm, where pupils learn particular processes, values, and attitudes to live effectively as citizens. Parker (2008) stated that schools are both "curricular and civic spaces...where people who come from numerous private worlds and social positions are congregated on common ground with shared interests" (p. 69). The school curriculum, he explained, can "afford opportunities for students to learn enlightened political engagement by exploiting school attendance—that is, by developing the public potential of schools to educated citizens" (2008, p. 70). Parker's conception of democratic citizenship education values direct involvement in public life, pluralism, and democracy as a way of life involving "deliberation, action, and reflection" (1996b, p. 121). He has argued for a discourse in school of "responsibility, negotiation, and obligation" aimed at creating a "broad political comradeship"—creating the political "one" out of the cultural "many" (1996b, p. 117). According to Parker, schools already possess the "bedrocks of democratic living—diversity and mutuality" (1996a, pp. 2, 10). The cultivation of their democratic potential entails increasing the opportunities for interaction among diverse students, and structuring this interaction so that "competent dialogue" is supported—i.e., dialogue that is purposeful, open, and inclusive (2008, p. 70). When schools offer such affordances, they are living up to what Parker (1996a) terms their "first moral obligation" to give children an education that will equip them to take advantage of their citizenship (p. 2).

INTERNET LITERACY AND ACTIVE CITIZENSHIP

How, then, can technology—and, more specifically, Internet literacy—be used to foster and promote this vision of active citizenship? Many argue that technology integration can assist in the "essential mission" of the social studies—preparing students for the responsibility of the office of citizen (e.g., VanFossen & Berson, 2008). This task, however, may be easier said than done, considering that both researchers and politicians recognize that digital technologies and the Internet are for many young people primarily a place to/for play—"a way to escape from offline constraint" (see Livingstone, 2010). Or, as President Obama suggested technology can serve as "a distraction, a diversion, a form of entertainment, rather than a tool of empowerment, rather than the means of emancipation" (Wiltmeyer, 2010). Within social studies education itself, research indicates that computer technology has not been seamlessly integrated into the classroom, nor has it transformed the teaching and learning process (Becker, 1999; Cuban, 2001; Ehman & Glenn, 1991). Internet use in social studies, according to a 2000 U.S. Department of Education study, is generally superficial in nature (VanFossen & Berson, 2008), despite the fact that nearly100 % of schools are currently connected to the Internet (Greenhow, Robelia, & Hughes, 2009). And, as Doolittle & Hicks (2003) observe, the social studies community has, for the most part, "side-stepped, or merely played lip service" to the need for a clear philosophical, theoretical, and pedagogical framework to think about technology and social studies education (p. 96). Yet if the mission of the social studies is to educate global citizens for the networked 21st century, we need to carefully consider what it means to teach students (and teachers) to learn how to critically engage in the type of systematic and sophisticated multimodal literacy work that Web 2.0 technologies require. Furthermore, it is essential to consider how Internet literacy can foster the understanding, knowledge, and skills for active citizenship—that is, when the contours of human interaction change—as is the case with Web 2.0 technologies—the ways of understanding civic life must change as well.

With the rapid expansion of networks for storing and moving information, citizens today have fewer limitations on how they can access information and how much information than can access. One recent estimate suggested that digital information is being created and stored at such a rapid rate that the amount of data stored is doubling every eleven hours (IBM, 2007). The consequences for democratic life are enormous. Citizens today have immediate access to billions of pages of information that may inform their civic attitudes. Beyond simple access, citizens need to engage that information and compose ideas that inform and guide their civic life. Citizens today need ways of understanding how to cope with the staggering amount of information, and more useful techniques for engaging this information in a critical and productive manner.

Expanded access to civic information has numerous implications for democratic life. Some concerns relate to the commercial control and monitoring of information online (Rosenzweig, 2001; Samoriski, 2000). Other issues involve the manner in which information access can influence political activity (Jiang & Xu, 2009; Lee, 2009; Tettey, 2001) and how democratic structures are affected by technological infrastructure (Groshek, 2009). More closely connected to education, others are focused upon the extent to which online information access affects civic dispositions and attitudes (Biddix, Somers, & Polman, 2009). Perhaps most important are issues related to how young people come to know and understand what it means to engage in civic democratic life in online environments.

In their 2008 survey of 2,251 adults, Smith, Schlozman, Veba, and Brady (2009) found that young citizens in the United States are increasingly making use of Internet resources to engage in political activities. Half of the respondents indicated that they engage in some form of online civic communication or action, including petitioning, editorializing, contacting government representatives, and networking with others. Most of this activity was concentrated among respondent ages 18–34. Seventy two percent of all political uses of social networking sites were among this youngest group, as was 55% of all political commentary posted on the Web. This, along with other research, indicates that youth are engaged in civic life, and that Internet and Web 2.0 technologies may offer new ways to learn about political life, to create civic communities across multiple boundaries (geographic, cultural, social, political), and to experience the complexity and challenge involved in civic life (Bers, 2008). Thus, the potential exists to engage in active citizenship, but only if citizens possess, on the one hand, Internet literacy skills and, on the other hand, civic knowledge. The two are inextricably linked; the nature of Web 2.0 technology requires unique ways of thinking, knowing, and doing.

Internet literacy, as well as a host of other terms for representing the literacies that emerge from uses of new technologies, suggest that two activities shape our ways of knowing, communicating, and processing information. Most certainly, methods of communicating have been transformed in a number of important ways with the introduction of new technologies such as Voice Over Internet (VOIP) protocol (e.g., Skype) and microblogging (e.g., Twitter). These new technologies and associated mediums make communication over distance easier and more dynamic, shaping ideas and enabling messages that are equally dynamic. At the same time, the mass of information created through new publishing and collaborative networks have dramatically increased demands on cognitive processing (Brand-Gruwel, Wopereis, & Vermetten, 2005; Duke, Schmar-Dobler, & Zhang, 2006; Walraven, Brand-Gruwel, & Boshuizen, 2009; c.f. Carr, 2010). The notion of Internet literacies is a helpful construct for managing and facilitating these emerging and, as Leu (2000) refers to them, deictic ways of knowing. Citizens must be conversant with new mediums and forms for communication, as well as with the mass of information and the opportunities to construct information.

But citizenship is much more. At the center of the idea of citizenship are beliefs and actions that improve the common good (Barton & Levstik, 2004). The question that needs to be answered is: How are new technologies and the myriad of literacies that have emerged alongside these technologies aimed at supporting or improving the common good? For us, the answer to this question lies not in how we use technology or even how we know or think about the activities supported by technologies. Instead, literacy for citizenship in the 21st century should be about being democratic and understanding the new literacies of democratic life writ large. The literacies of democratic life are both reflective of our current condition and pointed toward a better and more just social arrangement. Because new technologies play such a vital role in two lynchpin democratic activities, communication and the creation and uses of information, democratic citizens must have a clear understanding of how new technologies impact democratic life. Put another way, we need to expand our views of how to be democratic in contemporary life.

What does this look like in practical terms? Take a blog (i.e., weblog), which is a type of website that consists of journal-style entries that can provide commentary, descriptions of events, photographs, graphics, and video. These entries, created by an individual or group, are presented in reverse chronological order, and readers can comment on entries (Raynes-Goldie & Walker, 2008). Blogs can be used to disseminate information and/or for small groups to launch discussion around specific topics—both components of active citizenship. But in order to make sense of a blog and to use a blog for purposes of civic engagement, the user must possess Internet literacy skills. A user must be able to search the Internet to find a blog or possess the skills to create a blog; the user also needs to be able to critically analyze the content of the blog and to assess particular positions taken by the author of a blog. Moreover, creators of a blog need to understand the best ways to publicize/tag a blog designed to garner attention for a particular civic purpose. Blogs have quickly emerged as an alternative source for news information and as platforms for interest groups to organize and disseminate information. In American politics, multiuser blogs such as the progressive Daily Kos and the conservative Michelle Malkin provide political writers-activists with a public outlet that was, not too long ago, the exclusive purview of professional journalists and commentators (Schiffer, 2007).

Similarly, social networking tools can be used for active civic engagement but also require Internet literacy skills. Facebook and MySpace are two popular global social networking tools, operated and owned by private companies. On Facebook, for example, users can create personal profiles, add friends, send messages to friends, and join networks. Users can also mobilize their networks by posting links or information about issues, current events, and ways to get involved (Raynes-Goldie & Walker, 2007). In order to use Facebook effectively, however, users need to know how to access, create, and manage their profile. Additionally, they need to understand issues related to private and public knowledge access, be able to critically analyze information shared/published by friends, and understand ways of mobilizing their networks of friends through their profiles. As a space for enabling political activity, Facebook and MySpace have enjoyed some success (Donnelly-Smith, 2008). Preliminary studies show the potential of new technologies like social networks and blogs to engage young people in online civic life, and there is fertile ground for more research on how technology-based interventions can promote participation in a virtual and face-to-face world (Bers, 2008).

Anecdotal evidence of Web 2.0s potential for active citizenship is growing. The Navajo Nation in the southwestern United States provides a striking illustration of how the use of Web 2.0 and social networking technology can reflect Internet literacy and active citizenship. In 2008, a Navajo citizens' initiative called for a referendum on whether to reduce the number of members of the Navajo Nation Council (the legislative branch of the Navajo government) from 88 to 24. The rationale stemmed from a 2001 report that evaluated the efficiency of the legislature. The study found that Navajo Nation delegates represented an average of only 2,100 constituents—or about 26 times fewer constituents than those represented by Arizona legislators, but at 30 percent more cost per legislative item; in 2008, each Navajo Nation Council delegate represented an average of 3,409 constituents. According to proponents of the referendum, reducing the council to 24 delegates would reduce waste and inefficiency in the legislature but would still equate to 13 times the representation per constituent than the Arizona Legislature, and per capita the council would remain one of the highest levels of representation of any legislature in the country. In addition to the creation of an "88 to 24" website, proponents utilized Twitter, a MySpace blog, MySpace video, and Facebook to publicize their views on the issue, to explain how Navajos both on and off the reservation could register to vote, to obtain the required number of signatures for a petition to put the initiative to a vote, and to promote their "Get Out the Vote" efforts for the referendum, which took place in December 2009 and was the first time since 1934 that Navajos voted on the actual structure of their government. Voters approved the referendum by a large margin.

In Iran, another high profile and dramatic use of Web 2.0 technology unfolded after the Iranian presidential election of 2009. In the days and weeks after the election, makeshift human and technology networks on the ground in Iran were mobilized to distribute information within the country and to the outside world. Information coming out of Iran was almost completely unfiltered. Traditional news networks were confronted with the same issue that regular Internet information users face: How do we know whether information that is published online can be trusted? In this case, much of the information was disseminated using the microblogging website Twitter. Professional news organizations such as CNN made a critical decision to use the information from sites such as Twitter, in addition to their mainstream sources, for verification and corroboration (Palser, 2009). Gladwell (2010) quoting from an article in *Foreign Policy*, suggests that the use of Tweets—which were typically English language Tweets (not Farsi)—was more an example of a shallow journalism of convenience by reporters who could not reach or could not be bothered to reach anyone on the ground in Iran. However, what is important to note is that the media did pay attention to the Tweets in Iran, just as they also paid attention to bloggers and user-generated news sites in Kenya during the post election crisis in 2007–8 (Goldstein & Rotich, 2008), in Burma during the Saffron Revolution in 2007 (Chowdhury, 2008), in South Korea during the 2002 presidential elections (Joyce, 2007), in the Ukrainian Orange Revolution in 2004 (Goldstein, 2007), and most recently as a result of the Wikileaks release of the Afghanistan War Logs in the summer of 2010. This unfolding story of almost free-floating information illustrates in stark terms how citizens and mainstream information networks have to reconsider how they access and use information. In situations such as this, Internet literacies situated in dynamic social contexts are needed to use information meaningfully and critically. The need for critical uses of information, as exemplified in the case of Navajo nation in 2008, the 2009 presidential elections in Iran, and the other aforementioned flashpoints, is an area that could well be explored and fostered within and through K–16 settings if a key mission of education is to prepare children to engage in active citizenship. Case studies could also be developed and discussed in the social studies classroom regarding events surrounding the use of digital technologies and privacy, cyberbullying, and local activism and advocacy at varying scales of engagement.

ACTIVE CITIZENSHIP, INTERNET LITERACY, AND PEDAGOGY

The core skills and competencies required for both Internet literacy and active citizenship are not natural, easy, or intuitive; rather, they are complex, fluid, multi-layered, and ever-changing, much like democracy itself. This way of thinking about literacy, knowledge, and citizenship necessitates rethinking and asking questions of traditional curricula, pedagogies, and assessment and who has access to the use of and discussions regarding the use of digital technologies (see Livingstone, 2010). Bennett (2008) argues that civics education in the United States is in decline, and "where offered, the curriculum is often stripped of independent opportunities for young people to embrace and communicate about politics on their own terms" (p. 7). The result is that there is often "little connection between the academic presentation of politics and the acquisition of skills that might help develop engaged citizens" (Bennet, 2008, p. 7). Also, research indicates that while many young people have access to Web 2.0 tools that could facilitate active citizenship, they lack the critical Internet literacy skills that allow them to use the tools for meaningful civic engagement (Levine, 2008; Livingstone, 2008b). Education for citizenship and education for Internet literacy are both necessary, in conjunction with new ways of teaching with, about and for digital media.

Jenkins (2006) argues that educators should encourage and teach students the skills, knowledge, ethical frameworks, and self-confidence to be full participants in participatory, contemporary culture. But he warns that attention must be given to the fundamental inequalities in young people's access to Web 2.0 digital media—what he terms the "participation gap." He also identifies a "transparency problem" (young people are not actively reflecting on their media experiences) and an "ethics challenge" (ethical norms are not yet developed to cope with a complex and diverse social environment online). And, most importantly, he argues that the rhetoric and discussion of 21st century skills has obscured a fundamental truth— that textual literacy remains an essential skill, and that "before students can engage with the new participatory culture, they must be able to read and write" (Jenkins, 2006, p. 19). He notes that young people are already participating in Web 2.0 through affiliations (formal and informal online communities), expressions (producing new creative forms), collaborative problem solving (working together to complete tasks and develop new knowledge) and circulations (shaping the flow of media). Youth, however, fail to engage in critical dialogues to help them articulate how, why, and what skills they need for these experiences. Furthermore, educators are haphazard at best in incorporating Web 2.0 into teaching and learning and often fail to explicitly teach Internet literacy and engage students in critical dialogue. Jenkins (2006) calls for attention to a set of core social skills and cultural competencies that include play, experimentation, performance, simulation, appropriation, multitasking, distributed cognition, collective intelligence, judgment, networking, and negotiating (p. 56).

Kress (2003) suggests a shift from a "world told" where written communication was the predominant form of knowledge construction and exchange to a "world shown," where images and the screen have emerged as the primary form of meaning-making. Gee (2000) argues for a new set of pedagogical principles to support the teaching of multiple literacies in the formal educational setting. These include providing students with: (1) the room to engage in situated practices, where they can engage in hands-on, authentic learning experiences that involve relevant and meaningful talk, tools, and technologies; (2) explicit, overt instruction that helps students reflect upon patterns and themes in the language and practice being taught; (3) an understanding of how to critically frame what they are learning in terms of other domains and disciplines; and (4) the ability to produce and not just consume knowledge. Similarly, Levine (2008) asserts that students should have multiple opportunities to create digital media in schools, and that they should learn the effective use of a public voice in addition to political activism, deliberation, problem solving and participation. However, as Livingstone (2010) warns, care needs to be taken in designing such activities. If students are either uncertain of the value, purpose, and audience of teacher designed activities, or if such activities do not necessarily build on their own interests, curiosities, rights and responsibilities, it is likely students will resist such efforts and regard such formalized uses of digital technologies as little more than inauthentic attempts to dress up traditional classroom practices. In essence, the activities designed for the classroom must pay attention to the types of literacy questions that need to be asked of digital technologies writ large: who controls the technology, and for what purpose?

In short, education for both active citizenship and Internet literacy emphasizes: (1) explicit instruction in active citizenship; (2) incorporation of Web 2.0 in day-to-day instruction; (3) attention to Internet literacy—that is, how to access, understand, critique, and create information as well as how to critically reflect on one's use of technology; and (4) recognition and attention to questions of power and the democratic affordances and constraints of Internet technologies.

CONCLUSIONS AND QUESTIONS

Digital technologies are neither good nor bad; it is how we think of them and use them that make them so. There is a danger of teachers, educators, parents, and policy-makers succumbing to the idea that young people and adults are digital natives who as "produsers" (Bruns, 2008) know how to safely and meaningfully navigate within and through current and emerging digital technologies (see Buckingham, 2003; Livingstone, 2008a, 2008b). Issues of access (in terms of quality of access), the ethics of use and production, and understandings of how to navigate within and through the Internet (in order to collect, produce, distill, evaluate, and disseminate information) are complex and not naturally bestowed upon people simply because they are products of a specific era. As we have argued, learning to use technologies is a literacy issue that requires a broader understanding of literacy than the encoding and decoding of symbols—the ability to read and write—though this in itself is vital. Seeing the use of technology as a literacy issue makes it an educational concern, and tying this educational concern to the broader goal of educating for active democratic citizenship must be taken seriously across the K–16 spectrum as well as within informal educational settings. The provenance of our conceptualization of Internet literacy can be found in ongoing movements to conceptualize an expanded contemporary definition of literacy in terms of the work done in the areas of N/new literacy, multimodal literacy, and multiple literacies (Jewitt, 2008). What is clear from such work is that literacies are local and situated, and, as Jewitt (2008) reminds us, "the ways in which something is represented shape both what is to be learned, that is, the curriculum content, and how it is to be learned" (p. 241).

The need to develop a broader re-conceptualization of literacy is not simply the result of emerging digital technologies, but rather a recognition of the "new conditions of contemporary society," of which digital technologies are an important feature (Jewitt, 2008, p. 242). Thirty years ago, Daniel Bell (1976/1999) argued, "If capital and labor are the major structural features of industrial society, information and knowledge are those of the post-industrial society" (p. xci) Bell's predictions have proven true. With the rise of the network society, "the source of productivity lies in the technology of knowledge generation, information processing and symbolic communication" (Castells, 1996, p. 16–17). The very nature of how we interact with information to describe and read the contemporary world has dramatically changed our understanding of what it means to be literate. Literacy has been theoretically transformed by work in the fields of New literacies, multiliteracies, media literacy, information literacy, and multimodal literacies (Jewitt, 2008). The result is an ongoing and "increasingly pluralized and multiplied" understanding of the nature and definition of literacy (Jewitt, 2008, p. 244).

In terms of educating for Internet literacy and active citizenship, it becomes important to recognize that literacy in this context does not mean expending one's energies simply teaching children to use the plethora of digital technologies with their various software and platforms. Such a task is impossible, given the ever-changing face of the Internet and digital technologies. Rather, we have to recognize the importance of the principle of transfer when it comes to learning how to navigate the range of digital technologies. The first layer of engaging in systematic and sophisticated literacy work is to encourage quality access by instilling confidence, willingness, and the ability to play and explore both the benefits and drawbacks of technology. This goes beyond just physical access—though this is important in and of itself—but access here also includes an understanding of what the Internet is, how it is designed, how it functions, how the digital spaces that make up the Internet can be navigated, and what types of information and traces we as users leave as we visit sites to search for and upload information.

Moreover, it becomes important for users to understand and deliberately reflect upon the fact that the ways we move through virtual spaces shape our emerging identities as "produsers" (Bruns, 2008), and that while we may sit alone in front of a screen, we become nodes within and through a series of networks that connect us in multiple ways to diverse ideas, people, concepts, constructs, attitudes, and beliefs. We encounter ideas that are unfiltered, easily accessible and socially constructed; we find that ideas can be democratic and liberating as well as anti-democratic, small-minded, deceptive, or simply dangerous (c.f. Simon, Corrales, & Wolfensberger, 2002; Sunstein, 2009). Thus, another layer of Internet literacy is critical engagement with content and purposeful analysis of key issues of identity, power, aesthetics, ethics, and design and development that are embedded in the contexts of the Internet. Developing a reflective critical frame from which to engage and unpack information—while deliberately recognizing and being able to recreate and trace one's path through the Internet in order to understand how, where, and why one accesses certain ideas—is vital if young people are going to become thoughtful deliberative citizens capable of not only receiving and digesting information but also of producing, creating, and re-creating meanings and ideas across contexts.

Internet literacy requires recognition of the possibilities that come with the new spaces of information gathering, research, information creation, publication, and dissemination. It requires an understanding of the responsibilities one has for oneself and for others as a "produser." As Briggs (2005) contends:

> Unless we transform ideological constructions of how knowledge is produced, circulated, and received, routes of circulation, and how people are

positioned, we will be unlikely to promote effective alternative formulations or effectively support efforts by oppressed and marginalized populations to insert their voices into public debates. (p. 283)

The ability to be autonomous and self-regulating literate citizens who are capable of asking questions, connecting with multiple publics, examining varying agendas and perspectives, locating sources, searching for evidentiary warrant, constructing thoughtful and pragmatic arguments, and responding to others' ideas in order to enliven dialogue, debate, and democracy requires that we teach students to learn to ask several key questions about the information we and they seek out and produce:

- Who benefits from this point of view, argument, and/or product?
- Who will not benefit from these views and arguments?
- Whose perspectives and ideas are included, and whose are omitted in this argument and/or product?
- Is what I have downloaded or uploaded supported by evidence?
- How do these views benefit the greater good and promote democratic ideals?
- How do they recognize and support dialogue that is open and inclusive?
- How do these points of view or products shape one's emerging identity and ongoing interactions with others as an active democratic citizen?
- How will these ideas shape others' responses, perspectives, and ideas?
- How will others' responses impact one's own understanding of oneself and others?

We suggested earlier in this article that our work here would be a discussion, an effort to think about and extend existing scholarship and practice. Through our analysis, we suggest that critical Internet literacies are needed to support meaningful and active citizenship experiences. Clearly, a great deal more scholarship is required not only to conceptualize the intersections of citizenship education, literacy, and digital technologies, but also to design and evaluate pedagogies and pedagogical tools that seek to facilitate the teaching and learning of 21st century literacy skills necessary for engaged and enlightened active citizenship. Such work is essential to not only support the myriad of activities that compose democratic life, but to move forward our understanding of contemporary civic life and ensure a more just and productive democratic society.

REFERENCES

Barton, D., & Hamilton, M. (1998). *Local literacies: Reading and writing in one community*. London: Routledge.

Barton, K., & Levstik, L. (2004). *Teaching history for the common good*. Mahwah, NJ: Lawrence Erlbaum Associates.

Becker, H. (1999). *Internet use by teacher*. Retrieved from http://crito.uci.edu/papers/TLC/findings/internet-use/

Bell, D. (1976/1999). *The coming of post-industrial society: A venture in social forecasting*. NY: Basic Books.

Benkler, Y. (2006). *Wealth of networks: How social production transforms markets and freedom*. New Haven: Yale.

Bennett, S., Maton, K., & Kervin, L. (2008). The 'digital natives' debate: A critical review of the evidence. *British Journal of Educational Technology, 19*(5), 775–786.

Bennett, W. L. (2008). Changing citizenship in the digital age. In W. L. Bennett (Ed.), *Civic life online: Learning how digital media can engage youth* (pp. 1–24). The John D. and Catherine T. MacArthur Foundation Series on Digital Media and Learning. Cambridge, MA: The MIT Press.

Bers, M. U. (2008). Civic identities, online technologies: From designing civics curriculum to supporting civic experiences. In W. L. Bennett (Ed.), *Civic life online: Learning how digital media can engage youth* (pp. 139–160). The John D. and Catherine T. MacArthur Foundation Series on Digital Media and Learning. Cambridge, MA: The MIT Press.

Biddix, J., Somers, P., & Polman, J. (2009). Protest reconsidered: Identifying democratic and civic engagement learning outcomes. *Innovative Higher Education, 34*(3), 133–147.

Brand-Gruwel, S., Wopereis I., & Vermetten Y. (2005). Information problem solving: Analysis of a complex cognitive skill, *Computers in Human Behavior, 21*, 487–5.

Briggs, C. (2005). Communicability, racial discourse, and disease. *Annual Review of Anthropology, 34*, 269–291.

Bruns, A. (2008). *Blogs, Wikipedia, second life, and beyond: From production to produsage*. NY: Peter Lang.

Buckingham, D. (2003). *Media education: literacy, learning and contemporary culture*. Cambridge: Polity Press.

Buckingham, D. (2008). Introducing identity. In D. Buckingham (Ed.), *Youth, identity, and digital media* (pp. 1–24). Cambridge, MA: The MIT Press.

Bull, G., Thompson, A., Searson, M., Garofalo, J., Park, J., Younga, C., & Lee, J. (2008).Connecting informal and formal learning experiences in the age of participatory media. *Contemporary issues in technology and teacher education, 8*(2). Retrieved September 19, 2010 from http://www.citejournal.org/vol8/iss2/editorial/article1.cfm

Castells, M. (1996). *The rise of the network society*. Oxford: Blackwell.

Carr, N. (2010). *What the Internet is doing to our brains: The shallows*. NY: W.W. Norton.

Christensen, C., Johnson, C. W., & Horn, M. B. (2008). *Disrupting class: How disruptive innovation will change the way the world learns*. New York: McGraw Hill.

Chowdrey, M. (2008). The role of the Internet in Burma's Saffron Revolution. *Internet and democracy case study series*. Berkman Center research publication no

2008–08. Retrieved from http://cyber.law.harvard.edu/publications/2008/Role_of_the_Internet_in_Burmas_Saffron_Revolution

Clinton. H. (Jan 21st, 2010) *Remarks on Internet freedom. Speech at the Newseum,* Washington DC. Retrieved: http://www.state.gov/secretary/rm/2010/01/135519.htm

Cogan, J. J., & Derricott, R. (1998). *Citizenship for the 21st century: An international perspective on education.* London: Kogan Page.

Cuban, L. (2001). *Oversold and underused: Computers in the classroom.* Cambridge, MA: Harvard University Press.

Dahrendorf, R. (1997). *After 1989: Morals, revolution and civil society.* New York: St. Martin's Press.

Davies, L. (2006). Global citizenship: Abstraction or framework for action? *Educational Review, 58,* 5–25.

Davies, I., & Issitt, J. (2005). Reflections on citizenship education in Australia, England, and Canada. *Comparative Education, 41,* 389–410.

Dede, C. (2008). A seismic shift in epistemology. EDUCAUSE *Review,* 80–81. Retrieved September 22, 2010, from http://net.educause.edu/ir/library/pdf/ERM0837.pdf

DeWitt, S. W. (2007). Dividing the digital divide: Instructional use of computers in social studies. *Theory and Research in Social Education, 35(2),* 277–304.

Dewey, J. (1916). *Democracy and education.* New York: Macmillan.

Dewey, J. (1927). *The public and its problems.* Chicago: Swallow.

Donnelly-Smith, L. (2008). Political engagement in the age of Facebook: Student voices. *Peer Review, 10(2/3),* 37–39.

Doolittle, P., & Hicks, D. (2003). Constructivism as a theoretical foundation for the use of technology in Social Studies. *Theory and Research in Social Education, 31(1),* 72–104.

Duke, N.K., Schmar-Dobler, E., & Zhang, S. (2006). Comprehension and technology. In M. McKenna, L. D. Labbo, R. D. Kieffer, & D. Reinking, (Eds.), *International handbook of literacy and technology Vol. II* (pp. 317–326). Mahwah, NJ: Lawrence Erlbaum.

Ehman, L. H., & Glenn, A. D. (1991). Interactive technology in the social studies. In J. P. Shaver (Ed.), *Handbook of research on social studies teaching and learning* (pp. 513–522). NY: Macmillan.

Faris, R., & Etling, B. (2008). Madison and the smart mob: The promise and limitations of the Internet for democracy. *The Fletcher Forum of World Affairs, 32(2),* 65–85.

Friedman, A. M., & Hicks, D. (2006). The state of the field: Technology, social studies, and teacher education. *Contemporary Issues in Technology and Teacher Education, 6(2),* 246–258. Retrieved from http://www.citejournal.org/articles/v6i2socialstudies1.pdf

Gardner, H. (2009). *Five minds for the future.* Cambridge, MA: Harvard Business School Press.

Gee, J. (2000). New people in new worlds: Networks, capitalism and school. In B. Cope & M. Kalantzis (Eds.), *Multiliteracies: Literacy learning and the design of social futures* (pp. 43–68). London: Routledge.

Gladwell, M. (2010). Small change: Why the revolution will not be tweeted. *The New Yorker*. Retrieved http://www.newyorker.com/reporting/2010/10/04/101004fa_fact_gladwell

Goldstein J. (2007). The role of digital networked technologies in the Ukrainian Orange Revolution. *Internet and democracy case study series*. Berkman Center research publication no 2007-14. Retrieved from http://cyber.law.harvard.edu/publications/2007/The_Role_of_Digital_Networked_Technologies_in_the_Ukranian_Orange_Revolution

Goldstein, J., & Rotich, J. (2008). Digitally networked technology in Kenya's 2007–2008 post election crisis. *Internet and democracy case study series*. Berkman Center research publication no 2008–09. Retrieved from http://cyber.law.harvard.edu/publications/2008/Digitally_Networked_Technology_Kenyas_Post-Election_Crisis

Greenhow, C., Robelia, B., & Hughes, J. E. (2009). Web 2.0 and classroom research: What path should we take *now? Educational Researcher, 38*(4), 246–259.

Groshek, J. (2009). The democratic effects of the Internet, 1994–2003: A cross-national inquiry of 152 countries. *International Communication Gazette, 71*(3), 115–136.

Ibrahim, T. (2005). Global citizenship education: Mainstreaming the curriculum. *Cambridge Journal of Education, 35*, 177–194.

IBM Global Technology Services. (2007). *The toxic terabyte: How data-dumping threatens business efficiency*. Retrieved from, http://www-935.ibm.com/services/us/cio/leverage/levinfo_wp_gts_thetoxic.pdf

Jenkins, H. (2006). *Confronting the challenges of participatory culture: Media education for the 21ˢᵗ century*. White paper for the MacArthur Foundation. Retrieved September 24, 2009, from http://digitallearning.macfound.org

Jewitt, C. (2008). Multimodality and literacy in school classrooms. *Review of Research in Education, 32*, 241–267.

Jiang, M., & Xu, H. (2009). Exploring online structures on Chinese government portals: Citizen political participation and government legitimation. *Social Science Computer Review, 27*(2), 174–195.

Jones, E., & Gaventa, J. (2002). *IDS development bibliography 19: Concepts of citizenship*. Brighton, Sussex, England: Institute of Development Studies.

Joyce, M. (2007). The citizen journalism website "OhmyNews" and the 2002 South Korean Presidential election. *Internet and democracy case study series*. Berkman Center research publication no 2007–15. Retrieved from http://cyber.law.harvard.edu/publications/2007/The_Citizen_Journalism_Web_Site_Oh_My_News_and_the_South_Korean_Presidential_Election

Kress, G. (2003). Interpretation or design: From the world told to the world shown. In M. Styles & E. Bearne (Eds.), *Art, narrative and childhood* (pp.137–153). Stoke on Trent: Trentham Books.

Laverty, C. (2009). Our information literacy heritage: From evolution to revolution. *Feliciter, 3*(55), 88–91.

Lee, Y. (2009). Internet election 2.0? Culture, institutions, and technology in the Korean presidential elections of 2002 and 2007. *Journal of Information Technology & Politics, 6*(3/4), 312–325.

Leu, D. J., Jr. (2000). Literacy and technology: Deictic consequences for literacy education in an information age. In M. L. Kamil, P. Mosenthal, P. D. Pearson, & R. Barr (Eds.), *Handbook of reading research Vol. III* (pp. 743–770). Mahwah, NJ: Erlbaum.

Leu, D. J., O'Byrne, W. I., Zawilinski, L., McVerry, J. G., & Everett-Cacopardo, H. (2009). Comments on Greenhow, Robelia, and Hughes: Expanding the new literacies conversation. *Educational Researcher, 38*(4), 264–269.

Levine, P. (2008). A public voice for youth: The audience problem in digital media and online education. In W. L. Bennett (Ed.) *Civic life online: Learning how digital media can engage youth* (pp. 119–138). The John D. and Catherine T. MacArthur Foundation Series on Digital Media and Learning. Cambridge, MA: The MIT Press.

Livingstone, S. (2008a). Internet literacy: Young people's negotiation of new online opportunities. In T. McPherson (Ed.), *Digital youth, innovation, and the unexpected* (pp. 101–122). Cambridge, MA: The MIT Press.

Livingstone, S. (2008b). Taking risky opportunities in youthful content creation: teenager's use of social networking sites for intimacy, privacy, and self-expression. *New Media & Society, 10*(3), 393–411.

Livingstone, S. (2010). Youthful participation: What have we learned, what shall we ask? In *First annual digital media and learning conference: Diversifying participation, 18–22.* February, 2010, University of California San Diego, CA. Retrieved *http://eprints.lse.ac.uk/27219/1/Youthful_Participation_(LSERO_version).pdf*

Martorella, P. (1998) Technology and the social studies or which way to the sleeping giant? *Theory and Research in Social Education, 25,* 511–14.

McManus, R. (2005, August 6). Web 2.0 is not about version numbers or betas. *Read/Write/Web.* Retrieved September 12, 2010, from http://www.readwriteweb.com/archives/web_20_is_not_a.php

National Council for the Social Studies. (2009). *NCSS Position Statement on Media Literacy.* Washington, DC: Author. Retrieved from http://www.socialstudies.org/positions/medialiteracy

O'Reilly, T. (2007). What is Web 2.0: Design patterns and business modes for the next generation of software. *Communications & strategies, 65*(1st quarter, pp. 17–37).

Palser, B. (2009). Amateur content's star turn. *American Journalism Review, 31*(4), 42.

Parker, W. C. (1996a). Introduction. *Educating the democratic mind.* Albany, NY: State University of New York Press.

Parker, W. C. (1996b). "Advanced" ideas about democracy: Toward a pluralist conception of citizen education. *Teachers College Record, 98,* 104–125.

Parker, W.C. (2008). Knowing and doing in democratic citizenship education. In L.S. Levstik and C.A. Tyson (Eds.), *Handbook of research in social studies education* (pp. 65–80). NY: Routledge.

Raynes-Goldie, K. & Walker, L. (2008). Our space: Online civic engagement tools for youth. In W. L. Bennett's (Ed.) *Civic life online: Learning how digital media can engage youth* (pp. 161–188). The John D. and Catherine T. MacArthur Foundation Series on Digital Media and Learning. Cambridge, MA: The MIT Press.

Richardson, W. (2006). *Blogs, wikis, podcasts, and other powerful web tools for classrooms.* Thousand Oaks, CA.: Corwin Press.

Rosenzweig, R. (2001). The road to Xanadu: Public and private pathways on the history web. *Journal of American History 88*(2), 548–579.

Samoriski, J. H. (2000). Private spaces and public interests: Internet navigation, commercialism and the fleecing of democracy. *Communication Law & Policy,* 5(1), 93–113.

Schiffer, A. (2007). Between pajamas and Pulitzers: Distributed gatekeeping and the potential of blogs as news media. *Conference Papers—American Political Science Association,* 1–40.

Shulman, L.S. (2007). Practical wisdom in the service of professional practice. *Educational Researcher, 36,* 550–563.

Simon, L. D., Corrales, J., & Wolfensberger, D. (2002). *Democracy and the Internet. Allies or adversaries.* Washington D.C.: Woodrow Wilson Center Press.

Smith, A. Schlozman, K. H., Veba, S., & Brady, H. (2009). The Internet and civic engagement. *Pew Internet & American Life Project.* Retrieved from, http://www.pewinternet.org/Reports/2009/15—The-Internet-and-Civic-Engagement.aspx

Sunstein, C. (2009). *On rumors: How falsehoods spread, why we believe them, what can be done.* NY: Farrar, Straus & Giroux.

Tettey, W. J. (2001). Information technology and democratic participation in Africa. *Journal of Asian & African Studies, 36*(1), 133–153.

Torney-Purta, J. & Richardson, W. (2004). Anticipated political engagement among adolescents in Australia, England, Norway, and the United States. In J. Demaine (Ed.), *Citizenship and political education today* (pp. 41–58). Basingstoke, UK: Palgrave, Macmillan.

Torney-Purta, J., Lehmann, R., Oswald, H., & Schulz, W. (2001). *Citizenship and education in twenty-eight countries; Civic knowledge and engagement at age fourteen.* Amsterdam: The International Association for the Evaluation of Educational Achievement. Available: http://www.wam.umd.edu/~iea

VanFossen, P.J. & Berson, M. J. (Eds.) (2008). *The electronic republic? The impact of technology on education for citizenship.* Indiana: Purdue University Press.

Walraven, A., Brand-Gruwel, S., & Boshuizen, H. (2009). How students evaluate information and sources when searching the World Wide Web for information. *Computers & Education, 52*(1), 234–246,

Watts, M. (2006). Citizenship education revisited: Policy, participation, and problems. *Pedagogy, Culture, & Society, 14,* 83–97.

Wiltmeyer, P. Q. (2010, May 10). Obama at Hampton U.: 'Be role models. . . . be mentors'. *The Virginian—Pilot.* Retrieved from http://hamptonroads.com/2010/05/transcript-obamas-hampton-commencement-address

USING WEB 2.0 TO TRANSFORM A BRICK & MORTAR SCHOOL INTO A PARTICIPATORY MEDIA RICH CIVIC LEARNING ENVIRONMENT

Joseph O'Brien

Participatory media literacy is an active response to the as-yet-unsettled battles over political and economic power in the emerging mediasphere, and to the possibility that today's young people could have a say in shaping part of the world they live in—or might be locked out of that possibility.

—(Rheingold, p. 100)

In the 21ˢᵗ century, participatory media education and civic education are inextricable.

—(Rheingold, p. 103)

Online civic education at the local or school level requires the use of privately and commercially operated virtual places to serve public purposes.

Contemporary Social Studies: An Essential Reader, pages 493–526
Copyright © 2012 by Information Age Publishing
All rights of reproduction in any form reserved.

While the creation of an entire virtual world dedicated to civic education is the ideal situation (O'Brien, 2008), such is not likely to happen at the state and/or national level in the near future and localities lack the resources to create and maintain such a site. Civic educators have access to a host of for and non-profit sites, which offers users a wide range of participatory media services, but such sites rarely are designed with what is in the best interest of a student's civic education in mind. Even social action sites, such as Youth Noise, WireTap, and TakingITGlobal, which make rich use of participatory media and provide invaluable services to youth, typically are not designed with youth as students as the primary audience. As a result, teachers are forced to build a participatory media-rich civic learning environment for students on an ad hoc basis. This is quite a daunting task when one considers that participatory media includes: "blogs, wikis, RSS tagging and social bookmarking, music-photo-video sharing, mashups, podcasts, digital story-telling, virtual communities, social network services, virtual environments, and videoblogs" (Rheingold, p. 100). Such media is characterized as: "many-to-many media now make it possible for every person connected to the network to broadcast as well as receive text, images, audio, video, software, data, discussions, transactions, computations, tags, or links to and from every other person"; "social media whose values and power derives from the active participation of many people"; and, "social networks, when amplified by information and communications networks, enable broader, faster and lower cost coordination of activities" (Rheingold, p. 100). Given this, there is a need for a comprehensive, ongoing effort to translate research on youths' use of participatory media into meaningful formal and informal instructional practices, a need highlighted by: the importance of youths' civic education; the comprehensive nature of ongoing changes in information and communications technologies; the impact of these changes on youth; and the growing commercialization of the Internet.

As I explore civic learning in a participatory media rich environment, I am mindful of a caution voiced by Lankes (2008): "To put it bluntly, what users need in order to take charge of their own online decision making is at best an art and, more often than not, a series of trial-and-error solutions" (p. 103). At the same time I am sensitive to several constraints on incorporating Web 2.0 technology in schools identified by Bull, et al. (2008), two of which are relevant here: "Teachers have limited models for effective integration of media in their teaching; and, only limited research is available to guide best practice" (p. 2). I will draw upon the "limited research" to suggest a "model for effective integration" of blogs, wikis and online discussions in civic education, as well as discuss what I consider a critical but largely unaddressed aspect of civic education in the age of Web 2.0 technology, the civic socialization of youth in an increasingly commercialized online environment (Bull et al., 2008, p.2) [1] Prior to offering these suggestions on how to integrate several forms of participatory media so as to enable students to form an individual and group position on an issue of concern to them and to addressing the need to "socialize" students to the use of such media, I will discuss: different conceptions of citizenship and the importance of developing civic participatory skills; the growing digital disconnect between students' online out-of-school experiences and their offline in-school experiences; the blurring of the lines between the personal, public and commercial sectors of the "emerging mediasphere"; and, ways to transfer students' informal, social learning related to their use of participatory media to formal, academic learning.

BUILDING A CASE FOR THE DEVELOPMENT OF CIVIC PARTICIPATORY SKILLS: CITIZENSHIP WITHIN A POLITICAL, LEGAL AND SOCIAL CONTEXT

While Bull et al. (2008) noted that limited instructional models and research constrain the implementation of participatory media, civic educators also confront curricular constraints. State social studies standards fail to clearly articulate what constitutes citizenship, let alone the implications of youth's use of participatory media as emerging adult citizens. Typically, citizenship is defined as one's legal status relative to a nation-state "in terms of state boundaries, administrations, and rights" (Shaw, 2008, p. 154). Westheimer and Kahne (2004) contend that this is but a starting point, presenting three types of citizen, a personally responsible citizen, a participatory citizen, and a social justice citizen, which are based on "prominent theoretical perspectives," "important differences in the ways that educators conceive of democratic educational aims," and "ideas and ideals that resonate with practitioners" (p. 240). They argue that K–12 citizenship education focuses on the development of a "personally responsible citizen," with some attention to a "participatory citizen." Abowitz and Harnish (2006) "reviewed selected contemporary theoretical and more applied (curricular) texts focusing on citizenship or citizenship education" (p. 655). They "found a distinct dominance of the Enlightenment-inspired [civic republican and liberal] notions of citizenship [which] continue to define and powerfully shape how U.S. society understands citizenship and the ways in which the society's institutions, such as schools, thereby shape citizens" (pp., 656–657), the former most closely resembling Westheimer and Kahne's "personally responsible" citizen and the latter their "participatory" one. While they found evidence of "critical and transformative discourses of citizenship," such "discourses are marginalized in the curricular texts that define the standards and prominent meanings of citizenship taught in schools" (p. 657), a finding paralleling that of Westheimer and Kahne vis-à-vis the "social justice" citizen.

Not surprisingly, since social studies curricula fail to acknowledge different conceptions of citizenship and therefore the importance of citizenship as a discrete concept threaded throughout the entire curriculum, students typically do not learn about citizenship outside of civics or government courses.

The dominant types of citizenship identified above are defined in terms of an individual's legal and political relation with the U.S. government. T.H. Marshall (1964) concluded that there were three components of citizenship: civil (or legal), political, and social. Marshall's social citizenship "refers to an ability to have access to the society's resources and capacities that permit social mobility and comfort. Access to health care, education, employment opportunities, and nondiscriminatory housing are examples of the benefits that societal citizenship offers" (p. 69, Ladson-Billings as cited in Noddings, 2005). While Parsons (1965) theorized that African-Americans of his time most often were denied Marshall's social citizenship, today the economically disenfranchised are least likely to receive the full benefits of social citizenship. Simply voting and paying taxes or even becoming more adept at participating in the political process is unlikely to change one's economic status, yet most state standards are not designed to equip students with a broad range of civic participation skills. Given schools' reluctance to adopt a "social justice" or a "critical" citizen approach, Marshall's idea of social citizenship provides a theoretical basis for an expanded and richer conception of citizenship, one that would move us from an individualized to a group orientation toward citizenship and civic action and would align with Coleman's (2004) notion of a "networked" citizen.

A proponent of Marshall's social citizenship, Banks (2008) argues that "the conception of citizenship in a modern democratic nation-state should be expanded to include cultural rights and group rights within a democratic framework" (p. 129), a notion embedded in the United Nations Declaration of Human Rights (1948). Since the existing conception of citizenship not only is grounded in an "identification [with] soil, a state, the law, and fellow inhabitants" (DeRuyter & Spiecker, 2008, 352), but also in an "abstract individualism," then "[G]roup differences are not included in a universal conception of citizenship" (Banks, 2008, p. 131). This lends itself to a citizenship education curriculum that focuses on those included, rather than the excluded, which effectively eliminates learning about the struggles of the economically and ethnically disenfranchised. Drawing upon the work of Young (1989), Banks argues for a "differentiated conception of citizenship," for when "universal citizenship is determined, defined, and implemented by groups with power and when the interests of marginalized groups are not expressed or incorporated into civic discussions, the interests of the groups with power and influence will determine the definitions of universal citizenship and the public interest" (pp. 131–132). While Banks strives for a redefinition of citizenship and citizenship education, Rheingold (2008) suggests that participatory media literacy offers a means to act upon Banks' thinking:

> Participatory media literacy is an active response to the as-yet-unsettled battles over political and economic power in the emerging mediasphere, and to the possibility that today's young people could have a say in shaping part of the world they will live in—or might be locked out of that possibility (p. 100).

According to Rheingold "In the twenty-first century, participatory media education and civic education are inextricable" p. 103 in that participatory media provides civic educators with the means necessary to engage students in virtual democratic experiences and by so doing to cultivate the skills and dispositions necessary for civic engagement. While I realize that the most contentious public policy issues in U.S. history have concerned how the government and society have addressed distinct groups, which in turn have illustrated a continuing tension between an individual and group conception of citizenship, as Gloria Ladson-Billings (2004) has noted:

> The dynamic of the modern (or postmodern) nation-state makes identities as either an individual or a member of a group untenable. Rather than seeing the choice as either/or, the citizens of the nation-state operates in the realism of both/and. She is both an individual who is entitled to citizen rights that permit one to legally challenge infringement of those rights [and one who is] acting to a member of a group....

The distinction that she draws is critical. Those from de Tocqueville (1835) to Noveck (2005) have addressed the idea of how groups use the democratic process "to achieve together what we cannot achieve alone" (Noveck, p. 3). While I agree with Banks that a danger of a majoritarian system is that some groups might never find themselves part of a political majority, I also agree with Noveck that we cannot ignore "the collaborative nature of public life...and the way groups work today" (p. 5). While I will leave for another article whether adopting a group orientation to citizenship necessitates addressing the question of whether more influential groups have a responsibility to assist less influential ones, particularly when the less influential groups with a shared characteristic such as ethnicity, gender or economic condition fail to achieve full social citizenship, I do believe that K–12 citizenship education should prepare all youth for individual and group citizenship, particularly if they are to engage in Rheingold's "unsettled battles."

Torney-Purta & Lopez (2006) concluded that while traditional citizenship education is well suited to developing some of the intellectual skills necessary for civic and political participation, this is not true for individual let alone group civic participatory skills, particularly those that addressed either actual participation in the political system or substantive policy issues since such issues were likely to prove controversial and disquieting to the community, the latter a finding supported by Niemi & Niemi (2007). While Menezes (2003) argued that "citizenship education should...focus on students' empowerment for assuming an active role in the [democratic] process and defining and expanding citizenship itself" (p. 432), Torney-Purta and Lopez noted "there is hesitation about whether and how to incorporate enhanced opportunities for students' voice and input in their schools and classrooms" (p.15). Are not such opportunities though essential to helping "young people develop the ability to make informed and reasoned decisions for the public good as citizens of a culturally diverse, democratic society in an interdependent world" (National Council for the Social Studies, 1994, p. 3)? Also notable was that "because of the political nature of teaching and learning citizenship, teachers often are unsure of the boundaries around engaging students in political activities" (p. 17), a finding supported by Martin & Chiodo (2007). K–12 students are engaged in citizenship education that at best builds their knowledge base and promotes the acquisition of the intellectual skills necessary for life as a citizen, yet fails to develop civic participatory skills, due in part to a reluctance to immerse students in a non-school, civic setting where they seek to bring about social change. This reluctance extends to virtual participatory experiences as well. Whereas before such reluctance grew out of concerns related to the loss of instructional time and the logistics associated with community-based learning experiences, the difficulty in regulating and monitoring students' virtual experiences now fuel educators' reluctance to more fully use participatory media, resulting in a different kind of disconnect.

DIGITAL DISCONNECT, LEARNING AND THE DIGITAL GENERATION

New media allow for a degree of freedom and autonomy for youth that is less apparent in a classroom setting. Youth respect one another's authority online, and they are often more motivated to learn from peers than from adults. Their efforts are also largely self-directed, and the outcome emerges through exploration, in contrast to classroom learning that is oriented toward set, predefined goals.
—(Ito, et al., 2008)

As you read the title to this section you might have thought that I was giving a new name to the "old" idea of the digital divide, i.e. the divide between the "have" districts that supposedly wallow in high tech equipment and the "have-nots" districts that struggle to provide an overhead project let alone mobile labs with wireless access. Unquestionably, such a divide still exists and dramatically impacts student learning in some high-risk districts, though I wonder if the divide is as deep as we believe. If "digital" is defined primarily as access to and use of online resources via a computer, then the divide remains deep. What if our notion of digital though included cell phones, MP3 players and other personal devices? A survey of experts, for example, predict that the "mobile device will be "the primary connection tool to the Internet for most people in the world in 2020" (Anderson & Rainie, 2008, p.2). According to Jones & Fox (2009) about 75% of youth aged 12–17 own both a cell phone and a MP3 player. In addition, 93% regularly go online, 97 % play video games and 78% play online games; 75% have created online content and viewed online videos; 70% use social network sites; 59% download music; 55% create sns profile; 68% have broadband access at home; 50–60% post photos online; 40–50% tag online content; and, 25% have posted video online. If older youth either own or have access to such digital devices, then a more important issue for me is the digital disconnect, i.e. the separation between students' out-of-school access to the online environment and their in-school offline lives, especially given how Ito et al. (2008) described young people's online activity.

Just as Torney-Purta and Lopez's report eloquently confirmed what we already knew, i.e. that a dramatic distinction exists between what is occurring in the U.S. and worldwide and what actually is discussed in a typical civics or government classroom or is found the textbooks, so too we always have known that young people's in-school lives differs from their out-of-school lives. The digital disconnect though not only highlights the difference between youth's in and out of school lives, but also the pace at which the changes are occurring and deepening in the larger society and how quickly youth are integrating those changes not only into how they live but also how they identify themselves.

The National School Boards Association's "Creating & Connecting" report (2007) helps to illustrate the nature of the digital disconnect. At first blush the survey results (Figure 25.1) suggest that schools are seeking to minimize the social, while promoting the academic, use of participatory media. Stop though and reread the figures. Thirty-five percent of schools, for example, report using a blog. There is no indication though whether the use of blogs or an online collaborative project is occurring school-wide, across a grade level or simply in a single classroom on an ad hoc basis. Also, the results suggest that all schools are the same.

In some respects, the horses already are out of the barn though we would like to believe that we still are able to corral them. While some school districts initially sought a complete ban on cell phones, for example, such bans were unable to withstand the pressure from parents to permit students at least to bring the phones to school. School policies typically permit students to use phones before and after school and during lunch. Students are not permitted to have them turned on during class and teachers possess the

- Social and Educational Networking More than 80% of schools have rules against online chatting & IM
- 62% have rules against participating in bulletin boards or blogs
- 60% prohibit sending or receiving e mail in school
- 52% specifically prohibit the use of social networking sites
- ...yet, 69% of schools have student Web site programs.
- 49% say their schools participate in an online collaborative project with other schools
- 46% say their students participate in e pal projects
- 35% say either the school maintains a blog or one is found somewhere in an instructional program
- 22% say classroom involved in creating and maintaining a wiki (National School Boards Association, 2007)

FIGURE 25.1. Survey Results of Creating & Connecting: Research & Guidelines on Online

authority to seize them if students use them. Here is a test for you—how many of you are able to type and send a text message with your phone in your pocket? Given this situation, how likely is a teacher to try and seize a phone if s/he suspects the student is pocket texting? Are we now at a point where while we as educators are creating this digital disconnect so as to protect both students and instructional time, students very adeptly are working around it? What if as we craft a place for participatory media in civic classrooms we first acknowledge the "informal learning that occurs in the context of participatory media," since building upon such learning offers "significant opportunities for increased student engagement in formal learning settings," so as to connect their "experience with communication technologies" to sound "pedagogy...content...[and] learning objectives" (Bull et al., p. 6)? As part of this first step we need to recognize how this digital generation, those able to engage with media and technology in an intense, autonomous, and interest-driven way" (Ito et al., p. 28) learn differently

The continued evolution of the Internet's online-networking capacity is making learning in a sustained virtual environment a reality. Specifically referring to MMOG (massive multiple online games), Thomas & Brown (2009) indicate that such games share these characteristics: "a context for experiential learning"; "context for learning that is primarily social in nature"; permit "players who engage in the space to actually *create* and *change* and *evolve* the world they inhabit"; and, "produce a social space around the game that has a profound impact on the game's evolution" (p. 39). These characteristics also define virtual worlds such as Teen Life and some are present in participatory media such as blogs, wikis, and social networking sites. Thomas & Brown contend that a typical model of learning is for you to "learn about" something and then you "learn to be" something, such as learning about citizenship and then learning to be a citizen. A slightly more "complex" version of their model is that of "tell, model, and do." For many of us, prior to playing a board game we would learn the rules, i.e. learn about the game. If we had friends or older siblings familiar with the game, they might show us how to play and then we would play it. For youth and virtual games they start with "learning to be" by actually doing the game and using their play to figure out the rules or how a character moves, i.e. "learning about" the game.

For those not weaned on video games, how to operate in a virtual world often is so different from our real world experiences that we need to learn how "to be" in a virtual world. For example, talk with any adult of a certain age about their experience with trying to navigate an avatar in a place like Second Life and compare their experience with that of a 14 year old. The experiences for the older adults during their initial experiences in a virtual world are similar to experiences that we had as a child when first learning to walk or to ride a bike. While one could learn a lot about walking and riding a bike by observation or reading about it, we tended to learn both by doing it. Given our age at the time, this seemed like a natural way to approach learning. Only later did we come to believe in the importance of learning about it first and doing it later. In all fairness, early parts or stages of most games take the importance of learning about into account. Thus, your early interaction with an online game is intended for you to learn about the game, while you are doing or playing it. Stop and ask yourself—as an individual and a learner, which would you find more empowering? Reading a handbook of directions and then playing the game or immediately engaging with a game that enabled you to learn about it while you played it?

My point is simple—the digital disconnect is but the most obvious aspect of the challenge that we as civic educators confront in preparing youth for civic engagement in a participatory media rich world. We simply are not asking students to power down or even to relinquish much of the personal autonomy that their use of participatory media grants them. We are asking them to accept an approach to learning that runs counter to the way that they have used while exercising their digital independence. In coming to this realization I now am fully aware of how those during Galileo's time probably felt, except I cannot place myself in the position of Galileo and his supporters, but rather I must accept that my world view would more appropriately fit those that still believed that the sun revolved around the earth. Contrast a typical 30 minutes for a student in a social studies classroom where she probably receives a 20 minute lecture followed by an 10 minute small group activity with 30 minutes outside of class where the student exchanges 10–20 text messages with those on her favorites list, transfers several pictures from her cell phone to her social networking page, watches several YouTube videos, and works on a song using Garage Band.

In a classroom where students are expected to power down, I contend that civic educators are adhering to Coleman's (2008) "managed e-citizenship," where students are regarded as:

> apprentice citizens who are in a process of transition from the immaturity of childhood to the self-possession of adulthood. As apprentices, youth are in a state of dependency [which] means that they lack the powers of independent agency associated with self-determination. Civic apprenticeship entails learning the skills required to exercise responsible judgment in a risky and complex world (p. 191).

Those supportive of a "managed e-citizenship" approach assume that the Internet is "an anarchic realm in which unknown nodes perpetually collide, is an unsafe place for young people, not only because their social innocence might be exploited by predators, but because they are politically vulnerable to misinformation and misdirection" (Coleman, p. 191). Coleman argues that supporters of a "managed" approach "favor the establishment of safe, civilized, moderated [online] enclaves in which youth can learn and have their say" (p. 192), which complements Sharples et al. (2009) claim that, since the publication of a 1953 United Nations Educational, Scientific and Cultural Organization report of the effects of movies and radio on children, "adults have sought to protect children from the perceived dangers of the new media" (p. 71).

According to Coleman, an "autonomous e-citizenship approach," while recognizing youth's "limited experience or access to resources" assumes "they possess sufficiently autonomous agency to speak for themselves on agendas of their own making" (p. 191). Supporters of this approach perceive the Internet as a "relatively open public sphere in which the ideas and plans of protest can be exchanged with relative ease, speed and global scope." Coming full circle to Thomas & Brown's (2009) ideas about learning and this digital generation, Coleman contends that the "function of e-citizenship is to conceive, create and sustain members of a political community" (p.201), yet "the terms of citizenship are not static" and citizens need "to contest those terms" (p. 202). Considering Coleman's point in light of the earlier one about how students do not study the evolving nature of citizen and citizenship in U.S. history and how youth's use of participatory media affects how they approach learning, transforming informal online democratic experiences into formal academic ones is but a component of citizenship education in age of participatory media. Youth also must continually examine the changing role of citizen, citizenship, the relation between citizen, government and one's community, and how one participates individually and as a group, but in a way that provides for user agency or the ability for them to act autonomously. How can we not foster such user agency in a civic education program when youth routinely engage autonomously in a host of informal democratic experiences in an "indefinite and infinite" online environment where "all the places within it remain instantaneously accessible" (Greenhall & Fletcher, 2003)? At the same time, how do we ensure that we do not promote "participatory democracy...as an alternative to representative democracy but rather as a complement to it" (Schugurensky p. 615)? Prior to exploring in more depth how students engage in online participatory democratic experiences, the implications of them, and the roles they adopt, let me first explore the emerging participatory mediasphere.

COMMERCIAL OR PUBLIC PARTICIPATORY MEDIA?

So even though the Internet was initially based on a nonprofit philosophy, its recent history shows that market forces have established themselves as the hegemonic paradigm of the medium

—(Cammaerts, 2008, p. 363)

to territorialize cyberia as the public sphere is to determine in advance what sort of engagements and identities are proper to the political and to use this determination to homogenize political engagement, neutralize social space, and sanitize popular cultures.

—(Dean, 2001, pp. 246–47)

If, as Thomas and Brown argue (2009), "Virtual worlds are persistent, avatar-based social spaces that provide players or participants with the ability to engage in long-term, coordinated conjoined action" (p. 37), what are the implications of continued use of sites that have a commercial component? At some point do we as educators inadvertently become marketers for a site's owners? While less obvious with sites like Wikispaces, if teachers take advantage of the for-free subscription, might a student's constant exposure to Wikispaces cause them to use a for-free subscription with Wikispaces and then eventually move to a more robust, paid subscription? There is no question that teachers routinely make use of commercial products in their classrooms, the textbook represents the prime example. Obviously textbook companies are for for-profit businesses. I seriously question though whether any student, or teacher for that matter, ever went out and bought a textbook for pleasure reading. As a result, a student is unlikely to ever connect the textbook publisher to other product lines of any interest to them. Using the Internet simply to gather information, a Web 1.0 application, typically is a one-stop, one-act relation with an online information provider. Using Web 2.0 applications though changes the relation between the user and provider and how and why we use commercial resources for educational purpose, which necessitates understanding how the use of such resources might affect youth and redefine our role as teachers.

There are two ways to approach answering the section title question. First, in light of the textbook example, is to consider the effects that the development of participatory media has had on the traditional content producers and communications field. Second is to examine the use of the public and commercial applications of participatory media, and the potential effect of such use on youth. In response to the first, Carroll & Hackett (2006) argue that the democratization of the communications field has taken on four forms: finding ways to permit "oppositional voices" and "to change specific aspects of representation"; creation of "media reform coalitions"; "building independent, democratic and participatory media"; and, "changing the relationship between audiences and media, chiefly by empowering audiences." Two points to keep in mind as I proceed is that the democratization of the communications field does not necessarily make the field any less commercial and has redefined our role as audience, consumer and citizen.

"'Voice' [is] the unique style of personal expression that distinguishes one's communications" (Rheingold, p. 101), and one's online "public voice can be characterized not just as active, but as generative" (p. 102). While Carroll & Hackett argue that the democratization of the communications field has resulted in multiple opportunities for "oppositional voices" and "to change specific aspects of representation," the question is under what conditions and how well are students able to make sense of such "public voices." On a simple level, for example, how do users "source" these voices? Just as in the late 20th century non-news interests began to intrude upon the television newsroom, so too commercial interests are becoming intertwined with news reporting and expression of personal opinions on the Internet. The blogosphere best illustrates the "oppositional voices" aspect of the Internet. As certain bloggers have become recognized as credible and valid sources of information and opinion, commercial groups have financially courted them to use their blog to promote a product. There are instances though where a blogger portrays her/himself as an independent "voice" but actually has one or more commercial sponsors, known in the trade as a "flog," or a fake blog. Where goes the blogosphere? Are we witnessing a phenomenon akin to the early days of newspapers, where individuals periodically "published" a newssheet or a gazette, a commentary on public affairs, predecessors to daily newspapers? Are bloggers more like free lance editorialists and online news media like the newspapers of old, which gave the best ones space on the opinion page? Is the blogosphere developing a commercial sector but with most users remaining in the "public" sphere either out of choice or due to lack of commercial viability? If the latter, how do users come to distinguish the two and what are the implications for those "oppositional voices" that lack commercial viability, but could serve an invaluable public service?

Participatory media makes Carroll & Hackett's formation of coalitions a hallmark of Web 2.0 and reflects the associational nature of U.S. democracy very well. Just as within the communications field there are hosts of groups to promote critical media literacy, so too there are numerous groups, such as the Electronic Frontier Foundation (http://www.eff.org/), whose purpose is to maintain the democratic nature of the Internet so as to preserve a place for Coleman's "network empowered citizen." While sites such as MySpace and Facebook have come to define the participatory media's networking capacity, the Obama presidential campaign and use of Second Life for academic and professional purposes illustrated the non-social applications of such capacity.

"Building independent, democratic participatory media" is the third feature of Carroll and Hackett's democratization of the communications field. Is there an inherent tension between online social networking and commercial activity? What is a commercial service provider's responsibility to users of a social networking site, if a major purpose behind such networking is to share information and ideas? MySpace, for example, came under criticism late in 2005 for blocking links and content from competitor sites. One year later the News Corporation purchased MySpace, at which point Naples (2006)) cautioned: "Today, the purely linear, viral nature of the MySpace that is so much fun for users is anything but fun for advertisers who require more content security and targeting precision than MySpace can provide for their messages. That seems certain to change soon." Are we heading toward an online environment of what I call market-controlled online social networks? Once again, an analogy would prove apt. Commercial sites often are a gathering place for social groups and some businesses purposefully provide such space or promote their business as a place for social activities. How many bookstores have small "cafes" for drinks, books and friends? How about the super large retail stores with wide, open aisles suitable for weekend walkers? The difference though is that in the offline environment while similar places typically are found either in the public sector, such as a community center, or in the private sector, such as a church hall, there are few offline businesses that cater specifically to socializing, ala Facebook or MySpace.

Jenkins (2006) articulated very well Carroll & Hackett's fourth point: "Audiences, empowered by these new technologies, occupying a space at the intersection between old and new media, are demanding the right to participate within the culture" (p. 24). While only about 20% take on a content producer role, the traditional notion of audience does not apply to the participation of the other 80%. Compare a television or movie audience to an Internet user of media products. While your flexibility as an audience for television and movies has increased slightly, such as the ability to pay for a service that permits you to watch television shows at your leisure, you still possess few ways to actively participate other than to observe. Such is not the case with online media. You can upload your preferences and reviews to the media provider. You can chat with those not physically present with you while you watch the video. You can download the video and excise clips and combine them with other clips to make your own video, though you may never upload them. Compare the range of choices that you now have as part of "audience" with those you have while watching a movie. The user agency offered by participatory media thus subtly changes the role of even an audience member. While those out of college would consider such changes a novelty or privilege, those younger have grown up with this technology as it has emerged and as a result have come to expect it. And yet as noted by van Dijck (2009): "it is crucial to understand the new role of users as both *content providers* and *data providers*" (p. 47), which leads to consideration of the public and commercial applications of participatory media and the implications of such applications for youth and public policy.

For brevity's sake, I will focus on but six applications. First, online publishing applications and the use of service providers enable users to create and "publish" content. As Just (2009) notes: "Media products and services are simultaneously economic and cultural goods" (p. 98). Since users tend to consider a site such as YouTube as a means to an end, i.e. a way to upload one's creation and/or view that of others, do they fail to recognize this dual function? If they are not aware of the economic side of their relation with a provider such as YouTube, do they fail to recognize the "price" paid to use the service? Interestingly, the cultural nature of what users produce recently was recognized in international law by the UNESCO Convention on the Protection and Promotion of the Diversity of Cultural Expressions (2005): "cultural activities, goods and services have both an economic and a cultural nature ... and must therefore not be treated as solely having commercial value" (p. 2). If so, what are the implications for a site such as YouTube—do and/or should we consider YouTube as both an online democratic cultural commons and a commercial marketplace? While open source sites probably best approximate offline public spaces, does a site such as YouTube provide not simply a commercial but also a public service? Since 20% of adolescents already generate and publish content online, what if as this generation matures a majority evolve into content producers? Will this generation come to expect this service and hold YouTube accountable for it? What if this generation weaned on participatory democracy uses means other than commercial ones to hold YouTube accountable? What if YouTube and similar service providers took a different route and became more commercialized, such as YouTube's move to offer content providers the option to charge access to their videos, which was akin to the news media hiring widely read bloggers?

Second, while Carroll & Hackett note how the Internet provides a venue for "oppositional voices," there also is a corresponding trend occurring where commercial, private and public voices are merging to the point where they are becoming indistinguishable. Montgomery (2008) observed: "Incorporating social and political messages into the content of youth entertainment has already become a common practice in the social marketing and 'entertainment-education' campaigns of public health organizations" (p 32). In turn, there is the "growing practice of 'cause marketing,' in which companies link their products to causes and issues in order to build customer appreciation and loyalty" (Ibid). Montgomery wondered if the "ubiquitous and integrated nature of marketing in digital political engagement practices could serve to conflate civic identity and brand identity during this key formative stage" (p. 33).

Third, as Shah et al. (2001) noted: "it is not Internet use *per se*, but patterns of use featuring the exchange of information that matters." We leave digital footprints that are ever present, highly informative about us as a digital user, and readily available to those seeking the information. As a result, are we entering an era where digital voyeurism becomes highly profitable? How are we to know, for example, the intent of each and every person making use of participatory media? There rightly is a lot of concern over cyberbullies and cyber-predators. What about those individuals though that collect information about user interaction for commercial purposes? In this instance, what if I as a marketer cast a wide net on MySpace or Facebook by seeking ever wider and wider social networks and then using my access to individuals' profiles to create a marketing profile of the digital you. Place this in an offline context. How would you respond if after watching you go to your usual place of exercise 10 or 12 times, I came to realize the brand of pants, shirts, socks, shoes and equipment you wore, what perfume or aftershave you liked, and how you did your hair (or not!). What if I started posting coupons or ads where you exercised? While creepy offline, it is becoming increasingly acceptable online. Up to this point Internet use has been characterized by anonymity. As Solove (2004) suggests though, we need to consider our off-line selves as distinct from online or digital selves, particularly in light of van Dijck (2009) comments:

> Besides uploading content, users also willingly and unknowingly provide important information about their profile and behaviour to site owners and metadata aggregators. Before users can actually contribute uploads or comments to a site, they usually have to register with their name, email address and sometimes add more personal details such as gender, age, nationality or income. Their subsequent media behaviour can be minutely traced by means of databots. More importantly, all users of UGC sites unwittingly provide in-

formation because IP addresses—the majority of which can be connected to a user's name and address—can be mined and used without limit by platform owners. Permission to use metadata towards specific purposes are commonly regulated by a site's service agreements (Terms of Use), which users are required to sign. Metadata can be mined for various purposes, from targeted advertising to interface optimization, but the bottom line is that users have no power over data distribution (p.47)

Just as importantly, we often are not aware of what information is collected about us and how it is used. As Lessig (1999) argues: "Data is collected, but without your knowledge. Thus you cannot . . . choose whether you will participate in or consent to this surveillance . . . Nothing reveals whether you are being watched, so there is no real basis upon which to consent" (p. 505). As a result, the anonymity works two ways, while the privacy portions of the terms of use agreements with service providers ensure our personal anonymity, so too such agreements also permit the providers to collect information about our patterns of behavior to use for marketing purposes. Are we overly concerned with the privacy of the offline me at the expense of the online me? In one sense, do online marketers and other businesses really care and/or need to know about the offline me? Given this, who owns our digital footprints? What are the implications of behavioral advertising for youth? What is our obligation as civic educators to "protect" students' digital footprints?

Fourth, online networking not only builds social, but also commercial, capacity. "Marketers speak of "recruiting evangelists" by seeking out the:

influencing members of each social network" and turning them into 'brand breeders' or 'brand advocates' for products. Youth are offered incentives to incorporate brands into their user-generated content and distribute their work virally on the Internet, cell phones, and iPods. The rampant commercialization of these nascent digital communities raises serious questions about their future role as sites for political and civic engagement by youth (p. 34).

While we certainly can debate the appropriateness of such actions, this quickly is becoming accepted online business practice. What are the implications not only for how we use online sites but how we help young people act on the commercial and social uses of such sites?

Fifth, as the size and complexity of the Internet increases, many commercial interests are designing sites that provide greater uniformity and more closely regulate and monitor users' behavior. Interestingly, the situation is akin to the early days of the United States when due to their experience with the British government, many people were leery of a strong national government. Given this lack of a governmental, regulatory presence, commercial interests are filling the void. Consider the excerpt below from

Google's Terms of Use agreement that as a user you electronically sign prior to using many sites in light of point three.

> We may record information about your usage, such as when you use YouTube, the channels, groups, and favorites you subscribe to, the contacts you communicate with, and the frequency and size of data transfers, as well as information you display or click on in YouTube (including UI elements, settings, and other information). If you are logged in, we may associate that information with your account. We may use clear GIFs (a.k.a. 'Web Beacons') in HTML-based emails sent to our users to track which emails are opened by recipients. (http://youtube.com/t/terms)

Is access to our online patterns of behavior part of the price that we pay to participate in a personal information economy? As Karas (2002) noted: "The greatest harm to individuals from data collection is not disclosure of private information, but rather systematic exercise of power over them." According to Chester (2009):

> Sophisticated neuromarketing techniques, predictive algorithms, and other forms of artificial intelligence now permit marketers to *anticipate* our needs and interests—and to stimulate desire among especially vulnerable users (including children)—crossing the border that separates engagement from entrapment.

Creating a regulatory environment to ensure user safety or business efficiency is one thing, to use such an environment to subtly manipulate our commercial decisions is quite another, particularly if youth are the target of such manipulation. Consider the irony of this situation for youth who are attracted to the autonomy that participatory media apparently provides.

Sixth and finally, as Williamson (2009) states, while "the emergence of immersive digital media products for children, such as virtual worlds, creates an unprecedented opportunity for commercial marketing" (p. 9), "[U]nfortunately, as with social networks, advertising has not kept pace with usage of virtual worlds." This situation highlights the importance of the field taking a lead on providing guidance to those on the local level. To help illustrate this point, let me offer one example. Early childhood education, Sesame Street and public broadcasting are uniquely connected. Few either would argue against the contributions made by the Sesame Street Workshop for several decades or its importance to the vitality of public broadcasting. Some parents though might vividly recall the commercial side of Sesame Street several years ago, particularly if they were unable to deliver on an Elmo doll for the holidays. The dilemma with an organization like Sesame Street, one dependent upon the sale of products to continue to offer high quality educational services for youth, is determining the line between the commercial and educational parts of the organization. In "D is for Digital" report, sponsored by Joan Ganz Cooney Center at Sesame Workshop, Carly Shuler identified "consumer market trends" of which "the virtual world phenomenon" was one. To support this trend Shuler provided a chart with the URL and site description for 14 "examples of virtual worlds for children" (p. 19). The Virtual Worlds Association publishes "The Blue Book: A Consumer Guide to Virtual Worlds." Interestingly, of the 14 examples cited in Shuler's report, Sesame Street's Panwapa was the only one not listed in the guide. Just as young people need to learn about the blurring of the lines between the public, commercial and private realms within a digital environment, so too we as educators need to consider the implications of this blurring for access to, the quality of, and our use of digital learning resources.

What might the growing commercialization of the Internet mean for student use of participatory media? First, since the formation of personal identity becomes increasingly important as youth move into adolescence, we should remain mindful of the importance of user agency and role development. Participatory culture finds its economic equivalent in the notion of 'prosumption' or 'wikinomics', a theory in which user agency is increasingly defined in terms of production and less in terms of consumption (Tapscott and Williams, 2007). We need to recognize and prepare youth for the distinctiveness of certain roles in an online environment, such as that of a prosumer. For example, what if a young person's video went viral? Is global recognition of her or his work sufficient or should s/he receive some benefits from the site that hosts the video?

Second, as with any supposedly democratic process, a critical question to ask is who is able to make decisions, what are they able to make decisions about, what information is available to them to help make the decision, and how the architecture of the process might influence what, how and why decisions are made? YouTube, for example, is first and foremost a commercial site, not one whose primary purpose is to provide a means to share one's creations. If so, how does Google shape who does what on the site? The transition of the more popular user generated content sites from commons-like sites to commercially driven platforms is causing the roles of consumer and producer to take on more traditional tones. For example, while I still am able to create and upload videos, I now face more restrictions when doing so than in the past. Before I might not have concerned myself with what and how much I sampled given the difficulty of enforcing intellectual property laws online, at least until the Napster episode. Traditional content providers now are better able to direct their focus on several popular sites such as YouTube. Prior to its purchase by Google, users largely monitored YouTube. Due to intellectual property concerns Google/You-Tube employers had to take on more of a reviewer role. In turn, YouTube needs to remain responsive to advertisers and Google seeks to profit from use of "consumers'" personal data. In some respects, up to this point businesses like Google remind me of a vendor at an open-air market. Since admission to the "marketplace" is free and available to all, I wonder if we have come to consider the Internet as a public place. This might help explain the lack of public advocacy to promote the distinctiveness of civic education in a virtual environment and the need to ensure that students have equal and universal access to such an education.

While my portrayal of the growing commercialization of the Internet might seem overly dramatic, when you next browse the Internet ask yourself what is missing. Prior to doing so, drive around where you live and make note of all the examples of the public sector. Everywhere you go you will notice the services provided by the government and therefore supported by your taxes, such as roads, street lights, police protection, parks, schools, fire stations. Offline the public sector is visible and well defined. The lack of online "public" space relative to other types of space testifies to the efforts to minimize government's regulatory presence on the Internet. Are we simply replacing a governmental regulatory system for a commercial one? For example, are we moving to a system akin to cable television where you pay for different levels of access, so that lower levels customers are not able to access all sites? Will we move to a situation where those service providers that afford it will remain on the Internet freeway and those that can't are relegated to the Internet's "back roads"? The most important question for me is simple, in the online environment who and what represents the public interest? If nothing else, the Internet's commercialization raises public policy questions about privacy, personal autonomy, the price or value of personal information, and production and sale of personal goods such as videos all within the context of a participatory media rich environment—how appealing are such questions to today's adolescents?

YOUTH, PARTICIPATORY MEDIA, CIVIC & SOCIAL ENGAGEMENT, AND INFORMAL LEARNING: IMPLICATIONS FOR THE CIVIC CLASSROOM

Youths' participation in this networked world suggests new ways of thinking about the role of education. What would it mean to really exploit the potential of the learning opportunities available through online resources and networks? Rather than assuming that education is primarily about preparing for jobs and careers, what would it mean to think of it as a process guiding youths' participation in public life more generally?

—(Ito, et al., p. 3).

If we accept Marshall's notion of social citizenship and the goal of social studies to enable young people to make "informed and reasoned decisions for the public good as citizens of a culturally diverse, democratic society," then does "civic engagement include the production of culture, at least insofar as cultural expression shapes norms and priorities" (Levine, p. 121)? "Rather than conceptualize everyday media engagement as 'consumption' by 'audiences,' the term 'networked publics' places the active participation of a distributed social network in producing and circulating culture and knowledge in the foreground" (Ito, et al., p. 10). While young people start with friendship-driven online networks, many move to interest-driven ones. Given the collective nature of democracy, imagine drawing upon young people's online social and content generation experiences so as to guide them to pursue interest or, more appropriately for civic educators, policy-driven experiences. Consider the case of "fansubbers," which are "tight-knit work teams with jobs that include translators, timers, editors, typesetters, encoders, quality checkers, and distributors" (Ito et al., p. 30) that translate Japanese anime episodes. Fansubber or amateur subtitler groups illustrate "interest-driven participation [that] rely on peer-based learning dynamics, which have a different structure from formal instruction or parental guidance," (Ito et al., p. 11) and represent "interest-driven informal learning" that might translate into a civic participatory experience.

Fansubbers "often work faster and more effectively than professional localization industries, and their work is viewed by millions of anime fans around the world" whose members "pursue this work for the satisfaction of making anime available to fans overseas and for the pleasure they get in working with a close-knit production team that keeps in touch primarily on online chat channels and web forums" (Ibid). While on the one hand this is a specialized example, one used to illustrate the major attributes of participatory media, on the other hand it represents a form of cultural or civic action. Now, on a less complex level what are contributions to tagging sites, to a collaboratively maintained social networking site or to a site such as Wikipedia? At the very least should we not learn about students' digital lives so as better build upon their online informal learning?

Consider young people's experiences with online games, virtual worlds and social networking sites. While Runescape, a granddaddy of virtual worlds, was overwhelmingly the most popular virtual world in 2007, the next four most popular sites were Webkinz, Neopets, GaiaOnlline and Club Penguin (Prescott, 2007), which collectively appeal to 3–4 year olds to adolescents. If we stop to realize that 97% of teens play games and 48% use a cell phone to do so, then it becomes imperative to inquire about what youth learn while playing games. First, game play is a social affair with 65% indicating that they typically played with someone else present and 27% play with someone online. Interestingly, adolescents that socially interact during game play were more likely to become civically engaged (Lenhart, et al., 2008). While online games are often dismissed as just play, Erikson (1964) writes: "Play is to the child what thinking, planning, and blueprinting are to the adult" (p. 120). Such play though is likely to remain just that unless we heed Weigel, James & Gardner's recognition that a "key pedagogical challenge for informal learning is the learner's ability to apply lessons learned in the one context to related (and even unrelated) contexts" (2009, p. 9). Networked online environments, such as online role-playing games and virtual worlds, provide opportunities for youth to explore different identities (Kafai, et al., 2007; Ryberg & Larsen, (2007). How might we use or reshape such online experiences so as to foster the formation of a student's civic identity? Douglas & Brown studied users of *World of Warcraft* and learned that the game presents users with an "unprecedented degree of autonomy" and requires them "to provide and pass on certain pieces of knowledge that are essential for the functioning of the group" (pp. 41–42). Does this not parallel a critical civics lesson, i.e. the relation between personal autonomy and civic responsibility?

As we consider how to build upon this informal learning for academic purposes, Dwyer's study of MySpace users reminds us why youth use participatory media: "convenience, easy access, low cost and enjoyment are the main drivers when using electronic communications media to maintain social connections" (2007, p. 9). Given students' informal learning and what the literature suggests, a participatory media-classroom ought to build on students' online experience, so as not only to cultivate their civic intellectual skills, but also their participatory skills. This requires connecting important civic knowledge to student concerns, as well as providing opportunities not only to discuss controversial policy and social issues, but also to act upon them. As students engage in participatory media related experiences so as to "learn to be" citizens in a digital environment, as civic educators we must determine what they should learn about interacting in that environment. What follows first is a discussion about socializing youth in the use of commercial space for civic learning and followed by an example of how to integrate several participatory media tools to cultivate students' public voices and to provide them a platform for civic action.

ENABLING STUDENTS TO DEVELOP CIVIC AGENCY IN COMMERCIAL & PUBLIC ONLINE ENVIRONMENT

We are concerned about the lack of a public agenda that recognizes the value of youth participation in social communication and popular culture
—(Ito et al., p. 36)

First and foremost, students need to become socialized to civic and commercial life in an online environment, particularly given that the "growing salience of networked publics in young people's everyday lives is an important change in what constitutes the social groups and publics that structure young people's learning and identity" (Ito, p. 10). The risks associated with Web 2.0 technology, such as exposure to inappropriate content, cyberbullying and cyberpredators, led those such as Berson & Berson (2006) and Willard (2007) to advocate for cybersafety. "Sexting," "spamming," and "cyberbullying," while new words, they represent old inappropriate practices now conducted in a digital venue. Given the different contexts, we need to take the online environment into account and to determine how alike and different they are, and to develop online social norms accordingly. The very features of the Internet that make it a unique setting, also are the ones that help to illustrate that what is occurring is more than a generational divide. While always able to engage in most behavior replicated online, they never have in this manner. With sexting, for example, young people long have been able to engage in similar socially questionable acts. Even in the age of instant photography though, there still was a limited audience and life span of the act since eventually the photo faded. Today a digital picture can take on multiple lives in that the online display of the picture is but the simplest use of it. What then are the social norms and civic values considered acceptable in an online environment? While those such as Willard (2007) have addressed the social norms or ethical conduct part, few have considered what and how civic values are and should be articulated and acted upon in an online environment. At the very least, we as civic educators need to address a poignant question posed by O'Neill (2005, p. 4): "if social networks have migrated online, is it not logical to assume that the processes of differentiation, hierarchization, and control which, by all accounts, structure offline human interactions, have also done so?"

Given my earlier discussion about the blurring of the line between public and commercial online space, of more importance to me is the need to socialize students to the implications of civic, commercial and personal use of participatory media, particularly in light of the need to address what constitutes a civic identity in a digital environment. For example, civic educators should encourage students not only to evaluate the quality of a site relative to the content and/or service(s) provided, but also to peer behind the curtain to think more deeply about the "rules" and social norms governing the online community, how decisions are made at various levels, and the various roles they are capable of "playing" on the site. Consider the 2009 controversy surrounding Facebook. While having nearly 45 million more users than MySpace, Facebook was only generating about a third as much revenue. The difference was due, in part, to MySpace's limited license policy that permits MySpace:

to use, modify, delete from, add to, publicly perform, publicly display, reproduce, and distribute such Content solely on or through the MySpace Services, including without limitation distributing part or all of the MySpace Website in any media formats and through any media channels, except Content marked "private" will not be distributed outside the MySpace Website (http://www.myspace.com/Modules/Common/Pages/TermsConditions.aspx)

"MySpace is more explicitly a public place where friends hang out in the equivalent of a cafe or a club" whereas Facebook is more akin to a "private forum" where users "resent commercial intrusions," a situation reinforced by the site designers who "construct[ed] a commercial model that would preserve the intimacy of the site without filling it up with crude banner advertising." Facebook relies upon the "networks of friends for viral marketing of messages," but to make the most effective use of such marketing, the company needed to make more commercial use of personal information that users place on the site (Auchard, 2009). After much protest from users, Facebook not only withdrew the policy, but also adopted another policy that would permit input into new company policies, seemingly revolving the controversy. Less than a year later, Facebook once again revised its privacy policies and settings: "The default privacy setting for certain types of information you post on Facebook is set to 'everyone'..." (http://www.facebook.com/policy.php, 2010). While users initially proved successful, Facebook's desire for increased revenue override users' concerns.

Now, stop and consider the implications of this episode for civic education and the diverse ways to approach it. In light of Auchard's characterization of MySpace and Facebook, who decides how different online spaces are defined? Considering the users' concern over Facebook's use of their personal information, how is/should privacy be defined and acted upon in different types of online spaces? In economic terms, what is the value of one's personal information? Under what conditions should users not only generate, upload, and own such content, but also decide how such content is used? What role, if any, should users have in determining how service providers operate? Harking back to an unasked question from the Commercial or Public section, most importantly, given the nature of these questions, should we consider individuals not simply as users, but as citizens when seeking answer to these questions in an online context? A participatory media-rich classroom would serve as the ideal setting for students to engage these questions.

BLOGOSPHERE & WIKIWORLD: COLLABORATIVE PLATFORMS TO DEVELOP PUBLIC VOICES AND BUILD CIVIC NETWORKS

It is not yet clear whether the blogosphere...constitute the ideal of constructive debate...but if...many-to-many media afford a window of opportunity for

populations to exercise democratic power over would-be rulers—...education could play a pivotal role by equipping today's digital natives with [an] understanding [of] the connection between their power to publish online, their power to influence the circumstances of their own lives, and the health of democracy.
—(Rheingold, 2008, p 104)

Initially, I focus on the use of blogs so as to illustrate the role of participatory media in a civics classroom and then offer instructional suggestions on using blogs and wikis for students to explore and act upon a public policy issue. I recognize the irony of focusing on blogs and wikis, which are at best early generation Web 2.0 tools, in light of digital tools such as social networking sites, cloud computing, and video sharing, but unlike with blogs and wikis the use of most emerging forms of social media are not yet well grounded in research. Wikis and blogs share several characteristics: information sharing, virtual collaboration, and an intuitive, easy to use functionality. Wikis and blogs, and related digital tools such as podcasts, are a new generation of Web-based tools for virtual collaborative clinical practice and education (Boulos et al. 2006; Parker & Chao, 2007; & Trentin, 2008), ones that complement each other. In the past while civic educators discussed the importance of freedom of speech and public debate over crucial social and public policy issues, few opportunities existed to enable students either to develop a public voice or to engage in discussions about such issues beyond the classroom. Participatory media provides educators with the tools to do so, keeping in mind though that the use of such tools can serve personal, commercial and public interests. In considering those bloggers that typically address matters of public interests the "speed of publishing, the custom of using the hyperlink as in-text reference, the incorporation of comments into posts, and the current independence of most top bloggers from corporate ownership makes this form of political communication unique. As a discursive form blogs stand between traditional print and broadcast media and small group discussion" (Woodley, 2008, p. 115).

While on the surface blogs seem more akin to newspaper columns, Woodley (2008) notes that "reader comments almost never make it into the text of the column where they would become available to the whole population of readers for consideration, deliberation and evaluation" so that "the traditional newspaper column more closely resembles a regular monologue than an ongoing dialogue between author and readers" (p. 117). Since "bloggers tend to ask questions and make arguments by examining public facts or engaging with non-elite viewpoints that have been left out of traditional coverage in favor of elite he-said-she said" (Ibid, p.115), they demonstrate how public "[D]iscussion is a way of combining information and enlarging the range of arguments" (Rawls, 1971, p. 359). Due to "the structure of blogs as a communicative form" bloggers are "able to combine meticulous, fast-paced record keeping with equally speedy information aggregation and nearly instantaneous publicity" and "regularly ask their readers for information, especially specialized information, and their readers customarily respond" so that "the burden of finding-out is distributed among users on a voluntary basis..." (Woodly, 2008, p. 121). In that regard often bloggers "serve as 'intelligent filters' for their publics by selecting, contextualizing, and presenting links of particular interest for that public" though it "doesn't have to be political" (Rheingold, 2008, p. 107–108). A student could "choose to address...a public in the sense of a political public sphere that undergirds democracy," "an engaged community of interest—others who share" their "avocation, or obsession," or "a culture-producing public [by] remixing and sharing cultural content" (Ibid, p. 108).

Civic educators must recognize that adolescents are not drawn to participatory media in and of itself, but to what the use of such media provides them—the ability to act on what interests them and to interact with peers. Ravenscroft, et al. (2008) make this point well—"one of the problems with recent educational articulation of social software and Web 2.0 is the misalignment of social practices that are ostensibly oriented towards and motivated by 'interest' with those that oriented toward and motivated by learning..." (p. 433). If we accept Levine's (2008) notion that the creation of cultural artifacts is a form of civic engagement and that "the technology is not enough," then the challenge becomes how to cause students to "want to create—and...make products with public purposes—rather than use the Internet to get access to mass-produced culture" (p. 129). He offers several strategies for generating interest of which one is to "enable students to create digital media products with relatively low investments of time and expertise" (p. 132), which is an apt description both for blogs and wikis.

This represents but a starting point. Wikis and blogs might enable young people to develop what Levine describes as a public voice, which is "any style or tone that has a chance of persuading other people (outside of one's intimate circle) about shared matters, issues, or problems" (p. 121). According to Lennart and Madden (2008) though 62% of adolescents indicated that they only read their friends' blogs (p. 8), which results in what Levine terms an "audience problem." Students need to realize that they are addressing a "public" beyond their peers so as both to generate greater interest in "publishing" their thinking and to broaden the base of the public discussion. The interest driven, personalized nature of wikis and blogs support Bennett, Wells & Rank's (2008) thinking that efforts to encourage students to "appreciate the importance of government...must be combined with recognition of the interest of many younger citizens to approach politics from more personal standpoints that permit greater participation in the definition of issues, production of information and construction of action" (p. 10). Less clear is whether the blogosphere and wikiworld "lead to more isolated or more diverse conversations." Hargatti, Gallo, & Kane

(2008), for example, reviewed the sites of 20 conservative and 20 liberal bloggers. They discovered that 91% of links of blogrolls, i.e. the permanent links on the on home page of the site, were to sites of matching blogger's political ideology and that 12% of links, i.e. those embedded in blog itself, on conservative blog sites were to liberal sites and 16% on liberal blogs to conservative sites, though a "considerable proportion of these links are for straw-man arguments" (p. 85).

In light of the earlier discussion about the Internet's evolution as a commercial and public place, uncertainty abounds as to the future viability of the blogosphere and wikiworld as a means to cultivate students' public voices and collaborative skills. Is the blogosphere more akin to a host of small gatherings sites at such as the McDonalds or coffee shops around town where those of like mind gather to talk and, ultimately, to reinforce one another's thinking or a Hyde Park where speakers of all backgrounds and thinking gather and where people move from one speaker to another? For some of the more provocative and well-read bloggers, are they like your neighborhood real estate agent or Mary Kay person who chat you up while trying to sell you something? "Bloggers...often have only limited control over the content they produce and upload and embed themselves increasingly in the inherently hypercapitalist logic of the internet," particularly since "they need to pay between US$50 and US$900 per year for server space and the data traffic that they generate" if they choose not to carry ads on their blog (Cammaerts, p. 360). Is the blogosphere an example of narrowcasting? Typically, individuals outside of government needed some means, which usually involved association with an organization, to wield influence beyond an immediate area. For the bloggers that attract the most attention, have they become part of the Fourth Estate? The use of Blog Talk Radio (http://www.blogtalkradio.com) to report live the 2008 terrorist attack in Mumbai, India, for example, points in this direction.

Within the context of a civic education classroom, the purpose of a blog is not simply as a forum for personal expression, but as a platform for public discussion, just as a wiki is intended as a collaborative platform to formulate a collective position on an issue of substance. A key is for students to address substantive issues (Kahne & Middaugh, 2008), which are of interest to them (Sylversten, Flanigan, & Stout, 2007) and that they are able to act upon, while providing them multiple opportunities to exercise public voice in an open classroom environment. The last point is critical given Kahne and Middaugh's finding that students of low SES that "experienced many civic opportunities to learn, despite the lack of focus on these issues in the student's neighborhood and home, that same student would be expected to develop civic commitments that would place him/her well above average" (2008, p. 22).

Given our democracy's associational nature, the collaborative attributes of participatory media, and the need for students to address an "audience," civic educators should seek to create a sense of community when using social media. A "virtual social system" can emerge on a blog if there is a steady stream of public interaction not simply between the blogger and users but also between users (Pavicic, Alfirevic, & Gabelica, 2008, p. 166). When using a blog, the teacher and students need to establish a clear purpose for the blog, to consider an audience or community for the blog beyond the classroom so as to place the students' public voice in a more realistic, dynamic setting, and to consider the content and organization such as written comments, blogroll and embedded links. As Richardson (2006) notes, a "blog enables students "to connect ideas in ways that we could not do with paper, to distribute them in ways we could not do with the restrictiveness of html, and to engage in conversations and community in ways we could not do with newsgroups or other online communities before. As a result, students need to approach the public discussion that will occur via the blog not as single-focused and linear, but as complex and multi-layered. As the discussion unfolds and the comments and links are added, students will need guidance as they wrestle with the complexity of the issue both to maintain focus and to continue to move the discussion forward.

Doyle (2006) indicates that blogs and wikis differ in two ways: "how they organize information," and "the number of contributions and what those contributors hope to achieve." Elrufaie and Turner (2005) note that a wiki's greatest strengths also are its greatest weaknesses. For example, the fact that it is public and modifiable means that anyone in the group can make changes at any time, which might not work well for some students. Whereas blogs are more personal in that a single individual is primarily responsible for initiating and maintaining the blog, groups of students need to assume ownership of a wiki, which necessitates using wikis in group projects. With that in mind, Trentin recommends:

> redistribute authority for editing the overall document to all group members; spur each participant, through specific group work organization, to collaborate in the various stages in producing the overall work; and, establish an evaluation mechanism based on analysis of the interaction among participation, on evaluation of each individual's productions and on the reticular structuring of the final work—tasks performed using data from wiki default traces (comments, linkers, tags versioning) (p. 45).

According to Lowry et al. 2004 these stages or steps should include: "each individual reads assigned material; group members plan out design of final product and individual tasks; each individual designs own piece; review links created by others; peer review" (p. 47). Figure 25.2 outlines a series of steps students can follow when using social media and mobile devices. When using a wiki students create a digital history or record of their work, which includes: each person's contributions; peer review; and, links to work of others, which serves several purposes. Initially, students need to commit themselves to writing, which is different than participating in an oral discussion. Next, the teacher can review the digital record of each student's contributions to track and assess the evolution of the thinking both of individual students and of the group. Finally, if students track policy issues over time, they are able to assess their thinking over and to learn how discussions about public policy issues are framed and evolve.

Teachers and their students could use participatory media as a means to foster public discussion about and action on public policy issues, which focus on their community. Imagine using an online discussion forum as the means for a class of students not only to engage with each other in a richer and deeper discussion than is afforded either by a blog or wiki. As noted by Coflin, North & Martin (2009):

> unlike in spoken argumentation" asynchronous text-conferencing enables users "to more easily pick and choose which sub-topics they feel better informed or motivated to engage with, to track shifting points of view, to reflect on the accuracy and strength of the claims and the support put forward...to question and challenge such claims" and to bring "together diverse argument strands to reach a collective position on an issue (p. 94).

Unlike in a face-to-face classroom, as long as students have access to a computer or even a hand-held device as simple as a cell phone, each one can participate in a discussion. In a case study set in a high school social

---

- After initial class discussion about range of public policy issues raised by the use of participatory media, create an issues' interest survey using Survey Monkey (http://www.surveymonkey.com) or similar tool. Send survey's URL via a text message to students' cell phone (http://www.textmarks.com)
- Establish groups and create Ning (http://www.ning.com) for initial online discussion. Use the Ning's discussion forum to post questions for initial research by students using sites such as Newsvine. Also, each group can use rest of their students as sources of information. First, based on initial research create an online survey for other students to take. Second, use a blog (https://www.blogger.com/start) as a means for a representative from each of the other research groups to provide input
- Use cell phone to keep each other current on progress of work
- Use Wiki (http://www.wikispaces.com) as means for groups to craft a position on the issue. Ultimately, this statement needs to include ways to act upon their position.
- Use blog for group to present their views to rest of class—post weekly
- Post their position with suggestions on how to civically act upon the position on school website. Send notice to parents, school board and relevant groups in community.

Figure 25.2. Steps for Using Social Media and Mobile Devices

studies classroom, Larson (2003) found that introverted and second language students were more likely to participate in an electronic discussion. By extending the discussion to include other classes and possibly even community members, one addresses the need for an audience beyond the students. Here is where "learning about" plays a vital role, but one supported by those that did so while "learning to do," as students explore sites such as Youth Noise (http://www.youthnoise.com) and TakingITGlobal (http://www.tigweb.org) so as to extend their discussion beyond their classroom or school. By involving community members in the discussion, students can heighten the likelihood of taking action of the issue, particularly if they use the sites above for examples of how other youth have acted.

A CONCLUSION OR A BEGINNING?

Web 2.0 offers civic educators an unprecedented opportunity to transform brick and mortar schools into participatory media rich civic learning environments. Young people daily immerse themselves in an online social environment where they continuously create and upload multimedia content, exercise digital autonomy on an ongoing basis, socialize and share not only with local friends but with met and unmet global friends 24/7, enter into commercial agreements once only expected of adults, adopt and act on different responsibilities and roles as they undertake interest-driven group projects...and the list goes on. In conclusion, I leave you with the following question and thought—how much of what I just described relates to informal democratic practices? If such is the case, the challenge and beginning for us is how to "capitalize" upon young people's wealth of informal democratic experiences and translate them into more formal citizenship education, but in a way that best captures the online environment in which they are maturing into adult citizens.

REFERENCES

Abowitz, K. K., & Harnish, J. (Winter, 2006). Contemporary discourses of citizenship. *Review of Educational Research, 76*, 653–690.

Anderson, J., & Rainie, L. (2008). *The future of the Internet III*. Washington DC: Pew Internet & American Life Project.

Auchard, E. (February 24, 2009). Ad strategy at root of Facebook privacy row. *Reuters*. Retrieved May 27, 2010 from http://blogs.reuters.com/great-debate/2009/02/24/ad-strategy-at-root-of-facebook-privacy-row/

Banks, J. A. (2008). Diversity, group identify, and citizenship education in a global age. *Educational Researcher, 37*, 129–139.

Bennett, W. L., Wells, C., & Rank, C. (2008). *Young citizens and civic learning: Two paradigms of citizenship in the digital age.* Rank Center for Communication & Civic Engagement. Retrieved from http://www.engagedyouth.org/blog/wp-content/uploads/2008/08/youngcitizens_clo_finalaug_l.pdf

Berson, M. J., & Berson, I. R. (2003). Lessons learned about schools and their responsibility to foster safety online. *Journal of School Violence, 2,* 105–117.

Boulos, M. N. K., Maramba, I., & Wheeler, S. (2006). Wikis, blogs and podcasts: A new generation of Web-based tools for virtual collaborative clinical practice and education *BMC Medical Education, 6*(41), 1–8. doi:10.1186/1472–6920-6-41

Bull, G., Thompson, A., Searson, M., Garofalo, J., Park, J., Young, C., & Lee, J (2008). Connecting informal and formal learning: Experiences in the age of participatory media. *Contemporary Issues in Technology and Teacher Education, 8*(2). Retrieved from http://www.citejournal.org/vol8/iss2/editorial/article1.cfm

Cammaerts, B. (2008) Critiques on the participatory potentials of Web 2.0. *Communication, Culture & Critique, 1,* 358–377.

Carroll, W. K., & Hackett, R. A. (2006). Democratic media activism through the lens of social movement theory. *Media, Culture & Society, 28,* 83–104.

Center for the Digital Future. (2009). *Final report: Seventh annual digital future report.* Los Angeles: Annenberg School for Communication, University of Southern California.

Chester, J. (2009). *Behavioral targeting and the online assault on personal privacy.* Retrieved from http://www.democraticmedia.org/node/401

Chester, J. (2007). *Digital destiny: New media and the future of democracy.* New York: The New Press.

Cofflin. C., North, S., & Martin, D. (2009). Exchanging and countering points of view: A linguistic perspective on school students' use of electronic conferencing *Journal of Computer Assisted Learning, 25,* 85–98.

Coleman, S. (2004). *The networked-empowered citizen: How people share civic knowledge.* Retrieved from http://www.ippr.org.uk/uploadedFiles/research/projects/Digital_Society/the_networkempowered_citizen_coleman.pdf

Coleman, S. (2008). Doing IT for themselves: Management versus autonomy in youth e-citizenship. In Bennett, W. L. (Ed.), *Civic life online: Learning how digital media can engage youth.* (pp. 189–206). The John D. and Catherine T. MacArthur Foundation Series on Digital Media and Learning. Cambridge, MA: The MIT Press.

de Toqueville, A. (1835). *Democracy in America.* Online version located at http://xroads.virginia.edu/~HYPER/DETOC/toc_indx.html

Dean, J. (2001). Cybersalons and civil society: Rethinking the public sphere in transnational technoculture, *Public Culture 13,* 243–65.

de Ruyter, D., & Spieckler, B. The world citizens travels with a different view. In M.A. Peters, A. Britton, & H. Blee (Eds.), *Global education citizenship: Philosophy, theory and pedagogy.* (pp. 351–363). Rotterdam: Sense Publishers.

Doyle, B. (2006). *When to wiki, When to blog.* Retrieved from http://www.econtent-mag.com/?ArticleID=16900

Dwyer, C. (2007). *Digital Relationships in the 'MySpace' generation: Results from a qualitative study.* Proceedings of the 40th Annual Hawaii International Conference on System Sciences.

Elrufaie, E., & Turner, D. (2005) A Wiki paradigm for use in IT courses. *Proceedings of the International Conference on Information Technology: Coding and Computing* (ITCC'05, Vol. II). Washington, DC.

Erikson, E. (1964). *Insight and responsibility.* New York: W.W. Norton & Company. Human strength and the cycle of generations. Insight and responsibility. In (R. Coles, Ed.), *The Erik Erikson reader.* New York: W. W. Norton.

Greenhill, A., & Fletcher, G. (2003). Social construction of electronic space. Retrieved from http://www.spaceless.com/papers/12.htm

Hargittai, E., Gallo, J., & Kane, M. (2008). Cross-ideological discussions among conservative and liberal bloggers. *Public Choice, 134.* 67–86

Ito, M., Horst, H., Bittanti, M., boyd, d., Herr-Stephenson, B., Lange, P., C. J. Pasco, C. J., & Robinson, L. (2008). *Living and learning with new media: Summary of findings.* The John D. and Catherine T. MacArthur Foundation Reports on Digital Media and Learning. Chicago: IL.

Jenkins, H. (2006). Confronting the challenges of participatory culture: Media education for the twenty-first century. *The John D. and Catherine T. MacArthur Foundation Reports on Digital Media and Learning.* Chicago: IL.

Jonassen, D. H., & Kwon, H. I. (2001). Communication patterns in computer-mediated and face-to-face group problem-solving. *Educational Technology Research and Development, 49,* 35–51.

Jones, S. & Fox, S. (2009). Generations online in 2009. *Pew Internet & American Life Project.*

Just, N. (2009). Measuring media concentration and diversity: new approaches and instruments in Europe and the US. *Media Culture Society 31,* 97–117.

Kahne, J., & Middaugh, E. (2008). Democracy for some: The civic opportunity gap in high school. *The Center for Information and Research on Civic Learning & Engagement.*

Kafai, Y. B., Fields, D. A., & Cook, M. (2007). Your second selves: Avatar designs and identity play in a tween virtual world. *Proceedings from Situated Play: DiGRA 2007 Conference.* Retrieved from http://www.digra.org/dl/db/07311.32337.pdf

Karas, S. (2002). Enhancing the privacy discourse: Consumer information gathering as surveillance. *Journal of Technology, Law & Policy 7,* 29–64.

Kerawalla, L., Minocha, S., Kirkup, G., & Conole, G. (2009). Empirically grounded framework to guide blogging in higher education. *Journal of Computer Assisted Learning, 25,* 31–42

Ladson-Billings, G. (2004). Culture versus citizenship: The challenge of racialized citizenship in the United States. In J. A. Banks (Ed.), *Diversity and citizenship education: Global perspectives* (pp. 99–126), San Francisco: Jossey-Bass.

Lankes, R. D. (2008). Trusting the Internet: New approaches to credibility tools. In M. J. Metzger & A. J. Flanagin (Eds.), *Digital media, youth, and credibility.* (pp. 101–122). Cambridge, MA: The MIT Press.

Larson, B. E. (2003). Comparing face-to-face discussion and electronic discussion: A case study from high school social studies. *Theory and Research in Social Education, 31,* 349–365.

Lessig, L. (1999). The Law of the Horse: What Cyberlaw Might Teach, *Harvard Law Review, 113,* 501–546.

Lenhart, A., Kahne, J., Middaugh, E., Macgill, A., Evans, C., & Vitak, J. (2008). Teens, video games, and civics: Teens' gaming experiences are diverse & include significant social interaction and civic engagement. *Pew Internet & American Life Project.*

Lenhart, A., & Madden, M. (2008). Teen content creators and consumers. *Pew Internet & American Life Project.*

Levine, P. (2008). A Public voice for youth: The audience problem in digital media and civic education. In W. L. Bennett (Ed.), *Civic life online: Learning how digital media can engage youth.* (pp. 119–138). Cambridge, MA: The MIT Press.

Lowry P.B., Curtis A., & Lowry M.R. (2004) Building a taxonomy and nomenclature of collaborative writing to improve interdisciplinary research and practice. *Journal of Professional Communication 47,* 171–189.

MacKinnon, R. (2008). Flatter world and thicker walls? Blogs, censorship and civic discourse in China. *Public Choice, 134,* 31–46.

Marshall, T.H. (1964). *Class, citizenship, and social development: Essays of T. H. Marshall,* Westport, CT: Greenswood.

Martin, L. A., & Chiodo, J. J. (2007). Good citizenship: What students in rural students have to say about it. *Theory & Research in Social Education, 35,* 112–134.

Menezes, I. (2003). Participation experiences and civic concepts, attitudes and engagement: Implications for citizenship education projects. *European Educational Research Journal, 2,* 430–445.

Montgomery, K. C. (2008). Youth and digital democracy: Intersections of practice, policy, and the Marketplace. In W. L. Bennett (Ed.), *Civic life online: Learning how digital media can engage youth.* (pp. 25–50). Cambridge, MA: The MIT Press.

Naples, M. (2006) MySpace in the marketing mix, *United Online.* http://www.imediaconnection.com/content/10273.asp

National Council for the Social Studies. (1994). *Expectations for excellence: Curriculum standards for social Studies.* Washington, DC: National Council for the Social Studies.

National School Boards Association. (2007). *Creating and connecting: Research and guidelines on online social—and educational—networking,* Alexandria, VA: National School Boards Association.

Niemi, N.S., & Niemi, R.G. (2007). Partisanship, participation, and political trust as taught (or not) in high school history and government classes. *Theory & Research in Social Education, 35,* 32–61.

Noveck, B. S. (2005). Democracy of groups. *First Monday, 10* (11). Retrieved from http://www.uic.edu/htbin/cgiwrap/bin/ojs/index.php/fm/issue/view/190

O'Brien, J., (2008). Are we preparing young people for 21st century citizenship with 20th century thinking? Building a case for a virtual laboratory of democracy. *Contemporary Issues in Technology & Teacher Education.* Retrieved from http://www.citejournal.org/vol8/iss2/socialstudies/toc.cfm

O'Neil, M. (2005). *Weblogs and authority.* Paper presented at Blogtalk Downunder, Sydney, Australia. Retrieved from http://incsub.org/blogtalk/?page_id=107

Parker, K. R., & Chao, J.T. (2007). Wiki as a teaching tool. *Interdisciplinary Journal of Knowledge and Learning Objects, 3*, 57–72.

Parsons, T., 1965. Full citizenship for the Negro American? In T. Parsons & K. B. Clark (Eds.), *The Negro American* (pp. 709–754). Boston: Beacon Press.

Pavicic, J. Alfirevic, N., & Gabelica, N. (2008) Electronic Communities—Catalysts or Rotten Apples of Traditional Agents of Socialization for "Generation Y." *Wseas Transactions on Power Systems, 3*(4), 162–171.

Prescott, L. (2007). *Virtual worlds ranking: Runescape #1. Hitwise.* Retrieved from http://weblogs.hitwise.com/leeann-prescott/2007/04/virtual_worlds_ranking_runesca.html

Ravenscroft A., Wegerif R. B., & Hartley J. R. (2007) Reclaiming thinking: dialectic, dialogic and learning in the digital age. *British Journal of Educational Psychology Monograph Series II, Learning through Digital Technologies 5*, 39–57.

Rawls, J. (1971). *A theory of justice.* Cambridge: Belknap.

Rheingold, H. (2008). Using participatory media and public voice to encourage civic engagement. In W. L. Bennett (Ed.) *Civic life online: Learning how digital media can engage youth.* (pp. 97–118). Cambridge, MA: The MIT Press.

Richardson, W. (2005). *Connective writing.* Retrieved on May 26, 2010 from http://www.webcitation.org/5KPRYIBob

Ryberg, T., & Larsen, M.C. (2006). Networked identities—understanding different types of social organisation and movements between strong and weak ties In networked environments, Proceedings from the *Fifth International Conference on Networked Learning.* Lancaster, UK.

Schugurensky, D. (2004). The tango of citizenship learning and participatory democracy. In K. Mundel & D. Schugurensky (Eds.), *Lifelong Citizenship Learning.* (pp. 326–334). Transformative Learning Centre: OISE/UT.

Shah, D. V., McLeod J. M., & Yoon, S. H. (2001). Communication, context, and community: An exploration of print, broadcast, and Internet influences. *Communication Research, 28*, 464–506.

Sharples, M., Graber, R. Harrison, C., & Logan, K. (2009). E-safety and Web 2.0 for children aged 11–16. *Journal of Computer Assisted Learning, 25*, 70–84.

Shaw, R. (2008). The peculiar place of Enlightenment ideals in the governance concept of citizenship and democracy. In M.A. Peters, A. Britton, & H. Blee (Eds.), *Global education citizenship: Philosophy, theory and pedagogy.* (pp. 153–168). Rotterdam: Sense Publishers.

Shuler, C. (2007). *D is for Digital: An Analysis of the Children's Interactive Media Environment With a Focus on Mass Marketed Products that Promote Learning.* The Joan Ganz Cooney Center at Sesame Workshop. New York: NY. Retrieved from http://www.joanganzcooneycenter.org/upload_kits/disfordigital_reports.pdf

Solove, D. J. (2004). The digital person: Technology and privacy in the information age. New York City: New York University Press.

Syvertsen, A. K., Flanagin, C. A., & Stout, M. D., (2007). *Best practices in civic education: changes in students' civic outcome* [online]. CIRCLE Working Paper Series. Available from: http://www.civicyouth.org/PopUps/WorkingPapers/WP-57Flanagan.pdf

Tapscott, D., & Williams, A.D. (2007). *Wikinomics: How mass collaboration changes everything.* New York: Penguin.

Thomas, D., & Brown, J. (2009). Why virtual worlds can matter. *International Journal of Learning and Media, 1,* 37–49.

Torney-Purta, J., & Lopez, S. V. (2006). *Developing citizenship competencies from kindergarten through grade 12: A background paper for policymakers and educators.* Denver: Education Commission of the States and National Center for Learning and Citizenship.

Trentin, G. (2009). Using a wiki to evaluate individual contribution to a collaborative learning project, *Journal of Computer Assisted Learning, 25,* 43–55.

United Nations. (1948). *The universal declaration of human rights* Retrieved from http://www.un.org/en/documents/udhr/

United Nations Educational, Scientific and Cultural Organization. (2005). *Convention on the protection and promotion of the diversity of cultural expressions.* Retrieved from: http://portal.unesco.org/culture/en/ev.php-URL_ID=33232&URL_DO=DO_TOPIC&URL_SECTION=201.html#I

van Dijck, J. (2009). Users like you? Theorizing agency in user-generated content. *Media Culture Society. 31,* 41–58.

Virtual World Association. (2009). *The blue book: A consumer guide to virtual worlds,* 5th ed. Retrieved from http://www.associationofvirtualworlds.com/thebluebook/the_blue_book_january_2009_5th_edition.pdf

Weigel, M., James, C., & Gardner, H. (2009). Learning: Peering backward and looking forward in the digital era. *International Journal of Learning and Media, 1,* 1–18.

Westheimer, J., & Kahne, J. (2004). What kind of citizen? The politics of educating for democracy. *American Educational Research Journal, 41,* 237–269.

Willard, N. (2007). *Cyber-safe kids, cyber-savvy teens: Helping young people use the Internet safety and responsibly.* San Francisco, CA: Jossey-Bass.

Williamson, D. (2009). *Kids and Teens: Growing Up Virtual.* Retrieved from http://www.emarketer.com/Report.aspx?code=emarketer_2000568

Woodley, D. (2008). New competencies in democratic communication? *Public Choice, 134,*109–123

Young, I. M. (1989). Polity and group difference: A critique of the ideal of universal citizenship. *Ethics, 99,* 250–274.

CHAPTER 26

BROADENING SOCIAL STUDIES CURRICULA

Integrating Global Education in a Teacher Education Program

Lydiah Nganga and John Kambutu

Global education is essential, but it is relatively misunderstood. Given the growing global interdependence and awareness of common problems facing humanity, revolutionary advances in technology and transportation that have made our world a global village[1], it is important to prepare teachers who are globally minded. In this chapter, we explore meaning of global education, challenges of teaching global education in higher education and our own journey as global education supporters. Additionally, we explore our student teachers' understanding of global education and different approaches that we used to infuse global education in a teacher education program. Pre-teaching data from our pre-service teachers showed a narrow

---

[1] Village" in this study means a physical or virtual space that is void of all the "boundaries" that previously separated people... thanks to modern technologies. Thus, people are sharing the village for economic, political, social, and other benefits.

---

understanding of global education defining it as "a study of where we live." Post-teaching data, however, showed that a broadened curriculum enabled learners to develop a broader view.

Global education as a term has a different meaning for different people. According to Merryfield and Wilson (2005) global education is a systematic study of the interconnected nature of local, regional, national, and international events. Hicks (2003) defines global education as "the term used internationally to designate the academic field concerned with teaching and learning about global issues, events, and perspectives" (p. 274). Such a study necessitates that students read widely on a variety of humanistic topics. Equally helpful is the establishment of opportunities to immerse learners in unfamiliar "other"[2] cultural situations (Merryfield & Wilson, 2005). In this chapter, we discuss the definitions our pre-service teachers (students) provided for global education before and after they experienced our college courses. In addition, we discuss the challenges we experienced in our attempt to broaden our students' initial perceptions. For example, because our teacher education program is situated in a rural setting, isolated from multicultural cosmopolitans, our students were less motivated to study global education. As a result, we used an infused integration instructional model (Jacobs, 1991; Lakes, 2003) to not only boost our students' interest, but to also broaden their understanding and appreciation of global education. Specifically, we used the content-specific integration model as recommended by Davison, Miller, and Metheny (1997). This model attempts to integrate the content area objectives of one discipline with the content area objectives of a different discipline (in our case, Lydiah's Humanities Methods course and John's Foundations of Education course. See Appendix B). Additionally, our instructional process delved into the holistic nature of global education in that it explored the interconnectedness of different aspects of human life in different parts of the world (Burnouf, 2004; Dove, 2002; Zarrillo, 2008). As a result, localized events such as war and peace, or economic prosperity and decline are considered capable of producing global impacts. In other words, what happens in one part of the world, positively or negatively, has corresponding effects worldwide.

Learning about "other" cultures especially through immersion has many benefits. For example, an immersion experience designed to allow learners to be physically present in host cultures for purposes of study is likely to promote active interaction with host cultures through "talking, observing, listening, studying artifacts, reflecting, questioning and participating in meals, music, dances, religious activities and educational programs," (Kambutu & Nganga, 2008, p. 940). Learning from the locals, while tolerating the ambiguity(s) that might arise is likely to broaden learners' aware-

---

[2] "Other" denotes all cultures other than the ones a person or persons belongs to.

ness and understanding of the "other"— an essential component in global education (Rodriguez, 2000). Because global education is intended to expose learners to global challenges and shared cultural values and practices, learning through immersion is likely to illicit critical appreciation and understanding of pertinent opportunities and global complexities (Case, 1993; Merryfield & Wilson, 2005). Notwithstanding the purpose, however, Zarrillo, (2008) felt that to be effective, global education should help learners to acquire perceptual skills or to become empathetic world citizens in an ever-changing global society. Consequently, Zarrillo recommended broadening global education curricula. But a broadened global education, at the college level might encounter a myriad of challenges.

Among the challenges faced when teaching global education curricula at the college level are contested content standards (different colleges implement different outcomes and standards), and disagreements about definition and purpose(s) of global education in higher education (Bruce, Podemski, & Anderson, 1991). As a result, different foundational principles and ideologies are implemented at different colleges. Given the holistic nature of global education, it might not be necessary to agree on content after all, but an effective global curriculum helps learners to develop a deeper understanding and appreciation of the "other" in a global society (Parker, 2009). Thus, Alger and Harf (1986, p. 3) recommended that college students be exposed to an education that promotes the understanding, meaning, and purpose of global systems because "all people live their lives in a sea of transactions that link them continuously to worldwide systems of production, finance, communication, travel, education, military threats, and politics." Indeed, global education has a responsibility to equip learners with the knowledge and skills essential to effective participation in global systems. Therefore, a clear structure is needed in order to ensure the success of global education curricula (Bruce, Podemski, & Anderson, 1991).

STRUCTURED CURRICULUM

A structured global education curriculum has specific goals. In addition to developing clear outcomes and standards of study, program goals should address instructional and learning strategies. For example, curriculum designers should determine whether to infuse global education into an existing academic program or to create a new area of study that focuses purely on global education. Banks (1997) reasoned that infusing global education into existing curricula is most effective because such a curriculum helps students to "understand that knowledge is socially constructed and reflects researchers' personal experiences as well as the social, political, and economic contexts in which they live and work" (Banks, 2001, n.p). Additionally, this type of a curriculum encourages students to make decisions and take action related to the concepts, issues, or problems being explored (Banks, 2002). Subsequently, he recommended a four-level (Contribution, Additive, Transformational and Social Action) instructional model. At the Contribution level, global education is introduced following a fun, food, and fiesta (Three Fs) approach. The knowledge gained at the Contribution level is intended to familiarize learners with unfamiliar global practices in a non-threatening manner. At level two (Additive), global education topics are added to existing curricula. As a result, global topics are explored along with regular topics without changing curriculum structure. It is at level three (Transformative) that the existing curriculum is altered to allow learners to study global education topics from the perspective of the "other." When students see the perspective of other people, the oppressed especially, they are likely to recognize, speak out and take action against injustice as it occurs in their schools and communities and to develop a global consciousness with respect to human conditions and world issues (Western Canadian Protocol for Collaboration in Basic Education, 1993). Having an empathetic attitude is essential at level four (Social Action) because this level requires students to act in order to promote global justice (Zarrillo, 2008). Because effective global education requires faculty to think and teach in a different manner, it is essential for them to modify their teaching habits (Gilliom, 1993). Additionally, educators must themselves have a global consciousness/global perspective.

OUR JOURNEY AS GLOBAL EDUCATORS

As authors of this chapter, our journey to develop a global consciousness stems from our strong belief in the need to take a broader and critical view of other peoples' experiences. Our motivation to become global education proponents started with our own journey as higher education faculty of foreign descent (we were born in Kenya, Africa). In our teaching, we both received many questions regarding our country of origin. These questions revolved around issues of poverty, illnesses such as HIV and AIDS and wildlife. Generally, the questions showed a general lack of knowledge about the world, global connections and the interpretations of the process and effects of globalization. In addition, speaking English with an accent was looked upon as being deficient (we both have English as a second language), a predicament that has been documented in other research as evidenced in the quote below.

> Impossible to conceal as it is one's accent, especially the accent of third-world country faculty, provides a favorite topic to students who tend to show little tolerance for anything falling outside the boundaries defined by what their

social conditioning makes them believe is correct. And what they are familiar and feel comfortable with. (Dedoussis, 2007, p. 141)

Like many other higher education professors of foreign descent working in primarily white campuses, we were faced with the challenge of developing instruction strategies that would enable our pre-service teachers to acquire global perspectives. Our students viewed their cultures as better (modern schools, technological and medical advancements) and the Kenyan/African cultures as deficient (people live in huts, no food, plagued with HIV and AIDs, etc.). Given that our students considered their cultures to be superior when compared to other global cultures, they were generally less motivated to engage global education. Indeed, we find our students' refusal or resistance to global education to be a significant challenge in our teaching activities.

DEALING WITH RESISTANT STUDENTS

According to Manrique (2002) in many institutions, non-European immigrant faculty may represent the first significant personal contact that many students have with non-Europeans. This is especially true in rural communities in Wyoming, where the population is predominantly (88%) white. Consequently, because our pre-service teachers are mainly recruited from Wyoming, they tend to have little exposure to ethnic diversity or global issues, and are therefore, reluctant to engage in global education (Kambutu & Nganga, 2008). Additionally, because most of our students return to their rural communities to work, they do not consider global education a priority (Nganga & Kambutu, 2009). Consider, for example, the following reaction from a student in our Humanities Methods course: "I really do not know why we are learning stuff about cultures, countries and human differences. Wyoming does not have diversity. I feel this is a total waste of my time, and we should be learning other more important information."

It is true that Wyoming lacks the ethnic and racial diversity that is more common in states with major cities. Notwithstanding the lack of racial and ethnic diversity, however, other forms of human diversity (gender, religion, language, economic class, abilities/disabilities, etc.) are prevalent in Wyoming. Additionally, due to recent migration and immigration trends, the population of Wyoming is becoming increasingly diverse (Barron, 2007). The State of Wyoming Department of Administration and Information (2006), for example, reported a third of Wyoming's population growth between 2000 and 2006 was from minority groups, particularly immigrants of Hispanic origin. Another indication that the population of Wyoming is becoming diverse is the fact that the Teton County School District had 50 students enrolled in English as a Second Language (ESL) classes in 1999, but in 2004 that number had grown to 250 learners (Carmelita, Kambutu, & Rios, 2006). Indeed, an increase in student diversity in Wyoming's public schools (due to immigration) is a good reason for pre-service teachers in Wyoming to acquire the necessary global education knowledge and skills. Additionally, because modern technologies have eliminated the boundaries that previously separated humanity, we believe that the effects of global interconnectedness will be a constant reality worldwide, including Wyoming. Thus, we developed creative teaching strategies to help our students build interest in global education.

CREATIVE INSTRUCTIONAL APPROACHES

There are many ways to encourage students to study global education; for all of these, faculty commitment is crucial. Supportive faculty is likely to inculcate their students with the necessary global education knowledge and skills. For example, in the United States of America, where a melting pot ideology is popular, educators who are committed to the ideals of global education are likely to promote acculturation. Thus, instead of expecting "others" to adopt the "behaviors, values, beliefs, and the lifestyles of the dominant culture," educators implement a curriculum that calls for cultures living in close proximity to appreciate each other as equals, and when possible, to exchange cultural practices without giving-up first cultures entirely" (Diaz-Rico & Weed, 1993, p. 199). These exchanges provide for the development of new realities and favorable attitudes towards other cultures (Merryfield, 1995; Wilson, 1993). Notwithstanding the benefits of such a curriculum, however groups in positions of power and privilege are likely to resist any knowledge that teaches respect for "humanity's differences and cultural wealth" because such information is a threat to their positions of advantage (Gacel-Avila, 2005; Kambutu, Rios, & Carmelita, 2009). Given the importance of global education in a global "village," however, Sokolower (2006) urged educators to look for creative instructional approaches to motivate learners to study global education.

When learners are less motivated to study global education, the task of teaching can be unpleasant. As a result, educators should design creative ways to motivate their students. In our case, for example, we adopted faculty collaboration or teamwork for educators within and across academic disciplines (Bess, 2000). According to Taylor (1997, n.p.) "through collaboration with colleagues, teachers can increase the potential for developing integrated global units, creating global support networks, and conducting global service learning projects." As a result, although John teaches a Foundations of Education course in the department of Educational Studies, and Lydiah instructs a Humanities Methods course in the department of Elementary and Early Childhood, we collaborated to examine content in our courses, including our teaching approaches.

Consequently, we identified and infused democracy and global education strands in our two courses. For example, we adopted the following common readings:

1. *Developing a global dimension in the curriculum* (Graves, 2002)
2. *Teaching Students Whose Race, Class, Culture, or Language Differs from Your Own* (Pugach, 2006, pp. 175–212).
3. *Language, Literacy, and Biliteracy* (Prerez et al., 1998, pp. 21–48).

While the Foundations of Education course that John teaches lays the groundwork for global education, the Humanities Methods course taught by Lydiah expands on that foundation through service-learning, cultural immersion, problem-based learning, and reflective writing. In addition to expecting students to conduct library research on global topics of their choosing, they write research papers, and develop and teach global education lessons to their peers. In both courses we also use videos and music from other cultures, use multicultural children literature, discussions and journaling, and reflecting on the success and challenges experienced throughout the semester. But the use of learner-centered instruction was most beneficial.

Instructional approaches that are learner-centered focus more on the student rather than the instructor. Thus, the teacher facilitates learning instead of controlling and dispensing knowledge to inactive students (Angelis, 2003; Arends, 2008; Dewey, 1916; Papert, 1980; Wilson, 2002). When students are actively involved, they are likely to develop interest in a topic (Wenger, 1998). Although there are a variety of strategies that promote students' involvement, experiential and problem-based learning are usually helpful (Gordon, Roger, & Comfort, 2001; Johnson & Johnson, 2006). Also of value is any instructional strategy that contextualizes learning, i.e., linking abstract knowledge to real life experiences (Shoemaker, 1989). Learners are likely to contextualize knowledge that follows an "Infused Integration" model (Jacobs, 1991). For effective infused integration, Jacobs recommended instructional approaches that explore different subject areas and/or disciplines in a single unit of study. Needed also is instruction that combines different strands in a subject and/or academic discipline into a single subject or lesson. According to Dressel (1958), an integrative curriculum goes beyond linking disciplines to the creation of new models of understanding the world. Additionally, "the planned learning experiences not only provide the learners with a unified view of commonly held knowledge (by learning the models, systems, and structures of the culture) but also motivate and develop learners' power to perceive new relationships and thus to create new models, systems, and structures" (Dressel, 1958, pp. 3–4).

Perhaps because of adopting student-centered learning approaches, our students are showing broadened understanding and appreciation of global education. Equally helpful is the use of the "Infused Integration" model, and specifically, faculty collaboration.

As described earlier, we collaborated by adopting common instructional ideas including course syllabi and teaching resources. Examining faculty's instructional practices is, however, tricky because it is likely to infringe on faculty's academic freedom. Nonetheless, our commitment to help our students develop interest in global education, coupled with the fact that we work in a small program trumped all other concerns. Additionally, we were committed to the concept of curriculum integration and enjoyed the stimulation and challenge of collaboration across disciplines (Baloche, Hynes, & Berger, 1996). Thus, our teaching priority was to help our pre-service educators to acquire the right attitudes and professional practices in relation to global education. Having our students develop the right attitude is a welcome goal because educators, American teachers especially, are normally apathetic and ignorant of past and present global events (Cogan, 1984; Hill, 1981; Tucker & Cistone, 1991).

Faculty collaboration is an essential strategy to increase learner motivation. For example, Bess (2000, p. xiii) reported that faculty collaboration within a program and across academic disciplines transforms learning into a "communal human effort." Another benefit of collaboration is the likelihood of promoting the development of pedagogical bridges between different disciplines (Frost & Jean, 2003). Pedagogical bridges are likely to increase learners' interest, as well as knowledge retention and transfer from one academic discipline to another (Nganga & Kambutu, 2009).

Generally, educators, and mostly pre-service teachers lack the knowledge, skills, and expertise in global education. For example, Gilliom (1993) reported that newly trained teachers usually lack the essential knowledge and/or motivation to teach from a global perspective. Consequently, Gilliom suggested that all teacher education programs should infuse global education into exiting pre-service teacher education. A well planned global education curriculum is capable of helping learners to develop global knowledge such as social and economic injustice, the effects of war, prejudice, racism, discrimination, and other issues that prevents world citizens from achieving their dreams and aspirations (Merryfield, 2000).

GLOBAL EDUCATION FOR EDUCATORS

An education that prepares educators to be effective global education teachers is fully committed to global peace, fairness, justice, and the value of human life. Thus, in addition to implementing topics that focus on global opportunities and challenges, teacher education programs should adopt curriculum for cultural universals, i.e., exploring values and practices that humans share in common irrespective of their residence in the world.

Crucial also is providing a curriculum that eradicates ethnocentrism (using one's own culture to judge negatively all unfamiliar cultures) (Kambutu & Nganga, 2008). Such a curriculum explores global cultures and geographic regions using an additive lens, i.e., it examines unfamiliar cultures positively.

Indeed, an ideal global education curriculum encourages teachers to experience unfamiliar cultures, to borrow, and to contextualize unfamiliar ideas, events, cultural themes, and concepts. Additionally, topics that explore human rights, immigration, and conflict resolutions at local, regional, national, and international levels are examined (Anderson, 1990, Kniep, 1986). But of profound importance is a curriculum that enables learners to recognize the interconnection between local and international events. In other words, a global education curriculum that is designed specifically for teachers should show how the choices and decisions made at local levels affect other people around the world. An education thus designed allows learners to develop a holistic, and multiple perspective approach that is essential in the understanding of the self in relationship to global affairs (Tucker & Cistone, 1991). After receiving a holistic global education curriculum at the college level, educators are likely to have a similar focus while instructing their own students.

Herewith, therefore, we present the various aspects of global education curricula we have implemented in our teacher education program. Our work is grounded on the following principles: (a) that pre-service teachers must have a better understanding of the meaning of global education, (b) that pre-service teacher education programs should be charged with the responsibility(s) of cultivating global perspectives, and (c) that faculty in pre-service teacher education programs should be committed to global education in order to help their students acquire pertinent knowledge and skills.

BROADENED GLOBAL EDUCATION CURRICULUM

As stated earlier, we teach in a small teacher education program in Wyoming. Due to general lack of exposure to global events, our pre-service students are typically unmotivated to study global education. Thus, we adopted creative teaching approaches such as student-centered and infused "Integrated Infusion" instructional model to enhance their motivation to study global education. To measure the impact of our instructional efforts, we pre-tested (in writing) our pre-service teachers ($n=16$) at the beginning of the semester. In addition to focusing on their understanding and appreciation of global education, the pre-instruction survey they completed explored students' perceptions of "other" cultures particularly non-Western ones. At the end of the Humanities methods course (social studies for elementary education majors), students completed post-teaching questions. To develop our curriculum we used the United Nations Educational, Scientific and Cultural Organization (UNESCO) recommendations for global education as guiding principles which include providing learning opportunities that help students to "develop an understanding and respect for all peoples, their cultures, civilizations, values and ways of life, including domestic ethnic cultures and cultures of other nations...readiness on the part of individual to participate in solving the problems of his community and the world at large" (UNESCO, 1998, p. 2). Our common themes included; education and democracy, cultures of the world, and global issues (human rights, conflicts and wars, terrorism, foreign aid, poverty, global resources, immigration, and food and health). We framed both the pre- and post-teaching questions items on the following global education goals recommended by Bruce, Podemski and Anderson (1991): (a) that students should perceive and value cultural diversity, (b) that global education should be founded on up-to-date evidence, free from distortions, stereotype, prejudice, or romanticism, (c) that students should be knowledgeable about, and appreciate both Western and non-Western cultures, and (d) that students should learn about human interconnectedness, and should therefore be informed by research and scholarship from around the globe. A qualitative analysis of the data we collected (Bogdan & Biklen, 1998) had several themes that we collapsed into one robust theme, i.e., broadened views

BROADENED VIEWS

Pre-teaching data showed that our pre-service teachers had a wide range of views regarding global education, yet narrow (see Appendix A for pre- and post-instruction questions). For example, they defined global education as the awareness of "where we live." However, other definitions including the study of "Geography of the world, and learning about different cultures" showed a rather broader understanding of global education. Nonetheless, a majority of our pre-service teachers were possibly ethnocentric, i.e., after ethnocentrism, judging other cultures negatively using one's own culture as the norm (Kambutu & Nganga, 2008). For example, when asked to reflect, they described "other" cultures of the world as "peculiar or weird." Shockingly, they attributed the U.S. economic prosperity to "blessings from God" because while the "U.S. is a Christian nation, third world countries are poor because they are non-Christian." When we asked them what they wished to learn about foreign cultures, our students' interests were primarily on foods and holidays only. Banks (2002) argued against a "Three Fs curriculum, that is, a study that focuses on Food, Fun, and Fiesta" because it does not challenge the status-quo. Rather, it is superficial and touristy (Derman-Sparks & Edwards, 2010). Indeed, although our students were less interested in exploring global issues, they thought it would be fun to study foods and holiday practices from other countries. Considering that our students had a narrow view of global education, we implemented a variety of instructional strategies with positive results.

Engaging learners in a meaningful global education curriculum that does not focus either on local topics or foods and holidays from other countries only is not an easy task. As result, in addition to collaborative teaching and student-centered learning, we adopted Banks' (1997) curriculum model that recommends teaching global topics from simple to complex. For example, at the simple or Contribution level, we introduced global education following a "Three Fs" curriculum. Thus, our students studied global foods, music, holidays, and important people. This teaching led to level two (Additive level) in Banks' model that allowed us to add global content, concepts, ideas, and views to our existing traditional course contents. At level three (Transformative level), we encouraged our students to examine various global topics from "other" people's perspectives. This was important because it caused our students to become empathic about "Other" people's rights. At the final stage (Social Action) we required our students to do something (take action) to address the various local, regional, national and global challenges they studied. Although our pre-service students developed different actions for different issues, post-teaching data showed a preference for an inclusive global education curriculum, and more so a curriculum that promotes global mindedness (Merryfield, 2000).

Perhaps because of our instructional approaches, post-teaching data showed that our students had developed a deeper understanding of various aspects of global education. For example, their definitions for global education expanded from a study of local cultural issues to the study of various global phenomena as is evident in the following excerpts:

> Global education involves instructing students about the interconnections between themselves, where they live, and other parts of the world. It introduces students to other cultures, beliefs, and ideals. It helps them to develop knowledge and skills that will assist them in becoming active participants in an ever growing global society.

> Global education is holistic and involves being aware that we are neighbors who share the world. It is learning to accept and respect other people's differences even if one does not agree with them. It also involves taking time to educate ourselves about other cultures.

> Global education is going beyond regular classroom teaching and teaching about what is out in the world and how it relates to students. This stimulates the students to question what is happening and have the desire to get involved to make a difference.

Additionally, the different learning activities we incorporated (these included a research paper on a foreign country of their choosing, interviewing a person of another culture and presenting the findings from the perspectives of that culture, three weeks international cultural immersion service learning in Kenya, and analyzing children's books for global education) appeared to deepen our students' appreciation of global education. For example, after designing a unit on global education, the students distanced themselves from curricula that focused only on cultural tolerance, foods, fun, and fiesta. To that end, one student concluded that,

> A global education curriculum should include a wide variety of activities about other countries. Additionally, it should include the resources the world offers and how they contribute to the world. This curriculum makes the world a more interconnected place to students and allows them to see the many similarities that exist. It also helps students to be better adjusted and knowledgeable about other countries and how they rely upon one another. The curriculum helps students to see that they, themselves will very likely be interacting with other people from all over the world someday.

Other reflections also showed that perhaps due to our instructional process, our students developed critical perceptual knowledge. For example, post-teaching data indicated that our students developed an understanding that there is a positive link between global struggles for various resources, oil and other precious minerals especially, and the on-going international conflicts and wars. As a result, they advocated for an education for global justice and peace because, after all, humans are interconnected globally in many ways. Reflecting on the issue of global interconnectedness, one preservice student indicated that;

> Current events should be included in a global education curriculum because they show what is affecting people's lives locally and internationally. Local and international governments play a huge role in world conflicts and peace. To promote peace, we must teach how the different things countries or ethnicities do affect other people's lives in the world.

Helping students to develop perceptual knowledge is not an easy task. Because humans are creatures of habit, they tend to make sense of the world using existing and familiar phenomena (Kambutu & Nganga, 2008). Conversely, they resist or deny vehemently unfamiliar habits particularly those that are contrary to familiar ones. For example, a person who has internalized habits that consider a county's economic prosperity as a gift from a deity might resist strongly any idea that positively links injustice and historical events such as slavery, colonialism, and globalization to national economic success. Thus, Merryfield and Wilson (2005) recommended that any curriculum intended to promote perceptual understanding be designed carefully.

A learning experience that immerses learners in a new environment for a prolonged period of time is likely to reduce learners' resistance to new perceptions. For example, after visiting Kenya in one of our summer cultural immersion programs, a student reported that prior to visiting Kenya, he viewed globalization positively. However, after seeing all the "greenhouses that stretch for miles through some of the most fertile soil on the planet (land surrounding Lake Naivasha), constructed by international companies to grow flowers for export to benefit a few already privileged people while the food that should be grown there to feed the local people is imported," he had a change of perception. Instead, he considered globalization a tool of economic exploitation and added that, "being able to see the evidence makes it real, undeniable, and frustrating." In general, however, our pre-service teachers appeared to develop a deeper appreciation of the cultural values embraced in different parts of the world.

Our students were surprised at the similarities between different cultural practices around the world. As part of their lesson planning activity, we required them to study at least one culture from a country of their choosing. The cultural knowledge they gained from different parts of the world showed them that the world might have "universal cultural values and practices." For example, they singled out the protection of basic human needs, spirituality, and human rights as some universal cultural traditions. They also were able to identify the existing global connections in many areas including economy, historical events, politics, and technological advances. Also shared in common are global challenges, concerns, and conditions such as poverty, over population, health, terrorism, and drug trafficking. As a result, our students learned that historical questions raised in the context of new global realities can paint a clear picture of a country(s') historical and contemporary engagement with the rest of the world. Additionally, they understood that acquiring the necessary skills relative to global perspective might help some of the misconceptions they held regarding other countries (Duty, 2010; Merryfield, 2000; Tucher & Cistone, 1991). In a nutshell, learning "how aspects of culture, such as language, the arts, and belief systems, can both facilitate and impede global understanding, causes and possible solutions of global issues, such as health, security, and environmental quality" appears to be the major skill that our students acquired (Zarrillo, 2008, p. 341). To that end, one student concluded that an effective global education curriculum should focus on helping learners appreciate both Western and non-Western cultures.

DISCUSSION

Modern technologies are transforming the world into a "village" by blurring the boundaries that previously separated global cultures. As a result, an education that equips learners with the knowledge and skills that is essential in a global "village" is needed. In addition to developing an understanding and appreciation of "other" cultures, learners ought to become aware of the existing interconnectedness between different peoples in the world. Instead of embracing isolationism (studying local topics only), a broadened global education curricula is warranted. Designed carefully, a broad global education curriculum could easily motivate learners to develop a global mindset. Nonetheless, implementing broad global education is not necessarily free of challenges. For example, although we are preparing educators for a global "village," our students are generally less eager to study global issues.

As mentioned earlier, our education program is situated in a rural setting. Because our pre-service students seldom interact with the many aspects of globalization (such as immigration, cultural diversity, religious diversity among others) that are common in larger cosmopolitan areas, they are generally less motivated to study global education. Given that most of our graduates return to their rural homes to teach, they do not see the need for global education. Our challenge, therefore, has been to develop instructional strategies that motivate them to study global education. While different teaching approaches such as faculty collaboration were helpful, we believe that personalizing learning through student-centered learning, as well as immersing learners in global education was most meaningful. Indeed, Wenger (1998), argued that involving learners by encouraging them to decide what they want to learn, why they want to learn it, as well as how to learn it is likely to increase learners' interest and commitment. Learning thus designed is contextualized i.e., it links abstract knowledge to real life experiences (Shoemaker, 1989).

In our instructional efforts, we identified broad global education topics and asked our students to study the topic(s) of their choosing. Perhaps because of giving our students choices instead of forcing them to study any particular topic(s), our students appeared to develop an interest in and appreciation of global education. As our pre-service students explored different aspects of foreign countries and examined the similarities and differences between cultural practices, they learned about their cultural identities in a global context. Also as surprising, was our pre-service students' desire to not only shun isolationist local curricula, but to also teach broadened global education. To us this was a sign that our students were developing a global perspective. Generally, they seemed to understand that human events are interconnected, and that human experiences are a global phenomenon, in which people are constantly being influenced by transnational, cross-cultural, multicultural, multiethnic interactions, (Merryfield & Wilson, 2005). To amplify the value of global education, one student declared that "global education is essential because it prepares students to become sensitive citizens of the world."

CONCLUSIONS

Preparing public school educators for the 21st century and beyond who are equipped with the necessary cultural and global knowledge is an urgent priority. Nonetheless, implementing quality global education can be a daunting task especially when learners are unmotivated. In a global "village," however, the boundaries that previously separated cultures have been demolished. As a result, human events are more interconnected than at any other time in human history. An education that teaches to different global issues is therefore needed (Hanvey, 1975; Kirkwood, 2001). Meanwhile, to increase learner interest and commitment to global education, educators should adopt teaching strategies that promote knowledge ownership. Students are likely to study global education when they have a greater say in the learning process. Conversely, learners are likely to resist any curriculum that is imposed on them. For example, by using library research projects, service-learning with a cultural and global focus, and international cultural immersion, we not only motivated our students to study global education, but we also broadened their understanding and appreciation of global issues. Due to the knowledge and skills gained, our pre-service educators are now advocates of cultural and global education. Indeed, they developed a commitment to an education that not only validates every learner's culture, but also teaches them the necessary knowledge and skills to function effectively in a global "village." Meanwhile, we learned to value faculty collaboration.

Faculty collaboration is essential. In addition to promoting consistency within a program and across academic disciplines, faculty collaboration increases students' learning, knowledge retention, and transfer (Kambutu & Nganga, 2008). In our case, we collaborated by adopting common instructional ideas and resources, thus allowing our students to learn about global education sequentially from different faculty. After studying global education for a whole year, our students became familiar and receptive to it. Meanwhile, due to collaboration, we developed a team identity and a sense of purpose.

Working as a team deepened our understanding of global education. Although implementing global education can be challenging, teamwork is essential because it is likely to increase friendship and/or colleagueship. As colleagues, faculty are likely to mitigate proactively some of the stress involved in global education work. For example, although Gilliom (1993) reported a general lack of studies focusing on the implementation of effective global education in teacher education programs, collaborating faculty are better placed to design and implement strategies such as the ones we have presented in this chapter. As the saying goes, "two minds are better that one."

APPENDIX A: REFLECTIVE QUESTION USED BEFORE AND AFTER TEACHING GLOBAL EDUCATION.

1. What is your definition of global education?
2. How should an elementary education global education curriculum look like and why?

3. While selecting materials for global education, what consideration should be made and why?
4. What would you want to learn about foreign cultures?

APPENDIX B: COURSE: ELEMENTARY HUMANITIES EDUCATION (SOCIAL STUDIES)

This course focuses on the role of social studies education and humanities education in the elementary school curriculum. It is based on the premise that these areas of study enhance opportunities to facilitate inquiry, exploration, and understanding of the society and world in which we live. Secondly, it represents the thinking that the social studies and the humanities provide equally important contributions to the decisions which students must learn to make as intelligent and socially responsible citizens. A primary course goal will be to investigate innovative methods of initiating students into the world of the social sciences and the humanities (history, literature, sociology, art, and global education). As a member of this class, you are expected to familiarize yourself with the content and methodology of social studies instruction and to acquire strategies for integrating social studies education with other content areas.

The course focuses on the following objectives;

1. Develop a global education social studies unit that is original, meaningful, and engaging to both the teacher and students
2. Develop democratic learning environments
3. Become a reflective practitioner.

Course: Foundations of Education

Diverse Learners/Differentiated Instructions

The preservice teacher understands that schools are comprised of diverse learners who differ in their approaches to learning and that there are multiple theoretical models for understanding and addressing student diversity. He or she plans instruction with the assumptions that all students can learn and employs instructional methods in ways that connect learning with the students' diverse experiences and needs. The preservice teacher cultivates a mutually respectful learning community that values all students.

Democratic Learning Environments

The preservice teacher works to facilitate purposeful classroom and school learning environments that foster social interaction, active engagement, and collaboration with all stakeholders. The preservice teacher uses knowledge of the historical, social, and political roles of schooling in the U.S. to ensure equity for all children, especially given the relationship between schooling and the reproduction/mitigation of inequalities in the broader society. The preservice teacher knows and models principles of ethics, schooling for a democratic society, and social justice, especially in the development of mutual respect, support, and critical inquiry in the classroom. She or he is competent in behavior management that is reflective of the needs and practices of diverse students. This competence includes knowledge of classroom management skills, intervention strategies, motivational techniques, and monitoring and documenting student behavior. He or she critically reflects on personal history, beliefs, values, biases in relation to and as an agent of change within school and society.

Reflective Practitioner

The preservice teacher demonstrates self-assessment, individual and collective inquiry and life-long learning traits to support personal growth and professional development. The preservice teacher accesses resources such as literature, colleagues, observations, and/or classroom data to support her or his growth and development and that of colleagues.

REFERENCES

Alger, C. F., & Harf, J. E. (1986). Global education: Why? For whom? About what? In R. E. Freeman, (Ed.), *Promising practices in global education: A handbook with case studies* (pp. 1–13). NY: National Council on Foreign Language and International Studies.

Anderson, L. (1990). A rationale for global education. In K. A. Tye, (Ed.), *Global education from thought to action. The 1991 ASCD Yearbook* (pp. 13–34). Alexandria, VA: Association for Supervision and Curriculum Development.

Angelis, J. I. (2003). Conversation with the middle school classroom: Developing reading, writing, and other language abilities. *Middle School Journal, 34*(3), 57–61.

Arends, R. I. (2008). *Learning to teach* (7th ed.). New York: McGraw Hill.

Baloche, L., Hynes, J., & Berger H. (1996). Moving toward integration of professional and general education. *Action in Teacher Education, 18*(1), 1–9.

Barron, J. (2007, December 27th). Wyoming population climbs. *Star-Tribune Capital Bureau* trib.com. Retrieved From http://trib.com/news/state-and-regional/article_cf6d5176-d9ef-50b7-b4c5-d204b5432989.html.

Banks, J. A. (1997). Approaches to multicultural curriculum reform. In J. A. Banks & C. A McGee Banks (Eds.), *Multicultural education: Issues and perspective* (3rd ed.). Boston, MA: Allyn and Bacon.

Banks, J. (2001). *Diversity within unity: Essential principles for teaching and learning in a multicultural society.* Retrieved from http://www.marthalakecov.org/~building/strategies/multicultural/banks.htm

Banks, J. A. (2002. *An introduction to multicultural education.* Boston: Allyn and Bacon.

Bess, J.L. (2000). *Teaching alone, teaching together: Transforming the structure of teams forteaching.* San Francisco: Jossey-Bass.

Bogdan, R. C., & Biklen, S. K. (1998). *Qualitative research for education. An introduction to theory and methods* (2nd ed.). Boston: Allyn and Bacon.

Bruce M. G., Podemski R. S., & Anderson C. M. (1991). Developing a global perspective: Strategies for teacher education programs. *Journal of Teacher Education, 42*(1), 21–27.

Burnouf, L. (2004). Global awareness and perspectives in global education. *Canadian Social Studies, 38,* 3. Retrieved from http://www.quasar.ualberta.ca/css/Css_38_3 /Css_38_3/

Case, R. (1993). Key elements of a global perspective. *Social Education, 57,* 318–325.

Castaneda, R. C., Kambutu, J., & Rios, F. (2006, Summer). Speaking their truths: Teachers of color in diasporic contexts. *The Rural Educator, 27*(3), 13–23.

Cistone, P. J. (1991). Global perspectives for teachers: An urgent priority. *Journal of Teacher Education, 42*(1), 3–10.

Cogan, J. J. (9184). Should the U.S. mimic Japanese education? Let's look before we leap. *Phi Delta Kappan, 65*(7), 463.

Davison, D. M., Miller, K. W., & Metheny, D. L. (1995). What does integration of science and mathematics really mean? *School Science and Mathematics, 95*(5), 226–230.

Dedoussis, E.V. (2007). Issues of diversity in academia: Through the eyes of third-world country faculty. *High Education, 54,* 135–156.

Derman-Sparks, L., & Edwards, J. O. (2010). *Anti-bias education for young children and ourselves.* Washington, DC : National Association for the Education of Young Children (NAEYC).

Dewey, J. (1916). *Democracy and education.* New York: Macmillan

Diaz-Rico, L. (1993). From monocultural to multicultural teaching in inner-city middle school. In A. Woolfolk (Ed.), *Readings and cases in educational psychology.* Boston: Allyn and Bacon.

Diaz-Rico, L., & K. Z. Weed. (1995). *The cross-cultural, language, and academic developmenthandbook.* Needham Heights, MA: Allyn & Bacon

Dove, T. (2002). *Global Education: Seeing the world through many lenses.* Retrieved from http://www.ascd.org/publications/classroom_leadership/nov2002/Global_Education.aspxmportance.

Dressel, P. (1958). The meaning and significance of integration. In N. B. Henry (Ed.), *The integration of educational experiences, 57th yearbook of the National Society for the Study of Education* (pp. 3–25). Chicago: University of Chicago Press.

Duty, L. M. (2010). *Changing teacher's conceptualizations of teaching for citizenship in a globalized world.* (Doctoral dissertation, The Ohio State University). Retrieved from http://etd.ohiolink.edu/view

Frost, S. H., & Jean, P. M. (2003, March/April). Bridging the disciplines: Interdisciplinarydiscourse and faculty scholarship. *Journal of Higher Education, 74*(2), 119–149.

Gacel-Avila, J. (2005). The internationalization of higher education: A paradigm for global citizenry. *Journal of Studies in International Education, 9*(2), 121–136.

Gilliom, M. E. (1993, Winter). Mobilizing teacher educators to support global education in preservice programs. *Theory into Practice, 32*(1), 40–46.

Gordon, P., Rogers, A., & Comfort, M. (2001). A taste of problem-based learning increases achievement of urban minority middle-school students. *Educational Horizons, 79*(4),171–175.

Graves, J. (2002). Developing a global dimension in the curriculum. *The curriculum Journal, 13*(3), 303–311.

Hanvey, R. G. (1975). *An attainable global perspective.* Retrieved from http://eric.ed.gov/ERICDocs/data/ericdocs2sql/content_storage_01/

Hicks, D. (2003) Thirty years of global education: A reminder of key principles and precedents. *Educational Review, 55*(3), 265–275.

Hill, D. (1981). A survey of global understanding of American college students: A report to geographers. *The Professional Geographer,* (2), 237–245.

Jacobs, H. H. (1991). Planning for Curriculum Integration. *Educational Leadership, 49*(2), 27–28.

Johnson, D. W., & Johnson, F. P. (2006). *Joining together: Group theory and group skills* (9th. ed.). Englewood Cliffs, NJ: Prentice-Hall.

Kambutu, J. ,& Nganga, L. (2008). In these uncertain times: Educators build cultural awareness through planned international experiences. *Teaching and Teacher Education, 24*(4), 939–951.

Kambutu, J., Rios, F., & Castaneda, C. (2009). Stories deep within: Narratives of U.S. teachers of color from diasporic settings. *Diaspora, Indigenous, and Minority Education, 3,* 96–109.

Kirkwood, T. F. (2001). Our global age requires global education: Clarifying definitional ambiguities. *The Social Studies, 92*(1), 10–15.

Kniep, W. M. (1986). Defining a global education by its content. *Social Education, 50,* 437–446.

Lakes, K. (2003). *Integrated curriculum.* Northwest Regional Education Laboratory, School Improvement research series. Retrieved from http://www.small-schoolsproject.org/PDFS/Planning_Resources/summer2003/summer2003–integrating.pdf

Manrique, C. (2002). A foreign woman faculty's multiple whammies. In L. Vargas (Ed.), *Women faculty of color in the white classroom.* New York: Peter Lang.

Merryfield, M. M. (1995). Institutionalizing cross-cultural experiences and international expertise in teacher education: The development and potential of a global education PDS network. *Journal of Teacher Education, 46*(1), 19–27.

Merryfield, M. M. (2000). Why aren't American teachers being prepared to teach for diversity, equity, and interconnectedness? A study of lived experiences in the making of multicultural and global educators. *Teaching and Teacher Education, 16*(4), 429–443.

Merryfield, M. M., & Wilson A. (2005). *Social Studies and the world: Teaching global perspectives.* Silver Spring, MD: National Council of Social Studies.

Miller, K. W., Metheny, D. L., & Davison, D. M. (1997). Issues in integrating mathematics and science. *Science Educator, 6*(1), 16–21.

Nganga, L., & Kambutu, J. (2009). Teaching for democracy and social justice in isolated rural settings: Challenges and pedagogical opportunities. In S. Greonke & A. Hatch (Eds.), *Critical pedagogy and teacher education in the neoliberal era: Small openings.* Milton Keynes, U.K: Lighting Source UK Ltd.

Papert, S. (1980). *Mindstorms: Children, computers and powerful ideas.* New York, NY: Basic Books.

Parker, W. C. (2009). *Social studies in elementary education* (13th ed.). Boston: Allyn & Bacon.

Prerez, B. (1998). Language, literacy, and biliteracy. In Perez, B., MacCarty, T. L., Watahomigie, L. J., Dien, T. T., Chang, J. M., Smith, H. L., & Silva, A. D. (Eds.), *Sociocultural contexts of language and literacy*, pp. 21–48. Mahwah, New Jersey: Lawrence Erlbaum Associates, Publishers.

Pugach, M. L. (2006). Teaching students whose race, class, culture, or language differs from your own. In Paugch, M. L. (Ed.). *Because teaching matters* (pp. 175–212). Hoboken, NJ: John Wiley & Sons, Inc.

Rodriguez, K. (2000, May/June). Cultural immersion: Achieving the elusive perspective shift. *Transitions Abroad Magazine, XXIII*(6). Retrieved fromhttp://www.transitionsabroad.com/publications/magazine/0005/index.shtml

Shoemaker, B. (October 1989). Integrative education. A curriculum for the twenty-first century. *Oregon School Study Council (OSSC), Bulletin* 33, 2., Eugene, Oregon.

Sokolower, J. (2006, Fall). Bringing globalization home: A high school teacher helps immigrant students draw on their own expertise. *Rethinking Schools, 21*(1), 46–50.

State of Wyoming Department of Administration and Information (2006). *Wyoming's population in 2006 is the highest ever.* census.gov. 28 March 2007. http://www.eadiv.state.wy.us

Taylor, H. E. (1997). *Practical suggestions for teaching global education.* ERIC Digest. http://www.ericdigests.org/1997-1/global.html

Tucker, J. L., & Taylor, H. E. (1997). *Practical suggestions for teaching global education.* Eric Digest. Retrieved from http://www.ericdigests.org/1997-1/global.html

UNESCO (1974). *Recommendation concerning Education for international understanding, co-operation and peace and Education relating to human rights and fundamental freedoms.* UNESCO. Retrieved from http://www.unesco.org/education/nfsunesco/pdf/Peace_e.pdf

Western Canadian Protocol for Collaboration in Basic Education (1993). *Foundation document for the development of the common curriculum framework for Social Studies Kindergarten–Grade 12* . Retrieved from http://www.education.gov.ab.ca/wcp-socialfoundationdocument/index.html

Wenger, E. (1998). *Communities of practice. Learning as a social system.* Retrieved on 6-30-2008 from http://www.co-i-l.com/coil/knowledge-garden/cop/lss.shtml

Wilson, A. H. (1993). Conversation partners: Helping students gain a global perspective through cross-cultural experiences. *Theory into Practice, 32*(1), 21–26.

Wilson, H. C. (2002, Autumn). Discovery education: A definition. *Horizons, 19*, 25–29.

Zarrillo, J. J. (2008). *Teaching elementary social studies: Principles and applications* (3rd ed). Upper Saddle River, NJ: Pearson Merrill Prentice Hall.

CHAPTER 27

EXAMINING TEACHER DEVELOPMENT

The Role of Teacher Thinking, Observation, and Reflection

John Sturtz and Kevin Hessberg

INTRODUCTION

This chapter will explore the research on enhanced methods, practices, and models used to support pre-service and novice teachers in their teaching. Teacher education programs and school-based induction, or mentorship, programs across the country rely on classroom observations to improve instruction. However, there is little commonality among the observation models, frameworks, and programs that are used to support instruction. More recently, advances in technology combined with utilizing advanced protocols such as "think alouds" and Video Stimulated Recall (VSR) interviews are improving the feedback and support processes available to beginning teachers. These protocols allow teachers' implicit thoughts and decision-

Contemporary Social Studies: An Essential Reader, pages 547–564
Copyright © 2012 by Information Age Publishing
All rights of reproduction in any form reserved.

making to become explicit and enable the observation and feedback process to target deeper understandings of best practices. This chapter will cover the purposes of observation, examine various models used to provide feedback to pre-service and beginning teachers, and discuss the emerging role of technology in mentoring and field experience programs.

WHAT HAS BEEN DONE?

Scholars have concluded that learning to teach effectively is a difficult, complex, and time-intensive process (Burden, 1979; Cornett, 1990; Fuller, 1969; Fuller & Brown, 1975; Huberman, 1989; Rust, 1994; Ryan, 1986). Studies that have examined teacher development point to the importance of teacher thinking—in other words, gaining insight into how and what teachers are thinking about as they teach—so that proper support can be offered to foster the development of effective teaching strategies (Clark & Peterson, 1986). The research indicates that teachers make innumerable decisions every minute of every day (Clark & Peterson, 1986); including while planning, teaching, managing student behavior, making sense of the school context, and conversing with colleagues (Borko, Livingston, & Shavelson, 1990). Research also seems to indicate that the thought processes of beginning teachers are very different than the thought processes of expert teachers (Brandsford, Brown, & Cocking, 2001). The limited research conducted on beginning history teachers yields similar results (Bullough, 1989; Feiman-Nemser, 2001; van Hover & Yeager, 2004).

As much of the research pertaining to teacher thinking has been conducted at the elementary level, there is a paucity of research regarding secondary social studies teachers' thinking. Specifically, the current research does not explicitly explore what beginning teachers think about while engaged in instruction. Further, there is little research that attempts to examine social studies teachers' real-time decision-making within the field of social studies education.

Although specific, the question is an important one. More research needs to be done linking teacher decision-making to the increasingly common high-stakes testing environments of social studies classes in secondary schools. Many states now place an increased emphasis on factual recall of history, a notion seemingly at odds with the literature on best practices of social studies teaching (Grant, 2003). Examining feedback models such as "think aloud" and VSR can close this research gap by helping to scaffold professional development experiences for pre-service and beginning teachers and thus moving them towards ambitious teaching models.

RESEARCH ON EVALUATING AND
OBSERVING BEGINNING TEACHERS

Beginning teachers face many challenges as they enter K–12 classrooms. Heavy teaching loads, multiple preparations, minimal collegial or administrative support, lack of familiarity with the content, extracurricular duties, discipline and management issues, and high-stakes tests are just some of the hurdles novice teachers must surmount as they gain a foothold in the school environment (Darling-Hammond, 1998; Lawson, 1992, Rust, 1994; Yeager & van Hover, 2006). And, as Darling-Hammond (1997b) notes, in the current educational context, all teachers are being asked to teach more information, at higher cognitive levels, to an increasingly diverse student body, with decreased levels of support (Darling-Hammond, 1998; Darling-Hammond, 1997b; Lawson, 1992; Rust, 1994). A growing body of research supports the notion that "effective" teachers make a difference in student outcomes (Darling-Hammond, 1997a,b). Pillsbury (2005), for example, argues, "the common denominator in school improvement and student success is the teachers" (p. 49). The National Commission on Teaching and America's Future (as cited in Darling-Hammond, 1997) reports that teachers play the most significant part in determining student achievement and that teacher quality is a significant factor in closing the minority achievement gap.

The limited research on beginning social studies teachers yields similar results. A complex confluence of factors, including beliefs about students and content, educational background, teacher preparation, life experiences, and views towards high-stakes tests influences beginning social studies teachers' instructional decision-making (Bullough, 1989; Feiman-Nemser, 2001; van Hover & Yeager, 2004). Nonetheless, the current research in history education does not explicitly explore how and what beginning teachers think about while engaged *in* instruction. Examining how a teacher makes sense of social studies instruction, generally, and within a high-stakes testing environment, specifically, can provide insight into how teacher preparation and teacher induction can help foster effective teaching practices and advance teacher education programs (Bain, 2006). Darling-Hammond (1997a) observes that, "of beginners who enter teaching, about 30 percent leave within the first few years because they are left to sink or swim without support. Relatively few school districts offer intensive internships that provide the kind of learning support for teachers that new doctors, engineers, or architects enjoy" (p. 8).

Teachers, including beginning teachers, have a tough job. Administrators expect beginning teachers to enter the classroom with all of the required professional attributes necessary to teach in an increasingly complex environment (Darling-Hammond, 1997a; van Hover & Yeager, 2004; Wineburg, 2005). The research and literature suggests, however, that teachers need to have time and support to develop through a natural progression of professional development stages (Bullough, 1989; Moir, 1997). Ways the schools and educational systems support beginning teachers are through induction programs and various other professional development elements. Induction programs take on many forms, and tend to be characterized by a focus on helping beginning teachers assimilate into the teaching profession and school context (Wong, 2002). They are designed to help establish classroom management strategies, routines, and improve instruction (Wong, 2002). A vital element of these programs is the observation of the teacher's procedures and classroom teaching.

DEVELOPMENT OF BEGINNING TEACHERS

Several researchers have indicated that beginning teachers go through different stages during the early years of their teaching careers (Bullough, 1989; Feiman-Nemser, 2003; Fuller & Brown, 1975; Moir, 1997). Bullough (1989), for example, provides an in-depth examination of the characteristic stages beginning teachers go through in their first year of teaching in his year-long case study of a first-year teacher. Bullough argued this teacher, Kerrie, went through four stages of development: fantasy stage, survival stage, mastery stage, and impact stage. In the *fantasy stage*, the beginning teacher thinks he/she will become the next great teacher—changing every life they meet. In between the first and second stage is a period of shock where the classroom realities cause many beginning teachers to panic. In the *survival stage*, the beginning teacher struggles with management and discipline issues. Fortunately, this stage is followed closely by the mastery stage. In the mastery stage, the teacher continues to improve his/her management and discipline skills, making him/her able to move into the impact stage. In the *impact stage*, the teacher begins to concentrate on improving instruction.

Feiman-Nemser (2003) also asserts that many teachers progress through phases during their beginning teaching years. She argues that most new teachers progress through the initial shock of teaching, to isolation and survival, to disillusionment. These phases occur as teachers struggle to develop their teaching philosophy and integrate into the school culture. The school community, the support the beginning teacher receives, and attitudes of the other teachers in the school influence these phases. Similarly, Moir (1997) describes stages that include anticipation, disillusionment, survival, rejuvenation, reflection, and anticipation.

This notion of development stages can inform how administrators work with beginning teachers (Feiman-Nemser, 2003). Some researchers argue that administrators unfairly look at beginning teachers as finished products instead of recognizing the need for beginning teacher development (Feiman-Nemser, 2003; Wineburg, 2005). Feiman-Nemser (2003), for example, argues that variations exist in beginning teachers' readiness levels, and that administrators cannot think of beginning teachers as 100 percent ready to meet every challenge of the classroom. Her research meshes well with other researchers who emphasize the need to focus on a long-term trajectory of teachers as lifelong learners (Darling-Hammond, 1997a; Feiman-Nemser, 2003; van Hover & Yeager, 2004).

The research indicates that beginning teachers go through different stages during the early years of their professional development (Bullough, 1989; Feiman-Nemser, 2003; Moir, 1997). This research also notes that many administrators want beginning teachers to emerge from pre-service training with all of the required skills and abilities to teaching in a complex context. Beginning teacher development and administration expectations contribute to the challenges facing beginning teachers (van Hover & Yeager, 2004).

But what, then, makes an effective teacher? Many research-based frameworks include beginning teacher behaviors that fall under the category of "effective teaching." For example, the Interstate New Teacher Assessment and Support Consortium (INTASC)—an organization of state education agencies and national educational organizations working to reform teacher preparation and development—lists some generic criteria that they consider essential for new teachers. These criteria include an understanding of content pedagogy, student development, diverse learners, multiple instructional strategies, motivation and management, communication and technology, planning, assessment, reflective practice and professional growth, and school and community involvement. Other researchers cite additional characteristics such as student-centered teaching, effective classroom and behavior management, ethical role modeling, good prior academic performance, strong communication skills, creativity, an understanding of evaluation and assessment, self-development or lifelong learning, personality, and the ability to model concepts in their content area (Minor, Onwuegbuzie, & Witcher, 2002; Polk, 2006). These characteristics demonstrate the complexity of becoming an effective teacher.

DEVELOPING, OBSERVING, AND
SUPPORTING BEGINNING SOCIAL STUDIES TEACHERS

In the field of social studies education, researchers and educators continue to debate the content that is important to teach (Hirsch, 1988; Nash, Crabtree, & Dunn, 2000; Symcox, 2002). However, some consensus exists about what "effective" social studies teaching looks like. Scholars and educators agree that social studies education extends beyond factual knowledge and includes attention to more advanced habits of mind, such as critical thinking and analysis (Grant, 2001; Hartzler-Miller, 2001; Kantz, 2002; Seixas, 1998; Stearns, 2001; Wineburg, 1999; Yeager & Wilson, 1997). The intended goal, for a number of effective social studies teaching methods, is to prepare an educated citizenry (Barton & Levstik, 2004; Ferretti, MacArthur, & Okolo, 2001; Grant, 2003, 2005; Levstik & Barton, 2001). Thus, it is important for beginning teachers to develop teaching methodologies that move instruction beyond fact recall and towards instruction that promotes the skills and habits of mind vital to sustaining an educated citizenry.

How do teacher educators and school-based supervisory personnel help beginning social studies teachers teach in ways that reflect the literature on effective instruction? Johnston, Markle, and Boland (1985) wrote, "a major assumption of teacher effectiveness research is that teacher behavior is directly related to student achievement" (p. 4). Yet, a generation of scholars have concluded that learning to teach effectively is a difficult and complex process that cannot simply be measured by student achievement outcomes (Burden, 1979; Cornett, 1990; Fuller, 1969; Fuller & Brown, 1975; Huberman, 1989; Rust, 1994; Ryan, 1986). Studies that have examined teacher development point to the importance of teacher thinking—in other words, gaining insight into how and what teachers are thinking about as they teach—so that proper support and guidance can be offered to foster the development of effective teaching strategies (Clark & Peterson, 1986). The research indicates that teachers make innumerable decisions every minute of every day (Clark & Peterson, 1986) including while planning, teaching, managing student behavior, making sense of the school context, and conversing with colleagues (Borko, 1990). Beliefs, educational background, teacher training, and life experiences all influence how teachers think while planning, teaching, assessing, and interacting with students (Clark & Lampert, 1986). Additionally, studies show that beginning teachers engage in very different thought processes than expert teachers (Bransford, Brown, & Cocking, 2001). Gaining insight into what beginning teachers think about while teaching can have a positive impact on moving them towards expert teacher thinking.

WHAT BEGINNING TEACHERS REALLY NEED

Beginning social studies teachers encounter many new situations when they enter the classroom (Bullough, 1989; Darling-Hammond, 1997a,b; van Hover & Yeager, 2004) and often have limited experience to help inform their decisions (Bransford, Brown, & Cocking, 2001). Research indicates that a teacher's thought process dictates observable behaviors and influences how resources, curriculum, and lessons are implemented in the classroom (Clark & Peterson, 1986). Addressing the needs of beginning teachers can better prepare these teachers for classroom realities and thus improve the quality of their teaching (Feiman-Nemser, 2003). Feiman-Nemser outlined what beginning teachers need to learn for a better classroom experience. She wrote that, "addressing the learning needs of new teachers can improve both the rate of teacher retention and the quality of the teaching profession" (p. 25). Beginning teachers need to make their teaching meaningful for students, to construct an identity and personal teaching philosophy, and to react to situations properly. Gilbert (2005) surveyed 362 beginning K–12 grade teachers over two years in six different Georgia school districts to explore their perceptions on school support for beginning teachers. She found that the novice teachers asked for the following support:

1. The opportunity to observe other teachers
2. To be assigned smaller classes
3. To be assigned mentor teachers
4. To have co-planning time with other educators
5. To be provided feedback based on observation of their teaching (p. 36).

Mandel (2006) also recommends that traditional teacher education programs should ensure that pre-service teachers are made aware of classroom realities—specifically, that schools of education not only prepare pre-service teachers well in regards to teaching theories, but also provide more instruction about the teaching practice.

TEACHER THINKING

A teacher's thought process determines a teacher's classroom actions and instructional choices (Clark & Peterson, 1986) and, the teacher is the ultimate decision maker or "gatekeeper" in the classroom (Thornton, 1991). Internal and external classroom factors influence teachers' classroom decision-making—such as school policies, school organizational structures, teacher's background, and teacher beliefs about content, teaching and learning (Grant, 2003; van Hover & Yeager, 2004). And, ultimately, these teachers dictate what knowledge is presented and which methods used to do so in the classroom. Research on teacher thinking has been somewhat cyclical. Research on teaching in the 1960s focused on teacher behaviors, but the bulk of research in the last three decades of the twentieth century was focused on the thought processes that contributed to teacher behaviors (Calderhead, 1987). Early research in this field examined teacher effectiveness and sparked researchers to begin to examine what teachers think about and how teachers think during teaching and planning (Clark & Peterson, 1986). Hall and Smith (2006) reviewed the existing literature on the topic and discovered that a shift occurred in the last decade—research moved away from a focus on teacher thinking and moved to an examination of teacher reflection. Reflection is important in the developmental process of teachers in that it allows teachers to constantly modify their teaching.

BEGINNING TEACHERS, SOCIAL STUDIES & CLASSROOM PRACTICE

There exists a growing body of work which examines classroom teaching practices of secondary social studies teachers (Cornett, 1990; Fain, 1998; van Hover & Heinecke, 2005; van Hover & Yeager, 2004; Yeager & van Hover, 2006; Yeager & Wilson, 1997). Within this body of work, several researchers have narrowed their research focus to examine the practices of beginning social studies teachers (Gradwell, 2006; Grant, 2006; Hartzler-Miller, 2001; van Hover & Yeager, 2004; Yeager & Davis, 1995; Yeager & van Hover, 2006). For example Hartzler-Miller (2001) used qualitative methodology to study a beginning history teacher and found that though the teacher possessed the proper subject matter knowledge and beliefs necessary to teach historical inquiry, the teacher did not regularly stress historical thinking in instruction. This implies that there is a gap between the teacher's thinking and their instructional practices. Based on these findings, Hartzler-Miller argues for a practical professional education starting with questions about teachers' ideas of best practices for teaching history. These studies indicate that beginning social studies teachers' instructional practice is influenced by prior educational experience, beliefs about students, beliefs about content, and a complex confluence of other factors (Gradwell, 2006; Grant, 2003, 2005, 2006; van Hover & Heinecke, 2005; Yeager & van Hover, 2006).

In the era of No Child Left Behind, some researchers have begun examining how beginning teachers operate within the context of high-stakes testing (Gradwell, 2006; Grant, 2005, 2006; van Hover & Heinecke, 2005; Yeager & van Hover, 2006). Yeager and van Hover (2006) used case studies to examine how a beginning social studies teacher in Virginia and a beginning social studies teacher in Florida navigated the responsibilities of teaching in an environment dominated by high-stakes testing. They used case studies of two secondary history teachers and found similarities and differences between the two cases. They found that both teachers moved towards Grant's notion of ambitious teaching in classroom instruction by using interesting and engaging instructional strategies that connect the students to the content. They also suggest that the teachers' instructional approaches differed as a result of different influences of the state's end-of-year tests. Finally, they also wrote that the teachers' pre-service training and context influenced the teachers' instructional decisions. These researchers echo the Grant's (2001, 2003) notion that high-stakes test serve as an *uncertain lever* on beginning teachers' instructional practices. In his case studies, Grant (2001) notes that the effects of end-of-year exams on two teachers in New York are difficult to assess: "...the data from these two cases suggest that not only do tests not drive these teachers' pedagogy in any particular direction, but they may not drive much of anything at all" (p. 414). He argues that, in addition to state testing, there are many other pressures and influences on teachers with regard to instructional practices, including beliefs about the content, how students learn, and a teacher's beliefs about teaching.

An integral part of understanding how beginning teachers think is to examine the methods that the various stakeholders, such as teacher educators and school administrators, use to gather data for professional development purposes. Namely, what observational methods are employed and how is that data used to improve teaching and student outcomes? Gathering data on beginning teachers' thinking will help teacher educators and school administrators understand how these new teachers integrate their beliefs, thinking, past experiences, and context into their instructional decisions (Borko, Livingston, & Shavelson, 1990; Clark & Lampert, 1986; Clark & Peterson, 1986; Grant, 2003, 2005; van Hover & Heinecke, 2005; van Hover & Yeager, 2004). Understanding the decisions new teachers make and comparing those understandings to the field's conceptions of "effective" social studies teaching can provide a piece of data needed to improve teacher education experiences, professional development opportunities, and the resources offered to beginning teachers (Bain, 2006)

THE ROLE OF OBSERVATION IN MENTORING

Within the field of education, researchers and teachers educators have developed a solid understanding of the general thinking and various experiences that pre-service and beginning teachers have. However, there is little organized research that critically explores the observational methods and feedback protocols that are employed to help beginning and pre-service teachers' professional development (Bullough, 1989; Darling-Hammond, 1997a,b; Darling-Hammond & Youngs, 2002; Feiman-Nemser, 2001, 2003; Gilbert, 2005; Turley, Powers, & Nakai, 2006; van Hover & Yeager, 2004; Wineburg, 2005). Considerable research exists regarding teacher evaluation and feedback, though few have tried to recreate the teacher's real-time thinking (Clark & Peterson, 1986; Clark & Yinger, 1979; Hall & Smith, 2006). Hall and Smith (2006) note the importance and benefits of understanding a teacher's real-time thinking because it ties a teacher's observable behaviors to the cognitive processes that produced them. It is in trying to capture this thinking that researchers can begin to understand the motives behind the teachers' classroom behaviors.

At a time when social studies is at risk of losing its footing in the race of standards and accountability it is imperative that social studies teacher educators develop a firm understanding of the underlying thought processes of the beginning teacher. It is through the combination of measuring observable behaviors and the underlying motivations that teacher educators can make improvements to the programs that work to develop and maintain teachers. Drawing a clear connection between teacher thinking with student outcomes allows for the implicit to become explicit. Once this relationship is understood then teacher education professionals can develop experiences, opportunities, and methodologies to help link instructional thought to classroom practice. These innovations and enhanced observation methods work to uncover that which typically remains covered during the observation process.

PURPOSE OF OBSERVATIONS

Teacher educators and practitioners within the field of education use observations for two different, yet important jobs. Administrators use observation systems to collect evaluation data on teachers to improve teaching and make personnel decisions. Also, some professional development experiences for teachers require observations to help provide structure to the experience (Stodolsky, 1990). While current observational practices have been successful, pre-service and beginning teachers have a unique set of needs which necessitates a revision of the way researchers conceptualize observations. Observation systems alone might be effective as evaluation systems for experienced teachers but are at times inadequate as a professional development tool for pre-service and beginning teachers (Stodolsky, 1990). Observations often require evaluators to focus on teacher behavior while teaching. The presence or absence of these behaviors is the focus of the observation. Little attention is paid to the planning work that preceded the instructional behaviors. The assumption is that the process and habits of mind that lead to the demonstration of the behaviors is sufficient evidence to suggest that the teacher knows what he or she is doing. Unfortunately, this is not always the case. Beginning teachers report a tension between what they were exposed to during pre-service education and the realities they face in a school environment (Bullough, 1989; Darling-Hammond, 1997a,b; Darling-Hammond & Youngs, 2002; Feiman-Nemser, 2001, 2003; Gilbert, 2005; van Hover & Yeager, 2004).

Traditional observation requires a specific definition of good teaching (Stodolsky, 1990) and this definition provides the structure for many observation systems. The emphasis placed on high-stakes testing can lead to a tension between what social studies educators' consider good teaching and what administrators consider effective practice (Grant, 2003). The context of high-stakes testing has skewed the notion of good teaching (van Hover & Heinecke, 2005). Administrators in high-stakes testing environments might encourage teaching behaviors that improve student testing outcomes and thus develop observation systems that focus on characteristics associated with rote memorization and lower level thinking. This is often at odds with social studies programs that advocate for best teaching practices.

Observations protocols that rely solely on evaluating observed behavior fall short of the feedback pre-service and novice teachers need to develop into ambitious teachers (Stodolsky, 1990). Taken to the extreme, Scheeler and Lee (2002) used emerging technology to video record a teacher live while providing live feedback to the teacher as instruction was happening. The teacher had an earpiece ("Bug in the ear" technology) through which she could hear the observers who were watching live in another room. The observers, trained to provide corrective comments about the teacher's actions, provided feedback to the teacher live as she was teaching. Results indicated that "the immediate corrective feedback was more effective than a traditional delayed feedback procedure" (Scheeler & Lee, 2002, p. 239). For example, in their study, the immediate corrective feedback provided by earpiece each teacher wore correlated with increased feedback from the teachers to the students. This high-feedback ration led to increased scaffolding and encouragement. Scheeler and Lee write further that, the "findings support other research that demonstrate that immediate corrective feedback is effective in promoting acquisitions of effective teaching skills" (p. 239). Importantly, the link between immediate corrective feedback and an increase in effective teaching skills was made at the behavioral level. The research sought to influence teacher behaviors, rather than the underlying teacher-thinking. However, Hall and Smith (2006) note that this type of behaviorism is a start—it allows for an understanding of the origin of classroom behaviors, and what produce them. In turn, this affords teachers the ability to be more metacognitive in their teaching.

Research on effective teaching confirms the old cliché: teaching is more than what meets the eye (Black, 2001). For example, some beginning teachers experience numerous challenges as they learn to navigate an otherwise difficult context, including an increased emphasis on standards and accountability, an increasingly diverse student population, and lack of support or mentoring (van Hover & Yeager, 2004, p. 8). Without understanding the internal challenges, teacher-educators cannot begin to provide the most effective and beneficial development opportunities for our pre-service and beginning teachers. Traditional observation systems alone cannot gain access into teacher thinking (Stodolsky, 1990). Teacher development should be about changing thinking. Numerous technological advances make it attainable now more than ever.

OBSERVATION MODELS USING ADVANCED PROTOCOLS

Contemporary mentoring systems often utilize an outside observer who spends a short time observing the teacher (usually one lesson or less) to provide cursory feedback after a lesson. In a review of the issues associate with teacher mentoring, Zimpher and Rieger (2001) discussed the many ways that more experienced teachers assist in the professional development and mentoring of pre-service and novice teachers. Much of the review breaks down effective mentoring as a support structure, but does not focus on how the mentors provide feedback. This reflects common practice in the field in that feedback is often void of metacognitive modeling to scaffold the teacher's thinking. Often, both the mentor and the teacher rely on their memories to serve as the evidence to analyze the lesson (Welsh & Devlin, 2006). Instead, observations that utilize advanced protocols provide more targeted feedback to the pre-service or novice teacher. The term advanced protocol is being used to mean any observation system that focuses on observed behaviors as well as teacher thinking and decision-making. With advanced protocols such as think alouds and video stimulated recall interviews the outside observer prompts and navigates the teacher to better understand the thinking behind the observable actions. The protocols provide opportunities for intense meta-cognition and thus adjust teacher thinking and decision making. In essence, these techniques require the observed teacher to be more reflective; and a more reflective teacher often is a more effective teacher (Black, 2001; Ward & McCotter, 2004; Welsh & Devlin, 2006).

THINK ALOUDS

Another method that can be useful to uncover teachers' thought processes is known as "think-alouds." Think aloud methods ask the participant to speak out loud and continue to talk about any thoughts that entered their mind while trying to solve a problem (van Someren, Barnard, & Sandberg, 1994). Typically, there are no distractions, questions, or prompts from the researcher during these sessions. Think aloud methods are useful because the participant's thought process is not interrupted or disturbed during problem solving tasks, thus resulting in a more natural collection of real time data (van Someren, Barnard, & Sandberg, 1994).

The think-aloud allows the observer to focus on the planning that went into the observed instruction. Observers can utilize lesson plans, observation notes or video recorded lesson segments to ask reflective questions about the teaching. Ward and McCotter (2004) reviewed effective reflection practices and identified three main characteristics of reflection: reflection is situated in practice, is cyclic in nature, and makes use of multiple perspectives. The think-aloud allows for each of these characteristics to develop through a process that involves questioning teachers about their instruction and comparing it to their practice.

VIDEO STIMULATED RECALL INTERVIEWS

Advances in technology are providing the opportunity for better reflective practices during the observation cycle. For example, Video Stimulate Recall (VSR) is an example of a technological advance that seems particularly promising for teacher evaluators. The method typically involves replaying video taped segments to the teachers and asking these teachers questions about what they see and what they were thinking. The purpose of video stimulated recall is to gain insight into the participant's thought processes during a specific period of time. During the VSR interviews, participants watch themselves teach, and identify thought process and decision during the class. The participant can pause the tape at any time and talk about any aspect of the class while discussing any thoughts they had during the observation. Stimulated video recall procedures have been used in other fields but also in research on teacher-thinking (Clark & Peterson, 1986; McAlpine, Weston, & Berthiaume, 2006; Pirie, 1996). While stimulated video recall is not perfect, is has the potential to provide significant insights into research on teaching (Lyle, 2003; Welsch & Devlin, 2006).

A video based observation study conducted by Welsch and Devlin (2006) suggest that using video in observation and reflection increases the higher order nature of pre-service teachers' reflection. Though the study was not completely conclusive due to a small sample and inconsistently significant results across its data points, the study suggests that video based (as opposed to memory based) reflection contributes to higher order reflection. The authors arrived at this result by analyzing written responses to the following six question groups from the participants (Welsch & Devlin, 2006, p. 56):

1. To what extent did the students learn what you intended? How do you know?

2. In what ways were your teaching methods/activities effective? How do you know that?

3. If you were going to teach this class again to the same students (i.e., if you could go back in time), what would you do differently? What would you do the same? Why?

4. Based on what happened today, what would you plan to do next with this class?

5. Identify an individual or group of students who did well in today's lesson. How do you account for this individual or group's performance?

6. Identify an individual or group of students who had difficulty in today's lesson. What accounted for this individual or group's performance? How could you help this (these) student(s) achieve the learning goals?

More specifically, 92% of the participants reported that their ability to reflect on student learning and their instruction through these prompts was enhanced using the video compared to completing a reflection based on memory.

Think alouds and video stimulated recall interviews have been successfully used in complementary fields to education, such as psychology. However, they have seen limited use in classroom environments. Even more limited is the research on how the think-aloud and video stimulated recall methodology can be used as a way to enable pre-service and beginning teachers to systematically process through their thoughts, decisions, and actions employed in the classroom.

SUMMARY

This chapter explored the methods, practices, and models used to support pre-service and novice teachers' instruction. Classroom observations that rely on capturing overt teacher behaviors remain the preferred instrument for many teacher educators, reflected by the sheer number of teacher education programs and school-based induction programs that rely on observation. However, this paper has demonstrated that the assumptions underpinning these observation instruments are inadequate to support all of elements that should be explored with beginning social studies teachers. Beginning teachers require more that a cursory glance at their classroom behaviors and pedagogic methodologies. A look into their thinking is vital. In addition, the assumptions used to construct these instruments are developed within a high-stakes testing environment and often highlight behaviors that are at odds with the field's notion of good teaching characteristics.

Advances in technology and advanced protocols such as think-aloud and video-stimulated-recall interviews have enhanced the feedback and support process to beginning and novice teachers. These protocols allow implicit thoughts to become explicit and enable observation and feedback procedures that incorporate a deeper understanding of best practices.

Research within pre-service and novice teacher development is not new. Much has been done to improve the practices of teachers in the field. However, much work remains. More research in the realm of teacher observation should incorporate teacher-thinking. Also, research should move beyond a behaviorist approach to mentoring and integrate reflective practices in the observation model. The work being done in observation and supervision should include a component which accounts for the purpose of the observation. Pre-service and novice teachers need to be prompted to think, not just act, in new and relevant ways in the classroom to effectively meet the needs of our students in the 21st century.

REFERENCES

Bain, R. (2006). Paper presented at the National Council for the Social Studies, College and University Faculty Assembly, Washington, D.C.

Barton, K. C., & Levstik, L. S. (2004). *Teaching history for the common good.* Mahwah, NJ: Lawrence Erlbaum Associates.

Black, S. (2001). Thinking about teaching. *American School Board Journal, 108*(11), 42–44.

Borko, H., Livingston, C., & Shavelson, R. J. (1990). Teachers' thinking about instruction. *Remedial and Special Education, 11*(6), 40–53.

Bransford, J. D., Brown, A. L., & Cocking, R. R. (Eds.). (2001). *How people learn: Brain, mind, experience, and school.* Washington, DC: National Academy Press.

Bullough, R. V. (1989). *First-year teacher: A case study.* New York: Teachers College Press.

Burden, P. R. (1979). *Teacher's perceptions of the characteristics and influences on their personal and professional development.* Columbus, OH: Ohio State University Press.

Calderhead, J. (1987). *Exploring teachers' thinking.* London, England: Cassell Educational Limited.

Clark, C. M., & Lampert, M. (1986). The study of teacher thinking: Implications for teacher education. *Journal of Teacher Education, 37*(5), 27–31.

Clark, C. M., & Peterson, P. L. (1986). Teachers' thought processes. In M. C. Wittrock (Ed.), *Handbook of research on teaching* (pp. 255–296). New York, NY: Macmillan.

Clark, C. M., & Yinger, R. (1979). Teachers' thinking. In P. L. Peterson & H. J. Walberd (Eds.), *Research on teaching* (pp. 231–263). Berkeley, CA: McCutchan.

Cornett, J. W. (1990). Teacher thinking about curriculum and instruction: A case study of a secondary social studies teacher. *Theory and Research in Social Education, 28*(3), 248–273.

Darling-Hammond. (1998). Teacher learning that supports student learning. *Educational Leadership, 55*(5), 6–11.

Darling-Hammond, L. (1997a). Quality teaching: the critical key to learning. *Principal (Reston, Va.), 77*, 5–6.

Darling-Hammond, L. (1997b). What matters most: 21st-century teaching. *The Education Digest, 63*, 4–9.

Darling-Hammond, L., & Youngs, P. (2002). Defining "highly qualified teachers": What does "scientifically-based research" actually tell us?. *Educational Researcher, 31*(9), 13–25.

Fain, G. (1998). Teaching history. *The Clearing House, 72*(2), 68–69.

Feiman-Nemser, S. (2001). Helping novices learn to teach: lessons from an exemplary support teacher. *Journal of Teacher Education, 52*(1), 17–30.

Feiman-Nemser, S. (2003). What new teachers need to learn. *Educational Leadership, 60*(8), 25–29.

Ferretti, R. P., MacArthur, C. D., & Okolo, C. M. (2001). Teaching for historical understanding in inclusive classrooms. *Learning Disability Quarterly, 24*(1), 59–71.

Fuller, F. (1969). Concerns of teachers: A developmental conceptualization. *American Educational Research Journal, 6*(4), 207–226.

Fuller, F., & Brown, O. H. (1975). Becoming a Teacher. In K. Ryan (Ed.), *Teacher education.* Chicago, IL: University of Chicago Press.

Gilbert, L. (2005). What Helps Beginning Teachers? *Educational Leadership, 62*(8), 36–39.

Gradwell, J. (2006). Teaching in spite of, rather than because of, the test: A case of ambitious history teaching in New York State. In S. G. Grant (Ed.), *Measuring history: Cases of high-stakes testing across the states* (pp. 157–176). Greenwich, CT: Information Age Publishing.

Grant, S. G. (2001). An uncertain lever: Exploring the influence of state-level testing in New York State on teaching social studies. *Teachers College Record, 103*(3), 398–426.

Grant, S. G. (2003). *History Lessons: Teaching, Learning, and Testing in U.S. High School Classrooms.* Mahwah, NJ: Lawrence Erlbaum Associates.

Grant, S. G. (2005). More journey than end: A case study of ambitious teaching. In E. A. Yeager & O. L. Davis Jr. (Eds.), *Wise social studies teaching in an age of high-stakes testing: Essays on classroom practices and possibilities* (pp. 117–130).

Grant, S. G. (2006). *Measuring history: Cases of high-stakes testing across the states.* Greenwich, CT: Information Age Publishing.

Hall, T. J., & Smith, M. A. (2006). Teacher planning, instruction and reflection: What we know about teacher cognitive processes. *Quest, 58*(4), 424–442.

Hartzler-Miller, C. (2001). Making sense of "best practice" in teaching history. *Theory and Research in Social Education, 29*(4), 672–695.

Hirsch, E. D. (1988). *Cultural Literacy: What every American needs to know.* Boston, MA: Houghton Mifflin.

Huberman, A. M. (1989). The professional life cycle of teachers. *Teachers College Record, 91*(1), 31–56.

Johnston, J. H., Markle, G. C., & Boland, J. A. (1985). About teacher thinking. *Middle School Journal, 16*(2), 4–7.

Kantz, B. (2002). Historical Thinking and Other Unnatural Acts (Book Review). *The History Teacher (Long Beach, Calif.), 35*(4), 546–547.

Lawson, H. (1992). Beyond the new conception of teacher induction. *Journal of Teacher Education, 43*(3), 163–172.

Levstik, L. S., & Barton, K. C. (2001). *Doing history: investigating with children in elementary and middle schools* (2nd ed.). Mahwah, New Jersey: Lawrence Erlbaum Associates.

Lyle, J. (2003). Stimulated recall: A report on its use in naturalistic research. *British Education Research Journal, 29*(6), 861–878.

Mandel, S. (2006). What new teachers really need. *Educational Leadership, 63*(6), 66–69.

McAlpine, L., Weston, C., & Berthiaume, D. (2006). How do instructors explain their thinking when planning and teaching? *Higher Education, 51*(1), 125–155.

Minor, L. C., Onwuegbuzie, A. J., & Witcher, A. E. (2002). Pre-service teachers' educational beliefs and their perceptions of characteristics of effective teachers. *The Journal of Educational Research (Washington, D.C.), 96*(2), 116–127.

Moir, E. (1997). The stages of a teacher's first years. In M. Schurer (Ed.), *A better beginning: Supporting and mentoring teachers* (pp. 19–26). Alexandria: Association of Supervision and Curriculum Development.

Nash, G. B., Crabtree, C., & Dunn, R. E. (2000). *History on trial: Cultural wars and the teaching of the past.* New York: Vintage Books.

Pillsbury, P. (2005). Only the best: Hiring outstanding teachers. *Leadership, 35*(2), 36–38.

Pirie, S. E. B. (1996). *Classroom video recording: When, why and how it offers a valuable data source for qualitative research.* Paper presented at the Conference the Annual Meeting of the North American Chapter of the International Group for Psychology of Mathematics Education (Panama City, Florida). Retrieved from author January 31, 2007.

Polk, J. A. (2006). Traits of effective teachers. *Arts Education Policy Review, 107*(4), 23–29.

Rust, F. (1994). The first year of teaching: It's not what they expected. *Teaching & Teacher Education, 10*(2), 205–217.

Ryan, K. (1986). *The induction of new teachers.* Bloomington, IN: Phi Delta Kappa Educational Foundation.

Seixas, P. (1998). Student teachers thinking historically. *Theory and Research in Social Education, 26*(3), 310–341.

Scheeler, M. C., & Lee, D. L. (2002). Using technology to deliver immediate corrective feedback to pre-service teachers. *Journal of Behavioral Education, 11*(4), 231–241.

Stearns, P. N. (2001). {Historical Thinking and Other Unnatural Acts}. *American Journal of Education, 109*(4), 488–489.

Stodolksy, S. S. (1990). Classroom Observation. In J. Millman & L. Darling-Hammond (Eds.), *The New Handbook of Teacher Evaluation: Assessing Elementary and Secondary School Teachers* (pp. 175–190). Newbury Park: Sage Publications, Inc.

Symcox, L. (2002). *Whose history? The struggle for national standards in American classrooms.* New York: Teachers College Press.

Thornton, S. J. (1991). Teacher as Curricular-Instructional Gatekeeper in Social Studies. In J. P. Shaver (Ed.), *Handbook of Research on Social Studies Teaching and Learning* (pp. 237–248). New York: Macmillian.

Turley, S., Powers, K., & Nakai, K. (2006). Beginning teachers' confidence before and after induction. *Action in Teacher Education, 28*(1), 27–39.

van Hover, S. D., & Heinecke, W. F. (2005). The Impact of Accountability Reform on the "Wise Practice" of Secondary History Teachers. In E. A. Yeager & O. L. Davis Jr. (Eds.), *Wise social studies teaching in an age of high-stakes testing: Essays on classroom practices and possibilities* (pp. 89–115). Greenwich, Connecticut: Information Age Publishing.

van Hover, S. D., & Yeager, E. A. (2004). Challenges facing beginning history teachers: An exploratory study. *International Journal of Social Education, 19*(1), 8–26.

van Someren, M. W., Barnard, Y. F., & Sandberg, J. A. C. (1994). *The Think Aloud Method: A practical guide to modeling cognitive processes.* London: Academic Press.

Ward, J. R., & McCotter, S. S. (2004). Reflection as a visible outcome for pre-service teachers. *Teaching and Teacher Education, 20*(3), 243–257.

Welsch, R. G., & Devlin, P. A. (2006). Developing pre-service teachers' reflection: Examining the use of video. *Action in Teacher Education, 28*(4), 53–61.

Wineburg, S. (2005). What does NCATE have to say to future history teachers? Not much. *Phi Delta Kappan, 86*(9), 658–665.

Wineburg, S. S. (1999). Historical thinking and other unnatural acts. *Phi Delta Kappan, 80*(7), 488–499.

Wong, H. K. (2002). Induction: The Best Form of Professional Development. *Educational Leadership, 59*(6), 52–55.

Yeager, E. A., & Davis, O. L. (1995). Between campus and classroom: Secondary student-teachers' thinking about historical text. *Journal of Research and Development in Education, 29*(1), 1–8.

Yeager, E. A., & van Hover, S. (2006). Virginia vs. Florida: Two beginning history teachers' perceptions of the influence of high-stakes tests on their instructional decision-making. *Social Studies Research and Practice, 1*(3), 340–358.

Yeager, E. A., & Wilson, E. K. (1997). Teaching historical thinking in the social studies methods course: a case study. *The Social Studies, 88*(3), 121–126.

Zimpher, N. L. & Rieger, S. R. (2001). Mentoring teachers: What are the issues? *Theory into Practice, 27*(3), 175–182.

CHAPTER 28

A CAPSTONE COURSE IN A MASTER'S SOCIAL STUDIES PROGRAM IN AN AGE OF ACCOUNTABILITY AND TESTING

A Case Study

Jesus Garcia, Paula S. McMillen, and David To

INTRODUCTION

As we move into the second decade of the 21st century, America's schools are firmly guided by the goals of accountability and testing, and the present weak economic climate appears to be providing the fuel that propels K–12 education down this path. Pundits of all political stripes are calling for school systems to "trim the fat" from their budgets as no end is seen to depleting state revenues and shrinking federal assistance. And as schools

Contemporary Social Studies: An Essential Reader, pages 565–594
Copyright © 2012 by Information Age Publishing
565

move forward in pursuit of these two goals, they seem unable to please anyone. While much of the disparagement seems to be ideological, the climate is such that politicians, interest groups, business leaders, university officials, and parents are not above publically issuing scathing criticisms of public schools. These critics point to national and international test results and wonder out loud why students are not prepared for college, lack the knowledge and skills to transition into 21st century jobs, and appear not to be as strong as their international peers in the K–12 core subjects. These same critics, however, fail to inform the reader that international comparisons, while providing some insights into the performance of students across the globe, are not without their limitations (Koretz, 2002; Shiel & Eivers, 2009). Nevertheless, as a cross-section of Americans embrace a posture of fiscal tight-fistedness while demanding a change in the status quo, a major scapegoat in this worked-up frenzy is the classroom teacher. Who has not heard the lament, "Teachers are simply not doing the job required of them to prepare young adults for a 21st century job or college!"

Today the push is for a K–12 curriculum that is exceedingly lean and instruction that is teacher centered. It is not uncommon to hear of elementary schools that are de-emphasizing or ignoring the teaching of social studies and other core subjects, adopting scripted teaching and the memorization of discrete information, and minimizing the importance of risk-taking and creativity as legitimate forms of learning (Trilling & Fadel, 2009). These practices suggest that students are not being provided with basic foundations in social studies and in all probability matriculate into secondary schools lacking the knowledge, skills, and disposition to do well in their social science courses (in this essay we use social science and social studies interchangeably). Hence they often have a limited understanding of the value of a liberal education and the array of meanings associated with the phrase "rights and responsibilities of an active and progressive citizenry" (McEachron, 2010). Sadly, teachers entering the profession, who have themselves experienced this "new" form of education, are quickly socialized into these altered notions of teaching and learning. In short, the educational community is moving down a slippery path without revisiting fundamental questions that are the bedrock of American education: How can teachers promote learning so that students leave school inquisitive, creative, and prepared for educational opportunities beyond high school? What knowledge, skills, and dispositions are worth promoting in the 21st century? What knowledge, skills, and dispositions should K–12 teachers possess in order to prepare students to live locally and globally?

PURPOSE

The purpose of this chapter is two-fold. First, to establish the context of our case study, we explain the importance of social studies in the K–12 curriculum, its precipitous fall as a core subject in the K–6 curriculum, the state of social studies teaching in secondary schools, and the impact of the changing educational environment on the professional development of in-service social studies teachers. Second, we employ this background information to describe the redesign of a master's level capstone social studies course. The learning experiences offered to these social studies teachers in this course included the following: reflection on practice and consideration of the current status of social studies in K–12 schools; and increasing awareness of and capacity for actions available to professionals who find the present educational environment unacceptable and not in-keeping with basic tenets of good pedagogy. That is, since the 1960s, the educational community has advocated a form of social studies focusing on inquiry as a process that fosters students' intellectual curiosity to pursue knowledge (Smith & Cox, 1971). This approach is distinctly different from accountability driven prescriptive teaching and teaching to the test.

SOCIAL STUDIES AS A CORE SUBJECT AREA IN THE K–12 CURRICULUM

No political or educational leaders have taken a stance publically advocating the elimination of social studies from the K–12 curriculum. Nevertheless, its absence from the list of tested subjects has done much to diminish its standing. It seems appropriate, therefore, to provide a brief historical rationale for its place as a core subject in the schools. When the United States declared and gained its independence it quickly looked for ways to distinguish itself from England and the rest of Europe. In spite of dissension regarding *who* was to be educated, there was consensus that a curriculum for children and young adults would include history and geography, deference to the country's revolutionary leaders, and reverence for the political principles that led to the country's inception (Pulliam & Van Patten, 2007). The social studies would provide the knowledge and political beliefs that would bond and transform recent colonials into Americans.

As the new nation emerged and established a system of public education, it promoted the notion that the "schools of a democratic culture have a responsibility to socialize the younger generations according to the values and behavior patterns consistent with the ideals of that culture" (Lewenstein, 1963, p. 11). Over the years, educators concerned with the preparation of social studies teachers have endorsed this position (Ord, 1972, Garcia & Michaelis, 2001; Beal, Bolick, & Martorella, 2009; Parker, 2009). In the late 19th and early 20th century, as millions of European immigrants reached this country to begin a new life, political and educational leaders observed first-hand the cacophony of languages, cultural values, and political beliefs that characterized the growing population; they expressed alarm at these challenges to American Culture occurring in major cities across the country. These apprehensions were sufficiently acute that schools employed an assortment of programs aimed at acculturating the young and old into American society. In other instances, major events that challenged this country's political foundations (e.g., world wars, the Red Scare, civil rights movements) served to underscore the importance of social studies in the K–12 school curriculum. During times of war it is the schools that serve as the Liberty Pole for teachers to involve students in a variety of projects aimed at bringing the citizenry together in support of a common cause (Symcox, 2002).

In the last half of the 20th century, upheavals like those of the 1960s shook American society and motivated social studies educators to re-examine the goals of K–12 instructional programs. At the university level, social studies educators created a "new social studies" based on updated understandings of human behavior, enhanced learning theories, the structure of the social science disciplines, and a re-consideration of "society and the role of the individual." With this knowledge, K–12 teachers developed instructional programs where learners more actively investigated social studies issues, events, and personalities in the context of comprehending society (Smith & Cox, 1971). In addition, emphasis was placed on gaining broader insights into the country's founding political documents, learning about American's forgotten citizens, and exploring alternatives to commonly accepted societal practices.

Today, as educators observe the tension between nation state and globalization, social studies can provide the catalyst that brings overall meaning to the core subjects offered in the school curriculum. In the lower grades it establishes basic knowledge by introducing big ideas, skills, and dispositions that lead to a familiarity with the country's history, a commitment to democratic principles, and the initial connections between students' immediate environments and the world beyond. In the secondary schools, this foundational information is the prerequisite for continued development of students' critical thinking and information gathering skills, and for increasingly sophisticated understandings of nation state and the global community. The goal is to create learning environments where the big ideas in social studies are given meaning, and the country's core values are tested by students who construct knowledge in order to understand, appreciate, and value who we are as a nation.

The indefensible marginalization of social studies in the school curriculum is analogous to civic leaders abdicating their responsibility to productively guide conversations in local, state, national, and international forums. However, it appears our educational leaders have done just that— relinquished direction of social studies education to centers of political power—and have done so without providing the public an explanation. They don't appear to hear the concerns of classroom educators—particularly elementary teachers—and worried parents who attend school board meetings or write in the local newspapers about what are becoming common, yet troublesome, school practices: (1) principals who ask teachers to marginalize, subsume with literacy, or altogether delete social studies from the K–6 curriculum in response to special interest groups and (2) implementation of federal legislation which provide monies for instructional design and testing in reading, writing, and mathematics for grades 3–8; while no such efforts are made for social studies (Pederson, 2007; Zamosky, 2008). Middle school teachers are beginning to feel similar pressures (Vogler, 2003) and they too are also turning to direct instruction and other strategies that de-emphasize class discussion, learning by trial and error, and other forms of active learning (Bunting, 2006). Accountability is impacting the high schools as well. Although class discussion and other forms of active learning still occur, teachers sense the political climate and retreat to the textbook and direct instruction. It appears the emphasis on mastering discrete information will continue, and may increase as a prevalent form of instruction in today's high schools (Bain, 2006). While accountability has been part of school environments for many years (e.g., standards, objectives, school-wide guidelines for improving instruction), increased weight upon and consequences of standardized state and national testing have pushed state and district leaders to the brink as they search for fail-safe strategies that supposedly prepare students to perform well in reading, writing, and mathematics; no one wishes to see their school labeled "not making adequate yearly progress" (Costigan & Crocco, 2004). But this has often come at the expense of other subject areas, and it is the contention of many educational leaders that this testing frenzy has significantly changed the classroom behaviors and attitudes of K–6 and secondary social studies teachers (Bunting, 2006; Laguardia et al., 2002; Wills & Sandholtz, 2009).

CHANGING NATURE OF SOCIAL STUDIES TEACHERS IN THE SECOND HALF OF THE TWENTIETH CENTURY

The purpose of social studies is to promote our democratic ideals and develop "individuals who are active citizens in their communities and beyond" (Pulliam & Van Patten, 2007, p. 121). This understanding of social studies' purview has remained constant since the term was first introduced in 1916 (Ord, 1972; Jenness, National Council for the Social Studies, & American Historical Association, 1990; National Council for the Social Studies, 1994). What has changed over time is the interpretation of this charge (Thornton, 2008). In the late 1960s, with the advent of the "new social studies," researchers began identifying ideal characteristics of social studies teachers for the late 20th century and beyond. Smith and Cox (1971), in their seminal book, *New Strategies and Curriculum in Social Studies,* offer a set of characteristics that still serve as benchmarks to the social studies community on what constitutes excellence in teachers:

> a philosophical commitment to inquiry and the intellectual strength to meet the commitment; (2) a thorough knowledge of at least one discipline and a basic understanding of the interrelated disciplines which focus upon man as a political-social being; (3) an open mind which enables him (sic) to appreciate and tolerate the alternative points of view implicit in complex societal questions; and (4) the ability to design teaching strategies which will challenge students to become active inquirers rather than passive consumers of predigested facts, ideas, and generalizations (p. 153–54).

In the remaining part of this paper these characteristics are referred to as "markers of excellence."

In the late 1960s and for the next two decades many teachers entered master's programs or enrolled in professional development courses with a commitment to "becoming teachers." They embraced the belief that all Americans—young, old, and from all walks of life—could bring about change for a better society. In secondary schools across the country social studies teachers created programs that placed a stronger emphasis on the country's democratic ideals and employed a more active form of instruction that occasionally spilled out into local communities and influenced centers of political power. In this active environment, teachers encouraged K–12 students to employ America's founding documents and other relevant information to highlight instances of misalignment between the country's democratic values and everyday events. These served as fodder for societal change. Inspired by the 1960s Civil Rights Movement, teachers believed that young men and women would exit K–12 schools possessing a passion for change, and the appropriate social studies knowledge and skills to assume the role of concerned citizens committed to helping all Americans realize their dreams and aspirations. Shaver and National Council for the Social Studies (1991) provides an excellent look at the role of teachers in social studies education during this period.

Studies that looked specifically at K–12 teachers who embraced teaching, and entered university and graduate education with a vision and commitment to continue developing their professional role are difficult to identify. However there is some survey evidence suggesting that teachers were more liberal minded and that they addressed social justice issues of interest to them and their students (Ochoa, 1981; Adler, 1991; Vinson, 1998). Anecdotal evidence from social studies professors involved in graduate teacher education for over two decades further suggest that those teachers with a strong penchant for these markers of excellence enrolled in social science and humanities courses that provided them with additional resources to promote their programmatic goals. As they matriculated through their programs, they sharpened their use of content and pedagogy to better assist children and young adults in expressing their learning through active citizenship. And as they gained a greater sense of what it means to be a social studies teacher, they elevated their sense of professionalism by identifying novel approaches to informing the educational community and the public of the legitimate place of social studies as a core subject area in the K–12 curriculum. These in-service teachers took an active role in their post-baccalaureate education. When meeting with their advisors they took the lead and suggested what liberal arts and education courses they wished to take and, when they walked into their classes and looked at syllabi, they were first to offer suggestions or validate readings and assignments. They and their professors had similar visions (Hursh & Ross, 2000).

In the ensuing years other social studies educators have continued to support Smith and Cox's markers of excellence by elaborating and re-affirming their centrality in dialogues about the preparation of social studies teachers (Brophy, 1993; Leming, 1991; Newmann, 1991: Wineberg & Wilson, 1991). The National Council for the Social Studies (NCSS) also published two significant documents that re-affirmed these characteristics, "National Standards for Social Studies Teachers" (2002) and "A Vision of Powerful Teaching and Learning in the Social Studies: Building Social Understanding and Civic Efficacy" (2008).

Based on these generally accepted criteria for quality social studies educators, what dispositions, understandings of professionalism, content and pedagogical knowledge were expected of teachers as they exited undergraduate teacher education programs in the last three decades of the twentieth century? First, they embrace the markers described above, and assume the persona of "becoming teachers." In this state of intellectual ambiguity they are continuously learning; modifying their views on content and pedagogy; modeling information, media, and technology literacies; and demonstrating professionalism. The quest is to move ever closer to "becoming" but never quite reaching this elusive goal. They have a command of the foundations of social studies—its beginnings and how the field has evolved over time as it has matured. Novice teachers need to be familiar with the definition and purpose of social studies, politically sensitive to societal expectations in the 21st century (i.e., jobs, college, citizenship), and able to select instructional approaches that provide opportunities for learning in all three areas. They accept the responsibility that they are the education leaders responsible for learning in the classroom and view the materials provided to them as tools that help them facilitate that goal.

Second, these novice teachers should possess a fundamental command of content and be aware of the connection between content and pedagogy when assisting students in understanding concepts, themes, and generalizations related to the social studies. They also accept the basic precept that powerful learning is focused on the big ideas in social studies, such as how to sustain a viable form of democratic government that fosters participation from all citizens. Ideas drive the selection of content and the use of active forms of learning. Related to pedagogy, they must embrace the principle that having a strong understanding of students' backgrounds is fundamental to being a successful teacher. They understand that knowledge of students' cultural, socioeconomic, linguistic, and learning background is an integral element when reflecting on social studies approaches and developing instruction.

The third area is professionalism. Teachers committed to the markers of excellence believe that teaching is a *profession* and that they are *professionals*, not journeyman. Consistent with the stance of "becoming teachers," they view their initial preparation as an introduction to the profession. When they accept their first positions they are committed to gaining additional experiences in the areas of content, pedagogy and student knowledge. And once they gain a sense of competence, they learn how to become "ambassadors of social studies." Exhibiting a commitment to the markers of excellence in their teaching, they begin assuming leadership roles in their schools. They accept the roles of group leaders and department chairs and begin to internalize the importance of joining professional social science organizations. Increasingly, they realize that, in these new positions, they are obligated to inform the education community about the status of social studies in their school districts. And as they begin their post baccalaureate professional development, they accept the notion that presenting at professional organizations and writing for publication is one of the most powerful tools teachers can use to have their voices heard (Smiles & Short, 2006). Ultimately, they realize that there are many ways of "becoming teachers" and it is up to them to find the appropriate methods of informing K–12 education's stakeholders on the status of social studies instruction—its progress and the challenges—and what needs to be done to steer social studies education in directions that exemplify the markers of excellence.

THE CURRENT EDUCATIONAL ENVIRONMENT AND IMPLICATIONS FOR TEACHER PROFESSIONAL DEVELOPMENT

As the 1960s became historical legacy, the perceptions of the role of schools in society began changing as a growing segment of Americans raised concerns over contemporary educational innovations, the cost of education, and the preparation of students upon graduation. The 1983 publication of *A Nation at Risk* (National Commission on Excellence in Education, 1983) marked the beginning of a new direction for education.

Two somewhat countervailing responses emerged from these concerns. On the one hand, it seems that the liberal perspective, fundamental to the changes that occurred in the late 1960s and 1970s, succumbed to the voices of general and particular interest groups calling for holding schools, administrators, and teachers accountable. A cross section of citizens lobbied for conservative forms of education that placed the focus on raising test scores, preparing for 21st century jobs, and providing students with the appropriate experiences needed to transition successfully into top-tier colleges and universities. In a span of twenty years, educational leaders, the business community, the White House and key politicians used their persuasive powers in the form of blue ribbon committees, the standards movement, and withholding of state and federal monies to significantly change the K–12 school environment. As accountability gained traction, it was passage of No Child Left Behind legislation that enthroned testing as the ultimate goal and measure of student and teacher success. Today, it is the Common Core Standards and the Department of Education's initiative, "Race to the Top," that appear to define the purpose of public education. It seems at times that a liberal education, creativity, learning by doing, and student voice are becoming things of the past in many school systems.

However, there were still those voices in the educational conversation that maintained the importance and value for students of using active and inquiry based teaching approaches to foster curiosity, creativity and social engagement. These characteristics would become increasingly essential in the new information economy, some believed. With the explosion of technology onto both the business and education horizons in the late 1980s, national organizations identified information literacy (IL) as an essential set of student competencies for success in the "information economy" of the 21st century (American Association of School Librarians, 2007; American Library Association, 1989; Association of College & Research Libraries, 2000; Partnership for 21st Century Skills, 2009). Memorizing the contents of a single textbook is not consistent with this view for a number of reasons. Recent scandals surrounding the use of error-filled history texts in Virginia have demonstrated one potential set of problems that arises from reliance on a single source (Sieff, 2010). Even when textbooks are factually accurate, however, they typically represent one person's perspective which is influenced by numerous contextual factors (Loewen, 2007). The nearly ubiquitous access to information on the internet certainly challenges any assumptions that today's students will rely on the textbook alone, and it is vitally important that they understand how to triangulate sources of information on a topic and how to evaluate the authority and credibility of the sources they find. Well-grounded information seeking and evaluation strategies foster greater investment in a topic, and the opportunities to create new knowledge from various forms and types of information (e.g., primary sources like diaries, photographs, oral histories) can potentially spur creativity. The College Board's executive director of curriculum and content development was recently quoted as saying that, "the development of 21st-century skills... means less memorization and more emphasis on how to access information, evaluate it, and apply it properly to the topic at hand" (Davis, 2011).

What teachers need to know and be able to do depend on what we, as a society, define as essential learning outcomes for a student. Scripted teaching developed by publishing companies and test preparation as a primary role contribute to the de-professionalization of our teachers. However, if K–12 students are to master 21st century concepts and skills, teachers must be able to model these in their own work, as well as teach and assess them for their students. Some view the promotion of 21st century competencies as yet another set of skills for teachers to master, but these are really more appropriately considered as an adaptation of the markers of excellence, discussed earlier, to this new information and technology rich environment.

Professional library associations were the first to specify what students needed to master and, therefore, what teachers needed to be able to teach in order to cope with the evolving information landscape. The American Library Association (ALA) looked at how changing technologies were shifting the emphases for student learning by commissioning a committee to examine what skills would be essential for citizens to lead productive lives in the coming decades. This Presidential Committee report (1989) included the definition of information literacy that has stood as the touchstone for continuing discussion until the present day, i.e., "To be information literate, a person must be able to recognize when information is needed and have the ability to locate, evaluate, and use effectively the needed information" (ALA, 1989). Further, the committee posited that helping students become information literate in these ways was essential to creating an informed citizenry, which in turn is the foundation of a functioning democracy. Information literacy is, thus, very consistent with the long-held learning goals for social studies.

The report went on to provide recommendations that information literacy be a component of pre-service teacher education. For example, recommendation 5 begins:

> Teacher education and performance expectations should be modified to include information literacy concerns. Inherent in the concepts of information literacy and resource-based learning is the complementary concept of the teacher as a *facilitator of student learning rather than as presenter of ready-made information* (emphasis added) To be successful in such roles, teachers should

make use of an expansive array of information resources. They also should place a premium on problem solving and see that their classrooms are *extended outward to encompass the learning resources of the library media centers and the community* (emphasis added). They also should expect their students to become information literate (ALA, 1989).

Recommendation 5 goes on to specify what schools of teacher education should be doing to ensure training qualified teachers. These recommendations are not solely or even primarily about the use of technology, rather about using technologies to support conceptual and critical thinking abilities, noting, for example, the importance of problem-based strategies and cooperative learning as teaching approaches.

The American Association of School Librarians (AASL), in collaboration with the Association for Educational Communication and Technology (AECT) created standards for student learning in 1998 and updated them in 2007. The revised *Standards for the 21ˢᵗ Century Learner* acknowledge that, in addition to IL, new literacies have emerged from rapidly changing technologies—digital, visual, and technological—which are also key to success in the modern world. Not surprisingly, these new technologies continue to emphasize the critical thinking skills that are the hallmark of such foundational documents as the Association for College and Research Libraries' *Information Literacy Competency Standards for Higher Education* (2000). Generally students are expected to use technologies for research, productivity, communication, problem solving, and decision-making, and should understand the ethical issues surrounding the use of technology for these purposes. All of these learning outcomes are consistent with the goals promoted by the "new social studies."

Recently, the Partnership for 21ˢᵗ Century Skills, another coalition of business and education stakeholders, has developed a "vision for student success in the new global economy" (Partnership, 2004). This group and others (Hinchliffe, 2003; Rotherham & Willingham, 2009) believe that *fundamental* changes in society, business, and, therefore, education mean we must urgently refocus attention on skills that were needed in the past (e.g., critical thinking and problem solving) but which must be practiced in different ways today. Moreover, technological changes mean that we must develop and/or hone unfamiliar skills, e.g., digital media literacy (Trilling and Fadel, 2009, pp. xxiii–xxiv). Trilling and Fadel rightly point out that, with expanded access to information and the unprecedented ability to create and amplify information, we also have greater responsibilities (2009, p. 64). Included in their framework are information, media and ICT literacies, with some elaboration of the responsibilities around appropriate utilization of media tools to create communication products (Trilling & Fadel, 2009, pp. 61–71). They acknowledge that these literacies "power" the development of other essential 21ˢᵗ century skills: learning and innovation skills, life and career skills, core subjects and 21ˢᵗ century themes (Partnership, 2004). Not surprisingly, among the necessary support systems for this new model are teachers who are prepared to help students learn in inquiry-based and collaborative ways:

> ...professional development of both new and practicing teachers is a top priority...Teachers must become 21ˢᵗ century learners themselves, learning from inquiry, design and collaborative approaches that build a strong community of professional educators...These teaching methods are a break from the past...not commonly taught in schools of education (Trilling and Fadel, 2009, pp. 124–125).

Change is inevitable and, as society evolves over time, so too do our expectations of teachers. The role of social studies teachers in the 1940s was different from that for teachers in classrooms in the 1950s and 1960s. However, many of the changes schools are experiencing today are more profound than previously, and require modifications in the preparation of teachers at both the baccalaureate and master's levels. What seems inescapable in this new century is that the information explosion will continue and information technologies will play an increasingly critical role in almost every aspect of life—education, work, social and civic participation. Both the finding and creation of information call for enhanced skills in conceptual and critical thinking. In turn, these changes should and will shape the desired competencies for our K–12 students *and* the teachers who are preparing them for the future. It is heartening that some business and educational leaders still wish to promote a set of essential characteristics for teachers that resist the exclusive focus on teaching to the test. These leaders believe that teachers should be prepared to guide students in learning to ethically and effectively use technologies for the acquisition, critical evaluation and creation of information. Such knowledge and skills, they contend, will support lifelong learning and informed participation in society.

A CAPSTONE COURSE IN A
MASTER'S SOCIAL STUDIES PROGRAM

It is in this atmosphere that the first author's idea of re-designing a capstone experience in a master's program at a southwestern university took shape. Having taught such courses for well over twenty-five years, and in the last ten years coming to the realization that he was not satisfied with his teaching performance and the general outcomes of his students—mostly in-service K–12 teachers—he developed three reflective questions to gain insight into social studies at the master's level. In the last decade:

1. had societal expectations of teachers led to a transformation of the master's experience in social studies education?
2. had the instructor altered his expectations and those of his students in the capstone experiences?
3. had in-service teacher expectations of graduate work changed and influenced the development of the capstone experience?

This case study, arising out of these three questions, explores one instructor's experience teaching capstone courses in master's level programs and his efforts at developing and teaching a new capstone course that addressed the professional development of teachers through master's level social studies education.

The capstone experience as previously taught by the lead author required teachers to act out the role of professionals; reflect on their educational philosophy, purpose, and approaches to social studies; and to research and write short papers on issues and trends in social studies education. The culminating assignment, based on program requirements, was an instructional product that could be used in the classroom. This approach worked well because, historically, teachers viewed post-baccalaureate education as an opportunity to explore and expand their notions of content knowledge, pedagogy, and professionalism and, as a result, many exited the program more convinced that their classroom instruction was leading their students to view social studies as a preparation for active engagement in their communities.

In the 1990s NCLB wove its way through Congress, high stakes testing became a topic of discussion in Washington, and the accountability movement became a formidable force in public schools—all of which exerted pressure on teacher expectations of what they needed from continuing education (Cochran-Smith & Demers, 2008). According to the lead author, observations of teachers in graduate classes, conversations with colleagues directing other programs for teachers, and reviews of the literature suggested that teachers were narrowing their academic aspirations. As teachers matriculated through their course work and enrolled in the culminating experience of their master's program, many seemed fixated on accountability issues. Rather than being introspective about best practices, they commented to the instructor in so many words, "We know what material will be on the tests our students take, please show us how to get this content across to them and provide us with some test-taking techniques. We want them to do well in school."

In the view of the first author, teachers had succumbed to the socialization process and seem to have accepted a role as complacent and docile teachers and graduate students. For example, while they are aware of the importance of critical thinking, they also say things like, "We don't have time to help our students identify what they want to learn and take them through the inquiry process when we build instruction." Others assert that it is difficult to go against the grain when K–12 administrators, politicians, civic leaders, and parents place so much value on test scores. Many, who now speak of their teaching as a job, talk of being bullied by administrators to "get with the program." The thought of banding together and using their professional organizations to inform the various publics of what is occurring in schools only occasionally surfaces as an action available to them.

In the spring of 2009 the lead author decided to act on what he was reading in the literature on NCLB and high stakes testing, and on these tentative conclusions drawn from observing master's level graduate students. The goal was to build a 21st century capstone experience with the markers of excellence forming the foundation; content and pedagogy would inform teachers on how to improve classroom teaching; and professionalism—in the form of public speaking and writing for publication—would serve as the voice of teachers. The intent was to develop a contemporary course that would re-instill teachers' passion for the social studies and for the value of social studies instruction in the lives of K–12 students. He sought out the second author as a consultant on the course redesign because of her expertise in information literacy, resource-based learning, and knowledge of continually evolving technologies. The third author is a master's student who was enrolled in the course and volunteered to continue expressing his voice by participating in this project.

In developing the course syllabus (see Appendix A) the authors borrowed the terms "researchers, practitioners, and professionals" from documents developed by College of Education faculty and administrators (UNLV College of Education, 2007). The full meaning of these terms became clear as we reflected on the documents and synthesized the discussions that ensued as faculty from the various departments agreed on common goals in K–12 education. In master's programs where these terms are central, they refer to in-service teachers as research practitioners: (a) becoming well grounded in social science content, (b) honing their critical thinking and research skills, (c) using newly acquired knowledge and skills to adopt specialty areas within the social sciences, (d) sharpening their pedagogical skills to develop classroom instruction that makes use of research, library, and writing skills, and (e) demonstrating the application of their content areas in the context of community, country, and world. As teacher graduates in social studies , they are referred to as practitioners and professionals because they demonstrate the following dispositions: (a) striving to become outstanding teachers, (b) volunteering to become involved in a variety of activities (e.g., spokespersons for a grade level, assuming the role of department chair, increased activity in professional organizations), and (c) becoming spokespersons for social studies in K–12 schools (e.g., speaking at school department meetings and professional meetings, contributing writings to newsletters, newspapers, and professional journals).

Based on this model of "becoming teachers," the students in this redesigned capstone experience were going to re-establish their research skills to address discipline and pedagogy-based questions, and hone their abilities for writing research-based papers for publication. The goals of the course were to: (a) gauge their content knowledge in the social sciences and related disciplines, (b) ascertain their familiarity with the inquiry process to conceptualize a question, (c) assess their ability to conduct research using information sources critically, and (d) build their skills in writing persuasive research papers that could potentially be submitted as a manuscript for publication in a social studies journal or shaped into a school, district, or state publication. These goals were designed to integrate skills needed for the 21st century information economy into a revitalized syllabus which emphasized the value of inquiry based social studies education, and supported teachers as professionals who can shape—not just respond to—educational policy.

PERSPECTIVES OF THE TWO INSTRUCTORS AND A GRADUATE STUDENT

The lead author was acquainted with the twelve secondary teachers who enrolled in the social studies capstone experience in the spring of 2009. He was their major advisor and they had successfully completed other social studies courses he teaches in the Department of Curriculum and Instruction. They had completed numerous master's level courses in the Colleges of Education and Liberal Arts. The teachers had at least five years of teaching experience and some were considering other teaching and administrative positions in the district once they completed their master's degree.

In addition to requiring the completion of two research papers on topics of their choosing, students were exposed to other teaching professionals who had written for publication. They were also asked to reflect on both the research and writing process at the end of each project. A detailed description of the redesign process is provided in McMillen, Garcia, and Bolin's article (2010). At the conclusion of the course, we examined the formative and summative assessments, reviewed the students' research papers, and reflected on student anecdotal information. We also asked our student colleague, David To, to provide us with feedback by composing a reflective essay on his experiences (see Appendix B). All these sources of information confirmed that we had developed a capstone experience that promoted the development of the markers of excellence. Student reflections suggest that they were able to see the connection between content, pedagogy, and professionalism (see Appendix C). Most acknowledged the value of writing for publication, but were nevertheless challenged by the process. Five of the twelve teachers developed papers that could have been polished into publishable manuscripts for submission to state, regional, or national newsletters or journals. While both instructors offered to assist the teachers with editing, none wanted to pursue this independently. However, two of the teachers did agree to write with us on manuscripts related to the course re-design. Our intent is to again offer this capstone experience with a similar format and goals in spring 2011.

When we reflected on the original research questions, we agreed that they were all instrumental in influencing our actions and behaviors as we moved from the previous to the re-envisioned capstone experience. The evidence in the literature was corroborated by the lead author's experience as advisor to and instructor for the social studies program. We gained further insights as we guided the teachers in writing for publication and engaged them in informal conversations about teaching in the 21st century and about the status of social studies education in K–12 schools. We concluded from these interactions that these teachers were knowledgeable about societal demands on teachers, familiar with the historical foundations of education, and had experienced the negative effects of accountability both as they matriculated through K–12 schools and in their baccalaureate experiences. They entered the teaching profession knowing they would be held accountable to a standards-based teaching environment; however, most were not prepared for the criticism leveled at schools and the incessant demands that student performance be solely determined by test scores. One of the middle school teachers spoke of top down leadership styles and administrators who pressed her to reduce instructional time in social studies for the sake of teaching test-taking skills. What drives instruction, these teachers told us, is preparing student for tests. It was clear to some of the teachers that the recent call for changes in education and the manner in which they were implemented, particularly in response to NCLB, encouraged teachers to move from seeing themselves as "becoming teachers" to taskmasters. These societal perceptions of the role of schools in today's society in turn influenced teachers' views towards graduate work. A few were not happy with their professional lives and discussed with us the possibility of leaving the profession.

Colleges of Education have subsequently been affected by altered societal demands. School districts encouraged teachers to pursue professional development by earning master's degrees. Some teachers enrolled in mathematics and literacy workshops to become "highly qualified" in particular disciplines of the K–12 curriculum; while others enrolled in master's programs. Graduate schools of education experienced spikes in their enrollment as a growing number of teachers sought salary increases via continuing education. Education faculty encountered more teachers who were interested in a practical education than a liberal master's degree in education. The lead author's experiences and those of his colleagues suggest that, as teachers lobbied faculty for a different kind of master's education, faculty slowly and reluctantly accommodated. Like some of the teachers who enrolled in our master's program, these faculty felt they could fold in such teacher requests while still offering a social studies program that reflected the markers of excellence. The lead author certainly felt that way.

The authors have gained some valuable evidence as a result of teaching this capstone course. The course assessments and the informal discussions with the twelve teachers clearly identified weaknesses in the college's graduate social studies program. Most of these problems can be attributed to altered expectations on the part of the teacher preparation faculty. Over half of the in-service teachers demonstrated a less than adequate command of competent vocabulary, grammar, and writing skills. These teachers had trouble throughout the writing process. Many were unsophisticated in their research conceptualization and information evaluation skills. Some were not well grounded in the social sciences and showed difficulty in identifying a topic and using the writing process to move to a level of specificity and clearness that allowed for its examination within the constraints imposed by the instructor.

The social studies faculty will spend time looking at this case study and, we anticipate, suggest some programmatic changes. For example, the two authors will lobby for a mini writing-for-publication assignment in the introductory course of the program. Another need is to provide more robust discussion opportunities in all education courses on what is meant by professionalism and on what teachers can do to combat the marginalization of social studies in the K–12 curriculum. We are convinced, along with others (Smiles & Short, 2006; Vieth, 2007; Whitney, 2009), that research based writing for publication can be one of the most effective avenues for re-establishing teachers' role as professionals. At the same time we also need to be realistic and recognize that significant changes in the practice of K–12 education are impacting teachers. We firmly believe that master's programs in social studies education can have a level of practicality without abandoning markers of excellence. The process of continual change in the educational community is nothing new, although developments in technology have clearly shifted the emphasis on competencies needed to be an informed citizen in today's society. If we believe in the mantra of "becoming a teacher" then faculty in colleges of education need to continue working to ensure social studies education remains focused on the markers of excellence at the collegiate level and in K–12 social studies education.

APPENDIX A: SYLLABUS

Course: Seminar in Curriculum and Instruction: Social Studies

Purpose

The purpose of this course is to insert a research and writing experience into what you have learned in the areas of pedagogy and the social sciences.

In this course you will write two research papers—one 20+ and the other 15+ pages in length. The first one will be directed by the instructors and in the area of pedagogy and the other in the area of pedagogy and the social sciences and directed by the student. The course is divided into four parts: (1) we begin by spending the first three class meetings reviewing how to write a research paper and taking a trip to Lied Library, (2) move to reviewing purpose, approaches and major issues in social studies education and transition to research, its purpose and impact on social studies teaching, (3) begin the process of writing the first research paper directed by the instructors, and (4) transition to a paper written by the student with guidance from the instructors. We conclude the course by having you think of yourself as someone who can influence social studies education by writing in education journals and in the popular press. One of your papers will be a required artifact in your electronic portfolio that you will develop in the summer. Dr. Shim or I will describe the culminating experience in one of our class meetings.

Approach

During the first part of the class we will review what occurred in your masters program, take a trip to Lied Library, and transition to the second part of the course—writing research papers. In this part of the class you will follow a schedule that consists of submitting parts of your papers for instructor review and having you re-write each part once or twice before submitting your final papers. Writing in this fashion means spending time reflecting on the "problem" you are researching; using the library to identify pertinent research studies; reflecting, writing and revising; and further reflecting before submitting your final papers. Not following this schedule will result in loss of points and, in all probability, performing poorly on your papers. It is important for you to bring a laptop computer to each class meeting to take notes and to begin the writing process. If you look at the weekly schedule, there are ample opportunities for you to write and to seek feedback from the instructors and your peers. One behavior found among educators who wish to learn how to write is that they find a partner they can trust and establish a relationship that allows a discussion of writing goals and the sharing of positive reinforcement and constructive criticism on their writing.

Required Readings:

Booth, W.C and Others. (2008). *The Craft of Research.* 3rd Edition. Chicago, IL: University of Chicago Press.

Chastain, E. (2008). *How To Write a Research Paper.* New York: Spark Publishing.

You also will read four research articles and meet their authors to discuss fundamental questions relating to research and social studies education.

These readings are required and some are to be incorporated into your research papers.

Attendance: Each Tuesday class begins at 4:00p.m. An attendance sheet will be distributed at the beginning of each class meeting and collected ten minutes after the class begins. It is your responsibility to initial the sheet. If you arrive late you may sign the roster after class. If you know you are going to be absent on a given date, please let the instructor know in person, e-mail, or telephone. Please see a classmate on missed assignments and for weekly notes.

Written Assignments: Assignments are due at 4:00p.m. as you enter the classroom. They should be the best expression of the author's thoughts on a subject, and have few or no spelling, grammar, punctuation errors or poor content. If you do not understand any of the instructions concerning the submission of papers, it is your responsibility to speak to the instructors during the first two class meetings of the course.

Professionalism: Please show respect and listen courteously to others. You may criticize an idea, but refrain from outbursts directed at your peers and instructors. Students should raise their hand to be recognized by the instructors. Please refrain from dominating class discussion.

Grades:

1st Paper:	60 points
2nd Paper:	40 points
TOTAL:	100 points
Grading Scale:	
100—90	A
89—80	B
79—70	C
+ & – will be based on dispositions in class discussions and the quality of your work	

Weekly Schedule

Week 1: Introductions; a description of the syllabus with particular attention to requirements: attendance policy, reading assignments, and professional behavior in the classroom; a look at major issues in social studies education (e.g., multicultural education, social studies in the age of NCLB, core subjects, approaches to social studies, global education, standards-based teaching in the social studies); writing a research paper; identifying a problem to research and how to write a research question; instructors will offer the students a series of research questions to consider for their 1st paper; for next week read Chastain #1– #6.

Week 2: An introduction on writing a research paper—Introduction, Problem, Review of Literature, Results, Discussion, Implication to Education/Recommendations, Conclusion, Bibliography; major issues in social studies education; a look at pedagogy and content; doing research in social studies education, refining research questions developed by the instructors and by the students; submit a typewritten 1–3 sentence description of the problem you would like to research; how to write an introduction; for next week read Chastain #7–#11 and first research article.

Week 3: A trip to Lied Library to look at the social science and social studies collections; how to identify and order research journals; students are to meet with the instructors to further refine their research question; submit an introduction to your paper; how to write a review of the literature; for next week read Booth #1–#6; time to work on your paper.

Week 4: A meeting with Patrick Hinrichs to discuss RefWorks; What is educational research; research in the social sciences and social studies education; empirical and experimental research (qualitative and quantitative); a look at various examples of educational research; writing a research paper that focuses on pedagogy and the goals of social studies education; how to write a discussion; submit the beginnings of a review of research; for next week read Booth #7–11.

Week 5: Speak with the author of the 1st research article; a review of what has occurred over the last four weeks of the class; submit the beginnings of a discussion; how to write a conclusion or a set of recommendations; for next week read Booth #12–#17 and Feinstein research article, "Altering Perceptions Through Indigenous Studies: The Effects of Immersion in Hawaiian Traditional Ecological Knowledge (TEK) on Non-Native and Part-Native Students;" time to work on your research paper.

Week 6: An evening to review what you have put together as a research paper; instructors will review parts of a research paper; time to work on your paper.

Week 7: A second trip to Lied Library; research paper—problem, review of literature, results; meeting with the instructors to gain a sharper focus on your research paper; meet with Dr. Feinstein, the author of the 2nd research paper; submit a conclusion/recommendation and bibliography.

Week 8: Completing your 1st research paper; work time; distribute 3rd research article, "The March of Remembrance and Hope: Teaching about Diversity and Social Justice Through the Holocaust."

Week 9: Submit your paper to the instructors; half of the class will discuss their experiences based on a set of questions provided by the instructors; review writing a research paper in the social studies.

Week 10: Discuss research in social studies education with the authors of 3rd article; develop your own research question in the area of the social sciences or social studies education; review how to write a research paper.

Week 11: A third trip to Lied Library to begin the process of refining your problem and identifying research material; submit the problem you would like to research and an introduction.

Week 12: Review what is a literature review; meet with the instructors to bring focus to your problem; submit the beginnings of a review of literature; distribute 4th research article, "The Portrayal of African Americans and Hispanics at National Council for the Social Studies Annual Meetings (1997–2008).

Week 13: Meet with the authors to discuss 4th research paper; review discussion, implications/conclusions and bibliography; time to work on your paper.

Week 15: Writing your research paper—discussion, implications/conclusions, and bibliography; submit the beginnings of a discussion, conclusion/recommendation and bibliography.

Week 16: Submit your second research paper; second half of the class describes their experiences based on set of questions provided by the instructor.

APPENDIX B: DAVID TO'S REFLECTION

I entered the UNLV undergraduate secondary education social studies program in 2004 and earned my bachelor's degree in 2007. At the time of my graduation I was 21 years old and enjoying my part-time work as a substitute teacher. Instead of deciding to begin my full-time teaching career, I opted to pursue a master's in education as a full-time student and continue my various part-time jobs as a school district substitute, tutor, and university graduate assistant. I made this decision so that I could focus on my studies without having the stress of balancing a full-time teaching position as many education masters students do. My first year in the program was treated just like my undergraduate experience with classes that were eerily similar with maybe the exception of an extra paper here and there. It was not until I enrolled in Dr. Garcia's seminar course that I was truly challenged at a higher level than I was accustomed to.

At the time of the course, I was an Advancement via Individual Determination (AVID) tutor at Spring Valley High School in Las Vegas, NV. AVID is a program designed to help high school students get into college who normally would have trouble doing so. My job was to help students with schoolwork that they struggled with and to share my own experience getting into college and being a successful graduate. Part of this program involved helping high school students find and apply for financial aid and assisting them to fill out applications for different colleges around the country. This position was beneficial to me because, as a tutor, I served as an intermediary between teachers and students. Students would treat me as a teacher but also felt comfortable venting their frustrations about their teacher's failed methods. This job, in conjunction with Dr. Garcia's seminar course, helped me grow immensely as a person and as a professional.

When I entered Dr. Garcia's course, I realized that my fellow classmates were secondary social studies teachers. As a result, I was not surprised when they all groaned at the rigorous workload listed in the syllabus. Although I was looking forward to the challenge, I couldn't help but empathize with my classmates, knowing that they would have trouble completing the assignments with their full-time teaching duties. There was a clear difference in mentalities between my fellow students and myself. As contracted teachers, they felt that this course was an obligation that they had to complete in order to get a pay raise. For me, it was an experience that I could use to gain the knowledge that I needed in order to be successful in my future classroom. The seminar essentially required us to produce two papers of publishable quality. Dr. Garcia made it very clear from day one that these papers were not to be run of the mill research papers that we have been accustomed to doing. The thought of publishing initially excited me. Finally I felt like I was part of a graduate program rather than the same undergraduate courses with a slightly harder grading scale. At first, I did not quite know what it meant to publish but I knew that it was associated with accomplishment and professionalism. As someone who was seriously considering a doctorate degree, I felt that this experience would help me decide if I was capable of such an endeavor.

Growing up, the idea of college was a mystifying concept to me. My parents had divorced and left me to be raised by my grandparents who came over during the Vietnam War and could barely speak any English. Our groceries were bought using food stamps and my clothes were hand me downs from a younger cousin. The reality of college never occurred to me until I reached my sophomore year in high school when school officials announced that all Nevada students would earn a $10,000 scholarship for graduating from high school with a 3.0 GPA. With that amount of money, the distant notion of college became a reality to me. Always aware of my humble beginnings, I took full advantage of the opportunity and surprised even myself with a 3.75 undergraduate GPA. This confidence later allowed me to apply for a master's program. Despite already being in a graduate program, the idea of pursuing a doctoral degree was still intimidating. My professors seemed to be exceedingly knowledgeable in the various areas of their research and publications. This did not seem like something I was capable of doing at the time. Dr. Garcia's course opened up a door to this world for me that allowed me to see that I was capable of doing higher-level work.

Our first task was to choose a topic that had to do with either education or social studies. My choice came fairly easily to me as I had wondered why many schools in the area switched from traditional to block scheduling then back to traditional in a short period of time. The school where I was tutoring had switched to block and within five years had switched back to traditional scheduling apparently due to budget concerns. My students were tremendously concerned with the switch and many teachers at the school protested the switch because they had become accustomed to the longer class periods. The idea of change meant that teachers had to adjust all their lessons to the shorter class instruction time and students had to go back to having six classes a day as opposed to four. This made me very curious about whether scheduling formats had an effect on student school achievement. When I presented this topic to Dr. Garcia and Dr. McMillen, they both deemed the topic acceptable.

Once we had selected our topics, Dr. Garcia taught us the format for writing the paper, giving us guidelines in terms of introduction, problem statement, literature review, discussion, conclusion and recommendations. The text we were assigned also went into detail on how these sections should be written. From that point on, we had periodic due dates for the different sections of the paper. This helped out immensely as we were able to get weekly feedback on our work. Also, having weekly deadlines took away the stress of having a giant paper due at a last minute deadline. With this setup, it was hard to procrastinate because we actually had to have something every week for a grade.

Dr. McMillen was the co-instructor and she worked with us on research skills and how to use the library and its various tools. This aspect of the course I felt was crucial and was surprised that we hadn't learned this earlier in our graduate program. Now, it seems common sense to know how to find research articles from various databases but at the time this was new to a lot of us. Once I figured out how to find articles for my topic, the juices started flowing. As I began reading the different studies and arguments, I couldn't help but get more involved. Eventually the problem arose that I had too many sources and I had to learn how to sift through them and prioritize which ones were essential to my paper. As with the other sections, I met weekly with both instructors to help me through this process.

Once my research was established, I began to piece together the different parts of my paper. We were guided through each section and as each was submitted the instructors provided us with corrections and suggestions for improvement. That same process was repeated with all of the sections of the paper. By the time the first paper was due, we had already completed most of our work and had it reviewed by the instructors. When my first paper was complete, I was surprised at both how well it turned out and how much easier it was then I had initially thought. Our first paper was meant to be a process in which we were guided through. For our second paper, we were counted on to work more independently using a writing partner. By the time I had begun work on my second paper, I'd had already become familiar with the process from working on my first paper. I actually anticipated the opportunity to work on the second one on my own. It was clear that I needed much less help the second time around and I had no trouble completing the paper in time before the deadline.

During the course we were allowed to choose a writing partner to work with from our classmates. Partners were in charge of helping each other through editing, proofreading, and critiquing. Most chose a partner whom they were already close friends with from previous classes. My partner and I were also previous acquaintances. This writing buddy system seemed to be productive but also unproductive at times. We would quickly review each other's work in class during the allotted time but neither of us really contacted each other outside of class except for maybe a question we needed answered from being absent. Some pairs met outside of the class in the library to work while others spent most of the time chit chatting about unrelated topics. Overall, the writing buddy system was somewhat helpful but not absolutely essential.

In the end, this course offered me a lot more in terms of growth than many of the traditional graduate courses that I have taken at this university. Rather than being lectured to and forced to memorize information for an exam, this course allowed me to take control of my own learning. With the freedom to choose my own topic, I was able to pick content that I actually wanted to know about. I was responsible for learning this material through my own research of reliable sources. Writing all this information in the form of a publishable paper was an effective way of retaining the information that I had learned versus regurgitating it on a test. These papers also gave me a sense of empowerment. With the knowledge that I gained, it felt like I had power to use at my disposal. For example, if my administrator ever imposed a change upon me, I had the power to politely defend my stance with credible research. I believe that if all teachers gained this empowerment, then we would be taking the right step in turning teaching back in the direction of professionalism and away from a job in which a person functions as a cog in a machine being stripped of all creativity. In order to do this, graduate programs need to consider a course similar to this one that allows teachers the freedom to control their own learning and knowledge.

APPENDIX C: ASSESSMENT OF LEARNING

McMillen's Perspective: Reflection is a key aspect of meaningful learning. Therefore, in addition to receiving formative and summative feedback on the research papers themselves, Dr. Garcia and I crafted questions to promote student reflection on the research and writing processes and to assess self-perception of learning. For the first paper, students briefly reported on their chosen research topic in class, and orally responded to the following questions.

1. What did you find most satisfying about the writing experience?
2. What did you find most challenging?
3. What did you find helpful in going through the stages of writing the paper?
4. What would you like the instructors to do more of as you write your second paper?
5. What did you learn about your topic?
6. Have your views on this topic changed? Did they change as a result of your research?
7. How do you feel about the paper you have created?
8. How will this experience help you in your teaching? Your other responsibilities?
9. What have you learned about research in education?
10. Are you still interested in writing for publication?

Student comments were sufficiently thoughtful and rich to warrant repeating the process with the second paper. We made this a somewhat more formalized reflection activity by asking the students to write their responses to the questions and turn them in with the final paper. The questions were slightly different but asked them to consider similar areas.

As a result of writing your two research-based papers....

1. How has your overall view of education research changed?
2. What aspect of doing research on an educational topic proved the most unexpected or surprising?
3. How has your perspective of yourself as a participant in the creation and/or use of education research changed?
4. Has your understanding of how policy translates to practice in K–12 changed (think about how school boards, administrators, and teachers make decisions)?
5. Identify one way that you could change your behavior to become more of a researcher-practitioner in your profession:
6. Would you recommend this class to other teachers? Why or why not?

Comments from students in response to the questions indicated that they improved their sense of self-efficacy as researchers and writers, mastering some key information literacy competencies in the process. Sample comments include these:

- "Feel more capable of doing meaningful research."
- "I learned how to research critically." ALSO "I learned what a credible source is."
- "I became a better researcher and writer."
- "I have greater insight on how to look up answers to my questions…"
- "I feel confident that I would be able to produce more research on similar topics."
- "I feel more actively involved. I have more that I can bring to the table when collaborating with colleagues."

In spite of a nearly unanimous perception that education policies and practice seem to be disconnected from the relevant research on educational issues, comments suggest that the students saw how they *should* be connected.

- "Educational research is needed when making decisions. "
- "We need to challenge policies not based on research."
- "I will be more active in assessing policy in regards to data that is available."
- "…confident that my research can make change in my school."
- "More teachers need to ask critical questions about what we do."

It was encouraging that several students noted that their research process helped them rethink approaches in the classroom or school district setting.

- "I will do more research on best practices for what I'm teaching and implement them."
- "I feel better prepared for the classroom."
- "I need to do more assessment to create more evidence and support."
- "Reflected on my own work based on what I was reading."
- "I read about some strategies I could try"

There were also comments evidencing an experiential learning about the research process.

- "What surprised me most was the way my question evolved based on the research findings."
- "It was exciting to shift and move the question, even though also sometimes frustrating."
- "Process of research is not about predicting but about discovery."
- "It's helpful to talk out the possible research question."
- "Talking to others helped me push through the frustration."
- "Had to combine separate areas of research and that was a challenge."
- "Found a meta-analysis in a bibliography and used this to find additional resources."
- "Using bibliography trails is much better than searching."

- "Tolerating the unknown was difficult but essential to the process"
- "You have to find/read a lot of articles to answer a question due to the often conflicting nature of what you find."
- "Research is constantly building upon itself."
- The study itself needs to be evaluated, how it was conducted.

And finally, many voiced an increased sense of professionalism as a result of the research writing process.

- "I can continue to educate myself on education policy."
- "Read more about my profession and think about the holes I could fill."
- "I now understand the power of the pen. Writing for publication can truly have an impact in classrooms, schools and school districts."
- "Take time at beginning or end of school year to do research on questions I have about educational issues."
- "All educators need to be actively involved in trying to make education better. One way is by taking this course and learning how to write papers."
- "I can openly engage in discussion and research of key education issues and bring these items to the attention of administrators."

Overall, student responses provided a richer understanding of what they learned than a single grade on a paper can hope to give, and hopefully enhanced the students' own integration of their new knowledge.

REFERENCES

Adler, S. (1991). The education of social studies teachers. In J. P. Shaver (Ed.), *Handbook of research on social studies education* (pp. 210–221). New York: Macmillan.

American Association of School Librarians. (2007). *AASL standards for the 21st century learner.* No. 2010. Chicago, IL: American Library Association.

American Library Association Presidential Committee on Information Literacy. (1989). *Presidential committee on information literacy: Final report.* Chicago, IL: American Library Association.

Association of College and Research Libraries. (2000). *Information literacy competency standards for higher education.* Retrieved 3/9/2010, 2010, from http://www.ala.org/ala/mgrps/divs/acrl/standards/informationliteracycompetency.cfm

Bain, R. B. (2006). Rounding up unusual suspects: Facing the authority hidden in the history classroom. *Teachers College Record, 108*(10), 2080–2114.

Beal, C., Bolick, C. M., & Martorella, P. H. (2009). *Teaching social studies in middle and secondary schools* (5th ed.). Boston: Allyn & Bacon/Pearson.

Brophy, J. (Ed.). (1993). *Advances in research on teaching: Case studies of teaching and learning in social studies.* Greenwich, CT: JAI Press.

Bunting, C. (2006). Getting personal about teaching. *Phi Delta Kappan, 88*(1), 76–78.

Cochran-Smith, M., & Demers, K. E. (2008). How do we know what we know? Research and teacher education. In M. Cochran-Smith, S. Feiman-Nemser, D. J. McIntyre & Association of Teacher Educators (Eds.), *Handbook of research on teacher education :Enduring questions in changing contexts* (3rd ed., pp. 1009–1016). New York: Routledge and Association of Teacher Educators.

Costigan, A. T., & Crocco, M. S. (2004). *Learning to teach in an age of accountability.* Mahwah, NJ: Lawrence Erlbaum Associates.

Davis, M. R. (2011, 1/3/11). Schools examine content, delivery of online AP courses. *EdWeek,* Retrieved from http://www.edweek.org/ew/articles/2011/01/12/15edtech_ap.h30.html?tkn=SPLFSRniBmfYCPiTqEjM1wLXo5VQcXfjD7E%2F&cmp=clp-edweek

Garcia, J., & Michaelis, J. U. (2001). *Social studies for children: A guide to basic instruction* (12th ed.). Boston: Allyn & Bacon.

Hinchliffe, L. J. (2003). Technology and the concept of information literacy for pre-service teachers. *Behavioral & Social Sciences Librarian, 22*(1), 7–18. doi:10.1300/J103v22n01_02

Hursh, D. W., & Ross, E. W. (2000). *Democratic social education: Social studies for social change.* New York: Falmer Press.

Jenness, D., National Commission on Social Studies in the Schools, & American Historical Association. (1990). *Making sense of social studies.* New York, N.Y.: Macmillan.

Koretz, D. M. (2002). Limitations in the use of achievement tests as measures of educators' productivity. *Journal of Human Resources, 37*(4), 752–77.

Laguardia, A., Brink, B., Wheeler, M., Grisham, D., & Peck, C. (2002). From agents to objects: The lived experience of school reform. *Child Study Journal, 32*(1), 1–18.

Leming, J. S. (1991). Teacher characteristics and social studies education. In J. P. Shaver (Ed.), *Handbook of research on social studies teaching and learning* (pp. 222–236). New York: Macmillan.

Lewenstein, M. R. (1963). *Teaching social studies in junior and senior high schools, an ends and means approach.* Chicago: Rand McNally.

Loewen, J. W. (2007). *Lies my teacher told me: Everything your American history textbook got wrong.* New York: Simon & Schuster.

McEachron, G. (2010). Study of allocated social studies time in elementary classrooms in virginia: 1987–2009. *Journal of Social Studies Research, 34*(2), 208–228.

McMillen, P. S., Garcia, J., & Bolin, D. A. (2010). Promoting professionalism in master's level teachers through research based writing. *Journal of Academic Librarianship, 36*(5), 427–439. doi:10.1016/j.acalib.2010.06.007

National Commission on Excellence in Education. (1983). *A nation at risk: The imperative for educational reform.* Portland, OR: U.S.A. Research.

National Council for the Social Studies. (1994). *Expectations of excellence: Curriculum standards for social studies.* Washington, D.C.: National Council for the Social Studies.

National Council for the Social Studies. (2002). *National standards for social studies teachers.* Washington, DC: National Council for the Social Studies.

National Council for the Social Studies. (2008). *A vision of powerful teaching and learning in the social studies: Building social understanding and civic efficacy.* Washington, DC: National Council for the Social Studies.

Newmann, F. M. (1991). Promoting higher order thinking in social studies: Overview of a study of 16 high school departments. *Theory and Research in Social Education, 19*(4), 324–340.

Ochoa, A. S. (1981). A profile of social studies teachers. *Social Education, 45*(6), 401–04.

Ord, J. E. (1972). *Elementary school social studies for today's children.* New York: Harper & Row.

Parker, W. C. (2009). *Social studies in elementary education* (13th ed.). Boston, MA: Allyn & Bacon.

Partnership for 21st Century Skills. (2009). *Framework for 21st century learning.* Retrieved 3/11/2011, from http://www.p21.org/index.php?option=com_content&task=view&id=254&Itemid=120

Pederson, P. V. (2007). What is measured is treasured: The impact of the no child left behind act on nonassessed subjects. *Clearing House: A Journal of Educational Strategies, Issues and Ideas, 80*(6), 287–291.

Pulliam, J. D., & Van Patten, J. J. (2007). *History of education in America* (9th ed.). Columbus, OH: Pearson.

Rotherham, A. J., & Willingham, D. (2009). 21st century skills: The challenges ahead. *Educational Leadership, 67*(1), 16–21.

Shaver, J. P., & National Council for the Social Studies. (1991). *Handbook of research on social studies teaching and learning.* New York: Macmillan.

Shiel, G., & Eivers, E. (2009). International comparisons of reading literacy: What can they tell us? *Cambridge Journal of Education, 39*(3), 345–360.

Sieff, K. (2010, 12/29/2010). Virginia textbooks full of errors. *Washington Post.*

Smiles, T. L., & Short, K. G. (2006). Transforming teacher voice through writing for publication. *Teacher Education Quarterly, 33*(3), 133–147.

Smith, F. R., & Cox, C. B. (1971). *New strategies and curriculum in social studies.* Chicago, IL: Rand McNally.

Symcox, L. (2002). *Whose history? The struggle for national standards in American classrooms.* New York: Teachers College Press.

Thornton, S. J. (2008). Continuity and change in social studies curriculum. In L. S. Levstik, & C. A. Tyson (Eds.), *Handbook of research in social studies education* (pp. 15–32). New York: Routledge.

Trilling, B., & Fadel, C. (2009). *21st century skills: Learning for life in our times* (1st ed.). San Francisco, CA: Jossey-Bass.

UNLV College of Education. (2007). *Conceptual framework.* Retrieved 3/4, 2011, from http://education.unlv.edu/ncate/cf/pg7.html

Vieth, K. (2007). Celebrating student artwork through national publication: Developing worthy projects. *SchoolArts: The Art Education Magazine for Teachers, 106*(5), 40–41.

Vinson, K. D. (1998). The "traditions" revisited: Instructional approach and high school social studies teachers. *Theory and Research in Social Education, 26*(1), 50–82.

Vogler, K. (2003). Where does social studies fit in a high-stakes testing environment? *Social Studies, 94*(5), 207–211.

Whitney, A. E. (2009). Opening up the classroom door: Writing for publication. *Voices from the Middle, 16*(4), 17–24.

Wills, J. S., & Sandholtz, J. H. (2009). Constrained professionalism: Dilemmas of teaching in the face of test-based accountability. *Teachers College Record, 111*(4), 1065–1114.

Wineberg, S. S., & Wilson, S. M. (1991). Subject matter knowledge in the teaching of history. In J. E. Brophy (Ed.), *Advances in research on teaching. vol. 2* (pp. 305–347). Greenwich, CT: JAI Press.

Zamosky, L. (2008). Social studies: Is it history? *District Administration, 44*(3), 46–48.

BIOGRAPHIES

EDITOR BIOGRAPHY

William B. Russell III is Associate Professor of Social Science Education at The University of Central Florida. He teaches social studies related courses and serves as the Social Science Education Ph.D. track coordinator. Dr. Russell also serves as the director for The International Society for the Social Studies (www.TheISSS.org) and is the editor of *The Journal of Social Studies Research* (www.TheJSSR.com). His research interests include alternative methods for teaching social studies and teaching with film. Dr. Russell has authored over thirty-five peer-reviewed journal articles related to social studies education which have been featured in journals like *Action in Teacher Education, The Journal of Social Studies Research, Social Education, Social Studies and the Young Learner,* and *The Social Studies.* Dr. Russell has authored four books: *Reel Character Education: A Cinematic Approach to Character Development* (2010, co-author S. Waters), *Teaching Social Issues with Film* (2009), *Civil War Films for Teachers and Historians* (2008), and *Using Film in the Social Studies* (2007). Dr. Russell earned his Ph.D. in Social Science Education from Florida State University and prior to moving into higher education, taught middle and high school social studies.

Contemporary Social Studies: An Essential Reader, pages 595–604
Copyright © 2012 by Information Age Publishing
All rights of reproduction in any form reserved.

ABOUT THE AUTHORS

Keith C. Barton is Professor of Curriculum and Instruction and Adjunct Professor of History at Indiana University. His research investigates students' historical understanding, classroom contexts of teaching and learning, and the history of the social studies curriculum. He has conducted several studies in the United States, Northern Ireland, and New Zealand, and he has served as a visiting professor at Victoria University in Wellington, New Zealand, and the UNESCO Centre for Education in Pluralism, Human Rights, and Democracy at the University of Ulster. He is the author, with Linda S. Levstik, of *Doing History: Investigating with Children in Elementary and Middle Schools* (Routledge, 2011), *Teaching History for the Common Good* (Routledge, 2004), and *Researching History Education: Theory, Method, and Context* (Routledge, 2008), and editor of *Research Methods in Social Studies Education: Contemporary Issues and Perspectives* (Information Age Publishing, 2006). He teaches courses on secondary social studies methods, educational research, and curriculum history.

Beverly Milner (Lee) Bisland is an assistant professor of social studies education in the Elementary and Early Childhood Education Department at Queens College of the City University of New York. Dr. Bisland has been an active presenter at conferences including the College and University Faculty Assembly, International Assembly, the National Council for the Social Studies, and the American Educational Research Association. She has published scholarly articles in amongst others *Education and Urban Society, Journal of Social Studies Research, Teachers College Record, Theory and Research in Social Education, Social Studies Research and Practice* and *the Social Studies*. She is currently the editor of the *Journal of International Social Studies: the Official Journal of the International Assembly of the National Council for the Social Studies.*

Brad Burenheide is an assistant professor in the College of Education at Kansas State University. He is the program coordinator for secondary social studies education. His research focuses upon effective instruction in the disciplines of history and the social studies and also the use of instructional gaming

Prentice T. Chandler is an assistant professor of social studies education and Head of Secondary Education at Athens State University. Dr. Chandler taught secondary social studies (grades 6-12) in Alabama public schools for 6 years before joining the professoriate. His research and writing interests are in the areas of social studies education, critical race theory, academic freedom, and authentic social studies pedagogy. Some of his published work has appeared in *Social Education, The Journal of Social Studies Research, Social Studies Research and Practice,* and *Teacher Education Quarterly*. In 2007

Dr. Chandler was awarded the NCSS Defense of Academic Freedom Award for his work teaching alternative histories in Alabama public schools. His latest research has been with the Social Studies Inquiry Research Collaborative (SSIRC) examining Authentic Intellectual Work (AIW).

Jeremy Clabough is currently a doctoral student in Social Science Education at The University of Tennessee. He received his BA in Education from Maryville College and his masters in Social Science Education at The University of Tennessee. He is a former middle and high school teacher. His research interests include student engagement through role-playing activities and using primary sources in the social studies classroom.

Christine A. Draper is an assistant professor of middle grades education in the Deptartment of Teaching and Learning at Georgia Southern University. She currently researches and teaches classes on the nature and needs of middle grades learners, young adolescent literature, and language arts methods for the middle grades teacher.

Christy Folsom teaches in the Childhood Education Department at Lehman College of the City University of New York which is located in the Bronx. She uses the TIEL model in teaching curriculum development courses, student teaching seminars, and supervision of student teachers. She received her Ed.D. from Teachers College, Columbia University and has a broad and deep background in education. A former Oregonian, her teaching experience includes preschool, deaf, general, and gifted education. In addition she has worked as a staff developer and as an administrator. Influenced by her experiences as an educator and as a parent, she developed the conceptual framework of Teaching for Intellectual and Emotional Learning (TIEL®) during her doctoral studies. She has presented her work nationally and internationally. She also directs the TIEL Institute through which she works privately with students, schools, and districts. Dr. Folsom lives in New York City.

Paul G. Fitchett is assistant professor of social studies education in the Department of Middle, Secondary, and K12 Education at the University of North Carolina, Charlotte. His research interests include the influence of society and policy on social studies teaching and learning.

Jesus Garcia is Professor of Social Studies Education at the University of Nevada, Las Vegas and former President of the National Council for the Social Studies. He is co-author of *Social Studies for Children: A Guide to Basic Instruction* and *McDougal Littell's American History Program*. Jesus has written extensively in the area of the portrayal of societal groups in secondary U.S. history textbooks and social studies as a core subject area in the K-12 classroom. Dr. Garcia received his terminal degree from the University of California, Berkeley. He taught school in Fremont and in San Jose.

Kyle A. Greenwalt is an assistant professor in the Department of Teacher Education at Michigan State University. He is interested in the study of curriculum through the twin lenses of lived experience and identity. In the tradition of progressive education, his research, teaching and service all seek to contribute to the creation of schools that are sites of vibrant democratic living, where teachers and students are connected in a relationship of care. Kyle has published in such journals as *Teaching and Teacher Education, Education and Culture, Harvard Educational Review,* and *Phenomenology and Practice.* Prior to his appointment at Michigan State University, Kyle taught social studies in northern Minnesota and English in eastern Hungary.

Anne-Lise Halvorsen is an assistant professor of teacher education, specializing in social studies education, at Michigan State University. Halvorsen's work focuses on elementary social studies education, the history of education, and teacher preparation in the social studies. She teaches courses in elementary social studies education, field instruction, teacher education, quantitative methods, and the history of education. She is author and co-author of several journal articles and book chapters, and she is currently working on a book manuscript on the history of elementary social studies from 1850 to the present.

Tina Heafner is an associate professor of social studies in the Department of Middle, Secondary, and K-12 Education at the University of North Carolina at Charlotte. She earned her Ph.D. in Curriculum and Instruction from the University of North Carolina at Greensboro. At the University of North Carolina at Charlotte, her administrative responsibilities include coordinating the M.Ed. in Secondary Education and the Minor in Secondary Education. Tina's teaching and research focus on effective practices in social studies education such as technology integration, content literacy development, motivation, and service learning. Other research interests include policy and curriculum issues in social studies teaching and learning, online teaching and learning, and the impact of content-based applications of emerging technologies for K-12 learners.

Kevin Hessberg is a doctoral candidate and instructor in the Secondary Social Studies Education program in the Curry School of Education at the University of Virginia. He currently teaches in the Curriculum, Instruction, and Special Education Department. His academic and research interests include both civic education and global education. He is specifically interested in how authentic inquiry-based learning environments create active and engage citizens in a globalized world.

David Hicks is associate professor in the Department of Teaching and Learning at Virginia Polytechnic Institute and State University (Virginia Tech). David taught middle school social studies in New York and served as curator/educator for the Roanoke Valley History Museum before completing his Ph.D at Virginia Tech in 1999.

John Kambutu is Associate Professor of Educational Studies at the University of Wyoming, Casper College Center. His research work is in cultural diversity and transformative learning.

Patrick N. Leahy is a doctoral student in the Department of Teacher Education at Michigan State University. His research interests center on issues of religion, immigration, and identity in both national and local contexts of education. He holds a bachelor's and a master's degree in cultural anthropology.

John Lee is associate professor of social studies and middle grades education in the Department of Curriculum and Instruction at North Carolina State University. He earned his PhD from the University of Virginia. He research interests include digital history and the development of pedagogical content knowledge.

Timothy Lintner is an associate professor in the School of Education at the University of South Carolina, Aiken. He received his Ph.D. is Social Science and Comparative Education from UCLA. His current research focuses on understanding the perceptual and pedagogical relationships between social studies and special education.

J. B. Mayo, Jr., is an assistant professor of social studies education at the University of Minnesota. His research interests center on the inclusion of gender and GLBTQ issues and topics within the social studies and their intersections with multicultural education. He coordinates the M.Ed. program in social studies at the University of Minnesota and teaches an advanced methods course, a civic discourse class, and a course on multicultural and global issues, all within the context of secondary social studies. A former middle school teacher of six years, Mayo also serves on the executive board of the College and University Faculty Assembly (CUFA) of the National Council for the Social Studies.

Lance H. McConkey is a high school history teacher at Sequoyah High School. Madisonville, Tennessee. He received his BS in History from Tennessee Wesleyan College and his Masters in the Art of Teaching from Lee University. He later earned his Educational Specialist Degree in Social Science Education from the University of Tennessee at Knoxville where he is currently working on his PhD in Social Science Education.

Douglas McKnight is an associate professor of curriculum studies at the University of Alabama. He is the author of *Author of Schooling, the Puritan Imperative, and the Molding of an US National Identity*. His research includes how national narratives have shaped social education in the United States to preclude real race and class reform.

Paula McMillen has been an education and social sciences librarian for 11 years, first at Oregon State University and currently at the University of Nevada, Las Vegas. Her qualifications include a Master's degree in Library and Information Science and a PhD in Clinical Psychology. Scholarly interests include the therapeutic use of literature (bibliotherapy), the evolving practices for scholarly publishing, and the integration of the research and writing processes as an effective way to promote critical information competencies for students. She frequently collaborates on teaching, research and scholarship with faculty in the College of Education.

Merry M. Merryfield is a professor of social studies and global education at The Ohio State University. Her research interests include cross-cultural experiential learning online and face to face, internationalizing teacher education, and teacher decision-making in global education. In 2009 she won the NCSS Award for Global Understanding and the International Assembly's Global Scholar Award.

Jonathan Miller-Lane is an assistant professor of education at Middlebury College in Middlebury, VT. His teaching and research explores the skills of constructive disagreement that are a critical component of democratic life. Dr. Miller-Lane is also the founder and chief instructor of Blue Heron Aikido in Middlebury, VT.

Lydiah Nganga is an associate professor of humanities methods and early childhood education at the University of Wyoming, Casper Center. Her research work is in global education/international education, multicultural education and social justice.

Jason L. O'Brien is an assistant professor in the Department of Education at the University of Alabama in Huntsville. Before teaching at the university level, Jason taught upper elementary and high school classes in Tampa, Florida. Dr. O'Brien is a co-author of *Passport to Learning: Teaching Social Studies to ESL Students*, one of the first texts to specifically address how to teach social studies to ELLs.

Joseph O'Brien is an associate professor in the Department of Curriculum & Teaching at the University of Kansas. He teaches courses in middle and secondary social studies instructional practices, research and theory and has received numerous teaching awards. His research interests include the relation between digital participatory media and civic engagement and the use primary sources to promote students' ability to think historically.

Sarah Lewis Philpott is a PhD student in social science education at the University of Tennessee. She received her BS in Interdisciplinary Studies from Tennessee Wesleyan College and both her masters and educational specialist degree from Lincoln Memorial University. Sarak is a former elementary and middle school teacher and is currently involved in multiple research and writing projects at the University of Tennessee.

Anatoli Rapoport is assistant professor of Curriculum and Instruction in the College of Education at Purdue University. His scholarly interests include problems of citizenship education, international and global education, comparative aspects of education, and the impact of teachers' identities on their pedagogical practices. Dr. Rapoport is a Chair of Citizenship and Democratic Education Special Interest Group of Comparative and International Education Society (CIES). His scholarship has been published in *The Journal of Social Studies Research, International Journal of Social Education, Intercultural Education, International Education, The Social Studies, The Educational Forum,* and *Teachers and Teaching: Theory and Practice.*

Michelle Reidel is an assistant professor in the department of Teaching and Learning at Georgia Southern University. Her focus in social studies includes the affective dimensions of teaching and learning, critical literacy, democratic education, and social studies teacher education.

E. Wayne Ross is a professor of curriculum and pedagogy at the University of British Columbia. Dr. Ross was a Distinguished University Scholar and Chair of the Department of Teaching at the University of Louisville prior to his arrival at University of British Columbia in 2004. He earned his PhD at Ohio State University and is a former secondary social studies teacher.

Ellen Durrigan Santora, prior to retirement, directed the Secondary Social Studies Education Program and the *American History as Dialogue* (TAHG) professional development project at the University of Rochester and taught graduate and undergraduate courses in secondary social studies education, and the contexts of teaching and curriculum development at the Universities of Rochester and Alabama. Her teaching addresses the critical role of social studies education in preparing students for democratic citizenship in a culturally pluralistic society and an increasingly more interdependent global community. She received her Ph.D. from The Pennsylvania State University after 19 years as a middle school social studies and English teacher. Her research focuses on diversity in classroom interaction and in students' and teachers' understanding of history. It has appeared in journals including *Teaching Education, The Social Studies, The History Teacher, Education and Culture, Equity and Excellence in Education,* the *Social Science Docket,* and *Social Studies Research and Practice.*

Windy Schweder is an associate professor of Education at the University of South Carolina Aiken. She previously taught students with mild to profound disabilities in resource, self-contained, and inclusive settings. Her research interests include teaching students with disabilities in inclusive settings, faculty co-teaching in professional development schools, and identifying best practices for online learning in teacher education programs.

John Sturtz earned his doctoral degree from the University of Virginia and is currently an adjunct professor at Keene State College in Keene, New Hampshire. He teaches social studies methods courses and supervises various field experiences. His research interests include teacher education, beginning teacher development, and teaching history. He is specifically interested in advancing professional development opportunities for pre-service and beginning teacher through various feedback models.

David To is an English teacher in Seoul, Korea through the EPIK program. He received both a Bachelor of Science in Secondary Social Studies Education and a Master of Education in Curriculum & Instruction Social Studies from the University of Nevada Las Vegas. He also served as a graduate assistant in the UNLV Curriculum & Instruction department during his graduate studies. He has spent several years in the Clark County School District in Las Vegas, Nevada as a substitute teacher, student teacher, and AVID program tutor.

Reese H. Todd is an associate professor in Curriculum and Instruction in the College of Education at Texas Tech University. She teaches courses in social studies, geographic education, curriculum and instruction, and global awareness. Her research interests include the investigation of service-learning in teacher education and the development of geographic literacy in K-6 curriculum. She is currently partnering with National Geographic to bring the GIANT Traveling Map to rural schools in West Texas and Eastern New Mexico. She has more than 25 publications in professional journals including *Social Studies and the Young Learner* and *Research in Geographic Education.* She is an active member of the National Council for Geographic Education and the National Council for Social Studies.

Thomas N. Turner is a professor of education at the University of Tennessee. He received his BS in Elementary Education from the University of Cincinnati and his master's and doctorate in Social Science Education at The Pennsylvania State University. He is author of Essentials of Elementary

Social Studies as well as author or co-author of five other books and over a hundred chapters and journal articles. He is involved in storytelling and drama in schools and a writer of often lame, and occasionally intentionally humorous verse.

Stephanie van Hover is associate professor of Social Studies Education at the University of Virginia. Formerly a teacher in Fort Lauderdale, Florida, she earned her doctorate in social studies education from the University of Florida. Her research interests include technology, democracy and social studies education, and the teaching and learning of history.

Kevin D. Vinson is a senior lecturer at the University of the West Indies, Barbados. He earned his PhD in Curriculum and Instruction from the University of Maryland in 1996. He holds a BA in History from the University of Maryland, Baltimore County and an MA in Curriculum and Instruction from Loyola University. Dr. Vinson is the co-author of the book *Image and Education: Teaching in the Face of the New Disciplinarity* and the co-editor of *Defending Public Schools: Curriculum* (both with E. Wayne Ross). He is currently working on a new book tentatively entitled *iCitizenship: The Foundations of a Contemporary Critical Social Pedagogy*.

Trenia Walker is associate professor in social studies education at Texas Tech University. Current research explores transformative learning theories and the implications for inclusion, technology, popular culture, and globalization in social studies teaching and learning.

Elizabeth Yeager Washington is Professor of Social Studies Education in the School of Teaching and Learning at the University of Florida. She earned her Ph.D. from the University of Texas in Curriculum and Instruction, and an M.A.T. from Georgia State University in History. She received her B.A. in International Studies from the University of Alabama. Dr. Washington serves as an advisory board member for the International Society for the Social Studies and as a senior fellow for the Florida Joint Center for Citizenship.

Stewart Waters is an assistant professor of social science education at the University of Tennessee, Knoxville. He serves as the editorial assistant for the *Journal of Social Studies Research* and the Conference Coordinator for the International Society for the Social Studies Annual Conference. His research interests include 1) using film and other technology in the classroom to promote visual and media literacy, 2) powerful teaching methods (e.g. games/simulation, role playing, discussion) to help build decision-making and inquiry skills, as well as increase student achievement and interest, and 3) character education in schools and teacher preparation programs. He has authored several refereed journal articles related to social studies education and is the co-author of the book, *Reel Character Education: A Cinematic Approach to Character Development,* (2010), Information Age Publishing. He earned his doctorate in social science education from the University of Central Florida and taught middle school social studies before moving into higher education.

Cameron White is a professor of curriculum and instruction at the University of Houston. He earned his Ph.D. from the University of Texas.

Melissa B. Wilson is a lecturer of Early Childhood Studies at the University of the West Indies, Barbados. She earned her PhD at the University of Arizona.

CPSIA information can be obtained at www.ICGtesting.com
Printed in the USA
BVOW011258290412

288902BV00002B/25/P